Andrew Findlay / Alamy

CW00540488

PHILIP'S ROAD...

2017 BIG ATLAS BRITAIN & IRELAND

www.philips-maps.co.uk

First published in 2009 by Philip's
a division of Octopus Publishing Group Ltd
www.octopusbooks.co.uk
Carmelite House, 50 Victoria Embankment
London EC4Y 0DZ
An Hachette UK Company
www.hachette.co.uk

Eighth edition 2016
First impression 2016

ISBN 978-1-84907-415-5

Cartography by Philip's
Copyright © 2016 Philip's

Map data

This product includes mapping data licensed from Ordnance Survey®, with the permission of the Controller of Her Majesty's Stationery Office. © Crown copyright 2016. All rights reserved. Licence number 100011710

ORDNANCE SURVEY® OF NORTHERN IRELAND

The map of Ireland on pages XIV-XV is based upon the Crown Copyright and is reproduced with the permission of Land & Property Services under delegated authority from the Controller of Her Majesty's Stationery Office, © Crown Copyright and database right 2016, PMLPA No 100503, and on Ordnance Survey Ireland by permission of the Government © Ordnance Survey Ireland / Government of Ireland Permit number 9040.

Information for National Parks, Areas of Outstanding Natural Beauty, National Trails and Country Parks in Wales supplied by the Countryside Council for Wales.

Information for National Parks, Areas of Outstanding Natural Beauty, National Trails and Country Parks in England supplied by Natural England. Data for Regional Parks, Long Distance Footpaths and Country Parks in Scotland provided by Scottish Natural Heritage.

Gaelic name forms used in the Western Isles provided by Comhairle nan Eilean.

Data for the National Nature Reserves in England provided by Natural England. Data for the National Nature Reserves in Wales provided by Countryside Council for Wales. Darparwyd data'n ymwneud â Gwarchodfeydd Natur Cenedlaethol Cymru gan Gyngor Cefn Gwlad Cymru.

Information on the location of National Nature Reserves in Scotland was provided by Scottish Natural Heritage.

Data for National Scenic Areas in Scotland provided by the Scottish Executive Office. Crown copyright material is reproduced with the permission of the Controller of HMSO and the Queen's Printer for Scotland. Licence number C02W0003960.

Printed in China

*Data from Nielsen Total Consumer Market 2015, Weeks 1–48

CONTENTS

Inside back cover: **County and unitary authority boundaries**

Road map symbols

M6	Motorway, toll motorway
4 5	Motorway junction – full, restricted access
S S	Motorway service area – full, restricted access
	Motorway under construction
A453	Primary route – dual, single carriageway
S	Service area, roundabout, multi-level junction
4 5	Numbered junction – full, restricted access
	Primary route under construction
	Narrow primary route
Derby	Primary destination
A34	A road – dual, single carriageway
	A road under construction, narrow A road
B2135	B road – dual, single carriageway
	B road under construction, narrow B road
	Minor road – over 4 metres, under 4 metres wide
	Minor road with restricted access
2	Distance in miles
	Scenic route
TOLL	Toll, steep gradient – arrow points downhill
	Tunnel
	National trail – England and Wales
	Long distance footpath – Scotland
	Railway with station
	Level crossing, tunnel
	Preserved railway with station
	National boundary
	County / unitary authority boundary
	Car ferry, catamaran
	Passenger ferry, catamaran
	Hovercraft
CALAIS	Ferry destination
Ferry	Car ferry – river crossing
	Principal airport, other airport
	National park
	Area of Outstanding Natural Beauty – England and Wales
	National Scenic Area – Scotland
	forest park / regional park / national forest
	Woodland
	Beach
	Linear antiquity
	Roman road
1066	Hillfort, battlefield – with date
795	Viewpoint, nature reserve, spot height – in metres
	Golf course, youth hostel, sporting venue
	Camp site, caravan site, camping and caravan site
P&R	Shopping village, park and ride
29	Adjoining page number – road maps

Relief

Feet	metres
3000	914
2600	792
2200	671
1800	549
1400	427
1000	305
0	0

Road map scale 1: 200 000 • 3·15 miles to 1 inch

0 1 2 3 4 5 6 miles
0 1 2 3 4 5 6 7 8 9 10 km

Parts of Scotland 1: 250 000 • 3.94 miles to 1 inch

0 1 2 3 4 5 6 7 8 miles
0 1 2 3 4 5 6 7 8 9 10 11 12 km

Orkney and Shetland Islands 1:340 000, approximately 5.25 miles to 1 inch

Approach map symbols

M6	Motorway
	Toll motorway
6 5	Motorway junction – full, restricted access
S	Service area
	Under construction
A6	Primary route – dual, single carriageway
S	Service area
	Multi-level junction
	Roundabout
	Under construction
A195	A road – dual, single carriageway
B1288	B road – dual, single carriageway
	Minor road – dual, single carriageway
	Ring road
3	Distance in miles
COSELEY	Railway with station
LOXDALE	Tramway with station
M	Underground or metro station
	Congestion charge area

Town plan symbols

	Motorway
	Primary route – dual, single carriageway
	A road – dual, single carriageway
	B road – dual, single carriageway
	Minor through road
	One-way street
	Pedestrian roads
	Shopping streets
	Railway with station
City Hall	Tramway with station
	Bus or railway station building
	Shopping precinct or retail park
	Park
	Building of public interest
	Theatre, cinema
P	Parking, shopmobility
Bank	Underground station
West St	Metro station
H	Hospital, Police station
PO	Post office

Tourist information

Abbey, cathedral or priory	Church	House and garden	Safari park
Ancient monument	Country park England and Wales / Scotland	Motor racing circuit	Theme park
Aquarium	Farm park	Museum	Tourist information centre open all year, open seasonally
Art gallery	Garden	Picnic area	
Bird collection or aviary	Historic ship	Preserved railway	Zoo
Castle	House	Race course	Other place of interest
		Roman antiquity	

● Motorway service area

Kinross

M9
M90

Stirling
M80
Old Inns
M9
Bothwell
Hamilton
Heart of Scotland
M8

M74
Happendon
Abington

A74(M)

Annandale Water

Gretna Green
Todhills
Washington
Southwaite
Durham

M6
A1(M)

Tebay

Killington Lake

Burton-in-Kendal

A1(M)
Lancaster
Wetherby
M55
M6
M65
Hartshead
Blackburn with Darwen
Moor
Ferrybridge
Charnock Richard
M62
Birch
M62
Doncaster North
Rivington
Woolley Edge
M180
Burtonwood
M1
Blyth
Knutsford
Woodall
M56
Chester
Sandbach
Tibshelf
M1
Keele
Trowell
Stafford
Donington Park
M6
Leicester
Telford
Norton Canes
Leicester Forest East
M54
Hilton
Tamworth
Peterborough
Park
Corley
A1(M)
Frankley
M6
M1
Hopwood Park
Watford Gap
Warwick
Northampton
Strensham
M5
Newport Pagnell
M40
Baldock
M50
Cherwell Valley
M1
M11
Ross Spur
Gloucester
Toddington
A1(M)
Birchanger Green
M5
Pont Abraham
Oxford
South Mimms
Swansea
M25
M25
M4
Michaelwood
Beaconsfield
London Gateway
Cardiff
Magor
M4
Heston
Thurrock
Sarn Park
Gate
Severn
Membury
M4
Medway
View
Leigh
Reading
Cobham
M2
Cardiff West
Gordano
Delamere
Chieveley
M25
Maidstone
M5
M3
Clacket Lane
M20
Sedgemoor
Fleet
M23
Stop 24
Winchester
Bridgwater
Pease Pottage
M5
Taunton Deane
Rownhams
Tiverton
M27
Cullompton
M27

Exeter

Restricted motorway junctions

M1 Junction 34

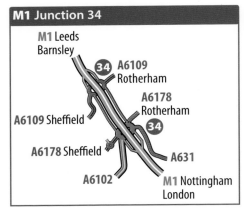

M1 Leeds Barnsley
34 A6109 Rotherham
A6178 Rotherham
A6109 Sheffield
A6178 Sheffield
34
A631
A6102
M1 Nottingham London

M1 Junctions 6, 6A
M25 Junctions 21, 21A

M1 The North Luton
A405 Hatfield St Albans
6A
21A
M25 (M40, M4) Heathrow
21
6
M25 (M11, M20) Dartford
A405 North Watford
M1 Watford Central London

M4 Junctions 25, 25A, 26

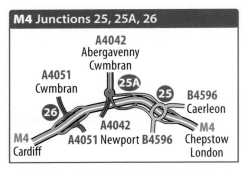

A4042 Abergavenny Cwmbran
A4051 Cwmbran
25A
25 B4596 Caerleon
26
A4042
A4051 Newport B4596
M4 Chepstow London
M4 Cardiff

M5 Junction 11A

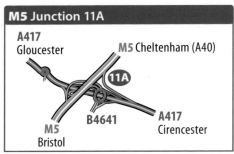

A417 Gloucester
M5 Cheltenham (A40)
11A
B4641
A417 Cirencester
M5 Bristol

M8 Junctions 8, 9 · M73 Junctions 1, 2 · M74 Junctions 2A, 3, 3A, 4

M8 Glasgow
9
M73 Stirling
8
2 A89 Coatbridge
A8 Edinburgh
B7058
A74
B765
1/4 M73
A74
B7001
M74 Glasgow
2A 3
M74
3A
A721
A763
B758
B7071
M74 Carlisle

M11 Junctions 13, 14

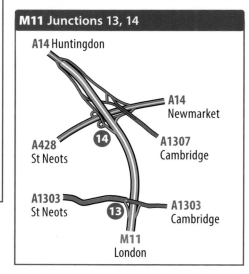

A14 Huntingdon
A14 Newmarket
A428 St Neots
14
A1307 Cambridge
A1303 St Neots
13
A1303 Cambridge
M11 London

M1	Northbound	Southbound
2	No exit	No access
4	No exit	No access
6A	No exit. Access from M25 only	No access. Exit to M25 only
7	No exit. Access from A414 only	No access. Exit to A414 only
17	No access. Exit to M45 only	No exit. Access from M45 only
19	No exit to A14	No access from A14
21A	No access	No exit
23A		Exit to A42 only
24A	No exit	No access
35A	No access	No exit
43	No access. Exit to M621 only	No exit. Access from M621 only
48	No exit to A1(M) southbound	

M3	Eastbound	Westbound
8	No exit	No access
10	No access	No exit
13	No access to M27 eastbound	
14	No exit	No access

M4	Eastbound	Westbound
1	Exit to A4 eastbound only	Access from A4 westbound only
2	Access from A4 eastbound only	Access to A4 westbound only
21	No exit	No access
23	No access	No exit
25	No exit	No access
25A	No exit	No access
29	No exit	No access
38		No access
39	No exit or access	No exit
41	No access	No access
41A	No exit	No access
42	Access from A483 only	Exit to A483 only

M5	Northbound	Southbound
10	No exit	No access
11A	No access from A417 eastbound	No exit to A417 westbound

M6	Northbound	Southbound
3A	No access. Exit to M42 northbound only	No exit. Access from M6 eastbound only
4A	No exit. Access from M42 southbound only	No access. Exit to M42 only
5	No access	No exit
10A	No access. Exit to M54 only	No exit. Access from M54 only
11A	No exit. Access from M6 Toll only	No access. Exit to M6 Toll only
20	No exit to M56 eastbound	No access from M56 westbound
24	No exit	No access
25	No access	No exit
30	No exit. Access from M61 northbound only	No access. Exit to M61 southbound only
31A	No access	No exit
45	No access	No exit

M6 Toll	Northbound	Southbound
T1		No exit
T2	No exit, no access	No access
T5	No access	No access
T7	No access	No exit
T8	No access	No exit

M8	Eastbound	Westbound
8	No exit to M73 northbound	No access from M73 southbound
9	No exit	No access
13	No exit southbound	Access from M73 southbound only
14	No access	No exit
16	No exit	No access
17	No exit	No access
18		No exit
19	No exit to A814 eastbound	No access from A814 westbound
20	No exit	No access
21	No access from M74	No exit
22	No exit. Access from M77 only	No access. Exit to M77 only
23	No exit	No access
25	Exit to A739 northbound only. Access from A739 southbound only	Access from A739 southbound only
25A	No exit	No access
28	No access	No exit
28A	No access	No access

M9	Eastbound	Westbound
1A	No exit	No access
2	No access	No exit
3	No exit	No access
6	No access	No exit
8	No exit	No access

M11	Northbound	Southbound
4	No exit. Access from A406 only	No access . Exit to A406 only
5	No access	No exit
9	No access	No exit
13	No access	No exit
14	No exit to A428 westbound	No exit. Access from A14 westbound only

M20	Eastbound	Westbound
2	No access	No exit
3	No exit. Access from M26 eastbound only	No access. Exit to M26 westbound only
11A	No access	No exit

M23	Northbound	Southbound
7	No exit to A23 southbound	No access from A23 northbound
10A		

M25	Clockwise	Anticlockwise
5	No exit to M26 eastbound	No access from M26 westbound
19	No access	No exit
21	No exit to M1 southbound. Access from M1 southbound only	No exit to M1 southbound. Access from M1 southbound only
31	No exit	No access

M27	Eastbound	Westbound
10	No exit	No access
12	No access	No exit

M40	Eastbound	Westbound
3	No exit	No access
7	No exit	No access
8	No exit	No access
13	No exit	No access
14	No access	No exit
16	No access	No exit

M42	Northbound	Southbound
1	No exit	No access
7	No access Exit to M6 northbound only	No exit Access from M6 northbound only
7A	No access. Exit to M6 southbound only	No exit
8	No exit. Access from M6 southbound only	Exit to M6 northbound only. Access from M6 southbound only

M45	Eastbound	Westbound
M1 J17	Access to M1 southbound only	No access from M1 southbound
With A45	No access	No exit

M48	Eastbound	Westbound
M4 J21	No exit to M4 westbound	No access from M4 eastbound
M4 J23	No access from M4 westbound	No exit to M4 eastbound

M49	Southbound	Northbound
18A	No exit to M5 northbound	No access from M5 southbound

M53	Northbound	Southbound
11	Exit to M56 eastbound only. Access from M56 westbound only	Exit to M56 eastbnd only. Access from M56 westbound only

M56	Eastbound	Westbound
2	No exit	No access
3	No access	No exit
4	No exit	No access
7	No access	No exit
8	No exit or access	No exit
9	No access from M6 northbound	No access to M6 southbound
15	No exit to M53	No access from M53 northbound

M57	Northbound	Southbound
3	No exit	No access
5	No exit	No access

M58	Eastbound	Westbound
1	No exit	No access

M60	Clockwise	Anticlockwise
2	No exit	
3	No exit to A34 northbound	No exit to A34 northbound
4	No access from M56	No exit to M56
5	No exit to A5103 southbound	No exit to A5103 northbound
14	No exit	No access
16	No exit	No access
20	No access	No exit
22		No access
25	No access	
26		No exit or access
27	No exit	No access

M61	Northbound	Southbound
2	No access from A580 eastbound	No exit to A580 westbound
3	No access from A580 eastbound. No access from A666 southbound	No exit to A580 westbound
M6 J30	No exit to M6 southbound	No access from M6 northbound

M62	Eastbound	Westbound
23	No access	No exit

M65	Eastbound	Westbound
9	No access	No exit
11	No exit	No access

M66	Northbound	Southbound
1	No access	No exit

M67	Eastbound	Westbound
1A	No access	No exit
2	No exit	No access

M69	Northbound	Southbound
2	No exit	No access

M73	Northbound	Southbound
2	No access from M8 or A89 eastbound. No exit to A89	No exit to M8 or A89 westbound. No access from A89

M74	Northbound	Southbound
3	No access	No exit
3A	No exit	No access
7	No exit	No access
9	No exit or access	No access
10		No exit
11	No exit	No access
12	No access	No exit

M77	Northbound	Southbound
4	No exit	No access
6	No exit	No access
7	No exit or access	
8	No access	No access

M80	Northbound	Southbound
4A	No access	No exit
6A	No exit	
8	Exit to M876 northbound only. No access	Access from M876 southbound only. No exit

M90	Northbound	Southbound
2A	No access	No exit
7	No exit	No access
8	No access	No access
10	No access from A912	No exit to A912

M180	Eastbound	Westbound
1	No access	No exit

M621	Eastbound	Westbound
2A	No exit	No access
4	No exit	
5	No exit	No access
6	No access	No exit

M876	Northbound	Southbound
2	No access	No exit

A1(M)	Northbound	Southbound
2	No access	No exit
3		No access
5	No exit	No access
14	No exit	No access
40	No access	No exit
43	No exit. Access from M1 only	No access. Exit to M1 only
57	No access	No exit
65	No access	No exit

A3(M)	Northbound	Southbound
1	No exit	No access
4	No access	No exit

A38(M)		Northbound	Southbound
With Victoria Rd, (Park Circus) Birmingham		No exit	No access

A48(M)	Northbound	Southbound
M4 Junc 29	Exit to M4 eastbound only	Access from M4 westbound only
29A	Access from A48 eastbound only	Exit to A48 westbound only

A57(M)	Eastbound	Westbound
With A5103	No access	No exit
With A34	No access	No exit

A58(M)		Southbound
With Park Lane and Westgate, Leeds		No access

A64(M)	Eastbound	Westbound
With A58 Clay Pit Lane, Leeds	No access	No exit
With Regent Street, Leeds	No access	No access

A74(M)	Northbound	Southbound
18	No access	No exit
22		No exit

A194(M)	Northbound	Southbound
A1(M) J65 Gateshead Western Bypass	Access from A1(M) northbound only	Exit to A1(M) southbound only

M3 Junctions 13, 14 · M27 Junction 4

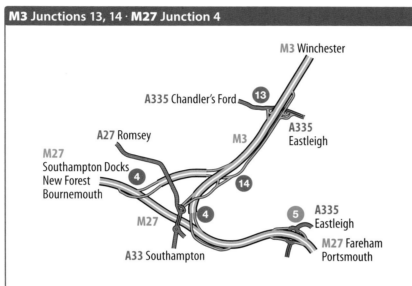

M6 Junctions 3A, 4A · M42 Junctions 7, 7A, 8, 9
M6 Toll Junctions T1, T2

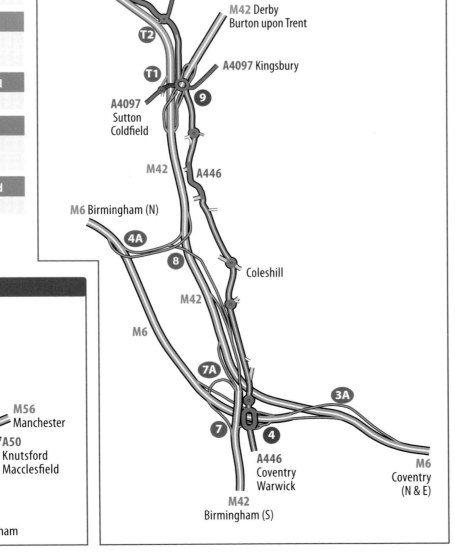

M6 Junction 20 · M56 Junction 4

M62 Junctions 32A, 33 · A1(M) Junctions 40, 41

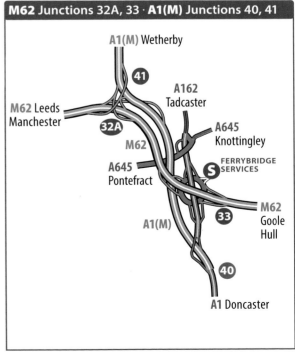

Mobile Layby Cafés – gourmet or gruesome?

Do you drive on by?

**Stephen Mesquita,
Philip's On the Road Correspondent**

Have you ever done this? You're driving along on one of Britain's A-Roads. It's sometime between 6am and 2pm. You're feeling a bit peckish. You see a layby coming up. There's a notice by the road. Something about hot food. There's a van flying a Union Jack. There are a couple of truck drivers there, queueing up. You might even catch a tempting whiff of something frying.

And you drive straight past. Not really for you? You've never eaten in a layby so you'll wait for a place you know and recognise. Or buy a sandwich at the next petrol station.

Well, that's what I've always done. Up until yesterday. That's when I set out, with my trusty accomplice (and Philip's Sales Supremo) Stuart, to see if my lifelong prejudices were justified.

Butty Vans

A quick word about terminology first. We're going to drop the 'Mobile Layby Cafés' and go with 'Butty Vans'. Stuart and I were out to beat The Breakfast Buns from Butty Vans in One Morning Record.

And so it was with some trepidation that we set off from Northampton and headed for our first Butty Van. Here's confession number one: as soon as we'd photographed the bacon roll that we'd ordered, we polished it off.

This was a good start – and in stark contrast to our Motorway Service Area research, where the fare was so unappetising that we tried only a tiny portion of each item and left the rest.

And as the day started, so it went on. Of the eight buns, only one really disappointed. The other seven were tasty, hot, great value and came with friendly chat. Stuart and I polished almost all of them off – and two especially good ones were down the gullets of Philip's intrepid breakfast critics before you could say 'another bacon roll please'.

▲ The first bacon butty of the day in a layby alongside the A43

Eight in a Day

Would I recommend eight in a day? As a gastronomic experience, no. It's too much salt intake (my car was littered with empty bottles of water by the end of the day). And I did long for a freshly made flat white by the end of the day.

But a Butty Van breakfast or snack every now and again? Absolutely. Now I've done it once, I'll be very happy to do it again. In fact, I'm rather ashamed I hadn't managed to overcome my prejudices before now.

So to answer my question. Gourmet: no. Gruesome: certainly not. A tasty roadside snack, piping hot, cooked to order and served with a smile – definitely. I'll have one of those.

Butty Vans vs. Motorway Service Areas – how they compare

If you're expecting Butty Vans to serve up the fare you get at your local deli, you probably don't need to read on. The buns are not made of artisanal sourdough ciabatta. The butter isn't Danish unsalted. The bacon didn't cost £15 a kilo. The eggs probably aren't fresh from the farm that morning. Butty Vans aren't posh.

But the point is this – all the Butty Vans we ate at were owned by people who took great pride in what they did. We met one real foody proprietor who told us he'd been to a burger fair the weekend before and always offered specials ('Codfinger'; 'Blue Burger Special'). All of them were aware that, to compete against the big brands, they had to offer good food at good prices.

The ingredients were perfectly decent. The bacon was almost universally of a better quality than we tasted last year in our Full English Breakfast campaign in Motorway Service Areas. And it was all cooked to order in front of you, which gave it one spectacular advantage over the Motorway Service Areas. It was hot.

And it was a fraction of the price.

The only disappointment was the tea and coffee. But at £0.70–£0.80 a cup, you should know what you're getting and you get what you pay for – although at one Butty Van, the teabags were Yorkshire Tea.

You can compare further in our **Butty Van vs. Motorway Service Area checklist:**

	Butty Vans	Motorway Services
Good Value for Money	✔	✗
Proud of what they do	✔	✗
Cooked to Order	✔	rarely
Meal Hot	✔	✗
Quality of ingredients	See above	See above
Quality of hot drinks	✗	✗
Friendly Service	✔	✗
Parking	✔	✔
Easy to find	✗	✔

Butty Vans – what you need to know

- **Layby cafes are licensed by the local authority**, normally annually, to do business in a particular layby.
- **Food Hygiene is an important part of their credibility** – most of them display their certificates prominently.
- **You can't go there for dinner.** Most open early (often around 6am) and shut up around 2pm (sometimes 3pm).
- **They aren't just found in laybys on A Roads.** Some are on industrial estates and business parks.
- **The good ones are there come rain or shine** (bad weather can be good for business) most days of the year.

- **Most of them have a name:** we sampled the fare at *Dom's Doorsteps, Taste Buds Snacks, Sizzlers, Delicias* and *Smell the Bacon.*
- **It's a competitive business** – and their regulars (mostly truck drivers and white van men on A Roads) are discerning customers who expect tasty food at reasonable prices. We heard one van driver say he draws the line at paying £1 for a cup of tea.
- **We were made very welcome**, even though it was obvious we weren't their usual clientele.

Our thanks to all the proprietors who answered our questions about their businesses so openly.

Eight Meals in a Bun between 9am and 2pm – how was it for me?

Meal in a Bun One:

Location	A43 West of Northampton
Meal	Bacon roll plus tea
Price	£2.50 plus £0.60

Verdict: Generous helping of tasty bacon, cooked in front of us and piping hot. The tea was wet and warm.

Meal in a Bun Two:

Location	A43 Brackley
Meal	Sausage and Bacon roll plus tea
Price	£3.20 plus £0.50

Verdict: A breakfast on its own served with a smile and lots of chat. The ingredients were nothing special but all tasty.

Meal in a Bun Three:

Location	A422 between Buckingham and Milton Keynes
Meal	Bacon and Egg roll plus coffee
Price	£3.00 plus £0.80

Verdict: Another very decent breakfast in a bun, with the egg cooked to order. Yorkshire Tea teabags spurned for instant coffee. Should have had the tea.

Meal in a Bun Four:

Location:	Harding Road, Milton Keynes
Meal:	Sausage and Egg roll plus tea
Price:	£2.25 plus £0.50

Verdict: Sausage and egg: not expensive ingredients but properly cooked, nice and hot and at a nugatory price.

Meal in a Bun Five:

Location	Yardley Road Industrial Estate, Olney
Meal	Double egg roll
Price	£2.50

Verdict: I was stupid. I had a double egg sandwich (which was tasty) but I was rightly berated by Mr Sizzler for not being more adventurous and having one of his speciality burgers or chicken dishes. The things I sacrifice to make these surveys fair.

Meal in a Bun Six:

Location	A505 West of Royston
Meal	Bacon Roll
Price	£2.00

Verdict: The best bread (slightly toasted) and loads of decent bacon for £2.00. I rest my case. I should have added: cooked by Italians. They know how to cook, the Italians. Even good old English Bacon butties. Buonissimo!

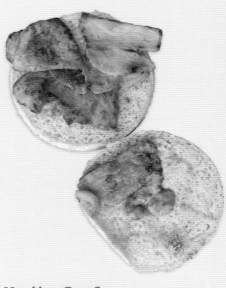

Meal in a Bun Seven:

Location	A505 West of Royston
Meal	Bacon Roll
Price	£2.50

Verdict: A bit disappointing. Bread tough, bacon tough. Our only below par experience of the day.

Meal in a Bun Eight:

Location:	A505 East of Royston
Meal:	Sausage roll
Price:	£3.00

Verdict: This café was called Smell the Bacon but the sausages were from Musks of Newmarket. They were delicious! They seemed to disappear remarkably quickly, Stuart.

How to find Butty Vans

Most Butty Vans are either an 'impulse buy' (you see them as you pass by) or have their regular customers who know where they are. But say you are planning a journey and you want to know for sure there's a Butty Van at a point on your route. Then you need the free app from Butty Van Finder (go to buttyvan.com). We don't even need to describe it: these screen grabs say it all.

Enter the Butty Van Competition

Send us your personal recommendations for *Breakfast On the Move* **(Butty Vans or anywhere else) by email, with pictures if possible, and tell us why you recommend them – or any amusing stories you have.**

Send them by 31st December 2017.

The 25 best entries in our opinion will each receive a free copy of the *Philip's Royal Geographical Society Essential World Atlas* (worth £25).

Email your entries to buttyvan@octopusbooks.co.uk

For terms and conditions, visit: www.octopusbooks.co.uk/assets/OctopusPublishingGroup/Downloads/ PhilipsNavigatorCompetitionTandCs.pdf

Matt Botwood / Alamy

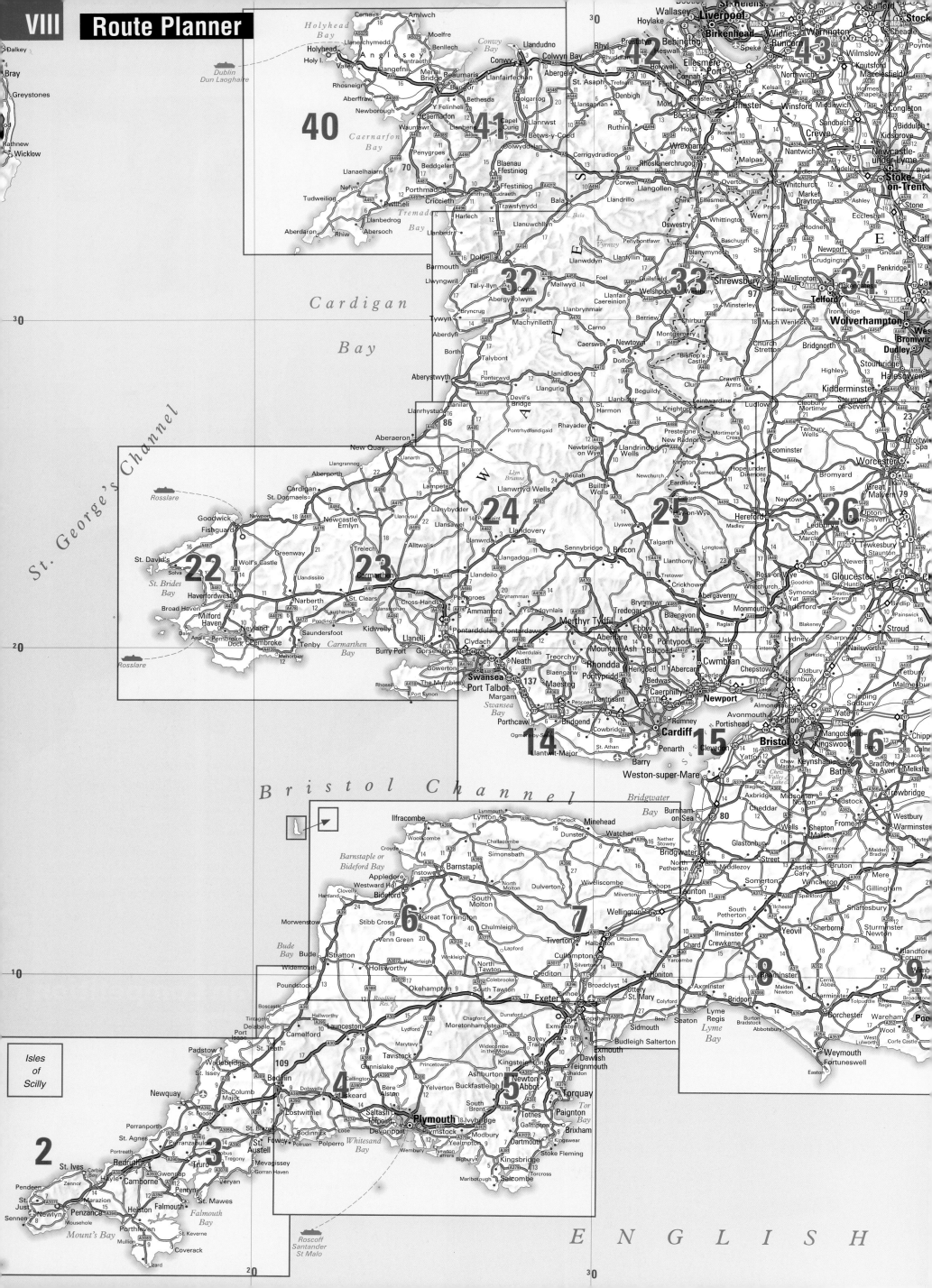

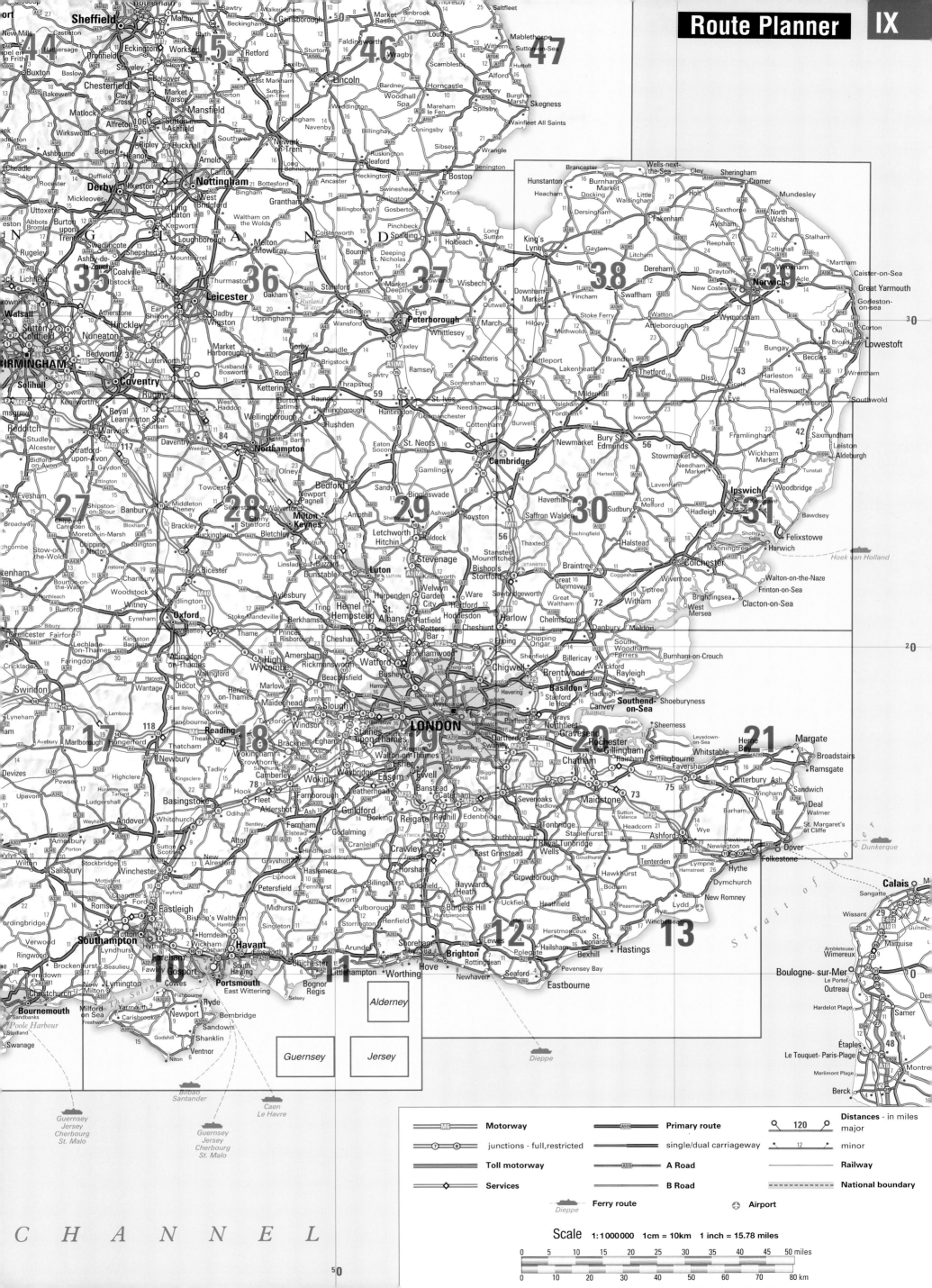

NORTH SEA

Amsterdam

Rotterdam Europoort Zeebrugge

Bridlington Bay

The Wash

71
63
58 **59**
51 **62** **53**
44 **45** **46** **47**
35 **36** **37** **38** **39**

Berwick-upon-Tweed
Scremerston
Belford
Bamburgh
Seahouses
Beadnell
Chatton
North Charlton
Embleton
Longhoughton
Alnwick
Lesbury
Alnmouth
Warkworth
Amble
Longhamington
Longhorsley
Ashington
Pegswood
Newbiggin-by-the-Sea
Hartburn
Morpeth
Bedlington
Belsay
Whalton
Ponteland
Blyth
Cramlington
Whitley Bay
Newcastle-upon-Tyne
Longbenton
Tynemouth
Blaydon
Jarrow
South Shields
Prudhoe
Whickham
Gateshead
Sunderland
Consett
Chester-le-Street
Washington
Houghton-le-Spring
Lanchester
Hetton-le-Hole
Seaham
Durham
Peterlee
Stanhope
Willington
Spennymoor
Ferryhill
Trimdon
Hartlepool
Bishop Auckland
Sedgefield
Newton Aycliffe
Billingham
Redcar
Marske-by-the-Sea
Staindrop
Stockton-on-Tees
Saltburn-by-the-Sea
Darlington
Thornaby on Tees
Middlesbrough
Loftus
Bowes
Yarm
Guisborough
Whitby
Richmond
Stokesley
Reeth
Scotch Corner
Catterick
Sleights
Robin Hood's Bay
Leyburn
Northallerton
Bedale
Masham
Thirsk
Kirkbymoorside
Scalby
Burniston
Scarborough
Kirkby Malzeard
Sowerby
Helmsley
Pickering
Thornton-le-Dale
Pateley Bridge
Ripon
Hovingham
Snainton
Filey
Stillington
Malton
Norton-on-Derwent
Boroughbridge
Sledmere
Rudston
Flamborough
Knaresborough
Stamford Bridge
Bridlington
Harrogate
York
Pocklington
Fridaythorpe
Driffield
Burton Agnes
Skipsea
Ilkley
Otley
Wetherby
Bainton
North Frodingham
Hornsea
Baildon
Collingham
Elvington
Hutton Cranswick
Bingley
Saltaire
Tadcaster
Escrick
Holme-on-Spalding Moor
Market Weighton
Leven
Aldbrough
Bradford
Leeds
Garforth
Selby
South Cave
Beverley
Sproatley
Halifax
Brighouse
Castleford
Howden
Cottingham
Hedon
Withernsea
Batley
Snaith
Goole
Kingston upon Hull
Keyingham
Dewsbury
Pontefract
Wakefield
Burton upon Stather
Barton-upon-Humber
Barrow upon Humber
Patrington
Huddersfield
Thorne
Scunthorpe
Easington
Meltham
Darton
Adwick le Street
Hatfield
Brigg
Immingham
Grimsby
Holmfirth
Barnsley
Epworth
Barnetby le Wold
Cleethorpes
Wombwell
Mexborough
Scotter
Haxey
Kirton in Lindsey
Caistor
Humberston
Stocksbridge
Rotherham
Bawtry
Walkeringham
Caenby
North Thoresby
North Somercotes
under-Lyne
Glossop
Doncaster
Gainsborough
Market Rasen
Binbrook
Saltfleet
Sheffield
Maltby
Retford
Sturton
Lea
Faldingworth
Louth
Mablethorpe
New Mills
Castleton
Eckington
Worksop
Blyth
Beckingham
Wragby
Scamblesby
Withern
Sutton-on-Sea
Hathersage
Staveley
East Markham
Wickenby
Horncastle
Alford
Buxton
Chesterfield
Bolsover
Lincoln
Bardney
Mareham le Fen
Burgh le Marsh
Baslow
Clay Cross
Tuxford
Sutton-on-Trent
Waddington
Woodhall Spa
Spilsby
Skegness
Bakewell
Market Warsop
Ollerton
Coningsby
Vainfleet All Saints
Matlock
Mansfield
Collingham
Navenby
Sibsey
Wirksworth
Alfreton
Sutton in Ashfield
Southwell
Billinghay
Wrangle
Ashbourne
Belper
Heanor
Ripley
Hucknall
Newark-on-Trent
Ruskington
Benington
Boston
Duffield
Arnold
Sleaford
Kirton
Rocester
Carlton
Long Bennington
Heckington
Swineshead
Uttoxeter
Mickleover
Nottingham
Grantham
Billingborough
Gosberton
Abbots Bromley
Derby
Ilkeston
West Bridgford
Bottesford
Bingham
Donington
Pinchbeck
Spalding
Burton upon Trent
Long Eaton
Ancaster
Bourne
Deeping St. Nicholas
Holbeach
Rugeley
Swadlincote
Ashby
Kegworth
Waltham on the Wolds
Colsterworth
Long Sutton
Lichfield
Shepshed
Melton Mowbray
Deeping St. James
Wisbech
Coalville
Loughborough
Mountsorrel
Stamford
Crowland
Downham
Ibstock
Thurmaston
Market Deeping
Oakham
Leicester

King's Lynn
Hunstanton
Heacham
Brancaster
Burnham Market
Docking
Dersingham
Little Walsingham
Wells-next-the-Sea
Cley
Holt
Sheringham
Cromer
Mundesley
North Walsham
Gayton
Litcham
Fakenham
Aylsham
Reepham
Stalham
Dereham
Swaffham
New Costessey
Norwich
Drayton
Acle
Great Yarmouth
Fincham
Martham
Caister-on-Sea

ENGLAND

50
60
50
40
60

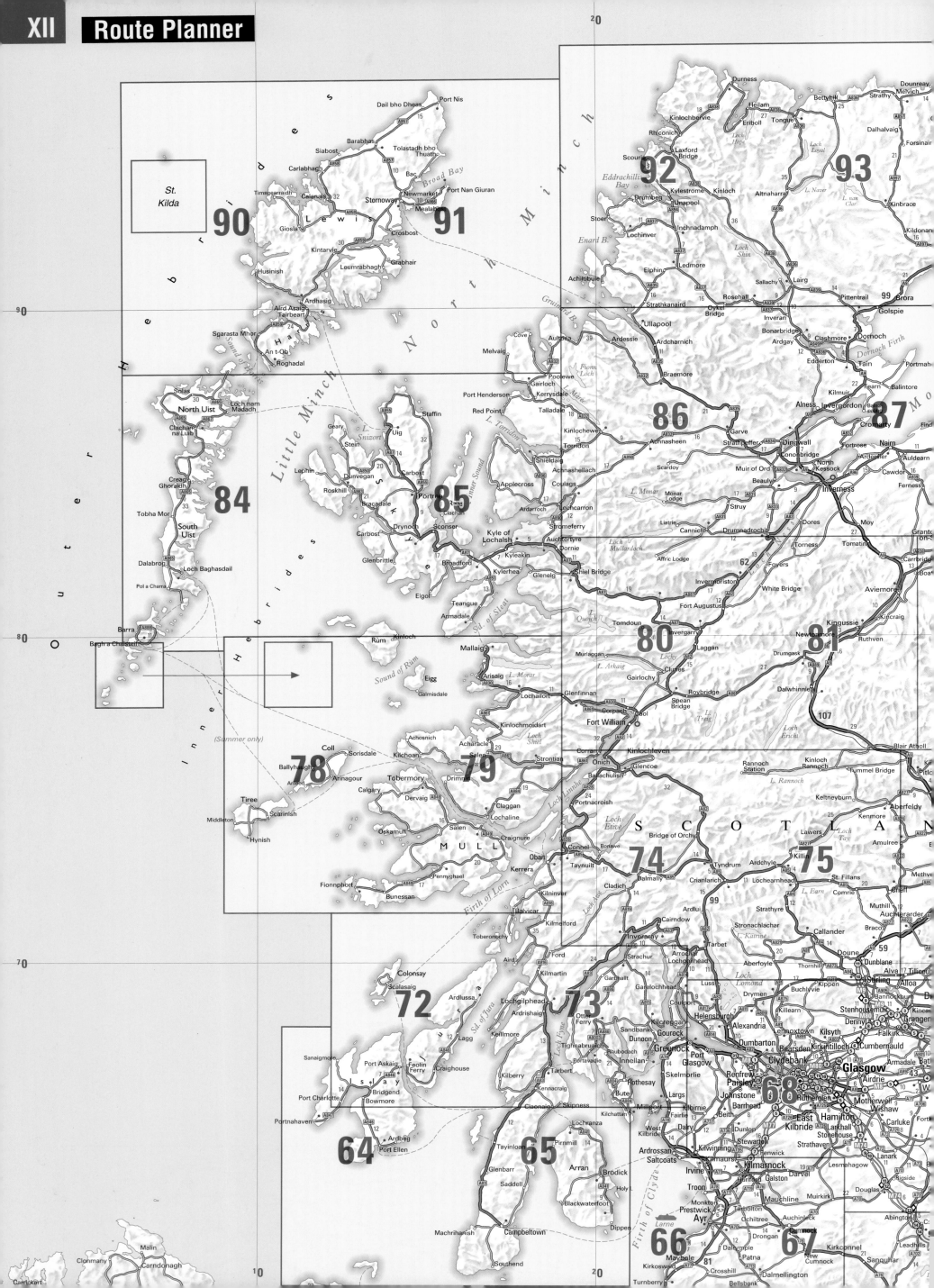

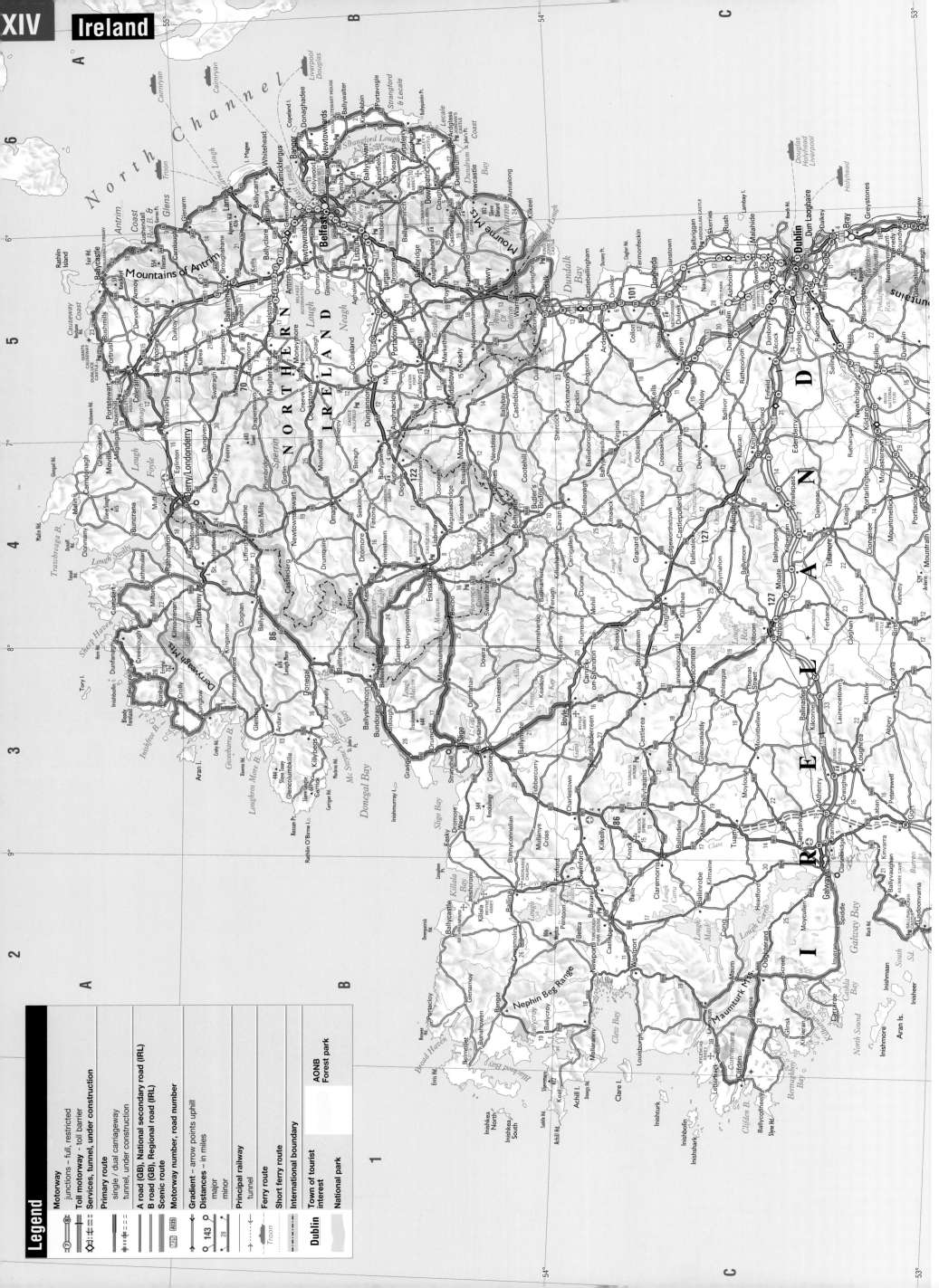

Legend

Motorway
junctions - full, restricted
Toll motorway - toll barrier
Services, tunnel, under construction

Primary route
single / dual carriageway
tunnel, under construction

A road (GB), National secondary road (IRL)
B road (GB), Regional road (IRL)
Scenic route
Motorway number, road number

Gradient - arrow points uphill
major
minor
Distances - in miles

Principal railway
tunnel

Ferry route
Short ferry route

International boundary

Dublin   Town of tourist interest

AONB
Forest park

National park

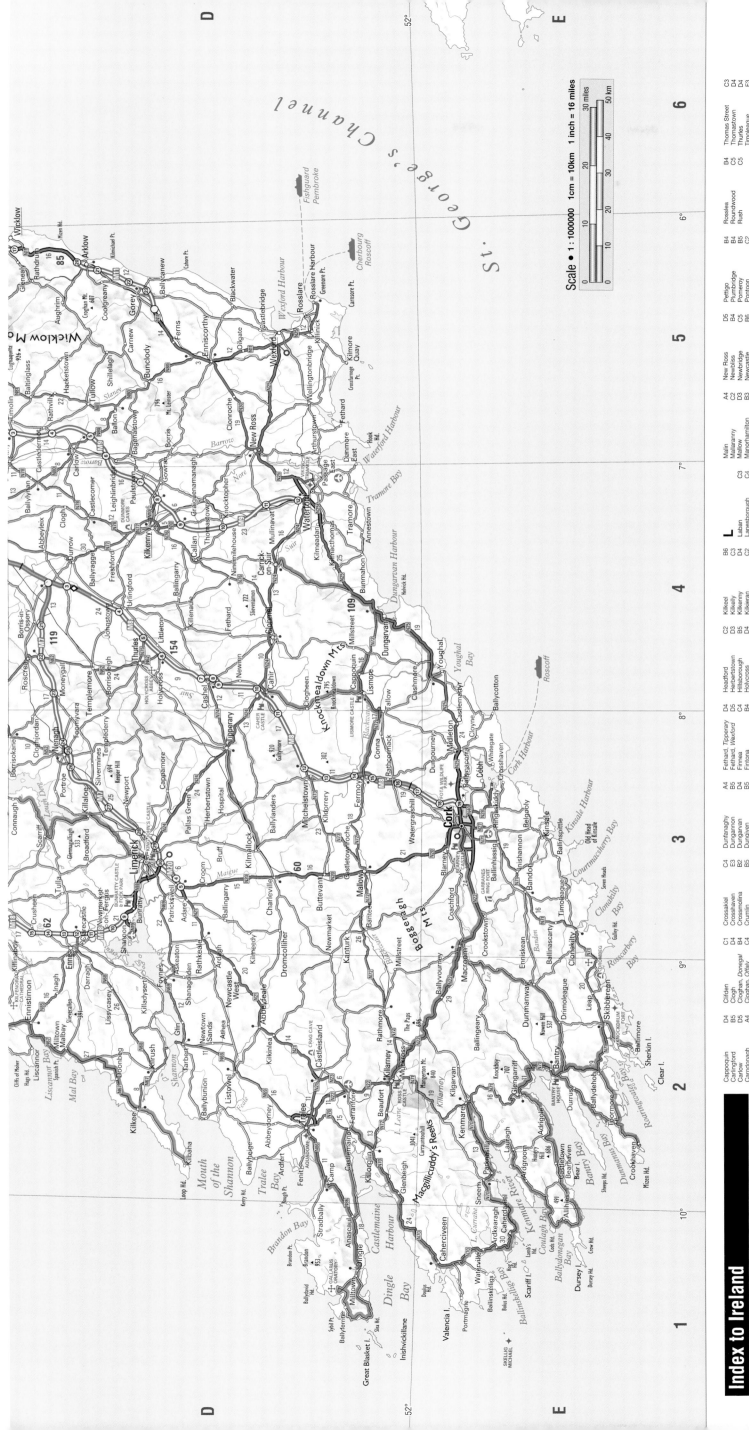

St. George's Channel

Wicklow Mts

Knockmealdown Mts

Galty Mts

Boggeragh Mts

Macgillycuddy's Reeks

Dingle Bay

Bantry Bay

Kenmare River

Castlemaine Harbour

Mouth of the Shannon

Scale • 1 : 1 000 000   1cm = 10km   1 inch = 16 miles

Index to Ireland

A
Abbey C3
Abbeydorney C2
Abbeyfeale C2
Abbeyleix D4
Abbeyleix D4
Adare C3
Adrigole B2
Aghabullogue B5
Aghada C5
Aghamore B5
Aghaville B5
Allihies B2
Anascaul B2
Annalong E3
Annestown D4
Antrim E2
Ardagh C2
Ardara D1
Ardee D2
Ardfert C2
Ardglass E3
Ardgroom B2
Arklow E4
Armagh D2
Arthurstown D4
Ashbourne D3
Askeaton C3
Athboy D3
Athea C2
Athenry C3
Athleague C3
Athlone C3
Athy D3
Augher D2
Aughnacloy D2
Aughrim, Galway C3
Aughrim, Wicklow E4

B
Balbriggan D3
Ballina, Mayo B2
Ballina, Tipperary C3
Ballinafad C2
Ballinakill D4
Ballinamallard D2
Ballinamore C2
Ballinascarty B5
Ballinasloe C3
Ballindine C2
Ballineen B5
Ballingarry, Limerick C3
Ballingarry, Tipperary D4
Ballingeary B5
Ballinhassig B5
Ballinlough C2
Ballinrobe C2
Ballinskelligs A2
Ballinspittle B5
Ballintober C2
Ballintra C1
Ballivor D3
Ballon D4
Ballybay D2
Ballybofey D1
Ballybunion C2
Ballycanew E4
Ballycarry E2
Ballycastle, Antrim E1
Ballycastle, Mayo B1
Ballyclare E2
Ballyconnell C2
Ballycotton C5
Ballydehob B5
Ballydonegan A2
Ballyferriter A2
Ballygawley D2

Ballygowan E2
Ballyhaise C2
Ballyhaunis C2
Ballyhean B2
Ballyheige C2
Ballyjamesduff D2
Ballylanders C3
Ballylongford C2
Ballylynan D3
Ballymacarbry D4
Ballymahon C3
Ballymena E2
Ballymoe C2
Ballymoney E1
Ballymore C3
Ballymote C2
Ballynacorra C5
Ballynahinch E2
Ballynure E2
Ballyragget D4
Ballysadare C2
Ballyshannon C1
Ballyvaughan C3
Ballyvourney B5
Ballywalter E2
Balrothery D3
Baltimore B5
Baltinglass D4
Banagher C3
Bandon B5
Bangor, Down E2
Bangor, Mayo B1
Bansha C4
Banteer B5
Bantry B5
Barntown D4
Beaufort B2
Belcoo C2
Belfast E2
Belgooly B5
Bellaghy D2
Belleek C1
Bellmullet B1

Beltra B2
Benburb D2
Beragh D2
Blackwater E4
Blarney B5
Blessington D3
Boris-in-Ossory D3
Borris D4
Borrisokane C3
Borrisoleigh D3
Boyle C2
Bracklin C3
Bracknagh D3
Broadford C3
Broughshane E2
Bruff C3
Bunbeg C1
Bunclody D4
Buncrana D1
Bundoran C1
Bunmahon D4
Bunnaboghal B1
Bunratty C3
Burnfort B5
Bushmills E1
Butler's Bridge C2
Buttevant B4

C
Caher C4
Caherciveen A2
Caherdaniel A2
Cahir C4
Callan D4
Camp B2
Cappamore C3
Cappoquin C4
Carlingford D2
Carlow D4
Carna B2
Carndonagh D1
Carnew D4
Carracastle C2
Carrick-on-Shannon C2
Carrick-on-Suir D4

Carrickart D1
Carrickfergus E2
Carrickmacross D2
Carrigahorig C3
Carrigaline B5
Carrigallen C2
Carrigtwohill C5
Cashel C4
Castlebar B2
Castlebellingham D2
Castleblayney D2
Castlebridge D4
Castlecomer D4
Castleconnell C3
Castledermot D4
Castlegregory B2
Castleisland C2
Castlemaine B2
Castlemartyr C5
Castleplunket C2
Castlepollard D3
Castlerea C2
Castletown D3
Castletownbere B2
Castletownroche B4
Castletownshend B5
Castlewellan E2
Cavan C2
Charlestown C2
Charleville B4
Clane D3
Clara D3
Clarecastle C3
Claremorris C2
Clarinbridge C3
Claudy D1

D
Daingean D3
Delvin D3
Derry D1
Derrygonnelly C2
Derrylin C2
Dingle B2
Doagh E2
Donaghadee E2
Donegal C1
Doneraile B4
Doonbeg C3
Downhill D1
Downpatrick E2
Dowra C2
Drimoleague B5
Dripsey B5
Drogheda D3
Dromahair C2
Dromcolliher B4
Dromore, Down E2
Dromore, Tyrone D2
Dromore West C2
Drumcliff C2
Drumkeeran C2
Drumlish C2
Drumquin D2
Drumshanbo C2
Dublin D3
Duleek D3
Dunboyne D3
Dundalk D2
Dunderrow B5
Dundrum, Down E2

E
Easky C2
Edenderry D3
Edgeworthstown C2
Eglinton D1
Emyvale D2
Enfield D3
Enniscorthy D4
Enniskean B5
Enniskillen D2
Ennistimon C3

F
Falcarragh C1
Farranfore B2
Fenagh C2
Fenit B2
Fermoy B4
Ferns D4
Fethard, Tipperary D4
Fethard, Wexford D4
Finnea C2
Fintona D2
Fivemiletown D2
Fontstown D3
Foxford C2
Frenchpark C2
Freshford D4

G
Galway C3
Garrison C1
Garvagh D1
Gilford D2
Glandore B5
Glanmire B5
Glanworth B4
Glaslough D2
Glenamoy B1
Glenamaddy C2
Glenarm E2
Glenavy E2
Glenbeigh B2
Glencolumbkille C1
Glendalough D3
Glengarriff B5
Glenties C1
Glin C3
Glinsk C2
Gorey E4
Gort C3
Gorumna B3
Gowran D4
Graiguenamanagh D4
Granard C2
Grange C2
Greencastle D1
Greenisland E2
Greystones E3

H
Hackettstown D4
Headford C2
Herbertstown C3
Hillsborough E2
Hilltown E2
Holycross D3
Holywood E2
Hospital C3

I
Inagh C3
Inishannon B5
Inver C1
Irvinestown D2

J
Johnstown D3
Julianstown D3

K
Keadew C2
Keady D2
Keel B2
Keenagh C2
Kells, Antrim E2
Kells, Meath D3
Kenmare B2
Kesh D2
Kilbeggan D3
Kilcar C1
Kilcock D3
Kilcolgan C3
Kilconnell C3
Kilcoole E3
Kilcormac D3
Kilcullen D3
Kildare D3
Kildorrery B4
Kilfenora C3
Kilfinnane C3
Kilgarvan B5
Kilkee C3
Kilkeel E3
Kilkelly C2
Kilkenny D4
Kilkieran B3
Kill D3
Killadysert C3
Killala B1
Killaloe C3
Killarney B2
Killashandra C2
Killeagh C5
Killeigh D3
Killenaule D4
Killimor C3
Killinaboy C3
Killinick D4
Killorglin B2
Killucan D3
Killybegs C1
Killyleagh E2
Killough E2
Kilmacanogue E3
Kilmacrenan D1
Kilmacthomas D4
Kilmaganny D4
Kilmaine C2
Kilmallock C3
Kilmeadan D4
Kilmeaden C5
Kilmichael B5
Kilmore Quay D4
Kilnaleck C2
Kilrea D1
Kilrush C3
Kiltamagh C2
Kiltealy D4
Kilworth B4
Kingscourt D2
Kinlough C1
Kinnegad D3
Kinnitty D3
Kinsale B5
Kinvarra C3
Kircubbin E2
Knock C2
Knockcroghery C2
Knocklong C3
Knocktopher D4

L
Laban C3
Lahinch C3
Lanesborough C2
Laragh D3
Larne E2
Lauragh B2
Laurencetown C3
Leap B5
Leenaun B2
Leighlinbridge D4
Leitrim C2
Letterfrack B2
Letterkenny D1
Lettermacaward C1
Lifford D1
Limavady D1
Limerick C3
Lisbellaw D2
Lisburn E2
Liscannor C3
Liscarroll B4
Lisdoonvarna B3
Lismore C4
Lisnaskea D2
Lispole B2
Lissycasey C3
Listowel C2
Littleton D4
Longford C2
Loughbrickland E2
Loughglinn C2
Loughrea C3
Louisburgh B2
Lucan D3
Lurgan E2

M
Macroom B5
Maghera E2
Magherafelt D2
Magilligan D1
Maguiresbridge D2
Malahide D3

Malin D1
Mallaranny B2
Mallow B4
Manorhamilton C2
Markethill D2
Maum B2
Middleton C5
Milford D1
Millstreet, Cork B5
Millstreet, Waterford D4
Milltown, Galway C2
Milltown, Kerry B2
Milltown Malbay C3
Mitchelstown C4
Moate C3
Mohill C2
Monaghan D2
Moneygall C3
Moneymore D2
Monivea C3
Mountbellew C3
Mountcharles C1
Mountmellick D3
Mountrath D3
Mountshannon C3
Moville D1
Moy D2
Moylough C2
Moynalty D2
Muckross B2
Muff D1
Mullany's Cross B2
Mullinavat D4
Mullingar C3

N
Naas D3
Navan D3
Naul D3
Nenagh C3

New Ross D4
Newbliss D2
Newbridge D3
Newcastle, Down E2
Newcastle West C3
Newinn C4
Newmarket B4
Newmarket-on-Fergus C3
Newport, Mayo B2
Newport, Tipperary C3
Newry D2
Newtown D4
Newtown Cunningham D1
Newtown Sands C2
Newtownabbey E2
Newtownards E2
Newtownbutler D2
Newtownhamilton D2
Newtown-mountkennedy E3
Newtownstewart D2
Nineimilehouse D4

O
Oilgate D4
Omagh D2
Oranmore C3
Oughterard C3

P
Pallas Green C3
Parknasilla B2
Partry C2
Passage East D4
Passage West B5
Patrickswell C3
Paulstown D4
Peterswell C3

Pettigo D2
Plumbridge D1
Pomeroy D2
Pontoon C2
Portadown D2
Portaferry E2
Portarlington D3
Portavogie E2
Portglenone D2
Portlaoise D3
Portmagee A2
Portnoo C1
Portrush D1
Portstewart D1
Portumna C3
Poyntz Pass D2

R
Randalstown D2
Raphoe D1
Rathcole D3
Rathcormack B4
Rathdrum E3
Rathfriland D2
Rathkeale C3
Rathmelton D1
Rathmolyon D3
Rathmore B2
Rathmullan D1
Rathnew E3
Rathowen C3
Ratoath D3
Recess B2
Ringaskiddy B5
Rockcorry D2
Roosky C2
Roscommon C3
Roscrea C3
Rosmult D3
Rosslare D4
Rosslare Harbour D4

Rosslea D2
Roundwood E3
Rush D3

S
Saint Johnstown D1
Sallins D3
Saltfield D2
Scarriff C3
Screeb B2
Seskinore D2
Shanagolden C3
Shercock D2
Shillelagh D4
Silvermines C3
Sion Mills D2
Skerries D3
Skibbereen B5
Slane D3
Sligo C2
Sneem B2
Stradbally D3
Strabane D1
Strandhill C2
Strangford E2
Strokestown C2
Swanlinbar D2
Swatragh D2
Swinford C2
Swords D3

T
Tallaght D3
Tallow C4
Tarbert C2
Templederry C3
Templemore D3
Templetouhy D3
Termonfeckin D3
Thomas Street C3
Thomastown D4
Thurles D3
Timoleague B5
Timolin D3
Tipperary C4
Tobercurry C2
Toomyvara C3
Tralee C2
Tramore D4
Trim D3
Tuam C2
Tuamgraney C3
Tubbercurry C2
Tulla C3
Tullamore D3
Tullow D4
Tulsk C2
Tyrrellspass D3

U
Urlingford D3

V
Virginia D2

W
Waterpoint B5
Waterford D4
Watergrasshill B5
Waterville A2
Wellingtonbridge D4
Westport B2
Wexford D4
Whitegate C5
Whitehead E2
Wicklow E3

Y
Youghal C5

Distance table

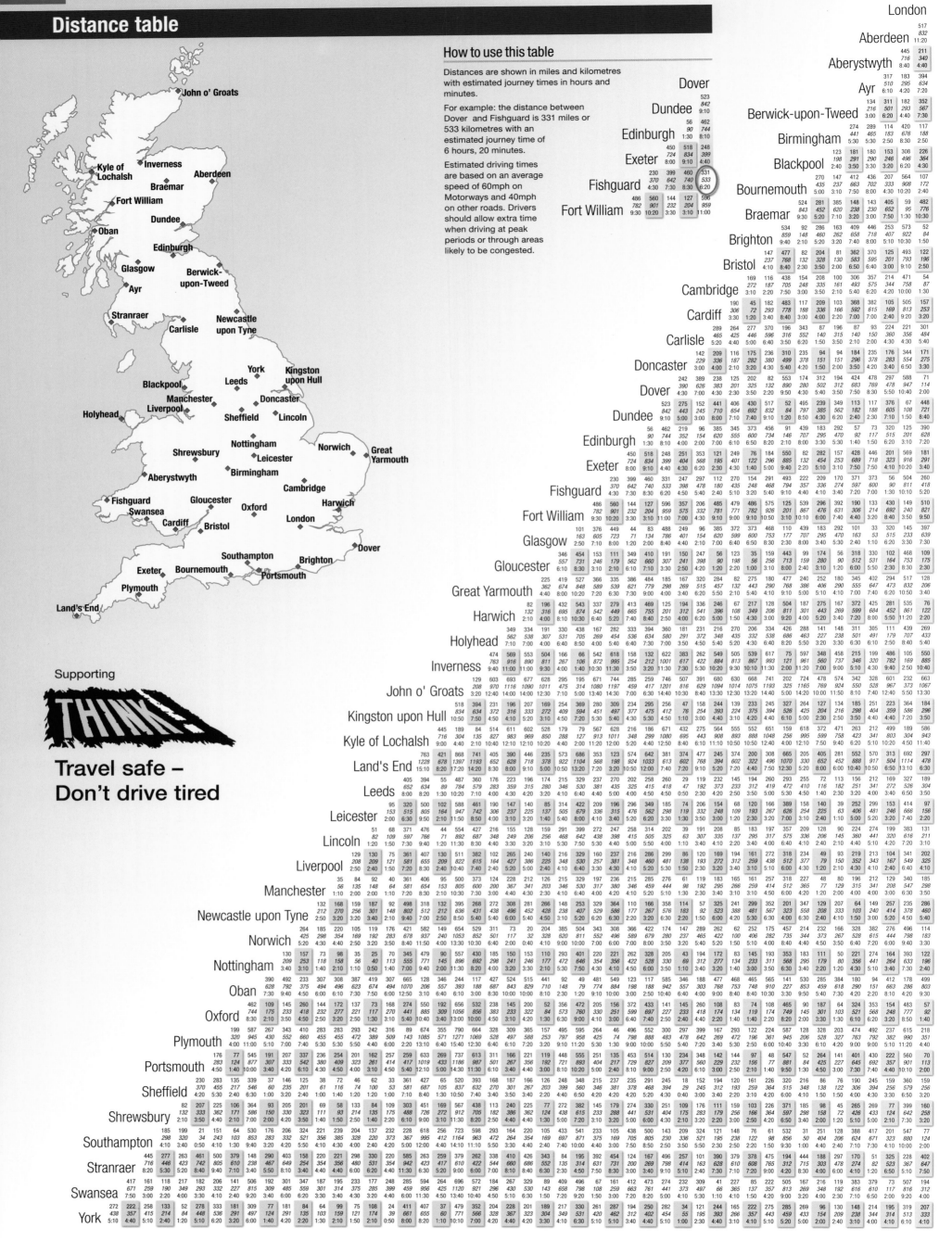

How to use this table

Distances are shown in miles and kilometres with estimated journey times in hours and minutes.

For example: the distance between Dover and Fishguard is 331 miles or 533 kilometres with an estimated journey time of 6 hours, 20 minutes.

Estimated driving times are based on an average speed of 60mph on Motorways and 40mph on other roads. Drivers should allow extra time when driving at peak periods or through areas likely to be congested.

Supporting

THINK!

Travel safe – Don't drive tired

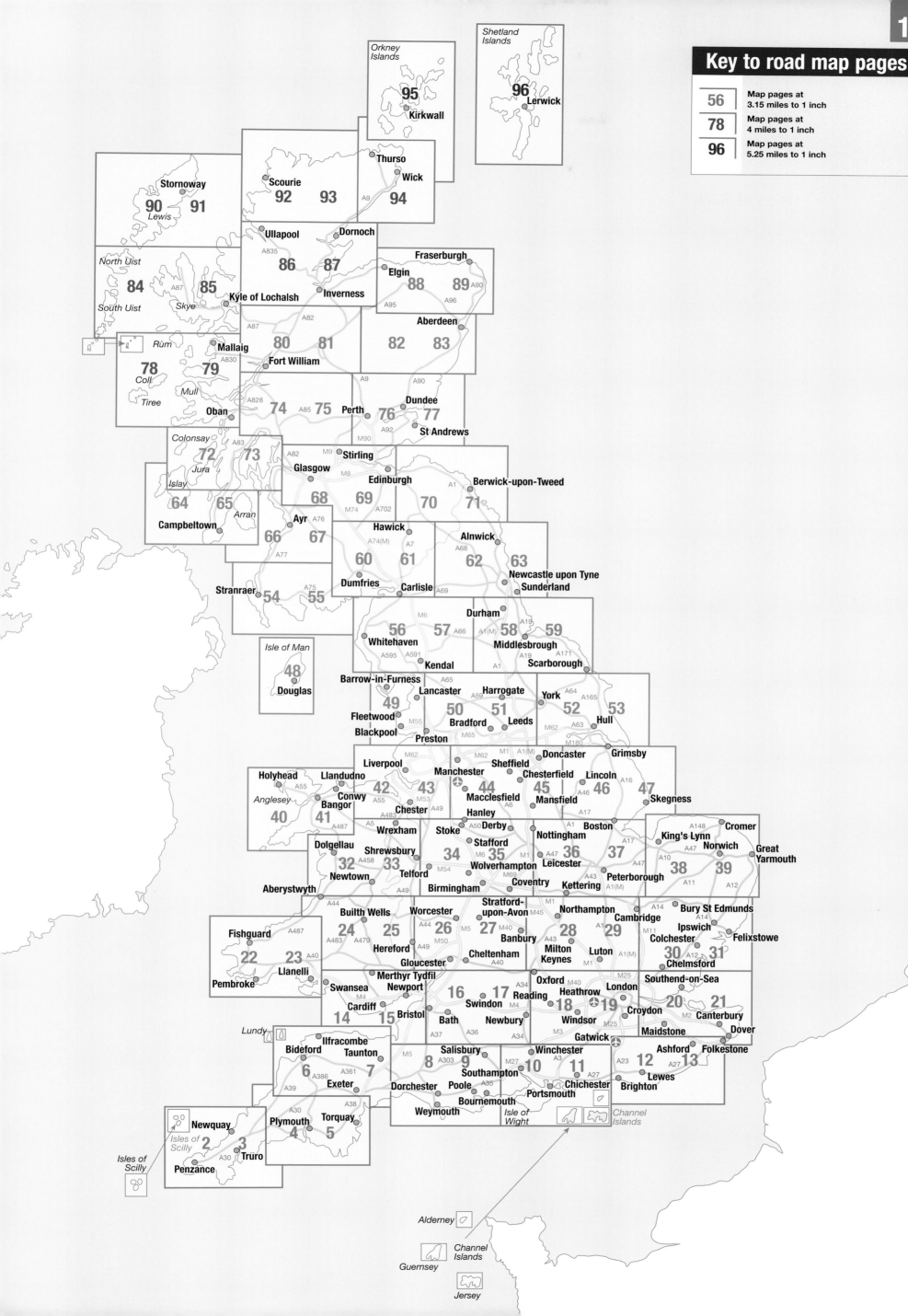

Key to road map pages

56	Map pages at 3.15 miles to 1 inch
78	Map pages at 4 miles to 1 inch
96	Map pages at 5.25 miles to 1 inch

Orkney Islands

Shetland Islands

95 Kirkwall

96 Lerwick

Stornoway
90 **91**
Lewis

Thurso
Scourie **92** **93** Wick
A9 **94**

North Uist

Ullapool Dornoch
84 **85** A835 **86** **87**
South Uist Skye Kyle of Lochalsh Inverness
A87

Rùm Mallaig
78 **79** A830 Fort William
Coll **80** **81** **82** **83**
Tiree Mull Oban A9

Fraserburgh
Elgin **88** **89** A90
A95 A96

Aberdeen

A9 A90

Dundee
74 A85 **75** Perth **76** **77**
A828 A82 M90 A92 St Andrews

Colonsay
72 **73** A82 M9 Stirling
Jura A83 Glasgow M8
Islay Edinburgh Berwick-upon-Tweed A1
64 **65** **68** **69** **70** **71**
Arran M74 A702
Campbeltown Ayr A76
66 **67** Hawick Alnwick
A77 **60** **61** A7 **62** A68 **63**
Dumfries Newcastle upon Tyne
Stranraer Carlisle A69 Sunderland
54 **55** A74(M)

Durham
M6 A66 A1(M) A19
56 **57** **58** **59**
Whitehaven Middlesbrough
A595 A591 A1 Scarborough
Isle of Man Kendal A19 A171
48 Barrow-in-Furness A65
Douglas Lancaster A59 Harrogate York A64 A165
49 **50** **51** **52** **53**
Fleetwood Bradford Leeds Hull
Blackpool M55 M62 A63
Preston M65 M180
Liverpool M62 Doncaster Grimsby
Holyhead Llandudno M62 Sheffield
42 **43** **44** Chesterfield Lincoln **47**
Anglesey Conwy Manchester **45** **46** A16
A55 Bangor Macclesfield A6 Mansfield A46 Skegness
40 **41** Chester A49 M53 A17
A487 Hanley A50 Boston
Wrexham Stoke Derby Nottingham A148 Cromer
Dolgellau A5 Shrewsbury Stafford A1 King's Lynn
32 **33** **34** **35** **36** **37** A47 Norwich **39**
Newtown A458 Telford M6 Leicester A47 A10 Great Yarmouth
Aberystwyth A49 Wolverhampton A47 **38** A47 A12
Birmingham M69 Kettering A11
Builth Wells M42 Peterborough A1(M)
24 **25** **26** **27** **28** **29** A14 Bury St Edmunds
A483 A479 Worcester Stratford- M45 Northampton A14
Fishguard A487 A44 upon-Avon Cambridge Ipswich
22 **23** A40 Hereford M5 Banbury A43 **30** **31** Felixstowe
Pembroke Llanelli A49 Cheltenham Milton Luton Colchester A12
M50 Keynes A1(M) Chelmsford
Swansea Merthyr Tydfil Gloucester A40 Oxford M40 London
Newport **16** **17** A34 Heathrow Southend-on-Sea
Cardiff **14** **15** Bristol Swindon Reading M4 **18** **19** **20** **21**
M4 Bath Newbury Windsor Croydon Canterbury
Lundy Newquay A37 A36 A34 M3 M25 Maidstone Dover
Ilfracombe M5 Gatwick
Bideford Taunton Salisbury Winchester Ashford Folkestone
6 **7** **8** A303 **9** **10** **11** **12** **13**
A386 Exeter A361 Southampton A3 Lewes A27
Dorchester Poole A35 Chichester Brighton
Plymouth Torquay Bournemouth Portsmouth
Newquay **4** **5** Weymouth Isle of Wight Channel Islands
2 **3**
Isles of Scilly Truro
Penzance A30

Isles of Scilly

Alderney

Channel Islands
Guernsey

Jersey

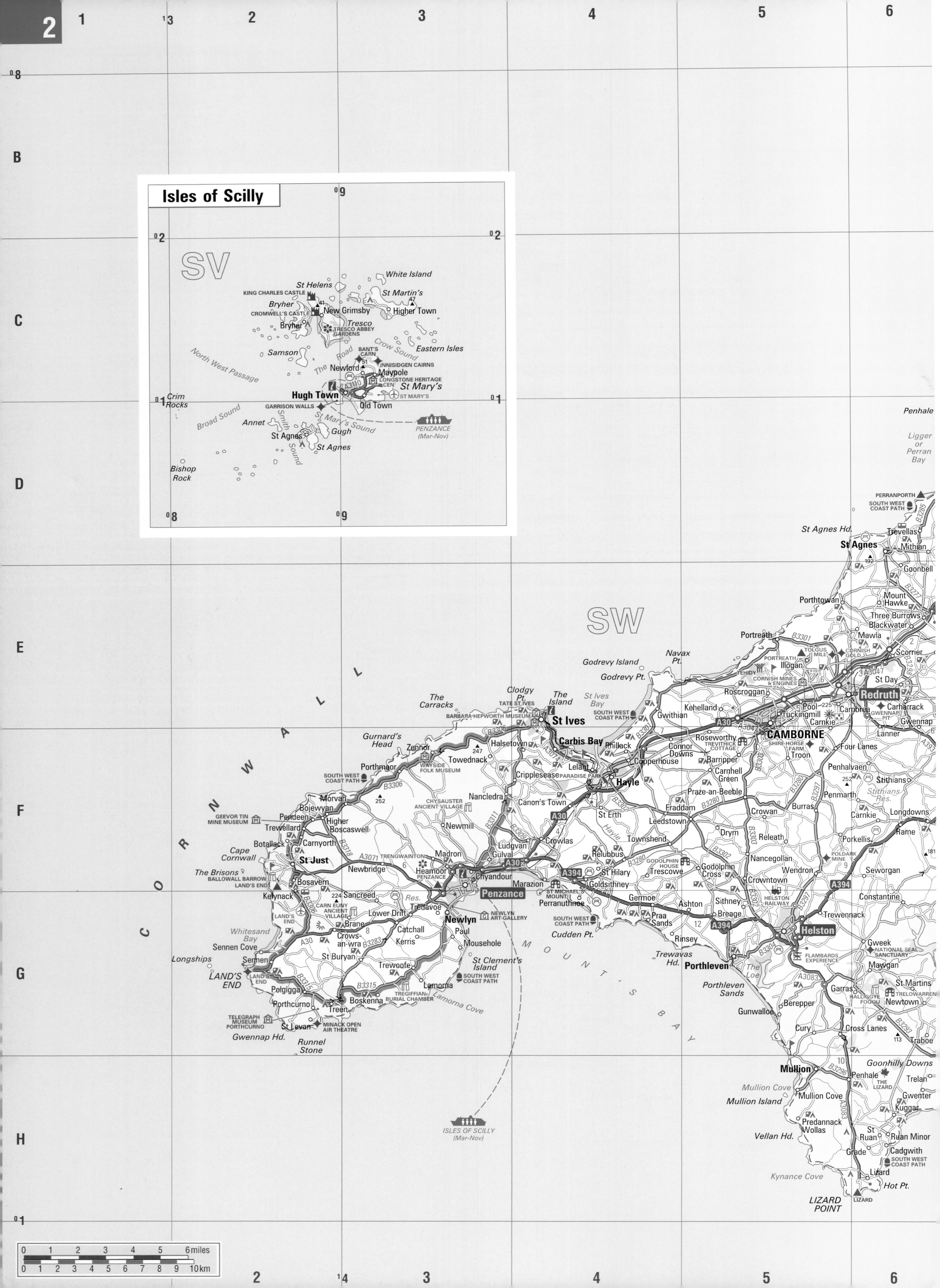

1   3   2   3   4   5   6

8

B

Isles of Scilly

9

2   2

SV

White Island

St Helens

KING CHARLES CASTLE   St Martin's
Bryher   41   47
CROMWELL'S CASTLE   New Grimsby   Higher Town
Bryher   Tresco
                    TRESCO ABBEY
C   GARDENS
Samson   Eastern Isles
                    Crow Sound
North West Passage   BANT'S
                    CARN
The Road   Newford   51   INNISIDGEN CAIRNS
                         Maypole
                    LONGSTONE HERITAGE
                    CEN   St Mary's
Crim   1   Hugh Town   1
Rocks   Old Town
         St Mary's   St Mary's
         GARRISON WALLS   Sound
Broad Sound   Penhale
Annet   Smith Sound   PENZANCE   Ligger
St Agnes   Gugh   (Mar-Nov)   or
         St Agnes   Perran
                         Bay
Bishop
Rock

D

8   9

PERRANPORTH
SOUTH WEST
COAST PATH

St Agnes Hd.   Trevellas
St Agnes   192   Mithian
                    Goonbell

Mount
Porthtowan   Hawke
Three Burrows
SW   Blackwater
Portreath   B3301   Mawla
PORTREATH   TEHIDY   Scorrier
PORTREATH   TOLGUS   CORNISH
MILL   GOLD   St Day
CORNISH MINES   A3047
Godrevy Island   Navax   & ENGINES   A3047
Pt.   Roscroggan   Pool   Redruth
Godrevy Pt.   Carn Brea
The   Clodgy   St Ives   Gwithian   Tuckingmill   Carharrack
Carracks   Pt.   TATE ST IVES   Bay   Kehelland   -225   Carn Brea   Carnkie
         The Island   SOUTH WEST   Gwennap
         St Ives   COAST PATH   Connor   PIT
E   BARBARA HEPWORTH MUSEUM   St Ives   A30   Downs   CAMBORNE   Gwennap
   B3306   St Ives   A304
Gurnard's   Halsetown   Carbis Bay   Phillack   Roseworthy   SHIRE HORSE   Four Lanes
Head   Zennor   Carbis Bay   Copperhouse   TREVITHICK   FARM &   Lanner
   WAYSIDE   Towednack   Lelant   Hayle   COTTAGE   Barripper   Troon   Penhalvaen
   FOLK MUSEUM   Connor   Praze-an-Beeble   Stithians
Porthmeor   Hayle   Carnhell   Stithians
SOUTH WEST   CHYSAUSTER   Nancledra   Canon's Town   Fraddam   Green   Res.
COAST PATH   ANCIENT VILLAGE   Crowan   Burras
Morvah   Newmill   St Erth   Leedstown   Carnkie
F   Bojewyan   252   Townshend   Drym   Releath   Porkellis   Rame
GEEVOR TIN   Higher   Ludgvan   Crowlas   POLDARK   Longdowns
MINE MUSEUM   Boscaswell   Madron   Gulval   Godolphin   MINE
Pendeen   Trewellard   Cross   Nancegollan
Botallack   Carnyorth   Heamoor   Chyandour   GODOLPHIN   Crowntown   Wendron   Sewargan
Cape   TRENGWAINTON   PENZANCE   HOUSE   TRESCOWE
Cornwall   St Just   A3071   Marazion   St Hilary   Goldsithney   Ashton   Sithney
The Brisons   Newbridge   ST MICHAEL'S   Germoe   Breage   A394   Trewennack
BALLOWALL BARROW   Bosavern   6   MOUNT   Praa   12   HELSTON   Constantine
LAND'S END   Perranuthnoe   Sands   Rinsey   RAILWAY   Helston
Kelynack   224   Sancreed   Tredavoe   NEWLYN   SOUTH WEST   Cudden Pt.   Gweek
LAND'S   CARN EUNY   Lower Drift   Newlyn   ART GALLERY   COAST PATH   NATIONAL SEAL
END   ANCIENT   Brane   Paul   FLAMBARDS   SANCTUARY
G   Whitesand   VILLAGE   Crows-   Catchall   Mousehole   EXPERIENCE   Mawgan
Bay   an-wra   B3283   Kerris   St Clement's   Trewavas   Garras   St Martins
Sennen Cove   St Buryan   Trewoofe   Island   Hd.   Porthleven   Treloweren
Longships   Sennen   Trewoofe   Lamorna   Porthleven   The   Berepper   Newtown
LAND'S   B3315   TREGIFFIAN   SOUTH WEST   Sands   Loe
END   Boskenna   BURIAL CHAMBER   COAST PATH   Gunwalloe   Cury   Cross Lanes
Polgigga   Porthcurno   Treen   Lamorna Cove   113   Traboe
TELEGRAPH   MINACK OPEN   MOUNT'S   Goonhilly Downs
MUSEUM   AIR THEATRE   BAY   Mullion   Penhale   Trelan
PORTHCURNO   St Levan   Mullion Cove   THE   Gwenter
Gwennap Hd.   Runnel   ISLES OF SCILLY   Mullion Cove   LIZARD   Kuggar
         Stone   (Mar-Nov)   Mullion Island
H   Predannack   St   Ruan Minor
                                    Wollas   Ruan   Cadgwith
                              Vellan Hd.   Grade   SOUTH WEST
                                          COAST PATH
                              Kynance Cove   Lizard
                                             Hot Pt.
1   LIZARD   LIZARD
                           POINT

0   1   2   3   4   5   6 miles
0 1 2 3 4 5 6 7 8 9 10km

2   4   3   4   5   6

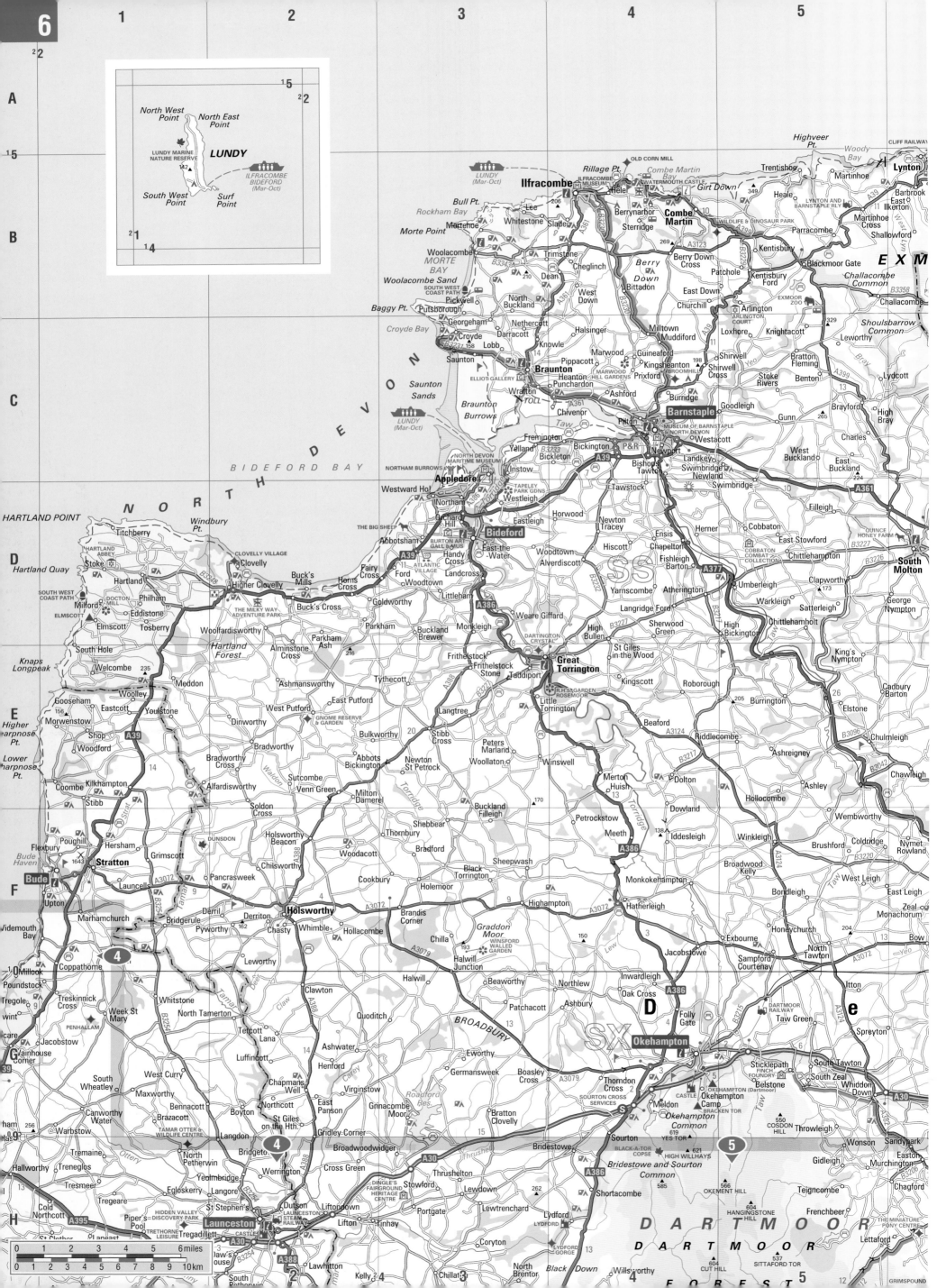

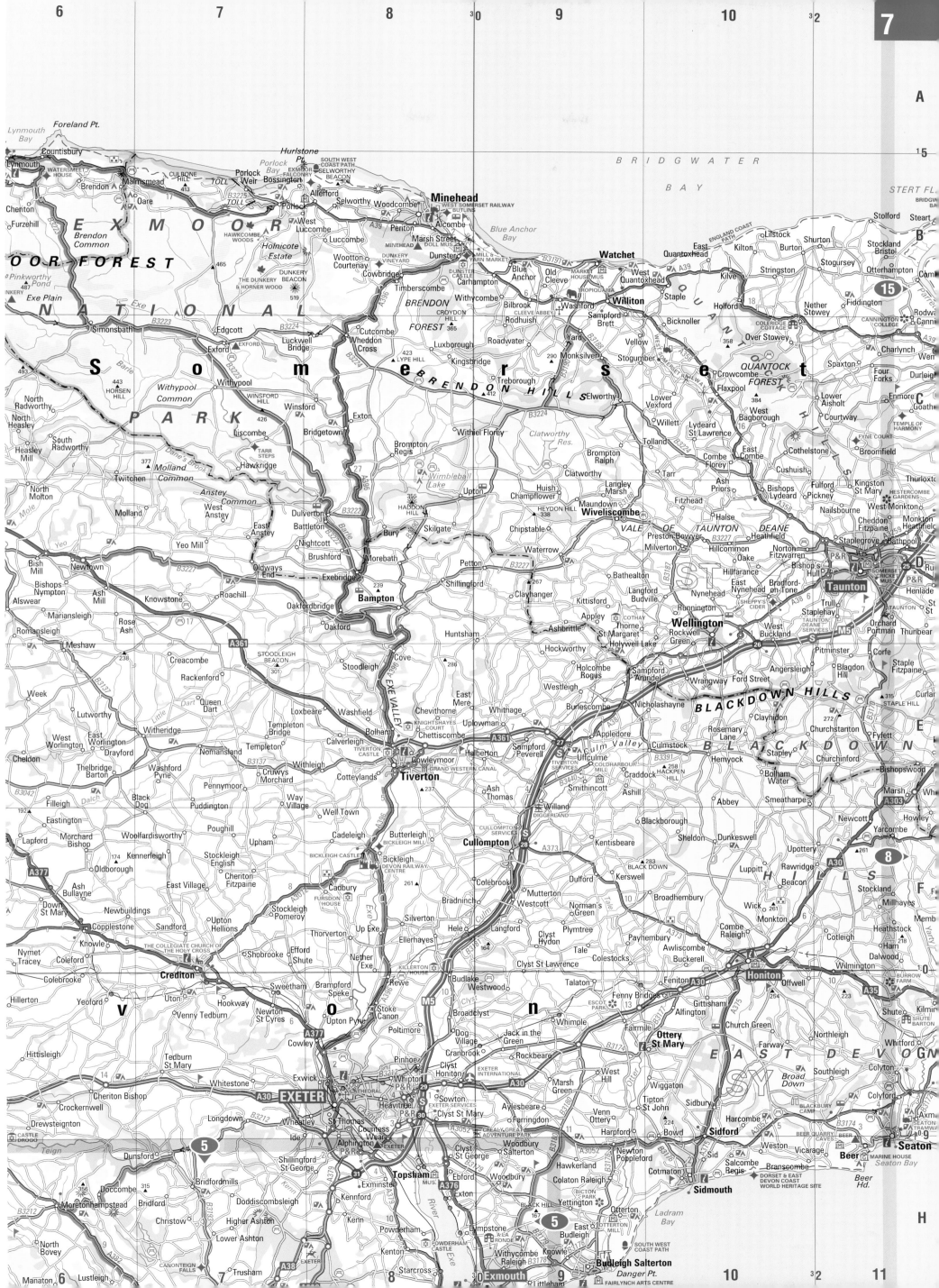

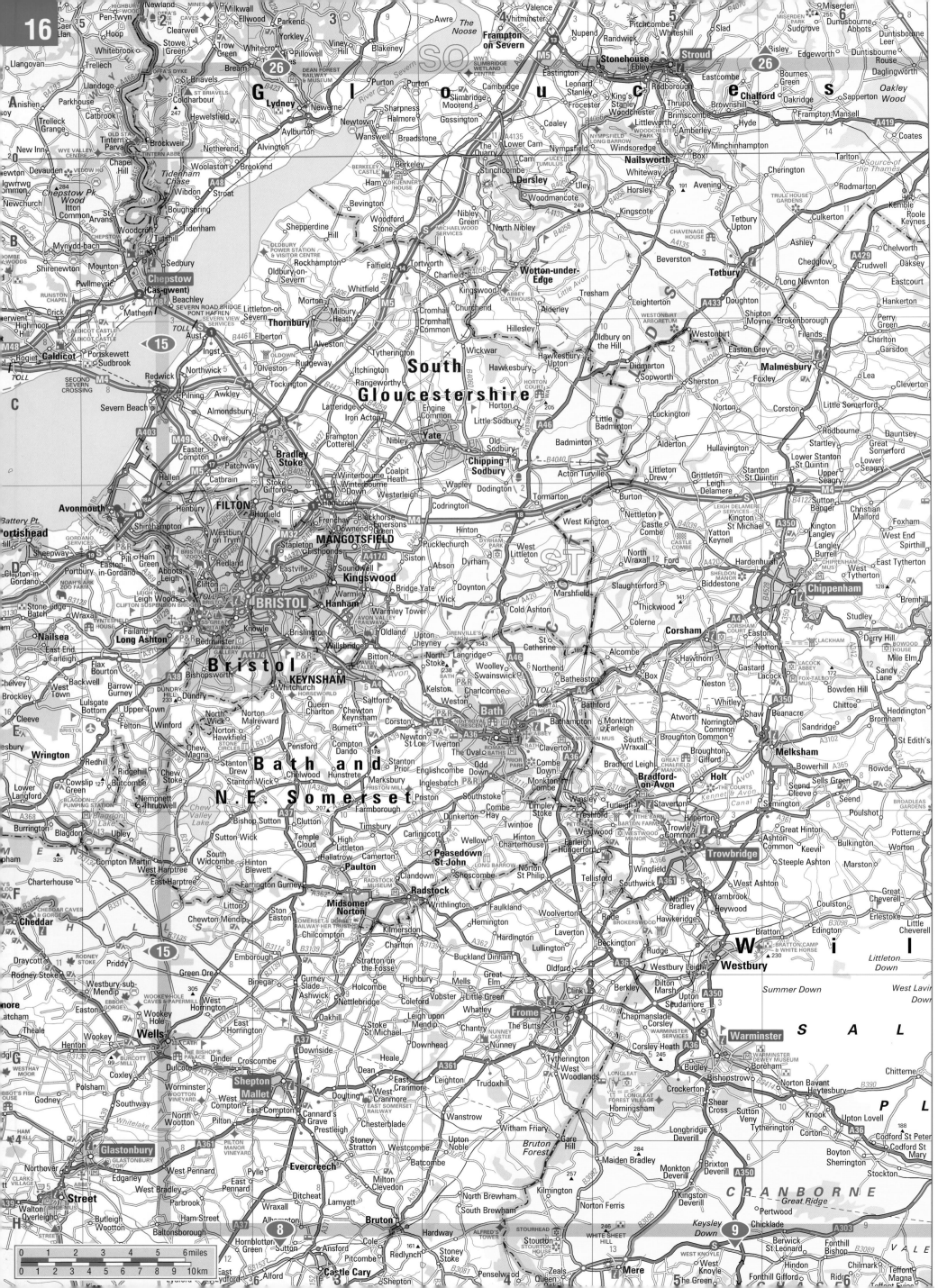

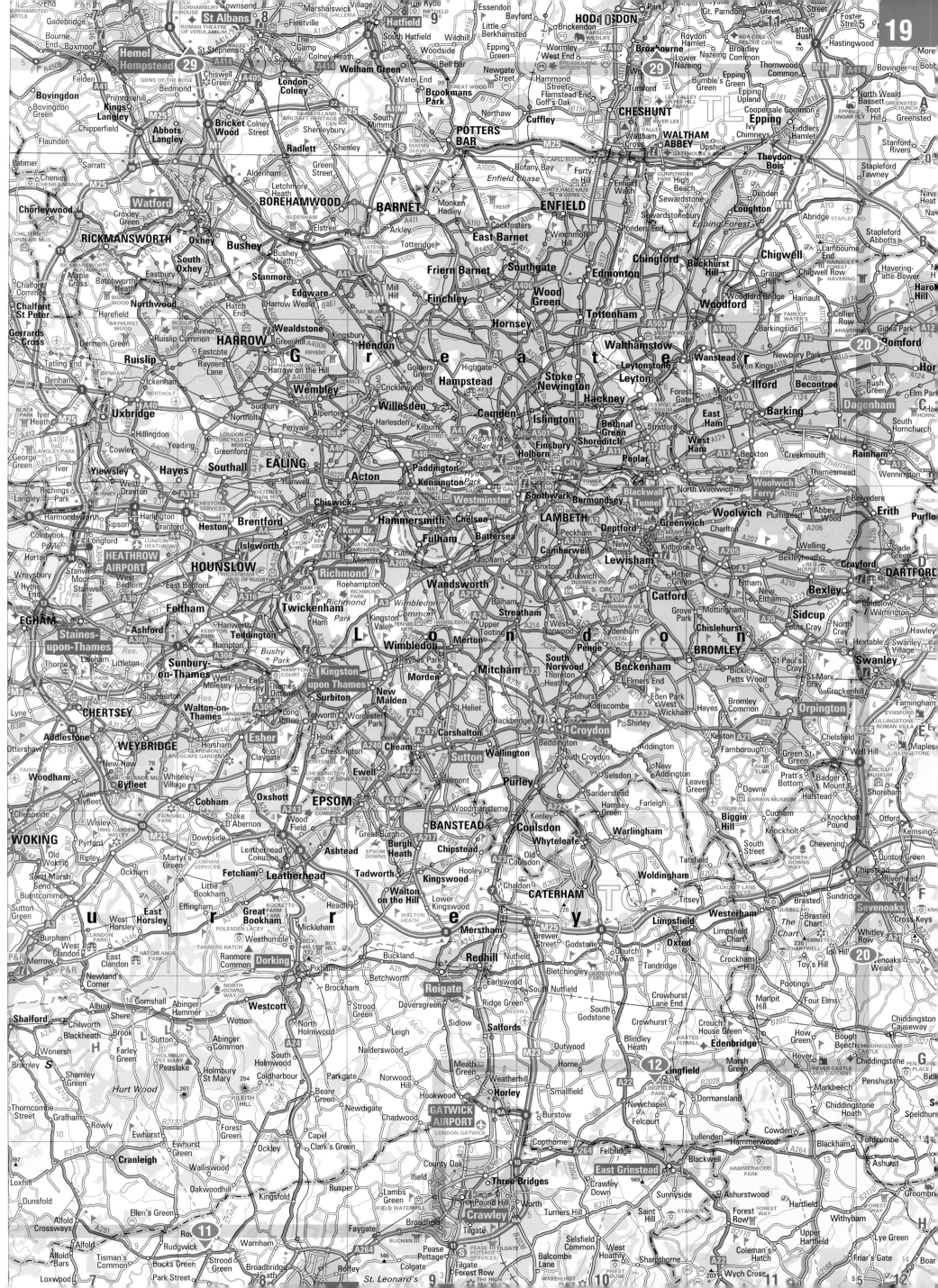

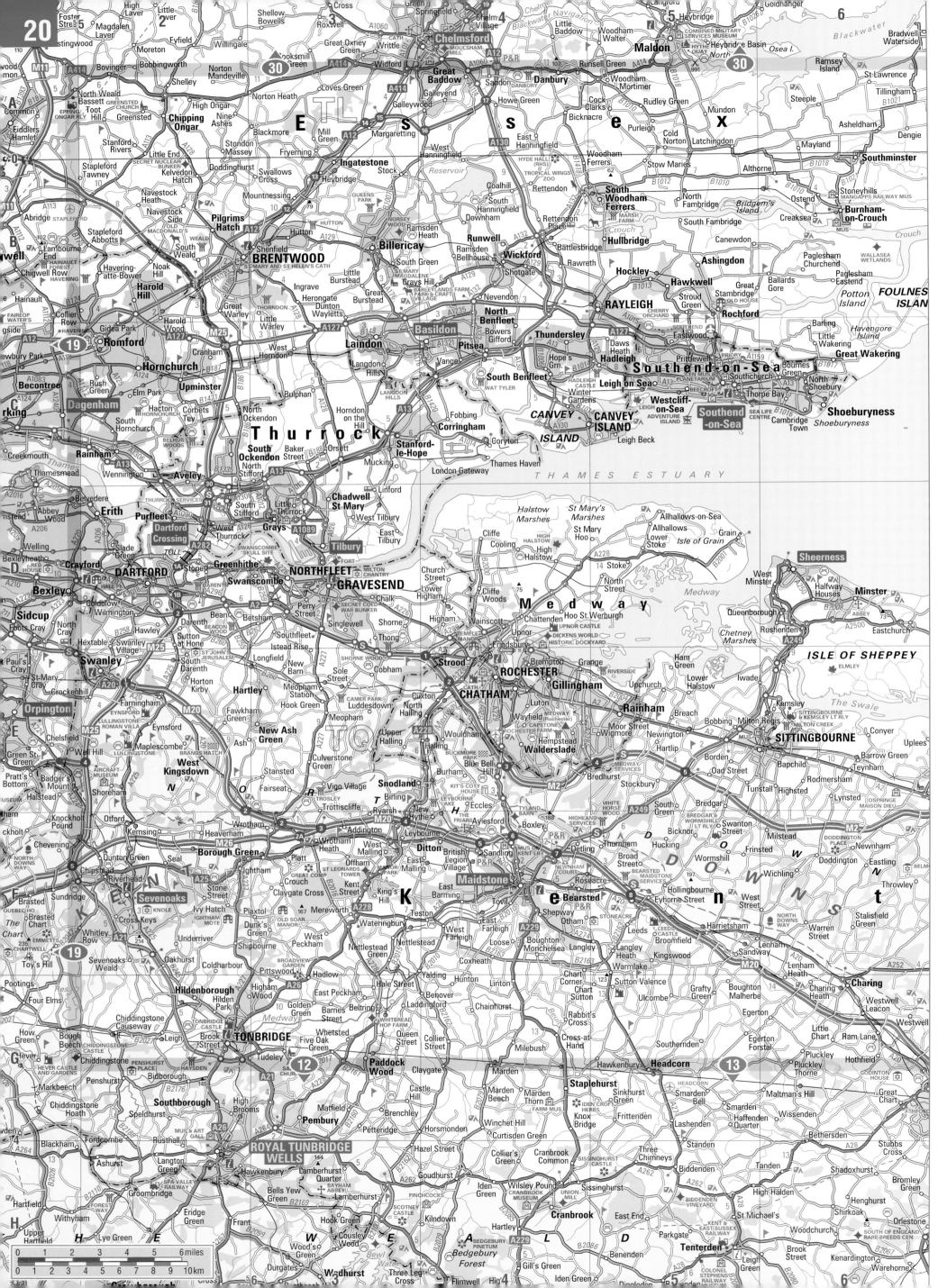

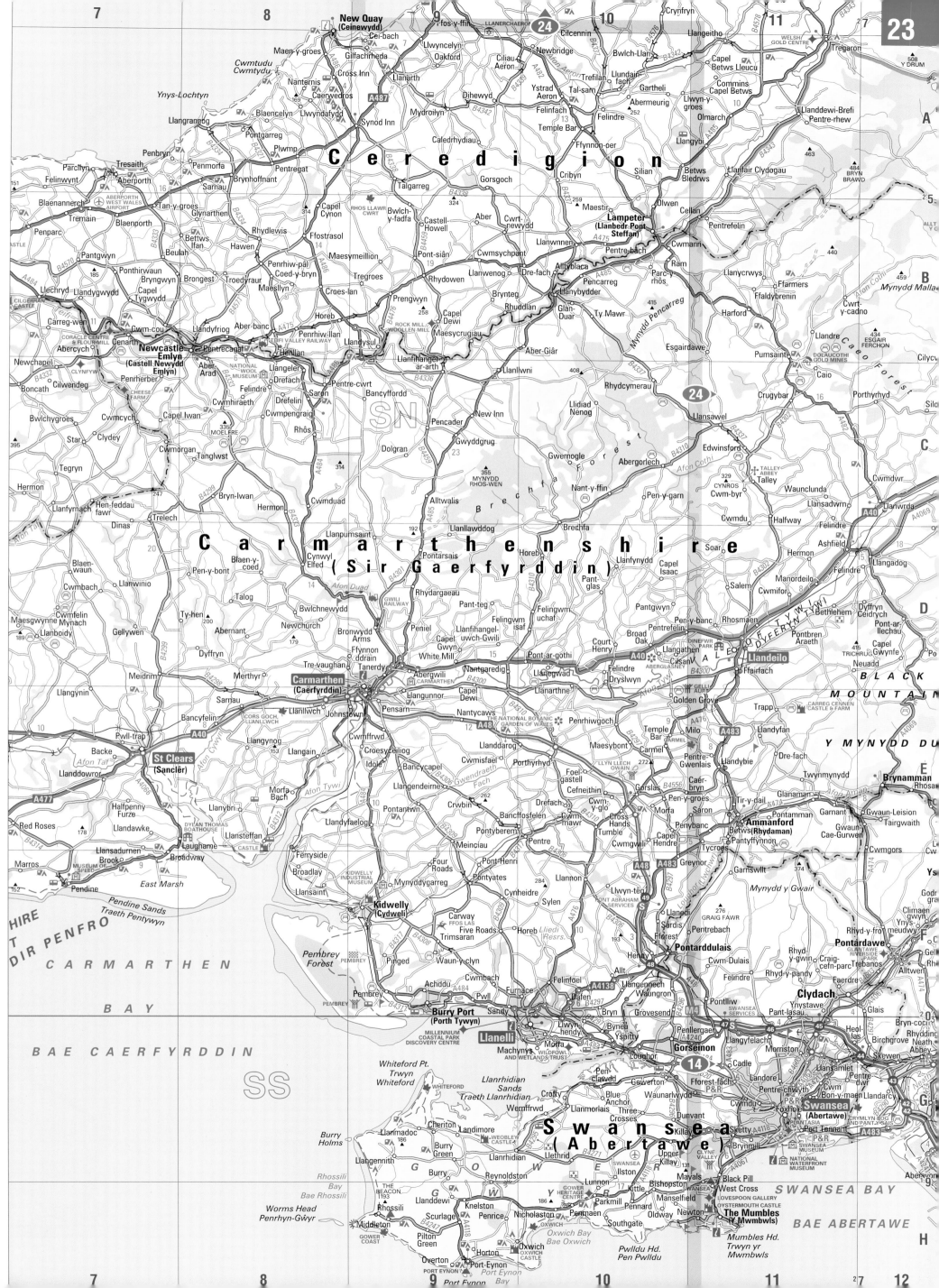

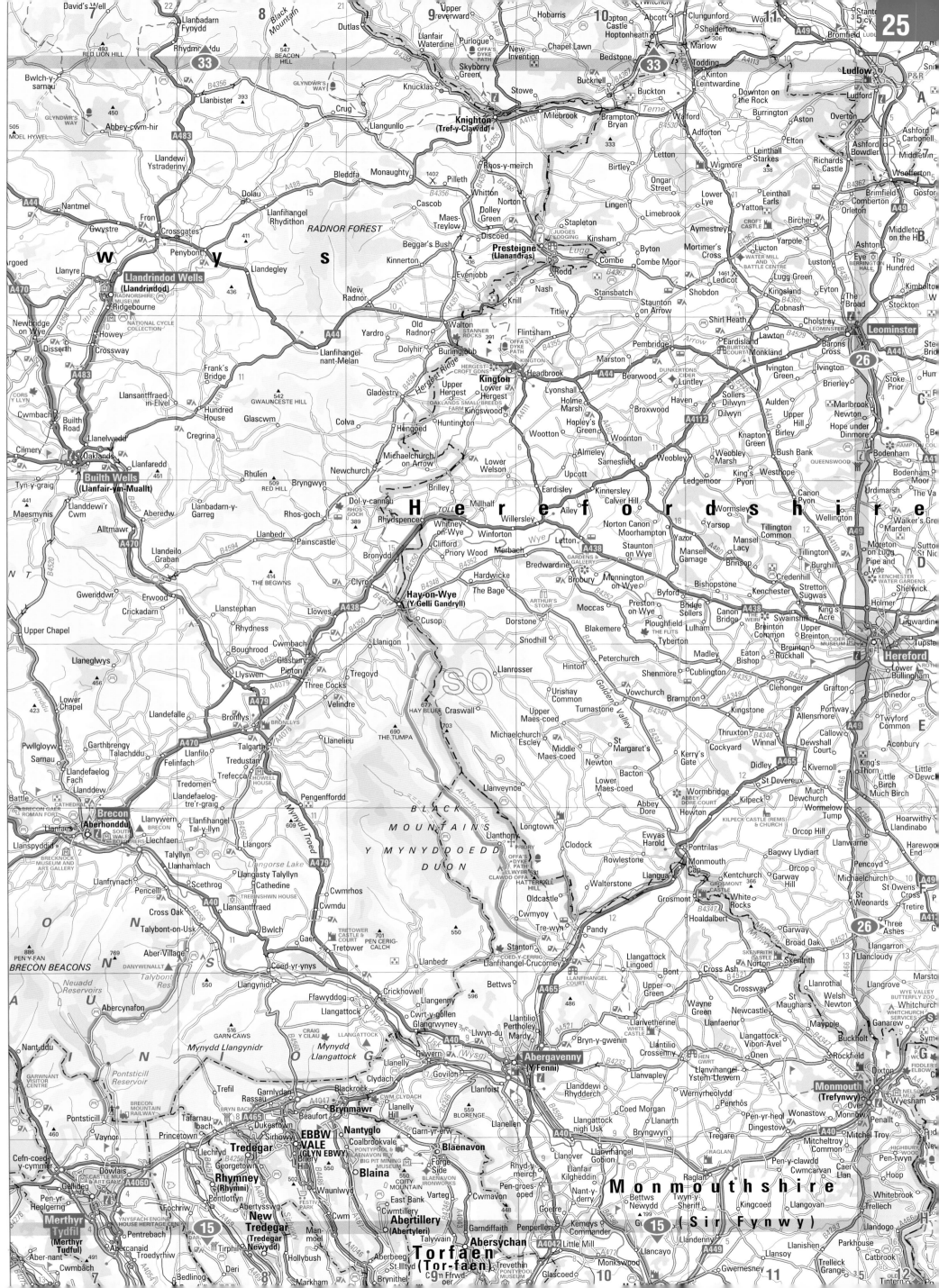

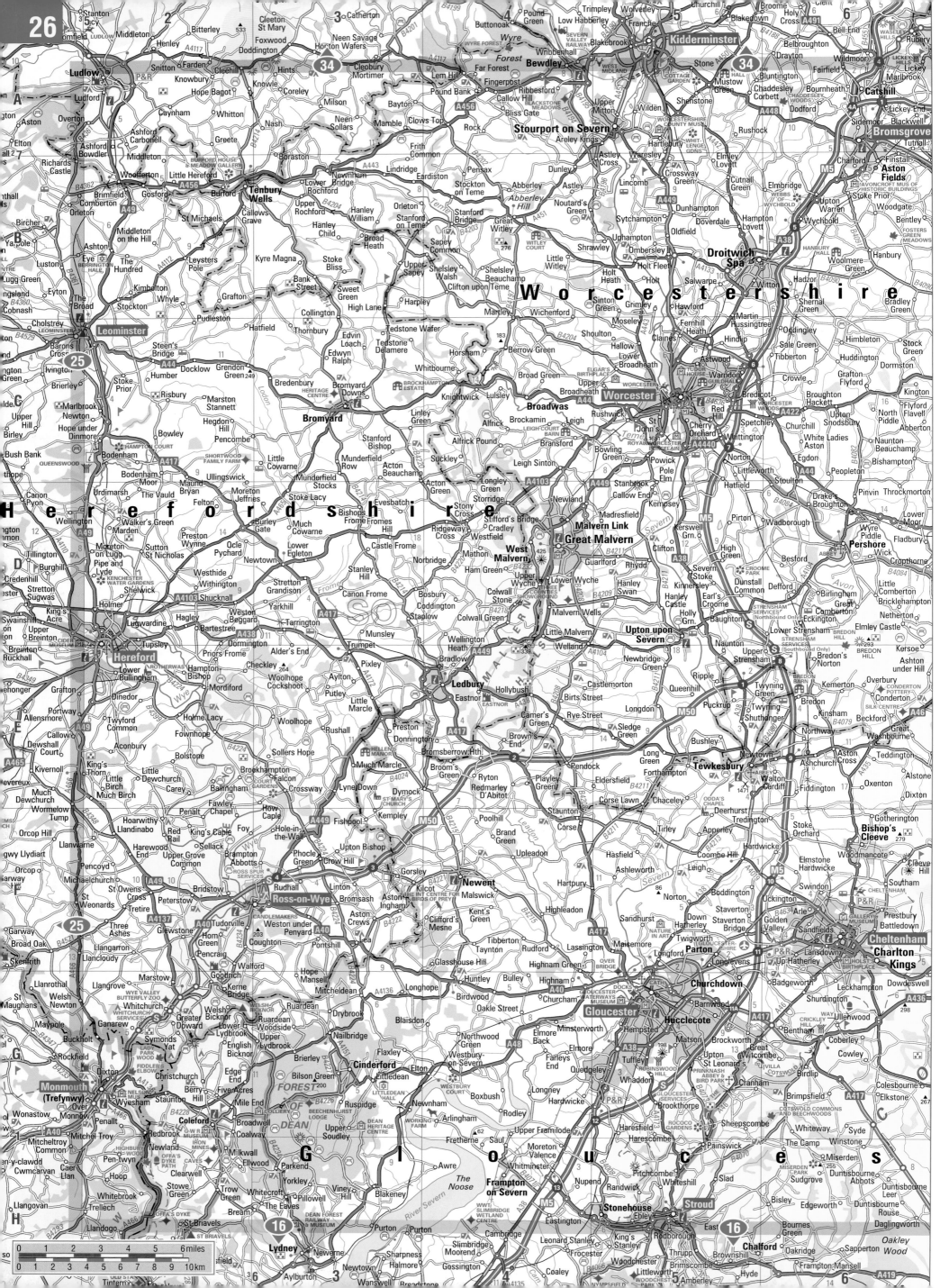

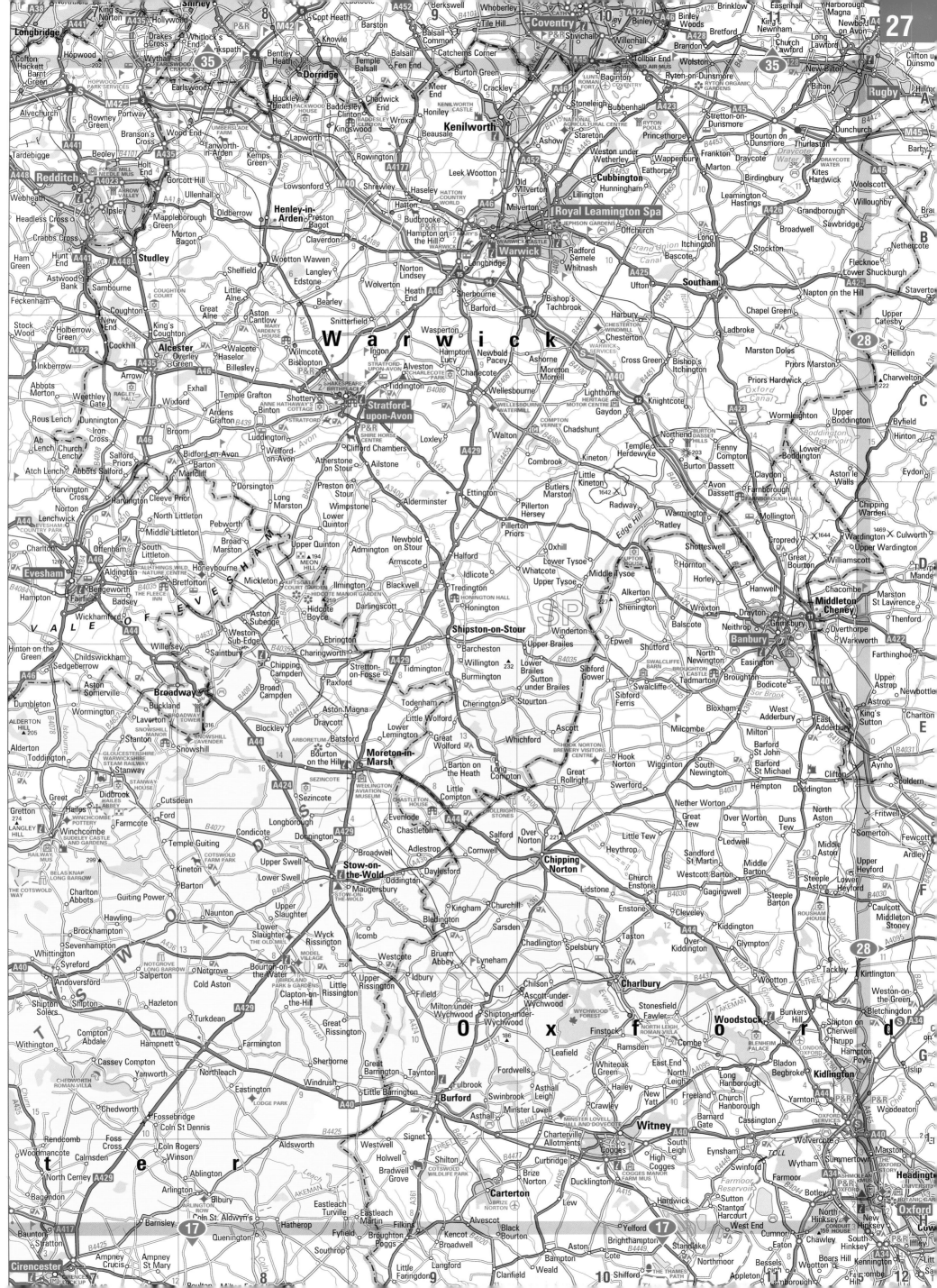

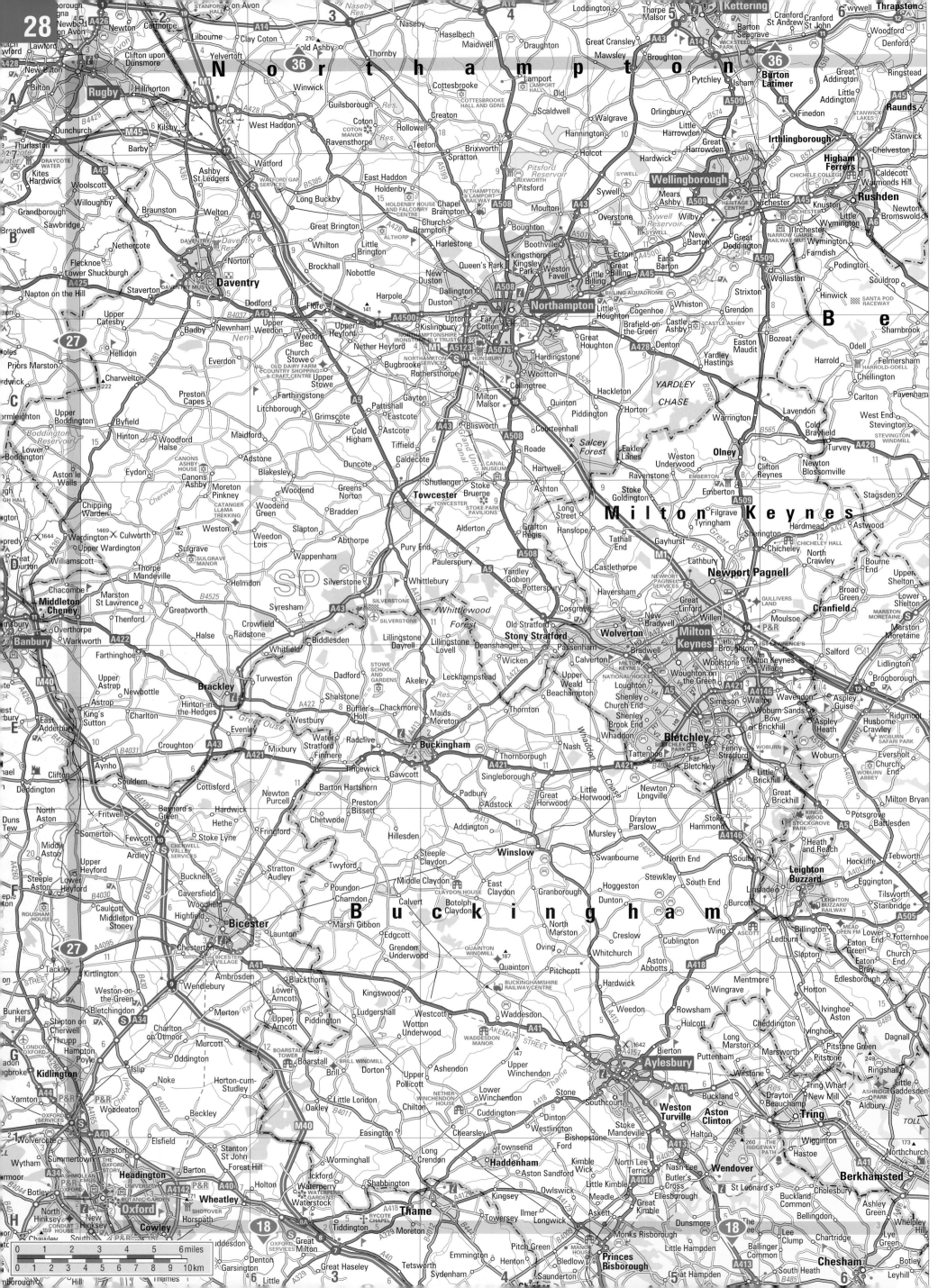

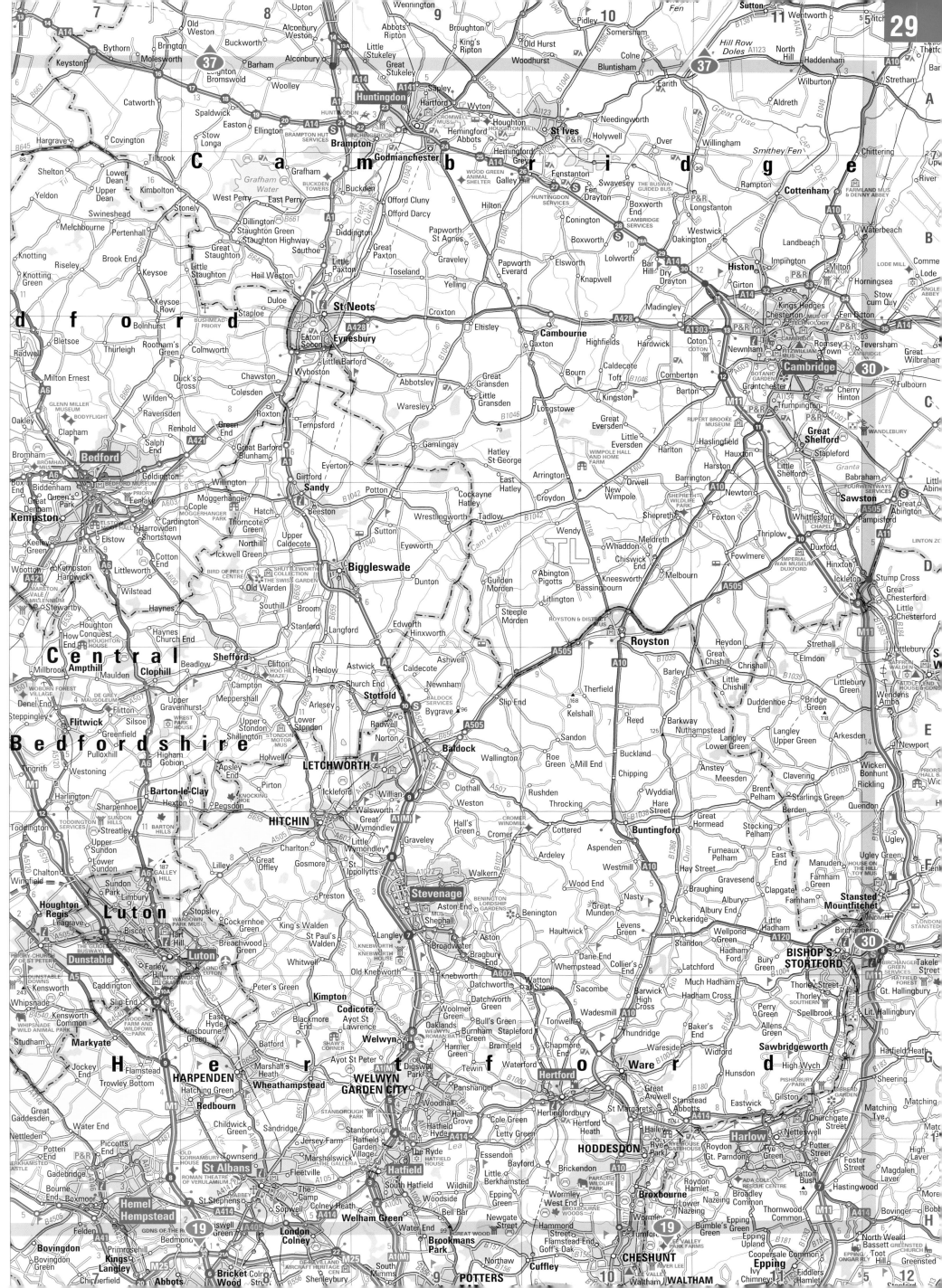

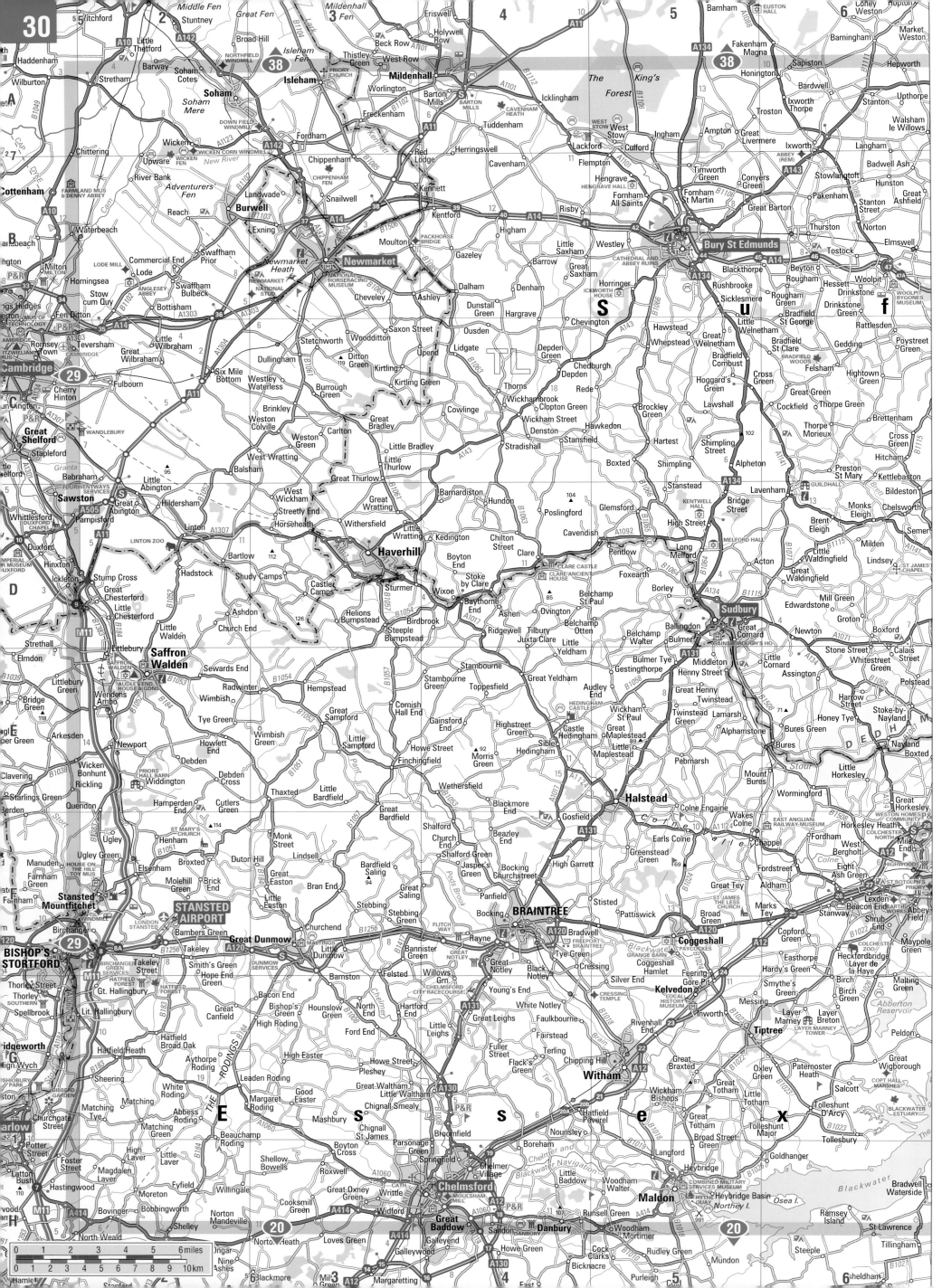

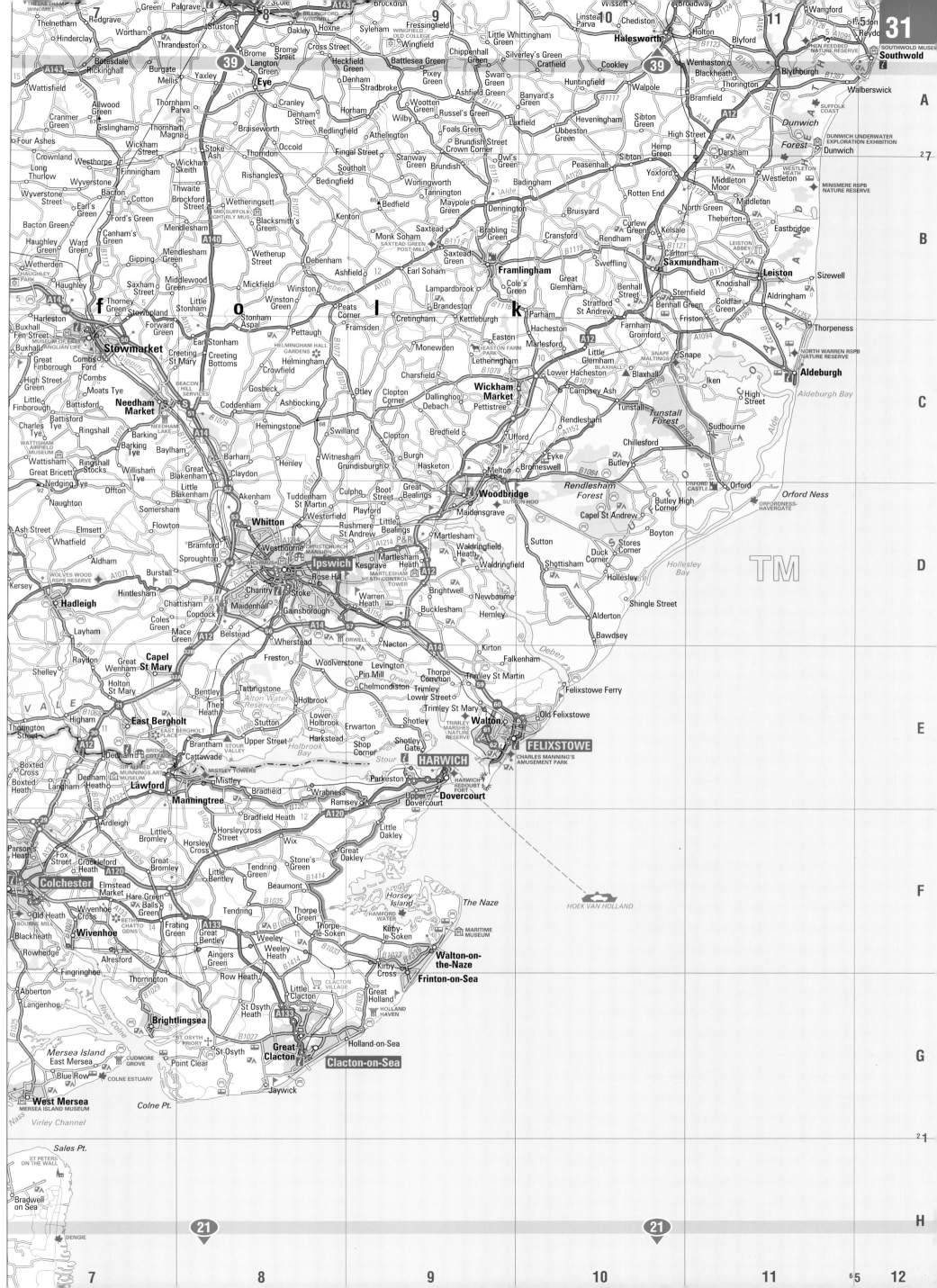

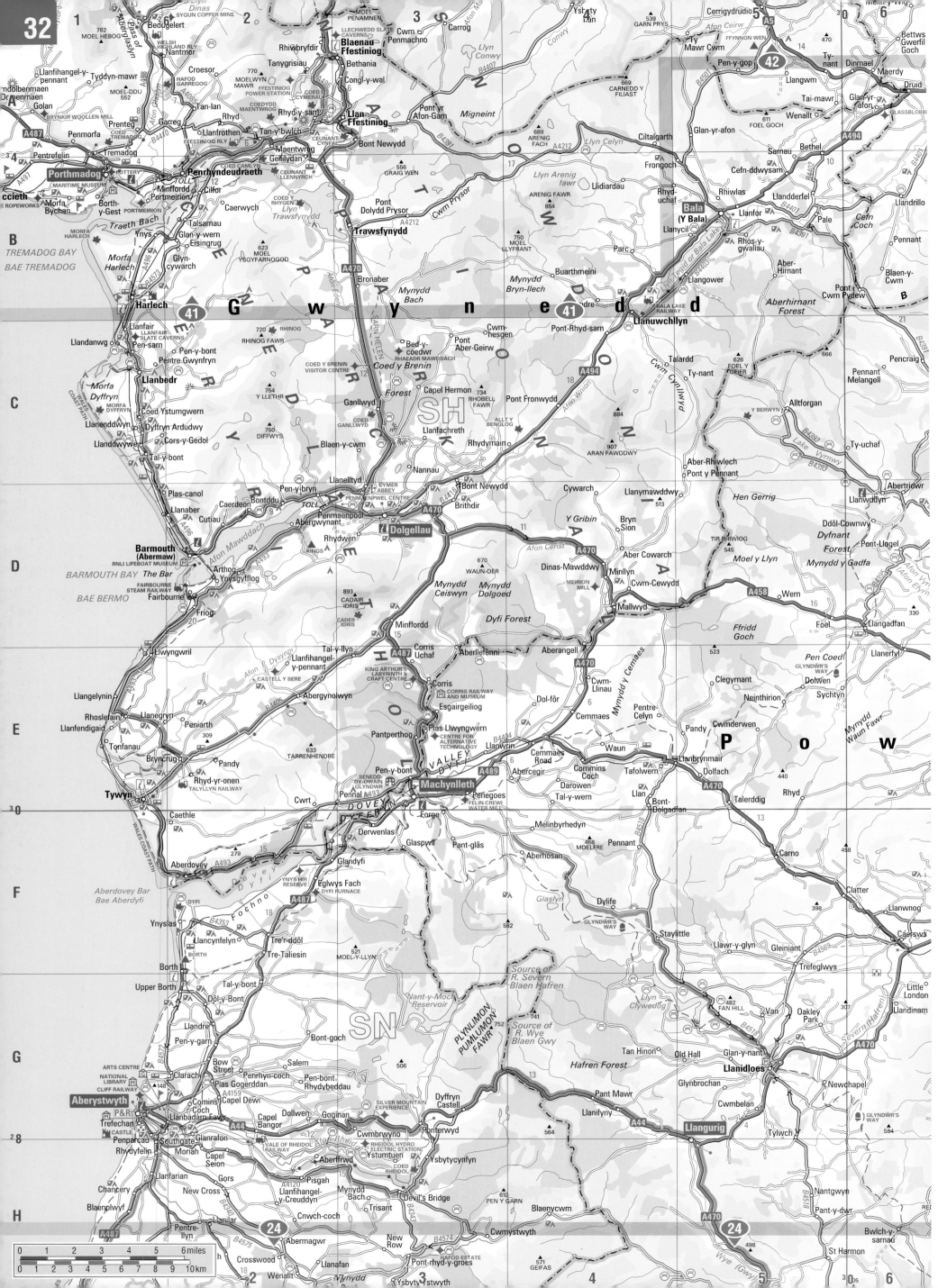

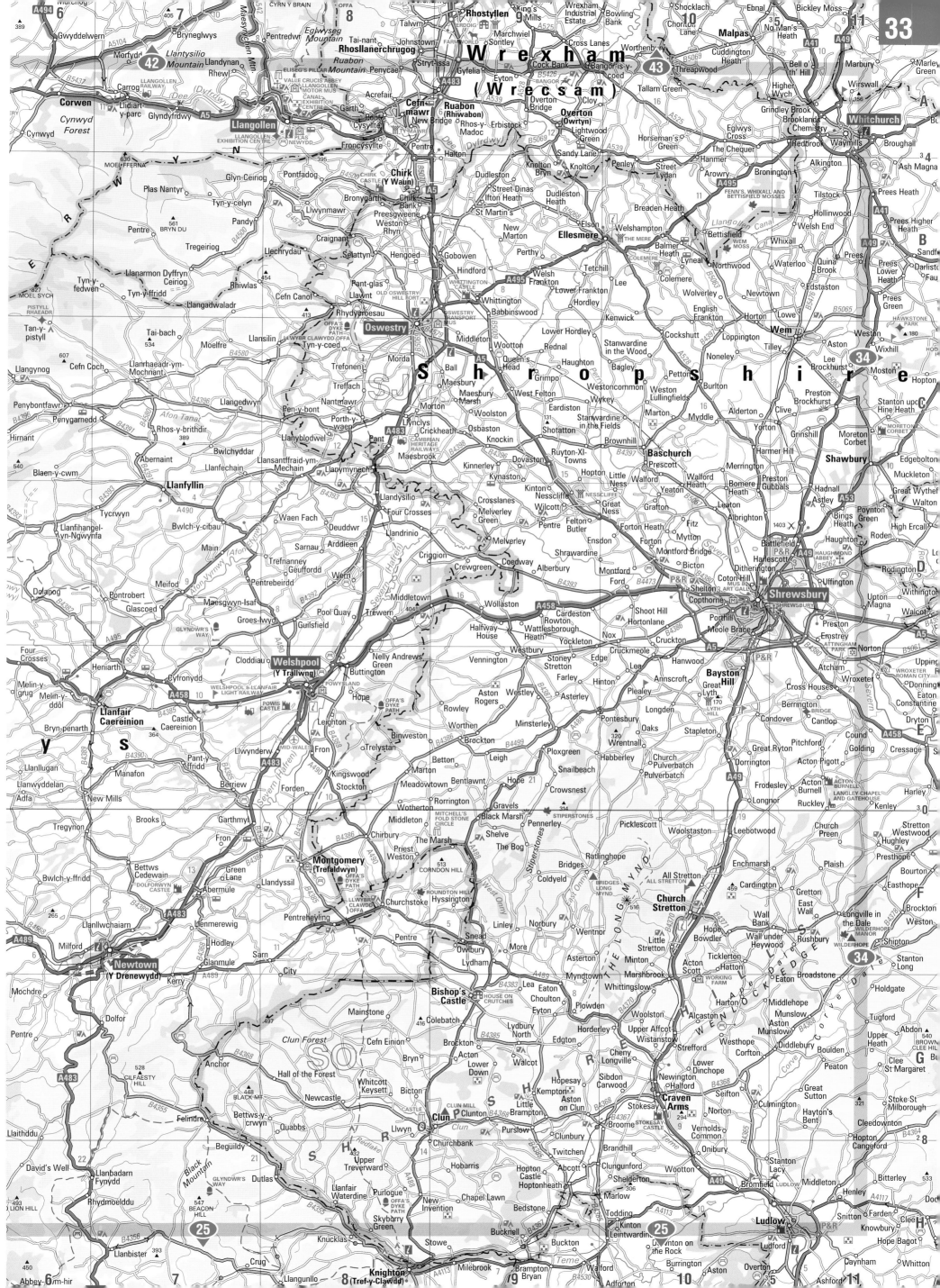

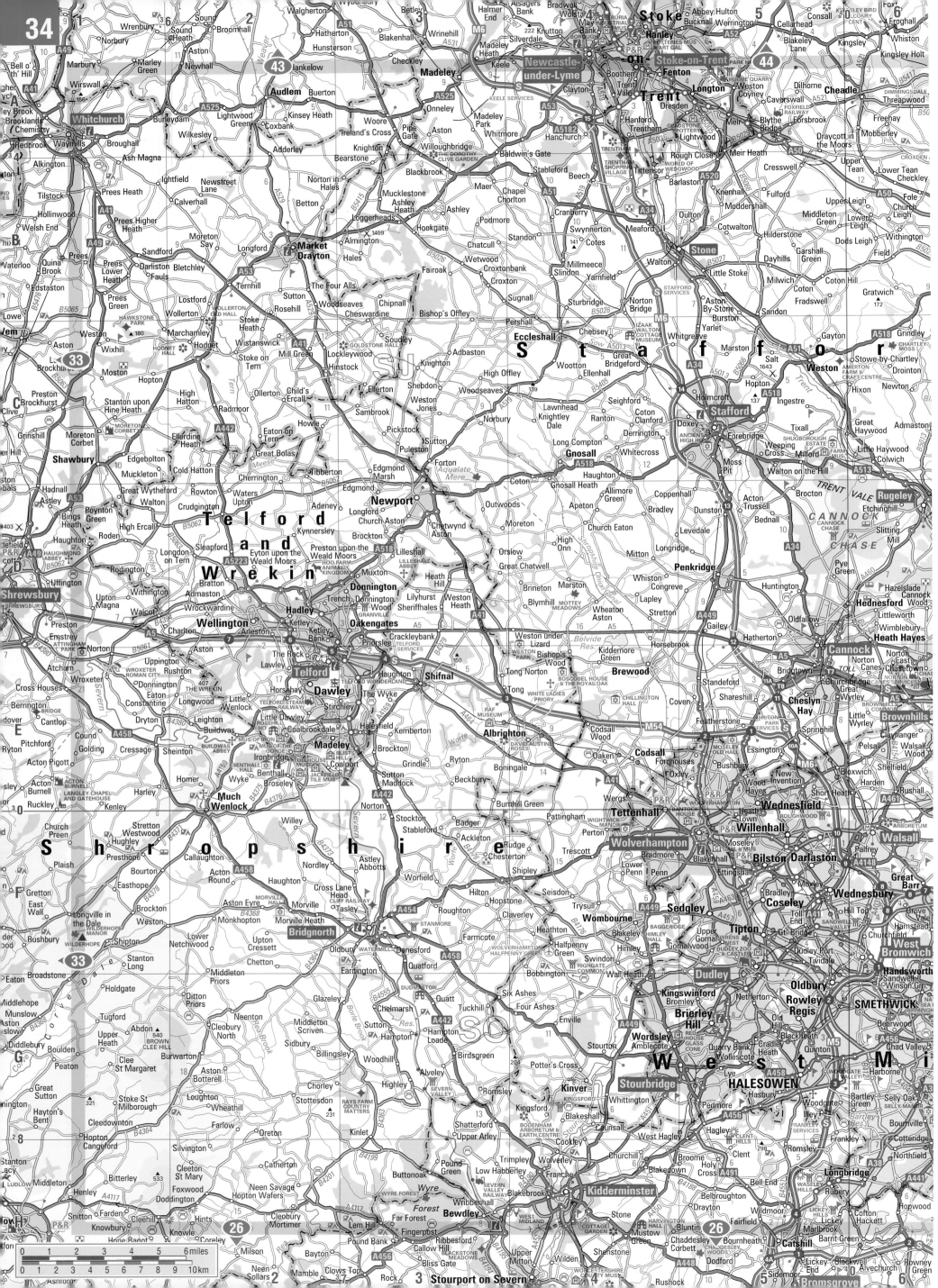

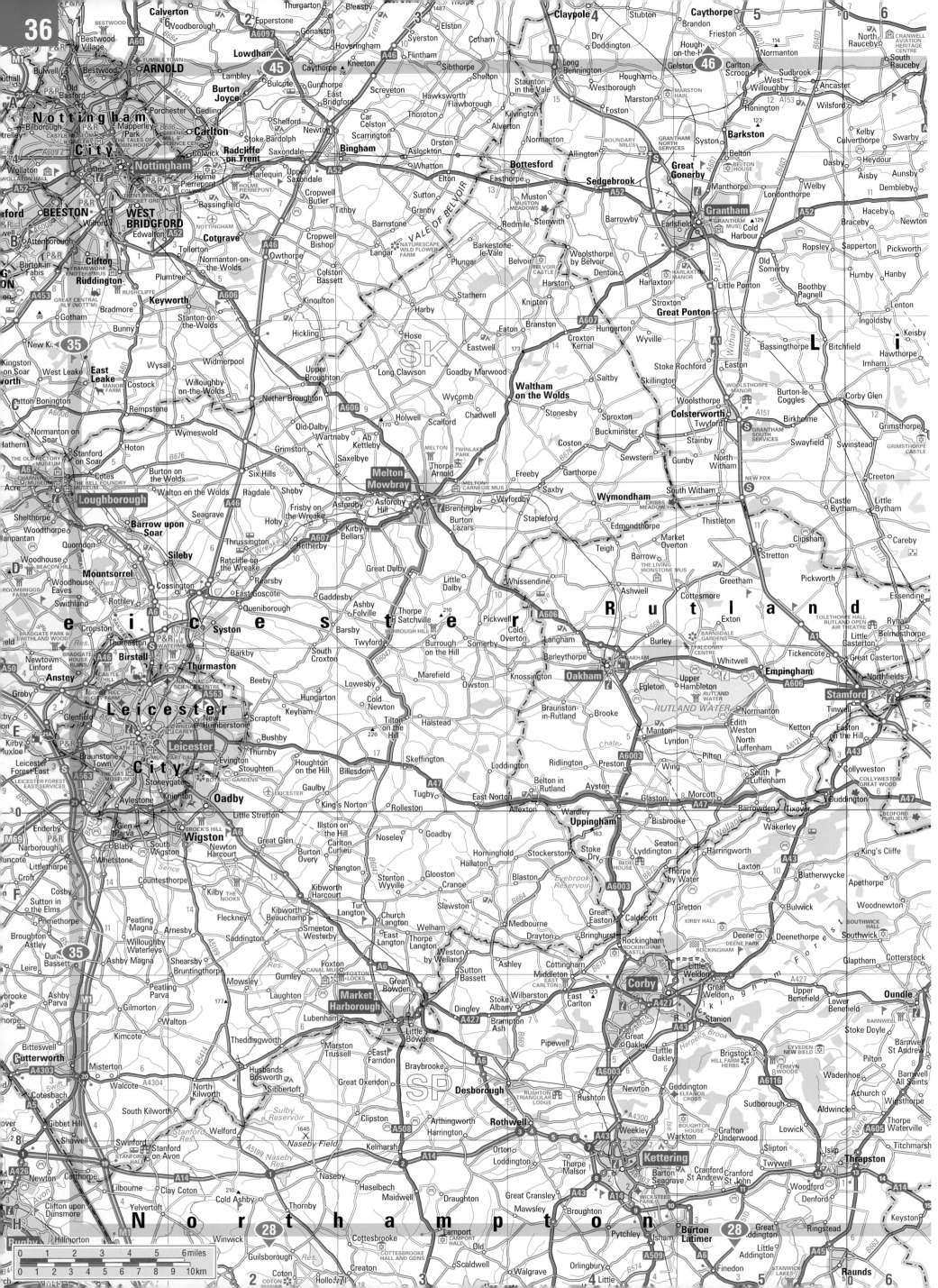

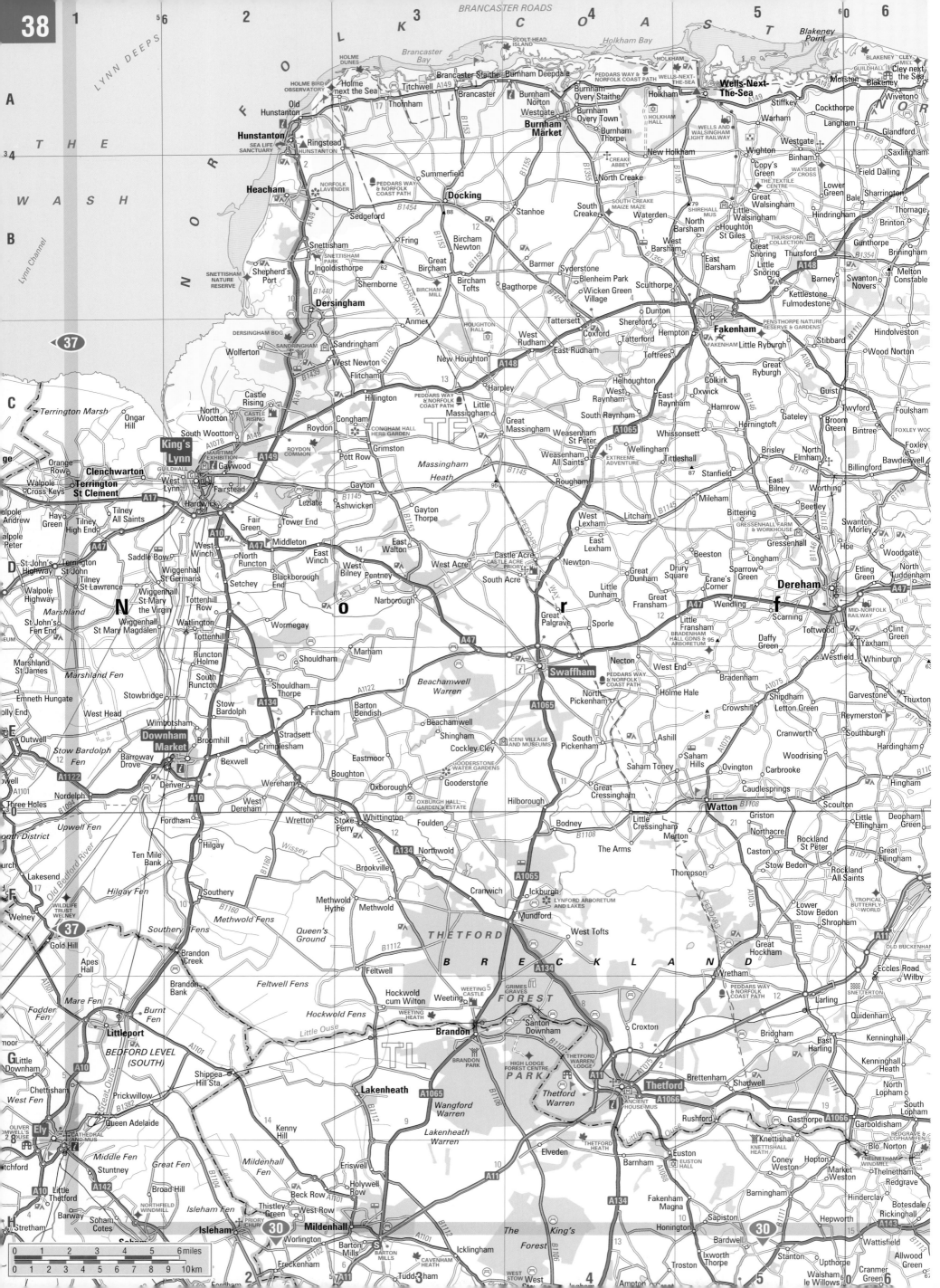

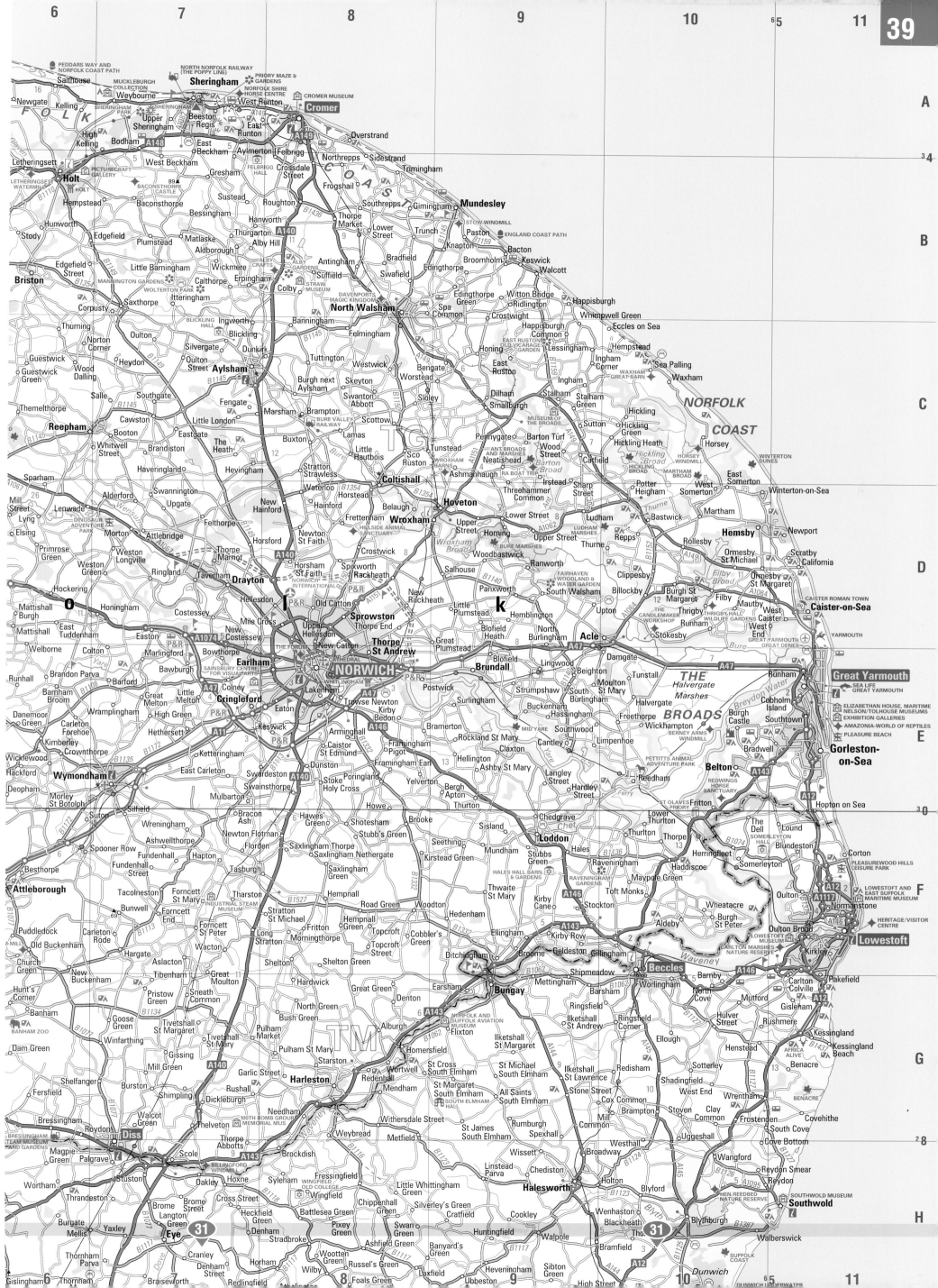

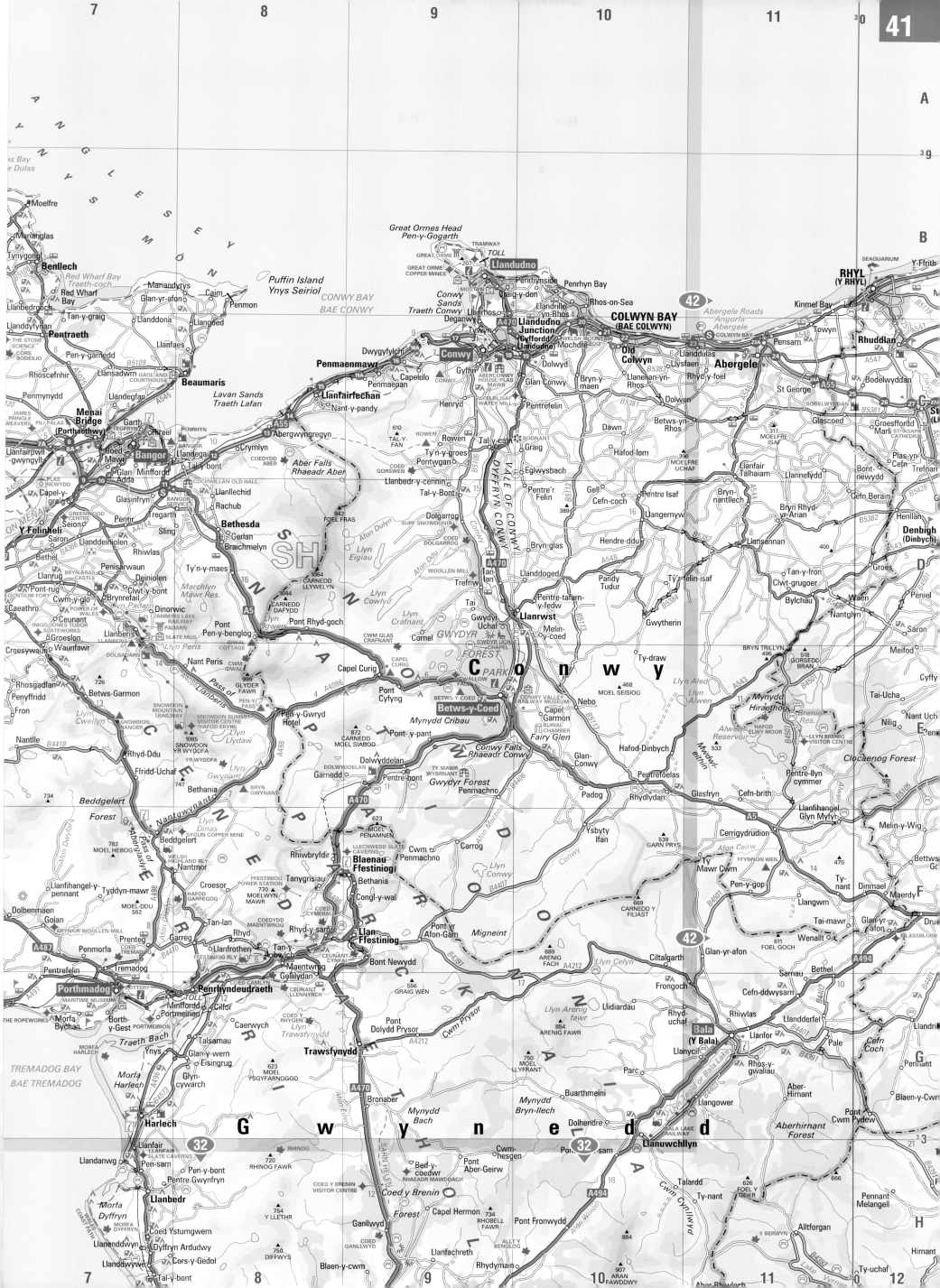

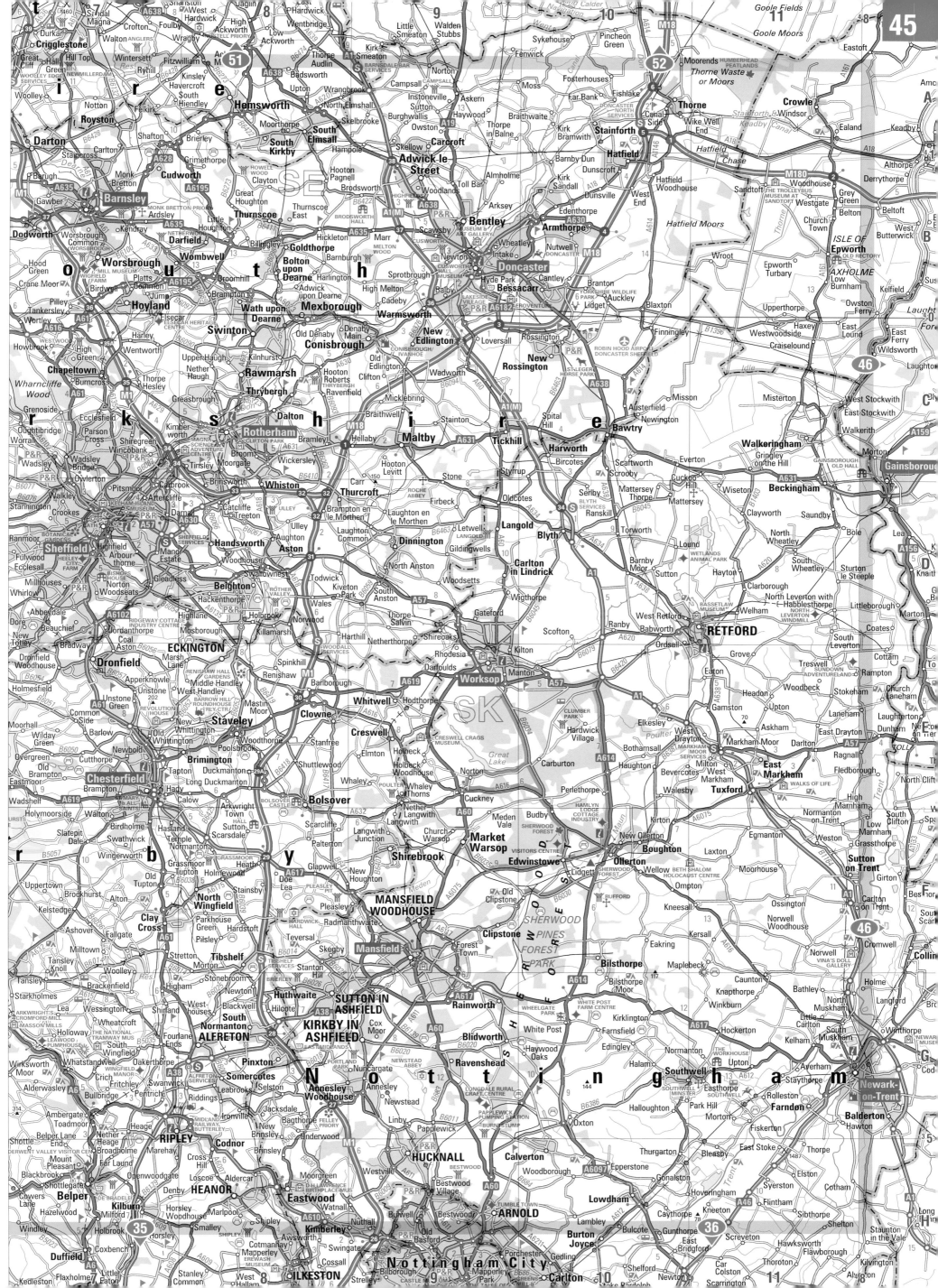

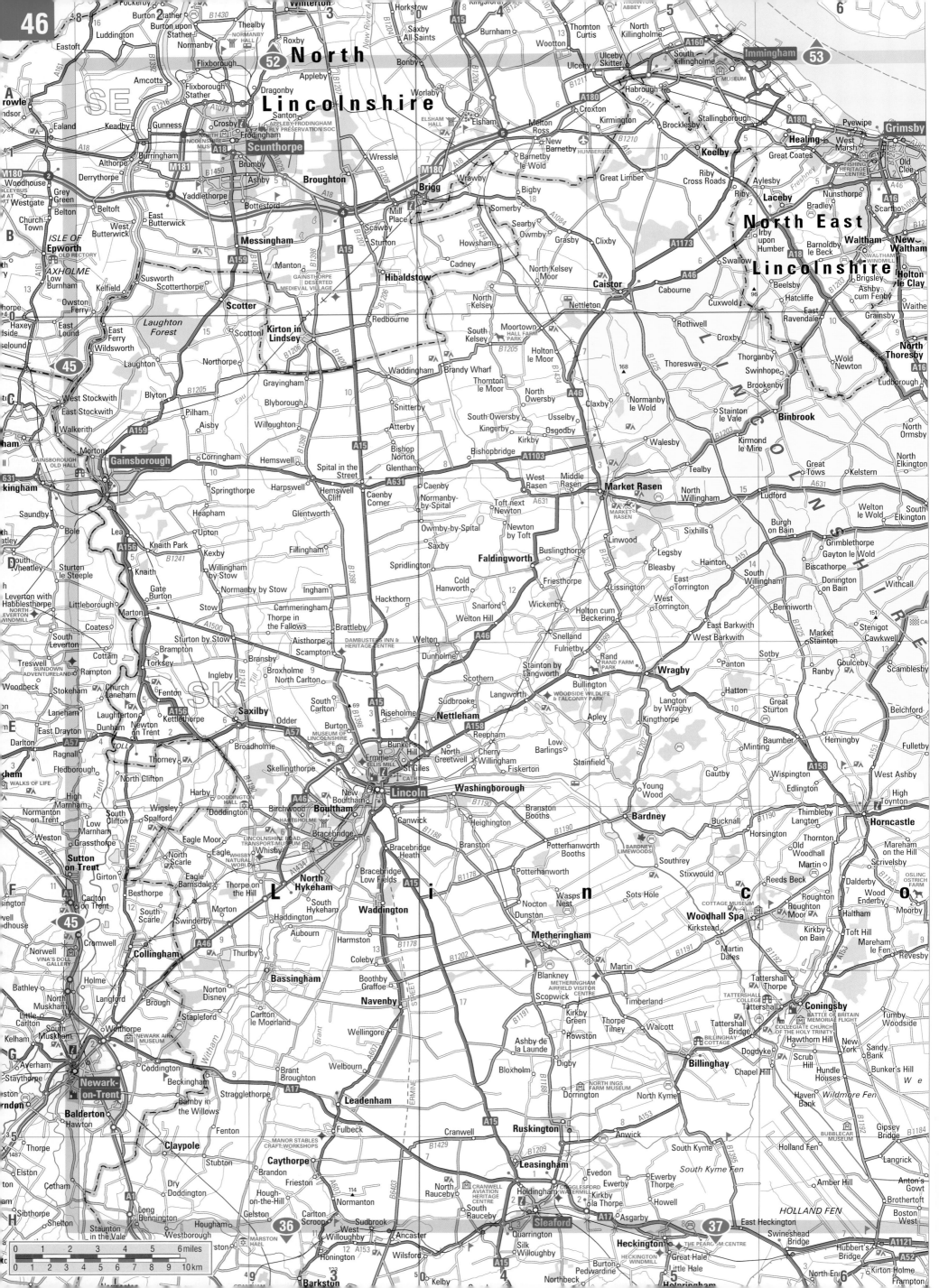

NX

I R I S H

S E A

POINT OF AYRE

Rue Pt.   The Ayres

Glentruan   Cranstal

A10   Dhowin   Bride

The Lhen   A19   A16

A10   A17

B3   A9

Andreas   A10

MANX CROSSES   Jurby   Jurby   Sandygate   MANX CROSSES   Regaby   A13   RAMSEY BAY

Jurby Head   SOUTH   East

Ballasalla   Jurby   St   A17   Dhoor   B7

West   Judes   A14   GROVE   Ramsey

The Cronk   A10   B9   Churchtown   MUSEUM   MANX ELECTRIC

CURRAGHS   Sulby   A3   RAILWAY

WILDLIFE PARK   B9   Port e Vullen

Orrisdale   Ballaugh   T.T. Course   Glen   A2   Maughold

Rhencullen   Ravensdale   A14   Auldyn   Dreemskerry   Maughold Head

MANX CROSSES   Kirk   A18   565   T.T. Course   MANX CROSSES

Michael   *I   s   l   e*   NORTH   Corrany   Ballajora

CELTIC   BARRULE

Ballaleigh   CRAFT   SNAEFELL   Glen Mona   Cornaa

Barregarrow   CENTRE   621   9

B10   *Druidale*   MURRAYS   Dhoon

MANX TRANSPORT MUSEUM   MOTORCYCLE MUSEUM   *o*   Agneash   LAXEY   Bulgham Bay

Knocksharry   A1   SNAEFELL   WHEEL

St Patrick's I.   Cronk-y-Voddy   644   MOUNTAIN   Ballaquine   AND MINES

PEEL   *M*   RAILWAY   Laxey

HOUSE OF MANANNAN   Peel   A20   487   *n*   LAXEY   Old Laxey

T.T. Course   COLDEN   BALLALHEANNAGH   WOOLLEN MILLS   Laxey Head

Contrary Head   TYNWALD   GARDENS   Fairy Cottage

KIPPER MUSEUM   CRAFT CENTRE   *Res.*   B12   Laxey Bay

TYNWALD HILL   Baldwin   Ballacannel

Patrick   A30   St John's   Creg-ny-Baa   Baldrine

A27   Greeba   B21   Clay Head

Glenmaye   333   T.T. Course   A23   Crosby

Dalby Pt.   Lower Foxdale   Glen Vine   A1   Strang   Onchan   MANX CROSSES

Dalby   Foxdale   B35   Union Mills   A22   Tromode   GROUDLE GLEN   *HEYSHAM*

Niarbyl   A24   Onchan   RAILWAY

Niarbyl Bay   Eairy   B36   Braaid   B32   Spring   Douglas   ONCHAN PLEASURE PARK   *LARNE*

483   222   Valley   (TT race period only)

SOUTH   Cooil   A5   Douglas Bay

BARRULE   Close   St Mark's   A6   Douglas

14   Clark   Newtown   Ballaveare   Ellenbrook   Head   *LIVERPOOL*

Ballamodha   B30   A25   CAMERA OBSCURA   (March-Nov)

Fleshwick Bay   Lingague   Ronague   Grenaby   A34   *Little Ness*   *BIRKENHEAD*

Surby   B40   Ballabeg   B25   (Nov-March)

Bradda Head   Bradda   Colby   RUSHEN   *Santon Head*   ISLE OF MAN

Port Erin   A1   ABBEY   STEAM RAILWAY

RAILWAY MUS   Four Roads   Ballasalla   *Port*

The Howe   A5   BILLOWN   *Greenaugh*

Cregneash   Castletown   Derbyhaven

Port   CASTLE RUSHEN   ISLE OF MAN

CREGNEASH VILLAGE   St Mary   NAUTICAL MUS   St Michael's I.

FOLK MUSEUM   SCARLETT VISITOR CENTRE   OLD

128   HOUSE OF KEYS

Calf of Man   *Spanish Head*   Scarlett   Dreswick Pt.   *BELFAST* (April-Sept)

Point   *DUBLIN* (April-Sept)

Chicken Rock

0   1   2   3   4   5   6 miles
0 1 2 3 4 5 6 7 8 9 10km

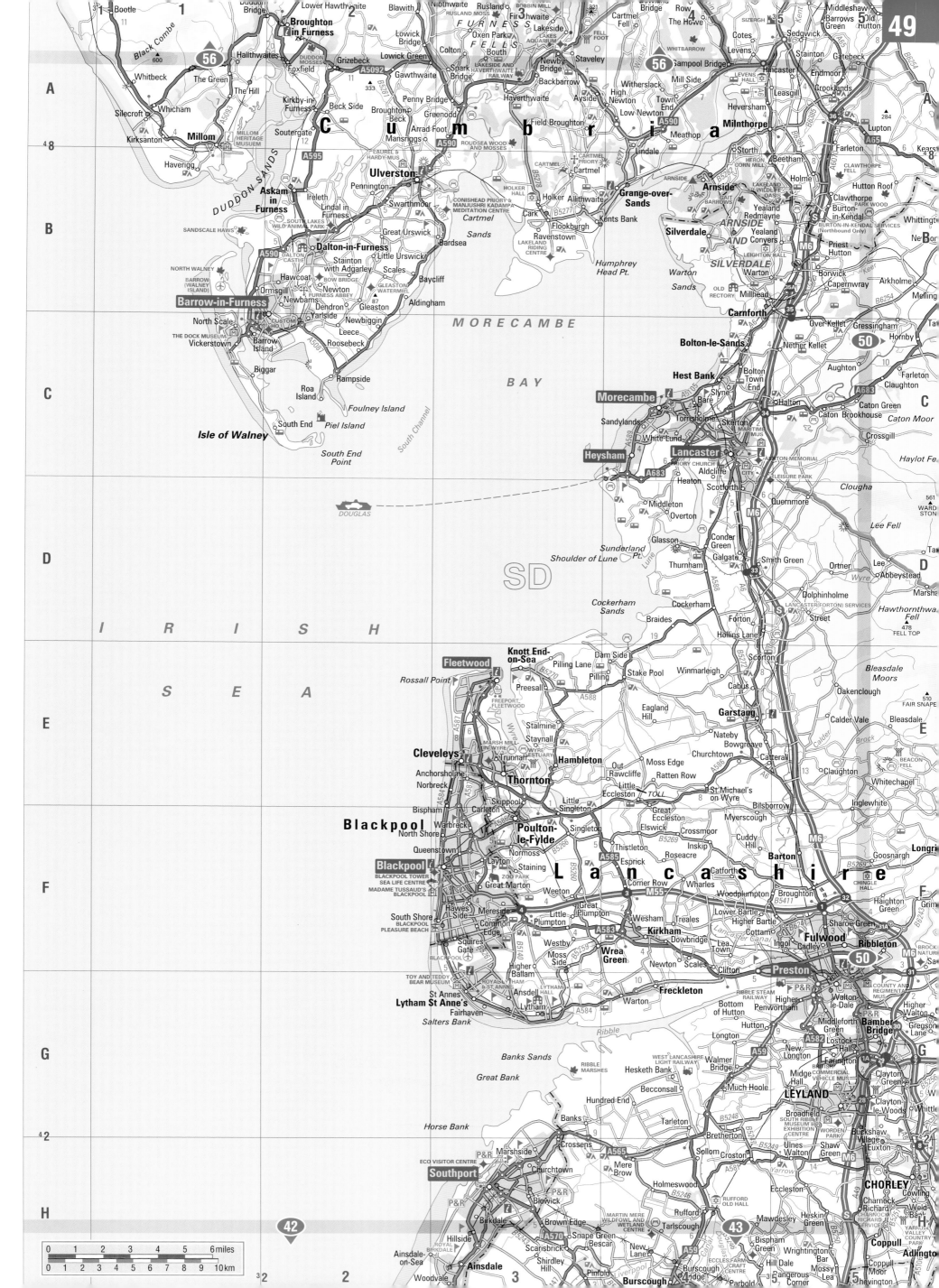

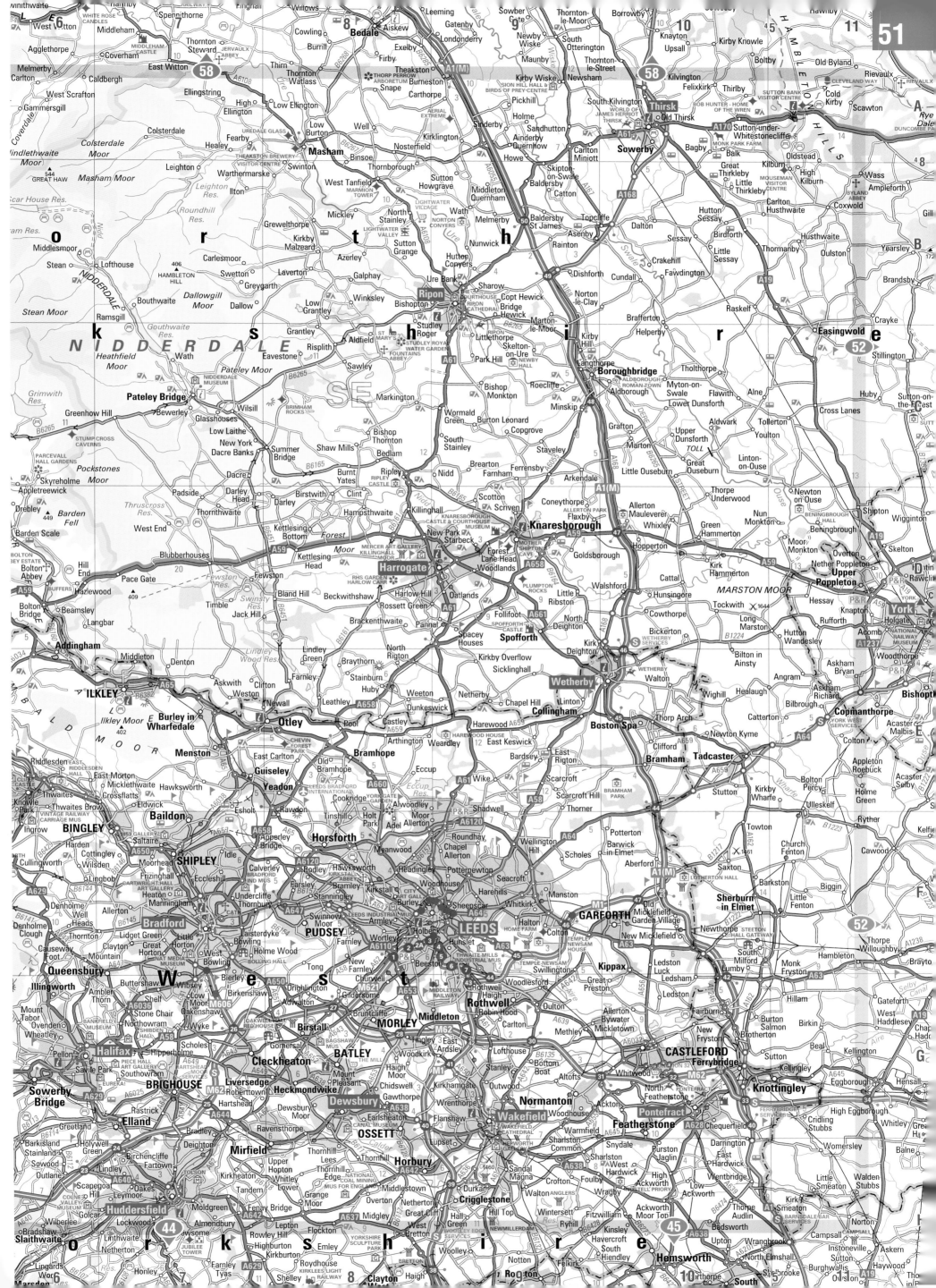

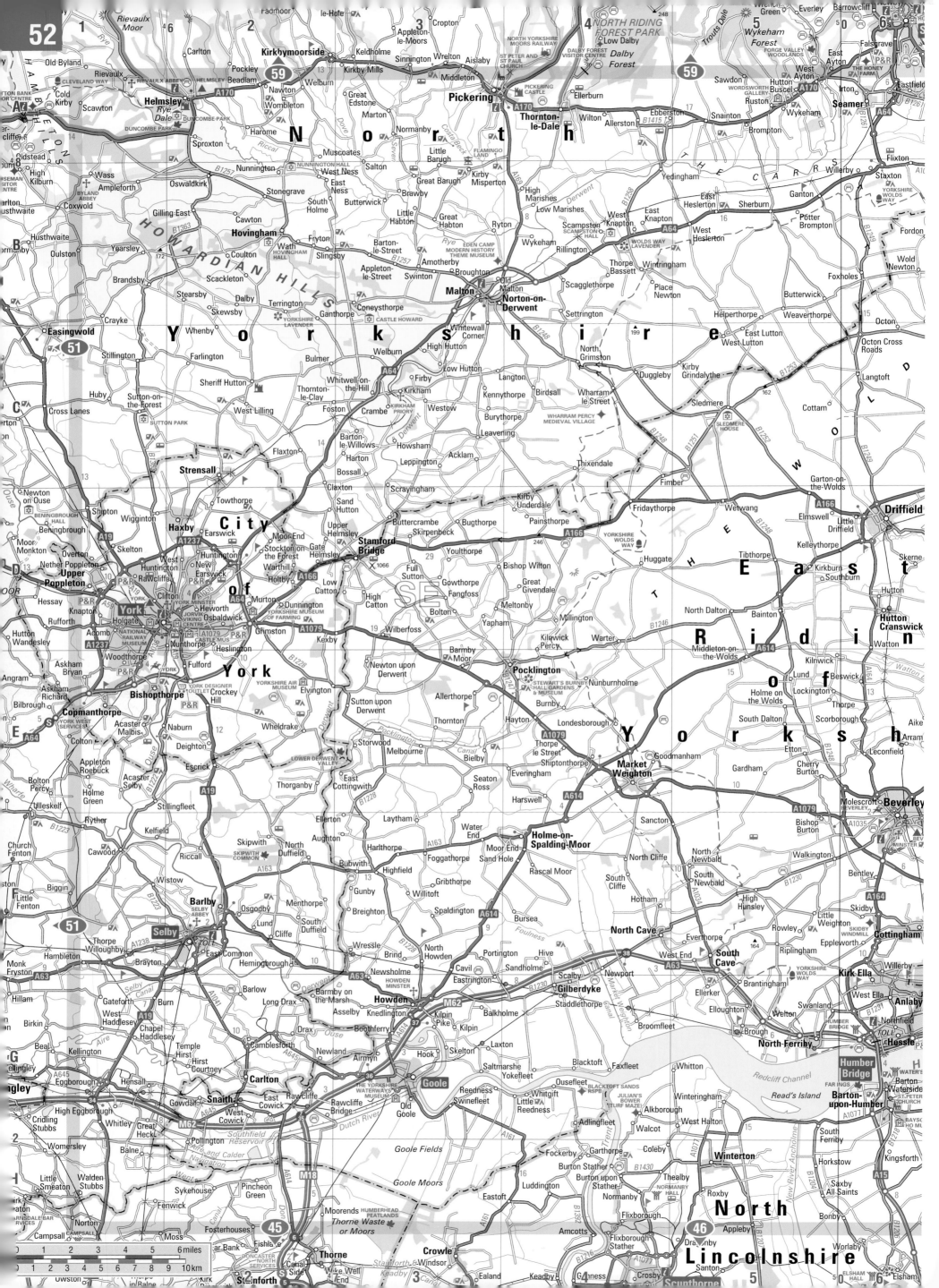

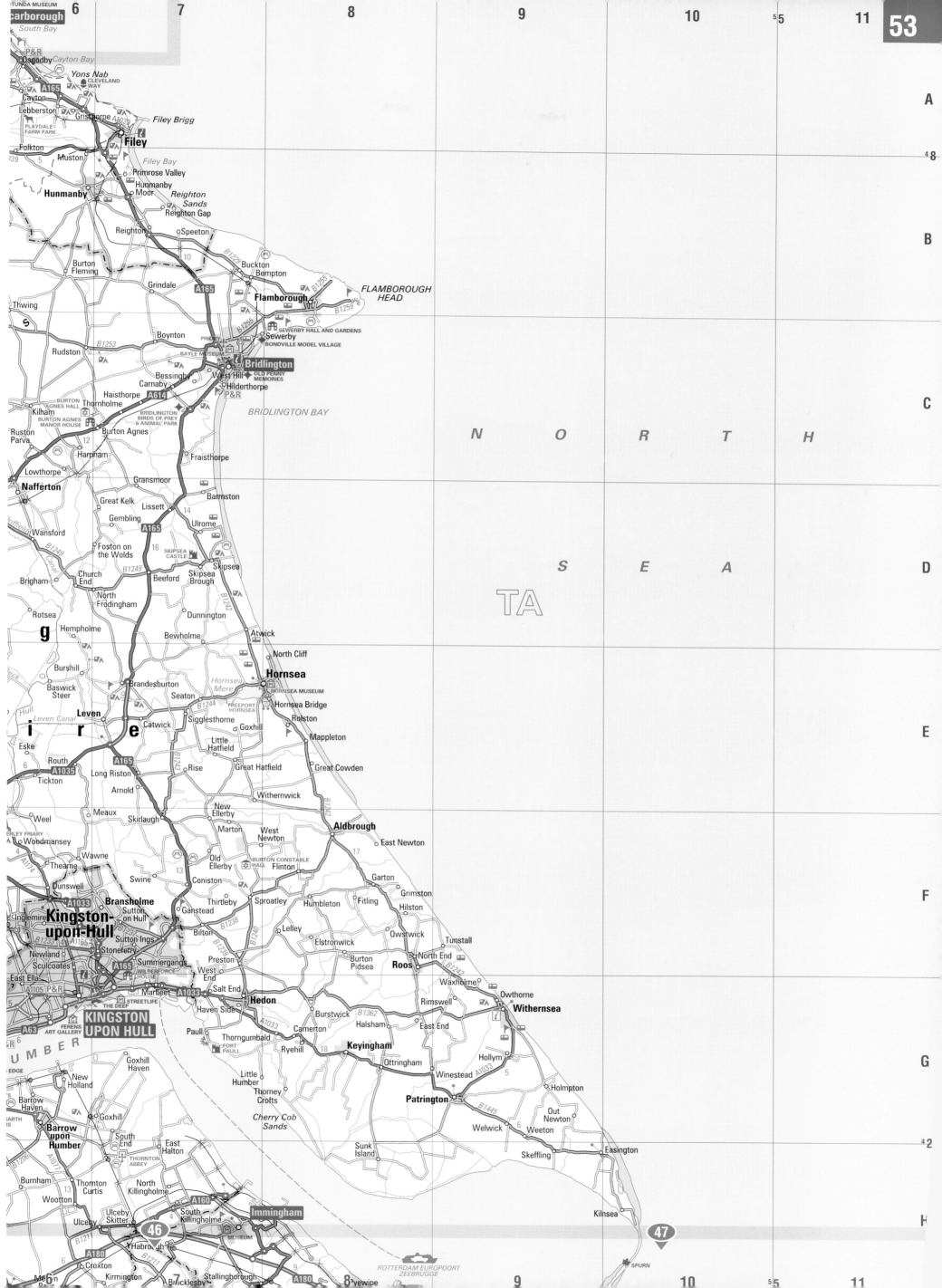

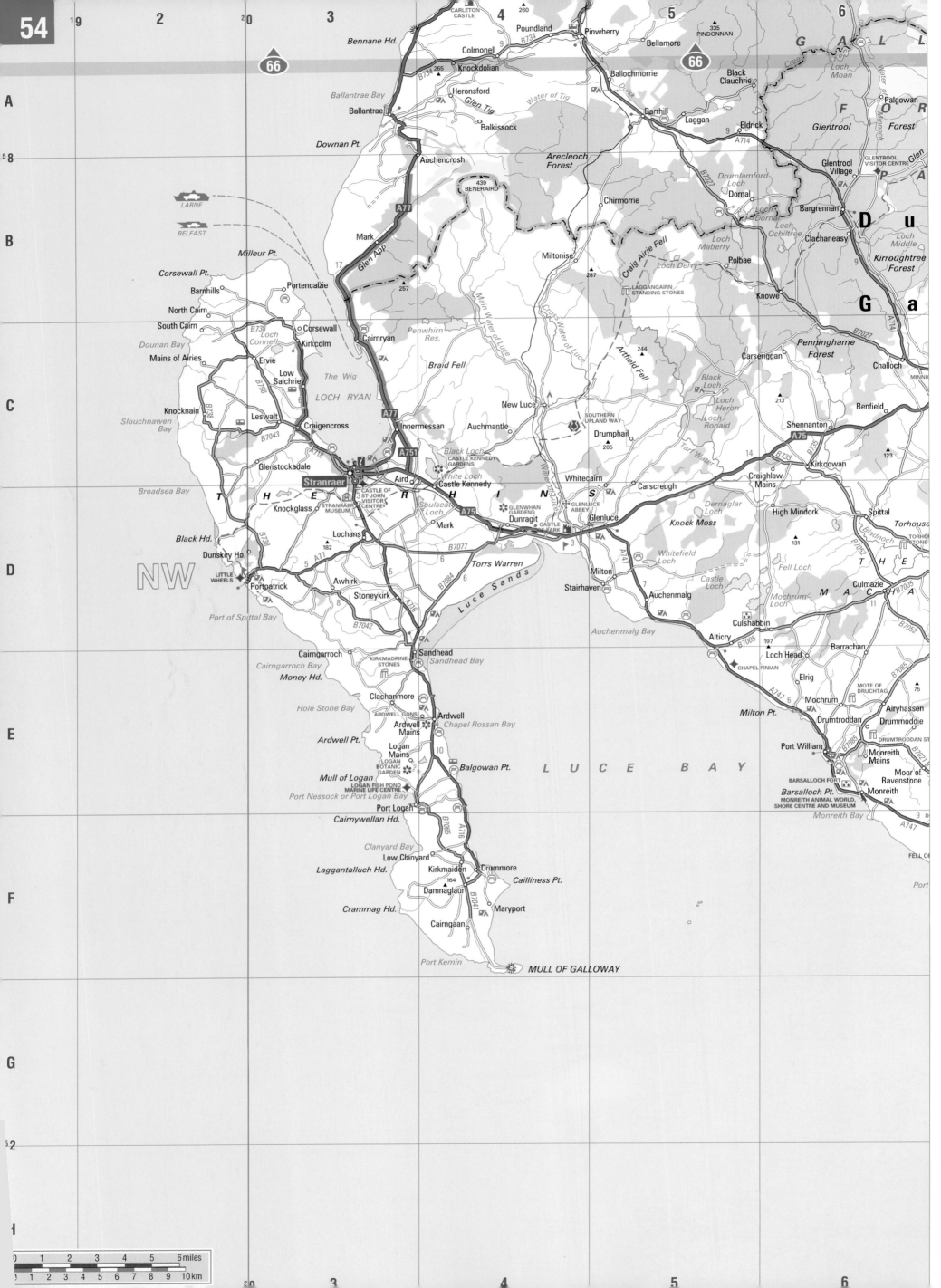

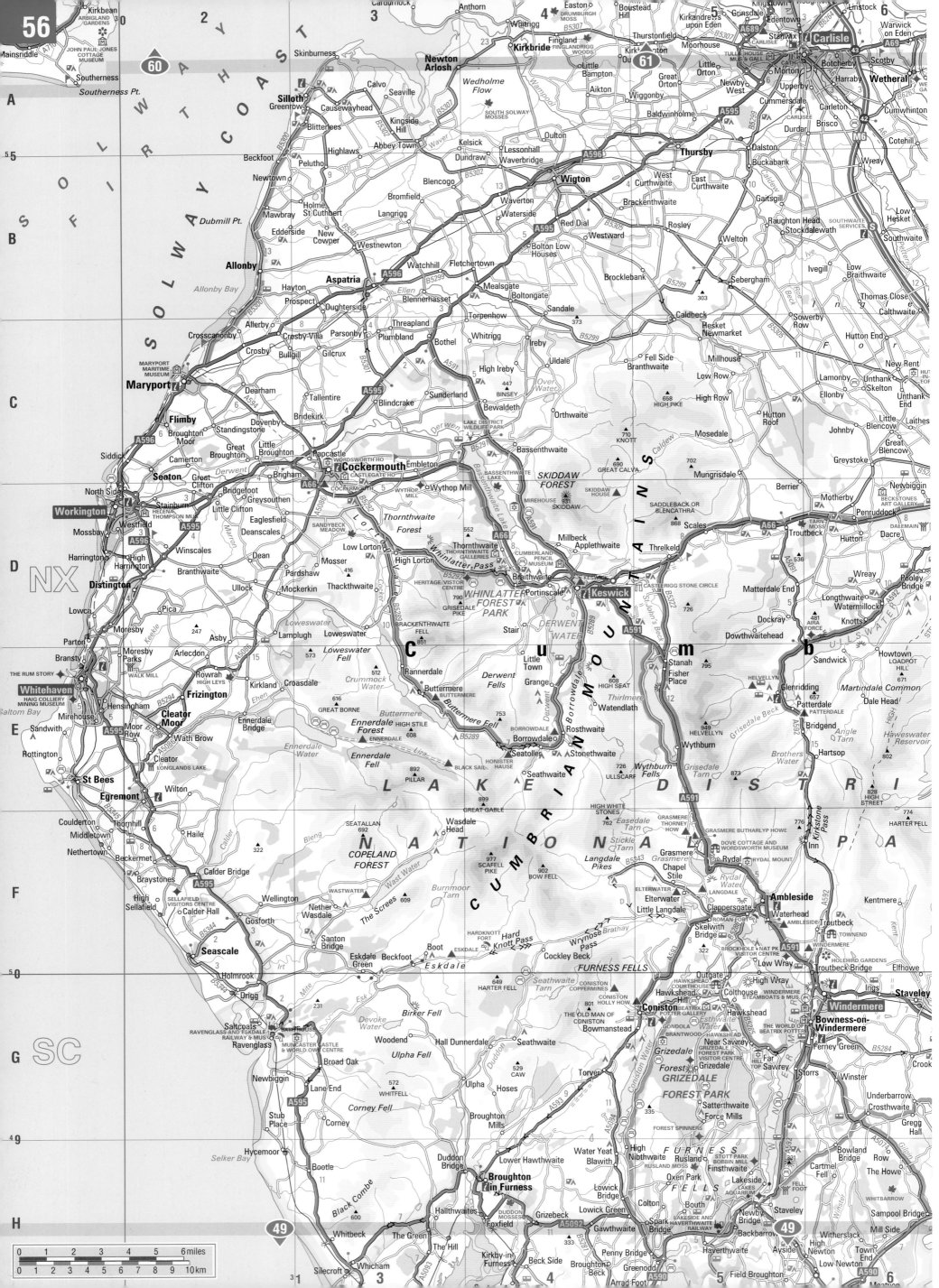

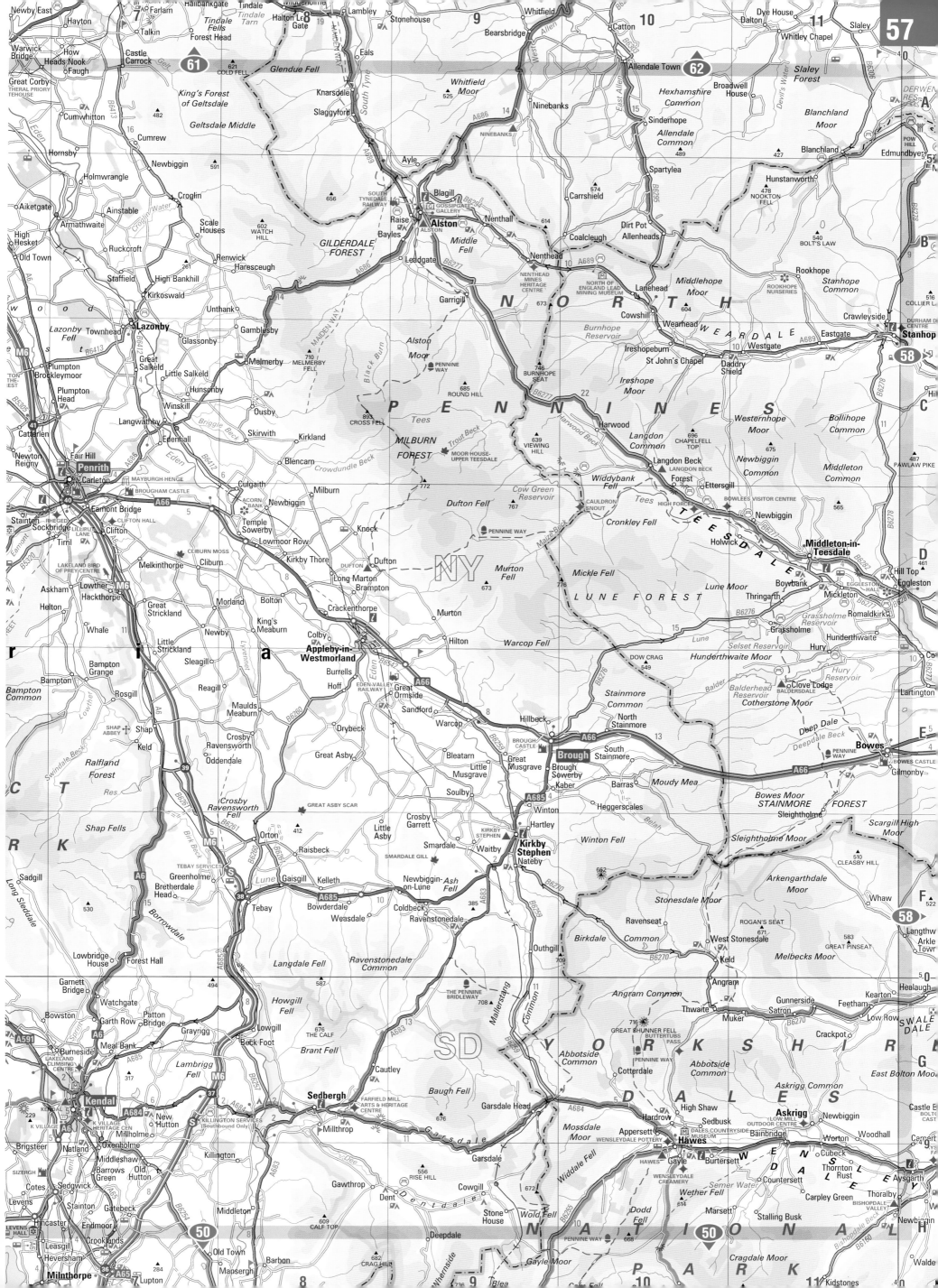

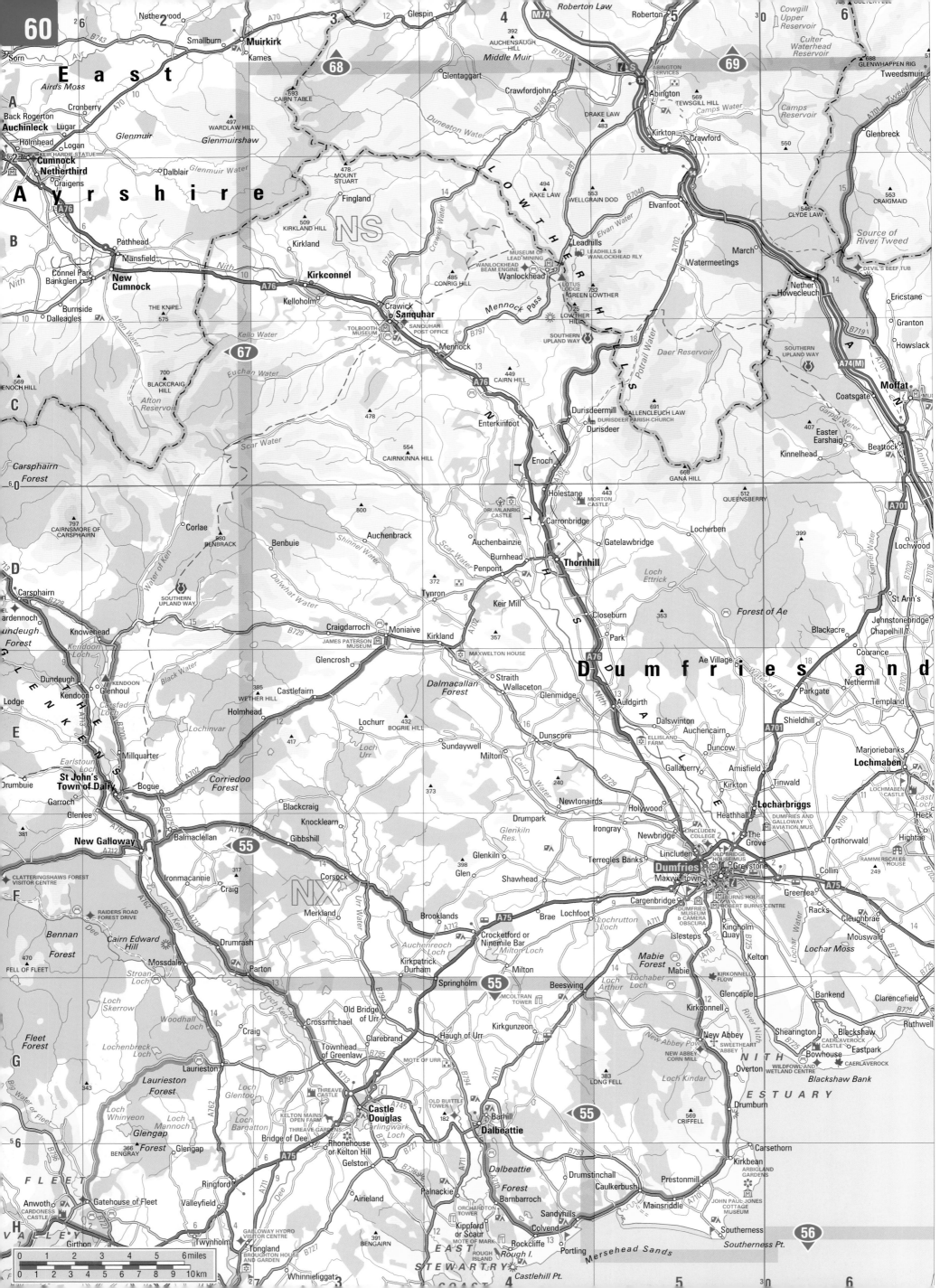

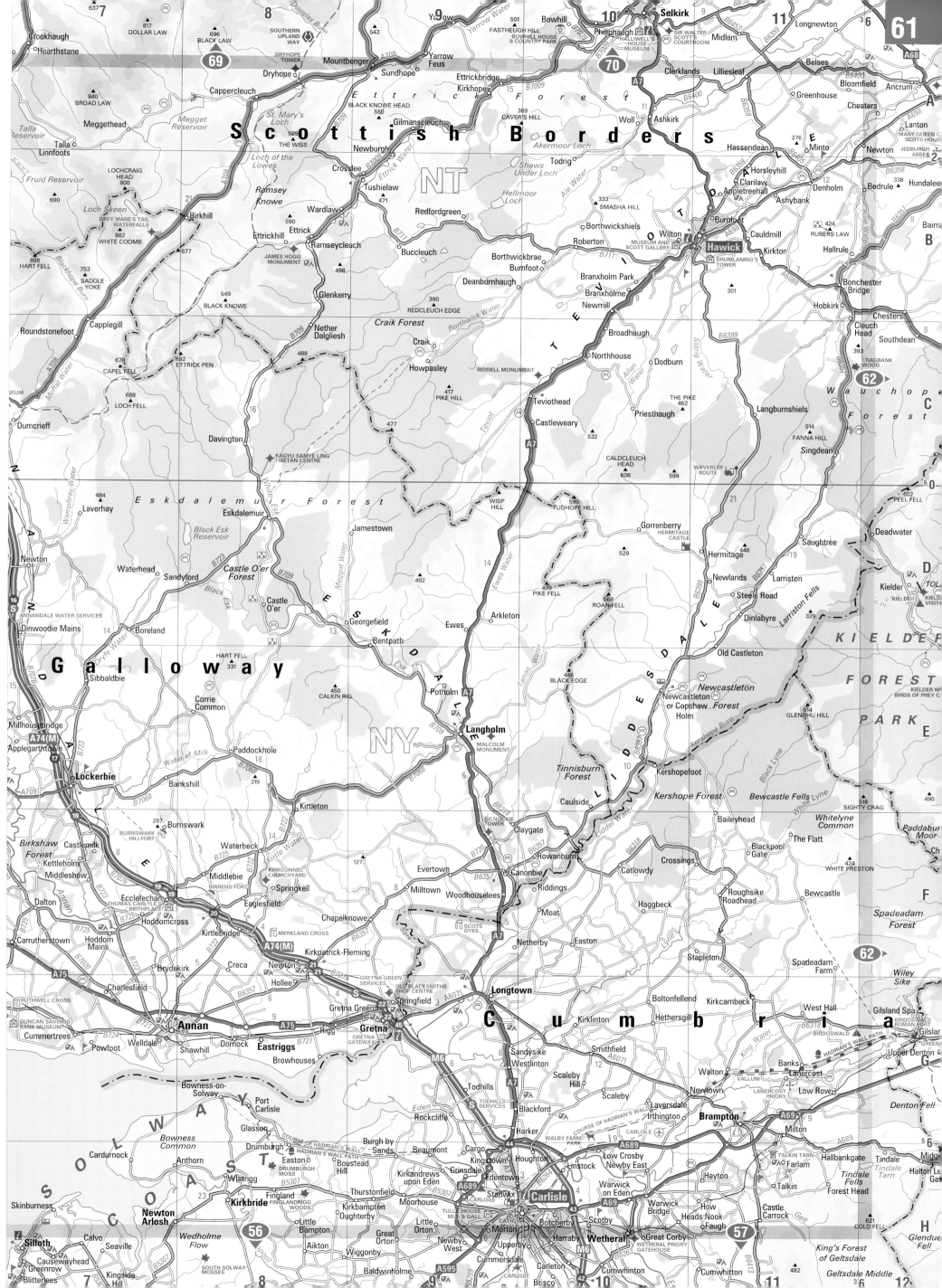

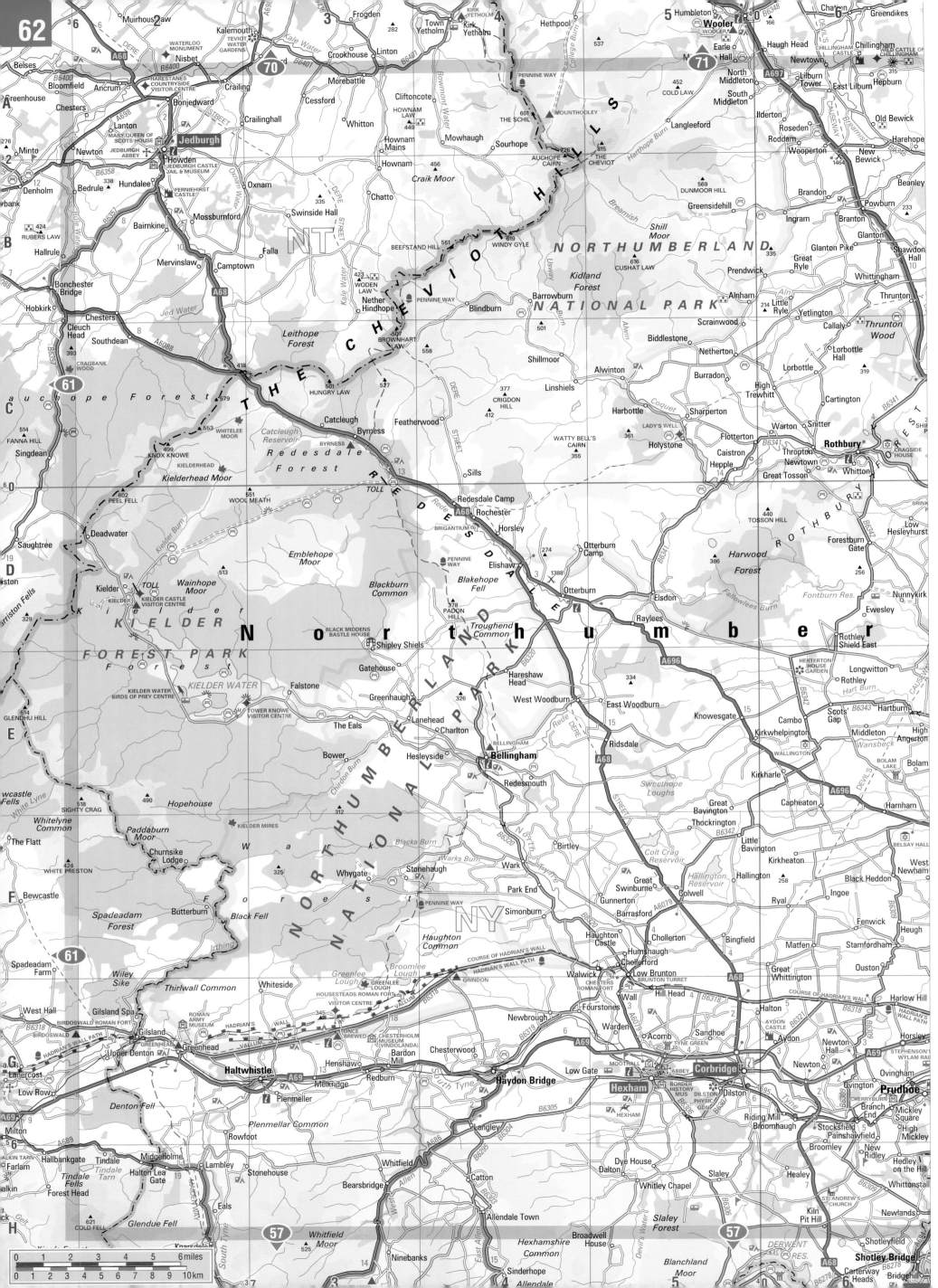

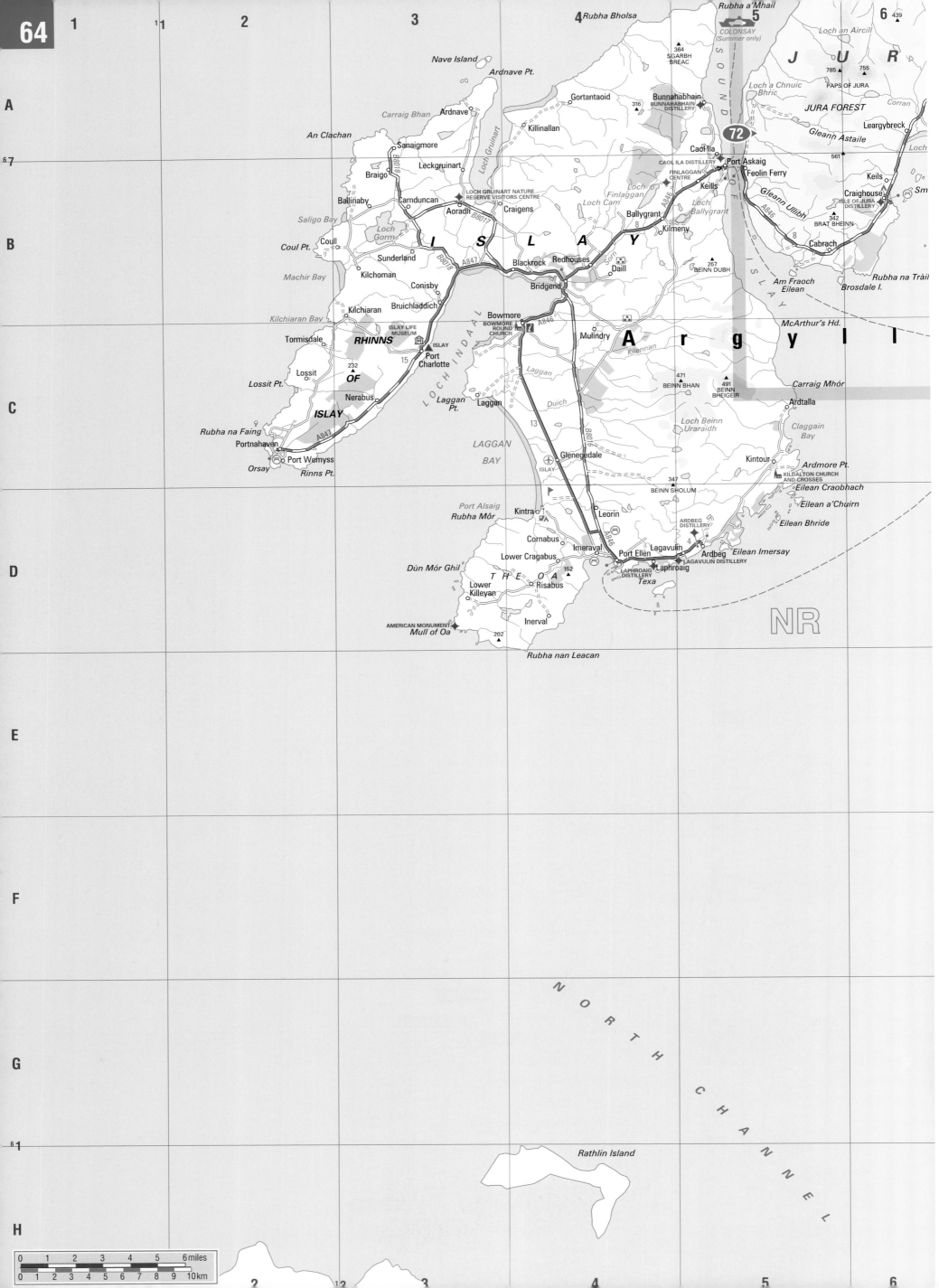

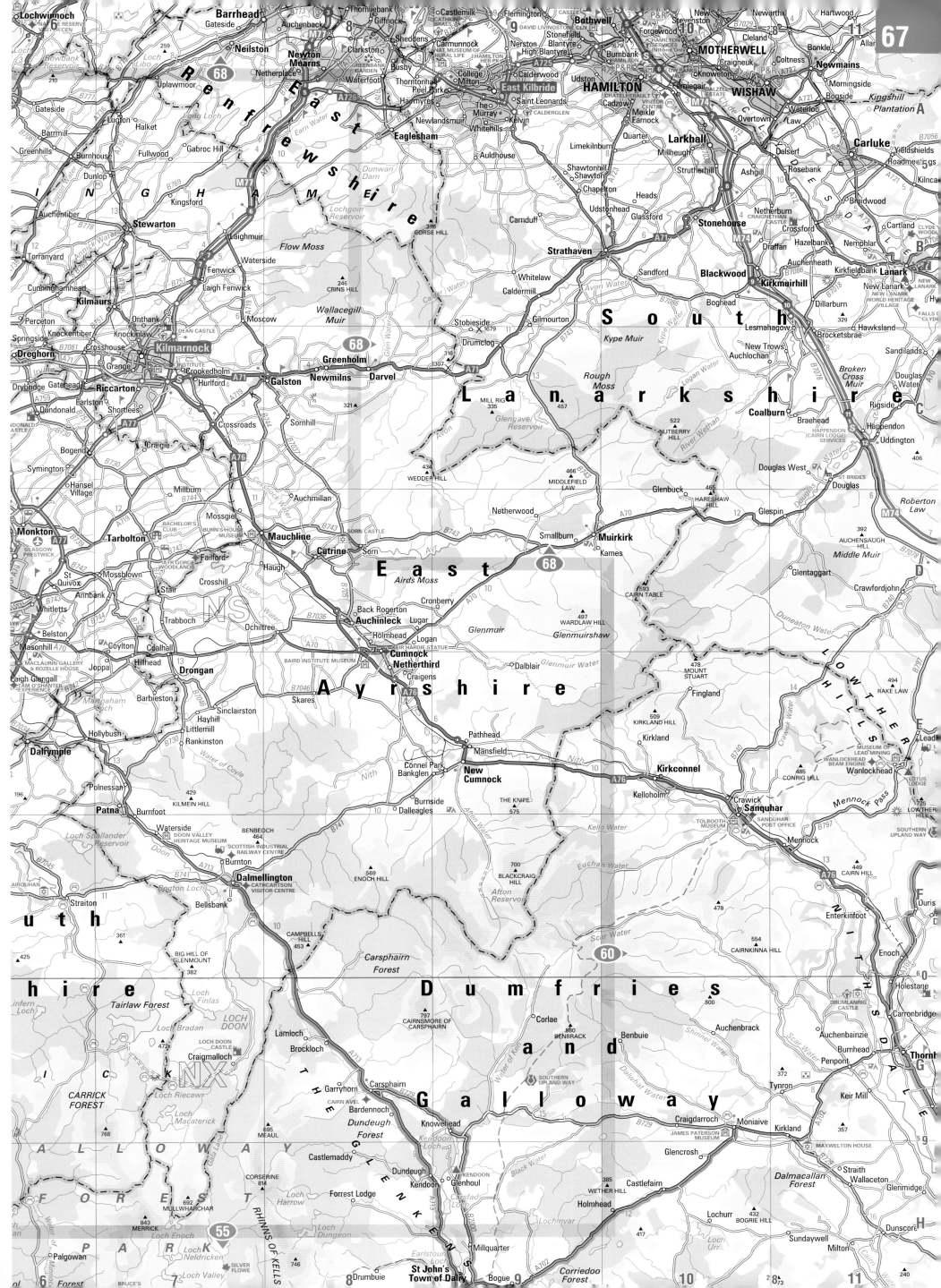

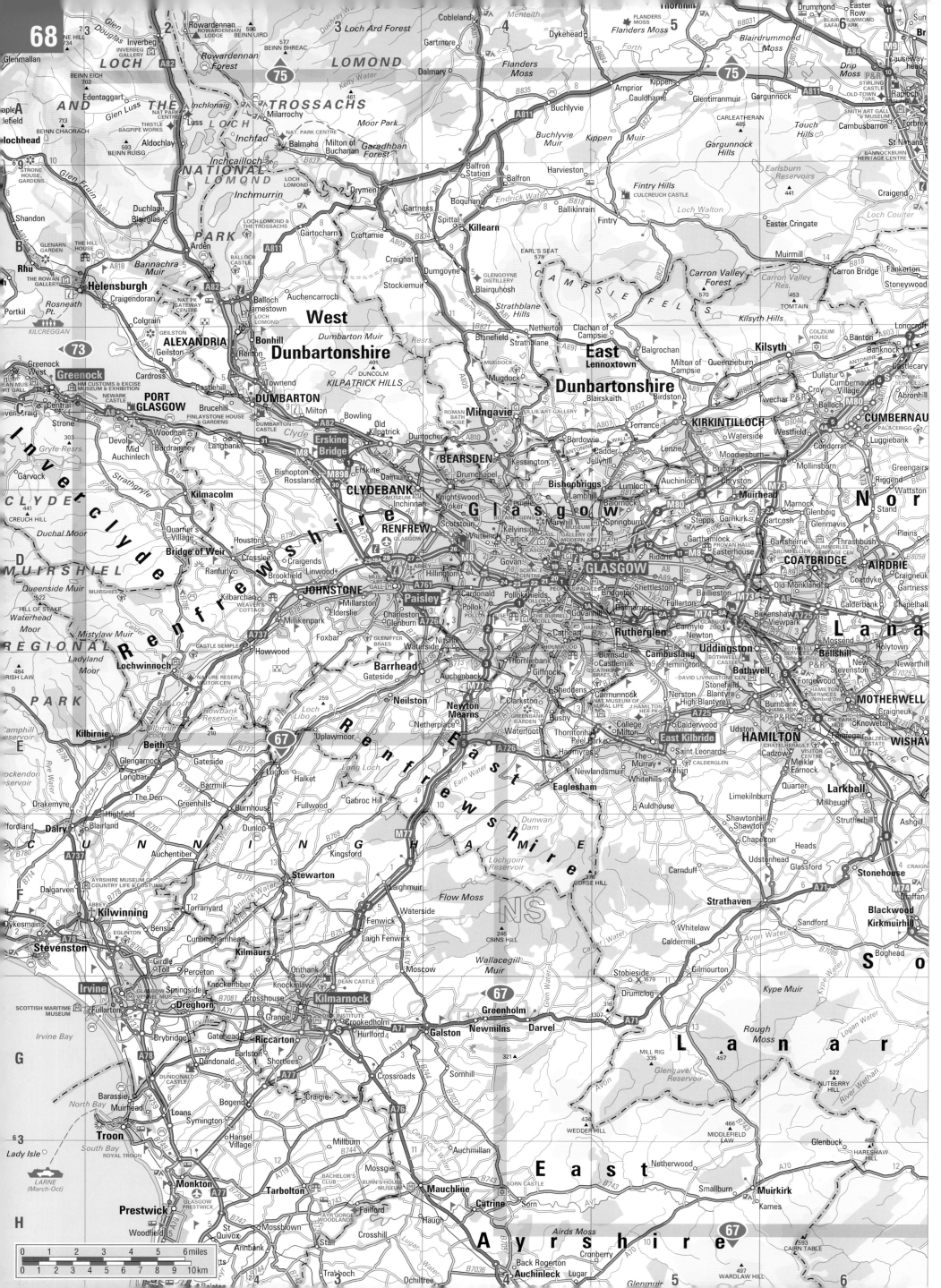

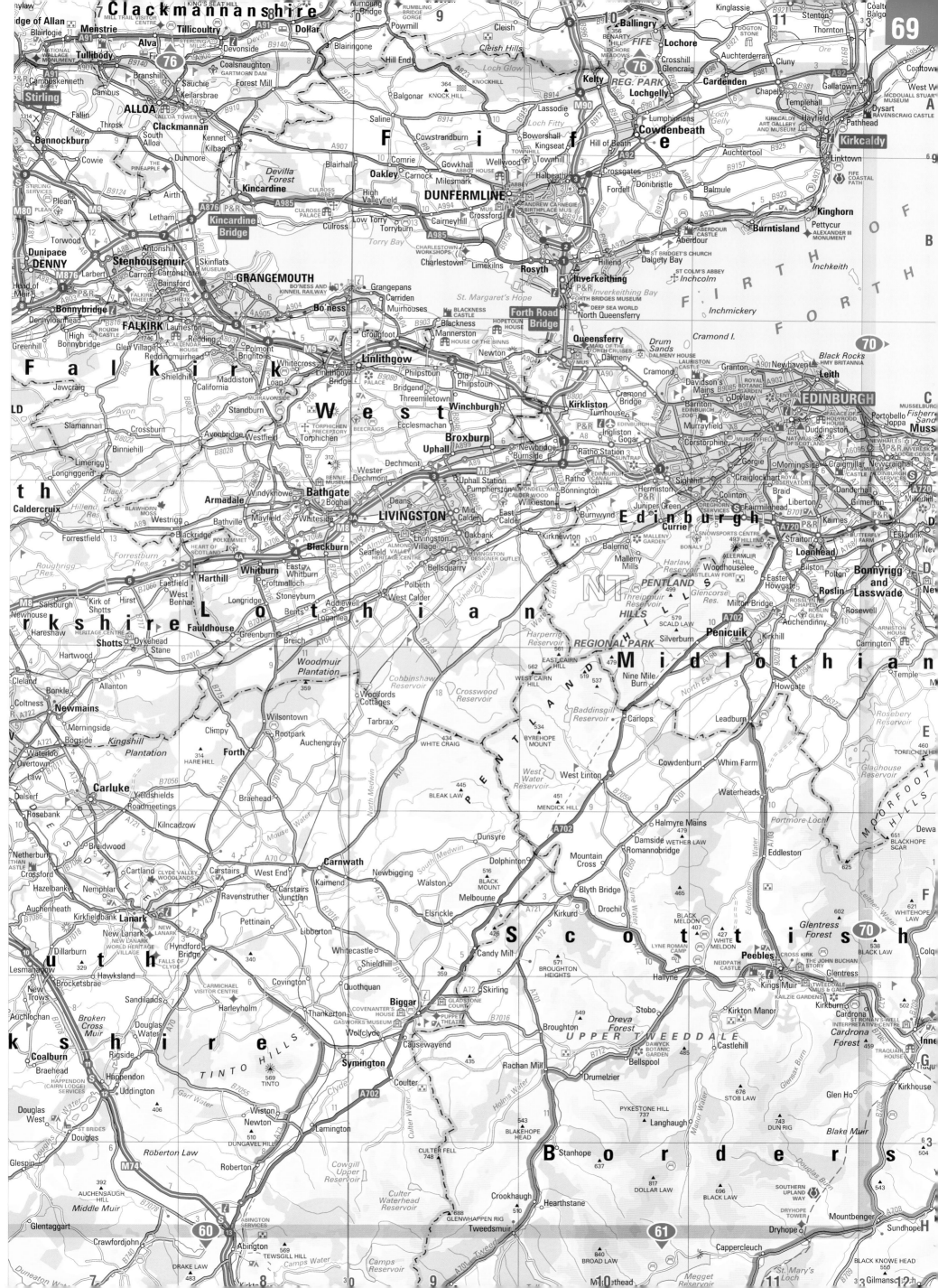

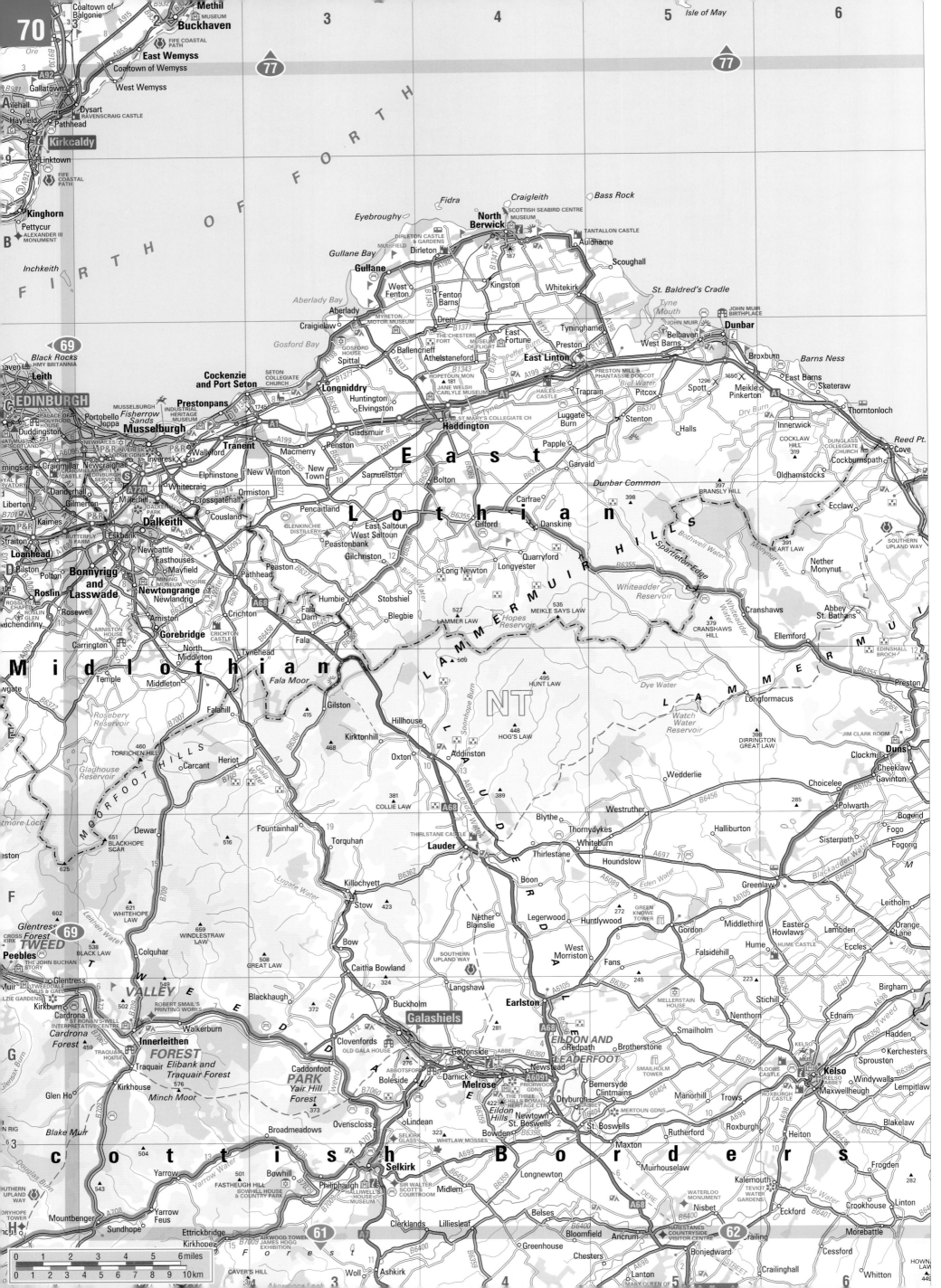

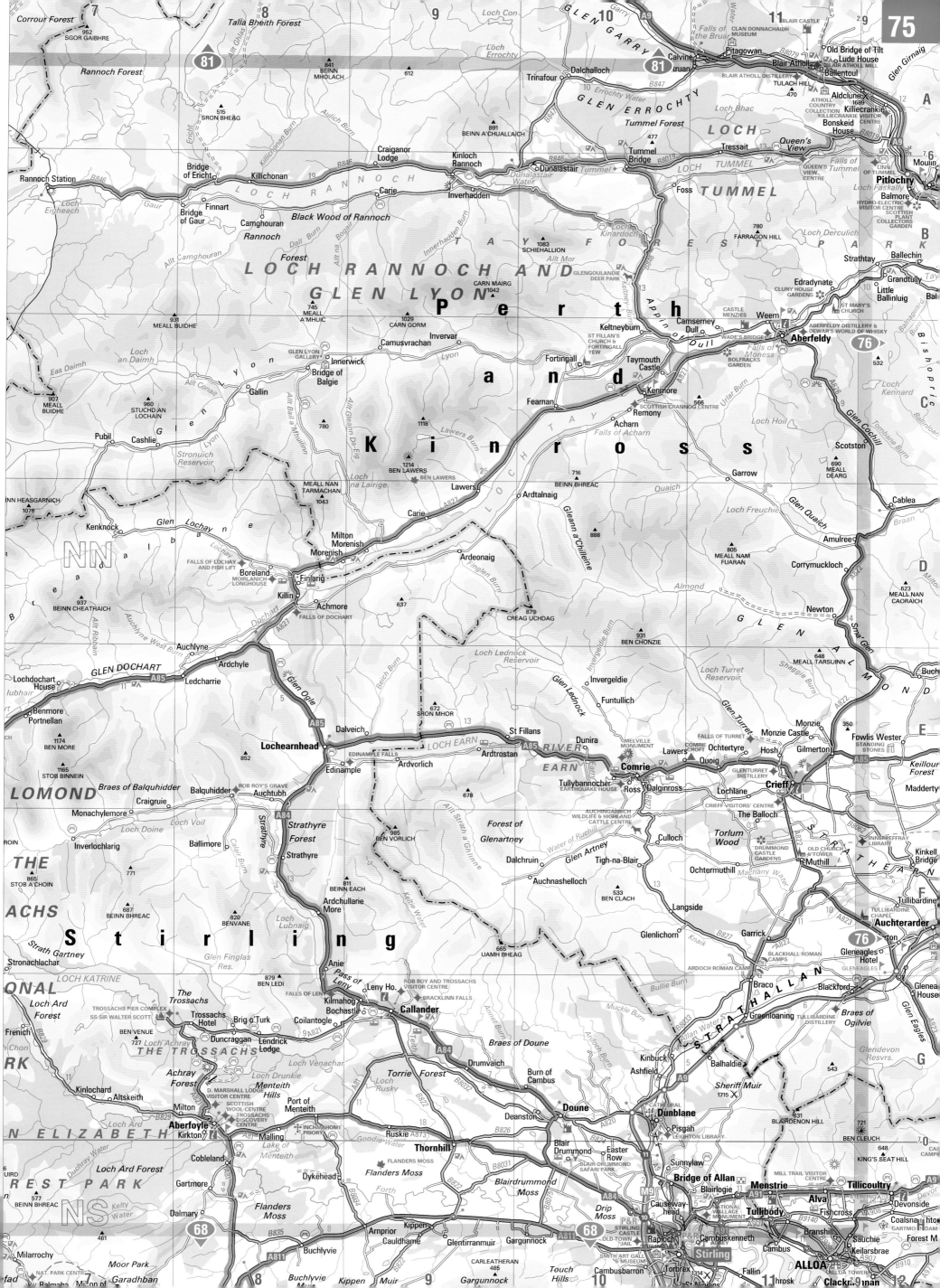

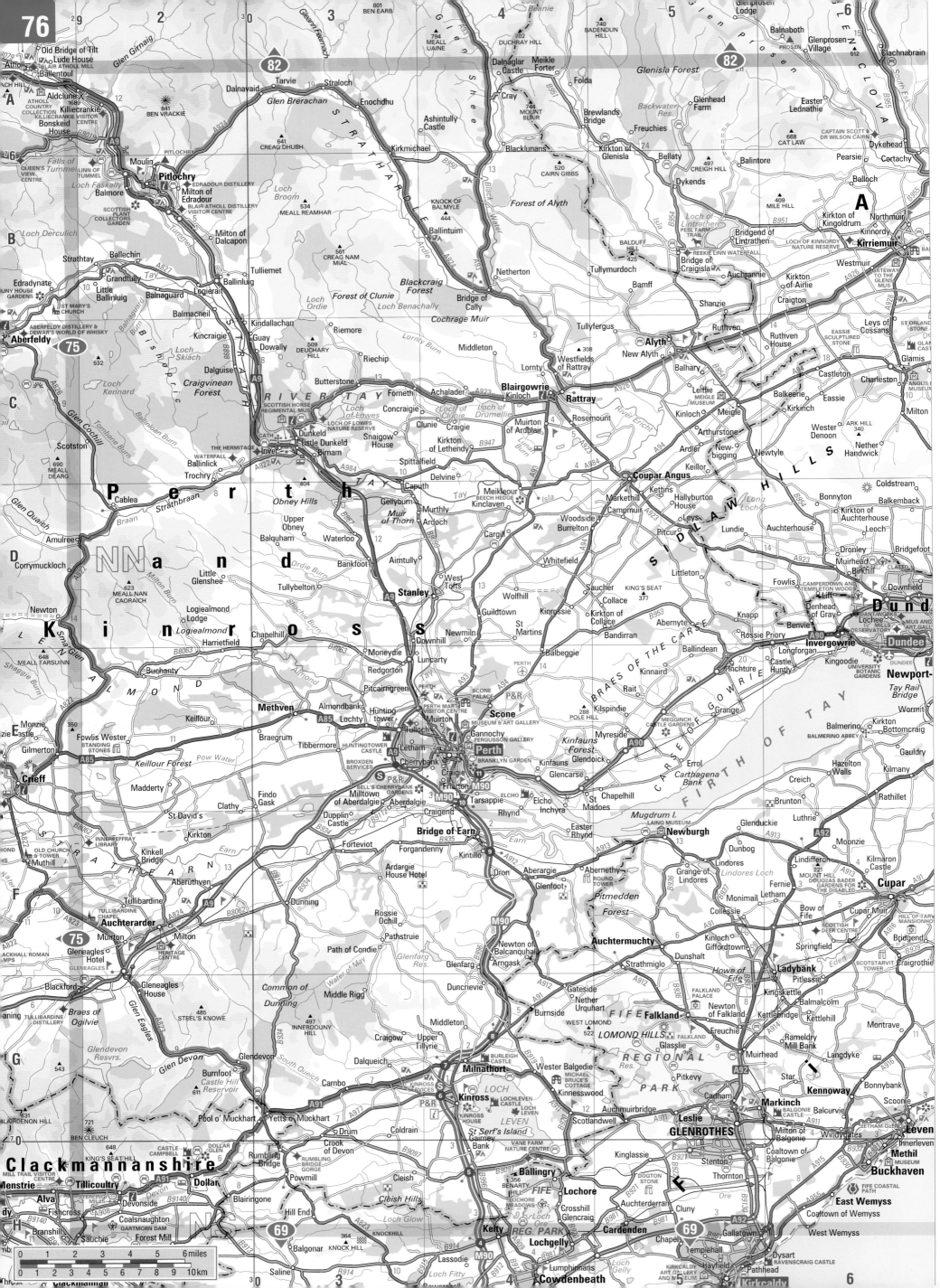

NF

The Small Isles

Canna
Garrisdale Pt.
A'Chill
Canna Harbour
Rubha Shamhnan Insir
Sanday
MALLAIG

84

85
388
Kinloch Glen
Kinloch
Loch Scresort
Rubha na Roinne
A'Bhrideanach
Schooner Pt.
571
ORVAL
R Ù M
KINLOCH CASTLE
Rubha Port na Caranean

Harris
Glen Harris
812
ASKIVAL
781
AINSHVAL
Rubha Sgorr an t-Snidhe

Rubha nam
Meirleach
Bay of Laig
Cleadale

Rubha an
Fhasaidh
Eigg
393
AN SGURR
Kildonnan

Galmisdale
Eilean

Eilean nan Each
SOUND OF EIGG

Muck
137
Port Mor

SOUND OF RÙM

Oigh-sgeir

Inset box (NL):

**Bhatarsaigh
(Vatersay)**
Ùidh
Bhatarsaigh
Bagh Bhatarsaigh

84

Flodaigh
(Flodday)
Caolas Shannraigh
207
**Sanndraigh
(Sandray)**

Lingeigh
(Lingay)
Greanamul
Caolas Phabaigh

Theisgeir
(Heiskers)
171
**Pabaidh
(Pabbay)**

Caolas Mhiui Laigh

NL

**Miùgh Laigh
(Mingulay)**
273

Bearnaraigh
(Berneray)
Caolas Bhearnaraigh

Barra Hd.

D

Sanna Point
Sanna Bay
Sanna
Portuairk
Achnaha
Point of
Ardnamurchan
ARDNAMURCHAN LIGHTHOUSE
Achosnich

Cairns of Coll
Ormsaigmore
Kilchoan
Ormsaigbeg
Kilchoan Bay

An Acairseid

E

Rubha Mor
Eilean Mor
Sorisdale
Bousd
Ardmore Bay
Ardmore Pt.
Bloody B

Cliad Bay
Arnabost
Gallanach
Grishipoll
73
Quinish Pt.
Glengorm
Castle
MULL MUSEUM
Ballyhaugh
Loch
Clad
COLL
OBAN
Hogh Bay
104
Arinagour
Rubha
an Aird
Quinish
Mishnish
S'AIRDE-BEINN
292

NL

Caliach Pt.
Totronald
Acha
Eilean Ornsay
Sunipol
Mornish
Penmore
Mill
MULL
THEATRE
Dervaig
Achnadrish
SPEINN

F

Feall
Bay
Arileod
Breachacha
Castle
Friesland
Loch
Eatharna
Calgary
THE OLD BYRE
HERITAGE CENTRE
Lettermore

CASTLEBAY
(Summer only)
Calgary Pt.
Gunna
Crossapol
Bay
Soa
Calgary Bay
Treshnish Pt.
Ensay
342
CARN MOR
Achnacraig

Rubh a'Chaoil
Haunn
Burg
Kilninian
Achleck
Fanmore
390
23

TIREE
Vaul
Bay
Salum
Caolas
Rubha Dubh
Ballygown

Hough
Skerries
Balephetrish
Bay
Vaul
Ruaig
Gott Bay
Soa
Treshnish Isles
Fladda
LOCH TUATH
EAS FORS
WATERFALL
Laggan
Bay
424
BEINN NA DRISE
Lagganulva

G

Balevullin
Kenovay
Scarinish
Eilean Dioghlum
Bearnus
313
Oskamull
R. Chraiginis
Kilkenneth
Moss
TIREE
Heanish
Lunga
Gometra
Ulva
Killiemor
Middleton
Heylipol
Crossapol
Rubha Traigh
an Duin
Ulva House
Balephuil
Loch
a'Phuill
Barrapol
Balemartine
Hynish Bay
Bac Mor
Little
Colonsay
LOCH NA KEAL
Eorsa
ISLE OF
Rinn
Thorbhais
141
Mannal
INCH KENNETH
CHAPEL
Inch
Kenneth
Derryguaig
Balephuil
Bay
Port Snoig
Hynish
Staffa
STAFFA
FINGAL'S CAVE
Balnahard

H

Erisgeir
MACKINNON'S CAVE
17
561

519
BEINN NA SREINE
ARDMEANACH
Killiemore
House
THE BURG
Kilfinichen
Bay

MACLEAN'S CROSS
Eilean
Annraidh
IONA ABBEY AND
CATHEDRAL
Rubha nan Cearc
LOCH SCRIDAIN

J

IONA HERITAGE CENTRE
100
ST COLUMBA EXHIBITION
& WELCOME CENTRE
Kintra
Torrans
Iona
Baile Mor
Aridhglas
Eorabus
Stac an
Aoineidh
Fionnphort
A849
Lee
18
BRO
Fidden
Tiraghoil
Bunessan
376
CRUACHAN MIN
Loch
Assapol
Erraid
ROSS OF MULL
Uisken
Soa I.
Ardalanish
Ardchiavaig
Scoor
125
Rubha nam
Braithrean
Eilean a'Chalmain
Malcolm's Pt.
Rubh Ardalanish

72

Torran Rocks

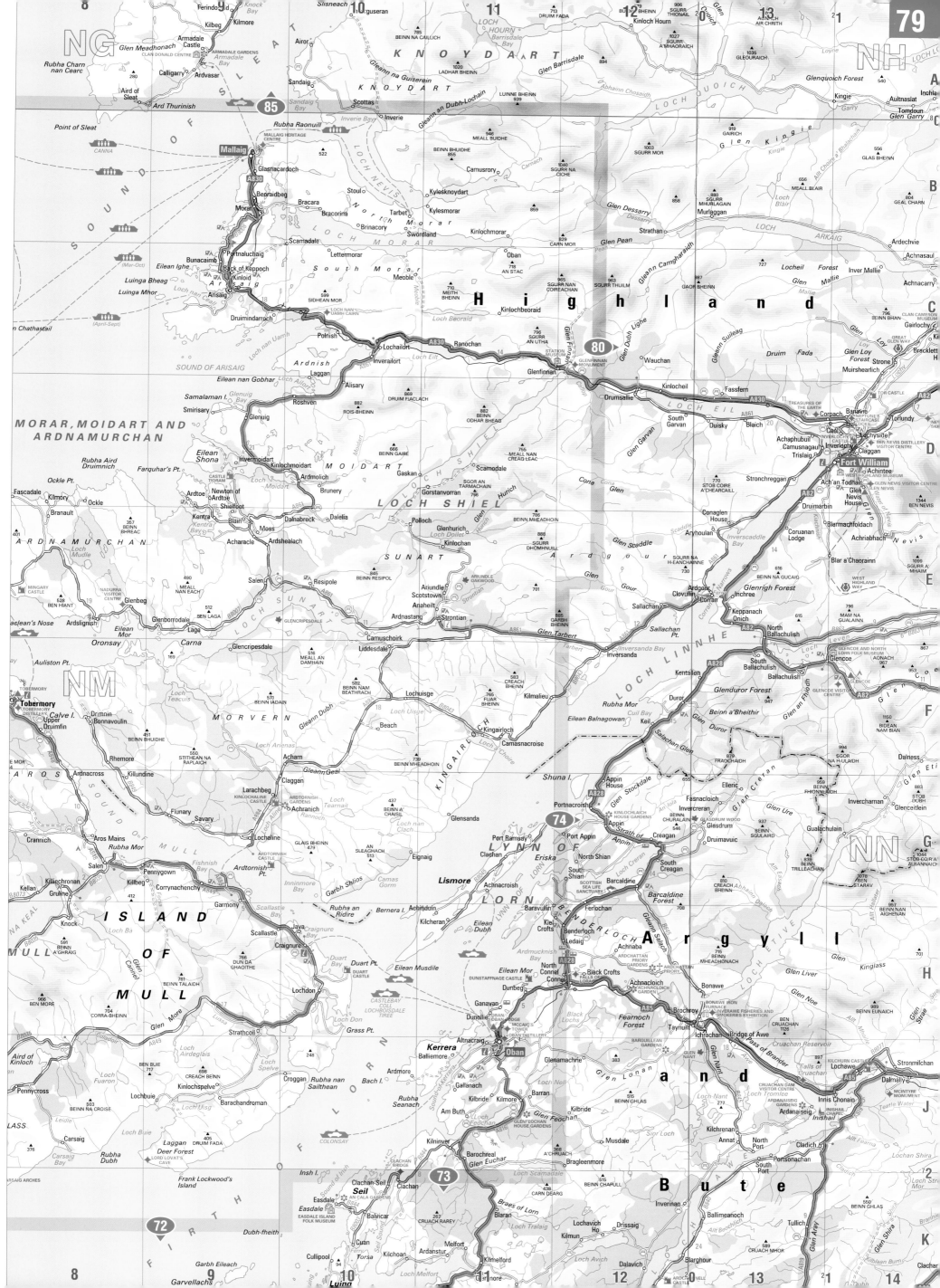

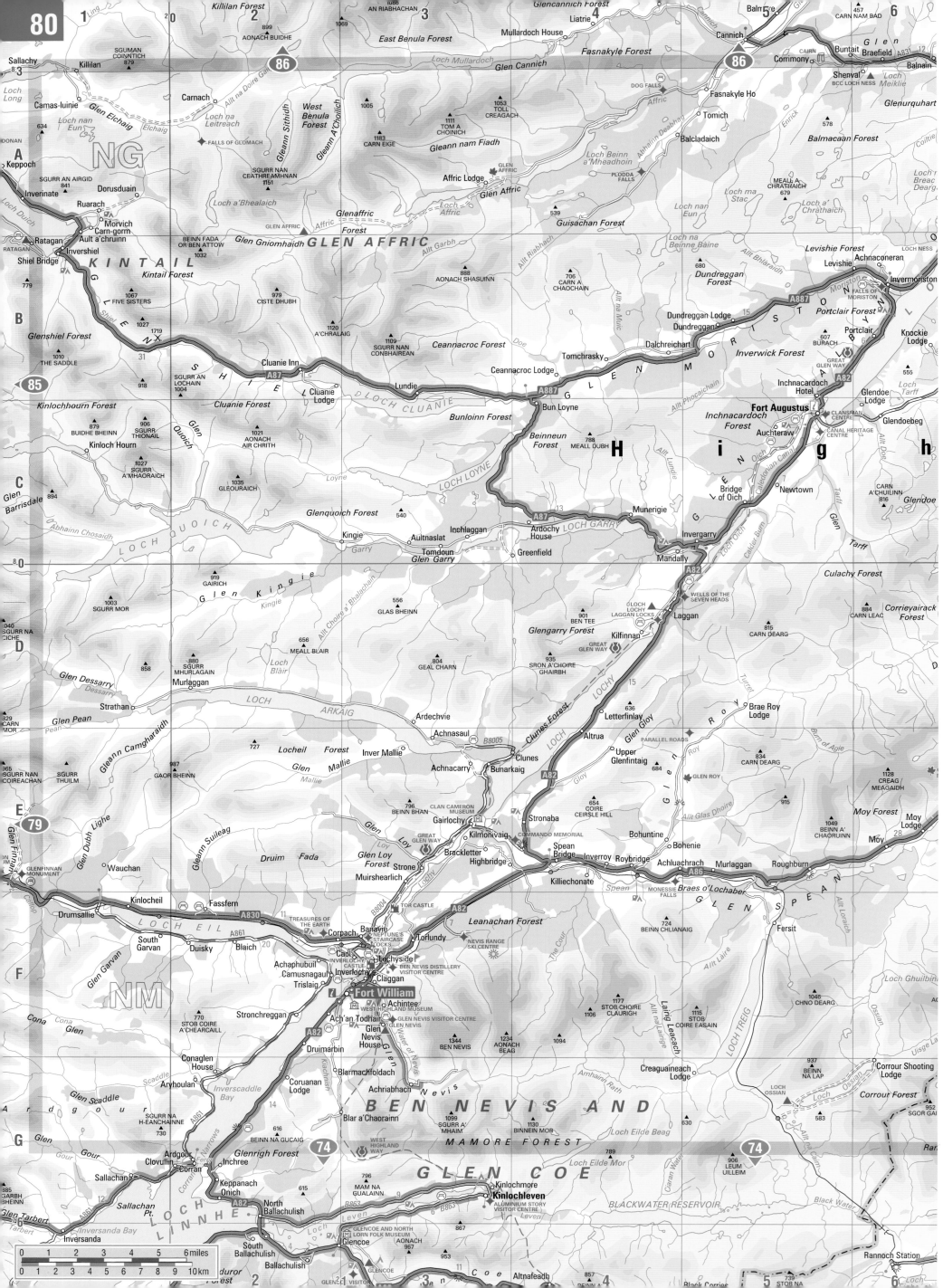

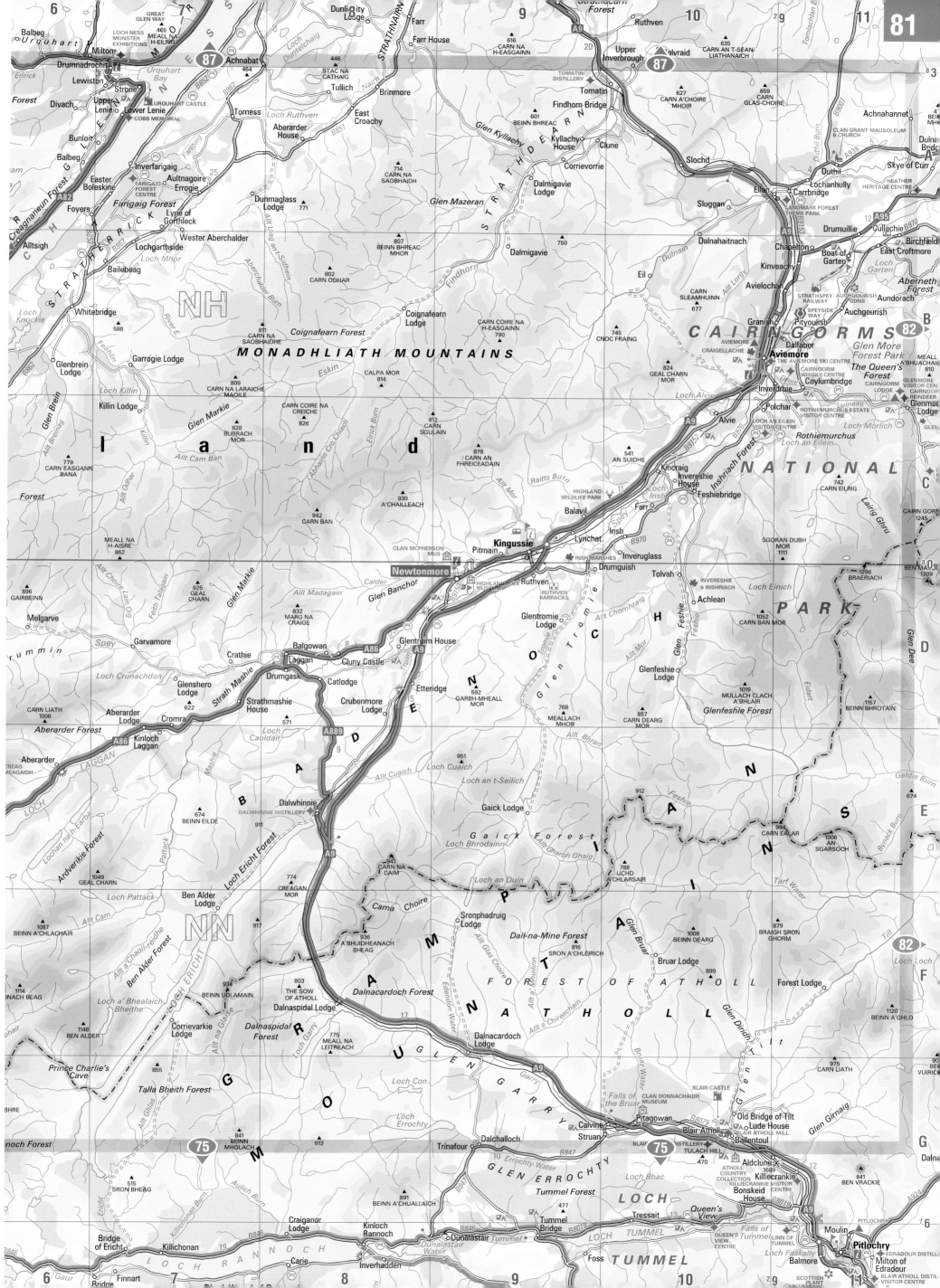

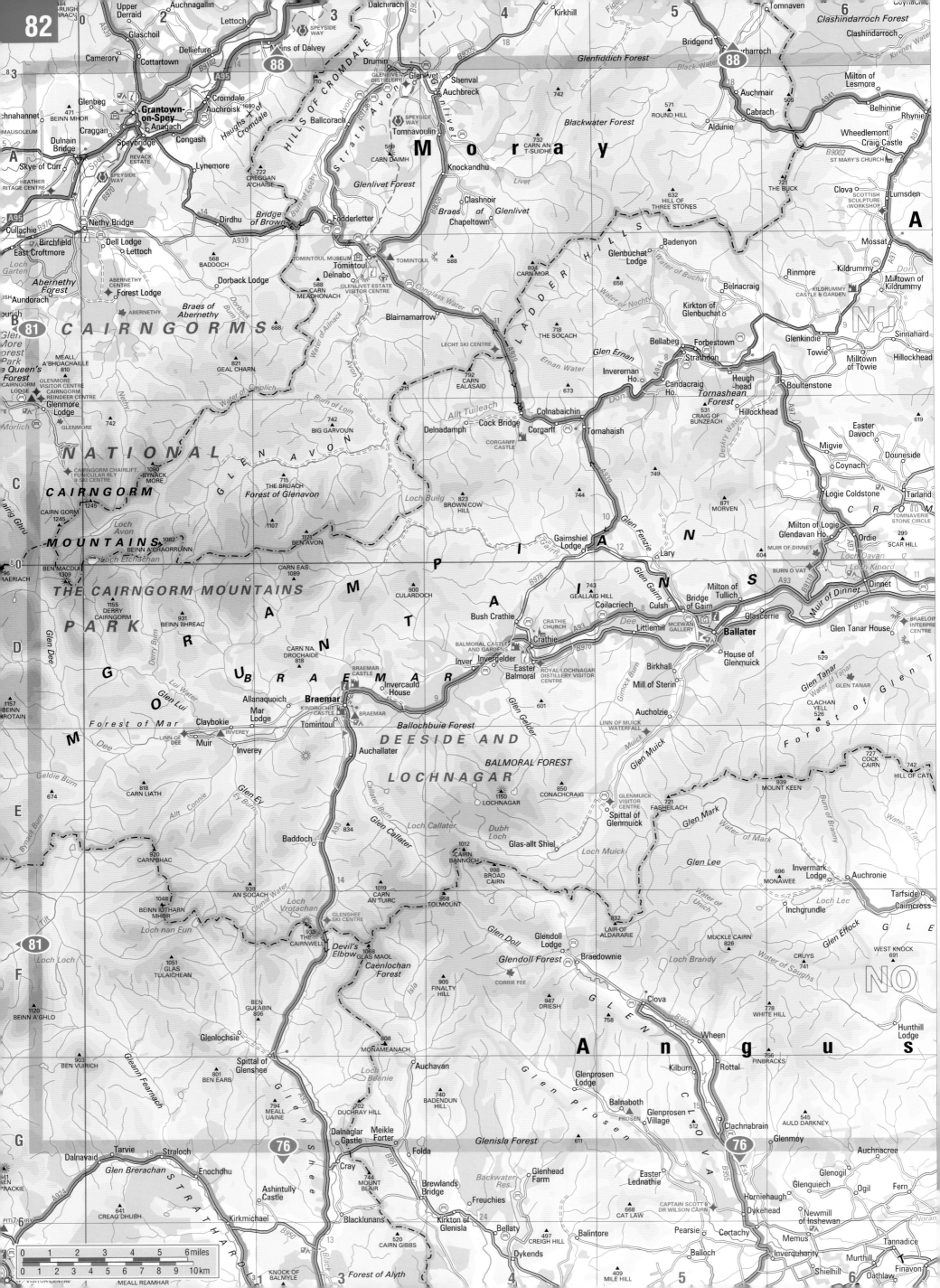

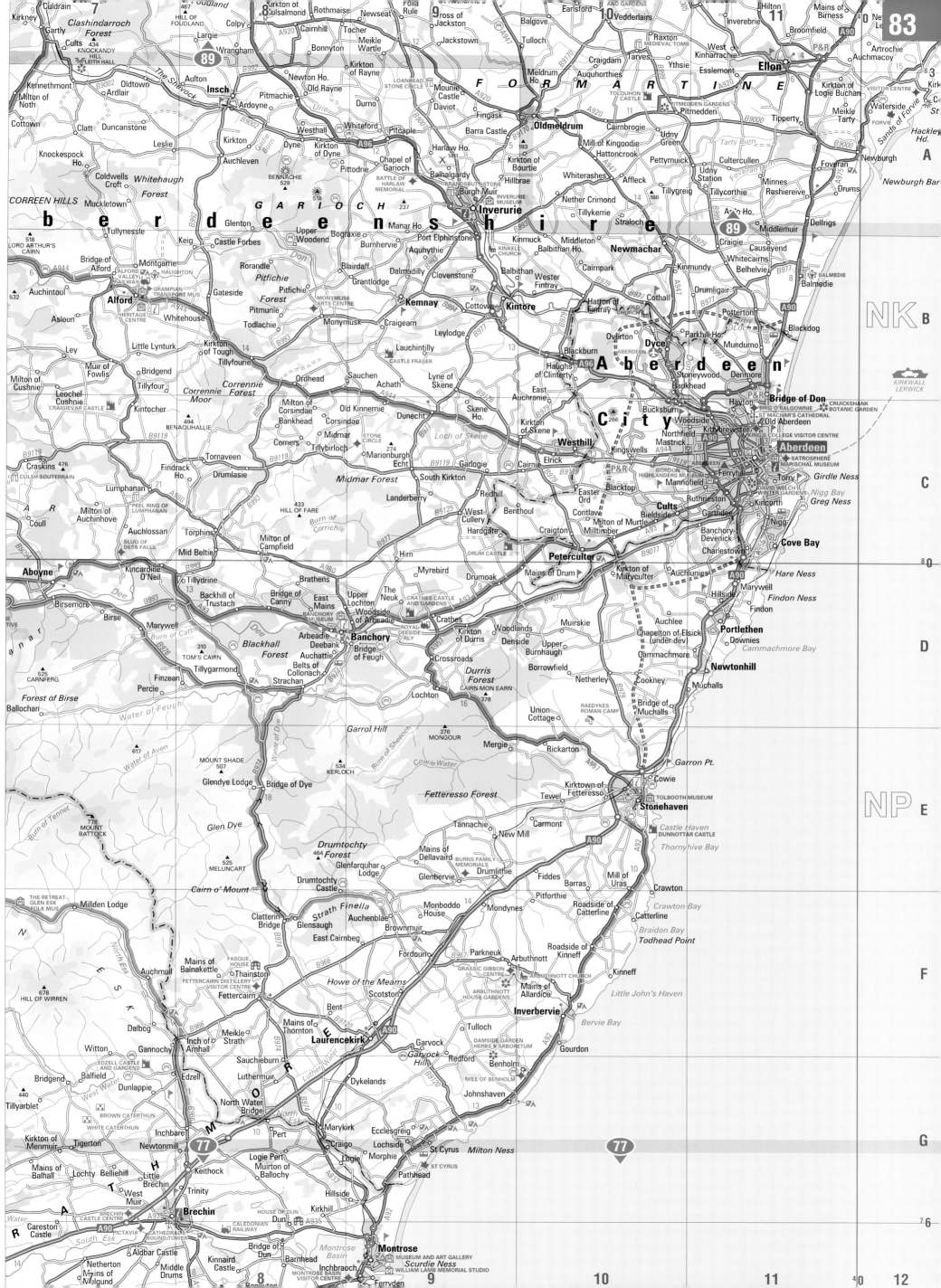

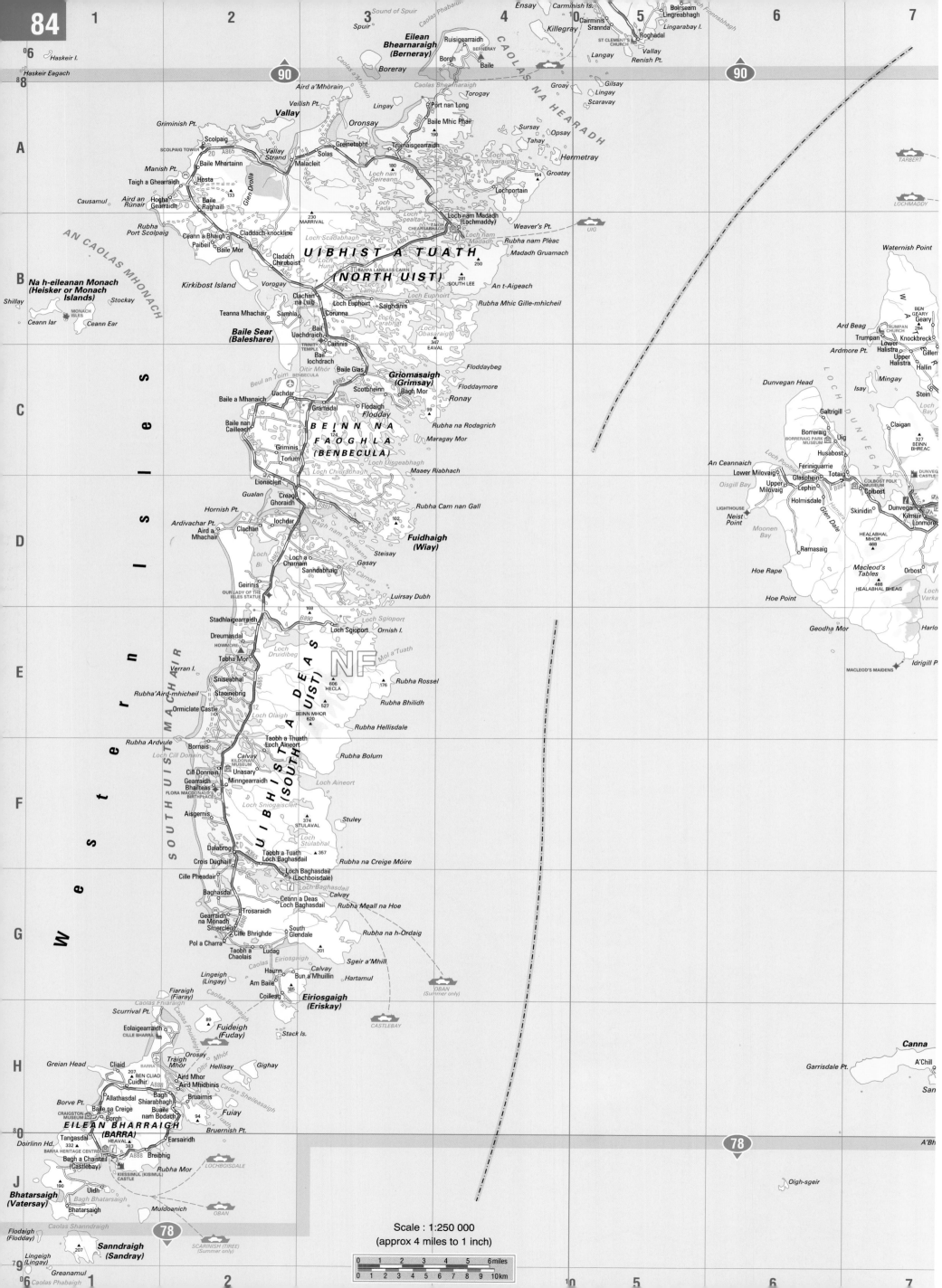

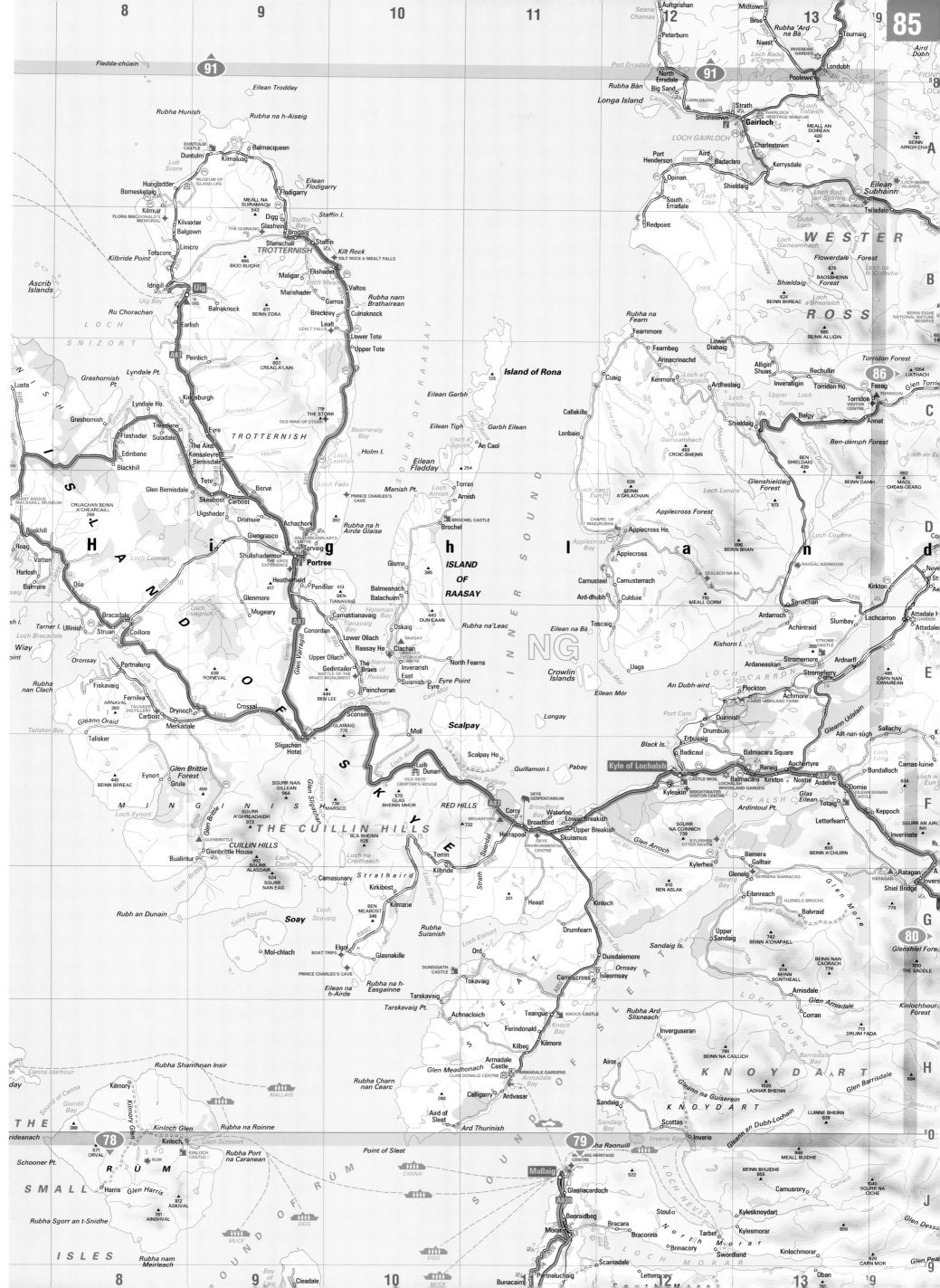

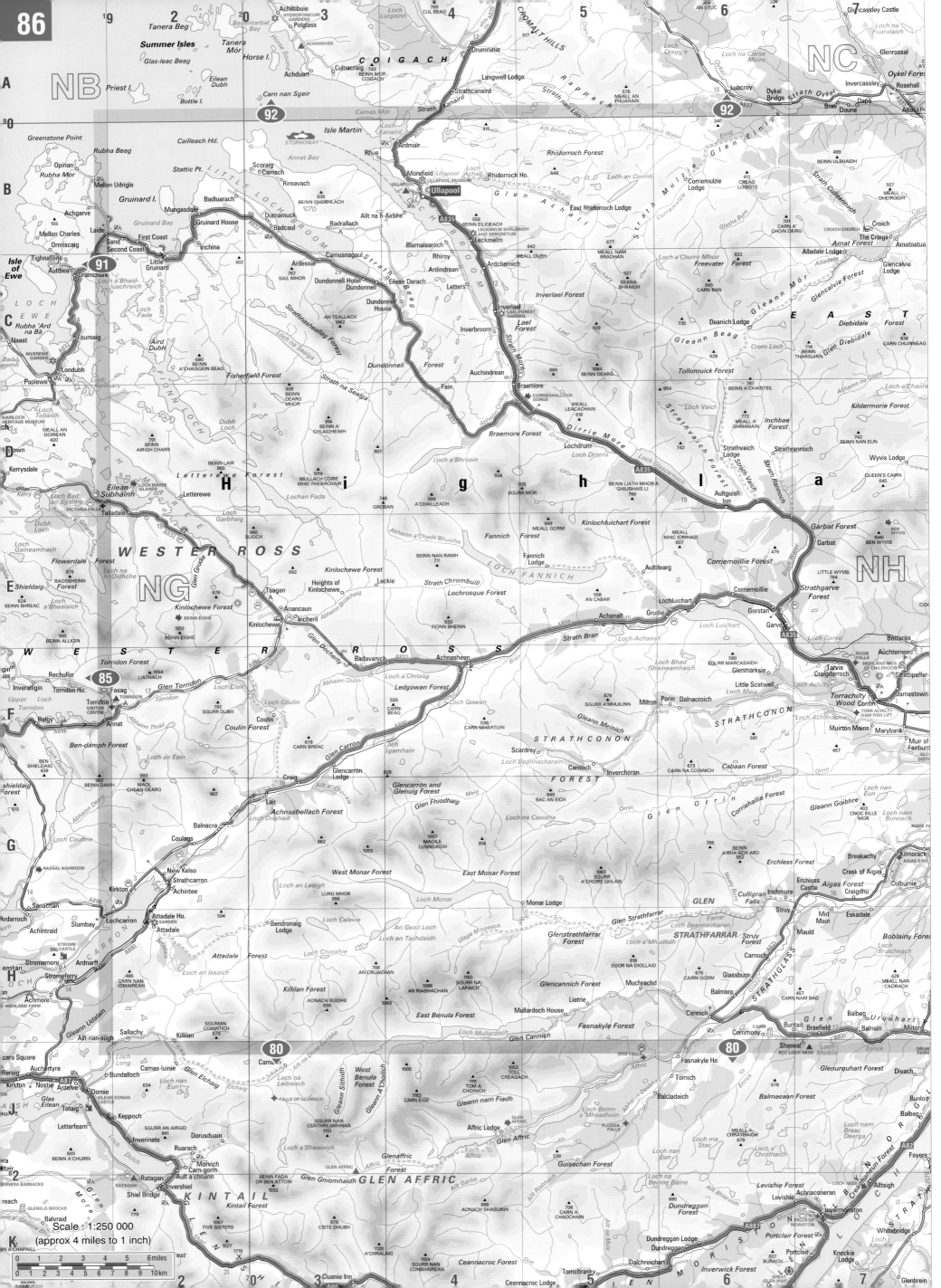

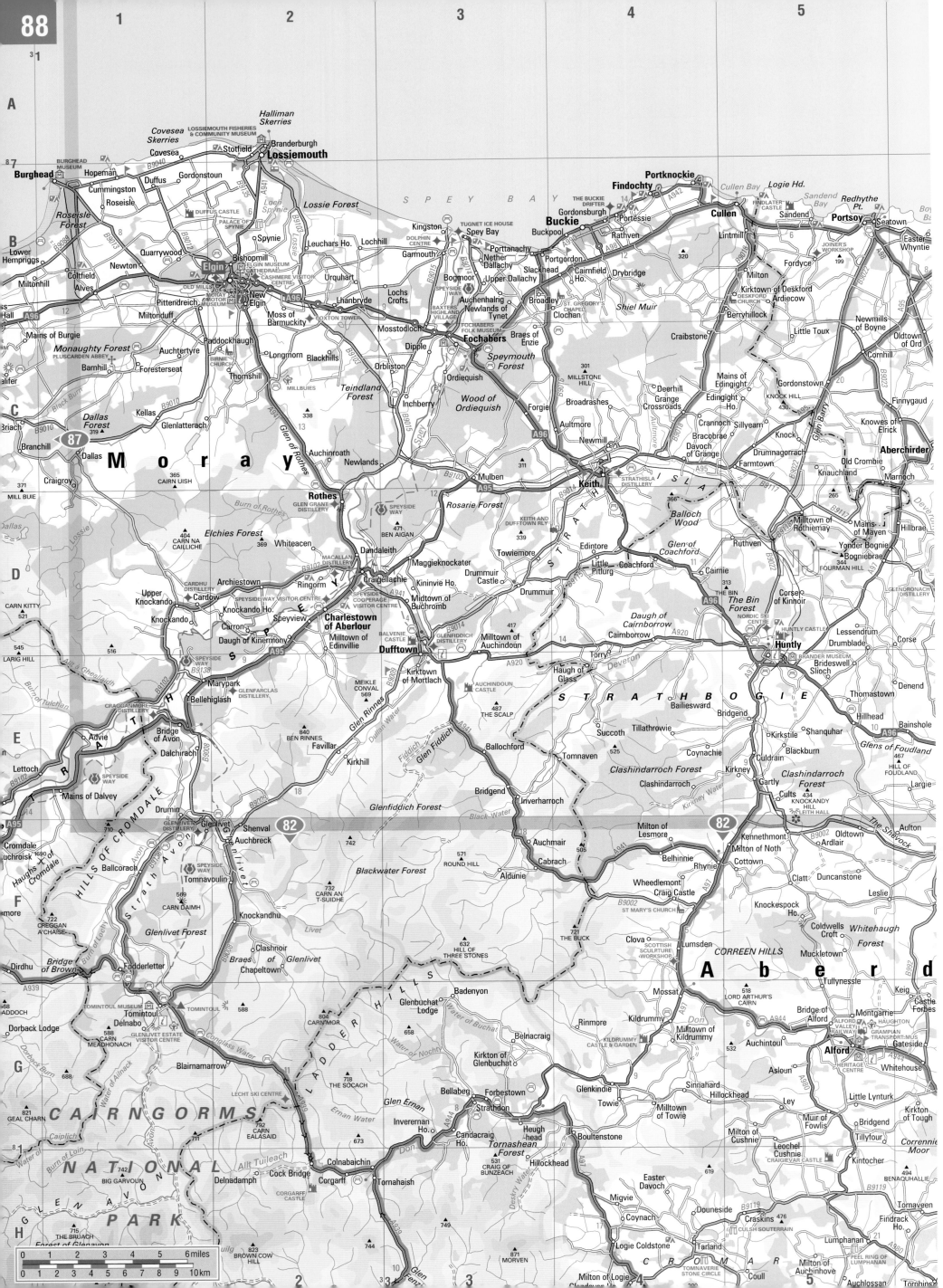

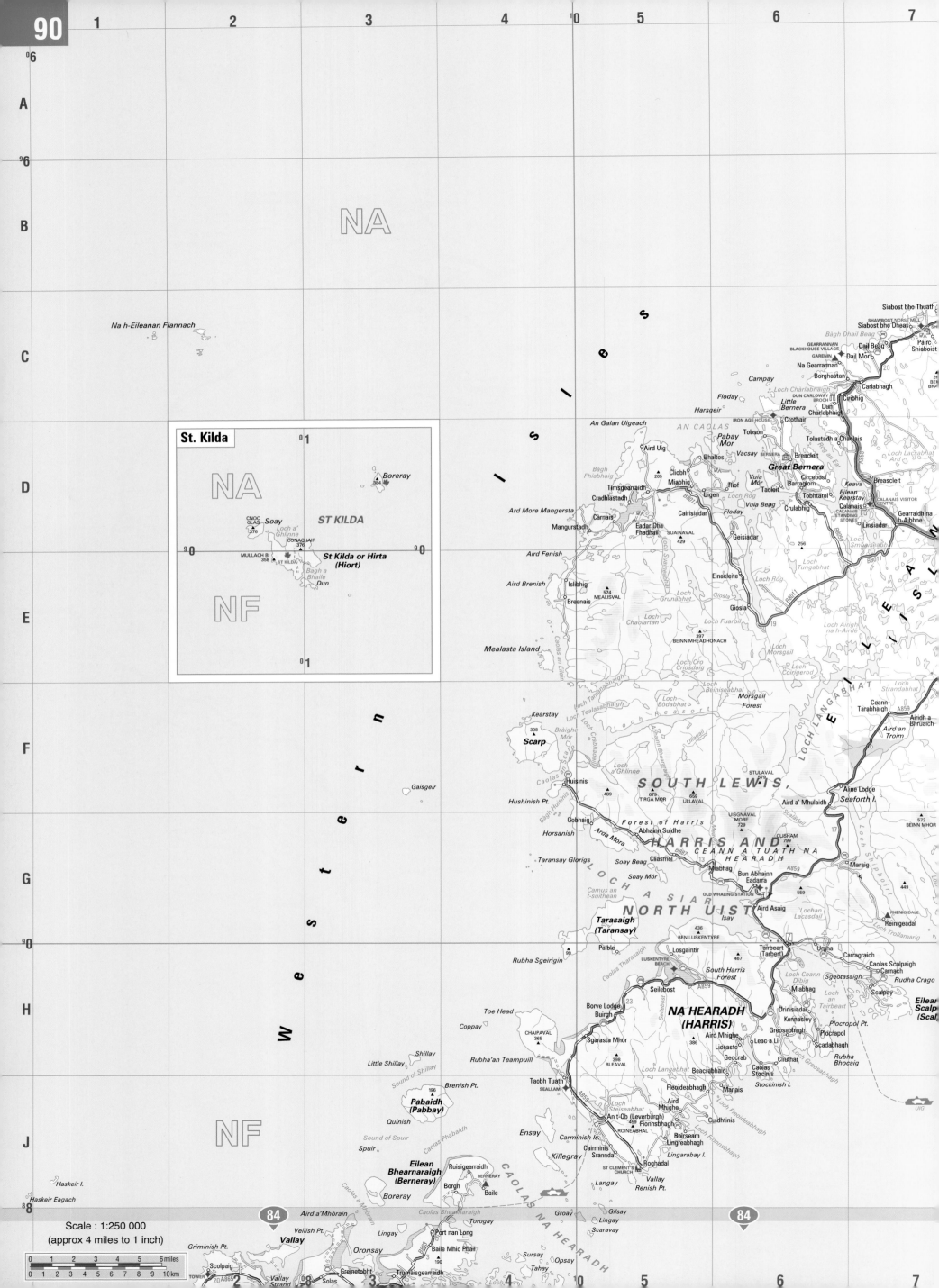

St. Kilda

NA

NF

ST KILDA

Boreray

CNOC
GLAS
376
Soay
Loch a'
Ghlinne
CONACHAIR
376
MULLACH BI
358
ST KILDA
St Kilda or Hirta
(Hiort)
Bàgh a
Bhaile
Dun

Na h-Eileanan Flannach

NA

Scale : 1:250 000
(approx 4 miles to 1 inch)

0   1   2   3   4   5   6 miles
0 1 2 3 4 5 6 7 8 9 10km

RUBHA ROBHANAIS
(BUTT OF LEWIS)

CHURCH OF ST MOULAG
Eòropaidh   Coig Peighinnean
Suainebost   Tàbost   Port Nis
Cross Sands   Cros   HARBOUR VIEW GALLERY
Aird Dhail   Lìonal
Dail bho Dheas   Dail bho Thuath   Sgiogarstaigh

Gabhsann bho Thuath
Gabhsann bho Dheas
Mealabost Bhuirgh   Cuiashader
Bail Àrd Bhuirgh   Cellar Head
Coig Peighinnean Bhuirgh
Rubha Leathann   Siadar
Siadar Ìarach
Aird Barvas   Siadar Uarach
Baile an Truiseil

Barabhas Ìarach   Barabhas Uarach
BLACK HOUSE MUSEUM   Bru   Barabhas
Labost   Arnol   Bail Ur Tholastaidh
Bragar   Tolastadh bho Thuath
WBOST MUSEUM   MUIRNEAG   Tolsta Head

Griais   Gleann Tholàstaidh
Col   Creag Fhraoch
Bac   Vatisker Pt.
Col Uarach   Breibhig
Coll Sands   Rubha an t-Siumpain
Aird Thunga   Port Nan Giùran
Grianan   Tunga   Cnoc   Aird
An Gleann Ur   Newmarket   Amhlaigh
Lacasdal   Sròn Ruadh   Port Mholair
MUSEUM NAN EILEAN   Sulaisiadar   Seisiadar
STORNOWAY   Garrabost   EYE
LEWIS LOFT CENTRE   Mealabost   PENINSULA
Sanndabhaig   Aiginis   Pabail Uarach
AN LANNTAIR GALLERY   ST COLUMBA'S   An Cnoc   Pabail Ìarach
Tolm   Suardail
Arnish Moor   Holm I.   Bàgh Phabail
Acha Mor   A'Chearc
Loch a'
Ghainmhich   ULLAPOOL
Griomsidar
Liurbost   Ben Casgro
Ranais   Raerinish Pt.
Soval Lodge   Crosbost
Barkin Is.   Tabhaidh Mhor
Ceos   Eilean Chaluim
Lacasaidh   Chille   Eilean Orasaidh
Baile   Gearraidh Bhaird   Cromar
Ailein   Cabharstadh   Eilean Thoraidh
Slidinis   Tabost   Marbhig
Ceann   KERSHADER   Calbost
Shiphoirt
Taobh a' Ghlinne   Grabhair
Kebock Head
PARK   Orasaigh
OR   Leumrabhagh
PAIRC   Eisgean
Loch Shell or Loch Sealg
Srianach
Eilean Iubhard
CRIONAIG
Mol Truisg
Gob Rubh'Uisenis
Rubha Bhrollum
Rubha
a'Bhaird

CAOLAS NAN EILEAN
Garbh
Eilean
Eilean Mhuire
Na h-Eileanan Mòra   Eilean an Tighe
(Shiant Islands)

NB

NG

Eilean Mullagrach

Glas-leac Mór

Glas-leac
Beag

Priest I.   Bottle I.

Greenstone Point
Rubha Beag
Opinan
Rubha Mór   Mellon Udrigle
Sròn a' Gheodha   Eilean   Gruinard I.
Dhuibh   Furadh Mór   Achgarve   Munga
Camas   Mellon Charles   Laide   Gruinard Bay
Rubha Reidh   Loch an   Ormiscaig   Sand   First Coast
Draing   Cove   Tighnafiline   Second Coast
AN CUAIDH   Isle   Aultbea   Drumchork   Little Gruinard
Melvaig   of
Ewe
Aultgrishan   Inverasdale
Midtown   LOCH
Brae   EWE
Seana   Rubha 'Ard
Chamas   na Bà
Peterburn   INVEREWE   Tournaig
GARDEN   Aird
Naast   Dubh
Port Erradale   Loch Bad
North   a'Chreamh   Londubh   Loch
Erradale   Poolewe   Kernsary
Rubha Bàn   Big Sand   FIONN
LOCH
Longa Island   Strath
CARN   GAIRLOCH   Smithstown   Gairloch   HERITAGE MUSEUM
Rubha Hunish   Rubha na h-Aiseig   LOCH GAIRLOCH   MEALL AN
DOIREAN   BEINN
Fladda-chùain   420   AIRIGH CHARR
Charlestown
DUNTULM   Port
CASTLE   Eilean Troddday   Henderson   Aird

85

92

86

85

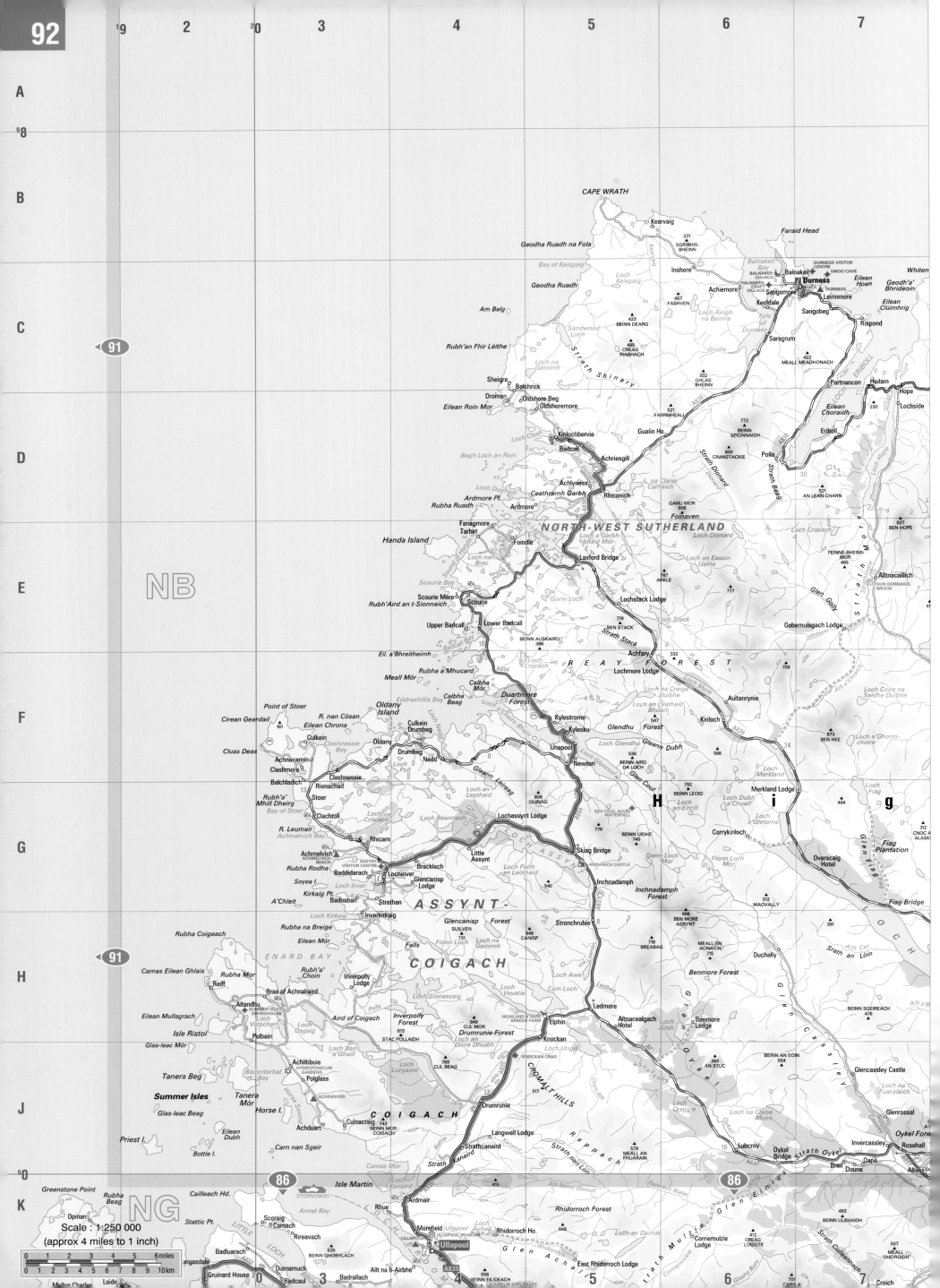

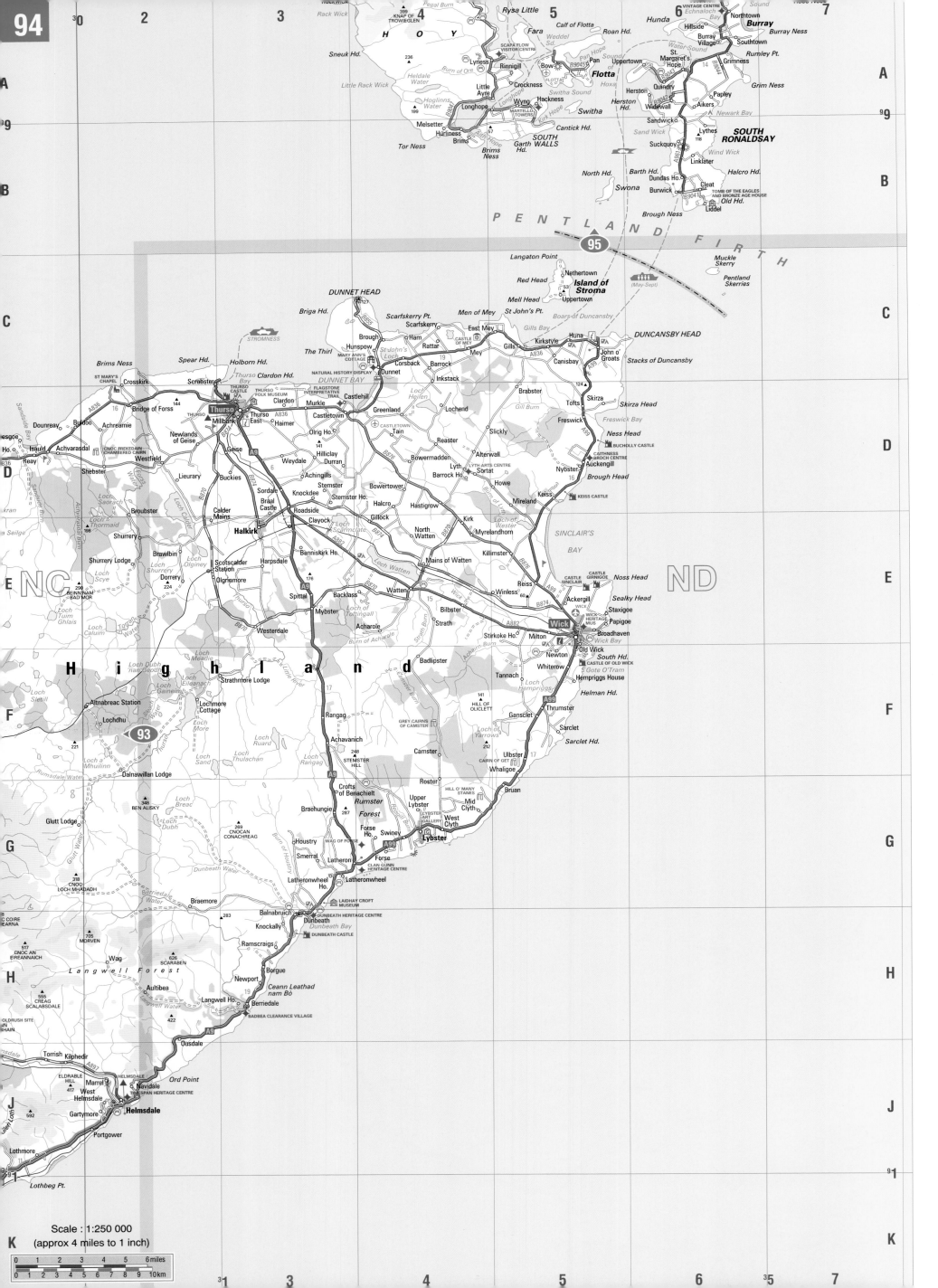

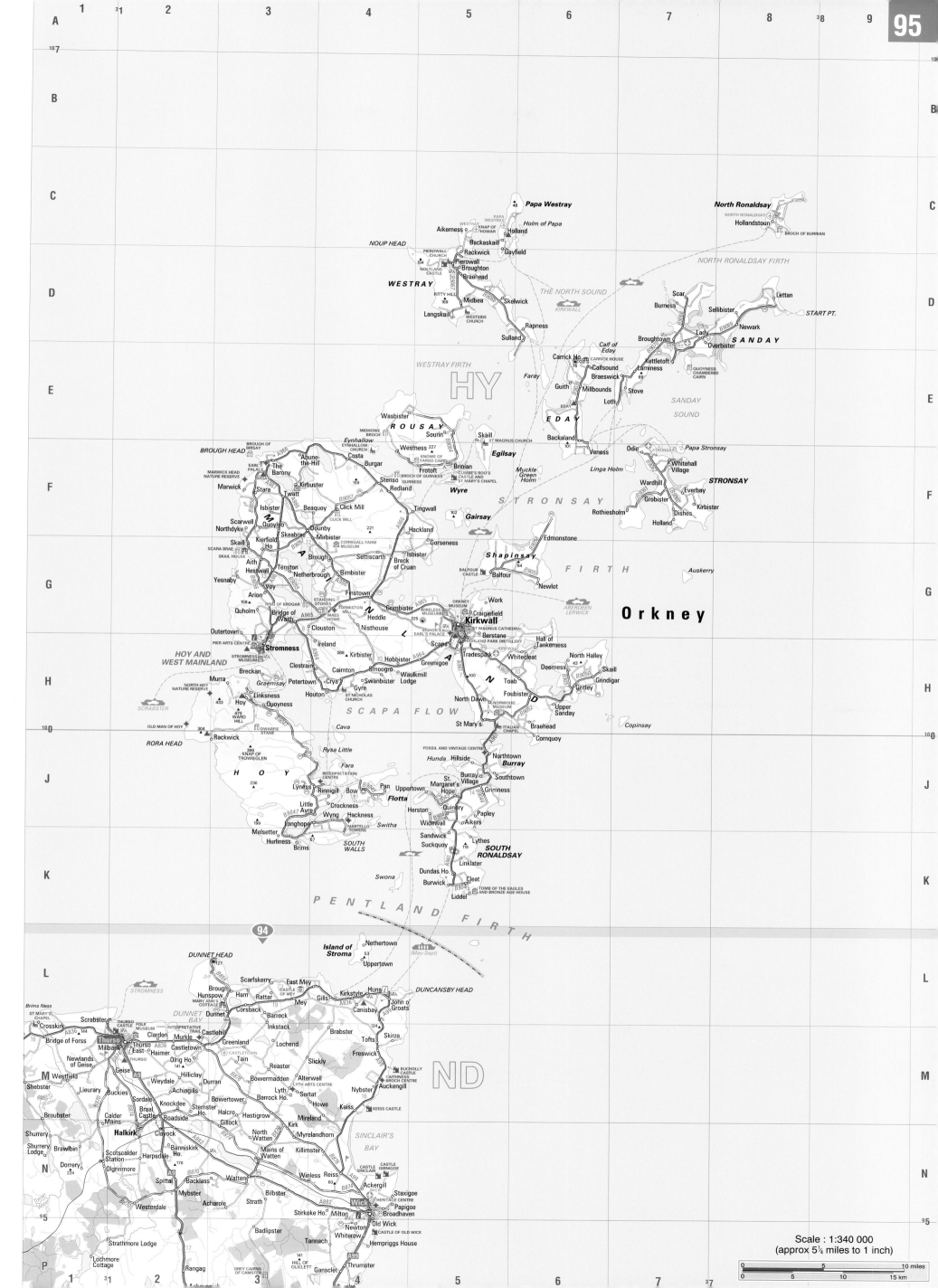

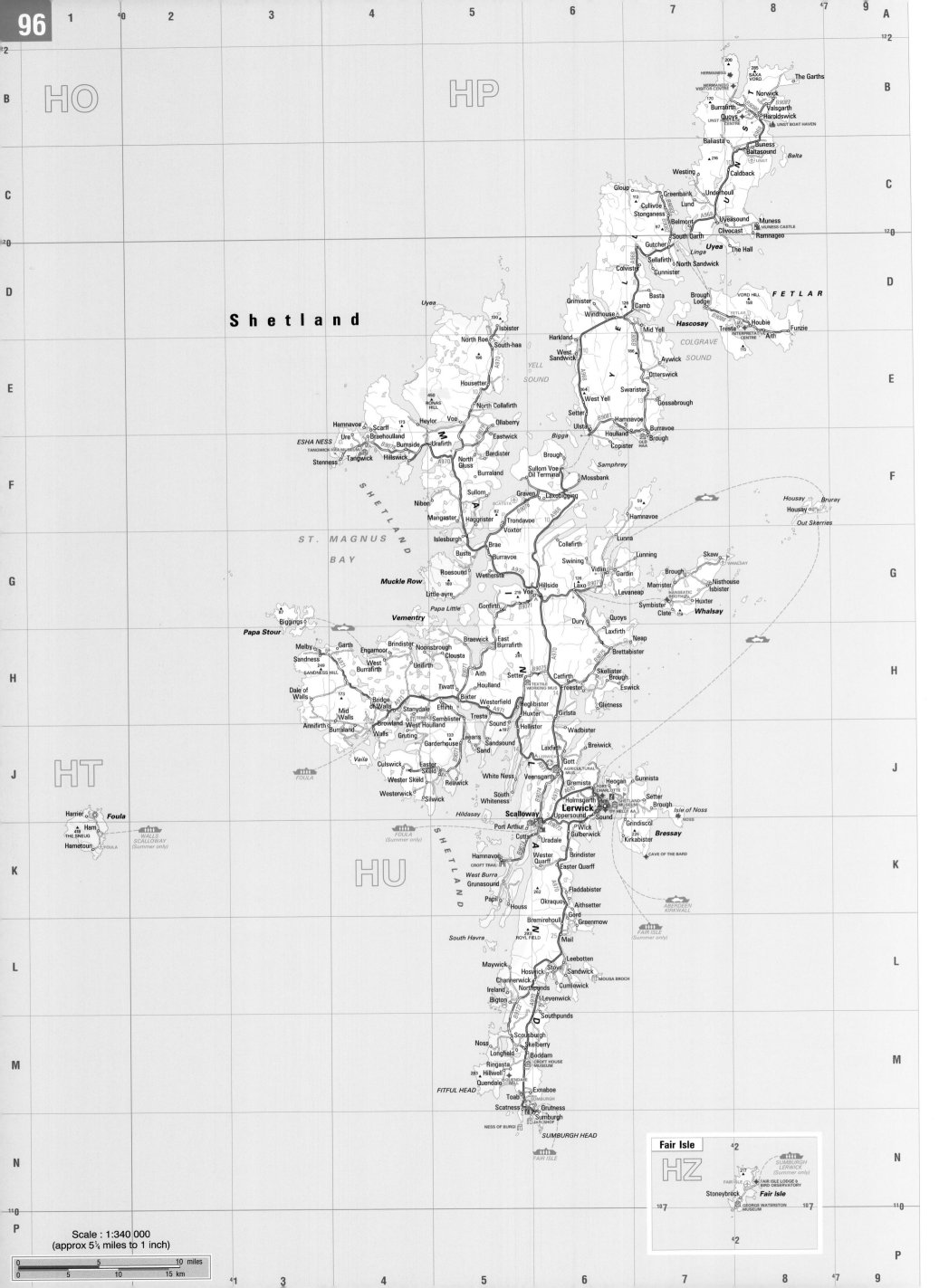

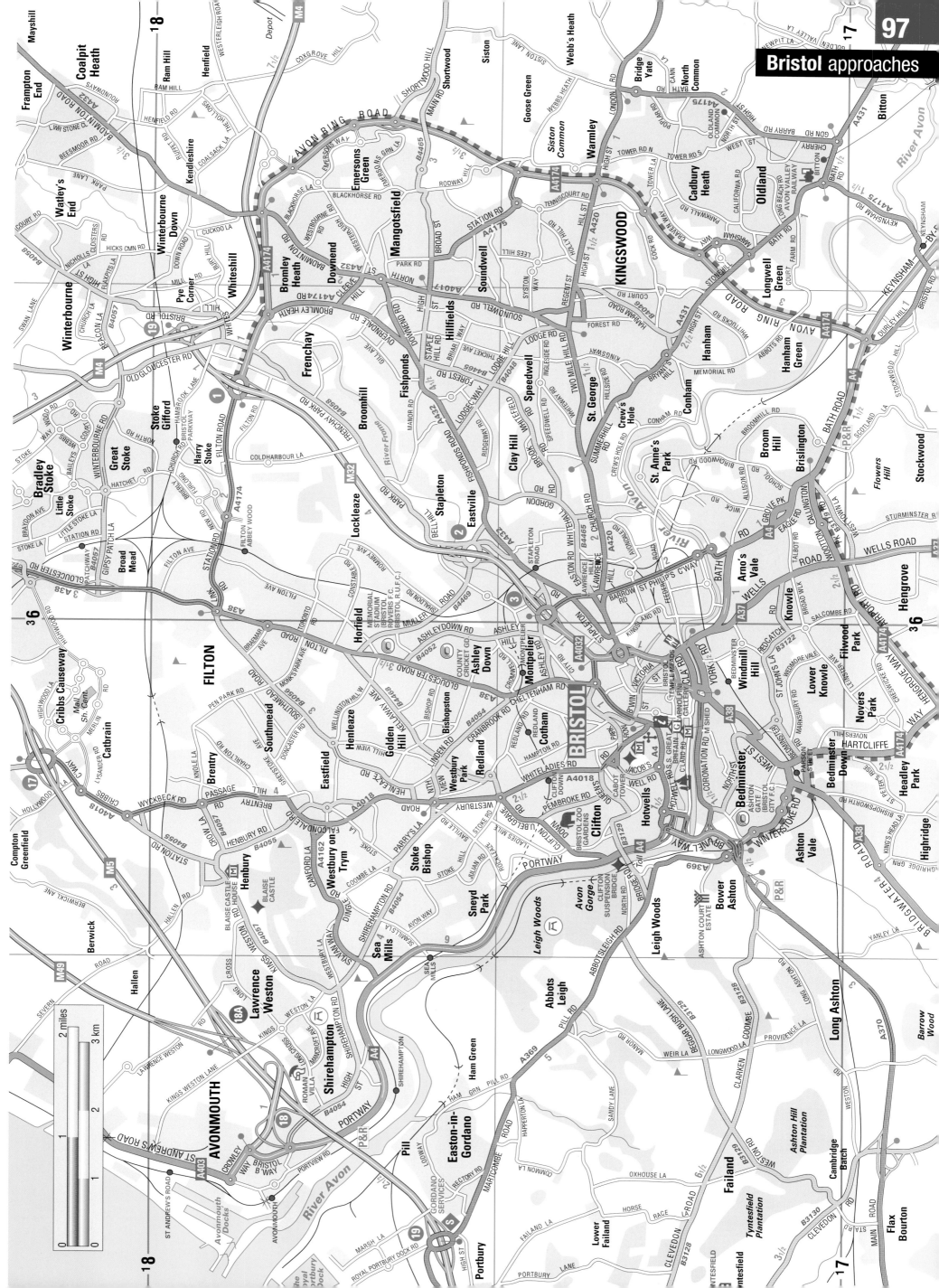

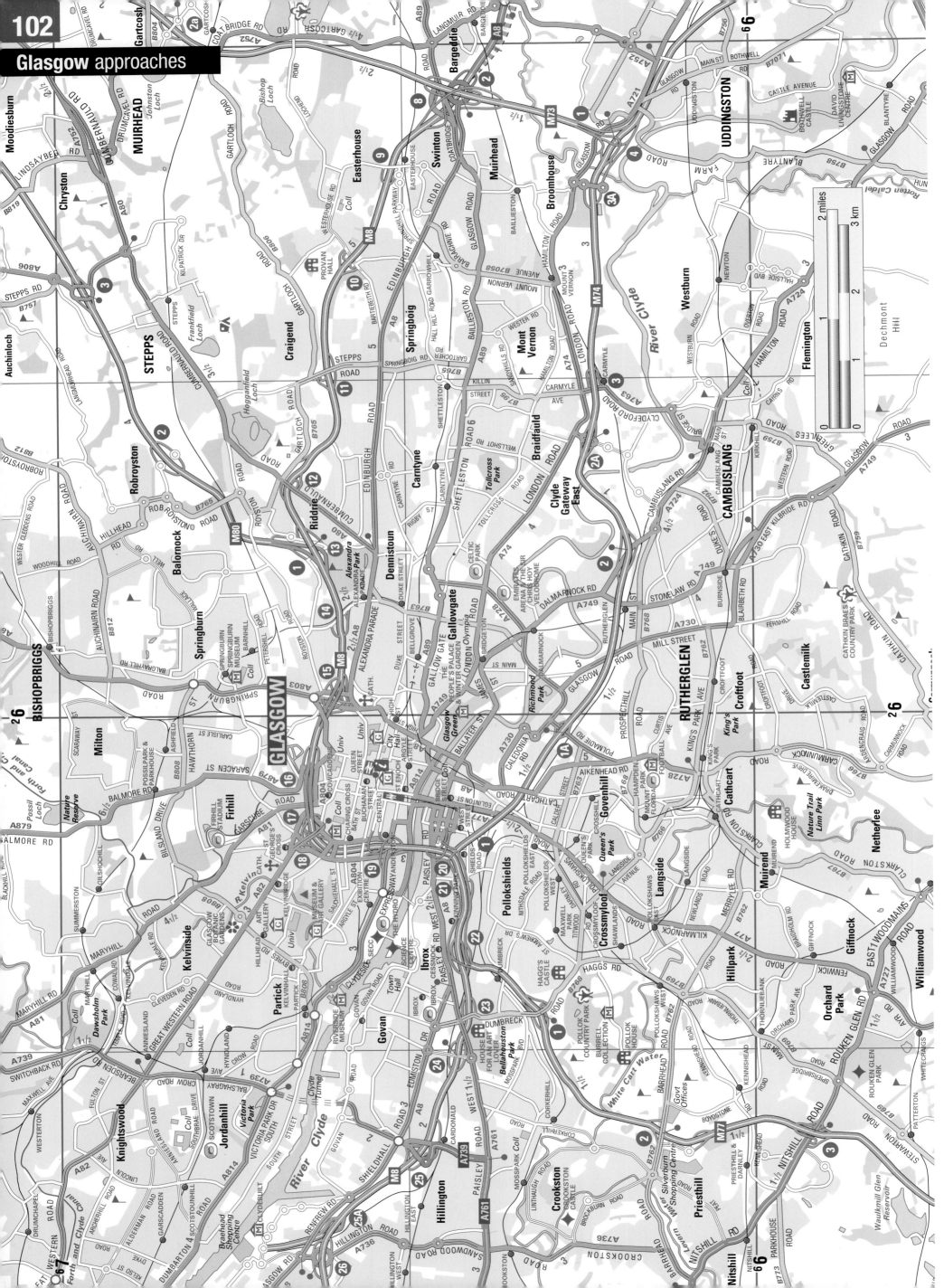

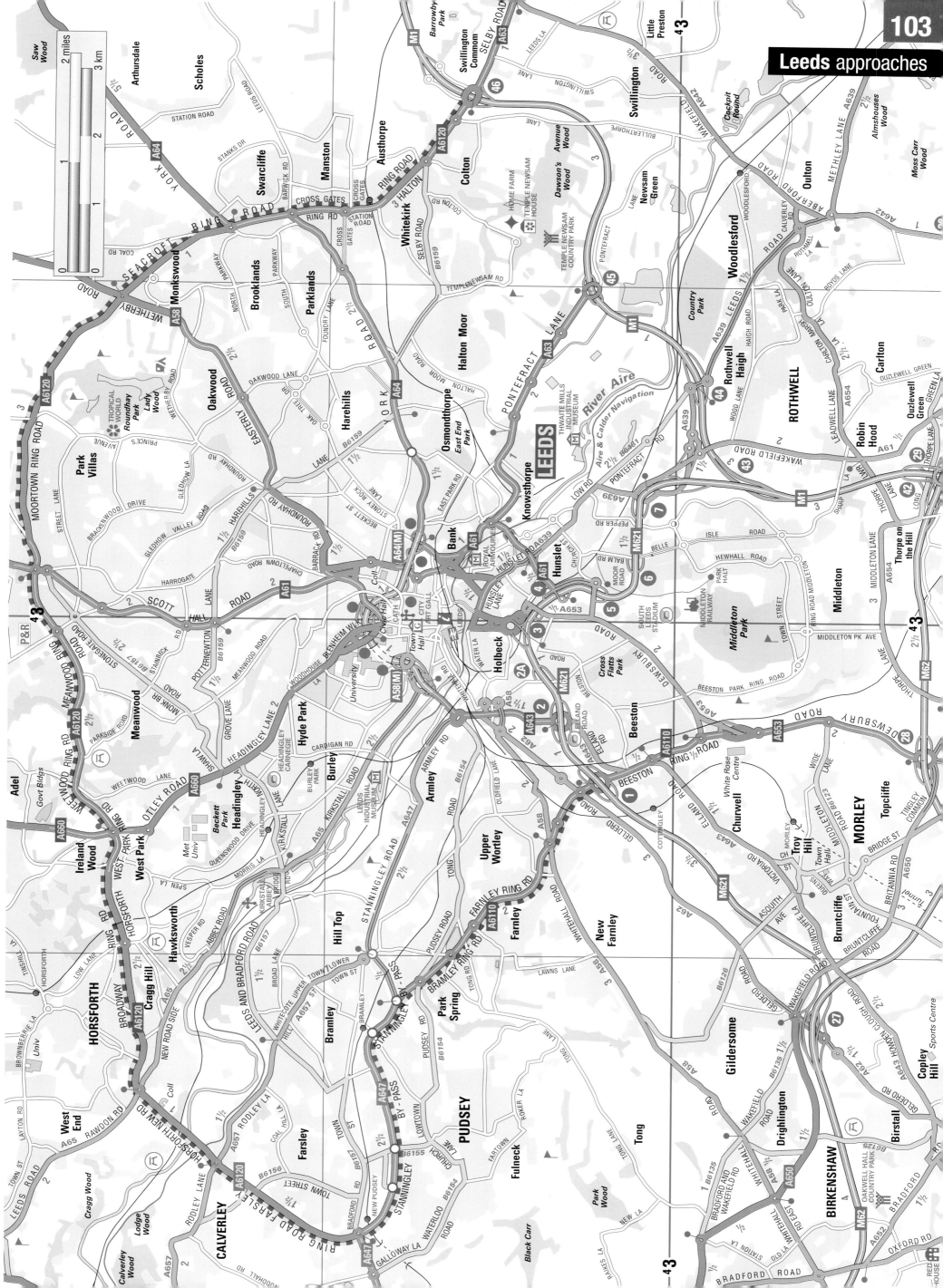

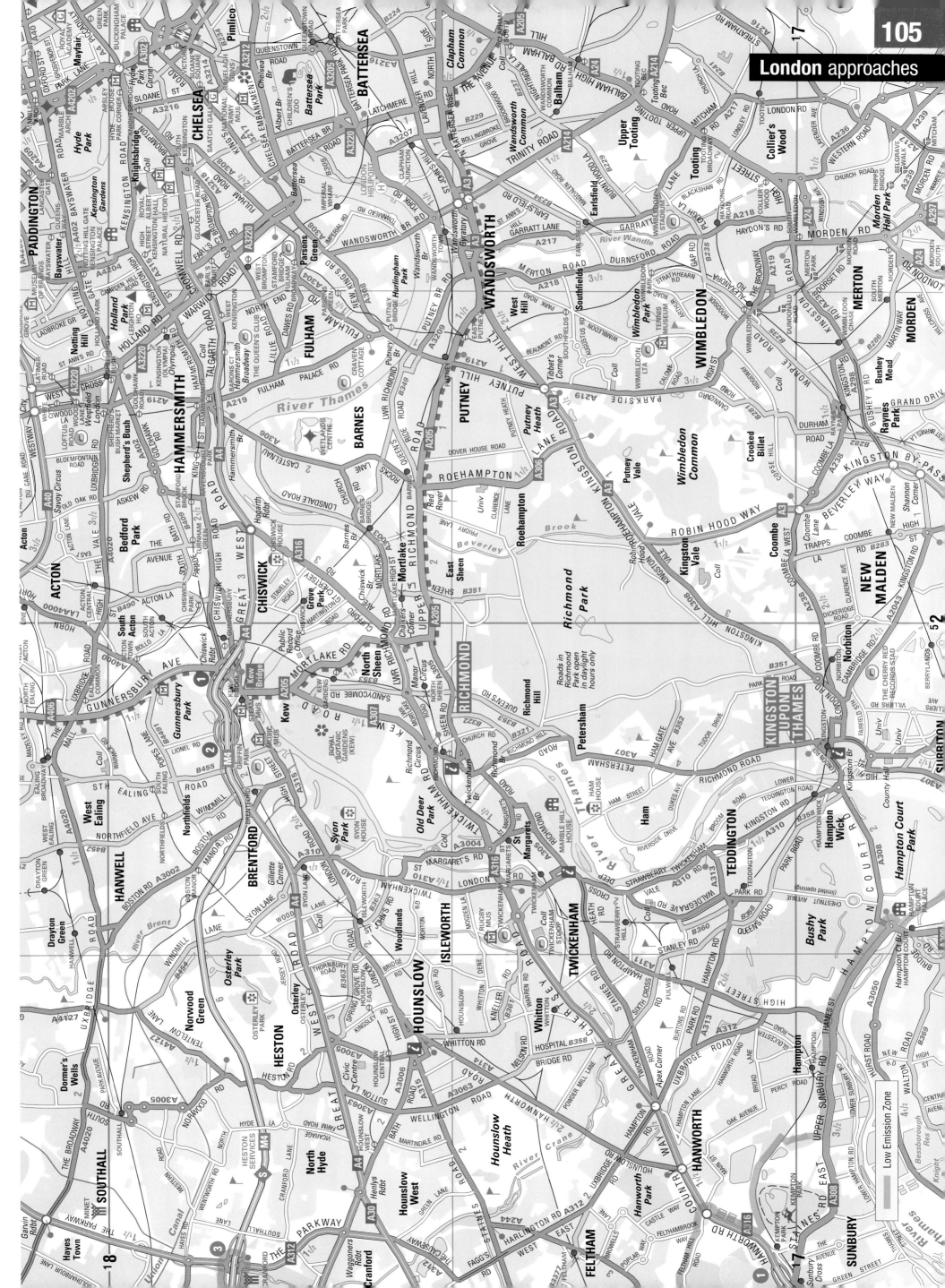

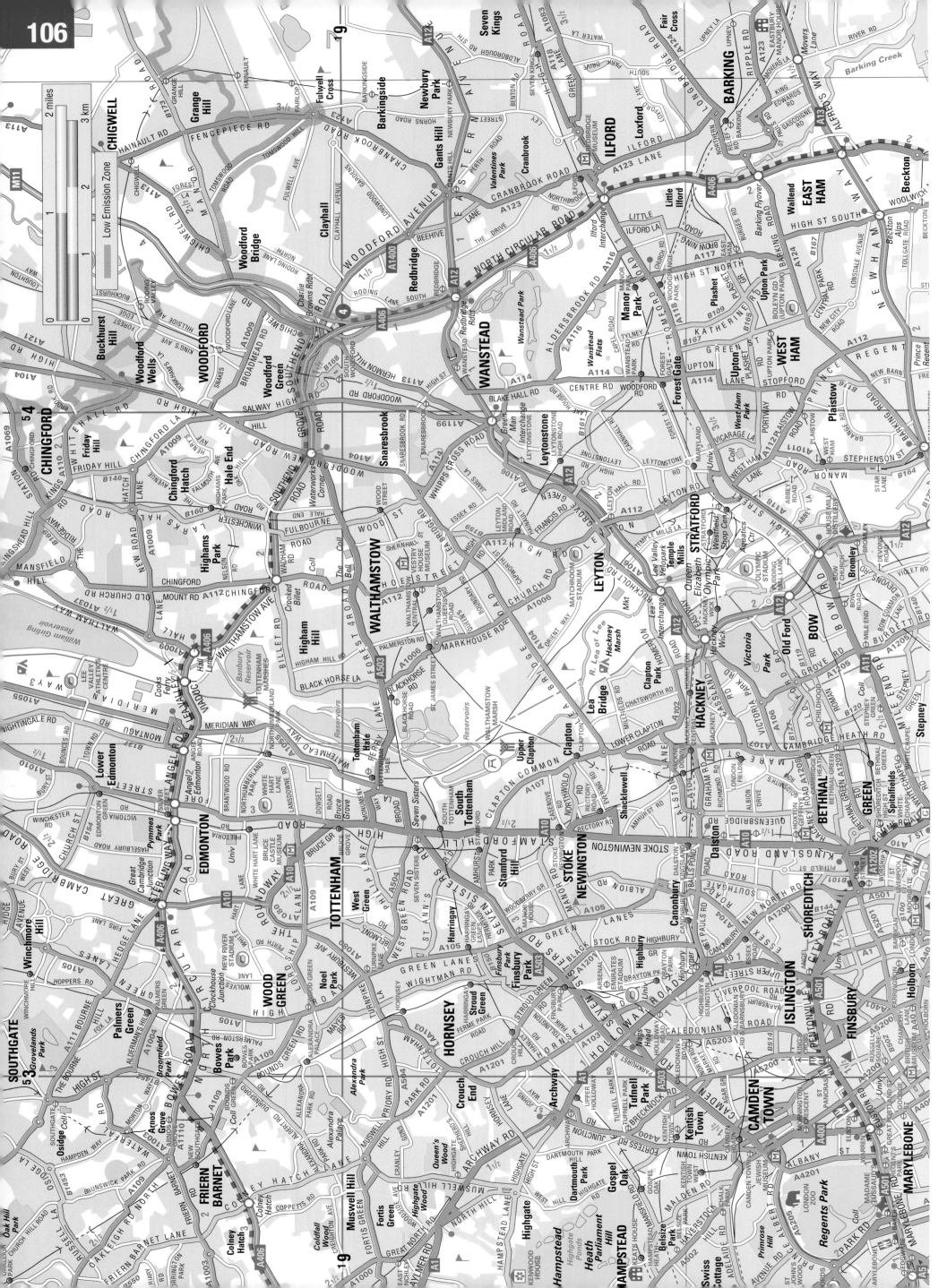

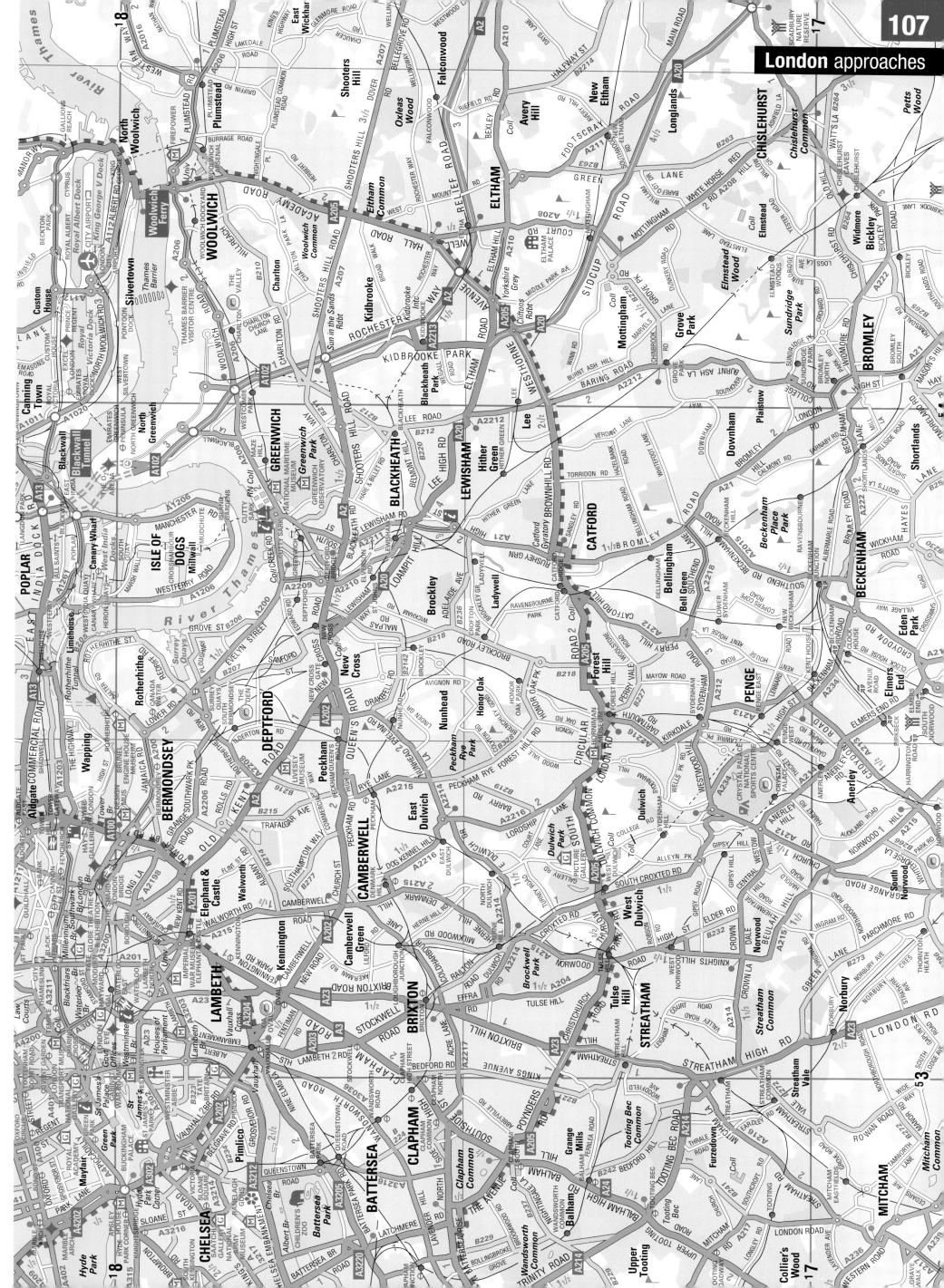

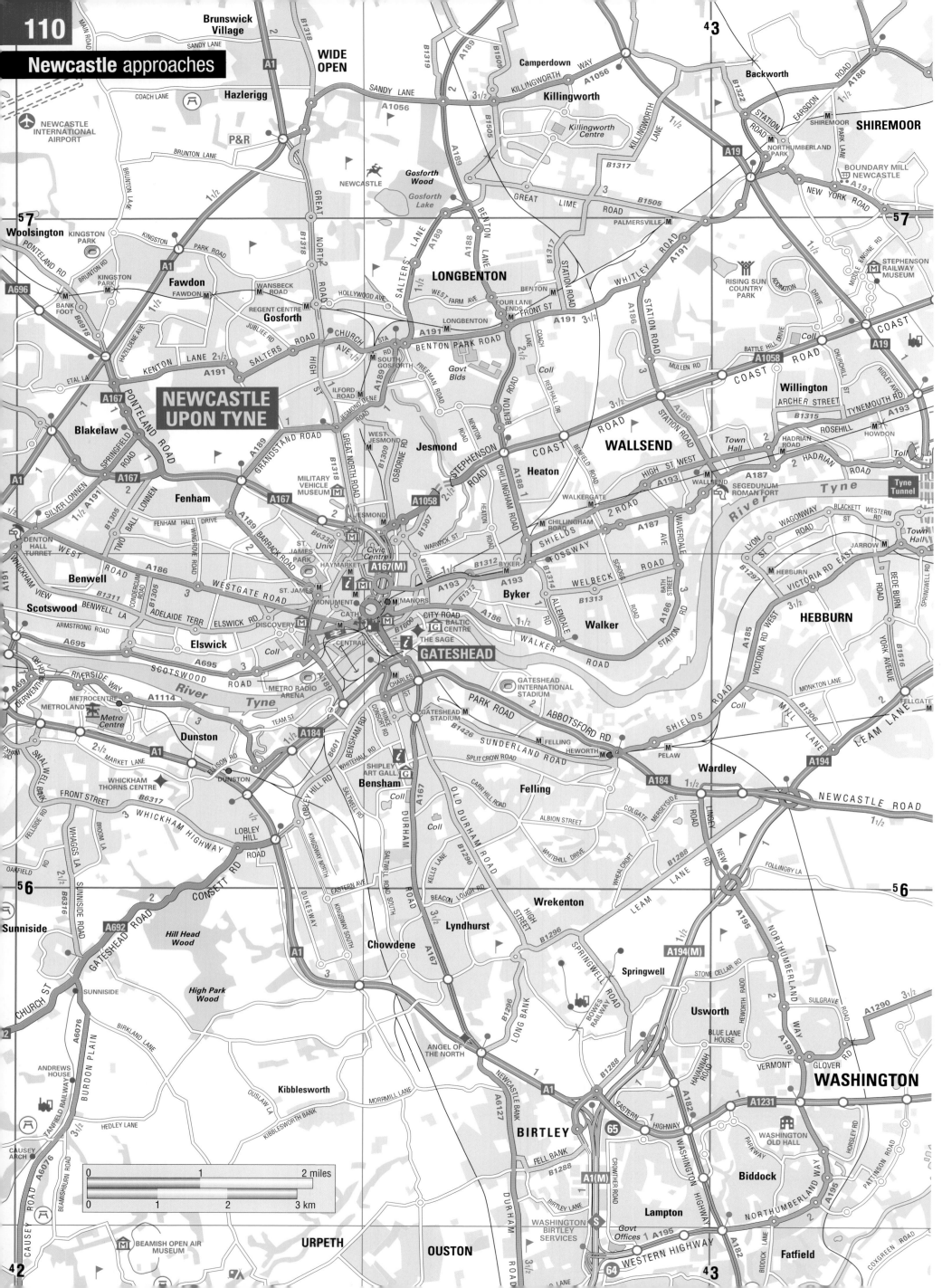

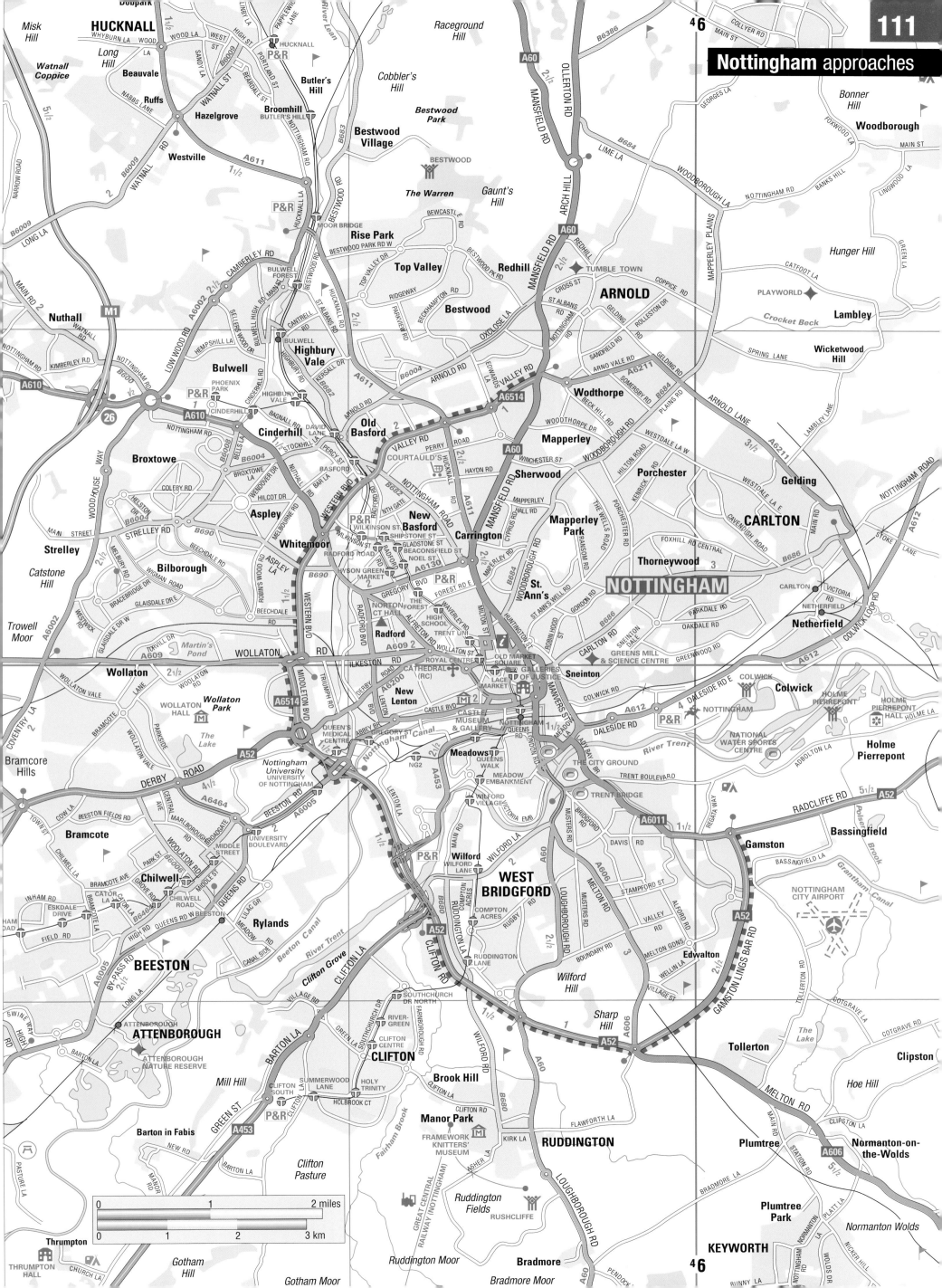

Bath

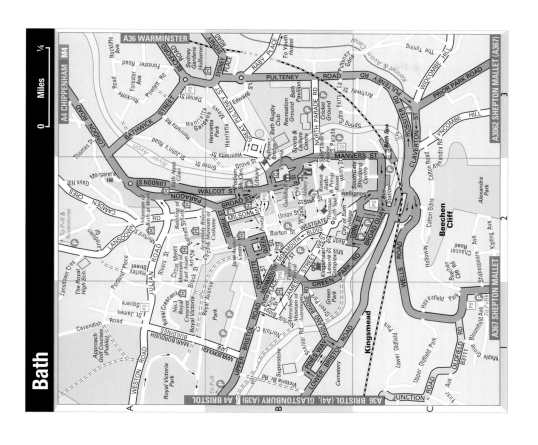

Blackpool

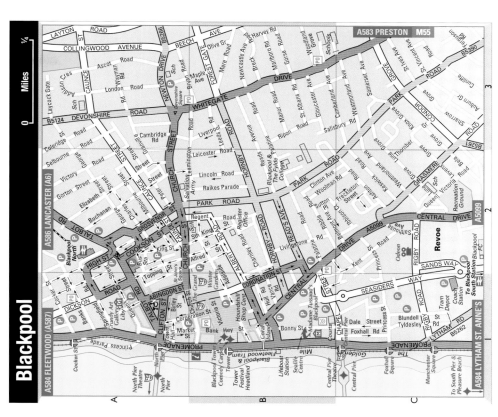

Aberdeen

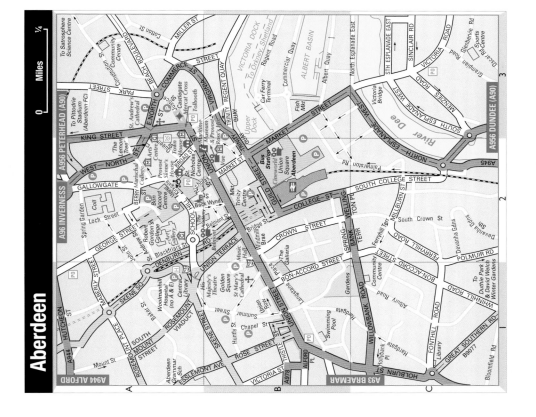

Town plan symbols

Motorway	
Primary route – dual, single carriageway	
A road – dual, single carriageway	
B road – dual, single carriageway	
Minor through road	
One-way street	
Pedestrian roads	
Shopping streets	
Railway with station	
Tramway with station	
Underground or Metro station	
Hospital	
Parking	
Police, Post Office	
Shopmobility	
Youth hostel	
Bus or railway station building	
Shopping precinct or retail park	
Park	
Congestion charge zone	

Abbey or cathedral
Ancient monument
Aquarium
Art gallery
Bird collection or aviary
Building of interest
Castle
Church of interest
Cinema
Garden
Historic ship
House
House and garden
Museum
Preserved railway
Roman antiquity
Safari park
Theatre
Tourist information centre
Zoo
Other place of interest

Birmingham

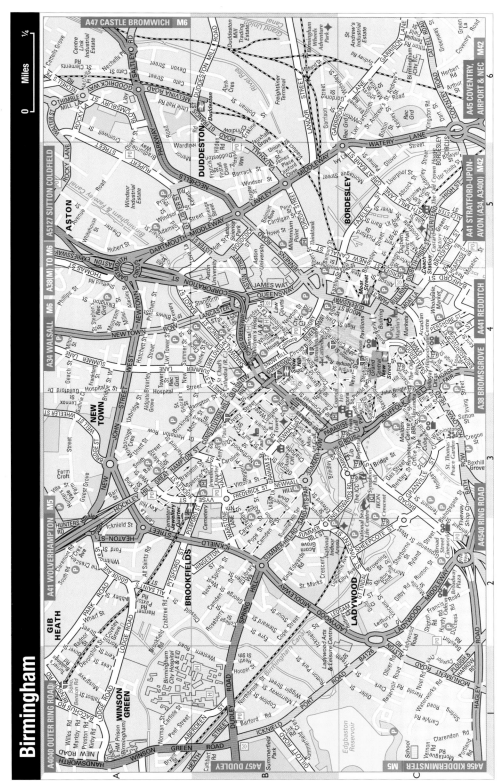

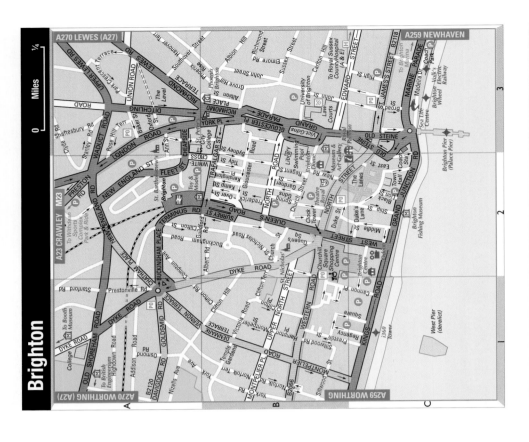

Brighton

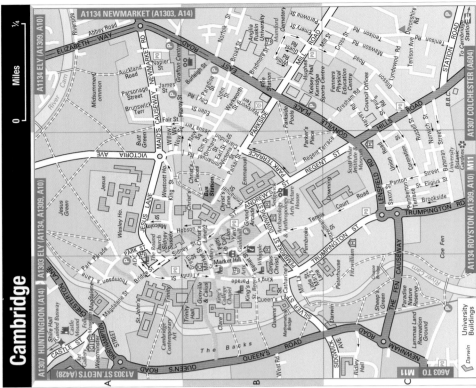

Cambridge

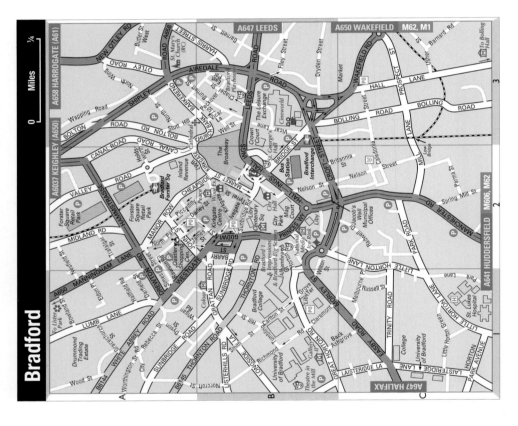

Bradford

Bournemouth

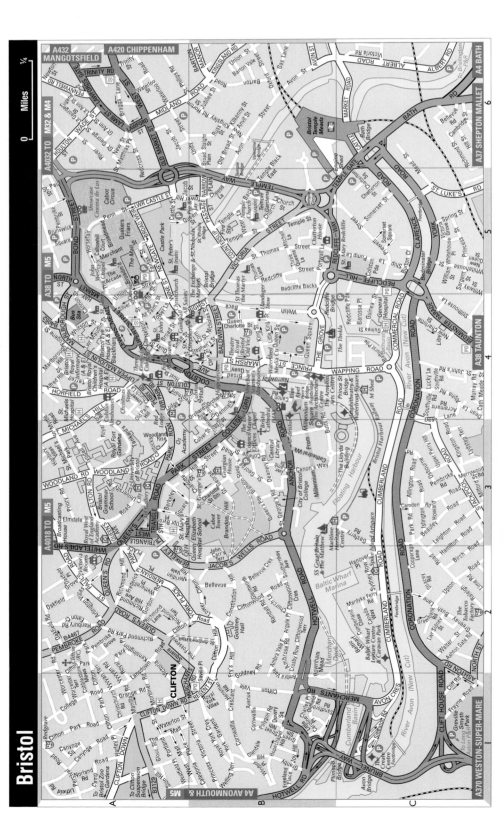

Bristol

Canterbury page 21 • **Cardiff** page 15 • **Cheltenham** page 26 • **Chester** page 43 • **Chichester** page 11 • **Colchester** page 31

115

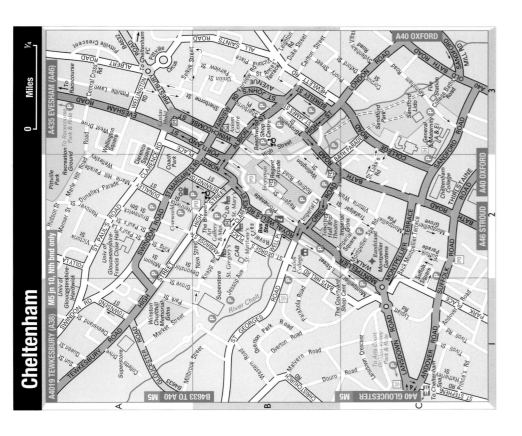

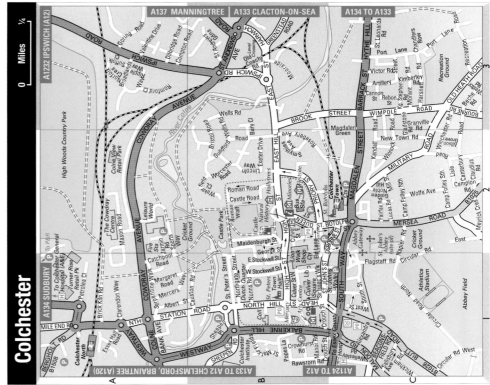

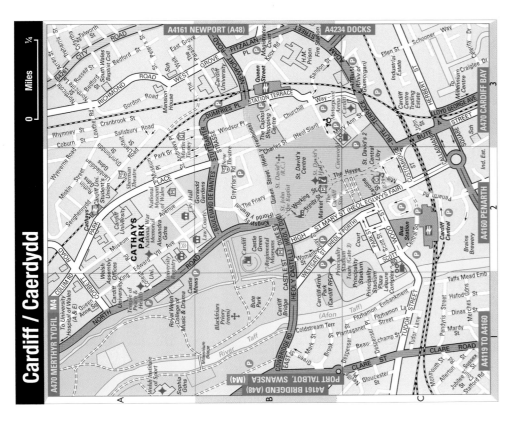

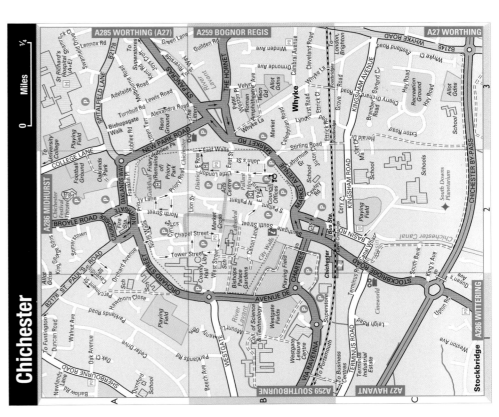

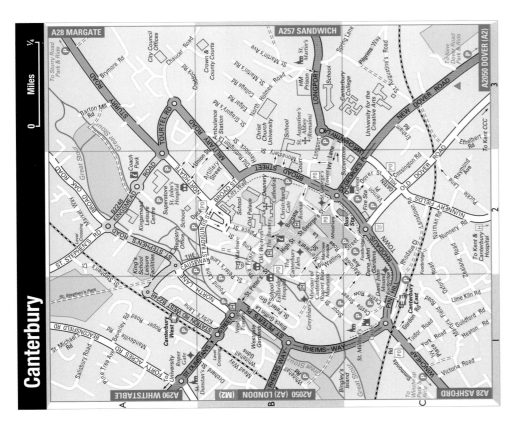

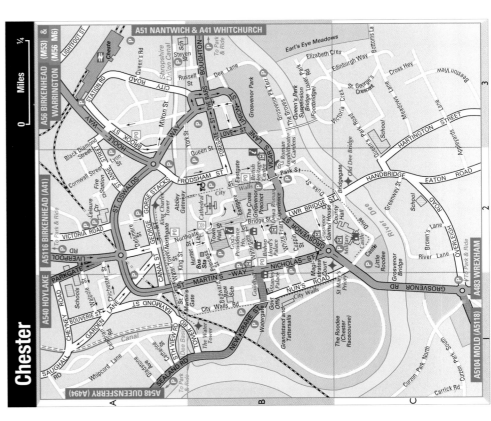

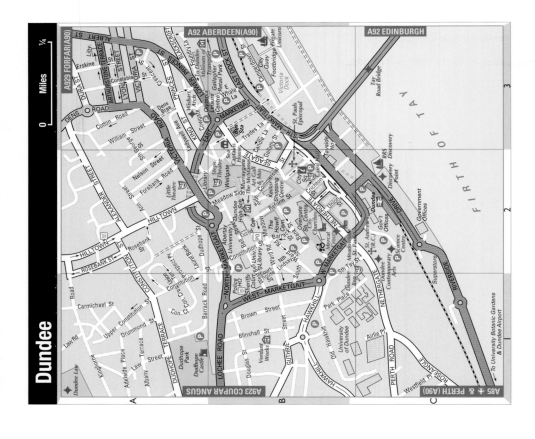

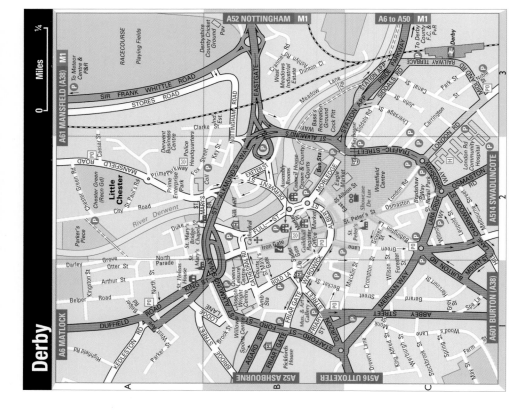

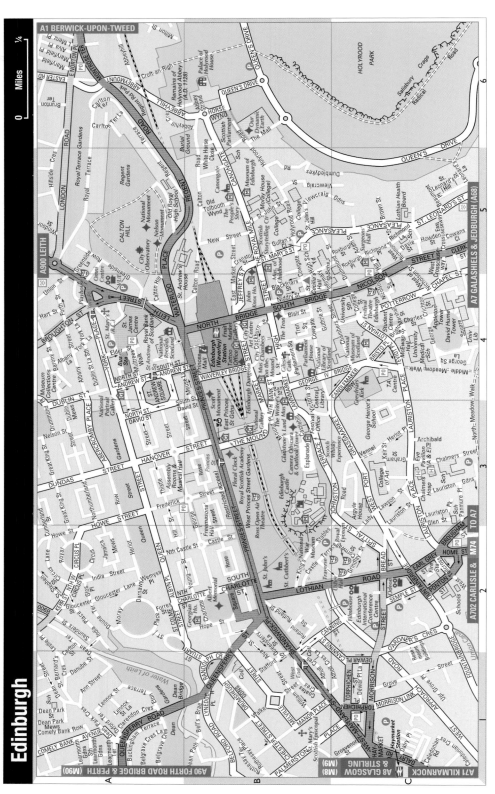

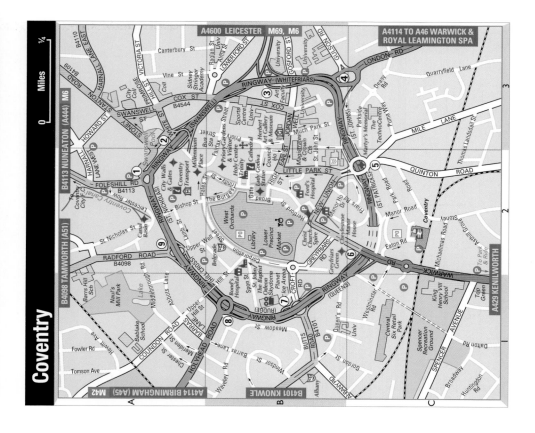

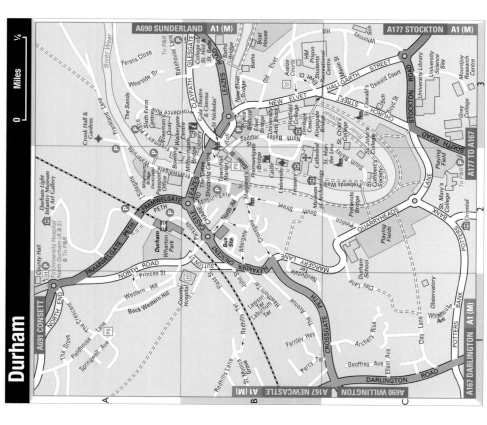

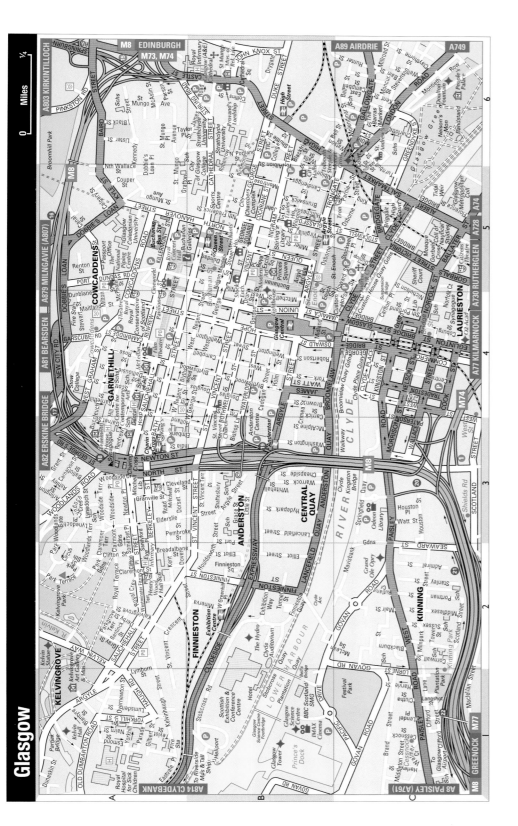

Glasgow

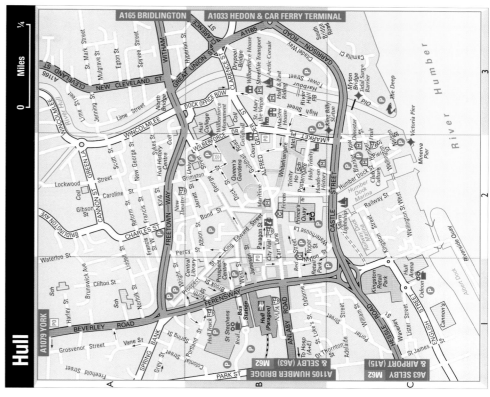

Hull

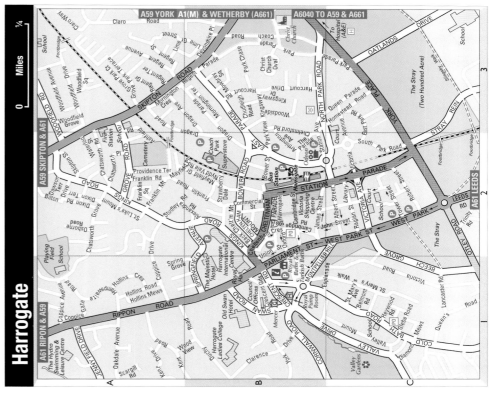

Harrogate

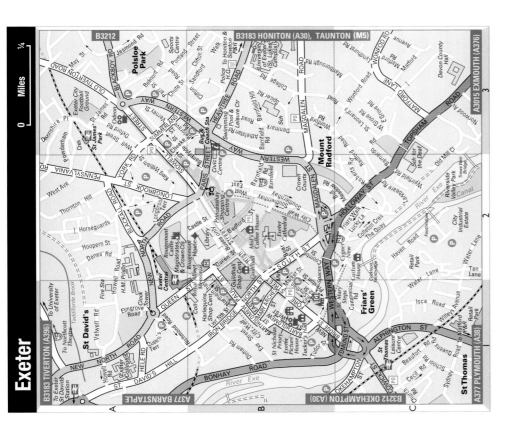

Exeter

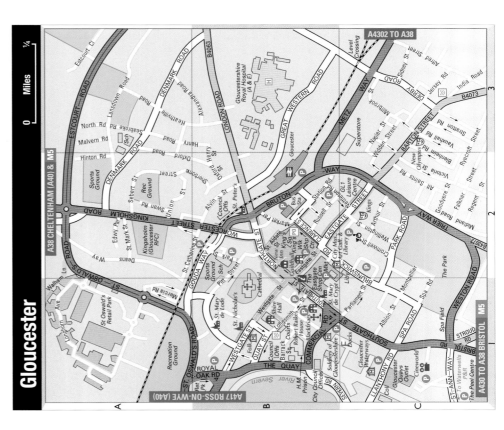

Gloucester

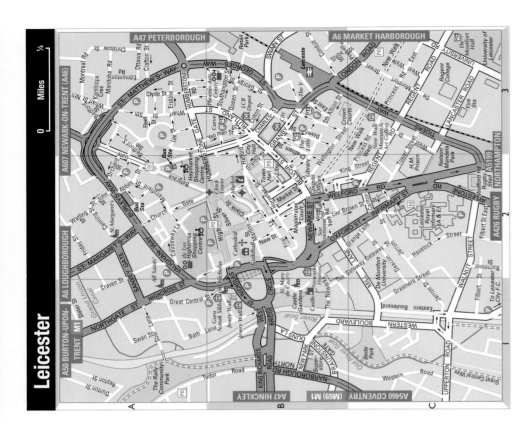

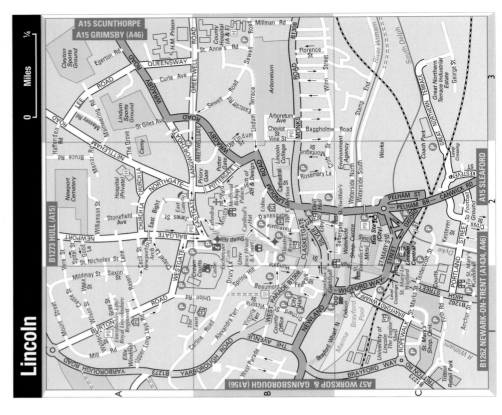

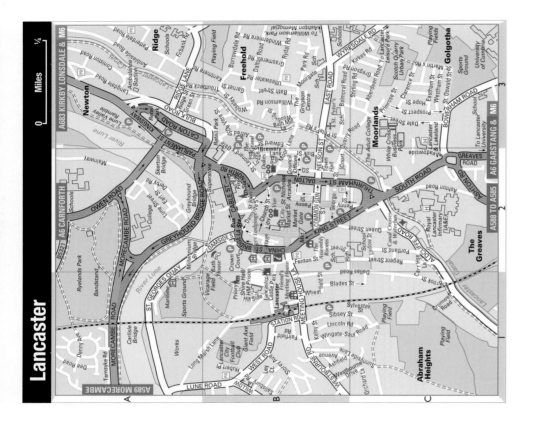

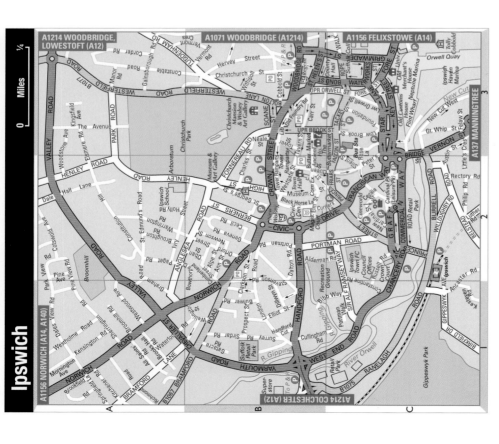

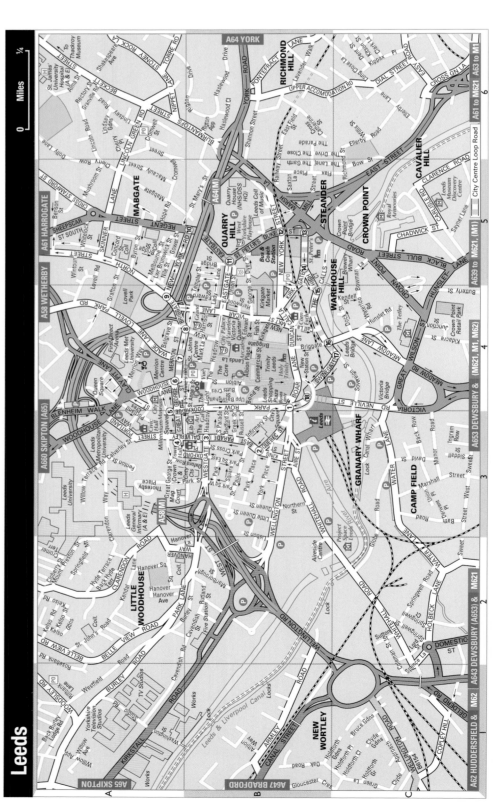

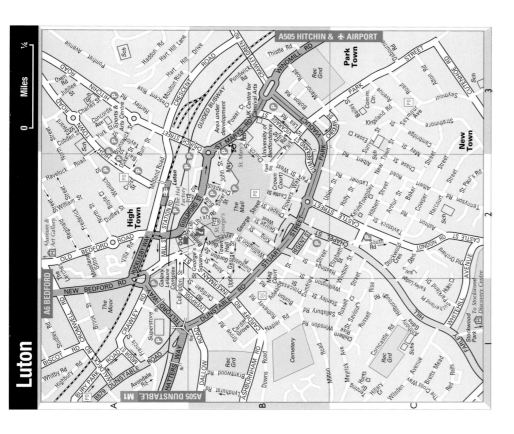

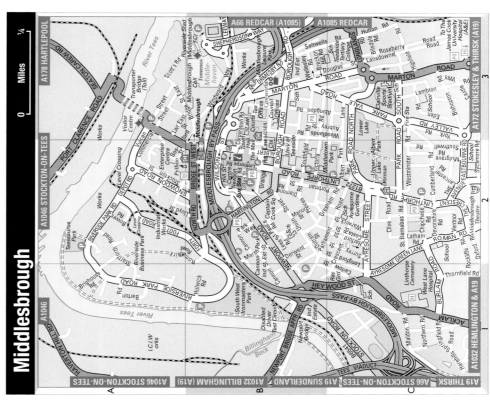

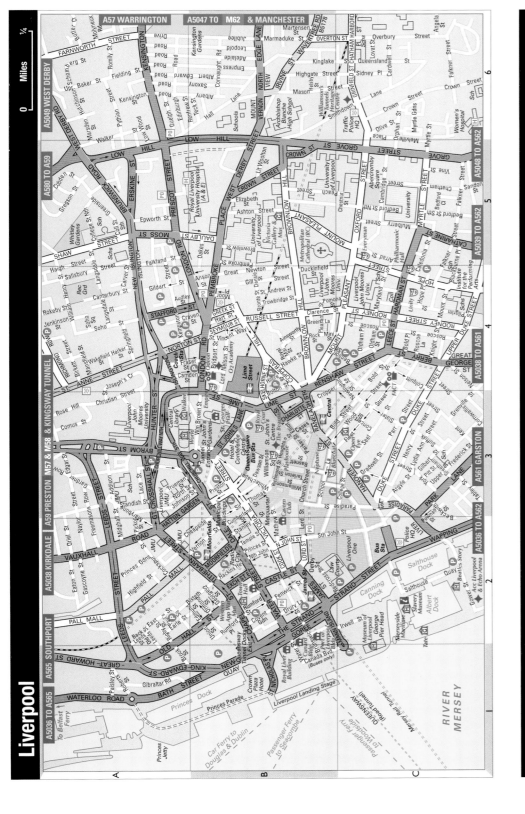

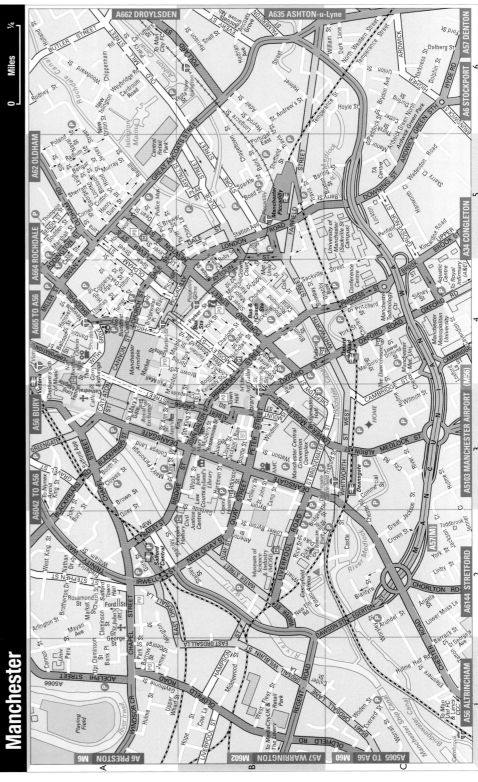

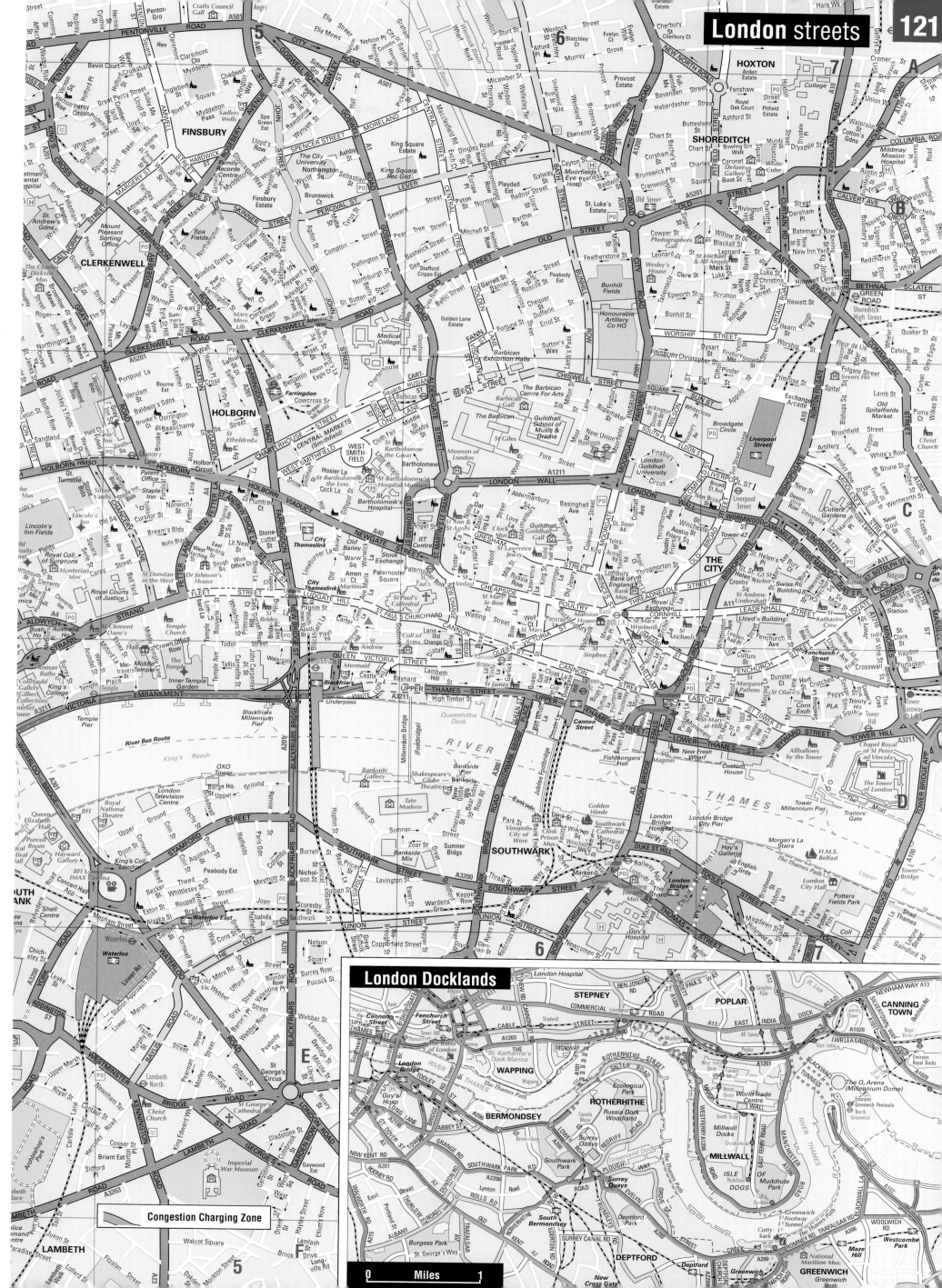

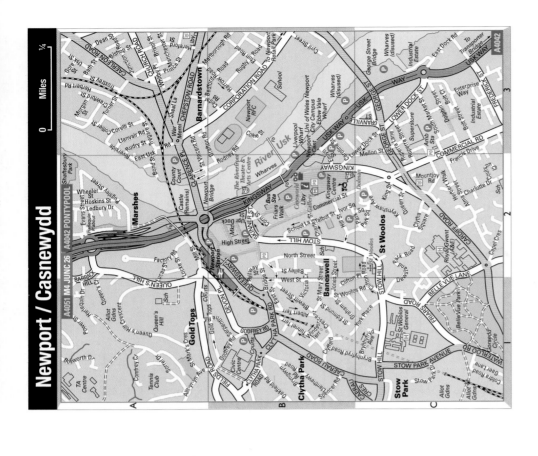

Newport / Casnewydd

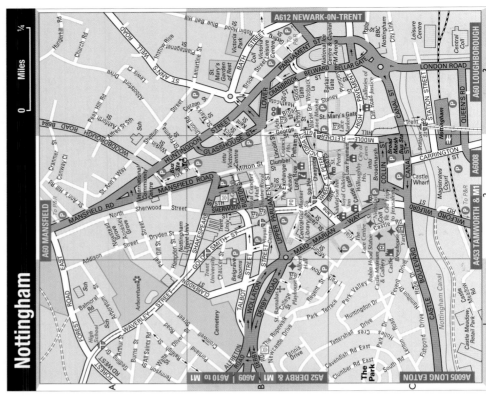

Nottingham

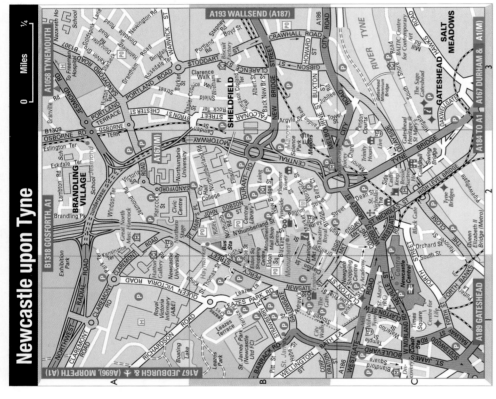

Newcastle upon Tyne

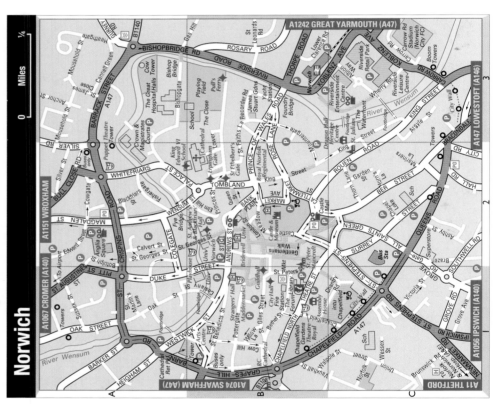

Norwich

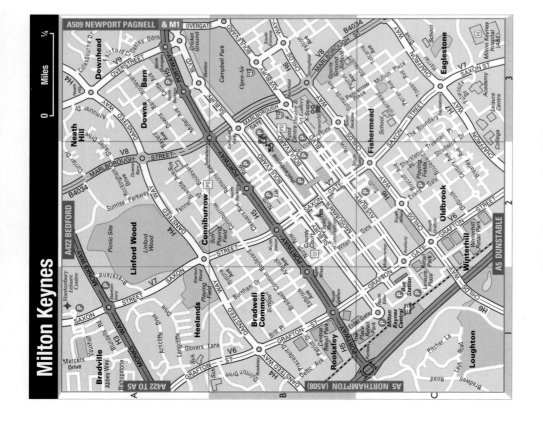

Milton Keynes

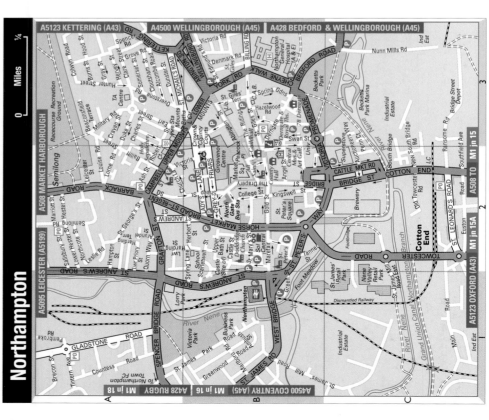

Northampton

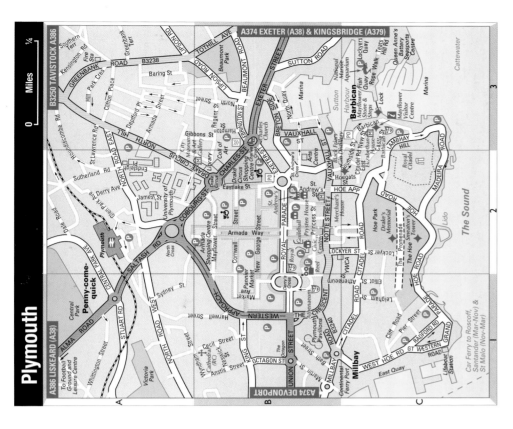

Plymouth

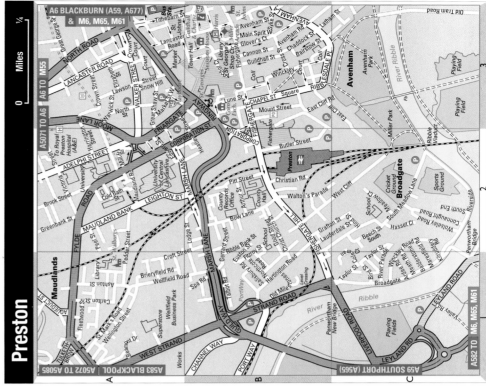

Preston

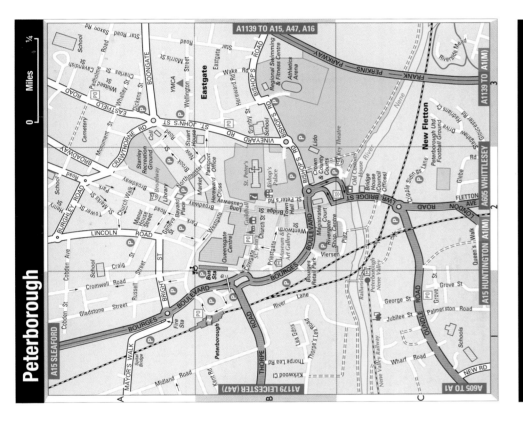

Peterborough

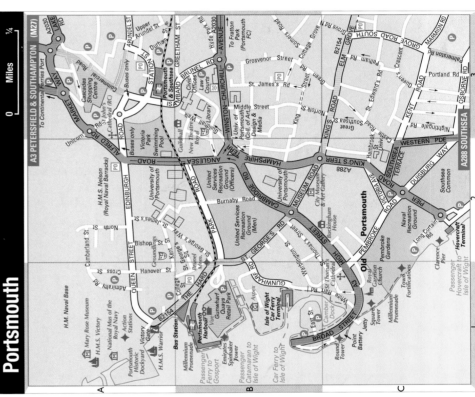

Portsmouth

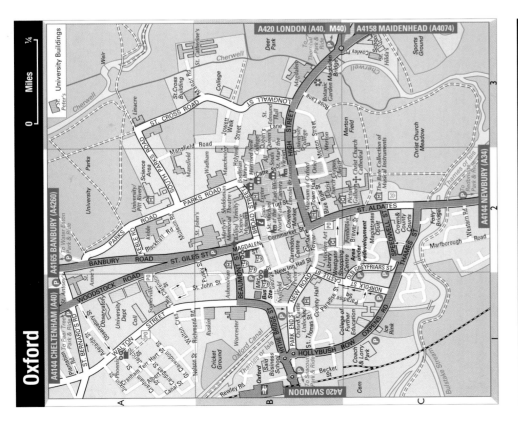

Oxford

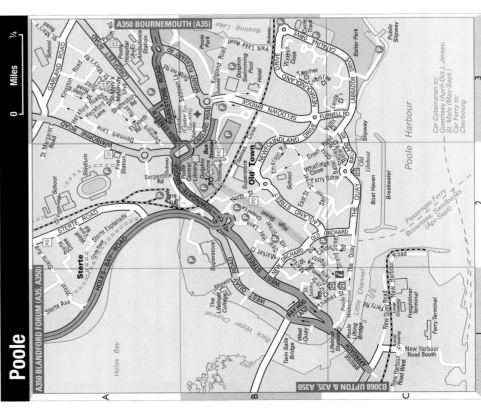

Poole

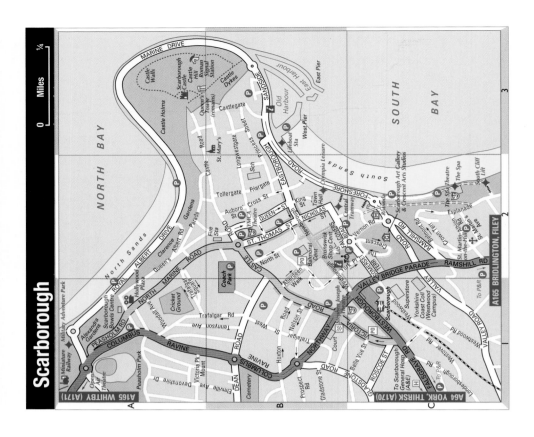

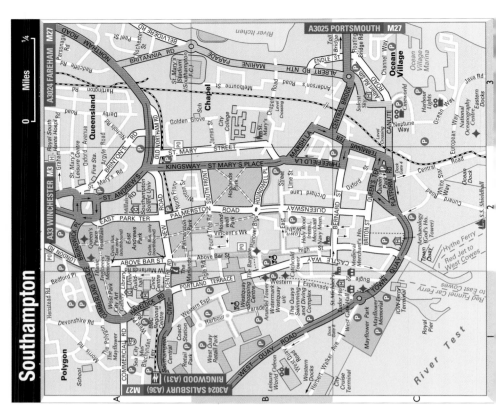

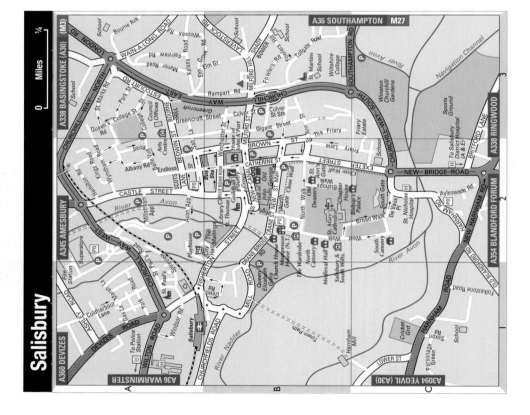

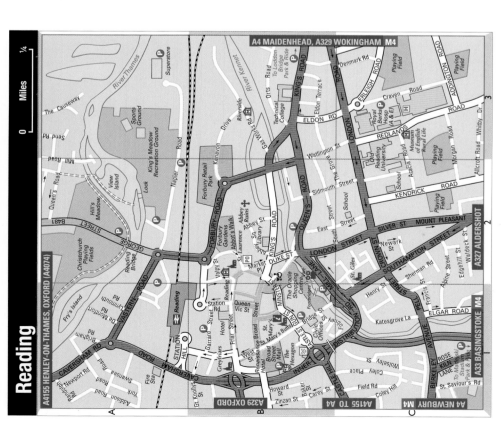

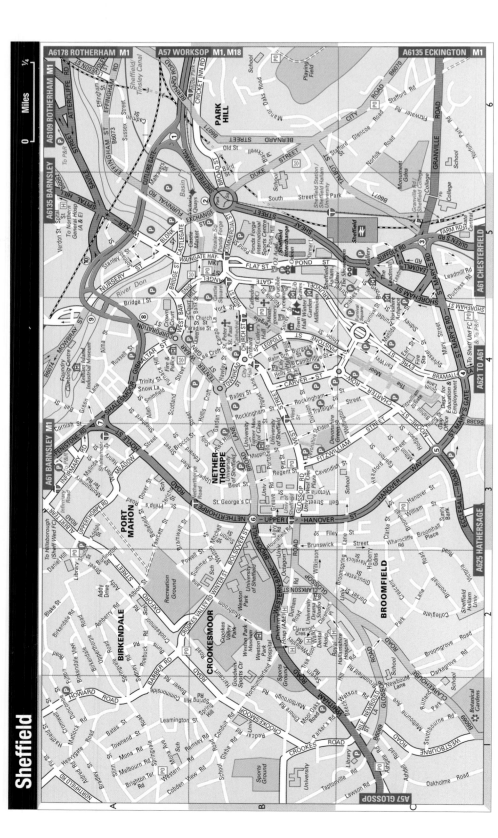

Southend-on-Sea page 20 • Stoke-on-Trent (Hanley) page 44 • Stratford-upon-Avon page 27 • Sunderland page 63 • Swansea page 14 • Swindon page 17

125

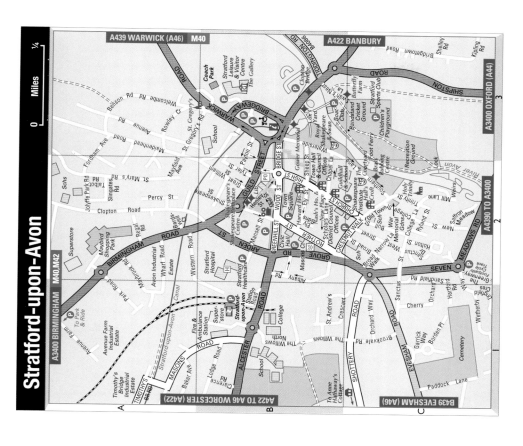

Stratford-upon-Avon

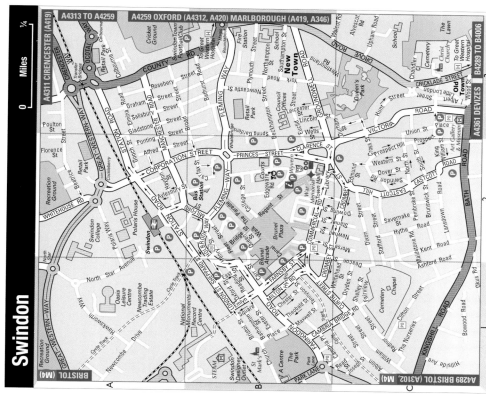

Swindon

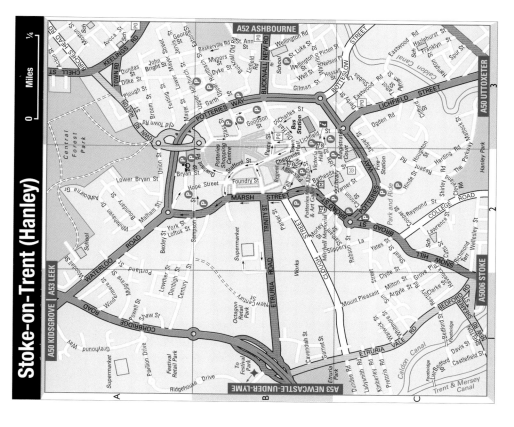

Stoke-on-Trent (Hanley)

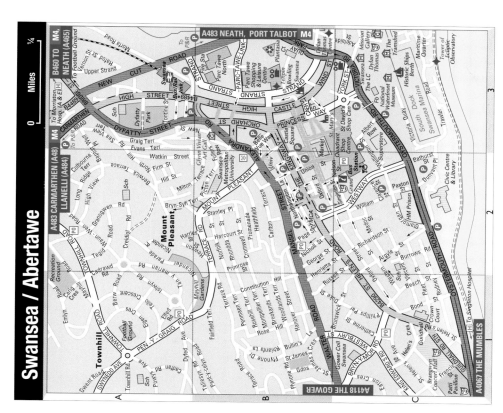

Swansea / Abertawe

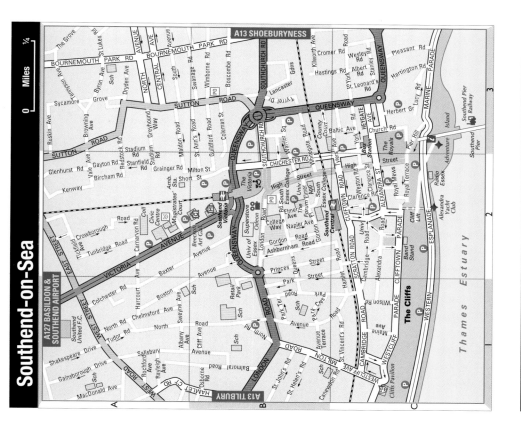

Southend-on-Sea

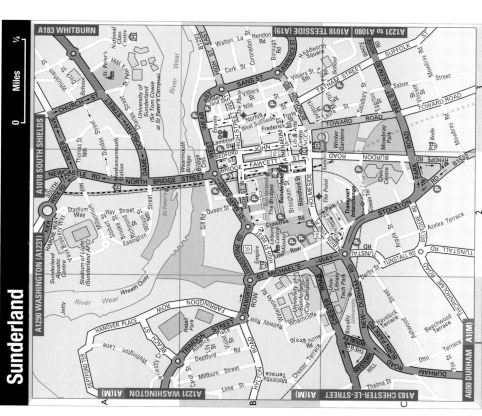

Sunderland

126

Telford page 34 • **Torquay** page 5 • **Winchester** page 10 • **Windsor** page 18 • **Worcester** page 26 • **York** page 52

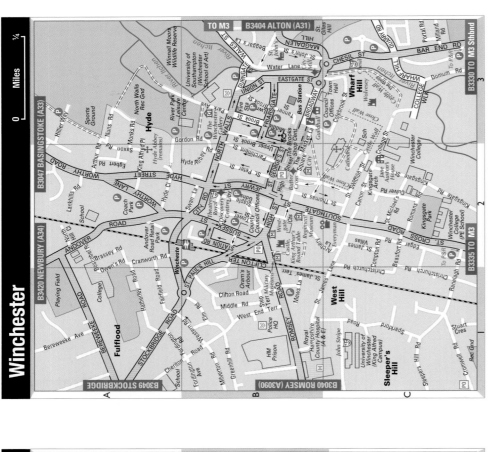

Winchester

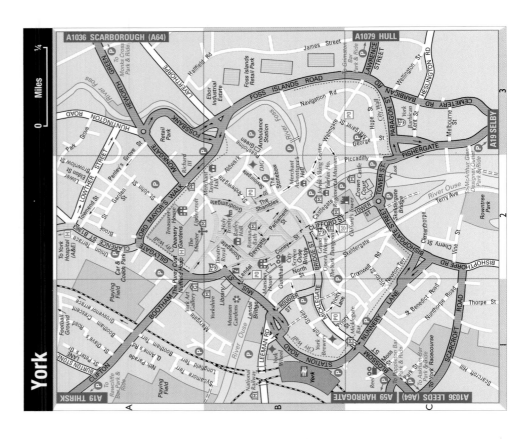

York

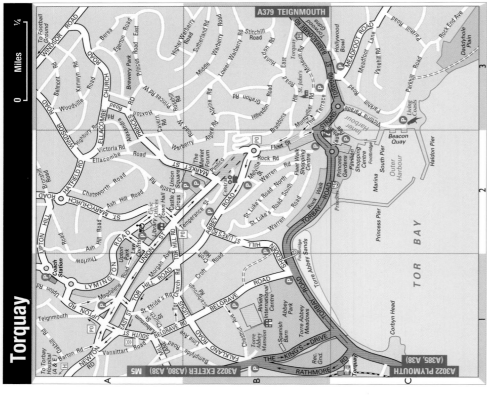

Torquay

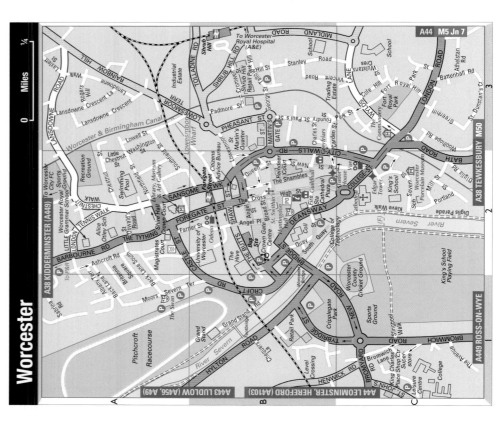

Worcester

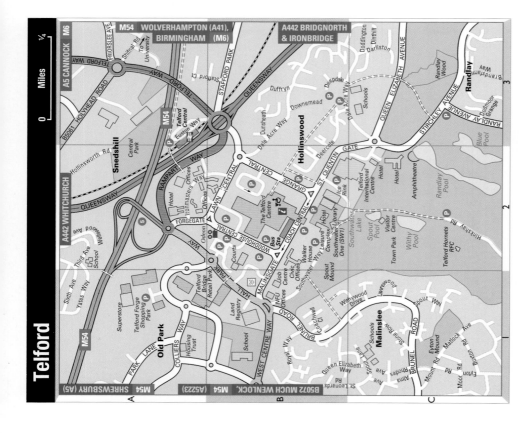

Telford

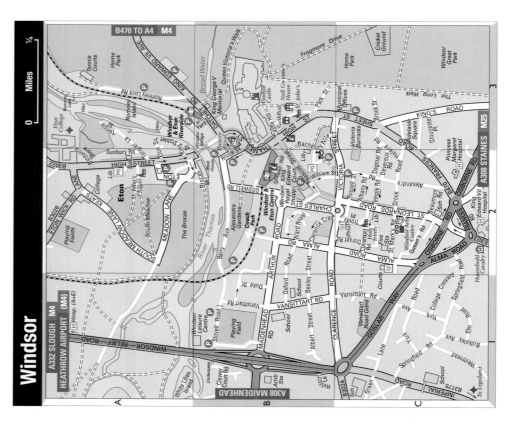

Windsor

Town plan indexes

St Paul's La A2
St Paul's Rd A2
St Paul's St A2
St Stephen's Rd C1
Sandford Lido C3
Sandford Mill Rd C3
Sandford Park C3
Sandford Rd C2
Selkirk St A3
Sherborne Pl B3
Sherborne St B3
Suffolk Pde C2
Suffolk Rd C1
Suffolk Sq C1
Sun St A1
Swindon Rd B2
Sydenham Villas Rd C3
Tewkesbury Rd A1
The Courtyard B1
Thirlstaine Rd C2
Tivoli Rd C1
Tivoli St C1
Town Hall & Theatre ☺ B2
Townsend St A1
Trafalgar St C2
Union St B3
Univ of Gloucestershire (Francis Cl Hall) A2
University of Gloucestershire (Hardwick) A1
Victoria Pl B3
Victoria St A2
Vittoria Walk C2
Wel Pl B2
Wellesley Rd A2
Wellington Rd A3
Wellington Sq A3
Wellington St B2
West Drive A3
Western Rd B1
Winchcombe St B3
Winston Churchill Meml Gardens ❁ A1

Chester 115

Abbey Gateway A2
Appleyards La C3
Bars, The B3
Bedward Row B1
Beeston View C3
Bishop Lloyd's Palace ⛫ B2
Black Diamond St A2
Bottoms La C3
Boughton B3
Bouverie St A1
Bridge St B2
Bridgegate C2
British Heritage Centre 🏛 B2
Brook St A3
Brown's La C2
Bus Station B2
Cambrian Rd A1
Canal St A2
Carrick Rd C1
Castle ♜ C2
Castle Dr C2
Cathedral ✝ B2
Catherine St A1
Chester ≥ A3
Cheyney Rd A1
Chichester St A1
City Rd A3
City Walls B1/B2
City Walls Rd B1
Cornwall St A2
County Hall C2
Cross Hey C3
Cross, The B2
Cuppin St B2
Curzon Park North C1
Curzon Park South C1
Dee Basin A1
Dee La B3
Delamere St A2
Dewa Roman Experience 🏛 B2
Duke St B2
Eastgate B2
Eastgate St B2
Eaton Rd C2
Edinburgh Way C3
Elizabeth Cr B3
Fire Station A2
Foregate St B2
Frodsham St B2
Gamul House B2
Garden La A1
George St A2
Gladstone Ave A1
God's Providence House ⛫ B2
Gorse Stacks A2
Greenway St C2
Grosvenor Bridge C1
Grosvenor Mus 🏛 B2
Grosvenor Park B3
Grosvenor Pk Terr C1
Grosvenor Prec B2
Grosvenor St B2
Groves Rd B3
Groves, The B3
Guildhall Mus 🏛 B1
Handbridge C2
Hartington St C3
Hoole Way A2
Hunter St B2
Information Ctr ℹ B2
King Charles' Tower ✦ A2
King St A2
Leisure Centre A2
Library B2
Lightfoot St A3
Little Roodee C2
Liverpool Rd A2
Love St B3
Lower Bridge St B2
Lower Park Rd B3
Lyon St A2
Magistrates Court B2
Meadows La C3
Meadows, The B3
Military Mus 🏛 C2
Milton St A3
New Crane St B1
Nicholas St B2
Northgate A2
Northgate St A2
Nun's Rd B1
Old Dee Bridge ✦ C2
Overleigh Rd C2
Park St B2
Police Station ☒ B2
Post Office ✉ A2/A3/B2
Princess St B2
Queen St B2
Queen's Park Rd C3
Queen's Rd A3
Race Course B1
Raymond St A1
River La C2
Roman Amphitheatre & Gardens ♠ B2
Roodee, The (Chester Racecourse) B1
Russell St A3
St Anne St A2
St George's Cr C3
St Martin's Gate A1
St Martin's Way B1
St Mary's Priory ✦ B2
St Oswalds Way A2
Saughall Rd A1
Sealand Rd A1
South View Rd A1
Stanley Palace ⛫ B1
Station Rd A3
Steven St A3
Tower Rd B1
Town Hall B2
Union St B3
Vicar's La B2
Victoria Cr C3
Victoria Rd A2
Walpole St A1
Water Tower St A1
Water Tower The ✦ B1
Watergate B1
Watergate St B2
Whipcord La A1
White Friars B2
York St B3

Chichester 115

Adelaide Rd A3
Alexandra Rd A3
Arts Centre B2
Ave de Chartres B1/B2
Barlow Rd A1
Basin Rd C2
Beech Ave B1
Bishops Palace Gardens B2
Bishopsgate Walk A3
Bramber Rd C3
Broyle Rd A2
Bus Station B2
Caledonian Rd B3
Cambrai Ave B3
Canal Wharf C2
Canon La B2
Cathedral ✝ B2
Cavendish St A1
Cawley Rd B2
Cedar Dr A1
Chapel St A2
Cherry Orchard Rd C3
Chichester ≥ B2
Chichester By-Pass C2/C3
Chichester Cinema 🎦 B3
Chichester Festival Theatre ☺ A2
Churchside A2
Cineworld 🎦 C1
City Walls B2
Cleveland Rd B3
Coll of Science & Technology B1
College La A2
Cory Cl C2
Council Offices B2
County Hall B2
Courts B2
District 🏛 B2
Duncan Rd A1
Durnford Cl A1
East Pallant B2
East Row B2
East St B2
East Walls B3
Eastland Rd C3
Ettrick Cl B3
Ettrick Rd B3
Exton Rd C3
Fire Station A2
Football Ground A2
Franklin Pl A2
Friary (Rems of) A2
Garland Cl C3
Green La A3
Grove Rd C3
Guilden Rd B3
Guildhall 🏛 A2
Hawthorn Cl A1
Hay Rd C3
Henty Gdns B1
Herald Dr C3
Hornet, The B3
Information Ctr ℹ B2
John's St B2
Joys Croft A3
Jubilee Pk A3
Jubilee Rd A3
Juxon Cl B2
Kent Rd A3
King George Gdns A2
King's Ave C2
Kingsham Ave C3
Kingsham Rd C2
Laburnum Gr B3
Leigh Rd C1
Lennox Rd A3
Lewis Rd A3
Library B2
Lion St B2
Litten Terr A3
Litten, The A3
Little London B2
Lyndhurst Rd B3
Market B3
Market Ave B2
Market Cross B2
Market Rd B3
Martlet Cl C2
Melbourne Rd A3
Mount La B1
New Park Rd A3
Newlands La A1
North Pallant B2
North St A2
North Walls A2
Northgate A2
Oak Ave A1
Oak Cl A1
Oaklands Park A2
Oaklands Way A2
Orchard Ave A1
Orchard St A1
Ormonde Ave B3
Pallant House 🏛 B2
Parchment St A1
Parklands Rd A1/B1
Peter Weston Pl B3
Police Station ☒ C2
Post Office ✉ A1/B2/B3
Priory La A2
Priory Park A2
Priory Rd A2
Queen's Ave C1
Riverside A3
Roman Amphitheatre B3
St Cyriacs A2
St Pancras A3
St Paul's Rd A2
St Richard's Hospital (A&E) H A3
Shamrock Cl A3
Sherbourne Rd A1
Somerstown A2
South Bank C2
South Downs Planetarium ✦ C2
South Pallant B2
South St B2
Southgate B2
Spitalfield La A3
Stirling Rd B3
Stockbridge Rd C1/C2
Swanfield Dr A3
Terminus Ind Est C1
Terminus Rd C1
Tower St A2
Tozer Way A3
Turnbull Rd A3
Upton Rd C1
Velyn Ave B3
Via Ravenna B1
Walnut Ave A1
West St B2
Westgate B1
Westgate Fields B1
Westgate L Ctr B1
Weston Ave C1
Whyke Cl C3
Whyke La B3
Whyke Rd C3
Winden Ave B3

Colchester 115

Abbey Gateway ✝ C2
Albert St A1
Albion Grove C2
Alexandra Rd C1
Artillery St C3
Arts Centre 🏛 B1
Balkerne Hill B1
Barrack St C3
Beaconsfield Rd C1
Beche Rd C3
Bergholt Rd A1
Bourne Rd C3
Brick Kiln Rd A1
Bristol Rd B2
Broadlands Way A3
Brook St B3
Bury Cl B2
Bus Sta B2
Butt Rd C1
Camp Folley North C2
Camp Folley South C2
Campion Rd C2
Cannon St C3
Canterbury Rd C2
Castle ♜ B2
Castle Park B2
Castle Rd B2
Catchpool Rd A1
Causton Rd B1
Chandlers Row C3
Circular Rd East C2
Circular Rd North C1
Circular Rd West C1
Clarendon Way A1
Claudius Rd C2
Colchester ≥ A1
Colchester Camp Abbey Field C1
Colchester Inst B1
Colchester Town ≥ C2
Colne Bank Ave A1
Colne View Ret Pk A2
Compton Rd A3
Cowdray Ave A1/A2
Cowdray Ctr, The A2
Crouch St B1
Crowhurst Rd B1
Culver Sq Sh Ctr B1
Culver St East B2
Culver St West B1
Dilbridge Rd A3
East Hill B2
East St B3
East Stockwell St B1
Eld La B1
Essex Hall Rd A1
Exeter Dr B2
Fairfax Rd C2
Fire Station A2
Firstsite 🏛 B2
Flagstaff Rd C1
George St B2
Gladstone Rd C2
Golden Noble Hill C2
Goring Rd A3
Granville Rd C3
Greenstead Rd B3
Guildford Rd B2
Harsnett Rd C3
Harwich Rd B3
Head St B1
High St B1/B2
High Woods Country Park A2
Hollytrees 🏛 B2
Hythe Hill C3
Information Ctr ℹ B2
Ipswich Rd A3
Jarmin Rd A2
Kendall Rd C2
Kimberley Rd C3
King Stephen Rd C3
Leisure World A2
Library B1
Lincoln Way B2
Lion Walk Sh Ctr B1
Lisle Rd C2
Lucas Rd C2
Magdalen Green C3
Magdalen St C2
Maidenburgh St B2
Maldon Rd C1
Manor Rd B1
Margaret Rd A1
Mason Rd A2
Mercers Way A1
Mercury ☺ B1
Mersea Rd C2
Meyrick Cr C2
Mile End Rd A1
Military Rd C2
Mill St C2
Minories 🏛 B2
Moorside B3
Morant Rd C3
Napier Rd C2
Natural History 🏛 B2
New Town Rd C2
Norfolk Cr A3
North Hill B1
North Station Rd A1
Northgate St B1
Nunns Rd B1
Odeon 🎦 B1
Old Coach Rd B3
Old Heath Rd C3
Osborne St B2
Petrolea Cl A1
Police Station ☒ C1
Popes La B1
Port La C3
Post Office ✉ B2/C1
Priory St B2
Queen St B2
Rawstorn Rd B1
Rebon St C3
Recreation Rd C3
Ripple Way A3
Roman Rd B2
Roman Wall B2
Romford Cl A3
Rosebery Ave B2
St Andrews Ave B3
St Andrews Gdns B3
St Botolph St B2
St Botolphs ⛪ B2
St John's Abbey (site of) ✝ C2
St John's St B1
St Johns Walk Shopping Centre B1
St Leonards Rd C3
St Marys Fields B1
St Peter's St B1
St Peters ⛪ B1
Salisbury Ave C1
Serpentine Walk A1
Sheepen Pl B1
Sheepen Rd B1
Sir Isaac's Walk B1
Smythies Ave B2
South St C1
South Way C1
Sports Way A2
Suffolk Cl A3
Town Hall B1
Turner Rise Ret Pk A1
Valentine Dr A3
Victor Rd C3
Wakefield Cl B2
Wellesley Rd C1
Wells Rd B2/B3
West St C1
West Stockwell St B1
Weston Rd C3
Westway A1
Wickham Rd C1
Wimpole Rd C3
Winchester Rd C2
Winnock Rd C2
Wolfe Ave C2
Worcester Rd B2

Coventry 116

Abbots La A1
Albany ☺ B1
Albany Rd B1
Alma St B3
Art Faculty B3
Asthill Grove C2
Bablake School A1
Barras La A1/B1
Barrs Hill School A1
Belgrade ☺ B2
Bishop St A2
Bond's Hospital ⛫ B1
Broad Gate B2
Broadway C1
Burges, The B2
Bus Station A3
Butts Radial B1
Canal Basin ✦ A2
Canterbury St A3
Cathedral ✝ B3
Central Six Ret Pk C1
Chester St A1
Cheylesmore Manor House ⛫ B2
Christ Church Spire ✦ B2
City Coll A3
City Walls & Gates ✦ A2
Corporation St B2
Council House B2
Coundon Rd A1
Coventry Sta ≥ C2
Coventry Transport Museum 🏛 A2
Cox St A3
Croft Rd B1
Dalton Rd C1
Deasy Rd C3
Earl St B2
Eaton Rd C2
Fairfax St B2
Foleshill Rd A2
Ford's Hospital ⛫ B2
Fowler Rd A1
Friars Rd C2
Gordon St C1
Gosford St B3
Greyfriars Gn ✦ B2
Greyfriars Rd B2
Gulson Rd B3
Hales St A2
Harnall Lane East A3
Harnall Lane West A2
Herbert Art Gallery & Museum 🏛 B3
Hertford St B2
Hewitt Ave A1
High St B2
Hill St B1
Holy Trinity ⛪ B2
Holyhead Rd A1
Howard St A3
Huntingdon Rd C1
Information Ctr ℹ B2
Jordan Well B3
King Henry VIII School C1
Lady Godiva Statue ✦ B2
Lamb St A2
Leicester Row A2
Library B2
Little Park St B2
London Rd C3
Lower Ford St B3
Lower Precinct Shop Ctr B2
Magistrates & Crown Courts B2
Manor House Drive B2
Manor Rd C2
Market B2
Martyr's Meml ✦ C2
Meadow St B1
Meriden St A1
Michaelmas Rd C2
Middleborough Rd A1
Mile La C3
Millennium Pl ✦ A2
Much Park St B3
Naul's Mill Park A1
New Union B2
Odeon 🎦 B1
Park Rd C2
Parkside C3
Planet Ice Arena B1
Post Office ✉ B2/C2
Primrose Hill St A3
Priory Gardens & Visitor Centre B2
Priory St B3
Puma Way C3
Quarryfield La C3
Queen's Rd B1
Quinton Rd C2
Radford Rd A2
Raglan St B3
Ringway (Hill Cross) A1
Ringway (Queens) B1
Ringway (Rudge) B1
Ringway (St Johns) B3
Ringway (St Nicholas) A2
Ringway (St Patricks) C2
Ringway (Swanswell) A2
Ringway (Whitefriars) B3
St John St B2
St John The Baptist ⛪ B2
St Nicholas St A2
Sidney Stringer Academy A3
Skydome B1
Spencer Ave C1
Spencer Rec Gnd C1
Spon St B1
Sports Centre B3
Stoney Rd C2
Stoney Stanton Rd A3
Swanswell Pool A3
Technocentre, The C3
Thomas Landsdail St C2
Tomson Ave A1
Top Green C1
Trinity St B2
University B3
Univ Sports Ctr B3
Upper Hill St A1
Upper Well St A2
Victoria St A3
Vine St A3
Warwick Rd C2
Waveley Rd B1
West Orchards Shopping Ctr B2
Westminster Rd C1
White St A3
Windsor St B1

Derby 116

Abbey St C1
Agard St B1
Albert St B2
Albion St B2
Ambulance Sta B1
Arthur St A1
Ashlyn Rd B3
Assembly Rooms ⛫ B2
Babington La C2
Becket St B1
Belper Rd A1
Bold La B1
Bradshaw Way C2
Bradshaw Way Retail Park C2
Bridge St B1
Brook St B1
Burton Rd C1
Bus Station B2
Caesar St A2
Canal St C3
Carrington St C3
Cathedral ✝ B2
Cathedral Rd B1
Charnwood St C2
Chester Green Rd A2
City Rd A2
Clarke St A3
Cock Pitt B3
Council House ⛫ B2
Courts B1
Cranmer Rd B3
Crompton St C1
Crown & County Courts B2
Curzon St B1
Darley Grove A1
Derby ≥ C3
Derbyshire County Cricket Ground B3
Derwent Bsns Ctr A2
Derwent St B2
Drewry La C1
Duffield Rd A1
Duke St A2
Dunton Cl B3
Eagle Market C2
East St B2
Eastgate B3
Exeter St B2
Farm St C1
Ford St B1
Forester St C1
Fox St A2
Friar Gate B1
Friary St B1
Full St B2
Gerard St C1
Gower St C2
Green La C2
Grey St C1
Guildhall ⛫ B2
Harcourt St C1
Highfield Rd A1
Hill La C2
Information Ctr ℹ B2
Iron Gate B2
John St C3
Joseph Wright Ctr B1
Kedleston Rd A1
Key St B2
King Alfred St C1
King St A1
Kingston St A1
Lara Croft Way C2
Leopold St C2
Library B1
Liversage St C3
Lodge La B1
London Rd C2
London Rd Com Hospl H C2
Macklin St C1
Mansfield Rd A2
Market B2
Market Pl B2
May St C1
Meadow La B3
Melbourne St C2
Mercian Way C1
Midland Rd C3
Monk St C1
Morledge B2
Mount St C1
Museum & Art Gallery 🏛 B1
Noble St C3
North Parade A1
North St A1
Nottingham Rd B3
Osmaston Rd C2
Otter St A1
Park St C3
Parker St A1
Pickfords Ho 🏛 B1
Playhouse ☺ C2
Police HQ ☒ A2
Police Station ☒ B2
Post Office ✉ A1/A2/B1/B2/C2/C3
Pride Parkway C3
Prime Enterprise Park A2
Prime Parkway A2
Queens Leisure Ctr B1
Racecourse A3
Railway Terr C3
Register Office B2
Sadler Gate B1
St Alkmund's Way B1/B2
St Helens House ✦ A1
St Mary's ⛪ A1
St Mary's Bridge A2
St Mary's Bridge Chapel ⛪ A2
St Mary's Gate B1
St Paul's Rd A2
St Peter's ⛪ C2
St Peter's St C2
Showcase De Lux 🎦 C2
Siddals Rd C3
Silk Mill 🏛 B2
Sir Frank Whittle Rd A3
Spa La C1
Spring St C1
Stafford St B1
Station Approach C3
Stockbrook St C1
Stores Rd A3
Traffic St C2
Wardwick B1
Werburgh St C1
West Ave A1
West Meadows Industrial Estate B3
Westfield Centre C2
Wharf Rd A2
Wilmot St C2
Wilson St C1
Wood's La C1

Dundee 116

Abertay University B2
Adelaide Pl A1
Airlie Pl C1
Albany Terr A1
Albert St A3
Alexander St A2
Ann St A2
Arthurstone Terr A3
Bank St B2
Barrack Rd A1
Barrack St B2
Bell St B2
Blackscroft A3
Blinshall St B1
Brown St B1
Bus Station B3
Caird Hall B2
Camperdown St B3
Candle La B3
Carmichael St A1
City Churches ⛪ B2
City Quay B3
City Sq B2
Commercial St B2
Constable St A3
Constitution Cres A1
Constitution Ct A1
Constitution St A1/B2
Cotton Rd A3
Courthouse Sq B1
Cowgate A3
Crescent St A3
Crichton St B2
Dens Brae A3
Dens Rd A3
Discovery Point ✦ C2
Douglas St B1
Drummond St A1
Dudhope Castle ♜ A1
Dudhope St A2
Dudhope Terr A1
Dundee ≥ C2
Dundee Contemporary Arts ✦ C2
Dundee High School B2
Dundee Law ✦ A1
Dundee Repertory ☺ C2
Dunhope Park A1
Dura St A3
East Dock St B3
East Marketgait B3
East Whale La B3
Erskine St A3
Euclid Cr B2
Forebank Rd A2
Foundry La A3
Frigate Unicorn ✦ B3
Gallagher Ret Pk B3
Gellatly St B3
Government Offices C2
Guthrie St B1
Hawkhill B1
Hilltown A2
Howff Cemetery, The B2
Information Ctr ℹ B2
Keiller Sh Ctr B2
Keillor Ctr, The B2
King St A3
Kinghorne Rd A1
Ladywell Ave A3
Laurel Bank A2
Law Rd A1
Law St A1
Library A2/A3
Library and Steps Theatre ☺ A2
Little Theatre ☺ A2
Lochee Rd B1
Lower Princes St A3
Lyon St A3
McManus Mus & Art Gallery, The 🏛 B2
Meadow Side B2
Meadowside St Pauls ⛪ B2
Mercat Cross ✦ B2
Murraygate B2
Nelson St A2
Nethergate B2/C1
North Lindsay St B2
North Marketgait B2
Old Hawkhill B1
Olympia L Ctr B3
Overgate Sh Ctr B2
Park Pl B1
Perth Rd C1
Police Sta ☒ A2/B1
Post Office ✉ B2
Princes St A3
Prospect Pl A2
Reform St B2
Riverside Dr C2
Roseangle C1
Rosebank St A2
RRS Discovery ⛴ C2
St Andrew's ✝ C2
St Pauls Episcopal ✝ B3
Science Centre ✦ C2
Seagate B2
Sheriffs Court B1
Shopmobility B2
South George St A2
South Marketgait B3
South Tay St B2
South Ward Rd B2
Tay Road Bridge ✦ C3
Tayside House B2
Trades La B3
Union St B2
Union Terr A1
University Library B2
Univ of Dundee B1
Upper Constitution St A1
Verdant Works ✦ B1
Victoria Dock B3
Victoria Rd A2
Victoria St A3
Ward Rd B1
Wellgate B2
West Bell St B1
West Marketgait B1/B2
Westfield Pl C1
William St A3
Wishart Arch ✦ A3

Durham 116

Alexander Cr B2
Allergate B2
Archery Rise C1
Assize Courts B3
Avenue, The B1
Back Western Hill A1
Bakehouse La A3
Baths B3
Baths Bridge B3
Boat House B3
Bowling A2
Boyd St C3
Bus Station B2
Castle ♜ B2
Castle Chare B2
Cathedral ✝ B2
Church St C3
Clay La C1
Claypath B3
College of St Hild & St Bede B3
County Hall A1
County Hospital H B1
Crescent, The A1
Crook Hall & Gardens ✦ A3
Crossgate B2
Crossgate Peth C1
Darlington Rd C1
Durham ≥ A2
Durham Light Infantry Museum & Arts Gallery 🏛 A2
Durham School C2
Ellam Ave C1
Elvet Bridge B3
Elvet Court B3
Farnley Hey B1
Ferens Cl A3
Fieldhouse La A1
Flass St B1
Framewelgate Bridge B2
Framwelgate A2
Framwelgate Peth A2
Framwelgate Waterside A2
Frankland La A3
Freeman's Pl A3
Freeman's Quay Leisure Centre A3
Gala Theatre & Cinema ☺ B3
Gates Sh Ctr, The B2
Geoffrey Ave C1
Gilesgate B3
Grey College C3
Grove, The A1
Hallgarth St C3
Hatfield College B3
Hawthorn Terr B1
Heritage Centre 🏛 B3
HM Prison B3
Information Ctr ℹ B3
John St B1
Kingsgate Bridge B3
Laburnum Terr B1
Lawson Terr B1
Leazes Rd B2/B3
Library B2
Margery La B2
Market B2
Mavin St C3
Millburngate B2
Millburngate Bridge B2
Millennium Bridge (foot/cycle) A2
Mountjoy Research Centre C3
Museum of Archaeology 🏛 B2
Nevilledale Terr B1
New Elvet B3
New Elvet Bridge B3
North Bailey B3
North End A1
North Rd A1/B2
Observatory C1
Old Elvet B3
Oriental Mus 🏛 C2
Oswald Court C3
Parkside B2
Passport Office A2
Percy Terr B1
Pimlico C2
Police Station ☒ B3
Post Office ✉ A1/B2
Potters Bank C1/C2
Prebends Bridge C2
Prebends Walk C2
Prince Bishops Shopping Centre B3
Princes St A1
Providence Row A3
Quarryheads La C2
Redhills La B1
Redhills Terr B1
Saddler St B3
St Chad's College C3
St Cuthbert's Society C2
St John's College C2
St Margaret's ⛪ B2
St Mary The Less ⛪ C2
St Mary's College C2
St Monica Grove B1
St Nicholas' ⛪ B3
St Oswald's ⛪ C3
Sands, The A3
Sidegate A2
Silver St B2
Sixth Form College A3
South Bailey C2
South Rd C3
South St B2
Springwell Ave A1
Stockton Rd C3
Students' Rec Ctr B3
Sutton St B2
Town Hall B2
Treasury Mus 🏛 B2
University ✦ B2
Univ Arts Block B3
University Library C3
Univ Science Site C3
Walkergate Centre A3
Wearside Dr A3
Western Hill A1
Wharton Park A2
Whinney Hill C3
Whitehouse Ave C1

Edinburgh 116

Abbey Strand B6
Abbeyhill A6
Abbeyhill Cr B6
Abbeymount A6
Abercromby Pl A3
Adam St C5
Albany La A4
Albany St A4
Albert Meml ✦ B2
Albyn Pl A2
Alva Pl A6
Alva St B1
Ann St A1
Appleton Tower C4
Archibald Pl C3
Argyle House C3
Assembly Rooms & Musical Hall A3
Atholl Cr B1
Atholl Crescent La C1
Bank St B4
Barony St A4
Beaumont Pl C5
Belford Rd B1
Belgrave Cr A1
Belgrave Cres La A1
Bell's Brae B1
Blackfriars St B4
Blair St B4
Bread St C2
Bristo Pl C4
Bristo St C4
Brougham St C2
Broughton St A4
Brown St C5
Brunton Terr A6
Buckingham Terr A1
Burial Ground A6
Bus Station A4
Caledonian Cr C1
Caledonian Rd C1
Calton Hill A4
Calton Hill A5
Calton Rd B4
Camera Obscura & Outlook Tower ✦ B3
Candlemaker Row C4
Canning St B2
Canongate B5
Canongate ⛪ B5
Carlton St A1
Carlton Terr A6
Carlton Terrace La A6
Castle St B2
Castle Terr B2
Castlehill B3
Central Library B4
Chalmers Hospl H C3
Chalmers St C3
Chambers St C4
Chapel St C4
Charles St C4
Charlotte Sq B2
Chester St B1
Circus La A2
Circus Pl A2
City Art Centre 🏛 B4
City Chambers ⛫ B4
City Observatory ✦ A5
Clarendon Cr A1
Clerk St C5
Coates Cr B1
Cockburn St B4
College of Art C3
Comely Bank Ave A1
Comely Bank Row A1
Cornwall St C2
Cowans Cl C5
Cowgate B4
Cranston St B5
Crichton St C4
Croft-An-Righ A6
Cumberland St A2
Dalry Pl C1
Dalry Rd C1
Danube St A1
Darnawy St A2
David Hume Tower C4
Davie St C5
Dean Bridge A1
Dean Gdns A1
Dean Park Cr A1
Dean Park Mews A1
Dean Park St A1
Dean Path B1
Dean St A1
Dean Terr A1
Dewar Pl C1
Dewar Place La C1
Doune Terr A2
Drummond Pl A3
Drummond St C5
Drumsheugh Gdns B1
Dublin Mews A3
Dublin St A4
Dublin St La South A4
Dumbiedykes Rd B5
Dundas St A3
Earl Grey St C2
East Crosscauseway C5
East Market St B4
East Norton Pl A6
East Princes St Gdns B3
Easter Rd A6
Edinburgh (Waverley) ≥ B4
Edinburgh Castle ♜ B3
Edinburgh Dungeon ✦ B4
Edinburgh Int Conference Ctr C2
Elder St A4
Esplanade B3
Eton Terr A1
Eye Pavilion H C3
Festival Office B3
Festival Theatre Edinburgh ☺ C4
Filmhouse 🎦 C2
Fire Station C2
Floral Clock ✦ B3
Forres St A2
Forth St A4
Fountainbridge C2
Frederick St A3
Freemasons' Hall B3
Fruit Market 🏛 B4
Gardner's Cr C2
George Heriot's School C3
George IV Bridge B4
George Sq C4
George Sq La C4
George St B3
Georgian House 🏛 B2
Gladstone's Land 🏛 B3
Glen St C3
Gloucester La A2
Gloucester Pl A2
Gloucester St A2
Graham St C3
Grassmarket C3
Great King St A3
Great Stuart B1
Greenside La A5
Greenside Row A5
Greyfriars Kirk ⛪ C4
Grindlay St C2
Grosvenor St C1
Grove St C1
Gullan's Cl B5
Guthrie St B4
Hanover St A3
Hart St A4
Haymarket C1
Haymarket Sta ≥ C1
Heriot Pl C3
Heriot Row A2
High School Yard B5
High St B4
Hill Pl C5
Hill St A2
Hillside Cr A5
Holyrood Abbey (remains of) A6
Holyrood Park C6
Holyrood Rd B5
Home St C2
Hope St B2
Horse Wynd B6
Howden St C5
Howe St A2
India Pl A2
India St A2
Infirmary St B4
Information Ctr ℹ B4
Jamaica Mews A2
Jeffrey St B4
John Knox Ho 🏛 B4
Johnston Terr C3
Keir St C3
Kerr St A2
King's Stables Rd B2
Lady Lawson St C3
Lauriston Gdns C3
Lauriston Park C3
Lauriston Pl C3
Lauriston St C3
Lawnmarket B3
Learmonth Gdns A1
Learmonth Terr A1
Leith St A4
Lennox St A1
Lennox St La A1

Middlesbrough • Milton Keynes • Newcastle upon Tyne • Newport • Northampton • Norwich 133

Chepstow St B3
Chester Rd C1/C2
Chester St C4
Chetham's School of Music A3
China La B5
Chippenham Rd A6
Chorlton Rd C2
Chorlton St B4
Church St A2
Church St A4
City Park A4
City Rd C3
Civil Justice Ctr B2
Cleminson St A2
Clowes St A3
College Land A3
Collier St B2
Commercial St C3
Conference Ctr C4
Cooper St B4
Copperas St A4
Corn Exchange, The A4
Cornbrook C1
Cornell St A5
Corporation St A4
Cotter St C6
Cotton St A5
Cow La B1
Cross St B3
Crown Court B4
Crown St C2
Dalberg St C6
Dale St A4/B5
Dancehouse, The C4
Dantzic St A4
Dark La C6
Dawson St C2
Dean St A5
Deansgate A3/B3
Deansgate Castlefield C3
Deansgate Sta C3
Dolphin St C6
Downing St C5
Ducie St B5
Duke Pl B2
Duke St B2
Durling St C6
East Ordsall La A2/B1
Edge St A4
Egerton St C2
Ellesmere St C1
Everard St C1
Every St B6
Fairfield St B5
Faulkner St B4
Fennel St A3
Ford St A2
Ford St C6
Fountain St B4
Frederick St A2
Gartside St B2
Gaythorne St A1
George Leigh St A5
George St A1
George St B4
Gore St A2
Goulden St A5
Granby Row B4
Gravel St A3
Great Ancoats St A5
Great Bridgewater St B3
Great George St A1
Great Jackson St C2
Great Marlborough St C4
Greengate A3
Grosvenor St C5
Gun St A5
Hadrian Ave B6
Hall St B3
Hampson St B1
Hanover St A4
Hanworth Cl C5
Hardman St B3
Harkness St C6
Harrison St B6
Hart St B4
Helmet St B6
Henry St A5
Heyrod St B6
High St A4
Higher Ardwick C6
Hilton St A4/A5
Holland St A6
HOME C3
Hood St A5
Hope St B1
Hope St B4
Houldsworth St A5
Hoyle St C6
Hulme Hall Rd C1
Hulme St A1
Hulme St C3
Hyde Rd C6
Information Ctr B3
Irwell St A2
Islington St A2
Jackson Cr C2
Jackson's Row B3
James St A1
Jenner Cl C2
Jersey St A5
John Dalton St B3
John Ryland's Library B3
John St A4
Kennedy St B3
Kincardine Rd C5
King St A3
King St West A3
Law Courts B3
Laystall St B5
Lever St A5
Library B3
Linby St C2
Little Lever St A4
Liverpool Rd B2
Liverpool St B1
Lloyd St B3
Lockton Cl C5
London Rd B5
Long Millgate A3
Longacre St B6
Loom St A5
Lower Byrom St B2
Lower Mosley St B3
Lower Moss La C2
Lower Ormond St C4
Loxford La C4
Luna St A5
Major St B4
Manchester Arndale A4
Manchester Art Gallery B4
Manchester Central Convention Complex B3
Manchester Metropolitan University B4/C4
Manchester Piccadilly Sta B5
Manchester Technology Ctr C4
Mancunian Way C3
Manor St C5
Marble St A4
Market St A2
Market St A4
Market St A4
Marsden St A3
Marshall St A5
Mayan Ave A2
Medlock St C3
Middlewood St B1
Miller St A4
Minshull St B4
Mosley St A4
Mount St B3
Mulberry St B3
Murray St A5
Museum of Science & Industry (MOSI) B2
Nathan Dr A2
National Football Mus A4
Naval St A5
New Bailey St A2
New Elm Rd B2
New Islington A6
New Islington Station B6
New Quay St B2
New Union St A6
Newgate St A4
Newton St A5
Nicholas St B4
North Western St C6
Oak St A4
Odeon A4
Old Mill St A6
Oldfield Rd A1/C1
Oldham Rd A5
Oldham St A4
Opera House B3
Ordsall La C1
Oxford Rd C4
Oxford Rd C4
Oxford St B4
Paddock St C6
Palace Theatre B4
Pall Mall A3
Palmerston St B6
Park St A1
Parker St B4
Peak St B5
Penfield Cl C5
Peoples' History Museum B2
Peru St A1
Peter St B3
Piccadilly A4
Piccadilly B5
Piccadilly Gdns B4
Piercy St A6
Poland St A5
Police Museum A5
Police Sta B3/B5
Pollard St B6
Port St A5
Portland St B4
Portugal St East B5
Post Office A1/A2/A4/A5/B3/B4
Potato Wharf B2
Princess St B3/C4
Pritchard St C4
Quay St A2
Quay St B2
Queen St B3
Radium St A5
Redhill St A5
Regent Rd B1
Retail Park A5
Rice St B2
Richmond St B4
River St C3
Roby St B5
Rodney St A6
Roman Fort B2
Rosamond St A2
Royal Exchange A3
Sackville St B4
St Andrew's St B6
St Ann St A3
St Ann's A3
St George's Ave C1
St James St B4
St John St B3
St John's Cathedral (RC) A2
St Mary's B3
St Mary's Gate A3
St Mary's Parsonage A3
St Peter's Sq B3
St Stephen St A2
Salford Approach A3
Salford Central A2
Sheffield St B5
Shepley St B5
Sherratt St A5
Shopmobility A4
Shudehill A4
Shudehill A4
Sidney St C4
Silk St A5
Silver St B4
Skerry Cl C5
Snell St B6
South King St B3
Sparkle St B5
Spear St A4
Spring Gdns A4
Stanley St A2/B2
Station Approach B5
Store St B5
Swan St A4
Tariff St B5
Tatton St C1
Temperance St B6/C6
Thirsk St C6
Thomas St A4
Thompson St A5
Tib La B3
Tib St A4
Town Hall (Manchester) B3
Town Hall (Salford) A2
Trafford St C3
Travis St B5
Trinity Way A2
Turner St A4
Union St C6
Univ of Manchester (Sackville St Campus) C5
Univ of Salford A1
Upper Brook St C5
Upper Cleminson St A1
Upper Wharf St A1
Vesta St B6
Victoria A4
Victoria Station A4
Wadesdon Rd C5
Water St B2
Watson St B3
West Fleet St B1
West King St A2
West Mosley St B4
Weybridge Rd A6
Whitworth St B4
Whitworth St West C3
Wilburn St B1
William St A2
William St C6
Wilmott St C3
Windmill St B3
Windsor Cr A1
Withy Gr A4
Woden St C1
Wood St B3
Woodward St A6
Worrall St C1
Worsley St C2
York St B4
York St C2
York St C4

Middlesbrough 119

Abingdon Rd C3
Acklam Rd C1
Albert Park C2
Albert Rd B2
Albert Terr C2
Aubrey St C3
Avenue, The C2
Ayresome Gdns C2
Ayresome Gn La C1
Ayresome St C2
Barton Rd A1
Bilsdale Rd C3
Bishopton Rd C3
Borough Rd B2/B3
Bowes Rd A2
Breckon Hill Rd B3
Bridge St East B3
Bridge St West B2
Brighouse Rd A1
Burlam Rd C1
Bus Station B2
Cannon Park B1
Cannon Park Way B2
Cannon St B1
Captain Cook Sq B2
Carlow St C1
Castle Way C3
Chipchase Rd C2
Cineworld B3
Clairville Sports Stadium C3
Cleveland Centre B2
Clive Rd C2
Commercial St A2
Corporation Rd B2
Costa St C2
Council Offices B3
Crescent Rd C2
Crescent, The C2
Cumberland Rd C2
Depot Rd A2
Derwent St B2
Devonshire Rd C2
Diamond Rd B2
Disabled Driver Test Circuit B1
Dorman Mus C2
Douglas St B3
Eastbourne Rd C2
Eden Rd C3
Enterprise Centre A2
Forty Foot Rd A2
Gilkes St B2
Gosford St A2
Grange Rd B2
Gresham Rd B2
Harehills Rd C1
Harford St C2
Hartington Rd B2
Haverton Hill Rd A1
Hey Wood St B1
Highfield Rd C3
Hill St Centre B2
Holwick Rd B1
Hutton Rd C3
ICI Works A1
Information Ctr B2
Lambton Rd C3
Lancaster Rd C2
Lansdowne Rd C3
Latham Rd C2
Law Courts B2/B3
Lees Rd B2
Leeway B3
Linthorpe Cemetery C1
Linthorpe Rd B2
Lloyd St B2
Longford St C2
Longlands Rd C3
Lower East St A3
Lower Lake C3
Maldon Rd C1
Manor St B2
Marsh St B2
Marton Rd B3
Middlehaven B3
Middlesbrough By-Pass B2/C1
Middlesbrough College B3
Middlesbrough Leisure Park B3
Middlesbrough Station B2
Middlesbrough Theatre C2
Middletown Park C2
MIMA B3
Mulgrave Rd C2
Newport Bridge B1
Newport Bridge Approach Rd B1
Newport Rd B2
North Ormesby Rd B3
North Rd B2
Northern Rd C1
Outram St B2
Oxford Rd C2
Park La C2
Park Rd North C2
Park Rd South C2
Park Vale Rd C3
Parliament Rd B1
Police Station A2
Port Clarence Rd A3
Portman St B2
Post Office B2/B3/C1/C2/C3
Princes Rd B2
Python A2
Riverside Bsns Pk A2
Riverside Park Rd A1
Riverside Stadium (Middlesbrough FC) B3
Rockliffe Rd C2
Romaldkirk Rd B1
Roman Rd C2
Roseberry Rd C3
St Barnabas' Rd C2
St Paul's Rd B2
Saltwells Rd B3
Scott's Rd A3
Seaton Carew Rd A3
Shepherdson Way B3
Snowdon Rd A2
South West Ironmasters Park B1
Southfield Rd B2
Southwell Rd C2
Springfield Rd C1
Startforth Rd A2
Stockton Rd C1
Stockton St A2
Surrey St C2
Sycamore Rd C2
Tax Offices B3
Tees Viaduct C1
Teessaurus Park A2
Teesside Tertiary College C3
Temenos B3
Thornfield Rd C1
Town Hall B2
Transporter Bridge (Toll) A3
Union St B2
Univ of Teesside B2
Upper Lake C2
Valley Rd C3
Ventnor Rd C2
Victoria Rd B2
Visitor Centre A3
Vulcan St A2
Warwick St C2
Wellesley Rd B3
West La Hospl C1
Westminster Rd C2
Wilson St B2
Windward Way B3
Woodlands Rd B2
York Rd C3

Milton Keynes 122

Abbey Way A1
Arbrook Ave B1
Armourer Dr A3
Arncliffe Dr A1
Avebury C2
Avebury Blvd C2
Bankfield B3
Bayard Ave A2
Belvedere A2
Bishopstone A1
Blundells Rd A1
Boundary, The C3
Boycott Ave C2
Bradwell Common Blvd B1
Bradwell Rd C1
Bramble Ave A2
Brearley Ave C2
Breckland A1
Brill Place B1
Burnham Dr B1
Bus Station C1
Campbell Park B3
Cantle Ave A3
Central Retail Pk C1
Century Ave C2
Chaffron Way C3
Childs Way C1
Christ the Cornerstone B2
Cineworld B2
Civic Offices B2
Cleavers Ave B2
Colesbourne Dr A3
Conniburrow Blvd B2
County Court B2
Currier Dr A2
Dansteed Way A2/A3/B1
Deltic Ave B1
Downs Barn A2
Downs Barn Blvd A3
Eaglestone C3
Eelbrook Ave B1
Elder Gate B1
Evans Gate C2
Fairford Cr A3
Falcon Ave B3
Fennel Dr A2
Fishermead Blvd C3
Food Centre B3
Fulwoods Dr C3
Glazier Dr A2
Glovers La A1
Grafton Gate C1
Grafton St A1/C2
Gurnards Ave B3
Harrier Dr C3
Ibstone Ave B1
Langcliffe Dr A1
Leisure Centre C3
Leisure Plaza C1
Leys Rd C1
Library B2
Linford Wood A2
Marlborough Gate B3
Marlborough St A2/B3
Mercers Dr A1
Midsummer C2
Midsummer Blvd B2
Milton Keynes Central C1
Milton Keynes Hospital (A&E) C3
Monks Way A1
Mullen Ave A3
Mullion Pl C3
Neath Hill A3
North Elder C1
North Grafton B1
North Overgate A3
North Row B2
North Saxon B2
North Secklow B2
North Skeldon A3
North Witan B1
Oakley Gdns A3
Oldbrook Blvd C2
Open-Air Theatre B3
Overgate A3
Overstreet A3
Patriot Dr B1
Pencarrow Pl B3
Penryn Ave B3
Perran Ave C3
Pitcher La C1
Pl Retail Pk, The C1
Police Station B2
Portway B2
Post Office A2/B2/B3
Precedent Dr B1
Quinton Dr B1
Ramsons Ave B2
Retail Park C2
Rockingham Dr A2
Rooksley B1
Saxon Gate B2
Saxon St A1/C3
Secklow Gate B2
Shackleton Pl C2
Shopmobility B2
Silbury Blvd B2
Skeldon A3
South Enmore B3
South Grafton C2
South Row C2
South Saxon C2
South Secklow B3
South Witan C2
Springfield B3
Stanton Wood A1
Stantonbury A1
Stantonbury Leisure Centre A1
Strudwick Dr C2
Sunrise Parkway A2
Theatre & Art Gallery B3
theCentre:mk B2
Tolcarne Ave C3
Tourist Information Centre B3
Towan Ave C3
Trueman Pl C2
Vauxhall A1
Winterhill Ret Pk C2
Witan Gate B2
X-Scape B3

Newcastle upon Tyne 122

Albert St B3
Argyle St B3
Back New Bridge St B3
BALTIC Centre for Contemporary Art C3
Barker St A3
Barrack Rd B1
Bath La B1
Bell's Court B2
Bessie Surtees House C2
Bigg Market C2
Biscuit Factory B3
Black Gate C2
Blackett St B2
Blandford Sq C1
Boating Lake A1
Boyd St B3
Brandling Park A2
Bus Station B2
Buxton St B3
Byron St A3
Camden St B2
Castle Keep C2
Central C1
Central Library B2
Central Motorway B2
Chester St A3
City Hall B2
City Rd B3/C3
City Walls C1
Civic Centre A2
Claremont Rd A1
Clarence St B3
Clarence Walk B3
Clayton St C1/B1
Clayton St West C1
Close, The C2
Coach Station C1
College St B2
Collingwood St C2
Copland Terr B3
Coppice Way B3
Corporation St B1
Courts C3
Crawhall Rd B3
Dean St C2
Dinsdale Pl A3
Dinsdale Rd A3
Discovery C1
Doncaster Rd A3
Durant Rd B2
Eldon Sq B1
Eldon Sq Sh Ctr B2
Ellison Pl B2
Empire B1
Eskdale Terr A2
Eslington Terr A2
Exhibition Park A1
Falconar St B3
Fenkle St C1
Forth Banks C1
Forth St C1
Gallowgate B1
Gate, The B1
Gateshead Heritage @ St Mary's C3
Gateshead Millennium Bridge C3
Gibson St B3
Goldspink La A3
Grainger Market B2
Grainger St B2
Grantham Rd A3
Granville Rd A3
Great North Mus:Hancock A2
Grey St B2
Groat Market C2
Guildhall C2
Hancock St A2
Hanover St C2
Hatton Gallery A1
Hawks Rd C3
Haymarket B2
Heber St B1
Helmsley Rd A3
High Bridge B2
High Level Bridge C2
Hillgate C3
Howard St B3
Hutton Terr A3
Information Ctr C3
Jesmond A2
Jesmond Rd A2/A3
John Dobson St B2
John George Joicey Museum C2
Jubilee Rd B3
Kelvin Gr A3
Kensington Terr A2
Laing Gallery B2
Lambton Rd A2
Leazes Cr B1
Leazes La B1
Leazes Park B1
Leazes Park Rd B1
Leazes Terr B1
Live C2
Low Friar St C1
Manor Chare C2
Manors B2
Manors Station B2
Market St B2
Melbourne St B2
Mill Rd C3
Mill Volvo Tyne C1
Monument B2
Monument Mall Shopping Centre B2
Morpeth St A2
Mosley St C2
Napier St A3
Nazareth House A3
New Bridge St B2/B3
Newcastle Central Station C1
Newcastle Univ A1
Newgate Sh Ctr C1
Newgate St B1
Newington Rd A3
Northern Stage Theatre A2
Northumberland Rd B2
Northumberland St B2
Northumbria Univ A2
Northwest Radial Rd A1
O2 Academy C1
Oakwellgate C3
Orchard St C2
Osborne Rd A2
Osborne Terr A3
Pandon C3
Pandon Bank B3
Park Terr A1
Percy St B1
Pilgrim St B2
Pipewellgate C2
Pitt St B1
Plummer Tower A2
Police Station B2
Portland Rd A3/B3
Portland Terr A3
Post Office A3/B1/B2/B3
Pottery La C1
Prudhoe Pl B1
Prudhoe St B1
Quayside C2
Queen Elizabeth II Bridge C2
Queen Victoria Rd A1
Richardson Rd A1
Ridley Pl B2
Rock Terr B3
Rosedale Terr A3
Royal Victoria Infirmary A1
Sage Gateshead, The C3
St Andrew's St B1
St James B1
St James' Blvd C1
St James' Park (Newcastle Utd FC) B1
St Mary's (RC) C1
St Mary's Place B2
St Nicholas C2
St Nicholas St C2
St Thomas' St B1
Sandyford Rd A2/A3
Science Park B2
Shield St B3
Shieldfield B3
Side, The C2
Simpson Terr B3
South Shore Rd C3
South St C1
Starbeck Ave A3
Stepney Rd B3
Stoddart St B3
Stowell St B1
Strawberry Pl B1
Swing Bridge C2
Temple St C1
Terrace Pl B1
Theatre Royal B2
Times Sq C1
Tower St B3
Trinity House C2
Tyne Bridge C2
Tyne Bridges C2
Tyneside B2
Victoria Sq A2
Warwick St A3
Waterloo St C1
Wellington St B1
Westgate Rd C1/C2
Windsor Terr A2
Worswick St B2
Wretham Pl B3

Newport
Casnewydd 122

Albert Terr B1
Allt-yr-Yn Ave A1
Alma St C2
Ambulance Sta C3
Bailey St B2
Barrack Hill A2
Bath St A3
Bedford Rd B3
Belle Vue La C1
Belle Vue Park C1
Bishop St A3
Blewitt St B1
Bolt Cl C3
Bolt St C3
Bond St A2
Bosworth Dr A1
Bridge St B1
Bristol St A3
Bryngwyn Rd B1
Brynhyfryd Ave C1
Brynhyfryd Rd C1
Bus Station B2
Caerau Cres C1
Caerau Rd B1
Caerleon Rd A3
Capel Cres C2
Cardiff Rd C2
Caroline St B3
Castle (Remains) A2
Cedar Rd B3
Charles St B2
Charlotte Dr C2
Chepstow Rd A3
Church Rd A3
Cineworld B2
Civic Centre B1
Clarence Pl A2
Clifton Pl B1
Clifton Rd C1
Clyffard Cres B1
Clytha Park Rd B1
Clytha Sq C2
Coldra Rd C1
Collier St A3
Colne St B3
Comfrey Cl A1
Commercial Rd C3
Commercial St B2
Corelli St A3
Corn St B2
Corporation Rd B3
Coulson Cl C2
County Court A2
Courts A1
Courts B1
Crawford St A3
Cyril St B3
Dean St A3
Devon Pl B1
Dewsland Park Rd C2
Dolman B2
Dolphin St C3
East Dock Rd C3
East St B1
East Usk Rd A3
Ebbw Vale Wharf B3
Emlyn St B2
Enterprise Way C3
Eton Rd B3
Evans St A2
Factory Rd A2
Fields Rd B1
Francis Dr C2
Frederick St C3
Friars Rd C1
Friars Walk B2
Gaer La C1
George St C3
George St Bridge C3
Godfrey Rd B1
Gold Tops B1
Gore St A3
Gorsedd Circle C1
Grafton Rd A3
Graham St B1
Granville St C3
Harlequin Dr A1
Harrow Rd B3
Herbert Rd A3
Herbert Walk C2
Hereford St A3
High St B2
Hill St B2
Hoskins St A2
Information Ctr B2
Ivor Sq B2
Jones St B1
Junction Rd A3
Keynshaw Ave C2
King St C2
Kingsway B2
Kingsway Centre B2
Ledbury Dr A2
Library A3
Library, Museum & Art Gallery B2
Liverpool Wharf B3
Llanthewy Rd B1
Llanvair Rd A3
Locke St A2
Lower Dock St C3
Lucas St A2
Manchester St A3
Market B2
Marlborough Rd B3
Mellon St C3
Mill St A2
Morgan St A3
Mountjoy Rd C2
Newport Bridge A2
Newport Ctr B2
Newport RFC B3
Newport Sta B2
North St B2
Oakfield Rd B1
Park Sq C2
Police Sta A3/C2
Post Office B2/C3
Power St A1
Prince St A3
Pugsley St A2
Queen St C2
Queen's Cl A1
Queen's Hill A1
Queen's Hill Cres A1
Queensway B2
Railway St B2
Riverfront Theatre & Arts Ctr, The B2
Riverside A3
Rodney Rd B2
Royal Gwent (A&E) C2
Rudry St A3
Rugby Rd B3
Ruperra La C3
Ruperra St C3
St Edmund St B1
St Mark's Cres A1
St Mary St B1
St Vincent Rd A3
St Woolos C2
St Woolos General (no A&E) C1
St Woolos Rd B1
School La B2
Serpentine Rd B1
Shaftesbury Park A2
Sheaf La A3
Skinner St B2
Sorrel Dr A1
South Market St C3
Spencer Rd B1
Stow Hill B2/C1/C2
Stow Park Ave C1
Stow Park Dr C1
TA Centre A1
Talbot St B2
Tennis Club A1
Tregare St A3
Trostrey St A3
Tunnel Terr B1
Turner St A3
Uni of Wales Newport City Campus B3
Upper Dock St B2
Usk St A3
Usk Way B3/C3
Victoria Cr B1
War Memorial A3
Waterloo Rd C1
West St B1
Wharves B2
Wheeler St A2
Whitby Pl A3
Windsor Terr B1
York Pl C1

Northampton 122

78 Derngate B3
Abingdon Sq B3
Abington St B3
Alcombe St A3
All Saints' B2
Ambush St B1
Angel St B2
Arundel St A2
Ash St A2
Auctioneers Way C2
Bailiff St A2
Barrack Rd A2
Beaconsfield Terr A3
Becketts Park C3
Becketts Park Marina C3
Bedford Rd B3
Billing Rd B3
Brecon St A1
Brewery C2
Bridge St C2
Broad St B2
Burns St A3
Bus Station B2
Campbell St A2
Castle (Site of) B2
Castle St B2
Cattle Market Rd C2
Central Museum & Art Gallery B2
Charles St A3
Cheyne Walk B3
Church La A2
Clare St A3
Cloutsham St A3
College St B2
Colwyn Rd A3
Cotton End C2
Countess Rd A1
County Hall B2
Court A2
Craven St A3
Crown & County Courts B3
Denmark Rd B3
Derngate B3
Derngate & Royal Theatres B3
Doddridge Church B2
Drapery, The B2
Duke St A3
Dunster St A3
Earl St A3
Euston Rd C2
Fire Station A3
Foot Meadow B2
Gladstone Rd A1
Gold St B2
Grafton St A2
Gray St A3
Green St B1
Greenwood Rd B1
Greyfriars B2
Grosvenor Centre B2
Grove Rd A3
Guildhall B2
Hampton St A2
Harding Terr A2
Hazelwood Rd B3
Herbert St B2
Hervey St A3
Hester St A2
Holy Sepulchre A2
Hood St A3
Horse Market B2
Hunter St A3
Information Ctr B1
Kettering Rd A3
Kingswell St B2
Lady's La B2
Leicester St A2
Leslie Rd A2
Library B3
Lorne Rd A2
Lorry Park A1
Louise Rd A2
Lower Harding St A2
Lower Hester St A2
Lower Mounts B3
Lower Priory St A2
Main Rd C1
Marefair B2
Market Sq B2
Marlboro Rd B1
Marriott St A2
Military Rd A3
Mounts Baths L Ctr A3
Nene Valley Ret Pk C1
New South Bridge Rd C2
Northampton General Hospital (A&E) B3
Northampton Station B1
Northcote St A2
Nunn Mills Rd C3
Old Towcester Rd C2
Overstone Rd A3
Peacock Pl B2
Pembroke Rd A1
Penn Court C2
Police Station B3
Post Office A1/A2/B3/C2
Quorn Way A2
Ransome Rd C3
Regent Sq A2
Ridings, The B3
Robert St A2
St Andrew's Rd B1
St Andrew's St A2
St Edmund's Rd B3
St George's St A2
St Giles B3
St Giles St B3
St Giles' Terr B3
St James Park Rd B1
St James Rd B1
St James Retail Pk C1
St James' Mill Rd B1
St James' Mill Rd East C1
St Leonard's Rd C2
St Mary's St B2
St Michael's Rd A3
St Peter's B2
St Peter's Square Shopping Prec B2
St Peter's Way B2
Salisbury St A2
Scarletwell St B2
Semilong Rd A2
Sheep St B2
Sol Central (L Ctr) B2
Somerset St A3
South Bridge C2
Southfield Ave C2
Spencer Bridge Rd A1
Spencer Rd A3
Spring Gdns B3
Spring La B2
Swan St B3
TA Centre A3
Tanner St B2
Tintern Ave A1
Towcester Rd C2
Upper Bath St B2
Upper Mounts A2
Victoria Park A1
Victoria Prom B2
Victoria Rd B3
Victoria St A2
Wellingborough Rd B3
West Bridge B1
York Rd B3

Norwich 122

Albion Way C3
All Saints Green C2
Anchor St A3
Anglia Sq A2
Argyle St C3
Arts Centre B1
Ashby St C2
Assembly Ho B1
Bank Plain B2
Barker St A1
Barn Rd A1
Barrack St A3
Ber St C2
Bethel St B1
Bishop Bridge A3
Bishopbridge Rd A3
Bishopgate A3
Blackfriars St A2
Botolph St A2
Bracondale C3
Brazen Gate C2
Bridewell B2
Brunswick Rd C1
Bull Close Rd A2
Bus Station C2
Calvert St A2
Cannell Green A3
Carrow Rd C3
Castle & Mus B2
Castle Mall B2
Castle Meadow B2
Cathedral B2
Cath Retail Park A1
Cattlemarket St B2
Chantry Rd C1
Chapel Loke C2
Chapelfield East B1
Chapelfield Gdns B1
Chapelfield North B1
Chapelfield Rd B1
City Hall B1
City Rd C2
City Wall C1/C3
Close, The B3
Colegate A2
Coslany St B1
Cow Hill B1
Cow Tower A3
Cowgate A2
Crown & Magistrates' Cts A2
Dragon Hall Heritage Centre C3
Duke St A1
Edward St A2
Elm Hill B2
Erpingham Gate B2
Fire Station B1
Fishergate A2
Forum, The B1
Foundry Bridge B3
Fye Bridge A2
Garden St C2
Gas Hill B3
Gentlemans Walk B2
Grapes Hill B1
Great Hospital Halls, The A3
Grove Ave C1
Grove Rd C1
Guildhall B1
Gurney Rd A3
Hall Rd C2
Heathgate A3
Heigham St A1
Horn's La C2
Information Ctr B1
intu Chapelfield C1
Ipswich Rd C1
James Stuart Gdns B3
King Edward VI School B2
King St B2
King St C3
Koblenz Ave C3
Library B1
London St B2
Lower Cl B3
Lower Clarence Rd B3
Maddermarket B1
Magdalen St A2
Mariners La C2
Market B2
Market Ave B2
Mountergate B3
Mousehold St A3
Newmarket Rd C1
Norfolk St C1
Norwich City FC C3
Norwich Gallery B2
Norwich Station B3
Oak St A1
Palace St A2
Pitt St A1
Playhouse B2

Police Station A3
Post Office A2/B2/C2
Pottergate B1
Prince of Wales Rd B2
Princes St B2
Pull's Ferry B3
Puppet Theatre A2
Queen St B2
Queens Rd C2
RC Cathedral B1
Recorder Rd B3
Riverside Entertainment Centre C3
Riverside L Ctr C3
Riverside Rd B3
Riverside Retail Pk C3
Rosary Rd B3
Rose La B2
Rouen Rd C2
Royal Norfolk Regimental Museum B2
St Andrews St B2
St Augustines St A1
St Benedicts St B1
St Ethelbert's Gate B2
St Faiths La B3
St Georges St A2
St Giles St B1
St James Cl A3
St Julians C2
St Leonards Rd B3
St Martin's La A1
St Peter Mancroft B2
St Peters St B1
St Stephens Rd C1
St Stephens St C1
Shopmobility C1
Silver Rd A2
Silver St A2
Southwell Rd C2
St. Andrew's & Blackfriars' Hall B2
Strangers' Hall B1
Superstore C2
Surrey St C2
Sussex St A1
Theatre Royal B1
Theatre St B1
Thorn La C2
Thorpe Rd B3
Tombland B2
Union St C1
Vauxhall St B1
Victoria St C1
Walpole St B1
Waterfront, The C3
Wensum St A2
Wessex St C1
Westwick St A1
Wherry Rd C3
Whitefriars A2
Willow La B1
Yacht Station B3

Nottingham 122

Abbotsford Dr A3
Addison St A1
Albert Hall B1
Alfred St South A3
Alfreton Rd B1
All Saints Rd A1
Annesley Gr A2
Arboretum A1
Arboretum St A1
Arthur St A1
Arts Theatre B3
Ashforth St A3
Balmoral Rd A1
Barker Gate B3
Bath St B3
BBC Nottingham C3
Belgrave Rooms B1
Bellar Gate B3
Belward St B3
Blue Bell Hill Rd B3
Brewhouse Yd C2
Broad Marsh Bus Station C2
Broad St B3
Brook St B3
Burns St A1
Burton St B2
Bus Station A2
Canal St C2
Carlton St B3
Carrington St C2
Castle C2
Castle Blvd C1
Castle Gate C2
Castle Meadow Rd C1
Castle Mdw Ret Pk C1
Castle Museum & Gallery C2
Castle Rd C2
Castle Wharf C2
Cavendish Rd East C1
Cemetery B1
Chaucer St B1
Cheapside B2
Church Rd A3
City Link C3
City of Caves C2
Clarendon St B1
Cliff Rd C3
Clumber Rd East C1
Clumber St B2
College St B1
Collin St C2
Conway Cl A2
Council House B2
Cranbrook St B3
Cranmer St A2
Cromwell St B1
Curzon St B3
Derby Rd B1
Dryden St A2
Exchange Ctr, The B2
Fishpond Dr C1
Fletcher Gate B3
Forest Rd East A1
Forest Rd West A1
Friar La C2
Galleries of Justice C3
Gedling Gr A1
Gedling St B3
George St B3
Gill St A2
Glasshouse St B2
Goldsmith St B2
Goose Gate B3
Great Freeman St A2
Guildhall B2
Hamilton Dr C1
Hampden St A1
Heathcote St B3
High Pavement C3
High School A1
Holles Cr C1
Hope Dr C1
Hungerhill Rd A3
Huntingdon Dr C1
Huntingdon St A2
Information Ctr B2
Instow Rise A3
Int Com Ctr A2
intu Broadmarsh C2
intu Victoria Ctr B2
Kent St B3
King St B2
Lace Centre, The C2
Lace Market B3
Lace Market Theatre C3
Lamartine St B3
Leisure Ctr C3
Lenton Rd C1
Lewis Cl A3
Lincoln St B2
London Rd C3
Long Row B2
Low Pavement C2
Lower Parliament St B3
Magistrates' Court C2
Maid Marian Way B2
Mansfield Rd A2/B2
Middle Hill C2
Milton St B2
Mount St B2
National Ice Ctr C3
Newcastle Dr B1
Newstead Gr A2
North Sherwood St A2
Nottingham Arena C3
Nottingham Sta C3
Nottingham Trent University A2/B2
Old Mkt Square B2
Oliver St A1
Park Dr C1
Park Row C1
Park Terr B1
Park Valley C1
Park, The C1
Peas Hill Rd A3
Peel St A1
Pelham St B2
Peveril Dr C1
Plantagenet St A3
Playhouse B1
Plumptre St C3
Police Sta B1/B2
Poplar St C3
Portland Rd B1
Post Office B2
Queen's Rd C3
Raleigh St A1
Regent St B1
Rick St B3
Robin Hood St B3
Robin Hood Statue C2
Ropewalk, The B1
Royal Centre B2
Royal Children Inn C2
Royal Concert Hall B2
St Ann's Hill Rd A2
St Ann's Way A2
St Ann's Well Rd A3
St Barnabas B1
St James' St B2
St Mark's St B3
St Mary's Garden of Rest B3
St Mary's Gate B3
St Nicholas C2
St Peter's C2
St Peter's Gate B2
Salutation Inn C2
Shakespeare St B2
Shelton St A2
Shopmobility A2
South Pde B2
South Rd C1
South Sherwood St B2
Station St C3
Station Street C3
Stoney St B3
Talbot St B1
Tattershall Dr C1
Tennis Dr B1
Tennyson St A1
Theatre Royal B2
Trent St C3
Trent University B2
Union Rd B3
Upper Parliament St B2
Victoria L Ctr B3
Victoria Park B3
Victoria St B2
Walter St A1
Warser Gate B3
Watkin St A2
Waverley St A1
Wheeler Gate B2
Wilford Rd C2
Wilford St C2
Willoughby Ho C2
Wollaton St B1
Woodborough Rd A2
Woolpack La B3
Ye Old Trip to Jerusalem C2
York St A2

Oxford 123

Adelaide St A1
Albert St A1
All Souls (Coll) B2
Ashmolean Mus B2
Balliol (Coll) B2
Banbury Rd A2
Bate Collection of Musical Instruments C2
Beaumont St B1
Becket St B1
Blackhall Rd A2
Blue Boar St B2
Bodleian Liby B2
Botanic Garden B3
Brasenose (Coll) B2
Brewer St C2
Broad St B2
Burton-Taylor Theatre B2
Bus Station B1
Canal St A1
Cardigan St A1
Carfax Tower B2
Castle B1
Castle St B1
Catte St B2
Cemetery C1
Christ Church (Coll) B2
Christ Church Cathedral C2
Christ Church Meadow C2
Clarendon Centre B2
Coach & Lorry Pk C1
College B3
Coll of Further Ed C1
Cornmarket St B2
Corpus Christi (Coll) B2
County Hall B1
Covered Market B2
Cowley Pl C3
Cranham St A1
Cranham Terr A1
Cricket Ground B1
Crown & County Courts C2
Deer Park B3
Exeter (Coll) B2
Folly Bridge C2
George St B1
Great Clarendon St A1
Hart St A1
Hertford (Coll) B2
High St B3
Hollybush Row B1
Holywell St B2
Hythe Bridge St B1
Ice Rink C1
Information Ctr B2
Jericho St A1
Jesus (Coll) B2
Jowett Walk B3
Juxon St A1
Keble (Coll) A2
Keble Rd A2
Library B2
Linacre (Coll) A3
Lincoln (Coll) B2
Little Clarendon St A1
Longwall St B3
Magdalen (Coll) B3
Magdalen Bridge B2
Magdalen St B2
Magistrate's Ct C2
Manchester (Coll) B2
Manor Rd B3
Mansfield (Coll) A2
Mansfield Rd A3
Market B1
Marlborough Rd C2
Martyrs' Meml B2
Merton (Coll) B3
Merton Field B3
Merton St B2
Museum of Modern Art B2
Mus of Oxford B2
Museum Rd A2
New College (Coll) B3
New Inn Hall St B2
New Rd B1
New Theatre B2
Norfolk St C1
Nuffield (Coll) B1
Observatory A1
Observatory St A1
Odeon B1/B2
Old Fire Station B1
Old Greyfriars St C2
Oriel (Coll) B2
Oxford Station B1
Oxford Story, The B2
Oxford University Research Ctrs A1
Oxpens Rd C1
Paradise Sq C1
Paradise St B1
Park End St B1
Parks Rd A2/B2
Pembroke (Coll) C2
Phoenix A1
Picture Gallery C2
Plantation Rd A1
Playhouse B2
Police Station C2
Post Office A1/B2
Pusey St B1
Queen's (Coll) B3
Queen's La B3
Radcliffe Camera B2
Rewley Rd B1
Richmond Rd A1
Rose La B3
Ruskin (Coll) B1
Saïd Bsns School B1
St Aldates C2
St Anne's (Coll) A1
St Antony's (Coll) A1
St Bernard's Rd A1
St Catherine's (Coll) B3
St Cross Building A3
St Cross Rd A3
St Edmund Hall (Coll) B3
St Giles St A2
St Hilda's (Coll) C3
St John St B2
St John's (Coll) B2
St Mary the Virgin B2
St Michael at the Northgate B2
St Peter's (Coll) B1
St Thomas St B1
Science Area A2
Science Mus B2
Sheldonian Theatre B2
Somerville (Coll) A1
South Parks Rd A2
Speedwell St C2
Sports Ground C3
Thames St C2
Town Hall B2
Trinity (Coll) B2
Turl St B2
Univ Coll (Coll) B3
Univ Mus & Pitt Rivers Mus A2
University Parks A2
Wadham (Coll) B2
Walton Cr A1
Walton St A1
Western Rd C2
Westgate Sh Ctr B2
Woodstock Rd A1
Worcester (Coll) B1

Peterborough 123

Athletics Arena B3
Bishop's Palace B2
Bishop's Rd B2/B3
Boongate A3
Bourges Bvd A1
Bourges Ret Pk B1/B2
Bridge House (Council Offices) C2
Bridge St B2
Bright St A1
Broadway A2
Broadway A2
Brook St A2
Burghley Rd A2
Bus Station B2
Cavendish St A3
Charles St A3
Church St B2
Church Walk A2
Cobden Ave A1
Cobden St A1
Cowgate B2
Craig St A2
Crawthorne Rd A2
Cripple Sidings La C2
Cromwell Rd A1
Dickens St A3
Eastfield Rd A3
Eastgate B3
Fire Station A1
Fletton Ave C2
Frank Perkins Parkway C3
Geneva St A2
George St C1
Gladstone St A1
Glebe Rd C2
Gloucester Rd C3
Granby St B3
Grove St C1
Guildhall B2
Hadrians Ct C3
Henry St A2
Hereward Cross (shopping) B2
Hereward Rd B3
Information Ctr B2
Jubilee St C1
Kent Rd B1
Key Theatre C2
Kirkwood Cl B1
Lea Gdns B1
Library A2
Lincoln Rd A2
London Rd C2
Long Causeway B2
Lower Bridge St C2
Magistrates Court B2
Manor House St A2
Mayor's Walk A1
Midland Rd A1
Monument St A2
Morris St A3
Museum & Art Gallery B2
Nene Valley Railway C1
New Rd A2
New Rd C1
Northminster A2
Old Customs Ho C2
Oundle Rd C1
Padholme Rd A3
Palmerston Rd C1
Park Rd A2
Passport Office B2
Peterborough Nene Valley C1
Peterborough B1
Peterborough United FC C2
Police Station B2
Post Office A3/B1/B2/B3/C1
Priestgate B2
Queen's Walk C2
Queensgate Ctr B2
Railworld C1
Regional Swimming & Fitness Centre B3
River La B1
Rivergate Sh Ctr B2
Riverside Mead C3
Russell St A1
St John's B2
St John's St A3
St Marks St A2
St Peter's B2
St Peter's Rd B2
Saxon Rd A3
Spital Bridge A1
Stagshaw Dr C3
Star Rd B3
Thorpe Lea Rd B1
Thorpe Rd B1
Thorpe's Lea Rd B1
Tower St A2
Town Hall B2
Viersen Platz B2
Vineyard Rd B3
Wake Rd B3
Wellington St A3
Wentworth St B2
Westgate B2
Whalley St A3
Wharf Rd C1
Whitsed St A3
YMCA A3

Plymouth 123

Alma Rd A1
Anstis St B1
Armada Shop Ctr B2
Armada St A3
Armada Way B2
Arts Centre B2
Athenaeum B1
Athenaeum St C1
Barbican C3
Barbican C3
Baring St A3
Bath St B1
Beaumont Park B3
Beaumont Rd B3
Black Friars Gin Distillery C2
Breton Side B3
Castle St C3
Cathedral (RC) B1
Cecil St B1
Central Park A1
Central Park Ave A2
Charles Church B3
Charles Cross B3
Charles St B2
Citadel Rd C2
Citadel Rd East C2
City Museum & Art Gallery B2
Civic Centre B2
Cliff Rd C1
Clifton Pl A3
Cobourg St A2
College of Art B2
Continental Ferry Port B1
Cornwall St B2
Crescent, The B1
Dale Rd A2
Deptford Pl A3
Derry Ave A2
Derry's Cross B1
Drake Circus B2
Drake Cir Sh Ctr B2
Drake's Meml C2
Eastlake St B2
Ebrington St B3
Elizabethan Ho C3
Elliot St C1
Endsleigh Pl A2
Exeter St B3
Fire Station A3
Fish Quay C3
Gibbons St A3
Glen Park Ave A2
Grand Pde C1
Great Western Rd C1
Greenbank Rd A3
Greenbank Terr A3
Guildhall B2
Hampton St B3
Harwell St B1
Hill Park Cr A3
Hoe Approach B2
Hoe Rd C2
Hoe, The C2
Hoegate St C2
Houndiscombe Rd A2
Information Ctr C3
James St A2
Kensington Rd A3
King St B1
Lambhay Hill C3
Leigham St C1
Library B2
Lipson Rd A3/B3
Lockyer St C1
Lockyers Quay C3
Madeira Rd C2
Marina C3
Market Ave B1
Martin St B1
Mayflower St B2
Mayflower Stone & Steps C3
Mayflower Visitor Centre C3
Merchant's Ho B2
Millbay Rd B1
National Marine Aquarium C3
Neswick St B1
New George St B2
New St C3
North Cross A2
North Hill A3
North Quay B2
North Rd East A2
North Rd West A1
North St B3
Notte St B2
Octagon, The B1
Octagon St B1
Pannier Market B1
Pennycomequick A1
Pier St C1
Plymouth Pavilions B1
Plymouth Sta A2
Police Station A3
Post Office C2
Princess St B2
Promenade, The C2
Prysten House B2
Queen Anne's Battery Seasports Centre C3
Radford Rd C1
Reel B2
Regent St B3
Rope Walk C3
Royal Citadel C2
Royal Pde B2
Royal Theatre B2
St Andrew's B2
St Andrew's Cross B2
St Andrew's St B2
St Lawrence Rd A2
Saltash Rd A2
Shopmobility B2
Smeaton's Tower C2
Southern Terr A3
Southside St C2
Stuart Rd A1
Sutherland Rd A2
Sutton Rd B3
Sydney St A1
Teats Hill Rd C3
Tothill Ave B3
Union St B1
Univ of Plymouth A2
Vauxhall St B2/3
Victoria Park A1
West Hoe Rd C1
Western Approach B1
Whittington St A1
Wyndham St B1
YMCA B2
YWCA C2

Poole 123

Ambulance Sta A3
Baiater Gdns C2
Baiter Park C3
Ballard Cl C2
Ballard Rd C2
Bay Hog La B1
Bridge Approach C1
Bus Station B2
Castle St B2
Catalina Dr B3
Chapel La B2
Church St B1
Cinnamon La B1
Colborne Cl B3
Dear Hay La B2
Denmark La A3
Denmark Rd A3
East St B2
Elizabeth Rd A3
Emerson Rd B2
Ferry Rd C1
Ferry Terminal C1
Fire Station A2
Freightliner Terminal C1
Furnell Rd B3
Garland Rd A3
Green Rd B2
Heckford La A3
Heckford Rd A3
High St B2
High St North A3
Hill St B2
Holes Bay Rd A1
Hospital (A&E) A3
Information Ctr C2
Kingland Rd B3
Kingston Rd A3
Labrador Dr C3
Lagland St B2
Lander Cl C3
Lifeboat Coll, The B2
Lighthouse – Poole Ctr for the Arts B3
Longfleet Rd A3
Maple Rd A3
Market Cl B2
Market St B2
Mount Pleasant Rd B3
New Harbour Rd C1
New Harbour Rd S C1
New Harbour Rd W C1
New Orchard B1
New Quay Rd C1
New St B2
Newfoundland Dr B2
North St B2
Old Lifeboat C2
Old Orchard B2
Parish Rd A3
Park Lake Rd B3
Parkstone Rd A3
Perry Gdns B2
Pitwines Cl B2
Police Station A2
Poole Central Liby B2
Poole Lifting Bridge C1
Poole Park B2
Poole Station A2
Poole Waterfront Museum C1
Post Office A2/B2
Quay, The C2
St John's Rd A3
St Margaret's Rd A2
St Mary's Maternity Unit A3
St Mary's Rd A3
Seldown Bridge B3
Seldown La B3
Seldown Rd B3
Serpentine Rd A2
Shaftesbury Rd A3
Skinner St B2
Slipway B1
Stanley Rd C2
Sterte Ave A2
Sterte Ave West A1
Sterte Cl A2
Sterte Esplanade A2
Sterte Rd A2
Strand St C2
Swimming Pool B3
Taverner Cl B3
Thames St B1
Towngate Bridge B2
Vallis Cl C3
Waldren Cl B3
West Quay B1
West Quay Rd B1
West St B1
West View Rd A2
Whatleigh Cl B2
Wimborne Rd A3

Portsmouth 123

Action Stations C1
Admiralty Rd A1
Alfred Rd A2
Anglesea Rd B2
Arundel St B3
Aspex B1
Bishop St A2
Broad St C1
Buckingham Ho C2
Burnaby Rd B2
Bus Station B1
Camber Dock C1
Cambridge Rd B2
Car Ferry to Isle of Wight B1
Cascades Sh Ctr A3
Castle Rd C3
City Museum & Art Gallery B2
Civic Offices B3
Clarence Pier C2
College St B1
Commercial Rd A3
Cottage Gr B3
Cross St A1
Cumberland St A2
Duisburg Way C2
Durham St A3
East St B1
Edinburgh Rd A2
Elm Gr C3
Emirates Spinnaker Tower B1
Great Southsea St C3
Green Rd B3
Greetham St B3
Grosvenor St B3
Groundlings A2
Grove Rd North C3
Grove Rd South C3
Guildhall B3
Guildhall Walk B3
Gunwharf Quays Retail Park B1
Gunwharf Rd B1
Hambrook St C2
Hampshire Terr B2
Hanover St A1
Hard, The B1
High St C2
HM Naval Base A1
HMS Nelson (Royal Naval Barracks) A2
HMS Victory A1
HMS Warrior A1
Hovercraft Terminal C2
Hyde Park Rd B3
Information Ctr A1/B3
Isambard Brunel Rd B3
Isle of Wight Car Ferry Terminal B1
Kent Rd C3
Kent St A2
King St B3
King's Rd C3
King's Terr C2
Lake Rd A3
Law Courts B3
Library B3
Long Curtain Rd C2
Market Way A3
Marmion Rd C3
Mary Rose Mus A1
Middle St B3
Millennium Promenade B1/C1
Museum Rd B2
National Museum of the Royal Navy A1
Naval Rec Gd C2
Nightingale Rd C3
Norfolk St B3
North St A2
Osborne Rd C3
Park Rd B2
Passenger Catamaran to Isle of Wight B1
Passenger Ferry to Gosport B1
Pelham Rd C3
Pembroke Gdns C2
Pier Rd C2
Point Battery C1
Police Station B3
Portsmouth & Southsea A3
Portsmouth Harbour B1
Portsmouth Historic Dockyard A1
Post Office A2/A3/B1/B3/C3
Queen St A1
Queen's Cr C3
Round Tower C1
Royal Garrison Church C1
St Edward's Rd C3
St George's Rd B2
St George's Sq B1
St George's Way B2
St James's Rd B3
St James's St A2
St John's Cathedral (RC) A3
St Thomas's Cathedral C1
St Thomas's St B2
Somers Rd B3
Southsea Common C2
Southsea Terr C2
Square Tower C1
Station St A3
Swimming Pool A3
Town Fortifications C1
Unicorn Rd A2
United Services Rec Gd B2
University of Portsmouth A2/B2
Univ of Portsmouth – Coll of Art, Design and Media B3
Upper Arundel St A3
Victoria Ave C2
Victoria Park A2
Victory Gate A1
Vue B1
Warblington St B1
Western Pde C2
White Hart Rd C1
Winston Churchill Ave B3

Preston 123

Adelphi St A2
Anchor Ct B3
Aqueduct St A1
Ardee Rd C1
Arthur St B2
Ashton St A1
Avenham La B3
Avenham Park C3
Avenham Rd B3
Avenham St B3
Bairstow St B3
Balderstone Rd C1
Beamont Dr A1
Beech St South C2
Bird St C1
Bow La B2
Brieryfield Rd A1
Broadgate C1
Brook St A2
Bus Station A3
Butler St B2
Cannon St B3
Carlton St A1
Chaddock St B3
Channel Way B1
Chapel St B3
Christ Church St B2
Christian Rd B2
Cold Bath St A2
Coleman Ct C1
Connaught Rd C2
Corn Exchange B3
Corporation St A2/B2
County Hall B2
County Records Office B2
Court A3
Court B3
Cricket Ground C2
Croft St A1
Cross St B3
Crown Court A3
Crown St A3
East Cliff C3
East Cliff Rd B3
Edward St A2
Elizabeth St A3
Euston St B1
Fishergate B2/B3
Fishergate Hill B2
Fishergate Sh Ctr B2
Fitzroy St B1
Fleetwood St A1
Friargate A3
Fylde Rd A1/A2
Gerrard St B2
Glover's Ct B3
Good St B2
Grafton St B2
Great George St A3
Great Shaw St A3
Greenbank St A2
Guild Way B1
Guildhall & Charter B3
Guildhall St B3
Harrington St A2
Harris Museum B3
Hartington Rd B1
Hasset Cl C2
Heatley St B2
Hind St C2
Information Ctr B3
Kilruddery Rd C1
Lancaster Rd A3/B3
Latham St B3
Lauderdale St C2
Lawson St A3
Leighton St A2
Leyland Rd C1
Library A1
Library B3
Liverpool Rd C1
Lodge St B2
Lune St B3
Main Sprit West B3
Maresfield Rd C1
Market St West A3
Marsh La B1/B2
Maudland Bank A2
Maudland Rd A2
Meadow Ct C2
Meath Rd C1
Mill Hill A2
Miller Arcade B3
Miller Park C3
Moor La A3
Mount St B3
North Rd A3
North St A3
Northcote Rd B1
Old Milestones B1
Old Tram Rd C3
Pedder St A1/A2
Peel St A2
Penwortham Bridge C2
Penwortham New Bridge C1
Pitt St B2
Playhouse A3
Police Station A3
Port Way B1
Post Office B3
Preston Station B2
Ribble Bank St B2
Ribble Viaduct C2
Ribblesdale Pl B3
Ringway B3
River Parade C1
Riverside C2
St George's Sh Ctr B3
St Georges B3
St Johns B3
St Johns Sh Ctr A3
St Mark's Rd A1
St Walburges A1
Salisbury Rd B1
Sessions House B3
Snow Hill A3
South End C2
South Meadow La C2
Spa Rd B1
Sports Ground C2
Strand Rd B1
Syke St B3
Talbot Rd B1
Taylor St C1
Tithebarn St A3
Town Hall B3
Tulketh Brow A1
University of Central Lancashire A2
Valley Rd C1
Victoria St A2
Walker St A3
Walton's Parade B2
Warwick St A3
Wellfield Bsns Pk A1
Wellfield Rd A1
Wellington St A1
West Cliff C2
West Strand A1
Winckley Rd C1
Winckley Square B3
Wolseley Rd C2

Reading 124

Abbey Ruins B2
Abbey Sq B2
Abbey St B2
Abbot's Walk B2
Acacia Rd C2
Addington Rd C3
Addison Rd A1
Allcroft Rd C3
Alpine St C2
Baker St B1
Berkeley Ave C1
Bridge St B1
Brigham Rd A1
Broad St B1
Broad Street Mall B1
Carey St B1
Castle Hill C1
Castle St B1
Causeway, The A3
Caversham Rd A1
Christchurch Playing Fields A2
Civic Offices B1
Coley Hill C1
Coley Pl C1
Craven Rd C3
Crown St C2
De Montfort Rd A1
Denmark Rd C3
Duke St B2
East St B2
Edgehill St C2
Eldon Rd B3
Eldon Terr B3
Elgar Rd C1
Erleigh Rd C3
Field Rd C1
Fire Station A1
Fobney St B1
Forbury Gdns B2
Forbury Rd B2
Forbury Retail Pk B2
Francis St C1
Friar St B1
Garrard St B1
Gas Works Rd B3
George St A2
Great Knollys St B1
Greyfriars B1
Grove, The B2
Gun St B1
Henry St C1
Hexagon Theatre, The B1
Hill's Meadow A2
Howard St B1
Information Ctr B1
Inner Distribution Rd B1
Katesgrove La C1
Kenavon Dr B2
Kendrick Rd C2
King's Mdw Rec Gd A2
King's Rd B2
Library B2
London Rd C3
London St B2
Lynmouth Rd A1
Magistrate's Ct B1
Market Pl B2
Mill La B2
Mill Rd A2
Minster St B1
Morgan Rd C3
Mount Pleasant C2
Museum of English Rural Life C3
Napier Rd A2
Newark St C2
Newport Rd A1
Old Reading Univ C3
Oracle Sh Ctr, The B1
Orts Rd B3
Pell St C1
Police Station B1
Post Office B2
Queen Victoria St B1
Queen's Rd A2
Queen's Rd B2
Randolph Rd A1
Reading Bridge A2
Reading Station A1
Redlands Rd C3
Renaissance Hotel B1
Riverside Mus B3
Rose Kiln La C1
Royal Berks Hospital (A&E) C3
St Giles C2
St Laurence B2
St Mary's B1
St Mary's Butts B1
St Saviour's Rd C1
Send Rd A3
Sherman Rd C2
Sidmouth St B2
Silver St C2
South St B2
Southampton St C2
Station Hill A1
Station Rd B1
Superstore A3
Swansea Rd A1
Technical College B3
Valpy St B2
Vastern Rd A1
Vue B2
Waldeck St C2
Watlington St B3
West St B1
Whitby Dr C3
Wolseley St C1
York Rd A1
Zinzan St B1

Salisbury 124

Albany Rd A2
Arts Centre A3
Ashley Rd A1
Avon Approach A2
Ayleswade Rd C2
Bedwin St A2
Belle Vue A2
Bishop's Palace C2
Bishops Walk B2
Blue Boar Row B2
Bourne Ave A3
Bourne Hill A3
Britford La C2
Broad Walk C2
Brown St B2
Bus Station B2
Castle St A2
Catherine St B2
Chapter House B2
Church House B2
Churchfields Rd B1
Churchill Way East B3
Churchill Way North A3
Churchill Way South C2
Churchill Way West A1
City Hall B2
Close Wall B2
Coldharbour La A1
College St A3
Council Offices A3
Court A1
Crane Bridge Rd B2
Crane St B2
Cricket Ground C1
Culver St South B3
De Vaux Pl C2
Devizes Rd A1
Dews Rd B1
Elm Grove B3
Elm Grove Rd A3
Endless St A2
Estcourt Rd A3
Exeter St C2
Fairview Rd A3
Fire Station A1
Fisherton St A1
Folkestone Rd C1
Fowlers Hill B3
Fowlers Rd B3
Friary Estate C3
Friary La B2
Friary, The B3
Gas La A1
Gigant St B3
Greencroft B3
Greencroft St A3
Guildhall B2
Hall of John Halle B2
Hamilton Rd A2
Harnham Mill B1
Harnham Rd C1/C2
High St B2
Hospital A1
House of John A'Port B2
Information Ctr B2

Scarborough • Sheffield • Southampton • Southend-on-Sea • Stoke-on-Trent • Stratford-upon-Avon • Sunderland 135

Kelsey Rd A3
King's Rd A2
Laverstock Rd B3
Library B2
London Rd A3
Lower St C1
Maltings, The B2
Manor Rd A3
Marsh La A1
Medieval Hall B2
Milford Hill B3
Milford St B3
Mill Rd B1
Millstream App A2
Mompesson House (NT) B2
New Bridge Rd C2
New Canal B2
New Harnham Rd C2
New St B2
North Canonry B2
North Gate B2
North Walk B2
Old Blandford Rd C1
Old Deanery B2
Old George Hall B2
Park St A3
Parsonage Green C1
Playhouse Theatre A2
Post Office A2/B2/C2
Poultry Cross B2
Queen Elizabeth Gdns B1
Queen's Rd A3
Rampart Rd B3
St Ann St B2
St Ann's Gate B2
St Marks Rd A3
St Martins B3
St Mary's Cath B2
St Nicholas Hospital C2
St Paul's A1
St Paul's Rd A1
St Thomas B2
Salisbury & South Wiltshire Mus B2
Salisbury General Hospital (A&E) C2
Salisbury Sta A1
Salt La A3
Saxon Rd C1
Scots La A2
Shady Bower B3
South Canonry C2
South Gate C2
Southampton Rd B2
Spire View A1
Sports Ground C3
Tollgate Rd B3
Town Path B1
Wain-a-Long Rd A3
Wardrobe, The B2
Wessex Rd A3
West Walk C2
Wilton Rd A1
Wiltshire College B3
Winchester St B3
Windsor Rd A1
Winston Churchill Gdns C3
Wyndham Rd A2
YHA B3
York Rd A1

Scarborough 124

Aberdeen Walk B2
Albert Rd A2
Albion Rd C2
Alexandra Gardens A1
Auborough St B2
Balmoral Ctr B2
Belle Vue St C1
Belmont Rd C2
Brunswick Shop Ctr B2
Castle Dykes B3
Castle Hill A3
Castle Holms A3
Castle Rd B2
Castle Walls A3
Castlegate B3
Cemetery B1
Central Tramway B2
Clarence Gardens A2
Coach Park B1
Columbus Ravine A1
Court B1
Crescent, The C2
Cricket Ground A1
Cross St B2
Crown Terr C2
Dean Rd B1
Devonshire Dr A1
East Harbour B3
East Pier B3
Eastborough B2
Elmville Ave B1
Esplanade C2
Falconers Rd B2
Falsgrave Rd C1
Fire Station B2
Foreshore Rd B2
Friargate B2
Gladstone Rd B1
Gladstone St B1
Hollywood Plaza A1
Hoxton Rd B1
Information Ctr B2/B3
King St B2
Library B2
Lifeboat Station B3
Londesborough Rd C1
Longwestgate B3
Marine Dr A3
Military Adventure Park A1
Miniature Railway A1
Nelson St B1
Newborough B2
Nicolas St B2
North Marine Rd A1
North St B2
Northway B1
Old Harbour B3
Olympia Leisure B2
Peasholm Park A1
Peasholm Rd A1
Police Station B1
Post Office B2/C1
Princess St B3
Prospect Rd B1
Queen St B2
Queen's Parade A2
Queen's Tower (Remains) A3
Ramshill Rd C2
Roman Signal Station A3
Roscoe St C1
Rotunda Mus C2
Royal Albert Dr A2
St Martin-on-the-Hill C2
St Martin's Ave C2
St Mary's B3
St Thomas St B2
Sandside B3
Scarborough C1
Scarborough Art Gallery and Crescent Art Studios C2
Scarborough Bowls Centre A1
Scarborough Castle A3
Shopmobility C2
Somerset Terr C2
South Cliff Lift C2
Spa Theatre, The C2
Spa, The C2
Stephen Joseph Theatre B1
Tennyson Ave B1
Tollergate B2
Town Hall B2
Trafalgar Rd B1
Trafalgar Square A1
Trafalgar St West B1
Valley Bridge Par C2
Valley Rd C1
Vernon Rd C2
Victoria Pk Mount A1
Victoria Rd B1
West Pier B3
Westborough C1
Westover Rd C1
Westwood C1
Woodall Ave A1
YMCA Theatre B2
York Pl B2
Yorkshire Coast College (Westwood Campus) C1

Sheffield 124

Addy Dr A2
Addy St A2
Adelphi St A3
Albert Terrace Rd A3
Albion St A2
Aldred Rd A1
Allen St A4
Alma St A4
Angel St B5
Arundel Gate B5
Arundel St C4
Ashberry Rd A2
Ashdell Rd C1
Ashgate Rd C1
Athletics Centre B2
Attercliffe Rd A6
Bailey St B4
Ball St A4
Balm Green B4
Bank St B4
Barber Rd A2
Bard St B5
Barker's Pool B4
Bates St A1
Beech Hill Rd C1
Beet St B3
Bellefield St A3
Bernard Rd A6
Bernard St B6
Birkendale A2
Birkendale Rd A2
Birkendale View A1
Bishop St C4
Blackwell Pl B6
Blake St A2
Blonk St A5
Bolsover St B2
Botanical Gdns C1
Bower Rd A1
Bradley St A1
Bramall La C4
Bramwell St A3
Bridge St A4/A5
Brighton Terr Rd A1
Broad La B3
Broad St B6
Brocco St A3
Brook Hill B3
Broomfield Rd C1
Broomgrove Rd C2
Broomhall Pl C3
Broomhall Rd C2
Broomhall St C3
Broomspring La C2
Brown St C5
Brunswick St B3
Burgess St B4
Burlington St A2
Burns Rd A2
Cadman St A6
Cambridge St B4
Campo La B4
Carver St B4
Castle Market B5
Castle Square B5
Castlegate A5
Cathedral B4
Cathedral (RC) B4
Cavendish St B3
Charles St C4
Charter Row C4
Children's Hospital (A&E) B2
Church St B4
City Hall B4
City Hall B4
City Rd C6
Claremont Cr B2
Claremont Pl B2
Clarke St C3
Clarkegrove Rd C2
Clarkehouse Rd C1
Clarkson St B2
Cobden View Rd A1
Collegiate Cr C2
Commercial St B5
Commonside A1
Conduit Rd B1
Cornish St A3
Corporation St A4
Court B4
Cricket Inn Rd B6
Cromwell St A1
Crookes Rd B1
Crookes Valley Pk B2
Crookes Valley Rd B2
Crookesmoor Rd A2
Crown Court A4
Crucible Theatre B5
Cutler's Hall B4
Cutlers Gate A6
Daniel Hill A2
Dental Hospital B2
Dept for Education & Employment C4
Devonshire Green B3
Devonshire St B3
Division St B4
Dorset St C2
Dover St A3
Duchess Rd C5
Duke St B5
Duncombe St A1
Durham Rd B2
Earl St C4
Earl Way C4
Ecclesall Rd C3
Edward St B3
Effingham Rd A6
Effingham St A6
Egerton St C3
Eldon St B3
Elmore Rd B1
Exchange St B5
Eyre St C4
Fargate B4
Farm Rd C5
Fawcett St A3
Filey St B3
Fir St A1
Fire & Police Museum A4
Fire Station C4
Fitzalan Sq/Ponds Forge B5
Fitzwater Rd C6
Fitzwilliam Gate C4
Fitzwilliam St B3
Flat St B5
Foley St A6
Foundry Climbing Centre A4
Fulton Rd A1
Furnace Hill A4
Furnival Rd A5
Furnival Sq C4
Furnival St C4
Garden St B3
Gell St B3
Gibraltar St A4
Glebe Rd B1
Glencoe Rd C6
Glossop Rd B2/B3/C1
Gloucester St C2
Granville Rd C6
Granville Rd/Sheffield Coll C5
Graves Gallery B5
Greave Rd B3
Green La A4
Hadfield St A1
Hanover St C3
Hanover Way C3
Harcourt Rd B1
Harmer La B5
Havelock St C2
Hawley St B4
Haymarket B5
Headford St C3
Heavygate Rd A1
Henry St A3
High St B4
Hodgson St C3
Holberry Gdns C2
Hollis Croft B4
Holly St B4
Hounsfield Rd B3
Howard Rd A1
Hoyle St A3
Hyde Park A6
Infirmary Rd A3
Infirmary Rd A3
Information Ctr B4
Jericho St A3
Johnson St A5
Kelham Island Ind Mus A4
Lawson Rd C1
Leadmill Rd C5
Leadmill St C5
Leadmill, The C5
Leamington St A1
Leavy Rd B3
Lee Croft B4
Leopold St B4
Leveson St A6
Library A2
Library B5
Library C1
Lyceum Theatre B5
Malinda St A3
Maltravers St A5
Manor Oaks Rd B6
Mappin St B3
Marlborough Rd B1
Mary St C4
Matilda St C4
Matlock Rd A1
Meadow St A3
Melbourn Rd A1
Melbourne Ave C1
Millennium Galleries B5
Milton St C3
Mitchell St B3
Mona Ave A1
Mona Rd A1
Montgomery Terrace Rd A3
Montgomery Theatre B4
Monument Gdns C6
Moor Oaks Rd B1
Moor, The C4
Moore St C3
Mowbray St A4
Mushroom La B2
Netherthorpe Rd B3
Netherthorpe Rd B3
Newbould La C1
Nile St C1
Norfolk Park Rd C6
Norfolk Rd C6
Norfolk St B4
North Church St B4
Northfield Rd A1
Northumberland Rd B1
Nursery St A5
O2 Academy B5
Oakholme Rd C1
Octagon B2
Odeon B5
Old St B6
Orchard Square B4
Oxford St A2
Paradise St B4
Park La C2
Park Sq B5
Parker's Rd B1
Pearson Building (Univ) C2
Penistone Rd A3
Pinstone St B4
Pitt St B3
Police Sta A4/B5
Pond Hill B5
Pond St B5
Ponds Forge Int Sports Ctr B5
Portobello St B3
Post Office A1/A2/B3/B4/B5/B6/C1/C3/C4/C6
Powell St A2
Queen St B4
Queen's Rd C5
Ramsey Rd B1
Red Hill B3
Redcar Rd B1
Regent St B3
Rockingham St B4
Roebuck Rd A2
Royal Hallamshire Hospital C2
Russell St A4
Rutland Park C1
St George's Cl B3
St Mary's Gate C3
St Mary's Rd C4/C5
St Peter & St Paul Cathedral B4
St Philip's Rd A3
Savile St A5
School Rd B1
Scotland St A4
Severn Rd B1
Shalesmoor A4
Shalesmoor A3
Sheaf St B5
Sheffield Hallam University B5
Sheffield Ice Sports Centre – Skate Central C5
Sheffield Interchange B5
Sheffield Parkway A6
Sheffield Sta C5
Sheffield Station/Sheffield Hallam University C5
Sheffield Univ B2
Shepherd St A3
Shipton St A2
Shoreham St C4
Showroom, The C5
Shrewsbury Rd C5
Sidney St C4
Site Gallery C5
Slinn St A1
Smithfield A4
Snig Hill A5
Snow La A4
Solly St B3
South La C4
South Street Park B5
Southbourne Rd C1
Spital Hill A5
Spital St A5
Spring Hill B1
Spring Hill Rd B1
Springvale Rd A1
Stafford Rd C6
Stafford St B6
Stanley St A5
Suffolk Rd C5
Summer St B2
Sunny Bank C3
Surrey St B4
Sussex St A6
Sutton St B3
Sydney Rd A2
Sylvester St C4
Talbot St B5
Taptonville Rd B1
Tax Office C4
Tenter St B4
Town Hall B4
Townend St A1
Townhead St B4
Trafalgar St B4
Tree Root Walk B2
Trinity St A4
Trippet La B4
Turner Museum of Glass B3
Union St B4
University Drama Studio B2
University of Sheffield B3
Upper Allen St A3
Upper Hanover St B3
Upperthorpe Rd A2/A3
Verdon St A5
Victoria Quays B5
Victoria Rd C2
Victoria St B3
Waingate B5
Watery St A3
Watson Rd C1
Wellesley Rd B2
Wellington St C3
West Bar A4
West Bar Green A4
West One Plaza B3
West St C3
West St B3
Westbourne Rd C1
Western Bank B2
Western Rd A1
Weston Park B2
Weston Park Hospital B2
Weston Pk Mus B2
Weston St B2
Wharncliffe Rd C3
Whitham Rd B1
Wicker A5
Wilkinson St B2
William St C3
Winter Garden B4
Winter St B2
York St B4
Yorkshire Artspace C5
Young St C4

Southampton 124

Above Bar St A2
Albert Rd North B3
Albert Rd South C3
Anderson's Rd B3
Archaeology Museum (God's House Tower) C2
Argyle Rd A2
Arundel Tower B1
Bargate, The B2
BBC Regional Ctr A1
Bedford Pl A1
Belvidere Rd A3
Bernard St C2
Blechynden Terr A1
Brinton's Rd A2
Britannia Rd A3
Briton St C2
Brunswick Pl A2
Bugle St C1
Canute Rd C3
Castle Way C2
Catchcold Tower B1
Central Bridge C3
Central Rd C2
Channel Way C3
Chapel Rd B3
Cineworld C3
City Art Gallery A1
City College B3
City Cruise Terminal C1
Civic Centre A1
Civic Centre Rd A1
Coach Station B1
Commercial Rd A1
Cumberland Pl A1
Cunard Rd C2
Derby Rd A3
Devonshire Rd A1
Dock Gate 4 C2
Dock Gate 8 B1
East Andrews Park A2
East Park Terr A2
East St B2
Endle St B3
European Way C2
Fire Station A2
Floating Bridge Rd C3
Golden Gr A3
Graham Rd A2
Guildhall A1
Hanover Bldgs B2
Harbour Lights C3
Harbour Pde B1
Hartington Rd A3
Havelock Rd A1
Henstead Rd A1
Herbert Walker Ave B1
High St B2
Hoglands Park B2
Holy Rood (Rems), Merchant Navy Memorial B2
Houndwell Park B2
Houndwell Pl B2
Hythe Ferry C2
Information Ctr A1
Isle of Wight Ferry Terminal C1
James St B3
Java Rd C3
Kingsway A2
Leisure World B1
Library A1
Lime St B2
London Rd A2
Marine Pde B3
Marlands Shop Ctr, The A1
Marsh La B2
Mayflower Memorial C1
Mayflower Park C1
Mayflower Theatre, The A1
Medieval Merchant's House C1
Melbourne St B3
Millais A2
Morris Rd A1
National Oceanography Centre C3
Neptune Way C3
New Rd A2
Nichols Rd A3
North Front A2
Northam Rd A3
Ocean Dock C2
Ocean Village Marina C3
Ocean Way C3
Odeon B1
Ogle Rd B1
Old Northam Rd A2
Orchard La B2
Oxford Ave A2
Oxford St C2
Palmerston Park A2
Palmerston Rd A2
Parsonage Rd A3
Peel St A3
Platform Rd C2
Polygon, The A1
Portland Terr B1
Post Office A2/A3/B2
Pound Tree Rd B2
Quays Swimming & Diving Complex, The B1
Queen's Park C2
Queen's Peace Fountain A2
Queen's Terr C2
Queensway B2
Radcliffe Rd A3
Rochester St A3
Royal Pier C1
Royal South Hants Hospital A2
St Andrew's Rd A2
St Mary St A2
St Mary's B3
St Mary's L Ctr A2
St Mary's Pl B2
St Mary's Rd A2
St Mary's Stadium (Southampton FC) A3
St Michael's C1
Sea City Mus A1
Solent Sky C3
South Front B2
Southampton Central Sta A1
Southampton Solent University A2
SS Shieldhall C2
Terminus Terr C2
Threefield La B2
Titanic Engineers' Memorial A2
Town Quay C1
Town Walls B2
Tudor House C1
Vincent's Walk B2
West Gate Hall C1
West Marlands Rd A1
West Park A1
West Park Rd A1
West Quay Rd B1
West Quay Ret Pk B1
Western Esplanade B1
Westquay Shop Ctr B1
White Star Way C2
Winton St A2

Southend-on-Sea 125

Adventure Island C3
Albany Ave A1
Albert Rd C3
Alexandra Rd C2
Alexandra St C2
Alexandra Yacht Club C2
Ashburnham Rd B2
Ave Rd B1
Avenue Terr B1
Balmoral Rd B1
Baltic Ave B3
Baxter Ave A2/B2
Beecroft Art Gallery B2
Bircham Rd A2
Boscombe Rd B3
Boston Ave A1/B2
Bournemouth Park Rd A3
Browning Ave A3
Bus Station C3
Byron Ave A3
Cambridge Rd C1/C2
Canewdon Rd B1
Carnarvon Rd A2
Central Ave A3
Chelmsford Ave A1
Chichester Rd B2
Church Rd C3
Civic Centre A2
Clarence Rd C2
Clarence St C2
Cliff Ave B1
Cliffs Pavilion C1
Clifftown Parade C2
Clifftown Rd C2
Colchester Rd A1
Coleman St B3
College Way B2
County Court B3
Cromer Rd B3
Crowborough Rd A2
Dryden Ave A3
East St A2
Elmer App B2
Elmer Ave B2
Forum, The B2
Gainsborough Dr A1
Gayton Rd A2
Glenhurst Rd A2
Gordon Pl B2
Gordon Rd B2
Grainger Rd A2
Greyhound Way A3
Grove, The A3
Guildford Rd B3
Hamlet Ct Rd B1
Hamlet Rd C1
Harcourt Ave A1
Hartington Rd C3
Hastings Rd B3
Herbert Gr C3
Heygate Ave C3
High St B2/C2
Information Ctr C3
Kenway A2
Kilworth Ave B3
Lancaster Gdns B3
London Rd B1
Lucy Rd C3
MacDonald Ave A1
Magistrates' Ct A2
Maine Ave C1
Maldon Rd A2
Marine Parade C3
Marine Rd C1
Milton Rd B1
Milton St B2
Napier Ave B2
North Ave A3
North Rd A1/B1
Odeon B2
Osborne Rd B1
Park Cres B1
Park Rd B1
Park St B1
Park Terr B1
Pier Hill C3
Pleasant Rd C3
Police Station A2
Post Office B2/B3
Princes St B2
Queens Rd B2
Queensway B2/B3/C3
Radio Essex C2
Rayleigh Ave A1
Redstock Rd A2
Rochford Ave A1
Royal Mews C2
Royal Terr C2
Royals Sh Ctr, The C3
Ruskin Ave A3
St Ann's Rd B3
St Helen's Rd B1
St John's Rd B1
St Leonard's Rd C3
St Lukes Rd A3
St Vincent's Rd C1
Salisbury Ave A1/B1
Scratton Rd C2
Shakespeare Dr A1
Shopmobility B2
Short St A2
South Ave A3
South Essex Coll B2
Southchurch Rd B3
Southend Central B2
Southend Pier Railway C3
Southend United FC A1
Southend Victoria B2
Stadium Rd A2
Stanfield Rd A2
Stanley Rd C3
Sutton Rd A3/B3
Swanage Rd B3
Sweyne Ave A1
Sycamore Gr A3
Tennyson Ave A3
Tickfield Ave A2
Tudor Rd A1
Tunbridge Rd A2
Tylers Ave B3
Tyrrel Dr B3
Univ of Essex B2/C2
Vale Ave A2
Victoria Ave A2
Victoria Shopping Centre, The B2
Warrior Sq B3
Wesley Rd C3
West Rd A1
West St A1
Westcliff Ave C1
Westcliff Parade C1
Western Esplanade C1
Weston Rd C2
Whitegate Rd B3
Wilson Rd C1
Wimborne Rd B3
York Rd C3

Stoke-on-Trent (Hanley) 125

Acton St A3
Albion St B2
Argyle St C1
Ashbourne Gr A2
Avoca St A3
Baskerville Rd B3
Bedford Rd C1
Bedford St C1
Bethesda St B2
Bexley St A2
Birches Head Rd A3
Botteslow St C3
Boundary St A2
Broad St C2
Broom St A3
Bryan St A2
Bucknall New Rd B3
Bucknall Old Rd B3
Bus Station B3
Cannon St C2
Castlefield St C1
Cavendish St B1
Central Forest Pk A2
Charles St B3
Cheapside B2
Chell St A3
Clarke St C1
Cleveland Rd C2
Clifford St C3
Clough St B2
Clyde St C1
College Rd C2
Cooper St C2
Corbridge Rd A1
Cutts St C2
Davis St C1
Denbigh St A1
Derby St C3
Dilke St A3
Dundas St A3
Dundee Rd C1
Dyke St B3
Eastwood Rd C3
Eaton St A3
Etruria Park B1
Etruria Rd B1
Etruria Vale Rd C1
Festing St A3
Festival Retail Pk A1
Fire Station C2
Foundry St B2
Franklyn St C3
Garnet St B1
Garth St B3
George St A3
Gilman St B3
Glass St B3
Goodson St B3
Greyhound Way A1
Grove Pl C1
Hampton St C3
Hanley Park C2
Hanley Park C2
Harding Rd C2
Hassall St B3
Havelock Pl C1
Hazlehurst St C3
Hinde St C2
Hope St B2
Houghton St C2
Hulton St A3
Information Ctr B3
Jasper St C2
Jervis St A3
John Bright St A3
John St B2
Keelings Rd A3
Kimberley Rd C1
Ladysmith Rd C1
Lawrence St C2
Leek Rd C3
Library C2
Lichfield St C3
Linfield Rd B3
Loftus St A2
Lower Bedford St C1
Lower Bryan St A2
Lower Mayer St A3
Lowther St A1
Magistrates Court C2
Malham St A2
Marsh St B2
Matlock St C3
Mayer St A3
Milton St C1
Mitchell Memorial Theatre B2
Morley St B2
Moston St A3
Mount Pleasant C1
Mulgrave St A1
Mynors St B3
Nelson Pl B3
New Century St B1
Octagon Retail Pk B1
Ogden Rd C3
Old Hall St B3
Old Town Rd A3
Pall Mall B2
Palmerston St C3
Park and Ride C2
Parker St B2
Parkway, The C2
Pavilion Dr A1
Pelham St C3
Percy St B2
Piccadilly B2
Picton St B3
Plough St A3
Police Station C2
Portland St A1
Post Office A3/B3/C3
Potteries Museum & Art Gallery B2
Potteries Sh Ctr B2
Potteries Way C2
Powell St A1
Pretoria Rd C1
Quadrant Rd B2
Ranelagh St C2
Raymond St C2
Rectory Rd C1
Regent Rd C2
Regent Theatre B2
Richmond Terr C2
Ridgehouse Dr A1
Robson St C2
St Ann St B3
St Luke St B3
Sampson St B2
Shaw St A1
Sheaf St C2
Shearer St C1
Shelton New Rd C1
Shirley Rd C2
Slippery La B2
Snow Hill C2
Spur St C3
Stafford St B2
Statham St B2
Stubbs La C3
Sun St C1
Supermarket A1/B2
Talbot St C3
Town Hall B2
Town Rd A3
Trinity St B2
Union St A2
Upper Hillchurch St A3
Upper Huntbach St B3
Victoria Hall Theatre B3
Warner St C2
Warwick St C1
Waterloo Rd A1
Waterloo St B3
Well St B3
Wellesley St C2
Wellington Rd B3
Wellington St B3
Whitehaven Dr A2
Whitmore St C1
Windermere St A1
Woodall St A1
Yates St C2
York St A2

Stratford-upon-Avon 125

Albany Rd B1
Alcester Rd B1
Ambulance Sta B1
Arden St B1
Avenue Farm A1
Ave Farm Ind Est A1
Avenue Rd A3
Avon Ind Est A2
Baker Ave A1
Bandstand C3
Benson Rd A3
Birmingham Rd A2
Boat Club B3
Borden Pl C1
Brass Rubbing Centre C2
Bridge St B2
Bridgetown Rd C3
Bridgeway B3
Broad St C2
Broad Walk C2
Brookvale Rd C1
Bull St C2
Butterfly Farm C3
Cemetery C1
Chapel La B2
Cherry Orchard C1
Chestnut Walk B2
Children's Playground C3
Church St C2
Civic Hall B2
Clarence Rd B1
Clopton Bridge B3
Clopton Rd A2
College B1
College La C2
College St C2
Com Sports Centre B1
Council Offices (District) B2
Courtyard, The C2
Cox's Yard B3
Cricket Ground C3
Ely Gdns B2
Ely St B2
Evesham Rd C1
Fire Station B1
Foot Ferry C3
Fordham Ave A2
Gallery, The B3
Garrick Way C1
Gower Meml B3
Great William St B2
Greenhill St B2
Greenway, The C2
Grove Rd B2
Guild St B2
Guildhall & School B2
Hall's Croft C2
Hartford Rd C1
Harvard House B2
Henley St B2
High St B2
Holton St C2
Holy Trinity C2
Information Ctr B3
Jolyffe Park Rd A2
Kipling Rd C3
Library B2
Lodge Rd B1
Maidenhead Rd A3
Mansell St B2
Masons Court B2
Masons Rd A1
Maybird Sh Pk A2
Maybrook Rd A1
Mayfield Ave A2
Meer St B2
Mill La C2
Moat House Hotel B3
Narrow La C2
Nash's House & New Place B2
New St C2
Old Town C2
Orchard Way C1
Paddock La C1
Park Rd A1
Payton St B2
Percy St A2
Police Station B2
Post Office B2
Recreation Gd C2
Regal Road A2
Rother St B2
Rowley Cr A3
Royal Shakespeare Theatre B3
Ryland St C2
Saffron Meadow C2
St Andrew's Cr B1
St Gregory's A3
St Gregory's Rd A3
St Mary's Rd A2
Sanctus Dr C2
Sanctus St C1
Sandfield Rd C2
Scholars La B2
Seven Meadows Rd C2
Shakespeare Centre B2
Shakespeare Inst C2
Shakespeare St B2
Shakespeare's Birthplace B2
Sheep St B2
Shelley Rd C3
Shipston Rd C3
Shottery Rd C1
Slingates Rd A2
Southern La C2
Station Rd B1
Stratford Healthcare B2
Stratford Hospl B2
Stratford Leisure & Visitor Centre B3
Stratford Sports Club B1
Stratford-upon-Avon Station B1
Swan Theatre B3
Swan's Nest La B3
Talbot Rd A2
Tiddington Rd B3
Timothy's Bridge Industrial Estate A1
Timothy's Bridge Rd A1
Town Hall & Council Offices B2
Town Sq B2
Trinity St C2
Tyler St B2
War Meml Gdns B3
Warwick Rd B3
Waterside B3
Welcombe Rd A3
West St C2
Western Rd A2
Wharf Rd A2
Willows North, The B1
Willows, The B1
Wood St B2

Sunderland 125

Albion Pl C2
Alliance Pl B1
Argyle St C2
Ashwood St C1
Athenaeum St B2
Azalea Terr C2
Beach St A1
Bede Theatre C3
Bedford St B2
Beechwood Terr C1
Belvedere Rd C2
Blandford St B2
Borough Rd B3
Bridge Cr B2
Bridge St B2
Bridges, The B2
Brooke St A2
Brougham St B2
Burdon Rd C2
Burn Park C1
Burn Park Rd C1
Burn Pk Tech Pk C1
Carol St B1
Charles St A3
Chester Rd C1
Chester Terr B1
Church St A3
Civic Centre C2
Cork St B3
Coronation St B3
Cowan Terr C2
Crowtree Rd B2
Dame Dorothy St A2
Deptford Rd B1
Deptford Terr A1
Derby St C2
Derwent St C2
Dock St A3
Dundas St A2
Durham Rd C1
Easington St A2
Egerton St C3
Empire B2
Empire Theatre B2
Farringdon Row B1
Fawcett St B2
Fox St C1
Foyle St B3
Frederick St B3
Gill Rd B2
Hanover Pl A1
Havelock Terr C1
Hay St A2
Headworth Sq B3
Hendon Rd B3
High St East B3
High St West B2/B3
Holmeside B2
Hylton Rd B1
Information Ctr B2
John St B3
Kier Hardie Way A2
Lambton St B3
Laura St C3
Lawrence St B3
Leisure Centre B2
Library & Arts Ctr B3
Lily St B1
Lime St B1

136 Swansea • Swindon • Telford • Torquay • Winchester • Windsor • Worcester • York

Livingstone Rd . . . B2
Low Row . . . B2
Matamba Terr . . . B1
Millburn St . . . B1
Millennium Way . . . A2
Minster . . . B2
Monkwearmouth Sta Mus . . . A2
Mowbray Park . . . C3
Mowbray Rd . . . C3
Murton St . . . C3
National Glass Centre . . . A3
New Durham Rd . . . C1
Newcastle Rd . . . A2
Nile St . . . B3
Norfolk St . . . B3
North Bridge St . . . A2
Northern Gallery for Contemporary Art . . . B3
Otto Terr . . . C1
Park La . . . C2
Park Lane . . . C2
Park Rd . . . C2
Paul's Rd . . . B3
Peel St . . . C3
Place, The . . . B3
Police Station . . . B2
Post Office . . . B2
Priestly Cr . . . A1
Queen St . . . B2
Railway Row . . . B1
Retail Park . . . B1
Richmond St . . . A2
Roker Ave . . . A2
Royalty Theatre . . . C1
Royalty, The . . . C1
Ryhope Rd . . . C2
St Mary's Way . . . B2
St Michael's Way . . . B2
St Peter's . . . A3
St Peter's . . . A2
St Peter's Way . . . A3
St Vincent St . . . C3
Salem Rd . . . C3
Salem St . . . C3
Salisbury St . . . C3
Sans St . . . B3
Silkworth Row . . . B1
Southwick Rd . . . A2
Stadium of Light (Sunderland AFC) . . . A2
Stadium Way . . . A2
Stobart St . . . A2
Stockton Rd . . . C2
Suffolk St . . . C3
Sunderland . . . B2
Sunderland Aquatic Centre . . . A2
Sunderland Museum . . . B3
Sunderland St . . . B3
Sunderland Sta . . . B2
Tatham St . . . C3
Tavistock Pl . . . B3
Thelma St . . . C1
Thomas St North . . . A2
Thornholme Rd . . . C1
Toward Rd . . . C3
Transport Interchange . . . C2
Trimdon St Way . . . B1
Tunstall Rd . . . C2
University . . . C1
University Library . . . C1
Univ of Sunderland (City Campus) . . . B1
Univ of Sunderland (Sir Tom Cowie at St Peter's Campus) . . . A3
Vaux Brewery Way . . . A2
Villiers St . . . B3
Villiers St South . . . B3
Vine Pl . . . C2
Violet St . . . B1
Walton La . . . B3
Waterworks Rd . . . B1
Wearmouth Bridge . . . B2
Wellington La . . . A1
West Sunniside . . . B3
West Wear St . . . B3
Westbourne Rd . . . B1
Western Hill . . . C1
Wharncliffe . . . B1
Whickham St . . . A3
White House Rd . . . C3
Wilson St North . . . A2
Winter Gdns . . . C3
Wreath Quay . . . A1

Swansea 125
Abertawe

Adelaide St . . . C3
Albert Row . . . C3
Alexandra Rd . . . B3
Argyle St . . . C1
Baptist Well Pl . . . A2
Beach St . . . C1
Belle Vue Way . . . B3
Berw Rd . . . A1
Berwick Terr . . . A2
Bond St . . . C1
Brangwyn Concert Hall . . . C1
Bridge St . . . A3
Brookands Terr . . . B1
Brunswick St . . . C1
Bryn-Syfi Terr . . . A2
Bryn-y-Mor Rd . . . C1
Bullins La . . . B1
Burrows Rd . . . C1
Bus Station . . . C2
Bus/Rail link . . . A3
Cadfan Rd . . . A1
Cadrawd Rd . . . A1
Caer St . . . B3
Carig Cr . . . A1
Carlton Terr . . . B2
Carmarthen Rd . . . A3
Castle Square . . . B3
Castle St . . . B3
Catherine St . . . C1
Cinema . . . C3
Civic Ctr & Library . . . C2
Clarence St . . . C2
Colbourne Terr . . . A2
Constitution Hill . . . B1
Court . . . B3
Creidiol Rd . . . A2
Cromwell St . . . B2
Crown Courts . . . C1
Duke St . . . B1
Dunvant Pl . . . C2
Dyfatty Park . . . A3
Dyfatty St . . . A3
Dyfed Ave . . . A1
Dylan Thomas Ctr . . . B3
Dylan Thomas Theatre . . . C3
Eaton Cr . . . C1
Eigen Cr . . . A1
Elfed Rd . . . A1
Emlyn Rd . . . A1
Evans Terr . . . A3
Fairfield Terr . . . B1
Ffynone Dr . . . B1
Ffynone Rd . . . B1
Fire Station . . . B3
Firm St . . . A2
Fleet St . . . C1
Francis St . . . C1
Fullers Row . . . B2
George St . . . B2
Glamorgan St . . . C2
Glynn Vivian Art Gall . . . B3
Gower Coll Swansea . . . C1
Graig Terr . . . A3
Grand Theatre . . . C2
Granogwen Rd . . . A2
Guildhall . . . C1
Guildhall Rd South . . . C1
Gwent Rd . . . A1
Gwynedd Ave . . . A1
Hafod St . . . A3
Hanover St . . . B1
Harcourt St . . . B2
Harries St . . . A2
Heathfield . . . B2
Henrietta St . . . B1
Hewson St . . . B2
High St . . . A3/B3
High View . . . A2
Hill St . . . A2
Historic Ships Berth . . . C3
HM Prison . . . C2
Information Ctr . . . C2
Islwyn Rd . . . A1
King Edward's Rd . . . C1
Kingsway, The . . . B2
LC, The . . . C3
Long Ridge . . . A2
Madoc St . . . C2
Mansel St . . . B2
Maritime Quarter . . . C3
Market . . . B3
Mayhill Gdns . . . B1
Mayhill Rd . . . A1
Milton Terr . . . A2
Mission Gallery . . . C3
Montpellier Terr . . . B1
Morfa Rd . . . A3
Mount Pleasant . . . B2
National Waterfront Museum . . . C3
Nelson St . . . C2
New Cut Rd . . . A3
New St . . . A3
Nicander Pde . . . A2
Nicander Pl . . . A2
Nicholl St . . . B2
Norfolk St . . . B2
North Hill Rd . . . A2
Northampton La . . . B2
Orchard St . . . B3
Oxford St . . . B2
Oystermouth Rd . . . C1
Page St . . . B2
Pant-y-Celyn Rd . . . B1
Parc Tawe Link . . . B3
Parc Tawe North . . . B3
Parc Tawe Shopping & Leisure Centre . . . B3
Patti Pavilion . . . C1
Paxton St . . . C2
Pen-y-Graig Rd . . . A1
Penmaen Terr . . . B1
Phillips Pde . . . C1
Picton Terr . . . B2
Plantasia . . . B3
Police Station . . . B2
Post Office . . . A1/A2/C1/C2
Powys Ave . . . A1
Primrose St . . . B2
Princess Way . . . B3
Promenade . . . B2
Pryder Gdns . . . A1
Quadrant Shop Ctr . . . C2
Quay Park . . . B3
Rhianfa La . . . B1
Rhondda St . . . B2
Richardson St . . . C2
Rodney St . . . C1
Rose Hill . . . B1
Rosehill Terr . . . B1
Russell St . . . B1
St David's Shop Ctr . . . C3
St Helen's Ave . . . C1
St Helen's Cr . . . C1
St Helen's Rd . . . C1
St James Gdns . . . B1
St James's Cr . . . B1
St Mary's . . . B3
Sea View Terr . . . A3
Singleton St . . . C2
South Dock . . . C3
Stanley Pl . . . B2
Strand . . . B3
Swansea Castle . . . B3
Swansea Metropolitan University . . . B2
Swansea Mus . . . C3
Swansea Sta . . . A3
Taliesyn Rd . . . B1
Tan y Marian Rd . . . A1
Tegid Rd . . . A2
Teilo Cr . . . A1
Tenpin Bowling . . . B3
Terrace Rd . . . B1/B2
Tontine St . . . A3
Tower of Ecliptic Observatory . . . C3
Townhill Rd . . . A1
Tramshed, The . . . C3
Trawler Rd . . . C3
Union St . . . B2
Upper Strand . . . A3
Vernon St . . . A3
Victoria Quay . . . C3
Victoria Rd . . . B3
Vincent St . . . C1
Walter Rd . . . B1
Watkin St . . . A2
Waun-Wen Rd . . . A2
Wellington St . . . C2
Westbury St . . . C1
Western St . . . C1
Westway . . . C2
William St . . . C2
Wind St . . . B3
Woodlands Terr . . . B1
YMCA . . . B2
York St . . . C3

Swindon 125

Albert St . . . C3
Albion St . . . C1
Alfred St . . . A2
Alvescot Rd . . . C3
Art Gallery & Museum . . . C3
Ashford Rd . . . C1
Aylesbury St . . . A2
Bath Rd . . . C2
Bathampton St . . . B1
Bathurst Rd . . . B3
Beatrice St . . . A2
Beckhampton St . . . B3
Bowood Rd . . . C1
Bristol St . . . B1
Broad St . . . A3
Brunel Arcade . . . B2
Brunel Plaza . . . B2
Brunswick St . . . C2
Bus Station . . . B2
Cambria Bridge Rd . . . B1
Cambria Place . . . B1
Canal Walk . . . B2
Carfax St . . . B2
Carr St . . . B1
Cemetery . . . C1/C3
Chandler Cl . . . C3
Chapel . . . C1
Chester St . . . B1
Christ Church . . . C3
Church Place . . . B1
Cirencester Way . . . A3
Clarence St . . . B2
Clifton St . . . C1
Cockleberry . . . A2
Colbourne . . . A3
Colbourne St . . . A3
College St . . . B2
Commercial Rd . . . B2
Corporation St . . . A2
Council Offices . . . B3
County Rd . . . A3
Courts . . . B2
Cricket Ground . . . A3
Cricklade Street . . . C3
Crombey St . . . B1/C2
Cross St . . . C2
Curtis St . . . B1
Deacon St . . . C1
Designer Outlet (Great Western) . . . B1
Dixon St . . . C2
Dover St . . . C2
Dowling St . . . C2
Drove Rd . . . C3
Dryden St . . . C1
Durham St . . . C3
East St . . . B1
Eastcott Hill . . . C2
Eastcott Rd . . . C2
Edgeware Rd . . . B2
Edmund St . . . C2
Elmina Rd . . . A3
Emlyn Square . . . B1
Euclid St . . . B3
Exeter St . . . B1
Fairview . . . C1
Faringdon Rd . . . B1
Farnsby St . . . B1
Fire Station . . . B3
Fleet St . . . B2
Fleming Way . . . B2/B3
Florence St . . . A2
Gladstone St . . . A3
Gooch St . . . A2
Graham St . . . A3
Great Western Way . . . A1/A2
Groundwell Rd . . . B3
Hawksworth Way . . . A1
Haydon St . . . A2
Henry St . . . B2
Hillside Ave . . . C1
Holbrook Way . . . B2
Hunt St . . . C3
Hydro . . . B1
Hythe Rd . . . C2
Information Ctr . . . B2
Joseph St . . . C1
Kent Rd . . . C2
King William St . . . C2
Kingshill Rd . . . C1
Lansdown Rd . . . C2
Lawn, The . . . C3
Leicester St . . . B3
Library . . . B2
Lincoln St . . . B3
Little London . . . C3
London St . . . B1
Magic . . . B3
Maidstone Rd . . . C2
Manchester Rd . . . A3
Maxwell St . . . B1
Milford St . . . B2
Milton Rd . . . B1
Morse St . . . C2
National Monuments Record Centre . . . B1
Newcastle St . . . B3
Newcombe Drive . . . A1
Newcombe Trading Estate . . . A1
Newhall St . . . C2
North St . . . C2
North Star . . . A1
North Star Ave . . . A1
Northampton St . . . B3
Nurseries, The . . . C1
Oasis Leisure Ctr . . . A1
Ocotal Way . . . A3
Okus Rd . . . C1
Old Town . . . C3
Oxford St . . . B1
Parade, The . . . B2
Park Lane . . . B1
Park Lane . . . B1
Park, The . . . B1
Pembroke St . . . C2
Plymouth St . . . B3
Polaris House . . . A2
Polaris Way . . . A2
Police Station . . . B2
Ponting St . . . A2
Post Office . . . B1/B2/C1/C3
Poulton St . . . A3
Princes St . . . B2
Prospect Hill . . . C2
Prospect Place . . . C2
Queen St . . . B2
Queen's Park . . . C3
Radnor St . . . C1
Read St . . . C1
Reading St . . . B1
Regent St . . . B2
Retail Park . . . A2/A3/B3
Rosebery St . . . A3
St Mark's . . . B1
Salisbury St . . . A3
Savernake St . . . C2
Shelley St . . . C1
Sheppard St . . . B1
South St . . . C2
Southampton St . . . B3
Spring Gardens . . . B3
Stafford Street . . . C2
Stanier St . . . C2
Station Road . . . A2
STEAM . . . B1
Swindon College . . . A2
Swindon Rd . . . C2
Swindon Sta . . . A2
Swindon Town Football Club . . . A3
T A Centre . . . B1
Tennyson St . . . B1
Theobald St . . . B1
Town Hall . . . B2
Transfer Bridges . . . A3
Union St . . . C2
Upham Rd . . . C3
Victoria Rd . . . C3
Walcot Rd . . . B3
War Memorial . . . B2
Wells St . . . B3
Western St . . . C2
Westmorland Rd . . . B3
Whalebridge . . . B2
Whitehead St . . . C1
Whitehouse Rd . . . A2
William St . . . C1
Wood St . . . C3
Wyvern Theatre & Arts Centre . . . B2
York Rd . . . B3

Telford 126

Alma Ave . . . C1
Amphitheatre . . . C2
Bowling Alley . . . B2
Brandsfarm Way . . . C3
Brunel Rd . . . B1
Bus Station . . . B2
Buxton Rd . . . C1
Central Park . . . A2
Civic Offices . . . B2
Coach Central . . . B2
Coachwell Cl . . . B1
Colliers Way . . . A1
Courts . . . B2
Dale Acre Way . . . B3
Darliston . . . C3
Deepdale . . . B3
Deercote . . . B2
Dinthill . . . C3
Doddington . . . C3
Dodmoor Grange . . . C3
Downemead . . . B3
Duffryn . . . B3
Dunsheath . . . B3
Euston Way . . . A3
Eyton Mound . . . C1
Eyton Rd . . . C1
Forgegate . . . A2
Grange Central . . . B2
Hall Park Way . . . B1
Hinkshay Rd . . . C2
Hollinsworth Rd . . . A2
Holyhead Rd . . . A3
Housing Trust . . . A1
Ice Rink . . . B2
Information Ctr . . . B2
Ironmasters Way . . . A2
Job Centre . . . B1
Land Registry . . . B1
Lawn Central . . . B2
Lawnswood . . . C1
Library . . . B2
Malinsgate . . . B1
Matlock Ave . . . C1
Moor Rd . . . C1
Mount Rd . . . C1
NFU Offices . . . B1
Odeon . . . B2
Park Lane . . . A1
Police Station . . . B1
Priorslee Ave . . . A3
Queen Elizabeth Ave . . . C3
Queen Elizabeth Way . . . B1
Queensway . . . A2/B3
Rampart Way . . . A2
Randlay Ave . . . C3
Randlay Wood . . . C3
Rhodes Ave . . . C1
Royal Way . . . B1
St Leonards Rd . . . B1
St Quentin Gate . . . B2
Shifnal Rd . . . A3
Sixth Ave . . . A1
Southwater One (SW1) . . . B2
Southwater Way . . . B1
Spout Lane . . . C1
Spout Mound . . . B1
Spout Way . . . C1
Stafford Court . . . B3
Stafford Park . . . B3
Stirchley Ave . . . C3
Stone Row . . . C1
Telford Bridge Retail Park . . . A1
Telford Central Station . . . A3
Telford Ctr, The . . . B2
Telford Forge Shopping Park . . . A1
Telford Hornets RFC . . . C2
Telford Int Ctr . . . C2
Telford Way . . . A3
Third Ave . . . A2
Town Park . . . C2
Town Pk Visitor Ctr . . . B2
Walker House . . . B2
Wellswood Ave . . . A2
West Centre Way . . . B1
Withywood Drive . . . C1
Woodhouse Central . . . B2
Yates Way . . . A1

Torquay 126

Abbey Rd . . . B2
Alexandra Rd . . . A2
Alpine Rd . . . B3
Ash Hill Rd . . . A2
Babbacombe Rd . . . B3
Bampfylde Rd . . . B1
Barton Rd . . . A1
Beacon Quay . . . C2
Belgrave Rd . . . A1/B1
Belmont Rd . . . A3
Berea Rd . . . A3
Braddons Hill Rd East . . . B3
Brewery Park . . . A3
Bronshill Rd . . . A2
Castle Circus . . . A2
Castle Rd . . . A2
Cavern Rd . . . A3
Central . . . B2
Chatsworth Rd . . . A2
Chestnut Ave . . . B1
Church St . . . A1
Civic Offices . . . A2
Coach Station . . . A1
Corbyn Head . . . C1
Croft Hill . . . B1
Croft Rd . . . B1
Daddyhole Plain . . . C3
East St . . . A1
Egerton Rd . . . A3
Ellacombe Church Rd . . . A3
Ellacombe Rd . . . A2
Falkland Rd . . . B1
Fleet St . . . B2
Fleet Walk Sh Ctr . . . B2
Grafton Rd . . . B3
Haldon Pier . . . C2
Hatfield Rd . . . A2
Highbury Rd . . . A2
Higher Warberry Rd . . . A3
Hillesdon Rd . . . B3
Hollywood Bowl . . . C3
Hoxton Rd . . . A3
Hunsdon Rd . . . B3
Information Ctr . . . B2
Inner Harbour . . . C3
Kenwyn Rd . . . A3
King's Drive, The . . . B1
Laburnum St . . . A1
Law Courts . . . A2
Library . . . A2
Lime Ave . . . B1
Living Coasts . . . C3
Lower Warberry Rd . . . B3
Lucius St . . . B1
Lymington Rd . . . A1
Magdalene Rd . . . A1
Marina . . . C2
Market Forum, The . . . B2
Market St . . . B2
Meadfoot Lane . . . C3
Meadfoot Rd . . . C3
Melville St . . . B2
Middle Warberry Rd . . . B3
Mill Lane . . . A1
Montpellier Rd . . . B3
Morgan Ave . . . A1
Museum Rd . . . B3
Newton Rd . . . A1
Oakhill Rd . . . A1
Outer Harbour . . . C2
Parkhill Rd . . . C3
Pavilion Sh Ctr . . . C2
Pimlico . . . B2
Police Station . . . A1
Post Office . . . A1/B2
Princes Rd . . . A3
Princes Rd East . . . A3
Princes Rd West . . . A3
Princess Gdns . . . C2
Princess Pier . . . C2
Princess Theatre . . . C2
Rathmore Rd . . . B1
Recreation Grd . . . B1
Riviera Int Ctr . . . B1
Rock End Ave . . . C3
Rock Rd . . . B2
Rock Walk . . . B2
Rosehill Rd . . . A3
St Efride's Rd . . . A1
St John's . . . B3
St Luke's Rd . . . B2
St Luke's Rd North . . . B2
St Luke's Rd South . . . B2
St Marychurch Rd . . . A2
Scarborough Rd . . . B1
Shedden Hill . . . B2
South Pier . . . C2
South St . . . A1
Spanish Barn . . . B1
Stitchill Rd . . . B3
Strand . . . B3
Sutherland Rd . . . B3
Teignmouth Rd . . . A1
Temperance St . . . B2
Terrace, The . . . B3
Thurlow Rd . . . A1
Tor Bay . . . B1
Tor Church Rd . . . A1
Tor Hill Rd . . . A1
Torbay Rd . . . B2
Torquay Mus . . . B3
Torquay . . . C1
Torre Abbey Mansion . . . B1
Torre Abbey Meadows . . . B1
Torre Abbey Sands . . . B1
Torwood Gdns . . . B3
Torwood St . . . C3
Town Hall . . . A2
Union Square . . . A2
Union St . . . A1
Upton Hill . . . A2
Upton Park . . . A1
Upton Rd . . . A1
Vanehill Rd . . . C3
Vansittart Rd . . . A1
Vaughan Parade . . . C2
Victoria Parade . . . C3
Victoria Rd . . . A2
Warberry Rd West . . . B2
Warren Rd . . . B2
Windsor Rd . . . A2/A3
Woodville Rd . . . A3

Winchester 126

Andover Rd . . . A2
Andover Rd Ret Pk . . . A2
Archery La . . . C2
Arthur Rd . . . A2
Bar End Rd . . . C3
Beaufort Rd . . . C2
Beggar's La . . . B3
Bereweeke Ave . . . A1
Bereweeke Rd . . . A1
Boscobel Rd . . . A2
Brassey Rd . . . A2
Broadway . . . B3
Brooks Sh Ctr, The . . . B3
Bus Station . . . B3
Butter Cross . . . B2
Canon St . . . C2
Castle Wall . . . C2/C3
Castle, King Arthur's Round Table . . . B2
Cathedral . . . C2
Cheriton Rd . . . A1
Chesil St . . . C3
Chesil Theatre . . . C3
Christchurch Rd . . . C1
City Mill . . . B3
City Museum . . . B2
City Rd . . . B2
Clifton Rd . . . B1
Clifton Terr . . . B2
Close Wall . . . C2/C3
Coach Park . . . A2
Colebrook St . . . C3
College St . . . C2
College Walk . . . C3
Compton Rd . . . C2
Council Offices . . . C3
County Council Offices . . . B2
Cranworth Rd . . . A2
Cromwell Rd . . . C1
Culver Rd . . . C2
Domum Rd . . . C3
Durngate Pl . . . B3
Eastgate St . . . B3
Edgar Rd . . . C2
Egbert Rd . . . A2
Elm Rd . . . B1
Everyman . . . C2
Fairfield Rd . . . A1
Fire Station . . . B3
Fordington Ave . . . B1
Fordington Rd . . . A1
Friarsgate . . . B3
Gordon Rd . . . B3
Greenhill Rd . . . B1
Guildhall . . . B3
Hatherley Rd . . . A1
High St . . . B2
Hillier Way . . . A3
HM Prison . . . B1
Hyde Abbey (Remains) . . . A2
Hyde Abbey Rd . . . B2
Hyde Cl . . . A2
Hyde St . . . A2
Information Ctr . . . B3
Jane Austen's House . . . C2
Jewry St . . . B2
John Stripe Theatre . . . C1
King Alfred Pl . . . A2
Kingsgate Arch . . . C2
Kingsgate Park . . . C2
Kingsgate Rd . . . C2
Kingsgate St . . . C2
Lankhills Rd . . . A2
Law Courts . . . B2
Library . . . B2
Lower Brook St . . . B3
Magdalen Hill . . . B3
Market La . . . B2
Mews La . . . B1
Middle Brook St . . . B3
Middle Rd . . . B1
Military Museums . . . B2
Milland Rd . . . C3
Milverton Rd . . . B1
Monks Rd . . . A3
North Hill Cl . . . A2
North Walls . . . B2
North Walls Rec Gnd . . . A3
Nuns Rd . . . A3
Oram's Arbour . . . B1
Owen's Rd . . . A2
Parchment St . . . B2
Park & Ride . . . C3
Park Ave . . . B3
Playing Field . . . A1
Police HQ . . . B1
Police Station . . . B3
Portal Rd . . . C3
Post Office . . . B2/C1
Quarry Rd . . . C3
Ranelagh Rd . . . C1
Regiment Mus . . . B2
River Park L Ctr . . . B3
Romans' Rd . . . C2
Romsey Rd . . . B1
Royal Hampshire County Hospital (A&E) . . . B1
St Cross Rd . . . C2
St George's St . . . B2
St Giles Hill . . . C3
St James Villas . . . C2
St James' La . . . B1
St James' Terr . . . B1
St John's . . . B3
St John's St . . . B3
St Michael's Rd . . . C2
St Paul's Hill . . . B1
St Peter St . . . B2
St Swithun St . . . C2
St Thomas St . . . C2
Saxon Rd . . . A2
School of Art . . . B3
Sleepers Hill Rd . . . C1
Southgate St . . . B2
Sparkford Rd . . . C1
Square, The . . . B2
Staple Gdns . . . B2
Station Rd . . . B2
Step Terr . . . B1
Stockbridge Rd . . . A1
Stuart Cres . . . C1
Sussex St . . . B2
Swan Lane . . . B2
Tanner St . . . B3
Theatre Royal . . . B2
Tower St . . . B2
Town Hall . . . C3
Union St . . . B3
Univ of Southampton (Winchester School of Art) . . . B3
University of Winchester (King Alfred Campus) . . . C1
Upper Brook St . . . B2
Wales St . . . B3
Water Lane . . . B3
Weirs, The . . . C3
West End Terr . . . B1
Western Rd . . . B1
Westgate . . . B2
Wharf Hill . . . C3
Winchester Coll . . . C2
Winchester Gallery, The . . . B3
Winchester Sta . . . A2
Winnall Moors Wildlife Reserve . . . A3
Wolvesey Castle . . . C3
Worthy Lane . . . A2
Worthy Rd . . . A2

Windsor 126

Adelaide Sq . . . C3
Albany Rd . . . C2
Albert St . . . B1
Alexandra Gdns . . . B2
Alexandra Rd . . . C2
Alma Rd . . . B2
Ambulance Sta . . . B1
Arthur Rd . . . B2
Bachelors Acre . . . B3
Barry Ave . . . B2
Beaumont Rd . . . C2
Bexley St . . . B1
Boat House . . . B2
Brocas St . . . B2
Brocas, The . . . A2
Brook St . . . C3
Bulkeley Ave . . . C1
Castle Hill . . . B3
Charles St . . . B2
Claremont Rd . . . C2
Clarence Cr . . . B2
Clarence Rd . . . B1
Clewer Court Rd . . . B1
Coach Park . . . B2
College Cr . . . C1
Courts . . . C2
Cricket Ground . . . C3
Dagmar Rd . . . C2
Datchet Rd . . . B3
Devereux Rd . . . C2
Dorset Rd . . . C2
Duke St . . . B1
Elm Rd . . . C1
Eton College . . . A3
Eton Ct . . . A2
Eton Sq . . . A2
Eton Wick Rd . . . A2
Farm Yard . . . B3
Fire Station . . . C2
Frances Rd . . . C2
Frogmore Dr . . . B3
Gloucester Pl . . . C3
Goslar Way . . . C1
Goswell Hill . . . B2
Goswell Rd . . . B2
Green La . . . C1
Grove Rd . . . C2
Guildhall . . . B3
Helena Rd . . . C2
Helston La . . . B1
High St . . . A2/B3
Holy Trinity . . . C2
Home Pk, The . . . A3/C3
Hospl (Private) . . . C2
Household Cavalry . . . C2
Imperial Rd . . . C1
Information Ctr . . . B2/B3
Keats La . . . A2
King Edward Ct . . . B2
King Edward VII Ave . . . A3
King Edward VII Hospital . . . C2
King George V Memorial . . . B3
King Stable St . . . A2
King's Rd . . . C3
Library . . . C2
Long Walk, The . . . C3
Maidenhead Rd . . . B1
Meadow La . . . A2
Municipal Offices . . . C3
Nell Gwynne's House . . . B3
Osborne Rd . . . C2
Oxford Rd . . . B1
Park St . . . B3
Peascod St . . . B2
Police Station . . . C2
Post Office . . . A2
Princess Margaret Hospital . . . C2
Queen Victoria's Walk . . . B3
Queen's Rd . . . C2
River St . . . B2
Romney Island . . . A3
Romney Lock . . . A3
Romney Lock Rd . . . A3
Russell St . . . C2
St John's . . . B3
St John's Chapel . . . A2
St Leonards Rd . . . C2
St Mark's Rd . . . C2
Sheet St . . . C3
South Meadow . . . A2
South Meadow La . . . A2
Springfield Rd . . . C1
Stovell Rd . . . B1
Sunbury Rd . . . A2
Tangier La . . . A2
Tangier St . . . A3
Temple Rd . . . C2
Thames St . . . B3
Theatre Royal . . . B3
Trinity Pl . . . C2
Vansittart Rd . . . B1/C1
Vansittart Rd Gdns . . . C1
Victoria Barracks . . . C2
Victoria St . . . C2
Ward Royal . . . B2
Westmead . . . C1
White Lilies Island . . . A1
William St . . . B2
Windsor & Eton Central . . . B2
Windsor & Eton Riverside . . . A3
Windsor Arts Centre . . . C2
Windsor Bridge . . . B3
Windsor Castle . . . B3
Windsor Great Pk . . . C3
Windsor L Ctr . . . B1
Windsor Relief Rd . . . A1
Windsor Royal Sh . . . B2
York Ave . . . C1
York Rd . . . C1

Worcester 126

Albany Terr . . . A1
Alice Otley School . . . A2
Angel Pl . . . B2
Angel St . . . B2
Ashcroft Rd . . . A2
Athelstan Rd . . . C3
Avenue, The . . . C1
Back Lane North . . . A1
Back Lane South . . . A1
Barbourne Rd . . . A2
Bath Rd . . . C2
Battenhall Rd . . . C3
Bridge St . . . B2
Britannia Sq . . . A1
Broad St . . . B2
Bromwich La . . . C1
Bromwich Rd . . . C1
Bromyard Rd . . . C1
Bus Station . . . B2
Butts, The . . . B2
Carden St . . . B3
Castle St . . . A2
Cathedral . . . C2
Cathedral Plaza . . . B2
Charles St . . . B3
Chequers La . . . B1
Chestnut St . . . A2
Chestnut Walk . . . A2
Citizens' Advice Bureau . . . B2
City Walls Rd . . . B2
Cole Hill . . . C3
Coll of Technology . . . B2
College St . . . C2
Commandery, The . . . C3
Cripplegate Park . . . B1
Croft Rd . . . B1
Cromwell St . . . B3
Cross, The . . . B2
CrownGate Ctr . . . B2
Deansway . . . B2
Diglis Pde . . . C2
Diglis Rd . . . C2
Edgar Tower . . . C2
Farrier St . . . A2
Fire Station . . . B2
Foregate St . . . B2
Foregate Street . . . B2
Fort Royal Hill . . . C3
Fort Royal Park . . . C3
Foundry St . . . B3
Friar St . . . C2
George St . . . B3
Grand Stand Rd . . . B1
Greenhill . . . C3
Greyfriars . . . B2
Guildhall . . . B2
Henwick Rd . . . B1
High St . . . B2
Hill St . . . B3
Hive, The . . . B2
Huntingdon Hall . . . B2
Hylton Rd . . . B1
Information Ctr . . . B2
King Charles Place Shopping Centre . . . C1
King's School . . . C2
King's School Playing Field . . . C2
Kleve Walk . . . C2
Lansdowne Cr . . . A3
Lansdowne Rd . . . A3
Lansdowne Walk . . . A3
Laslett St . . . A3
Leisure Centre . . . A3
Library, Museum & Art Gallery . . . A2
Little Chestnut St . . . A2
Little London . . . A2
London Rd . . . C3
Lowell St . . . A3
Lowesmoor . . . B2
Lowesmoor Terr . . . A3
Lowesmoor Wharf . . . A3
Magistrates Court . . . A2
Midland Rd . . . B3
Mill St . . . C2
Moors Severn Terr . . . A1
New Rd . . . C1
New St . . . B2
Northfield St . . . A2
Odeon . . . B2
Padmore St . . . B3
Park St . . . C3
Pheasant St . . . B3
Pitchcroft Racecourse . . . A1
Police Station . . . A2
Portland St . . . C2
Post Office . . . B2
Quay St . . . B2
Queen St . . . B2
Rainbow Hill . . . A3
Recreation Gd . . . A2
Reindeer Court . . . B2
Rogers Hill . . . A3
Sabrina Rd . . . A1
St Dunstan's Cr . . . C3
St John's . . . C1
St Martin's Gate . . . B3
St Martin's Quarter . . . B3
St Oswald's Rd . . . A2
St Paul's St . . . B3
St Swithin's Church . . . B2
St Wulstans Cr . . . C3
Sansome Walk . . . A2
Severn St . . . C2
Shambles, The . . . B2
Shaw St . . . B2
Shire Hall Crown Court . . . A2
Shrub Hill . . . B3
Shrub Hill Rd . . . B3
Shrub Hill Ret Pk . . . B3
Slingpool Walk . . . C1
South Quay . . . B2
Southfield St . . . A2
Sports Ground . . . A2/C1
Stanley Rd . . . B3
Swan, The . . . A1
Swimming Pool . . . A2
Tallow Hill . . . B3
Tennis Walk . . . A2
Tolladine Rd . . . B3
Tudor House . . . B2
Tybridge St . . . B1
Tything, The . . . A2
Univ of Worcester . . . B2
Vincent Rd . . . B3
Vue . . . C2
Washington St . . . A3
Woolhope Rd . . . C3
Worcester Bridge . . . B2
Worcester County Cricket Ground . . . C1
Worcester Porcelain Museum . . . C2
Worcester Royal Grammar School . . . A2
Wylds La . . . C3

York 126

Aldwark . . . B2
Ambulance Sta . . . B3
Barbican Rd . . . C3
Barley Hall . . . B2
Bishopgate St . . . C2
Bishopthorpe Rd . . . C2
Blossom St . . . C1
Bootham . . . A1
Bootham Cr . . . A1
Bootham Terr . . . A1
Bridge St . . . B2
Brook St . . . A2
Brownlow St . . . A2
Burton Stone La . . . A1
Castle Museum . . . C2
Castlegate . . . B2
Cemetery Rd . . . C3
Cherry St . . . C2
City Screen . . . B2
City Wall . . . A2/B1/C3
Clarence St . . . A2
Clementhorpe . . . C2
Clifford St . . . B2
Clifford's Tower . . . B2
Clifton . . . A1
Coach park . . . A2
Coney St . . . B2
Cromwell Rd . . . C2
Crown Court . . . C2
Davygate . . . B2
Deanery Gdns . . . A2
DIG . . . B2
Ebor Industrial Est . . . B3
Fairfax House . . . B2
Fishergate . . . C3
Foss Islands Rd . . . B3
Foss Islands Ret Pk . . . B3
Fossbank . . . A3
Garden St . . . A2
George St . . . C3
Gillygate . . . A2
Goodramgate . . . B2
Grand Opera Ho . . . B2
Grosvenor Terr . . . A1
Guildhall . . . B2
Hallfield Rd . . . A3
Heslington Rd . . . C3
Heworth Green . . . A3
Holy Trinity . . . B2
Hope St . . . C3
Huntington Rd . . . A3
Information Ctr . . . B2
James St . . . B3
Jorvik Viking Centre . . . B2
Kent St . . . C3
Lawrence St . . . C3
Layerthorpe . . . A3
Leeman Rd . . . B1
Lendal . . . B2
Lendal Bridge . . . B1
Library . . . B1
Longfield Terr . . . A1
Lord Mayor's Walk . . . A2
Lower Eldon St . . . A2
Lowther St . . . A2
Mansion House . . . B2
Margaret St . . . C3
Marygate . . . A1
Melbourne St . . . C3
Merchant Adventurer's Hall . . . B2
Merchant Taylors' Hall . . . B2
Micklegate . . . B1
Micklegate Bar . . . C1
Minster, The . . . A2
Monkgate . . . A2
Moss St . . . C1
Museum Gdns . . . B1
Museum St . . . B1
National Railway Museum . . . B1
Navigation Rd . . . B3
Newton Terr . . . C2
North Pde . . . A1
North St . . . B2
Nunnery La . . . C1
Nunthorpe Rd . . . C1
Ouse Bridge . . . B2
Paragon St . . . C3
Park Gr . . . A3
Park St . . . C1
Parliament St . . . B2
Peasholme Green . . . B3
Penley's Grove St . . . A2
Piccadilly . . . B2
Police Station . . . B2
Post Office . . . B1/B2/C3
Priory St . . . B1
Purey Cust Nuffield Hospital, The . . . A2
Queen Anne's Rd . . . A1
Quilt Museum . . . B3
Reel . . . C1
Regimental Museum . . . B2
Richard III Museum . . . A2
Roman Bath . . . B2
Rowntree Park . . . C2
St Andrewgate . . . B2
St Benedict Rd . . . C1
St John St . . . A2
St Olave's Rd . . . A1
St Peter's Gr . . . A1
St Saviourgate . . . B2
Scarcroft Hill . . . C1
Scarcroft Rd . . . C1
Shambles, The . . . B2
Skeldergate . . . C2
Skeldergate Bridge . . . C2
Station Rd . . . B1
Stonebow, The . . . B2
Stonegate . . . B2
Sycamore Terr . . . A1
Terry Ave . . . C2
Theatre Royal . . . B2
Thorpe St . . . C1
Toft Green . . . B1
Tower St . . . C2
Townend St . . . A2
Treasurer's Ho . . . A2
Trinity La . . . B1
Undercroft Mus . . . A2
Union Terr . . . A2
Victor St . . . C2
Vine St . . . C2
Walmgate . . . B3
Wellington St . . . C3
York Art Gallery . . . A1
York Barbican . . . C3
York Brewery . . . B1
York Dungeon, The . . . B2
York Station . . . B1

Abbreviations used in the index

Aberdeen	Aberdeen City
Aberds	Aberdeenshire
Ald	Alderney
Anglesey	Isle of Anglesey
Angus	Angus
Argyll	Argyll and Bute
Bath	Bath and North East Somerset
Bedford	Bedford
Bl Gwent	Blaenau Gwent
Blackburn	Blackburn with Darwen
Blackpool	Blackpool
Bmouth	Bournemouth
Borders	Scottish Borders
Brack	Bracknell
Bridgend	Bridgend
Brighton	City of Brighton and Hove
Bristol	City and County of Bristol
Bucks	Buckinghamshire
Caerph	Caerphilly
Cambs	Cambridgeshire
Cardiff	Cardiff
Carms	Carmarthenshire
Ceredig	Ceredigion
Ches E	Cheshire East
Ches W	Cheshire West and Chester
Clack	Clackmannanshire
Conwy	Conwy
Corn	Cornwall
Cumb	Cumbria
Darl	Darlington
Denb	Denbighshire
Derby	City of Derby
Derbys	Derbyshire
Devon	Devon
Dorset	Dorset
Dumfries	Dumfries and Galloway
Dundee	Dundee City
Durham	Durham
E Ayrs	East Ayrshire
E Dunb	East Dunbartonshire
E Loth	East Lothian
E Renf	East Renfrewshire
E Sus	East Sussex
E Yorks	East Riding of Yorkshire
Edin	City of Edinburgh
Essex	Essex
Falk	Falkirk
Fife	Fife
Flint	Flintshire
Glasgow	City of Glasgow
Glos	Gloucestershire
Gtr Man	Greater Manchester
Guern	Guernsey
Gwyn	Gwynedd
Halton	Halton
Hants	Hampshire
Hereford	Herefordshire
Herts	Hertfordshire
Highld	Highland
Hrtlpl	Hartlepool
Hull	Hull
IoM	Isle of Man
IoW	Isle of Wight
Invclyd	Inverclyde
Jersey	Jersey
Kent	Kent
Lancs	Lancashire
Leicester	City of Leicester
Leics	Leicestershire
Lincs	Lincolnshire
London	Greater London
Luton	Luton
M Keynes	Milton Keynes
M Tydf	Merthyr Tydfil
Mbro	Middlesbrough
Medway	Medway
Mers	Merseyside
Midloth	Midlothian
Mon	Monmouthshire
Moray	Moray
N Ayrs	North Ayrshire
N Lincs	North Lincolnshire
N Lanark	North Lanarkshire
N Som	North Somerset
N Yorks	North Yorkshire
NE Lincs	North East Lincolnshire
Neath	Neath Port Talbot
Newport	City and County of Newport
Norf	Norfolk
Northants	Northamptonshire
Northumb	Northumberland
Nottingham	City of Nottingham
Notts	Nottinghamshire
Orkney	Orkney
Oxon	Oxfordshire
Pboro	Peterborough
Pembs	Pembrokeshire
Perth	Perth and Kinross
Plym	Plymouth
Poole	Poole
Powys	Powys
Ptsmth	Portsmouth
Reading	Reading
Redcar	Redcar and Cleveland
Renfs	Renfrewshire
Rhondda	Rhondda Cynon Taff
Rutland	Rutland
S Ayrs	South Ayrshire
S Glos	South Gloucestershire
S Lanark	South Lanarkshire
S Yorks	South Yorkshire
Scilly	Scilly
Shetland	Shetland
Shrops	Shropshire
Slough	Slough
Som	Somerset
Soton	Southampton
Staffs	Staffordshire
Stirling	Stirling
Stockton	Stockton-on-Tees
Stoke	Stoke-on-Trent
Suff	Suffolk
Sur	Surrey
Swansea	Swansea
Swindon	Swindon
T&W	Tyne and Wear
Telford	Telford and Wrekin
Thurrock	Thurrock
Torbay	Torbay
Torf	Torfaen
V Glam	The Vale of Glamorgan
W Berks	West Berkshire
W Dunb	West Dunbartonshire
W Isles	Western Isles
W Loth	West Lothian
W Mid	West Midlands
W Sus	West Sussex
W Yorks	West Yorkshire
Warks	Warwickshire
Warr	Warrington
Wilts	Wiltshire
Windsor	Windsor and Maidenhead
Wokingham	Wokingham
Worcs	Worcestershire
Wrex	Wrexham
York	City of York

Index to road maps of Britain

How to use the index

Example: **Thornton-le-Beans** N Yorks **58 G4**
- grid square
- page number
- county or unitary authority

Austrey Warks 35 E8
Austwick N Yorks 50 C3
Authorpe Lincs 47 D8
Authorpe Row Lincs 47 E9
Avebury Wilts 17 E8
Aveley Thurrock 20 C2
Avening Glos 16 B5
Averham Notts 45 G11
Aveton Gifford Devon 5 G7
Avielochan Highld 81 B11
Aviemore Highld 81 B10
Avington Hants 10 A4
Avington W Berks 17 E10
Avoch Highld 87 F10
Avon Hants 9 E10
Avon Dassett Warks 27 D11
Avonbridge Falk 69 C8
Avonmouth Bristol 15 D11
Avonwick Devon 5 F8
Awbridge Hants 10 B2
Awhirk Dumfries 54 D3
Awkley S Glos 16 C2
Awliscombe Devon 7 F10
Awre Glos 26 H4
Awsworth Notts 35 A10
Axbridge Som 15 F10
Axford Hants 18 G3
Axford Wilts 17 D9
Axminster Devon 8 E1
Axmouth Devon 8 E1
Axton Flint 42 D4
Aycliff Kent 21 G10
Aycliffe Durham 58 D3
Aydon Northumb 62 G6
Aylburton Glos 16 A3
Ayle Northumb 57 B9
Aylesbeare Devon 7 G9
Aylesbury Bucks 28 G5
Aylesby NE Lincs 46 B6
Aylesford Kent 20 F4
Aylesham Kent 21 F9
Aylestone Leicester 36 E1
Aylmerton Norf 39 B7
Aylsham Norf 39 C7
Aylton Hereford 26 E3
Aymestrey Hereford 25 B11
Aynho Northants 28 E2
Ayot St Lawrence Herts 29 G8
Ayot St Peter Herts 29 G9
Ayr S Ayrs 66 D6
Aysgarth N Yorks 58 H1
Ayside Cumb 49 A3
Ayston Rutland 36 E4
Aythorpe Roding Essex 30 G2
Ayton Borders 71 D8
Aywick Shetland 96 E7
Azerley N Yorks 51 B8

B

Babbacombe Torbay 5 E10
Babbinswood Shrops 33 B9
Babcary Som 8 B4
Babel Carms 24 E5
Babell Flint 42 E4
Babraham Cambs 30 C2
Babworth Notts 45 D10
Bac W Isles 91 C9
Bachau Anglesey 40 B6
Back of Keppoch Highld 79 C9
Back Rogerton E Ayrs 67 D8
Backaland Orkney 95 E6
Backaskaill Orkney 95 C5
Backbarrow Cumb 49 A3
Backe Carms 23 E7
Backfolds Aberds 89 C10
Backford Ches W 43 E7
Backford Cross Ches W 43 E6
Backhill Aberds 89 E10
Backhill Aberds 89 E7
Backhill of Clackriach Aberds 89 D9
Backhill of Fortree Aberds 89 D9
Backhill of Trustach Aberds 83 D8
Backies Highld 93 J11
Backlass Highld 94 E4
Backwell N Som 15 E10
Backworth T&W 63 F9
Bacon End Essex 30 G3
Baconsthorpe Norf 39 B7
Bacton Hereford 25 E10
Bacton Norf 39 B9
Bacton Suff 31 B7
Bacton Green Suff 31 B7
Bacup Lancs 50 G4
Badachro Highld 85 A12
Badanloch Lodge Highld 93 F10
Badavanich Highld 86 F4
Badbury Swindon 17 C8
Badby Northants 28 C2
Badcall Highld 92 D5
Badcaul Highld 86 B3
Baddeley Green Stoke 44 G3
Baddesley Clinton Warks 27 A9
Baddesley Ensor Warks 35 F8
Baddidarach Highld 92 G3
Baddoch Aberds 82 E3
Baddock Highld 87 F10
Badenscoth Aberds 89 E7
Badenyon Aberds 82 B5
Badger Shrops 34 F3
Badger's Mount Kent 19 E11
Badgeworth Glos 26 G6
Badgworth Som 15 F9
Badicaul Highld 85 F12
Badingham Suff 31 B10
Badlesmere Kent 21 F7
Badlipster Highld 94 F4
Badluarach Highld 86 B2
Badminton S Glos 16 C5
Badnaban Highld 92 G3
Badninish Highld 87 B10
Badrallach Highld 86 B3
Badsey Worcs 27 D7
Badshot Lea Sur 18 G5
Badsworth W Yorks 45 A8
Badwell Ash Suff 30 B6
Bae Colwyn = Colwyn Bay Conwy 41 C10
Bag Enderby Lincs 47 E7
Bagby N Yorks 51 A10
Bagendon Glos 27 H7
Bagh a Chaisteil = Castlebay W Isles 84 J1
Bagh Mor W Isles 84 C3
Bagh Shiarabhagh W Isles 84 H2
Baghasdal W Isles 84 G2
Bagillt Flint 42 E5
Baginton Warks 27 A10
Baglan Neath 14 B3
Bagley Shrops 33 C10
Bagnall Staffs 44 G3
Bagnor W Berks 17 E11
Bagshot Sur 18 E6
Bagshot Wilts 17 E10
Bagthorpe Norf 38 B3
Bagthorpe Notts 45 G8
Bagworth Leics 35 E10
Bagwy Llydiart Hereford 25 F11
Bail àrd Bhuirgh W Isles 91 B9
Bail' Iochdrach W Isles 84 C3
Bail Uachdraich W Isles 84 B3
Bail' Ur Tholastaidh W Isles 91 C10
Baildon W Yorks 51 F7
Baile W Isles 90 J4
Baile a Mhanaich W Isles 84 C2
Baile Ailein W Isles 91 E7
Baile an Truiseil W Isles 91 B8
Baile Boidheach Argyll 72 F6
Baile Glas W Isles 84 C3
Baile Mhartainn W Isles 84 A2
Baile Mhic Phail W Isles 84 A3
Baile Mor Argyll 78 J5
Baile Mor W Isles 84 B2
Baile na Creige W Isles 84 H1
Baile nan Cailleach W Isles 84 C2
Baile Raghaill W Isles 84 A2
Bailebeag Highld 81 B7
Baileyhead Cumb 61 F11
Bailiesward Aberds 88 E4
Baillieston Glasgow 68 D5
Bainbridge N Yorks 57 G11
Bainsford Falk 69 B7
Bainshole Aberds 88 E6
Bainton E Yorks 52 D5
Bainton Pboro 37 E6
Bairnkine Borders 62 B2
Baker Street Thurrock 20 C3
Baker's End Herts 29 G10
Bakewell Derbys 44 F6
Bala = Y Bala Gwyn 32 B5
Balachuirn Highld 85 D10
Balavil Highld 81 C9
Balbeg Highld 81 A6
Balbeg Highld 86 H7
Balbeggie Perth 76 E4
Balbithan Aberds 83 B9
Balbithan Ho. Aberds 83 B10
Balblair Highld 87 B8
Balblair Highld 87 E10
Balby S Yorks 45 B9
Balchladich Highld 92 F3
Balchraggan Highld 87 G8
Balchraggan Highld 87 H8
Balchrick Highld 92 D4
Balchrystie Fife 77 G7
Balcladaich Highld 80 A4
Balcombe W Sus 12 C2
Balcombe Lane W Sus 12 C2
Balcomie Fife 77 F9
Balcurvie Fife 76 G6
Baldersby N Yorks 51 B9
Baldersby St James N Yorks 51 B9
Balderstone Lancs 50 F2
Balderton Ches W 42 F6
Balderton Notts 46 G2
Baldhu Corn 3 E6
Baldinnie Fife 77 F7
Baldock Herts 29 E9
Baldovie Dundee 77 D7
Baldrine IoM 48 D4
Baldslow E Sus 13 E6
Baldwin IoM 48 D3
Baldwinholme Cumb 56 A5
Baldwin's Gate Staffs 34 A3
Bale Norf 38 B6
Balearn Aberds 89 C10
Balemartine Argyll 78 G2
Balephuil Argyll 78 G2
Balerno Edin 69 D10
Balevullin Argyll 78 G2
Balfield Angus 83 G7
Balfour Orkney 95 G5
Balfron Stirling 68 B4
Balfron Station Stirling 68 B4
Balgaveny Aberds 89 D6
Balgavies Angus 77 B8
Balgonar Fife 69 A9
Balgove Aberds 89 E8
Balgowan Highld 81 D8
Balgown Highld 85 B8
Balgrochan E Dunb 68 C5
Balgy Highld 85 C13
Balhaldie Stirling 75 G11
Balhalgardy Aberds 83 A9
Balham London 19 D9
Balhary Perth 76 C5
Baliasta Shetland 96 C8
Baligill Highld 93 C11
Balintore Angus 76 B5
Balintore Highld 87 D11
Balintraid Highld 87 D10
Balk N Yorks 51 A10
Balkeerie Angus 76 C6
Balkemback Angus 76 D6
Balkholme E Yorks 52 G3
Balkissock S Ayrs 54 A4
Ball Shrops 33 C9
Ball Haye Green Staffs 44 G3
Ball Hill Hants 17 E11
Ballabeg IoM 48 E2
Ballacannel IoM 48 D4
Ballachulish Highld 74 B3
Ballajora IoM 48 C4
Ballaleigh IoM 48 D3
Ballamodha IoM 48 E2
Ballantrae S Ayrs 54 A3
Ballaquine IoM 48 D4
Ballards Gore Essex 20 B6
Ballasalla IoM 48 C3
Ballasalla IoM 48 E2
Ballater Aberds 82 D5
Ballaugh IoM 48 C3
Ballaveare IoM 48 E3
Ballcorach Moray 82 A3
Ballechin Perth 76 B2
Balleigh Highld 87 C10
Ballencrieff E Loth 70 C3
Ballentoul Perth 81 G10
Ballidon Derbys 44 G6
Balliemore Argyll 73 E9
Balliemore Argyll 79 J11
Ballikinrain Stirling 68 B4
Ballimeanoch Argyll 73 B9
Ballimore Argyll 73 E8
Ballimore Stirling 75 F8
Ballinaby Argyll 64 B3
Ballindean Perth 76 E5
Ballingdon Suff 30 D5
Ballinger Common Bucks 18 A6
Ballingham Hereford 26 E2
Ballingry Fife 76 H4
Ballinlick Perth 76 C2
Ballinluig Perth 76 B2
Ballintuim Perth 76 B4
Balloch Angus 76 B6
Balloch Highld 87 G10
Balloch N Lanark 68 C6
Balloch W Dunb 68 B2
Ballochan Aberds 83 D7
Ballochford Moray 88 E3
Ballochmorrie S Ayrs 54 A5
Balls Cross W Sus 11 B8
Balls Green Essex 31 F7
Ballygown Argyll 78 G7
Ballygrant Argyll 64 B4
Ballyhaugh Argyll 78 F4
Balmacara Highld 85 F13
Balmacara Square Highld 85 F13
Balmaclellan Dumfries 55 B9
Balmacneil Perth 76 B2
Balmacqueen Highld 85 A9
Balmae Dumfries 55 E9
Balmaha Stirling 68 A3
Balmalcolm Fife 76 G6
Balmeanach Highld 85 D10
Balmedie Aberds 83 B11
Balmer Heath Shrops 33 B10
Balmerino Fife 76 E6
Balmerlawn Hants 10 D2
Balmichael N Ayrs 66 C2
Balmirmer Angus 77 D8
Balmore Highld 85 D7
Balmore Highld 86 H6
Balmore Highld 87 G11
Balmore Perth 76 B2
Balmule Fife 69 B11
Balmullo Fife 77 E7
Balmungie Highld 87 F10
Balnaboth Angus 82 G5
Balnabruaich Highld 87 E10
Balnabruich Highld 94 H3
Balnacoil Highld 93 H11
Balnacra Highld 86 G2
Balnafoich Highld 87 H9
Balnagall Highld 87 C11
Balnaguard Perth 76 B2
Balnahard Argyll 72 D3
Balnahard Argyll 78 H7
Balnain Highld 86 H7
Balnakeil Highld 92 C6
Balnaknock Highld 85 B9
Balnapaling Highld 87 E10
Balne N Yorks 52 H1
Balochroy Argyll 65 C8
Balone Fife 77 F7
Balornock Glasgow 68 D5
Balquharn Perth 76 D3
Balquhidder Stirling 75 E8
Balsall W Mid 35 H8
Balsall Common W Mid 35 H8
Balsall Hth. W Mid 35 G6
Balscott Oxon 27 D10
Balsham Cambs 30 C2
Baltasound Shetland 96 C8
Balterley Staffs 43 G10
Baltersan Dumfries 55 C7
Balthangie Aberds 89 C8
Baltonsborough Som 8 A4
Balvaird Highld 87 F8
Balvicar Argyll 72 B6
Balvraid Highld 85 G13
Balvraid Highld 87 H11
Bamber Bridge Lancs 50 G1
Bambers Green Essex 30 F2
Bamburgh Northumb 71 G10
Bamff Perth 76 B5
Bamford Derbys 44 D6
Bamford Gtr Man 44 A2
Bampton Cumb 57 E7
Bampton Devon 7 D8
Bampton Oxon 17 A10
Bampton Grange Cumb 57 E7
Banavie Highld 80 F3
Banbury Oxon 27 D11
Bancffosfelen Carms 23 E9
Banchory Aberds 83 D8
Banchory-Devenick Aberds 83 C11
Bancycapel Carms 23 E9
Bancyfelin Carms 23 E8
Bancyffordd Carms 23 C9
Bandirran Perth 76 D5
Banff Aberds 89 B6
Bangor Gwyn 41 C7
Bangor-is-y-coed Wrex 43 H6
Banham Norf 39 G6
Bank Hants 10 D1
Bank Newton N Yorks 50 D5
Bank Street Worcs 26 B3
Bankend Dumfries 60 G6
Bankfoot Perth 76 D3
Bankglen E Ayrs 67 E9
Bankhead Aberdeen 83 B10
Bankhead Aberds 83 C8
Banknock Falk 68 C6
Banks Cumb 61 G11
Banks Lancs 49 G3
Bankshill Dumfries 61 E7
Banningham Norf 39 C8
Banniskirk Ho. Highld 94 E3
Bannister Green Essex 30 F3
Bannockburn Stirling 69 A7
Banstead Sur 19 F9
Bantham Devon 5 G7
Banton N Lanark 68 C6
Banwell N Som 15 F9
Banyard's Green Suff 31 A9
Bapchild Kent 20 E6
Bar Hill Cambs 29 B10
Barabhas W Isles 91 C8
Barabhas Iarach W Isles 91 C8
Barabhas Uarach W Isles 91 B8
Barachandroman Argyll 79 J9
Barassie S Ayrs 66 C6
Baravullin Argyll 79 H11
Barbaraville Highld 87 D10
Barber Booth Derbys 44 D5
Barbieston S Ayrs 67 E7
Barbon Cumb 50 A2
Barbridge Ches E 43 G9
Barbrook Devon 6 B6
Barby Northants 28 A2
Barcaldine Argyll 74 C2
Barcheston Warks 27 E9
Barcombe E Sus 12 E3
Barcombe Cross E Sus 12 E3
Barden N Yorks 58 G2
Barden Scale N Yorks 51 D6
Bardennoch Dumfries 67 G8
Bardfield Saling Essex 30 F3
Bardister Shetland 96 F5
Bardney Lincs 46 F5
Bardon Leics 35 D10
Bardon Mill Northumb 62 G3
Bardowie E Dunb 68 C4
Bardrainney Invclyd 68 C2
Bardsea Cumb 49 B3
Bardsey W Yorks 51 E9
Bardwell Suff 30 A6
Bare Lancs 49 C4
Barfad Argyll 73 G7
Barford Norf 39 E7
Barford Warks 27 B9
Barford St John Oxon 27 E11
Barford St Martin Wilts 9 A9
Barford St Michael Oxon 27 E11
Barfrestone Kent 21 F9
Bargod = Bargoed Caerph 15 B7
Bargoed = Bargod Caerph 15 B7
Bargrennan Dumfries 54 B6
Barham Cambs 37 H7
Barham Kent 21 F9
Barham Suff 31 C8
Barharrow Dumfries 55 D9
Barhill Dumfries 55 C11
Barholm Lincs 37 D6
Barkby Leics 36 E2
Barkestone-le-Vale Leics 36 B3
Barkham Wokingham 18 E4
Barking London 19 C11
Barking Suff 31 C7
Barking Tye Suff 31 C7
Barkingside London 19 C11
Barkisland W Yorks 51 H6
Barkston Lincs 36 A5
Barkston N Yorks 51 F10
Barkway Herts 29 E10
Barlaston Staffs 34 B4
Barlavington W Sus 11 C8
Barlborough Derbys 45 E8
Barlby N Yorks 52 F2
Barlestone Leics 35 E10
Barley Herts 29 E10
Barley Lancs 50 E4
Barley Mow T&W 58 A3
Barleythorpe Rutland 36 E4
Barling Essex 20 C6
Barlow Derbys 45 E7
Barlow N Yorks 52 G2
Barlow T&W 63 G7
Barmby Moor E Yorks 52 E3
Barmby on the Marsh E Yorks 52 G2
Barmer Norf 38 B4
Barmoor Castle Northumb 71 G8
Barmoor Lane End Northumb 71 G9
Barmouth = Abermaw Gwyn 32 D2
Barmpton Darl 58 E4
Barmston E Yorks 53 D7
Barnack Pboro 37 E6
Barnacle Warks 35 G9
Barnard Castle Durham 58 E1
Barnard Gate Oxon 27 G11
Barnardiston Suff 30 D4
Barnbarroch Dumfries 55 D11
Barnburgh S Yorks 45 B8
Barnby Suff 39 G10
Barnby Dun S Yorks 45 B10
Barnby in the Willows Notts 46 G2
Barnby Moor Notts 45 D10
Barnes Street Kent 20 G3
Barnet London 19 B9
Barnetby le Wold N Lincs 46 B4
Barney Norf 38 B5
Barnham Suff 38 H4
Barnham W Sus 11 D8
Barnham Broom Norf 39 E6
Barnhead Angus 77 B9
Barnhill Ches W 43 G7
Barnhill Dundee 77 D7
Barnhill Moray 88 C1
Barnhills Dumfries 54 B2
Barningham Durham 58 E1
Barningham Suff 38 H5
Barnoldby le Beck NE Lincs 46 B6
Barnoldswick Lancs 50 E4
Barns Green W Sus 11 B10
Barnsley Glos 27 H7
Barnsley S Yorks 45 B7
Barnstaple Devon 6 C4
Barnston Essex 30 G3
Barnston Mers 42 D5
Barnstone Notts 36 B3
Barnt Green Worcs 27 A7
Barnton Ches W 43 E9
Barnton Edin 69 C10
Barnwell All Saints Northants 36 G6
Barnwell St Andrew Northants 36 G6
Barnwood Glos 26 G5
Barochreal Argyll 79 J11
Barons Cross Hereford 25 C11
Barr S Ayrs 66 G5
Barra Castle Aberds 83 A9
Barrachan Dumfries 54 E6
Barrack Aberds 89 D8
Barraglom W Isles 90 D6
Barrahormid Argyll 72 E6
Barran Argyll 79 J11
Barrapol Argyll 78 G2
Barras Aberds 83 E10
Barras Cumb 57 E10
Barrasford Northumb 62 F5
Barravullin Argyll 73 C7
Barregarrow IoM 48 D3
Barrhead E Renf 68 E3
Barrhill S Ayrs 54 A5
Barrington Cambs 29 D10
Barrington Som 8 C2
Barripper Corn 2 F5
Barrmill N Ayrs 67 A6
Barrock Highld 94 C4
Barrock Ho. Highld 94 D4
Barrow Lancs 50 F3
Barrow Rutland 36 D4
Barrow Suff 30 B4
Barrow Green Kent 20 E6
Barrow Gurney N Som 15 E11
Barrow Haven N Lincs 53 G6
Barrow-in-Furness Cumb 49 C2
Barrow Island Cumb 49 C1
Barrow Nook Lancs 43 B7
Barrow Street Wilts 9 A7
Barrow upon Humber N Lincs 53 G6
Barrow upon Soar Leics 36 D1
Barrow upon Trent Derbys 35 C9
Barroway Drove Norf 38 E1
Barrowburn Northumb 62 B4
Barrowby Lincs 36 B4
Barrowcliff N Yorks 59 H11
Barrowden Rutland 36 E5
Barrowford Lancs 50 F4
Barrows Green Ches E 43 G9
Barrows Green Cumb 57 H7
Barrow's Green Mers 43 D8
Barry Angus 77 D8
Barry = Y Barri V Glam 15 E7
Barry Island V Glam 15 E7
Barsby Leics 36 D2
Barsham Suff 39 G9
Barston W Mid 35 H8
Bartestree Hereford 26 D2
Barthol Chapel Aberds 89 E8
Barthomley Ches E 43 G10
Bartley Hants 10 C2
Bartley Green W Mid 34 G6
Bartlow Cambs 30 D2
Barton Cambs 29 C11
Barton Ches W 43 G7
Barton Glos 27 F8
Barton Lancs 42 B6
Barton Lancs 49 F5
Barton N Yorks 58 F3
Barton Oxon 28 H2
Barton Torbay 5 E10
Barton Warks 27 C8
Barton Bendish Norf 38 E3
Barton Hartshorn Bucks 28 E3
Barton in Fabis Notts 35 B11
Barton in the Beans Leics 35 E9
Barton-le-Clay C Beds 29 E7
Barton-le-Street N Yorks 52 B3
Barton-le-Willows N Yorks 52 C3
Barton Mills Suff 30 A4
Barton on Sea Hants 9 E11
Barton on the Heath Warks 27 E9
Barton St David Som 8 A4
Barton Seagrave Northants 36 H4
Barton Stacey Hants 17 G11
Barton Turf Norf 39 C9
Barton-under-Needwood Staffs 35 D7
Barton-upon-Humber N Lincs 52 G6
Barton Waterside N Lincs 52 G6
Barugh S Yorks 45 B7
Barway Cambs 37 H11
Barwell Leics 35 F10
Barwick Herts 29 G10
Barwick Som 8 C4
Barwick in Elmet W Yorks 51 F9
Baschurch Shrops 33 C10
Bascote Warks 27 B11
Basford Green Staffs 44 G3
Bashall Eaves Lancs 50 E2
Bashley Hants 9 E11
Basildon Essex 20 C4
Basingstoke Hants 18 F3
Baslow Derbys 44 E6
Bason Bridge Som 15 G9
Bassaleg Newport 15 C8
Bassenthwaite Cumb 56 C4
Bassett Soton 10 C3
Bassingbourn Cambs 29 D10
Bassingfield Notts 36 B2
Bassingham Lincs 46 F3
Bassingthorpe Lincs 36 C5
Basta Shetland 96 D7
Baston Lincs 37 D7
Bastwick Norf 39 D10
Baswick Steer E Yorks 53 E6
Batchworth Heath Herts 19 B7
Batcombe Dorset 8 D5
Batcombe Som 16 H3
Bate Heath Ches E 43 E9
Batford Herts 29 G8
Bath Bath 16 E4
Bathampton Bath 16 E4
Bathealton Som 7 D9
Batheaston Bath 16 E4
Bathford Bath 16 E4
Bathgate W Loth 69 D8
Bathley Notts 45 G11
Bathpool Corn 4 D3
Bathpool Som 8 B1
Bathville W Loth 69 D8
Batley W Yorks 51 G8
Batsford Glos 27 E8
Battersby N Yorks 59 F6
Battersea London 19 D9
Battisborough Cross Devon 5 G6
Battisford Suff 31 C7
Battisford Tye Suff 31 C7
Battle E Sus 12 E6
Battle Powys 25 E7
Battledown Glos 26 F6
Battlefield Shrops 33 D11
Battlesbridge Essex 20 B4
Battlesden C Beds 28 F6
Battlesea Green Suff 39 H8
Battleton Som 7 D8
Battram Leics 35 E10
Battramsley Hants 10 E2
Baughton Worcs 26 D5
Baughurst Hants 18 F2
Baulking Oxon 17 B10
Baumber Lincs 46 E6
Baunton Glos 17 A7
Baverstock Wilts 9 A9
Bawburgh Norf 39 E7
Bawdeswell Norf 38 C6
Bawdrip Som 15 H9
Bawdsey Suff 31 D10
Bawtry S Yorks 45 C10
Baxenden Lancs 50 G3
Baxterley Warks 35 F8
Baybridge Hants 10 B4
Baycliff Cumb 49 B2
Baydon Wilts 17 D9
Bayford Herts 29 H10
Bayford Som 8 B6
Bayles Cumb 57 B9
Baylham Suff 31 C8
Baynard's Green Oxon 28 F2
Bayston Hill Shrops 33 E10
Baythorn End Essex 30 D4
Bayton Worcs 26 A3
Beach Highld 79 F10
Beachampton Bucks 28 E4
Beachamwell Norf 38 E3
Beachans Moray 87 G13
Beacharr Argyll 65 D7
Beachborough Kent 21 H8
Beachley Glos 16 B2
Beacon Devon 7 F10
Beacon End Essex 30 F6
Beacon Hill Sur 18 H5
Beacon's Bottom Bucks 18 B4
Beaconsfield Bucks 18 C6
Beacrabhaic W Isles 90 H6
Beadlam N Yorks 52 A2
Beadlow C Beds 29 E8
Beadnell Northumb 71 H11
Beaford Devon 6 E4
Beal N Yorks 51 G11
Beal Northumb 71 F9
Beamhurst Staffs 35 B6
Beaminster Dorset 8 D3
Beamish Durham 58 A3
Beamsley N Yorks 51 D6
Bean Kent 20 D2
Beanacre Wilts 16 E6
Beanley Northumb 62 B6
Beaquoy Orkney 95 F4
Bear Cross Bmouth 9 E9
Beardwood Blackburn 50 G2
Beare Green Sur 19 G8
Bearley Warks 27 B8
Bearnus Argyll 78 G6
Bearpark Durham 58 B3
Bearsbridge Northumb 62 H3
Bearsden E Dunb 68 C4
Bearsted Kent 20 F4
Bearstone Shrops 34 B3
Bearwood Hereford 25 C10
Bearwood Poole 9 E9
Bearwood W Mid 34 G6
Beattock Dumfries 60 C6
Beauchamp Roding Essex 30 G2
Beauchief S Yorks 45 D7
Beaufort Bl Gwent 25 G8
Beaufort Castle Highld 87 G8
Beaulieu Hants 10 D2
Beauly Highld 87 G8
Beaumaris Anglesey 41 C8
Beaumont Cumb 61 H9
Beaumont Essex 31 F8
Beaumont Hill Darl 58 E3
Beausale Warks 27 A9
Beauworth Hants 10 B4
Beaworthy Devon 6 G3
Beazley End Essex 30 F4
Bebington Mers 42 D6
Bebside Northumb 63 E8
Beccles Suff 39 F10
Becconsall Lancs 49 G4
Beck Foot Cumb 57 G8
Beck Hole N Yorks 59 F9
Beck Row Suff 38 H2
Beck Side Cumb 49 A2
Beckbury Shrops 34 E3
Beckenham London 19 E10
Beckermet Cumb 56 F2
Beckfoot Cumb 56 B2
Beckfoot Cumb 56 F3
Beckford Worcs 26 E6
Beckhampton Wilts 17 E7
Beckingham Lincs 46 G2
Beckingham Notts 45 D11
Beckington Som 16 F5
Beckley E Sus 13 D7
Beckley Hants 9 E11
Beckley Oxon 28 G2
Beckton London 19 C11
Beckwithshaw N Yorks 51 D8
Becontree London 19 C11
Bed-y-coedwr Gwyn 32 C3
Bedale N Yorks 58 H3
Bedburn Durham 58 C2
Bedchester Dorset 9 C7
Beddau Rhondda 14 C6
Beddgelert Gwyn 41 F7
Beddingham E Sus 12 F3
Beddington London 19 E10
Bedfield Suff 31 B9
Bedford Bedford 29 C7
Bedham W Sus 11 B9
Bedhampton Hants 10 D6
Bedingfield Suff 31 B8
Bedlam N Yorks 51 C8
Bedlington Northumb 63 E8
Bedlington Station Northumb 63 E8
Bedlinog M Tydf 14 A6
Bedminster Bristol 16 D2
Bedmond Herts 19 A7
Bednall Staffs 34 D5
Bedrule Borders 62 B2
Bedstone Shrops 33 H9
Bedwas Caerph 15 C7
Bedworth Warks 35 G9
Bedworth Heath Warks 35 G9
Beeby Leics 36 E2
Beech Hants 18 H3
Beech Staffs 34 B4
Beech Hill Gtr Man 43 B8
Beech Hill W Berks 18 E3
Beechingstoke Wilts 17 F7
Beedon W Berks 17 D11
Beeford E Yorks 53 D7
Beeley Derbys 44 F6
Beelsby NE Lincs 46 B6
Beenham W Berks 18 E2
Beeny Corn 4 B2
Beer Devon 7 H11
Beer Hackett Dorset 8 C4
Beercrocombe Som 8 B2
Beesands Devon 5 G9
Beesby Lincs 47 D8
Beeson Devon 5 G9
Beeston C Beds 29 D8
Beeston Ches W 43 G8
Beeston Norf 38 D5
Beeston Notts 35 B11
Beeston W Yorks 51 F8
Beeston Regis Norf 39 A7
Beeswing Dumfries 55 C11
Beetham Cumb 49 B4
Beetley Norf 38 D5
Begbroke Oxon 27 G11
Begelly Pembs 22 F6
Beggar's Bush Powys 25 B9
Beguildy Powys 33 H7
Beighton Norf 39 E9
Beighton S Yorks 45 D8
Beighton Hill Derbys 44 G6
Beith N Ayrs 66 A6
Bekesbourne Kent 21 F8
Belaugh Norf 39 D8
Belbroughton Worcs 34 H5
Belchamp Otten Essex 30 D5
Belchamp St Paul Essex 30 D4
Belchamp Walter Essex 30 D5
Belchford Lincs 46 E6
Belford Northumb 71 G10
Belhaven E Loth 70 C5
Belhelvie Aberds 83 B11
Belhinnie Aberds 82 A6
Bell Bar Herts 29 H9
Bell Busk N Yorks 50 D5
Bell End Worcs 34 H5
Bell o' th' Hill Ches W 43 H8
Bellabeg Aberds 82 B5
Bellamore S Ayrs 66 H5
Bellanoch Argyll 72 D6
Bellaty Angus 76 B5
Belleau Lincs 47 E8
Bellehiglash Moray 88 E1
Bellerby N Yorks 58 G2
Bellever Devon 5 D7
Belliehill Angus 77 A8
Bellingdon Bucks 28 H6
Bellingham Northumb 62 E4
Belloch Argyll 65 E7
Bellochantuy Argyll 65 E7
Bells Yew Green E Sus 12 C5
Bellsbank E Ayrs 67 F7
Bellshill N Lanark 68 D6
Bellshill Northumb 71 G10
Bellspool Borders 69 G10
Bellsquarry W Loth 69 D9
Belmaduthy Highld 87 F9
Belmesthorpe Rutland 36 D6
Belmont Blackburn 50 H2
Belmont London 19 E9
Belmont S Ayrs 66 D6
Belmont Shetland 96 C7
Belnacraig Aberds 82 B5
Belowda Corn 3 C8
Belper Derbys 45 H7
Belper Lane End Derbys 45 H7
Belsay Northumb 63 F7
Belses Borders 70 H4
Belsford Devon 5 F8
Belstead Suff 31 D8
Belston S Ayrs 67 D6
Belstone Devon 6 G5
Belthorn Blackburn 50 G3
Beltinge Kent 21 E8
Beltoft N Lincs 46 B2
Belton Leics 35 C10
Belton Lincs 36 B5
Belton N Lincs 45 B11
Belton Norf 39 E10
Belton in Rutland Rutland 36 E4
Beltring Kent 20 G3
Belts of Collonach Aberds 83 D8
Belvedere London 19 D11
Belvoir Leics 36 B4
Bembridge IoW 10 F5
Bemersyde Borders 70 G4
Bemerton Wilts 9 A10
Bempton E Yorks 53 B7
Ben Alder Lodge Highld 81 F7
Ben Armine Lodge Highld 93 H10
Ben Casgro W Isles 91 E9
Benacre Suff 39 G11
Benbuie Dumfries 60 D3
Benderloch Argyll 74 D2
Bendronaig Lodge Highld 86 H3
Benenden Kent 13 C7
Benfield Dumfries 54 C6
Bengate Norf 39 C9
Bengeworth Worcs 27 D7
Benhall Green Suff 31 B10
Benhall Street Suff 31 B10
Benholm Aberds 83 G10
Beningbrough N Yorks 51 D11
Benington Herts 29 F9
Benington Lincs 47 H7
Benllech Anglesey 41 B7
Benmore Argyll 73 E10
Benmore Stirling 75 E7
Benmore Lodge Highld 92 H6
Bennacott Corn 6 G1
Bennan N Ayrs 66 D2
Benniworth Lincs 46 D6
Benover Kent 20 G4
Bensham T&W 63 G8
Benslie N Ayrs 66 B6
Benson Oxon 18 B3
Bent Aberds 83 F8
Bent Gate Lancs 50 G3
Benthall Northumb 71 H11
Benthall Shrops 34 E2
Bentham Glos 26 G6
Benthoul Aberdeen 83 C10
Bentlawnt Shrops 33 E9
Bentley E Yorks 52 F6
Bentley Hants 18 G4
Bentley S Yorks 45 B9
Bentley Suff 31 E8
Bentley Warks 35 F8
Bentley Worcs 26 B6
Bentley Heath W Mid 35 H7
Benton Devon 6 C5
Bentpath Dumfries 61 D9
Bents W Loth 69 D8
Bentworth Hants 18 G3
Benvie Dundee 76 D6
Benwick Cambs 37 F9
Beoley Worcs 27 B7
Beoraidbeg Highld 79 B9
Bepton W Sus 11 C7
Berden Essex 29 F11
Bere Alston Devon 4 E5
Bere Ferrers Devon 4 E5
Bere Regis Dorset 9 E7
Berepper Corn 2 G5
Bergh Apton Norf 39 E9
Berinsfield Oxon 18 B2
Berkeley Glos 16 B3
Berkhamsted Herts 28 H6
Berkley Som 16 G5
Berkswell W Mid 35 H8
Bermondsey London 19 D10
Bernera Highld 85 F13
Bernice Argyll 73 D10
Bernisdale Highld 85 C9
Berrick Salome Oxon 18 B3
Berriedale Highld 94 H3
Berrier Cumb 56 D5
Berriew Powys 33 E7
Berrington Northumb 71 F9
Berrington Shrops 33 E11
Berrow Som 15 F9
Berrow Green Worcs 26 C4
Berry Down Cross Devon 6 B4
Berry Hill Glos 26 G2
Berry Hill Pembs 22 B5
Berry Pomeroy Devon 5 E9
Berryhillock Moray 88 B5
Berrynarbor Devon 6 B4
Bersham Wrex 42 H6
Berstane Orkney 95 G5
Berwick E Sus 12 F4
Berwick Bassett Wilts 17 D7
Berwick Hill Northumb 63 F7
Berwick St James Wilts 17 H7
Berwick St John Wilts 9 B8
Berwick St Leonard Wilts 9 A8
Berwick-upon-Tweed Northumb 71 E8
Bescar Lancs 43 A6
Besford Worcs 26 D6
Bessacarr S Yorks 45 B10
Bessels Leigh Oxon 17 A11
Bessingby E Yorks 53 C7
Bessingham Norf 39 B7
Bestbeech Hill E Sus 12 C5
Besthorpe Norf 39 F6
Besthorpe Notts 46 F2
Bestwood Nottingham 36 A1
Bestwood Village Notts 45 H9
Beswick E Yorks 52 E6
Betchworth Sur 19 G9
Bethania Ceredig 24 B2
Bethania Gwyn 41 E8
Bethania Gwyn 41 F9
Bethel Anglesey 40 C5
Bethel Gwyn 32 B5
Bethel Gwyn 41 D7
Bethersden Kent 13 B8
Bethesda Gwyn 41 D8
Bethesda Pembs 22 E5
Bethlehem Carms 24 F3
Bethnal Green London 19 C10
Betley Staffs 43 H10
Betsham Kent 20 D3
Betteshanger Kent 21 F10
Bettiscombe Dorset 8 E2
Bettisfield Wrex 33 B10
Betton Shrops 33 E9
Betton Shrops 34 B2
Bettws Bridgend 14 C5
Bettws Mon 25 G9
Bettws Newport 15 B8
Bettws Cedewain Powys 33 F7
Bettws Gwerfil Goch Denb 42 H3
Bettws Ifan Ceredig 23 B8
Bettws Newydd Mon 25 H10
Bettws-y-crwyn Shrops 33 G8
Bettyhill Highld 93 C10
Betws Carms 24 G3
Betws Bledrws Ceredig 23 A10
Betws-Garmon Gwyn 41 E7
Betws-y-Coed Conwy 41 E9
Betws-yn-Rhos Conwy 42 E2
Beulah Ceredig 23 B7
Beulah Powys 24 C6
Bevendean Brighton 12 F2
Bevercotes Notts 45 E10
Beverley E Yorks 52 F6
Beverston Glos 16 B5
Bevington Glos 16 B3
Bewaldeth Cumb 56 C4
Bewcastle Cumb 61 F11
Bewdley Worcs 34 H3
Bewerley N Yorks 51 C7
Bewholme E Yorks 53 D7
Bexhill E Sus 12 F6
Bexley London 19 D11
Bexleyheath London 19 D11
Bexwell Norf 38 E2
Beyton Suff 30 B6
Bhaltos W Isles 90 D5
Bhatarsaigh W Isles 84 J1
Bibury Glos 27 H8
Bicester Oxon 28 F2
Bickenhall Som 8 C1
Bickenhill W Mid 35 G7
Bicker Lincs 37 B8
Bickershaw Gtr Man 43 B9
Bickerstaffe Lancs 43 B7
Bickerton Ches E 43 G8
Bickerton N Yorks 51 D10
Bickington Devon 5 D8
Bickington Devon 6 C4
Bickleigh Devon 4 E6
Bickleigh Devon 7 F8
Bickleton Devon 6 C4
Bickley London 19 E11
Bickley Moss Ches W 43 H8
Bicknacre Essex 20 A4
Bicknoller Som 7 C10
Bicknor Kent 20 F5
Bickton Hants 9 C10
Bicton Shrops 33 D10
Bicton Shrops 33 G8
Bidborough Kent 12 B4
Biddenden Kent 13 C7
Biddenham Bedford 29 D7
Biddestone Wilts 16 D5
Biddisham Som 15 F9
Biddlesden Bucks 28 D3
Biddlestone Northumb 62 C5
Biddulph Staffs 44 G2
Biddulph Moor Staffs 44 G3
Bideford Devon 6 D3
Bidford-on-Avon Warks 27 C8
Bidston Mers 42 C5
Bielby E Yorks 52 E3
Bieldside Aberdeen 83 C10
Bierley IoW 10 G4
Bierley W Yorks 51 F7
Bierton Bucks 28 G5
Big Sand Highld 85 A12
Bigbury Devon 5 G7
Bigbury on Sea Devon 5 G7
Bigby Lincs 46 B4
Biggar Cumb 49 C1
Biggar S Lanark 69 G9
Biggin Derbys 44 G5
Biggin Derbys 44 H6
Biggin N Yorks 51 F11
Biggin Hill London 19 F11
Biggings Shetland 96 G3
Biggleswade C Beds 29 D8
Bighouse Highld 93 C11
Bighton Hants 10 A5
Bignor W Sus 11 C8
Bigton Shetland 96 L5
Bilberry Corn 3 C9
Bilborough Nottingham 35 A11
Bilbrook Som 7 B9
Bilbrough N Yorks 51 E11
Bilbster Highld 94 E4
Bildershaw Durham 58 D3
Bildeston Suff 30 D6
Billericay Essex 20 B3
Billesdon Leics 36 E3
Billesley Warks 27 C8
Billingborough Lincs 37 B7
Billinge Mers 43 B8
Billingford Norf 38 C6
Billingham Stockton 58 D5
Billinghay Lincs 46 G5
Billingley S Yorks 45 B8
Billingshurst W Sus 11 B9
Billingsley Shrops 34 G3
Billington C Beds 28 F6
Billington Lancs 50 F3
Billockby Norf 39 D10
Billy Row Durham 58 C2
Bilsborrow Lancs 49 F5
Bilsby Lincs 47 E8
Bilsham W Sus 11 D8
Bilsington Kent 13 C9
Bilson Green Glos 26 G3
Bilsthorpe Notts 45 F10
Bilsthorpe Moor Notts 45 G10
Bilston Midloth 69 D11
Bilston W Mid 34 F5
Bilstone Leics 35 E9
Bilting Kent 21 G7
Bilton E Yorks 53 F7
Bilton Northumb 63 B8
Bilton Warks 27 A11
Bilton in Ainsty N Yorks 51 E10
Bimbister Orkney 95 G4
Binbrook Lincs 46 C6
Binchester Blocks Durham 58 C3
Bincombe Dorset 8 F5
Bindal Highld 87 C12
Binegar Som 16 G3
Binfield Brack 18 D5
Binfield Hth. Oxon 18 D4
Bingfield Northumb 62 F5
Bingham Notts 36 B3
Bingley W Yorks 51 F7
Bings Heath Shrops 33 D11
Binham Norf 38 B5
Binley Hants 17 F11
Binley W Mid 35 H9
Binley Woods Warks 35 H9
Binniehill Falk 69 C7
Binsoe N Yorks 51 B8
Binstead IoW 10 E4
Binsted Hants 18 G4
Binton Warks 27 C8
Bintree Norf 38 C6
Binweston Shrops 33 E9
Birch Essex 30 G6
Birch Gtr Man 44 B2
Birch Green Essex 30 G6
Birch Heath Ches W 43 F8
Birch Hill Ches W 43 E8
Birch Vale Derbys 44 D4
Bircham Newton Norf 38 B3
Bircham Tofts Norf 38 B3
Birchanger Essex 30 F2
Birchencliffe W Yorks 51 H7
Bircher Hereford 25 B11
Birchgrove Cardiff 15 D7
Birchgrove Swansea 14 B3
Birchington Kent 21 E9
Birchmoor Warks 35 E8
Birchover Derbys 44 F6
Birchwood Lincs 46 F3
Birchwood Warr 43 C9
Bircotes Notts 45 C10
Birdbrook Essex 30 D4
Birdforth N Yorks 51 B10
Birdham W Sus 11 E7
Birdholme Derbys 45 F7
Birdingbury Warks 27 B11
Birdlip Glos 26 G6
Birds Edge W Yorks 44 B6
Birdsall N Yorks 52 C4
Birdsgreen Shrops 34 G3
Birdsmoor Gate Dorset 8 D2
Birdston E Dunb 68 C5
Birdwell S Yorks 45 B7
Birdwood Glos 26 G4
Birgham Borders 70 G6
Birkby N Yorks 58 F4
Birkdale Mers 49 H3
Birkenhead Mers 42 D6
Birkenhills Aberds 89 D7
Birkenshaw N Lanark 68 D5
Birkenshaw W Yorks 51 G8
Birkhall Aberds 82 D5
Birkhill Angus 76 D6
Birkhill Borders 61 B8
Birkholme Lincs 36 C5
Birkin N Yorks 51 G11
Birley Hereford 25 C11
Birling Kent 20 E3
Birling Northumb 63 C8
Birling Gap E Sus 12 G4
Birlingham Worcs 26 D6
Birmingham W Mid 35 G6
Birnam Perth 76 C3
Birse Aberds 83 D7
Birsemore Aberds 83 D7
Birstall Leics 36 E1
Birstall W Yorks 51 G8
Birstwith N Yorks 51 D8
Birthorpe Lincs 37 B7
Birtley Hereford 25 B10
Birtley Northumb 62 F4
Birtley T&W 63 H8
Birts Street Worcs 26 E4
Bisbrooke Rutland 36 F4
Biscathorpe Lincs 46 D6
Biscot Luton 29 F7
Bish Mill Devon 7 D6
Bisham Windsor 18 C5
Bishampton Worcs 26 C6
Bishop Auckland Durham 58 D3
Bishop Burton E Yorks 52 F5
Bishop Middleham Durham 58 C4
Bishop Monkton N Yorks 51 C9
Bishop Norton Lincs 46 C3
Bishop Sutton Bath 16 F2
Bishop Thornton N Yorks 51 C8
Bishop Wilton E Yorks 52 D3
Bishopbridge Lincs 46 C4
Bishopbriggs E Dunb 68 D5
Bishopmill Moray 88 B2
Bishops Cannings Wilts 17 E7
Bishop's Castle Shrops 33 G9
Bishop's Caundle Dorset 8 C5
Bishop's Cleeve Glos 26 F6
Bishops Frome Hereford 26 D3
Bishop's Green Essex 30 G3
Bishop's Hull Som 7 D11
Bishop's Itchington Warks 27 C10
Bishops Lydeard Som 7 D10
Bishops Nympton Devon 7 D6
Bishop's Offley Staffs 34 C3
Bishop'S Stortford Herts 29 F11
Bishop's Sutton Hants 10 A5
Bishop's Tachbrook Warks 27 B10
Bishops Tawton Devon 6 C4
Bishop's Waltham Hants 10 C4
Bishop's Wood Staffs 34 E4
Bishopsbourne Kent 21 F8
Bishopsteignton Devon 5 D10
Bishopstoke Hants 10 C3
Bishopston Swansea 23 H10
Bishopstone Bucks 28 G5
Bishopstone E Sus 12 F3
Bishopstone Hereford 25 D11
Bishopstone Swindon 17 C9
Bishopstone Wilts 9 B9
Bishopstrow Wilts 16 G5
Bishopswood Som 8 C1
Bishopsworth Bristol 16 E2
Bishopthorpe York 52 E1
Bishopton Darl 58 D4
Bishopton Dumfries 55 E7
Bishopton N Yorks 51 B9
Bishopton Renfs 68 C3
Bishopton Warks 27 C8
Bishton Newport 15 C9
Bisley Glos 26 H6
Bisley Sur 18 F6
Bispham Blackpool 49 E3
Bispham Green Lancs 43 A7
Bissoe Corn 3 E6
Bisterne Close Hants 9 D11
Bitchfield Lincs 36 C5
Bittadon Devon 6 B4
Bittaford Devon 5 F7
Bittering Norf 38 D5
Bitterley Shrops 34 H1
Bitterne Soton 10 C3
Bitteswell Leics 35 G11
Bitton S Glos 16 E3
Bix Oxon 18 C4
Bixter Shetland 96 H5
Blaby Leics 36 F1
Black Bourton Oxon 17 A9
Black Callerton T&W 63 G7
Black Clauchrie S Ayrs 54 A5
Black Corries Lodge Highld 74 B5
Black Crofts Argyll 74 D2
Black Dog Devon 7 F7
Black Heddon Northumb 62 F6
Black Lane Gtr Man 43 B10
Black Marsh Shrops 33 F9
Black Mount Argyll 74 C5
Black Notley Essex 30 F4
Black Pill Swansea 14 B2
Black Tar Pembs 22 F4
Black Torrington Devon 6 F3
Blackacre Dumfries 60 D6
Blackadder West Borders 71 E7
Blackawton Devon 5 F9
Blackborough Devon 7 F9
Blackborough End Norf 38 D2
Blackboys E Sus 12 D4
Blackbrook Derbys 45 H7
Blackbrook Mers 43 C8
Blackbrook Staffs 34 B3
Blackburn Aberds 83 B10
Blackburn Aberds 88 E5
Blackburn Blackburn 50 G2
Blackburn W Loth 69 D8
Blackcraig Dumfries 60 E3
Blackden Heath Ches E 43 E10
Blackdog Aberds 83 B11
Blackfell T&W 63 H8
Blackfield Hants 10 D3
Blackford Cumb 61 G9
Blackford Perth 75 G11
Blackford Som 8 B5
Blackford Som 15 G10
Blackfordby Leics 35 D9
Blackgang IoW 10 G3
Blackhall Colliery Durham 58 C5
Blackhall Mill T&W 63 H7
Blackhall Rocks Durham 58 C5
Blackham E Sus 12 C3
Blackhaugh Borders 70 G3
Blackheath Essex 31 F7
Blackheath Suff 31 A11
Blackheath Sur 19 G7
Blackheath W Mid 34 G5
Blackhill Aberds 89 C10
Blackhill Aberds 89 D10
Blackhill Highld 85 C8
Blackhills Highld 87 F12
Blackhills Moray 88 C2
Blackhorse S Glos 16 D3
Blackland Wilts 17 E7
Blacklaw Aberds 89 C6
Blackley Gtr Man 44 B2
Blacklunans Perth 76 A4
Blackmill Bridgend 14 C5
Blackmoor Hants 11 A6
Blackmoor Gate Devon 6 B5
Blackmore Essex 20 A3
Blackmore End Essex 30 E4
Blackmore End Herts 29 G8
Blackness Falk 69 C9
Blacknest Hants 18 G4
Blacko Lancs 50 E4
Blackpool Blackpool 49 F3
Blackpool Devon 5 G9
Blackpool Pembs 22 E5
Blackpool Gate Cumb 61 F11
Blackridge W Loth 69 D7
Blackrock Argyll 64 B4
Blackrock Mon 25 G9
Blackrod Gtr Man 43 A9
Blackshaw Dumfries 60 G6
Blackshaw Head W Yorks 50 G5
Blacksmith's Green Suff 31 B8
Blackstone W Sus 11 C11
Blackthorn Oxon 28 G3
Blackthorpe Suff 30 B6
Blacktoft E Yorks 52 G4
Blacktop Aberdeen 83 C10
Blacktown Newport 15 C8
Blackwall Tunnel London 19 C10
Blackwater Corn 2 E6
Blackwater Hants 18 F5
Blackwater IoW 10 F4
Blackwaterfoot N Ayrs 66 D1
Blackwell Darl 58 E3
Blackwell Derbys 44 E5
Blackwell Derbys 45 G8
Blackwell W Sus 12 C2
Blackwell Warks 27 D9
Blackwell Worcs 26 A6
Blackwood = Coed Duon Caerph 15 B7
Blackwood S Lanark 68 F6
Blackwood Hill Staffs 44 G3
Blacon Ches W 43 F6
Bladnoch Dumfries 55 D7
Bladon Oxon 27 G11
Blaen-gwynfi Neath 14 B4
Blaen-waun Carms 23 D7
Blaen-y-coed Carms 23 D8
Blaen-y-Cwm Denb 32 B6
Blaen-y-cwm Gwyn 32 C3
Blaen-y-cwm Powys 33 C6
Blaenannerch Ceredig 23 B7
Blaenau Ffestiniog Gwyn 41 F9
Blaenavon Torf 25 H9
Blaencelyn Ceredig 23 A8
Blaendyryn Powys 24 E6
Blaenffos Pembs 22 C6
Blaengarw Bridgend 14 B5
Blaengwrach Neath 24 H5
Blaenpennal Ceredig 24 B3
Blaenplwyf Ceredig 32 H1
Blaenporth Ceredig 23 B7
Blaenrhondda Rhondda 14 A5
Blaenycwm Ceredig 32 H4
Blagdon N Som 15 F11
Blagdon Torbay 5 E9
Blagdon Hill Som 7 E11
Blagill Cumb 57 B9
Blaguegate Lancs 43 B7
Blaich Highld 80 F2
Blain Highld 79 E9
Blaina Bl Gwent 25 H9
Blair Atholl Perth 81 G10
Blair Drummond Stirling 75 H10
Blairbeg N Ayrs 66 C3
Blairdaff Aberds 83 B8
Blairglas Argyll 68 B2
Blairgowrie Perth 76 C4
Blairhall Fife 69 B9
Blairingone Perth 76 H2
Blairland N Ayrs 66 B6
Blairlogie Stirling 75 H11
Blairlomond Argyll 74 H4
Blairmore Argyll 73 E10
Blairnamarrow Moray 82 B4
Blairquhosh Stirling 68 B4
Blair's Ferry Argyll 73 G8
Blairskaith E Dunb 68 C4
Blaisdon Glos 26 G4
Blakebrook Worcs 34 H4
Blakedown Worcs 34 H4
Blakelaw Borders 70 G6
Blakeley Staffs 34 F4
Blakeley Lane Staffs 44 H3
Blakemere Hereford 25 D10
Blakeney Glos 26 H3
Blakeney Norf 38 A6
Blakenhall Ches E 43 H10
Blakenhall W Mid 34 F5
Blakeshall Worcs 34 G4
Blakesley Northants 28 C3
Blanchland Northumb 57 A11
Bland Hill N Yorks 51 D8
Blandford Forum Dorset 9 D7
Blandford St Mary Dorset 9 D7
Blanefield Stirling 68 C4
Blankney Lincs 46 F4
Blantyre S Lanark 68 E5
Blar a'Chaorainn Highld 80 G3
Blaran Argyll 73 B7
Blarghour Argyll 73 B8
Blarmachfoldach Highld 80 G2
Blarnalearoch Highld 86 B4
Blashford Hants 9 D10
Blaston Leics 36 F4
Blatherwycke Northants 36 F5
Blawith Cumb 56 H4
Blaxhall Suff 31 C10
Blaxton S Yorks 45 B10
Blaydon T&W 63 G7
Bleadon N Som 15 F9
Bleak Hey Nook Gtr Man 44 B4
Blean Kent 21 E8
Bleasby Lincs 46 D5
Bleasby Notts 45 H11
Bleasdale Lancs 50 E1
Bleatarn Cumb 57 E9
Blebocraigs Fife 77 F7
Bleddfa Powys 25 B9
Bledington Glos 27 F9
Bledlow Bucks 18 A4
Bledlow Ridge Bucks 18 B4
Blegbie E Loth 70 D3
Blencarn Cumb 57 C8
Blencogo Cumb 56 B3
Blendworth Hants 10 C6
Blenheim Park Norf 38 B4
Blennerhasset Cumb 56 B3
Blervie Castle Moray 87 F13
Bletchingdon Oxon 28 G2
Bletchingley Sur 19 F10
Bletchley M Keynes 28 E5
Bletchley Shrops 34 B2
Bletherston Pembs 22 D5
Bletsoe Bedford 29 C7
Blewbury Oxon 18 C2
Blickling Norf 39 C7
Blidworth Notts 45 G9
Blindburn Northumb 62 B4
Blindcrake Cumb 56 C3
Blindley Heath Sur 19 G10
Blisland Corn 4 D2
Bliss Gate Worcs 26 A4
Blissford Hants 9 C10
Blisworth Northants 28 C4
Blithbury Staffs 35 C6
Blitterlees Cumb 56 A3
Blo' Norton Norf 38 H6
Blockley Glos 27 E8
Blofield Norf 39 E9
Blofield Heath Norf 39 D9
Bloomfield Borders 61 A11
Blore Staffs 44 H5
Blount's Green Staffs 35 B6
Blowick Mers 49 H3
Bloxham Oxon 27 E11
Bloxholm Lincs 46 G4
Bloxwich W Mid 34 E5
Bloxworth Dorset 9 E7
Blubberhouses N Yorks 51 D7
Blue Anchor Som 7 B9
Blue Anchor Swansea 23 G10
Blue Row Essex 31 G7
Blundeston Suff 39 F11
Blunham C Beds 29 C8
Blunsdon St Andrew Swindon 17 C8
Bluntington Worcs 26 A5
Bluntisham Cambs 29 A10
Blunts Corn 4 E4
Blyborough Lincs 46 C3
Blyford Suff 39 H10
Blymhill Staffs 34 D4
Blyth Northumb 63 E9
Blyth Notts 45 D10
Blyth Bridge Borders 69 F10
Blythburgh Suff 39 H10
Blythe Borders 70 F4
Blythe Bridge Staffs 34 A5
Blyton Lincs 46 C2
Boarhills Fife 77 F8
Boarhunt Hants 10 D5
Boars Head Gtr Man 43 B8
Boars Hill Oxon 17 A11
Boarshead E Sus 12 C4
Boarstall Bucks 28 G3
Boasley Cross Devon 6 G3
Boat of Garten Highld 81 B11
Boath Highld 87 D8
Bobbing Kent 20 E5
Bobbington Staffs 34 F4
Bobbingworth Essex 30 H2
Bocaddon Corn 4 F2
Bochastle Stirling 75 G9
Bocking Essex 30 F4
Bocking Churchstreet Essex 30 F4
Boddam Aberds 89 D11
Boddam Shetland 96 M5
Boddington Glos 26 F5
Bodedern Anglesey 40 B5
Bodelwyddan Denb 42 E3
Bodenham Hereford 26 C2
Bodenham Wilts 9 B10
Bodenham Moor Hereford 26 C2
Bodermid Gwyn 40 H3
Bodewryd Anglesey 40 A5
Bodfari Denb 42 E3
Bodffordd Anglesey 40 C6
Bodham Norf 39 A7
Bodiam E Sus 13 D6
Bodicote Oxon 27 E11
Bodieve Corn 3 B8
Bodinnick Corn 4 F2
Bodle Street Green E Sus 12 E5
Bodmin Corn 4 E1
Bodney Norf 38 F4
Bodorgan Anglesey 40 D5
Bodsham Kent 21 G8
Boduan Gwyn 40 G5
Bodymoor Heath Warks 35 F7
Bogallan Highld 87 F9
Bogbrae Aberds 89 E10
Bogend Borders 70 F6
Bogend S Ayrs 67 C6
Boghall W Loth 69 D8
Boghead S Lanark 68 F6
Bogmoor Moray 88 B3
Bogniebrae Aberds 88 D5
Bognor Regis W Sus 11 E8
Bograxie Aberds 83 B9
Bogside N Lanark 69 E7
Bogton Aberds 89 C6
Bogue Dumfries 55 A9
Bohenie Highld 80 E4
Bohortha Corn 3 F7
Bohuntine Highld 80 E4
Boirseam W Isles 90 J5
Bojewyan Corn 2 F2
Bolam Durham 58 D2
Bolam Northumb 62 E6
Bolberry Devon 5 H7
Bold Heath Mers 43 D8
Boldon T&W 63 G9
Boldon Colliery T&W 63 G9
Boldre Hants 10 E2
Boldron Durham 58 E1
Bole Notts 45 D11
Bolehill Derbys 44 G6
Boleside Borders 70 G3
Bolham Devon 7 E8
Bolham Water Devon 7 E10
Bolingey Corn 3 D6
Bollington Ches E 44 E3
Bollington Cross Ches E 44 E3
Bolney W Sus 12 D1
Bolnhurst Bedford 29 C7
Bolshan Angus 77 B9
Bolsover Derbys 45 E8
Bolsterstone S Yorks 44 C6
Bolstone Hereford 26 E2
Boltby N Yorks 58 H5
Bolter End Bucks 18 B4
Bolton Cumb 57 D8
Bolton E Loth 70 C4
Bolton E Yorks 52 D3
Bolton Gtr Man 43 B10
Bolton Northumb 63 B7
Bolton Abbey N Yorks 51 D6
Bolton Bridge N Yorks 51 D6
Bolton-by-Bowland Lancs 50 E3
Bolton-le-Sands Lancs 49 C4
Bolton Low Houses Cumb 56 B4
Bolton-on-Swale N Yorks 58 G3
Bolton Percy N Yorks 51 E11
Bolton Town End Lancs 49 C4
Bolton upon Dearne S Yorks 45 B8
Boltonfellend Cumb 61 G10
Boltongate Cumb 56 B4
Bolventor Corn 4 D2
Bomere Heath Shrops 33 D10
Bon-y-maen Swansea 14 B2
Bonar Bridge Highld 87 B9
Bonawe Argyll 74 D3
Bonby N Lincs 52 H6
Boncath Pembs 23 C7
Bonchester Bridge Borders 61 B11
Bonchurch IoW 10 G4
Bondleigh Devon 6 F5
Bonehill Devon 5 D8
Bonehill Staffs 35 E7
Bo'ness Falk 69 B8
Bonhill W Dunb 68 C2
Boningale Shrops 34 E4
Bonjedward Borders 62 A2
Bonkle N Lanark 69 E7
Bonnavoulin Highld 79 F8
Bonnington Edin 69 D10
Bonnington Kent 13 C9
Bonnybank Fife 76 G6
Bonnybridge Falk 69 B7
Bonnykelly Aberds 89 C8
Bonnyrigg and Lasswade Midloth 70 D2
Bonnyton Aberds 89 E6
Bonnyton Angus 76 D6
Bonnyton Angus 77 B9
Bonsall Derbys 44 G6
Bonskeid House Perth 75 A11
Bont Mon 25 G10
Bont-Dolgadfan Powys 32 E4
Bont-goch Ceredig 32 G2
Bont-newydd Conwy 42 E3
Bont Newydd Gwyn 32 C3
Bont Newydd Gwyn 41 F9
Bontddu Gwyn 32 D2
Bonthorpe Lincs 47 E8
Bontnewydd Ceredig 24 B3
Bontnewydd Gwyn 40 E6
Bontuchel Denb 42 G3
Bonvilston V Glam 14 D6
Booker Bucks 18 B5
Boon Borders 70 F4
Boosbeck Redcar 59 E7
Boot Cumb 56 F3
Boot Street Suff 31 D9
Booth W Yorks 50 G6
Booth Wood W Yorks 50 H6
Boothby Graffoe Lincs 46 G3
Boothby Pagnell Lincs 36 B5
Boothen Stoke 34 A4
Boothferry E Yorks 52 G3
Boothville Northants 28 B4
Bootle Cumb 56 H3
Bootle Mers 42 C6
Booton Norf 39 C7
Boquhan Stirling 68 B4
Boraston Shrops 26 A3
Borden Kent 20 E5
Borden W Sus 11 B7
Bordley N Yorks 50 C5
Bordon Hants 18 H5
Bordon Camp Hants 18 H4
Boreham Essex 30 H4
Boreham Wilts 16 G5
Boreham Street E Sus 12 E5
Borehamwood Herts 19 B8
Boreland Dumfries 61 D7
Boreland Stirling 75 D8
Borgh W Isles 84 H1
Borgh W Isles 90 J4
Borghastan W Isles 90 C7
Borgie Highld 93 D9
Borgue Dumfries 55 E9
Borgue Highld 94 H3
Borley Essex 30 D5
Bornais W Isles 84 F2
Bornesketaig Highld 85 A8
Borness Dumfries 55 E9
Borough Green Kent 20 F3
Boroughbridge N Yorks 51 C9
Borras Head Wrex 42 G6
Borreraig Highld 84 C6
Borrobol Lodge Highld 93 G11
Borrowash Derbys 35 B10
Borrowby N Yorks 58 H5
Borrowdale Cumb 56 E4
Borrowfield Aberds 83 D10
Borth Ceredig 32 F2
Borth-y-Gest Gwyn 41 G7
Borthwickbrae Borders 61 B10
Borthwickshiels Borders 61 B10
Borve Highld 85 D9
Borve Lodge W Isles 90 H5
Borwick Lancs 49 B5
Bosavern Corn 2 F2
Bosbury Hereford 26 D3
Boscastle Corn 4 B2
Boscombe Bmouth 9 E10
Boscombe Wilts 17 H9
Boscoppa Corn 3 D9
Bosham W Sus 11 D7
Bosherston Pembs 22 G4
Boskenna Corn 2 G3
Bosley Ches E 44 F3
Bossall N Yorks 52 C3
Bossiney Corn 4 C1
Bossingham Kent 21 G8
Bossington Som 7 B7
Bostock Green Ches W 43 F9
Boston Lincs 37 A9
Boston Long Hedges Lincs 47 H7
Boston Spa W Yorks 51 E10
Boston West Lincs 46 H6
Boswinger Corn 3 E8
Botallack Corn 2 F2
Botany Bay London 19 B9
Botcherby Cumb 61 H10
Botcheston Leics 35 E10
Botesdale Suff 38 H6
Bothal Northumb 63 E8
Bothamsall Notts 45 E10
Bothel Cumb 56 C3
Bothenhampton Dorset 8 E3
Bothwell S Lanark 68 E6
Botley Bucks 18 A6
Botley Hants 10 C4
Botley Oxon 27 H11
Botolph Claydon Bucks 28 F4
Botolphs W Sus 11 D10
Bottacks Highld 86 E7
Bottesford Leics 36 B4
Bottesford N Lincs 46 B2
Bottisham Cambs 30 B2
Bottlesford Wilts 17 F8
Bottom Boat W Yorks 51 G9
Bottom House Staffs 44 G4
Bottom o' th' Moor Gtr Man 43 A9
Bottom of Hutton Lancs 49 G4
Bottomcraig Fife 76 E6
Botusfleming Corn 4 E5
Botwnnog Gwyn 40 G4
Bough Beech Kent 19 G11
Boughrood Powys 25 E8
Boughspring Glos 16 B2
Boughton Norf 38 E2
Boughton Northants 28 B4
Boughton Notts 45 F10
Boughton Aluph Kent 21 G7
Boughton Lees Kent 21 G7
Boughton Malherbe Kent 20 G5
Boughton Monchelsea Kent 20 F4
Boughton Street Kent 21 F7
Boulby Redcar 59 E8
Boulden Shrops 33 G11
Boulmer Northumb 63 B8
Boulston Pembs 22 E4
Boultenstone Aberds 82 B6
Boultham Lincs 46 F3
Bourn Cambs 29 C10
Bourne Lincs 37 C6
Bourne End Bucks 18 C5
Bourne End C Beds 28 D6
Bourne End Herts 29 H7
Bournemouth Bmouth 9 E9
Bournes Green Glos 16 A6
Bournes Green Southend 20 C6
Bournheath Worcs 26 A6
Bournmoor Durham 58 A4
Bournville W Mid 34 G6
Bourton Dorset 9 A6
Bourton N Som 15 E9
Bourton Oxon 17 C9
Bourton Shrops 34 F1
Bourton on Dunsmore Warks 27 A11
Bourton on the Hill Glos 27 E8
Bourton-on-the-Water Glos 27 F8
Bousd Argyll 78 E5
Boustead Hill Cumb 61 H8
Bouth Cumb 56 H5
Bouthwaite N Yorks 51 B7
Boveney Bucks 18 D6
Boverton V Glam 14 E5
Bovey Tracey Devon 5 D9
Bovingdon Herts 19 A7
Bovingdon Green Bucks 18 C5
Bovingdon Green Herts 19 A7
Bovinger Essex 30 H2
Bovington Camp Dorset 9 F7
Bow Borders 70 F3
Bow Devon 6 F6
Bow Orkney 95 J4
Bow Brickhill M Keynes 28 E6
Bow of Fife Fife 76 F6
Bow Street Ceredig 32 G2
Bowbank Durham 57 D11
Bowburn Durham 58 C4
Bowcombe IoW 10 F3
Bowd Devon 7 G10
Bowden Borders 70 G4
Bowden Devon 5 G9
Bowden Hill Wilts 16 E6

Bowderdale Cumb 57 F8
Bowdon Gtr Man 43 D10
Bower Northumb 62 E3
Bower Hinton Som 8 C3
Bowerchalke Wilts 9 B9
Bowerhill Wilts 16 E6
Bowermadden Highld 94 D4
Bowers Gifford Essex 20 C4
Bowershall Fife 69 A9
Bowertower Highld 94 D4
Bowes Durham 57 E11
Bowgreave Lancs 49 E4
Bowgreen Gtr Man 43 D10
Bowhill Borders 70 H3
Bowhouse Dumfries 60 G6
Bowland Bridge Cumb 56 H6
Bowley Hereford 26 C2
Bowlhead Green Sur 18 H6
Bowling W Dunb 68 C3
Bowling W Yorks 51 F7
Bowling Bank Wrex 43 H6
Bowling Green Worcs 26 C5
Bowmanstead Cumb 56 G5
Bowmore Argyll 64 C4
Bowness-on-Solway Cumb 61 G8
Bowness-on-Windermere Cumb 56 G6
Bowsden Northumb 71 F8
Bowside Lodge Highld 93 C11
Bowston Cumb 57 G6
Bowthorpe Norf 39 E7
Box Glos 16 A5
Box Wilts 16 E5
Box End Bedford 29 D7
Boxbush Glos 26 G4
Boxford Suff 30 D6
Boxford W Berks 17 D11
Boxgrove W Sus 11 D8
Boxley Kent 20 F4
Boxmoor Herts 29 H7
Boxted Essex 30 E6
Boxted Suff 30 C5
Boxted Cross Essex 31 E7
Boxted Heath Essex 31 E7
Boxworth Cambs 29 B10
Boxworth End Cambs 29 B10
Boyden Gate Kent 21 E9
Boylestone Derbys 35 B7
Boyndie Aberds 89 B6
Boynton E Yorks 53 C7
Boysack Angus 77 C9
Boyton Corn 6 G2
Boyton Suff 31 D10
Boyton Wilts 16 H6
Boyton Cross Essex 30 H3
Boyton End Suff 30 D4
Bozeat Northants 28 C6
Brù W Isles 91 C8
Braaid IoM 48 E3
Braal Castle Highld 94 D3
Brabling Green Suff 31 B9
Brabourne Kent 13 B9
Brabourne Lees Kent 13 B9
Brabster Highld 94 D5
Bracadale Highld 85 E8
Bracara Highld 79 B10
Braceborough Lincs 37 D6
Bracebridge Lincs 46 F3
Bracebridge Heath Lincs 46 F3
Bracebridge Low Fields Lincs 46 F3
Braceby Lincs 36 B6
Bracewell Lancs 50 E4
Brackenfield Derbys 45 G7
Brackenthwaite Cumb 56 B4
Brackenthwaite N Yorks 51 D8
Bracklesham W Sus 11 E7
Brackletter Highld 80 E3
Brackley Argyll 65 D8
Brackley Northants 28 E2
Brackloch Highld 92 G4
Bracknell Brack 18 E5
Braco Perth 75 G11
Bracobrae Moray 88 C5
Bracon Ash Norf 39 F7
Bracorina Highld 79 B10
Bradbourne Derbys 44 G6
Bradbury Durham 58 D4
Bradda IoM 48 F1
Bradden Northants 28 D3
Braddock Corn 4 E2
Bradeley Stoke 44 G2
Bradenham Bucks 18 B5
Bradenham Norf 38 E5
Bradenstoke Wilts 17 D7
Bradfield Essex 31 E8
Bradfield Norf 39 B8
Bradfield W Berks 18 D3
Bradfield Combust Suff 30 C5
Bradfield Green Ches E 43 G9
Bradfield Heath Essex 31 F8
Bradfield St Clare Suff 30 C6
Bradfield St George Suff 30 B6
Bradford Corn 4 D2
Bradford Derbys 44 F6
Bradford Devon 6 F3
Bradford Northumb 71 G10
Bradford W Yorks 51 F7
Bradford Abbas Dorset 8 C4
Bradford Leigh Wilts 16 E5
Bradford-on-Avon Wilts 16 E5
Bradford-on-Tone Som 7 D10
Bradford Peverell Dorset 8 E5
Brading IoW 10 F5
Bradley Derbys 44 H6
Bradley Hants 18 G3
Bradley NE Lincs 46 B6
Bradley Staffs 34 D4
Bradley W Mid 34 F5
Bradley W Yorks 51 G7
Bradley Green Worcs 26 B6
Bradley in the Moors Staffs 35 A6
Bradley Stoke S Glos 16 C3
Bradlow Hereford 26 E4
Bradmore Notts 36 B1
Bradmore W Mid 34 F4
Bradninch Devon 7 F9
Bradnop Staffs 44 G4
Bradpole Dorset 8 E3
Bradshaw Gtr Man 43 A10
Bradshaw W Yorks 44 A4
Bradstone Devon 4 C4
Bradwall Green Ches E 43 F10
Bradway S Yorks 45 D7
Bradwell Derbys 44 D5
Bradwell Essex 30 F5
Bradwell M Keynes 28 E5
Bradwell Norf 39 E11
Bradwell Staffs 44 H2
Bradwell Grove Oxon 27 H9
Bradwell on Sea Essex 31 H7
Bradwell Waterside Essex 30 H6
Bradworthy Devon 6 E2
Bradworthy Cross Devon 6 E2
Brae Dumfries 60 F4
Brae Highld 91 J13
Brae Highld 92 J7
Brae Shetland 96 G5
Brae of Achnahaird Highld 92 H3
Brae Roy Lodge Highld 80 D5
Braeantra Highld 87 D8
Braedownie Angus 82 F4
Braefield Highld 86 H7
Braegrum Perth 76 E3
Braehead Dumfries 55 D7
Braehead Orkney 95 D5
Braehead Orkney 95 H6
Braehead S Lanark 69 E8
Braehead S Lanark 69 G7
Braehead of Lunan Angus 77 B9
Braehoulland Shetland 96 F4
Braehungie Highld 94 G3
Braelangwell Lodge Highld 87 B8
Braemar Aberds 82 D3
Braemore Highld 86 D4
Braemore Highld 94 G2
Braes of Enzie Moray 88 C3
Braeside Invclyd 73 F11
Braeswick Orkney 95 E7
Braewick Shetland 96 H5
Brafferton Darl 58 D3
Brafferton N Yorks 51 B10
Brafield-on-the-Green Northants 28 C5
Bragar W Isles 91 C7
Bragbury End Herts 29 F9
Bragleenmore Argyll 74 E2
Braichmelyn Gwyn 41 D8
Braid Edin 69 D11
Braides Lancs 49 D4
Braidley N Yorks 50 A6
Braidwood S Lanark 69 F7
Braigo Argyll 64 B3
Brailsford Derbys 35 A8
Brainshaugh Northumb 63 C8
Braintree Essex 30 F4
Braiseworth Suff 31 A8
Braishfield Hants 10 B2
Braithwaite Cumb 56 D4
Braithwaite S Yorks 45 A10
Braithwaite W Yorks 50 E6
Braithwell S Yorks 45 C9
Bramber W Sus 11 C10
Bramcote Notts 35 B11
Bramcote Warks 35 G10
Bramdean Hants 10 B5
Bramerton Norf 39 E8
Bramfield Herts 29 G9
Bramfield Suff 31 A10
Bramford Suff 31 D8
Bramhall Gtr Man 44 D2
Bramham W Yorks 51 E10
Bramhope W Yorks 51 E8
Bramley Hants 18 F3
Bramley S Yorks 45 C8
Bramley Sur 19 G7
Bramley W Yorks 51 F8
Bramling Kent 21 F9
Brampford Speke Devon 7 G8
Brampton Cambs 29 A9
Brampton Cumb 57 D8
Brampton Cumb 61 G11
Brampton Derbys 45 E7
Brampton Hereford 25 E11
Brampton Lincs 46 E2
Brampton Norf 39 C8
Brampton S Yorks 45 B8
Brampton Suff 39 G10
Brampton Abbotts Hereford 26 F3
Brampton Ash Northants 36 G3
Brampton Bryan Hereford 25 A10
Brampton en le Morthen S Yorks 45 D8
Bramshall Staffs 35 B6
Bramshaw Hants 10 C1
Bramshill Hants 18 E4
Bramshott Hants 11 A7
Bran End Essex 30 F3
Branault Highld 79 E8
Brancaster Norf 38 A3
Brancaster Staithe Norf 38 A3
Brancepeth Durham 58 C3
Branch End Northumb 62 G6
Branchill Moray 87 F13
Brand Green Glos 26 F4
Branderburgh Moray 88 A2
Brandesburton E Yorks 53 E7
Brandeston Suff 31 B9
Brandhill Shrops 33 H10
Brandis Corner Devon 6 F3
Brandiston Norf 39 C7
Brandon Durham 58 C3
Brandon Lincs 46 H3
Brandon Northumb 62 B6
Brandon Suff 38 G3
Brandon Warks 35 H10
Brandon Bank Cambs 38 G2
Brandon Creek Norf 38 F2
Brandon Parva Norf 39 E6
Brandsby N Yorks 52 B1
Brandy Wharf Lincs 46 C4
Brane Corn 2 G3
Branksome Poole 9 E9
Branksome Park Poole 9 E9
Bransby Lincs 46 E2
Branscombe Devon 7 H10
Bransford Worcs 26 C4
Bransgore Hants 9 E10
Branshill Clack 69 A7
Bransholme Hull 53 F7
Branson's Cross Worcs 27 A7
Branston Leics 36 C4
Branston Lincs 46 F4
Branston Staffs 35 C8
Branston Booths Lincs 46 F4
Branstone IoW 10 F4
Bransty Cumb 56 E1
Brant Broughton Lincs 46 G3
Brantham Suff 31 E8
Branthwaite Cumb 56 C4
Branthwaite Cumb 56 D2
Brantingham E Yorks 52 G5
Branton Northumb 62 B6
Branton S Yorks 45 B10
Branxholm Park Borders 61 B10
Branxholme Borders 61 B10
Branxton Northumb 71 G7
Brassey Green Ches W 43 F8
Brassington Derbys 44 G6
Brasted Kent 19 F11
Brasted Chart Kent 19 F11
Brathens Aberds 83 D8
Bratoft Lincs 47 F8
Brattleby Lincs 46 D3
Bratton Telford 34 D2
Bratton Wilts 16 F6
Bratton Clovelly Devon 6 G3
Bratton Fleming Devon 6 C5
Bratton Seymour Som 8 B5
Braughing Herts 29 F10
Braunston Northants 28 B2
Braunston-in-Rutland Rutland 36 E4
Braunstone Town Leicester 36 E1
Braunton Devon 6 C3
Brawby N Yorks 52 B3
Brawl Highld 93 C11
Brawlbin Highld 94 E2
Bray Windsor 18 D6
Bray Shop Corn 4 D4
Bray Wick Windsor 18 D5
Braybrooke Northants 36 G3
Braye Ald 11
Brayford Devon 6 C5
Braystones Cumb 56 F2
Braythorn N Yorks 51 E8
Brayton N Yorks 52 F2
Brazacott Corn 6 G1
Breach Kent 20 E5
Breachacha Castle Argyll 78 F4
Breachwood Green Herts 29 F8
Breacleit W Isles 90 D6
Breaden Heath Shrops 33 B10
Breadsall Derbys 35 B9
Breadstone Glos 16 A4
Breage Corn 2 G5
Breakachy Highld 86 G7
Bream Glos 26 H3
Breamore Hants 9 C10
Brean Som 15 F8
Breanais W Isles 90 E4
Brearton N Yorks 51 C9
Breascleit W Isles 90 D7
Breaston Derbys 35 B10
Brechfa Carms 23 C10
Brechin Angus 77 A8
Breck of Cruan Orkney 95 G4
Breckan Orkney 95 H3
Breckrey Highld 85 B10
Brecon = Aberhonddu Powys 25 F7
Bredbury Gtr Man 44 C3
Brede E Sus 13 E7
Bredenbury Hereford 26 C3
Bredfield Suff 31 C9
Bredgar Kent 20 E5
Bredhurst Kent 20 E4
Bredicot Worcs 26 C6
Bredon Worcs 26 E6
Bredon's Norton Worcs 26 E6
Bredwardine Hereford 25 D10
Breedon on the Hill Leics 35 C10
Breibhig W Isles 84 J1
Breibhig W Isles 91 D9
Breich W Loth 69 D8
Breightmet Gtr Man 43 B10
Breighton E Yorks 52 F3
Breinton Hereford 25 E11
Breinton Common Hereford 25 D11
Breiwick Shetland 96 J6
Bremhill Wilts 16 D6
Bremirehoull Shetland 96 L6
Brenchley Kent 12 B5
Brendon Devon 7 B6
Brenkley T&W 63 F8
Brent Eleigh Suff 30 D6
Brent Knoll Som 15 F9
Brent Pelham Herts 29 E11
Brentford London 19 D8
Brentingby Leics 36 D3
Brentwood Essex 20 B2
Brenzett Kent 13 D9
Brereton Staffs 35 D6
Brereton Green Ches E 43 F10
Brereton Heath Ches E 44 F2
Bressingham Norf 39 G6
Bretby Derbys 35 C8
Bretford Warks 35 H10
Bretforton Worcs 27 D7
Bretherdale Head Cumb 57 F7
Bretherton Lancs 49 G4
Brettabister Shetland 96 H6
Brettenham Norf 38 G5
Brettenham Suff 30 C6
Bretton Derbys 44 E6
Bretton Flint 42 F6
Brewer Street Sur 19 F10
Brewlands Bridge Angus 76 A4
Brewood Staffs 34 E4
Briach Moray 87 F13
Briants Puddle Dorset 9 E7
Brick End Essex 30 F2
Brickendon Herts 29 H10
Bricket Wood Herts 19 A8
Bricklehampton Worcs 26 D6
Bride IoM 48 B4
Bridekirk Cumb 56 C3
Bridell Pembs 22 B6
Bridestowe Devon 4 C6
Brideswell Aberds 88 E5
Bridford Devon 5 C9
Bridfordmills Devon 5 C9
Bridge Kent 21 F8
Bridge End Lincs 37 B7
Bridge Green Essex 29 E11
Bridge Hewick N Yorks 51 B9
Bridge of Alford Aberds 83 B7
Bridge of Allan Stirling 75 H10
Bridge of Avon Moray 88 E1
Bridge of Awe Argyll 74 E3
Bridge of Balgie Perth 75 C8
Bridge of Cally Perth 76 B4
Bridge of Canny Aberds 83 D8
Bridge of Craigisla Angus 76 B5
Bridge of Dee Dumfries 55 D10
Bridge of Don Aberdeen 83 B11
Bridge of Dun Angus 77 B9
Bridge of Dye Aberds 83 E8
Bridge of Earn Perth 76 F4
Bridge of Ericht Perth 75 B8
Bridge of Feugh Aberds 83 D9
Bridge of Forss Highld 93 C13
Bridge of Gairn Aberds 82 D5
Bridge of Gaur Perth 75 B8
Bridge of Muchalls Aberds 83 D10
Bridge of Oich Highld 80 C5
Bridge of Orchy Argyll 74 D5
Bridge of Waith Orkney 95 G3
Bridge of Walls Shetland 96 H4
Bridge of Weir Renfs 68 D2
Bridge Sollers Hereford 25 D11
Bridge Street Suff 30 D5
Bridge Trafford Ches W 43 E7
Bridge Yate S Glos 16 D3
Bridgefoot Angus 76 D6
Bridgefoot Cumb 56 D2
Bridgehampton Som 8 B4
Bridgehill Durham 58 A1
Bridgemary Hants 10 D4
Bridgemont Derbys 44 D4
Bridgend Aberds 83 B7
Bridgend Aberds 88 E5
Bridgend Angus 83 G7
Bridgend Argyll 64 B4
Bridgend Argyll 65 E8
Bridgend Argyll 73 D7
Bridgend = Pen-y-bont ar Ogwr Bridgend 14 D5
Bridgend Cumb 56 E5
Bridgend Fife 76 F6
Bridgend Moray 88 E3
Bridgend N Lanark 68 C5
Bridgend Pembs 22 B6
Bridgend W Loth 69 C9
Bridgend of Lintrathen Angus 76 B5
Bridgerule Devon 6 F1
Bridges Shrops 33 F9
Bridgeton Glasgow 68 D5
Bridgetown Corn 4 C4
Bridgetown Som 7 C8
Bridgham Norf 38 G5
Bridgnorth Shrops 34 F3
Bridgtown Staffs 34 E5
Bridgwater Som 15 H9
Bridlington E Yorks 53 C7
Bridport Dorset 8 E3
Bridstow Hereford 26 F2
Brierfield Lancs 50 F4
Brierley Glos 26 G3
Brierley Hereford 25 C11
Brierley S Yorks 45 A8
Brierley Hill W Mid 34 G5
Briery Hill Bl Gwent 25 H8
Brig o'Turk Stirling 75 G8
Brigg N Lincs 46 B4
Briggswath N Yorks 59 F9
Brigham Cumb 56 C2
Brigham E Yorks 53 D6
Brighouse W Yorks 51 G7
Brighstone IoW 10 F3
Brightgate Derbys 44 G6
Brighthampton Oxon 17 A10
Brightling E Sus 12 D5
Brightlingsea Essex 31 G7
Brighton Brighton 12 F2
Brighton Corn 3 D8
Brighton Hill Hants 18 G3
Brightons Falk 69 C8
Brightwalton W Berks 17 D11
Brightwell Suff 31 D9
Brightwell Baldwin Oxon 18 B3
Brightwell cum Sotwell Oxon 18 B2
Brignall Durham 58 E1
Brigsley NE Lincs 46 B6
Brigsteer Cumb 57 H6
Brigstock Northants 36 G5
Brill Bucks 28 G3
Brilley Hereford 25 D9
Brimaston Pembs 22 D4
Brimfield Hereford 26 B2
Brimington Derbys 45 E8
Brimley Devon 5 D8
Brimpsfield Glos 26 G6
Brimpton W Berks 18 E2
Brims Orkney 95 K3
Brimscombe Glos 16 A5
Brimstage Mers 42 D6
Brinacory Highld 79 B10
Brind E Yorks 52 F3
Brindister Shetland 96 H4
Brindister Shetland 96 K6
Brindle Lancs 50 G2
Brindley Ford Stoke 44 G2
Brineton Staffs 34 D4
Bringhurst Leics 36 F4
Brington Cambs 37 H6
Brinian Orkney 95 F5
Briningham Norf 38 B6
Brinkhill Lincs 47 E7
Brinkley Cambs 30 C3
Brinklow Warks 35 H10
Brinkworth Wilts 17 C7
Brinmore Highld 81 A8
Brinscall Lancs 50 G2
Brinsea N Som 15 E10
Brinsley Notts 45 H8
Brinsop Hereford 25 D11
Brinsworth S Yorks 45 D8
Brinton Norf 38 B6
Brisco Cumb 56 A6
Brisley Norf 38 C5
Brislington Bristol 16 D3
Bristol Bristol 16 D2
Briston Norf 39 B6
Britannia Lancs 50 G4
Britford Wilts 9 B10
Brithdir Gwyn 32 D3
British Legion Village Kent 20 F4
Briton Ferry Neath 14 B3
Britwell Salome Oxon 18 B3
Brixham Torbay 5 F10
Brixton Devon 5 F6
Brixton London 19 D10
Brixton Deverill Wilts 16 H5
Brixworth Northants 28 A4
Brize Norton Oxon 27 H10
Broad Blunsdon Swindon 17 B8
Broad Campden Glos 27 E8
Broad Chalke Wilts 9 B9
Broad Green C Beds 28 D6
Broad Green Essex 30 F5
Broad Green Worcs 26 C4
Broad Haven Pembs 22 E3
Broad Heath Worcs 26 B3
Broad Hill Cambs 38 H1
Broad Hinton Wilts 17 D8
Broad Laying Hants 17 E11
Broad Marston Worcs 27 D8
Broad Oak Carms 23 D10
Broad Oak Cumb 56 G3
Broad Oak Dorset 8 E3
Broad Oak Dorset 9 C6
Broad Oak E Sus 12 D5
Broad Oak E Sus 13 E7
Broad Oak Hereford 25 F11
Broad Oak Mers 43 C8
Broad Street Kent 20 F5
Broad Street Green Essex 30 H5
Broad Town Wilts 17 D7
Broadbottom Gtr Man 44 C3
Broadbridge W Sus 11 D7
Broadbridge Heath W Sus 11 A10
Broadclyst Devon 7 G8
Broadfield Gtr Man 44 A2
Broadfield Lancs 49 G5
Broadfield Pembs 22 F6
Broadfield W Sus 12 C1
Broadford Highld 85 F11
Broadford Bridge W Sus 11 B9
Broadhaugh Borders 61 C10
Broadhaven Highld 94 E5
Broadheath Gtr Man 43 D10
Broadhembury Devon 7 F10
Broadhempston Devon 5 E9
Broadholme Derbys 45 H7
Broadholme Lincs 46 E2
Broadland Row E Sus 13 E7
Broadlay Carms 23 F8
Broadley Lancs 50 H4
Broadley Moray 88 B3
Broadley Common Essex 29 H11
Broadmayne Dorset 8 F6
Broadmeadows Borders 70 G3
Broadmere Hants 18 G3
Broadmoor Pembs 22 F5
Broadoak Kent 21 E8
Broadrashes Moray 88 C4
Broadsea Aberds 89 B9
Broadstairs Kent 21 E10
Broadstone Poole 9 E9
Broadstone Shrops 33 G11
Broadtown Lane Wilts 17 D7
Broadwas Worcs 26 C4
Broadwater Herts 29 F9
Broadwater W Sus 11 D10
Broadway Carms 23 F7
Broadway Pembs 22 E3
Broadway Som 8 C2
Broadway Suff 39 H9
Broadway Worcs 27 E7
Broadwell Glos 26 G2
Broadwell Glos 27 F9
Broadwell Oxon 17 A9
Broadwell Warks 27 B11
Broadwell House Northumb 57 A11
Broadwey Dorset 8 F5
Broadwindsor Dorset 8 D3
Broadwood Kelly Devon 6 F5
Broadwoodwidger Devon 4 C5
Brobury Hereford 25 D10
Brochel Highld 85 D10
Brochloch Dumfries 67 G8
Brochroy Argyll 74 D3
Brockamin Worcs 26 C4
Brockbridge Hants 10 C5
Brockdam Northumb 63 A7
Brockdish Norf 39 H8
Brockenhurst Hants 10 D2
Brocketsbrae S Lanark 69 G7
Brockford Street Suff 31 B8
Brockhall Northants 28 B3
Brockham Sur 19 G8
Brockhampton Glos 27 F7
Brockhampton Hereford 26 E2
Brockholes W Yorks 44 A5
Brockhurst Derbys 45 F7
Brockhurst Hants 10 D5
Brocklebank Cumb 56 B5
Brocklesby Lincs 46 A5
Brockley N Som 15 E10
Brockley Green Suff 30 C5
Brockleymoor Cumb 57 C6
Brockton Shrops 33 E9
Brockton Shrops 33 G9
Brockton Shrops 34 E3
Brockton Shrops 34 F1
Brockton Telford 34 D3
Brockweir Glos 15 A11
Brockwood Hants 10 B5
Brockworth Glos 26 G5
Brocton Staffs 34 D5
Brodick N Ayrs 66 C3
Brodsworth S Yorks 45 B9
Brogaig Highld 85 B9
Brogborough C Beds 28 E6
Broken Cross Ches E 44 E2
Broken Cross Ches W 43 E9
Brokenborough Wilts 16 C6
Bromborough Mers 42 D6
Brome Suff 39 H7
Brome Street Suff 39 H7
Bromeswell Suff 31 C10
Bromfield Cumb 56 B3
Bromfield Shrops 33 H10
Bromham Bedford 29 C7
Bromham Wilts 16 E6
Bromley London 19 E11
Bromley W Mid 34 G5
Bromley Common London 19 E11
Bromley Green Kent 13 C8
Brompton Medway 20 E4
Brompton N Yorks 52 A5
Brompton N Yorks 58 G4
Brompton-on-Swale N Yorks 58 G3
Brompton Ralph Som 7 C9
Brompton Regis Som 7 C8
Bromsash Hereford 26 F3
Bromsberrow Hth. Glos 26 E4
Bromsgrove Worcs 26 A6
Bromyard Hereford 26 C3
Bromyard Downs Hereford 26 C3
Bronaber Gwyn 41 G9
Brongest Ceredig 23 B8
Bronington Wrex 33 B10
Bronllys Powys 25 E8
Bronnant Ceredig 24 B3
Bronwydd Arms Carms 23 D9
Bronydd Powys 25 D9
Bronygarth Shrops 33 B8
Brook Carms 23 F7
Brook Hants 10 B2
Brook Hants 10 C1
Brook IoW 10 F2
Brook Kent 13 B9
Brook Sur 18 H6
Brook Sur 19 G7
Brook End Bedford 29 B7
Brook Hill Hants 10 C1
Brook Street Kent 13 C8
Brook Street Kent 20 G2
Brook Street W Sus 12 D2
Brooke Norf 39 F8
Brooke Rutland 36 E4
Brookenby Lincs 46 C6
Brookend Glos 16 B2
Brookfield Renfs 68 D3
Brookhouse Lancs 49 C5
Brookhouse Green Ches E 44 F2
Brookland Kent 13 D8
Brooklands Dumfries 60 F4
Brooklands Gtr Man 43 C10
Brooklands Shrops 33 A11
Brookmans Park Herts 19 A9
Brooks Powys 33 F7
Brooks Green W Sus 11 B10
Brookthorpe Glos 26 G5
Brookville Norf 38 F3
Brookwood Sur 18 F6
Broom C Beds 29 D8
Broom S Yorks 45 C8
Broom Warks 27 C7
Broom Worcs 34 H5
Broom Green Norf 38 C5
Broom Hill Dorset 9 D9
Broome Norf 39 F9
Broome Shrops 33 G10
Broome Park Northumb 63 B7
Broomedge Warr 43 D10
Broomer's Corner W Sus 11 B10
Broomfield Aberds 89 E9
Broomfield Essex 30 G4
Broomfield Kent 20 F5
Broomfield Kent 21 E8
Broomfield Som 7 C11
Broomfleet E Yorks 52 G4
Broomhall Ches E 43 H9
Broomhall Windsor 18 E6
Broomhaugh Northumb 62 G6
Broomhill Norf 38 E2
Broomhill Northumb 63 C8
Broomhill S Yorks 45 B8
Broomholm Norf 39 B9
Broomley Northumb 62 G6
Broompark Durham 58 B3
Broom's Green Glos 26 E4
Broomy Lodge Hants 9 C11
Brora Highld 93 J12
Broseley Shrops 34 E2
Brotherhouse Bar Lincs 37 D8
Brotherstone Borders 70 G5
Brothertoft Lincs 46 H6
Brotherton N Yorks 51 G10
Brotton Redcar 59 E7
Broubster Highld 93 C13
Brough Cumb 57 E9
Brough Derbys 44 D5
Brough E Yorks 52 G5
Brough Highld 94 C4
Brough Notts 46 G2
Brough Orkney 95 G4
Brough Shetland 96 F7
Brough Shetland 96 F6
Brough Shetland 96 G7
Brough Shetland 96 H6
Brough Shetland 96 J7
Brough Lodge Shetland 96 D7
Brough Sowerby Cumb 57 E9
Broughall Shrops 34 A1
Broughton Borders 69 G10
Broughton Cambs 37 H8
Broughton Flint 42 F6
Broughton Hants 10 A2
Broughton Lancs 49 F5
Broughton M Keynes 28 D5
Broughton N Lincs 46 B3
Broughton N Yorks 50 D5
Broughton N Yorks 52 B3
Broughton Northants 36 H4
Broughton Orkney 95 D5
Broughton Oxon 27 E11
Broughton V Glam 14 D5
Broughton Astley Leics 35 F11
Broughton Beck Cumb 49 A2
Broughton Common Wilts 16 E5
Broughton Gifford Wilts 16 E5
Broughton Hackett Worcs 26 C6
Broughton in Furness Cumb 56 H4
Broughton Mills Cumb 56 G4
Broughton Moor Cumb 56 C2
Broughton Park Gtr Man 44 B2
Broughton Poggs Oxon 17 A9
Broughtown Orkney 95 D7
Broughty Ferry Dundee 77 D7
Browhouses Dumfries 61 G8
Browland Shetland 96 H4
Brown Candover Hants 18 H2
Brown Edge Lancs 42 A6
Brown Edge Staffs 44 G3
Brown Heath Ches W 43 F7
Brownhill Aberds 89 D8
Brownhill Aberds 89 D6
Brownhill Blackburn 50 F2
Brownhill Shrops 33 C10
Brownhills Fife 77 F8
Brownhills W Mid 34 E6
Brownlow Ches E 44 F2
Brownlow Heath Ches E 44 F2
Brownmuir Aberds 83 F9
Brown's End Glos 26 E4
Brownshill Glos 16 A5
Brownston Devon 5 F7
Brownyside Northumb 63 A7
Broxa N Yorks 59 G10
Broxbourne Herts 29 H10
Broxburn E Loth 70 C5
Broxburn W Loth 69 C9
Broxholme Lincs 46 E3
Broxted Essex 30 F2
Broxton Ches W 43 G7
Broxwood Hereford 25 C10
Broyle Side E Sus 12 E3
Bruairnis W Isles 84 H2
Bruan Highld 94 G5
Bruar Lodge Perth 81 F10
Brucehill W Dunb 68 C2
Bruera Ches W 43 F7
Bruern Abbey Oxon 27 F9
Bruichladdich Argyll 64 B3
Bruisyard Suff 31 B10
Brumby N Lincs 46 B2
Brund Staffs 44 F5
Brundall Norf 39 E9
Brundish Suff 31 B9
Brundish Street Suff 31 A9
Brunery Highld 79 D10
Brunshaw Lancs 50 F4
Brunswick Village T&W 63 F8
Bruntcliffe W Yorks 51 G8
Bruntingthorpe Leics 36 F2
Brunton Fife 76 E6
Brunton Northumb 63 A8
Brunton Wilts 17 F9
Brushford Devon 6 F5
Brushford Som 7 D8
Bruton Som 8 A5
Bryanston Dorset 9 D7
Brydekirk Dumfries 61 F7
Bryher Scilly 2 C2
Brymbo Wrex 42 G5
Brympton Som 8 C4
Bryn Carms 23 F10
Bryn Gtr Man 43 B8
Bryn Neath 14 B4
Bryn Shrops 33 G8
Bryn-coch Neath 14 B3
Bryn Du Anglesey 40 C5
Bryn Gates Gtr Man 43 B8
Bryn-glas Conwy 41 D10
Bryn Golau Rhondda 14 C5
Bryn-Iwan Carms 23 C8
Bryn-mawr Gwyn 40 G4
Bryn-nantllech Conwy 42 F2
Bryn-penarth Powys 33 E7
Bryn Rhyd-yr-Arian Conwy 42 F2
Bryn Saith Marchog Denb 42 G3
Bryn Sion Gwyn 32 D4
Bryn-y-gwenin Mon 25 G10
Bryn-y-maen Conwy 41 C10
Bryn-yr-eryr Gwyn 40 F5
Brynamman Carms 24 G4
Brynberian Pembs 22 C6
Brynbryddan Neath 14 B3
Brynbuga = Usk Mon 15 A9
Bryncae Rhondda 14 C5
Bryncethin Bridgend 14 C5
Bryncir Gwyn 40 F6
Bryncroes Gwyn 40 G4
Bryncrug Gwyn 32 E2
Bryneglwys Denb 42 H4
Brynford Flint 42 E4
Bryngwran Anglesey 40 C5
Bryngwyn Ceredig 23 B7
Bryngwyn Mon 25 H10
Bryngwyn Powys 25 D8
Brynhenllan Pembs 22 C5
Brynhoffnant Ceredig 23 A8
Brynithel Bl Gwent 15 A8
Brynmawr Bl Gwent 25 G8
Brynmenyn Bridgend 14 C5
Brynmill Swansea 14 B2
Brynna Rhondda 14 C5
Brynrefail Anglesey 40 B6
Brynrefail Gwyn 41 D7
Brynsadler Rhondda 14 C6
Brynsiencyn Anglesey 40 D6
Brynteg Anglesey 40 B6
Brynteg Ceredig 23 B9
Buaile nam Bodach W Isles 84 H2
Bualintur Highld 85 F9
Buarthmeini Gwyn 41 G10
Bubbenhall Warks 27 A10
Bubwith E Yorks 52 F3
Buccleuch Borders 61 B9
Buchanhaven Aberds 89 D11
Buchanty Perth 76 E2
Buchlyvie Stirling 68 A4
Buckabank Cumb 56 B5
Buckden Cambs 29 B8
Buckden N Yorks 50 B5
Buckenham Norf 39 E9
Buckerell Devon 7 F10
Buckfast Devon 5 E8
Buckfastleigh Devon 5 E8
Buckhaven Fife 76 H6
Buckholm Borders 70 G3
Buckholt Mon 26 G2
Buckhorn Weston Dorset 9 B6
Buckhurst Hill Essex 19 B11
Buckie Moray 88 B4
Buckies Highld 94 D3
Buckingham Bucks 28 E3
Buckland Bucks 28 G5
Buckland Devon 5 G7
Buckland Glos 27 E7
Buckland Hants 10 E2
Buckland Herts 29 E10
Buckland Kent 21 G10
Buckland Oxon 17 B10
Buckland Sur 19 F9
Buckland Brewer Devon 6 D3
Buckland Common Bucks 28 H6
Buckland Dinham Som 16 F4
Buckland Filleigh Devon 6 F3
Buckland in the Moor Devon 5 D8
Buckland Monachorum Devon 4 E5
Buckland Newton Dorset 8 D5
Buckland St Mary Som 8 C1
Bucklebury W Berks 18 D2
Bucklegate Lincs 37 B9
Bucklerheads Angus 77 D7
Bucklers Hard Hants 10 E3
Bucklesham Suff 31 D9
Buckley = Bwcle Flint 42 F5
Bucklow Hill Ches E 43 D10
Buckminster Leics 36 C4
Bucknall Lincs 46 F5
Bucknall Stoke 44 H3
Bucknell Oxon 28 F2
Bucknell Shrops 25 A10
Buckpool Moray 88 B4
Buck's Cross Devon 6 D2
Bucks Green W Sus 11 A9
Bucks Horn Oak Hants 18 G5
Buck's Mills Devon 6 D2
Bucksburn Aberdeen 83 C10
Buckshaw Village Lancs 50 G1
Buckskin Hants 18 F3
Buckton E Yorks 53 B7
Buckton Hereford 25 A10
Buckton Northumb 71 G9
Buckworth Cambs 37 H7
Budbrooke Warks 27 B9
Budby Notts 45 F10
Budd's Titson Corn 4 A3
Bude Corn 6 F1
Budlake Devon 7 G8
Budle Northumb 71 G10
Budleigh Salterton Devon 7 H9
Budock Water Corn 3 F6
Buerton Ches E 34 A2
Buffler's Holt Bucks 28 E3
Bugbrooke Northants 28 C3
Buglawton Ches E 44 F2
Bugle Corn 3 D9
Bugley Wilts 16 G5
Bugthorpe E Yorks 52 D3
Buildwas Shrops 34 E2
Builth Road Powys 25 C7
Builth Wells = Llanfair-ym-Muallt Powys 25 C7
Buirgh W Isles 90 H5
Bulby Lincs 37 C6
Bulcote Notts 36 A2
Buldoo Highld 93 C12
Bulford Wilts 17 G8
Bulford Camp Wilts 17 G8
Bulkeley Ches E 43 G8
Bulkington Warks 35 G9
Bulkington Wilts 16 F6
Bulkworthy Devon 6 E2
Bull Hill Hants 10 E2
Bullamoor N Yorks 58 G4
Bullbridge Derbys 45 G7
Bullbrook Brack 18 E5
Bulley Glos 26 G4
Bullgill Cumb 56 C2
Bullington Hants 17 G11
Bullington Lincs 46 E4
Bull's Green Herts 29 G9
Bullwood Argyll 73 F10
Bulmer Essex 30 D5
Bulmer N Yorks 52 C2
Bulmer Tye Essex 30 E5
Bulphan Thurrock 20 C3
Bulverhythe E Sus 13 F6
Bulwark Aberds 89 D9
Bulwell Nottingham 45 H9
Bulwick Northants 36 F5
Bumble's Green Essex 29 H11
Bun Abhainn Eadarra W Isles 90 G6
Bun a'Mhuillin W Isles 84 G2
Bun Loyne Highld 80 C4
Bunacaimb Highld 79 C9
Bunarkaig Highld 80 E3
Bunbury Ches E 43 G8
Bunbury Heath Ches E 43 G8
Bunchrew Highld 87 G9
Bundalloch Highld 85 F13
Buness Shetland 96 C8
Bunessan Argyll 78 J6
Bungay Suff 39 G9
Bunker's Hill Lincs 46 E3
Bunker's Hill Lincs 46 G6
Bunkers Hill Oxon 27 G11
Bunloit Highld 81 A7
Bunnahabhain Argyll 64 A5
Bunny Notts 36 C1
Buntait Highld 86 H6
Buntingford Herts 29 F10
Bunwell Norf 39 F7
Burbage Derbys 44 E4
Burbage Leics 35 F10
Burbage Wilts 17 E9
Burchett's Green Windsor 18 C5
Burcombe Wilts 9 A9
Burcot Oxon 18 B2
Burcott Bucks 28 F5
Burdon T&W 58 A4
Bures Suff 30 E6
Bures Green Suff 30 E6
Burford Ches E 43 G9
Burford Oxon 27 G9
Burford Shrops 26 B2
Burg Argyll 78 G6
Burgar Orkney 95 F4
Burgate Hants 9 C10
Burgate Suff 39 H6
Burgess Hill W Sus 12 E2
Burgh Suff 31 C9
Burgh by Sands Cumb 61 H9
Burgh Castle Norf 39 E10
Burgh Heath Sur 19 F9
Burgh le Marsh Lincs 47 F9
Burgh Muir Aberds 83 A9
Burgh next Aylsham Norf 39 C8
Burgh on Bain Lincs 46 D6
Burgh St Margaret Norf 39 D10
Burgh St Peter Norf 39 F10
Burghclere Hants 17 E11
Burghead Moray 87 E14
Burghfield W Berks 18 E3
Burghfield Common W Berks 18 E3
Burghfield Hill W Berks 18 E3
Burghill Hereford 25 D11
Burghwallis S Yorks 45 A9
Burham Kent 20 E4
Buriton Hants 10 B6
Burland Ches E 43 G9
Burlawn Corn 3 B8
Burleigh Brack 18 E5
Burlescombe Devon 7 E9
Burleston Dorset 9 E6
Burley Hants 9 D11
Burley Rutland 36 D4
Burley W Yorks 51 F8
Burley Gate Hereford 26 D2
Burley in Wharfedale W Yorks 51 E7
Burley Lodge Hants 9 D11
Burley Street Hants 9 D11
Burleydam Ches E 34 A2
Burlingjobb Powys 25 C9
Burlow E Sus 12 E4
Burlton Shrops 33 C10
Burmarsh Kent 13 C9
Burmington Warks 27 E9
Burn N Yorks 52 G1
Burn of Cambus Stirling 75 G10
Burnaston Derbys 35 B8
Burnbank S Lanark 68 E6
Burnby E Yorks 52 E4
Burncross S Yorks 45 C7
Burneside Cumb 57 G7
Burness Orkney 95 D7
Burneston N Yorks 58 H4
Burnett Bath 16 E3
Burnfoot Borders 61 B11
Burnfoot Borders 61 B10
Burnfoot E Ayrs 67 F7
Burnfoot Perth 76 G2
Burnham Bucks 18 C6
Burnham N Lincs 53 H6
Burnham Deepdale Norf 38 A4
Burnham Green Herts 29 G9
Burnham Market Norf 38 A4
Burnham Norton Norf 38 A4
Burnham-on-Crouch Essex 20 B6
Burnham-on-Sea Som 15 G9
Burnham Overy Staithe Norf 38 A4
Burnham Overy Town Norf 38 A4
Burnham Thorpe Norf 38 A4
Burnhead Dumfries 60 D4
Burnhead S Ayrs 66 F5
Burnhervie Aberds 83 B9
Burnhill Green Staffs 34 E3
Burnhope Durham 58 B2
Burnhouse N Ayrs 67 A6
Burniston N Yorks 59 G11
Burnlee W Yorks 44 B5
Burnley Lancs 50 F4
Burnley Lane Lancs 50 F4
Burnmouth Borders 71 D8
Burnopfield Durham 63 H7
Burnsall N Yorks 50 C6
Burnside Angus 77 B8
Burnside E Ayrs 67 E8
Burnside Fife 76 G4
Burnside S Lanark 68 D5
Burnside Shetland 96 F4
Burnside W Loth 69 C9
Burnside of Duntrune Angus 77 D7
Burnswark Dumfries 61 F7
Burnt Heath Derbys 44 E6
Burnt Houses Durham 58 D2
Burnt Yates N Yorks 51 C8
Burntcommon Sur 19 F7
Burnthouse Corn 3 F6
Burntisland Fife 69 B11
Burnton E Ayrs 67 F7
Burntwood Staffs 35 E6
Burnwynd Edin 69 D10
Burpham Sur 19 F7
Burpham W Sus 11 D9
Burradon Northumb 62 C5
Burradon T&W 63 F8
Burrafirth Shetland 96 B8
Burraland Shetland 96 F5
Burraland Shetland 96 J4
Burras Corn 2 F5
Burravoe Shetland 96 F7
Burravoe Shetland 96 G5
Burray Village Orkney 95 J5
Burrells Cumb 57 E8
Burrelton Perth 76 D5
Burridge Devon 6 C4
Burridge Hants 10 C4
Burrill N Yorks 58 H3
Burringham N Lincs 46 B2
Burrington Devon 6 E5
Burrington Hereford 25 A11
Burrington N Som 15 F10
Burrough Green Cambs 30 C3
Burrough on the Hill Leics 36 D3
Burrow-bridge Som 8 B2
Burrowhill Sur 18 E6
Burry Swansea 23 G9
Burry Green Swansea 23 G9
Burry Port = Porth Tywyn Carms 23 F9
Burscough Lancs 43 A7
Burscough Bridge Lancs 43 A7
Bursea E Yorks 52 F4
Burshill E Yorks 53 E6
Bursledon Hants 10 D3
Burslem Stoke 44 H2
Burstall Suff 31 D7
Burstock Dorset 8 D3
Burston Norf 39 G7
Burston Staffs 34 B5
Burstow Sur 12 B2
Burstwick E Yorks 53 G8
Burtersett N Yorks 57 H10
Burtle Som 15 G9
Burton Ches W 42 E6
Burton Ches W 43 F8
Burton Dorset 9 E10
Burton Lincs 46 E3
Burton Northumb 71 G10
Burton Pembs 22 F4
Burton Som 7 B10
Burton Wilts 16 D5
Burton Agnes E Yorks 53 C7
Burton Bradstock Dorset 8 F3
Burton Dassett Warks 27 C10
Burton Fleming E Yorks 53 B6
Burton Green W Mid 35 H8
Burton Green Wrex 42 G6
Burton Hastings Warks 35 F10
Burton-in-Kendal Cumb 49 B5
Burton in Lonsdale N Yorks 50 B2
Burton Joyce Notts 36 A2
Burton Latimer Northants 28 A6
Burton Lazars Leics 36 D3
Burton-le-Coggles Lincs 36 C5
Burton Leonard N Yorks 51 C9
Burton on the Wolds Leics 36 C1
Burton Overy Leics 36 F2
Burton Pedwardine Lincs 37 A7
Burton Pidsea E Yorks 53 F8
Burton Salmon N Yorks 51 G10
Burton Stather N Lincs 52 H4
Burton upon Stather N Lincs 52 H4
Burton upon Trent Staffs 35 C8
Burtonwood Warr 43 C8
Burwardsley Ches W 43 G8
Burwarton Shrops 34 G2
Burwash E Sus 12 D5
Burwash Common E Sus 12 D5
Burwash Weald E Sus 12 D5
Burwell Cambs 30 B2
Burwell Lincs 47 E7
Burwen Anglesey 40 A6
Burwick Orkney 95 K5
Bury Cambs 37 G8
Bury Gtr Man 44 A2
Bury Som 7 D8
Bury W Sus 11 C9
Bury Green Herts 29 F11
Bury St Edmunds Suff 30 B5
Burythorpe N Yorks 52 C3
Busby E Renf 68 E4
Buscot Oxon 17 B9
Bush Bank Hereford 25 C11
Bush Crathie Aberds 82 D4
Bush Green Norf 39 G8
Bushbury W Mid 34 E5
Bushby Leics 36 E2
Bushey Herts 19 B8
Bushey Heath Herts 19 B8
Bushley Worcs 26 E5
Bushton Wilts 17 D7
Buslingthorpe Lincs 46 D4
Busta Shetland 96 G5
Butcher's Cross E Sus 12 D4
Butcombe N Som 15 E11
Butetown Cardiff 15 D7
Butleigh Som 8 A4
Butleigh Wootton Som 15 H11
Butler's Cross Bucks 28 H5
Butler's End Warks 35 G8
Butlers Marston Warks 27 C11
Butley Suff 31 C10
Butley High Corner Suff 31 D10
Butt Green Ches E 43 G9
Butterburn Cumb 62 F2
Buttercrambe N Yorks 52 D3
Butterknowle Durham 58 D2
Butterleigh Devon 7 F8
Buttermere Cumb 56 E3
Buttermere Wilts 17 E10
Buttershaw W Yorks 51 G7
Butterstone Perth 76 C3
Butterton Staffs 44 G4
Butterwick Durham 58 D4
Butterwick Lincs 47 H7
Butterwick N Yorks 52 B5
Butterwick N Yorks 52 B3
Buttington Powys 33 E8
Buttonoak Worcs 34 H3
Butt's Green Hants 10 B2
Buttsash Hants 10 D3
Buxhall Suff 31 C7
Buxhall Fen Street Suff 31 C7
Buxley Borders 71 E7
Buxted E Sus 12 D3
Buxton Derbys 44 E4
Buxton Norf 39 C8
Buxworth Derbys 44 D4
Bwcle = Buckley Flint 42 F5
Bwlch Powys 25 F8
Bwlch-Llan Ceredig 23 A10
Bwlch-y-cibau Powys 33 D7
Bwlch-y-fadfa Ceredig 23 B9
Bwlch-y-ffridd Powys 33 F6
Bwlch-y-sarnau Powys 25 A7
Bwlchgwyn Wrex 42 G5
Bwlchnewydd Carms 23 D8
Bwlchtocyn Gwyn 40 H5
Bwlchyddar Powys 33 C7
Bwlchygroes Pembs 23 C7
Byermoor T&W 63 H7
Byers Green Durham 58 C3
Byfield Northants 28 C2
Byfleet Sur 19 E7
Byford Hereford 25 D10
Bygrave Herts 29 E9
Byker T&W 63 G8
Bylchau Conwy 42 F2
Byley Ches W 43 F10
Bynea Carms 23 G10
Byrness Northumb 62 C3
Bythorn Cambs 37 H6
Byton Hereford 25 B10
Byworth W Sus 11 B8

C

Cabharstadh W Isles 91 E8
Cablea Perth 76 D2
Cabourne Lincs 46 B5
Cabrach Argyll 72 G3
Cabrach Moray 82 A5
Cabrich Highld 87 G8
Cabus Lancs 49 E4
Cackle Street E Sus 12 D3
Cadbury Devon 7 F8
Cadbury Barton Devon 6 E5
Cadder E Dunb 68 C5
Caddington C Beds 29 G7
Caddonfoot Borders 70 G3
Cade Street E Sus 12 D5
Cadeby Leics 35 E10
Cadeby S Yorks 45 B9
Cadeleigh Devon 7 F8
Cadgwith Corn 2 H6
Cadham Fife 76 G5
Cadishead Gtr Man 43 C10
Cadle Swansea 14 B2
Cadley Lancs 49 F5
Cadley Wilts 17 E9
Cadley Wilts 17 F9
Cadmore End Bucks 18 B4
Cadnam Hants 10 C1
Cadney N Lincs 46 B4
Cadole Flint 42 F5
Cadoxton V Glam 15 E7
Cadoxton-Juxta-Neath Neath 14 B3
Cadshaw Blackburn 50 H3
Cadzow S Lanark 68 E6
Caeathro Gwyn 41 D7
Caehopkin Powys 24 G5
Caenby Lincs 46 D4
Caenby Corner Lincs 46 D3
Caér-bryn Carms 23 E10
Caer Llan Mon 25 H11
Caerau Bridgend 14 B4
Caerau Cardiff 15 D7
Caerdeon Gwyn 32 D2
Caerdydd = Cardiff Cardiff 15 D7
Caerfarchell Pembs 22 D2
Caerffili = Caerphilly Caerph 15 C7
Caerfyrddin = Carmarthen Carms 23 D9
Caergeiliog Anglesey 40 C5
Caergwrle Flint 42 G6
Caergybi = Holyhead Anglesey 40 B4
Caerleon = Caerllion Newport 15 B9
Caerllion = Caerleon Newport 15 B9
Caernarfon Gwyn 40 D6
Caerphilly = Caerffili Caerph 15 C7
Caersws Powys 32 F6
Caerwedros Ceredig 23 A8
Caerwent Mon 15 B10
Caerwych Gwyn 41 G8
Caerwys Flint 42 E4
Caethle Gwyn 32 F2
Caim Anglesey 41 B8
Caio Carms 24 E3
Cairinis W Isles 84 B3
Cairisiadar W Isles 90 D5
Cairminis W Isles 90 J5
Cairnbaan Argyll 73 D7
Cairnbanno Ho. Aberds 89 D8
Cairnborrow Aberds 88 D4
Cairnbrogie Aberds 89 F8
Cairnbulg Castle Aberds 89 B10
Cairncross Angus 82 F6
Cairncross Borders 71 D7
Cairndow Argyll 74 F4
Cairness Aberds 89 B10
Cairneyhill Fife 69 B9
Cairnfield Ho. Moray 88 B4
Cairngaan Dumfries 54 F4
Cairngarroch Dumfries 54 E3
Cairnhill Aberds 89 E6
Cairnie Aberds 83 C10
Cairnie Aberds 88 D4
Cairnorrie Aberds 89 D8
Cairnpark Aberds 83 B10
Cairnryan Dumfries 54 C3
Cairnton Orkney 95 H4
Caister-on-Sea Norf 39 D11
Caistor Lincs 46 B5
Caistor St Edmund Norf 39 E8
Caistron Northumb 62 C5
Caitha Bowland Borders 70 F3
Calais Street Suff 30 E6
Calanais W Isles 90 D7
Calbost W Isles 91 F9
Calbourne IoW 10 F3
Calceby Lincs 47 E7
Calcot Row W Berks 18 D3
Calcott Kent 21 E8
Caldback Shetland 96 C8
Caldbeck Cumb 56 C5
Caldbergh N Yorks 58 H1
Caldecote Cambs 29 C10
Caldecote Cambs 37 G7
Caldecote Herts 29 E9
Caldecote Northants 28 C3
Caldecott Northants 28 B6
Caldecott Oxon 17 B11
Caldecott Rutland 36 F4
Calder Bridge Cumb 56 F2
Calder Hall Cumb 56 F2
Calder Mains Highld 94 E2
Calder Vale Lancs 49 E5
Calderbank N Lanark 68 D6
Calderbrook Gtr Man 50 H5
Caldercruix N Lanark 69 D7
Caldermill S Lanark 68 F5
Calderwood S Lanark 68 E5
Caldhame Angus 77 C7
Caldicot Mon 15 C10
Caldwell Derbys 35 D8
Caldwell N Yorks 58 E2
Caldy Mers 42 D5
Caledrhydiau Ceredig 23 A9
Calfsound Orkney 95 E6
Calgary Argyll 78 F6
Califer Moray 87 F13
California Falk 69 C8
California Norf 39 D11
Calke Derbys 35 C9
Callakille Highld 85 C11
Callaly Northumb 62 C6
Callander Stirling 75 G9
Callaughton Shrops 34 F2
Callestick Corn 3 D6
Calligarry Highld 85 H11
Callington Corn 4 E4
Callow Hereford 25 E11
Callow End Worcs 26 D5
Callow Hill Wilts 17 C7
Callow Hill Worcs 26 A4
Callows Grave Worcs 26 B2
Calmore Hants 10 C2
Calmsden Glos 27 H7
Calne Wilts 17 D7
Calow Derbys 45 E8
Calshot Hants 10 D3
Calstock Corn 4 E5
Calstone Wellington Wilts 17 E7
Calthorpe Norf 39 B7
Calthwaite Cumb 56 B6
Calton N Yorks 50 D5
Calton Staffs 44 G5
Calveley Ches E 43 G8
Calver Derbys 44 E6
Calver Hill Hereford 25 D10
Calverhall Shrops 34 B2
Calverleigh Devon 7 E8
Calverley W Yorks 51 F8
Calvert Bucks 28 F3
Calverton M Keynes 28 E4
Calverton Notts 45 H10
Calvine Perth 81 G10
Calvo Cumb 56 A3
Cam Glos 16 B4
Camas-luinie Highld 80 A1
Camasnacroise Highld 79 F11
Camastianavaig Highld 85 E10
Camasunary Highld 85 G10
Camault Muir Highld 87 G8
Camb Shetland 96 D7
Camber E Sus 13 E8
Camberley Sur 18 E5
Camberwell London 19 D10
Camblesforth N Yorks 52 G2
Cambo Northumb 62 E6
Cambois Northumb 63 E9
Camborne Corn 2 E5
Cambourne Cambs 29 C10
Cambridge Cambs 29 C11
Cambridge Glos 16 A4
Cambridge Town Southend 20 C6
Cambus Clack 69 A7
Cambusavie Farm Highld 87 B10
Cambusbarron Stirling 68 A6
Cambuskenneth Stirling 69 A7
Cambuslang S Lanark 68 D5
Cambusmore Lodge Highld 87 B10
Camden London 19 C9
Camelford Corn 4 C2
Camelsdale Sur 11 A7
Camerory Highld 87 H13
Camer's Green Worcs 26 E4
Camerton Bath 16 F3
Camerton Cumb 56 C2
Camerton E Yorks 53 G8
Camghouran Perth 75 B8
Cammachmore Aberds 83 D11
Cammeringham Lincs 46 D3
Camore Highld 87 B10
Camp Hill Warks 35 F9
Campbeltown Argyll 65 F8
Camperdown T&W 63 F8
Campmuir Perth 76 D5
Campsall S Yorks 45 A9
Campsey Ash Suff 31 C10
Campton C Beds 29 E8
Camptown Borders 62 B2
Camrose Pembs 22 D4
Camserney Perth 75 C11
Camster Highld 94 F4
Camuschoirk Highld 79 E10
Camuscross Highld 85 G11
Camusnagaul Highld 80 F2
Camusnagaul Highld 86 C3
Camusrory Highld 79 B11
Camusteel Highld 85 D12
Camusterrach Highld 85 D12
Camusvrachan Perth 75 C9
Canada Hants 10 C1
Canadia E Sus 12 E6
Canal Side S Yorks 45 A10
Candacraig Ho. Aberds 82 B5
Candlesby Lincs 47 F8
Candy Mill S Lanark 69 F9
Cane End Oxon 18 D3
Canewdon Essex 20 B5
Canford Bottom Dorset 9 D9
Canford Cliffs Poole 9 F9
Canford Magna Poole 9 E9
Canham's Green Suff 31 B7
Canholes Derbys 44 E4
Canisbay Highld 94 C5
Cann Dorset 9 B7
Cann Common Dorset 9 B7
Cannard's Grave Som 16 G3
Cannich Highld 86 H6
Cannington Som 15 H8
Cannock Staffs 34 E5
Cannock Wood Staffs 34 D6
Canon Bridge Hereford 25 D11
Canon Frome Hereford 26 D3
Canon Pyon Hereford 25 D11
Canonbie Dumfries 61 F9
Canons Ashby Northants 28 C2
Canonstown Corn 2 F4
Canterbury Kent 21 F8
Cantley Norf 39 E9
Cantley S Yorks 45 B10
Cantlop Shrops 33 E11
Canton Cardiff 15 D7
Cantraybruich Highld 87 G10
Cantraydoune Highld 87 G10
Cantraywood Highld 87 G10
Cantsfield Lancs 50 B2
Canvey Island Essex 20 C4
Canwick Lincs 46 F3
Canworthy Water Corn 4 B3
Caol Highld 80 F3
Caol Ila Argyll 64 A5
Caolas Argyll 78 G3
Caolas Scalpaigh W Isles 90 H7
Caolas Stocinis W Isles 90 H6
Capel Sur 19 G8
Capel Bangor Ceredig 32 G2
Capel Betws Lleucu Ceredig 24 C3
Capel Carmel Gwyn 40 H3
Capel Coch Anglesey 40 B6
Capel Curig Conwy 41 E9
Capel Cynon Ceredig 23 B8
Capel Dewi Carms 23 D9
Capel Dewi Ceredig 23 B9
Capel Dewi Ceredig 32 G2
Capel Garmon Conwy 41 E10
Capel-gwyn Anglesey 40 C5
Capel Gwyn Carms 23 D9
Capel Gwynfe Carms 24 F4
Capel Hendre Carms 23 E10
Capel Hermon Gwyn 32 C3
Capel Isaac Carms 23 D10
Capel Iwan Carms 23 C7
Capel le Ferne Kent 21 H9
Capel Llanilltern Cardiff 14 C6
Capel Mawr Anglesey 40 C6
Capel St Andrew Suff 31 D10
Capel St Mary Suff 31 E7
Capel Seion Ceredig 32 H2
Capel Tygwydd Ceredig 23 B7
Capel Uchaf Gwyn 40 F6
Capel-y-graig Gwyn 41 D7
Capelulo Conwy 41 C9
Capenhurst Ches W 42 E6
Capernwray Lancs 49 B5
Capheaton Northumb 62 E6
Cappercleuch Borders 61 A8
Capplegill Dumfries 61 C7
Capton Devon 5 F9
Caputh Perth 76 D3
Car Colston Notts 36 A3
Carbis Bay Corn 2 F4
Carbost Highld 85 D9
Carbost Highld 85 E8
Carbrook S Yorks 45 D7
Carbrooke Norf 38 E5
Carburton Notts 45 E10
Carcant Borders 70 E2
Carcary Angus 77 B9
Carclaze Corn 3 D9
Carcroft S Yorks 45 A9
Cardenden Fife 69 A11
Cardeston Shrops 33 D9
Cardiff = Caerdydd Cardiff 15 D7
Cardigan = Aberteifi Ceredig 22 B6
Cardington Bedford 29 D7
Cardington Shrops 33 F11
Cardinham Corn 4 E2
Cardonald Glasgow 68 D4
Cardow Moray 88 D1
Cardrona Borders 70 G2
Cardross Argyll 68 C2
Cardurnock Cumb 61 H7
Careby Lincs 36 D6
Careston Castle Angus 77 B8
Carew Pembs 22 F5
Carew Cheriton Pembs 22 F5
Carew Newton Pembs 22 F5
Carey Hereford 26 E2
Carfrae E Loth 70 D4
Cargenbridge Dumfries 60 F5
Cargill Perth 76 D4
Cargo Cumb 61 H9
Cargreen Corn 4 E5
Carham Northumb 71 G7
Carhampton Som 7 B9
Carharrack Corn 2 E6
Carie Perth 75 B9
Carie Perth 75 D9
Carines Corn 3 D6
Carisbrooke IoW 10 F3
Cark Cumb 49 B3
Carlabhagh W Isles 90 C7
Carland Cross Corn 3 D7
Carlby Lincs 37 D6
Carlecotes S Yorks 44 B5
Carlesmoor N Yorks 51 B7
Carleton Cumb 56 A6
Carleton Cumb 57 D7
Carleton Lancs 49 F3
Carleton N Yorks 50 E5
Carleton Forehoe Norf 39 E6
Carleton Rode Norf 39 F7
Carlin How Redcar 59 E8
Carlingcott Bath 16 F3
Carlisle Cumb 61 H10
Carlops Borders 69 E10
Carlton Bedford 28 C6
Carlton Cambs 30 C3
Carlton Leics 35 E9
Carlton N Yorks 51 A6
Carlton N Yorks 52 G2
Carlton N Yorks 58 E2
Carlton N Yorks 59 H7
Carlton Notts 36 A2
Carlton S Yorks 45 A7
Carlton Stockton 58 D4
Carlton Suff 31 B10
Carlton W Yorks 51 G9
Carlton Colville Suff 39 G11
Carlton Curlieu Leics 36 F2
Carlton Husthwaite N Yorks 51 B10
Carlton in Cleveland N Yorks 58 F6
Carlton in Lindrick Notts 45 D9
Carlton le Moorland Lincs 46 G3
Carlton Miniott N Yorks 51 A9
Carlton on Trent Notts 45 F11
Carlton Scroop Lincs 36 A5
Carluke S Lanark 69 E7
Carmarthen = Caerfyrddin Carms 23 D9
Carmel Anglesey 40 B5
Carmel Carms 23 E10
Carmel Flint 42 E4
Carmel Guern 11
Carmel Gwyn 40 E6
Carmont Aberds 83 E10
Carmunnock Glasgow 68 E5
Carmyle Glasgow 68 D5
Carmyllie Angus 77 C8
Carn-gorm Highld 80 A1
Carnaby E Yorks 53 C7
Carnach Highld 80 A2
Carnach Highld 86 B3
Carnach W Isles 90 H7
Carnachy Highld 93 D10
Càrnais W Isles 90 D5
Carnbee Fife 77 G8
Carnbo Perth 76 G3
Carnbrea Corn 2 E5
Carnduff S Lanark 68 F5
Carnduncan Argyll 64 B3
Carne Corn 3 F8
Carnforth Lancs 49 B4
Carnhedryn Pembs 22 D3
Carnhell Green Corn 2 F5
Carnkie Corn 2 F5
Carnkie Corn 2 F6
Carno Powys 32 F5
Carnoch Highld 86 F5
Carnoch Highld 86 H6
Carnock Fife 69 B9
Carnon Downs Corn 3 E6
Carnousie Aberds 89 C6
Carnoustie Angus 77 D8
Carnwath S Lanark 69 F8
Carnyorth Corn 2 F2
Carperby N Yorks 58 H1
Carpley Green N Yorks 57 H11
Carr S Yorks 45 C9
Carr Hill T&W 63 G8
Carradale Argyll 65 E9
Carragraich W Isles 90 H6
Carrbridge Highld 81 A11
Carrefour Selous Jersey 11
Carreg-wen Pembs 23 B7
Carreglefn Anglesey 40 B5
Carrick Argyll 73 E8
Carrick Fife 77 E7
Carrick Castle Argyll 73 D10
Carrick Ho. Orkney 95 E6
Carriden Falk 69 B9
Carrington Gtr Man 43 C10
Carrington Lincs 47 G7
Carrington Midloth 70 D2
Carrog Conwy 41 F9
Carrog Denb 33 A7
Carron Falk 69 B7
Carron Moray 88 D2
Carron Bridge Stirling 68 B6
Carronbridge Dumfries 60 D4
Carronshore Falk 69 B7
Carrshield Northumb 57 B10
Carrutherstown Dumfries 61 F7
Carrville Durham 58 B4
Carsaig Argyll 72 E6
Carsaig Argyll 79 J8
Carscreugh Dumfries 54 D5
Carse Gray Angus 77 B7
Carse Ho. Argyll 72 G6
Carsegowan Dumfries 55 D7
Carseriggan Dumfries 54 C6
Carsethorn Dumfries 60 H5
Carshalton London 19 E9
Carsington Derbys 44 G6
Carskiey Argyll 65 H7
Carsluith Dumfries 55 D7
Carsphairn Dumfries 67 G8
Carstairs S Lanark 69 F8
Carstairs Junction S Lanark 69 F8
Carswell Marsh Oxon 17 B10
Carter's Clay Hants 10 B2
Carterton Oxon 27 H9
Carterway Heads Northumb 58 A1
Carthew Corn 3 D9
Carthorpe N Yorks 51 A9
Cartington Northumb 62 C6
Cartland S Lanark 69 F7
Cartmel Cumb 49 B3
Cartmel Fell Cumb 56 H6
Carway Carms 23 F9
Cary Fitzpaine Som 8 B4
Cas-gwent = Chepstow Mon 15 B11
Cascob Powys 25 B9
Cashlie Perth 75 C7
Cashmoor Dorset 9 C8
Casnewydd = Newport Newport 15 C9
Cassey Compton Glos 27 G7
Cassington Oxon 27 G11
Cassop Durham 58 C4
Castell Denb 42 F4
Castell-Howell Ceredig 23 B9

Castell-Nedd = Neath Neath 14 B3
Castell Newydd Emlyn = Newcastle Emlyn Carms 23 B8
Castell-y-bwch Torf 15 B8
Castellau Rhondda 14 C6
Casterton Cumb 50 B2
Castle Acre Norf 38 D4
Castle Ashby Northants 28 C5
Castle Bolton N Yorks 58 G1
Castle Bromwich W Mid 35 G7
Castle Bytham Lincs 36 D5
Castle Caereinion Powys 33 E7
Castle Camps Cambs 30 D3
Castle Carrock Cumb 61 H11
Castle Cary Som 8 A5
Castle Combe Wilts 16 D5
Castle Donington Leics 35 C10
Castle Douglas Dumfries 55 C10
Castle Eaton Swindon 17 B8
Castle Eden Durham 58 C5
Castle Forbes Aberds 83 B8
Castle Frome Hereford 26 D3
Castle Green Sur 18 E6
Castle Gresley Derbys 35 D8
Castle Heaton Northumb 71 F8
Castle Hedingham Essex 30 E4
Castle Hill Kent 12 B5
Castle Huntly Perth 76 E6
Castle Kennedy Dumfries 54 D4
Castle O'er Dumfries 61 D8
Castle Pulverbatch Shrops 33 E10
Castle Rising Norf 38 C2
Castle Stuart Highld 87 G10
Castlebay = Bagh a Chaisteil W Isles 84 J1
Castlebythe Pembs 22 D5
Castlecary N Lanark 68 C6
Castlecraig Highld 87 E11
Castlefairn Dumfries 60 E3
Castleford W Yorks 51 G10
Castlehill Borders 69 G11
Castlehill Highld 94 D3
Castlehill W Dunb 68 C2
Castlemaddy Dumfries 67 H8
Castlemartin Pembs 22 G4
Castlemilk Dumfries 61 F7
Castlemilk Glasgow 68 E5
Castlemorris Pembs 22 C4
Castlemorton Worcs 26 E4
Castleside Durham 58 B1
Castlethorpe M Keynes 28 D5
Castleton Angus 76 C6
Castleton Argyll 73 E7
Castleton Derbys 44 D5
Castleton Gtr Man 44 A2
Castleton N Yorks 59 F7
Castleton Newport 15 C8
Castletown Ches W 43 G7
Castletown Highld 87 G10
Castletown Highld 94 D3
Castletown IoM 48 F2
Castletown T&W 63 H9
Castleweary Borders 61 C10
Castley N Yorks 51 E8
Caston Norf 38 F5
Castor Pboro 37 F7
Catacol N Ayrs 66 B2
Catbrain S Glos 16 C2
Catbrook Mon 15 A11
Catchall Corn 2 G3
Catchems Corner W Mid 35 H8
Catchgate Durham 58 A2
Catcleugh Northumb 62 C3
Catcliffe S Yorks 45 D8
Catcott Som 15 H9
Caterham Sur 19 F10
Catfield Norf 39 C9
Catfirth Shetland 96 H6
Catford London 19 D10
Catforth Lancs 49 F4
Cathays Cardiff 15 D7
Cathcart Glasgow 68 D4
Cathedine Powys 25 F8
Catherington Hants 10 C5
Catherton Shrops 34 H2
Catlodge Highld 81 D8
Catlowdy Cumb 61 F10
Catmore W Berks 17 C11
Caton Lancs 49 C5
Caton Green Lancs 49 C5
Catrine E Ayrs 67 D8
Cat's Ash Newport 15 B9
Catsfield E Sus 12 E6
Catshill Worcs 26 A6
Cattal N Yorks 51 D10
Cattawade Suff 31 E8
Catterall Lancs 49 E4
Catterick N Yorks 58 G3
Catterick Bridge N Yorks 58 G3
Catterick Garrison N Yorks 58 G2
Catterlen Cumb 57 C6
Catterline Aberds 83 F10
Catterton N Yorks 51 E11
Catthorpe Leics 36 H1
Cattistock Dorset 8 E4
Catton N Yorks 51 B9
Catton Northumb 62 H4
Catwick E Yorks 53 E7
Catworth Cambs 29 A7
Caudlesprings Norf 38 E5
Caulcott Oxon 28 F2
Cauldcots Angus 77 C9
Cauldhame Stirling 68 A5
Cauldmill Borders 61 B11
Cauldon Staffs 44 H4
Caulkerbush Dumfries 60 H5
Caulside Dumfries 61 E10
Caunsall Worcs 34 G4
Caunton Notts 45 G11
Causeway End Dumfries 55 C7
Causeway Foot W Yorks 51 F6
Causeway-head Stirling 75 H10
Causewayend S Lanark 69 G9
Causewayhead Cumb 56 A3
Causey Park Bridge Northumb 63 D7
Causeyend Aberds 83 B11
Cautley Cumb 57 G8
Cavendish Suff 30 D5
Cavendish Bridge Leics 35 C10
Cavenham Suff 30 B4
Caversfield Oxon 28 F2
Caversham Reading 18 D4
Caverswall Staffs 34 A5
Cavil E Yorks 52 F3
Cawdor Highld 87 F11
Cawkwell Lincs 46 E6
Cawood N Yorks 52 F1
Cawsand Corn 4 F5
Cawston Norf 39 C7
Cawthorne S Yorks 44 B6
Cawthorpe Lincs 37 C6
Cawton N Yorks 52 B2
Caxton Cambs 29 C10
Caynham Shrops 26 A2
Caythorpe Lincs 46 H3
Caythorpe Notts 45 H10
Cayton N Yorks 53 A6
Ceann a Bhaigh W Isles 84 B2
Ceann a Deas Loch Baghasdail W Isles 84 G2
Ceann Shiphoirt W Isles 91 F7
Ceann Tarabhaigh W Isles 90 F7
Ceannacroc Lodge Highld 80 B4
Cearsiadair W Isles 91 E8
Cefn Berain Conwy 42 F2
Cefn-brith Conwy 42 G2
Cefn Canol Powys 33 B8
Cefn-coch Conwy 41 D10
Cefn Coch Powys 33 C7
Cefn-coed-y-cymmer M Tydf 25 H7
Cefn Cribbwr Bridgend 14 C4
Cefn Cross Bridgend 14 C4
Cefn-ddwysarn Gwyn 32 B5
Cefn Einion Shrops 33 G8
Cefn-gorwydd Powys 24 D6
Cefn-mawr Wrex 33 A8
Cefn-y-bedd Flint 42 G6
Cefn-y-pant Carms 22 D6
Cefneithin Carms 23 E10
Cei-bach Ceredig 23 A9
Ceinewydd = New Quay Ceredig 23 A8
Ceint Anglesey 40 C6
Cellan Ceredig 24 D3
Cellarhead Staffs 44 H3
Cemaes Anglesey 40 A5
Cemmaes Powys 32 E4
Cemmaes Road Powys 32 E4
Cenarth Carms 23 B7
Cenin Gwyn 40 F6
Central Invclyd 73 F11
Ceos W Isles 91 E8
Ceres Fife 77 F7
Cerne Abbas Dorset 8 D5
Cerney Wick Glos 17 B7
Cerrigceinwen Anglesey 40 C6
Cerrigydrudion Conwy 42 H2
Cessford Borders 62 A3
Ceunant Gwyn 41 D7
Chaceley Glos 26 E5
Chacewater Corn 3 E6
Chackmore Bucks 28 E3
Chacombe Northants 27 D11
Chad Valley W Mid 34 G6
Chadderton Gtr Man 44 B3
Chadderton Fold Gtr Man 44 B2
Chaddesden Derby 35 B9
Chaddesley Corbett Worcs 26 A5
Chaddleworth W Berks 17 D11
Chadlington Oxon 27 F10
Chadshunt Warks 27 C10
Chadwell Leics 36 C3
Chadwell St Mary Thurrock 20 D3
Chadwick End W Mid 27 A9
Chadwick Green Mers 43 C8
Chaffcombe Som 8 C2
Chagford Devon 5 C8
Chailey E Sus 12 E2
Chain Bridge Lincs 37 A9
Chainbridge Cambs 37 E10
Chainhurst Kent 20 G4
Chalbury Dorset 9 D9
Chalbury Common Dorset 9 D9
Chaldon Sur 19 F10
Chaldon Herring Dorset 9 F6
Chale IoW 10 G3
Chale Green IoW 10 G3
Chalfont Common Bucks 19 B7
Chalfont St Giles Bucks 18 B6
Chalfont St Peter Bucks 19 B7
Chalford Glos 16 A5
Chalgrove Oxon 18 B3
Chalk Kent 20 D3
Challacombe Devon 6 B5
Challoch Dumfries 54 C6
Challock Kent 21 F7
Chalton C Beds 29 F7
Chalton Hants 10 C6
Chalvington E Sus 12 F4
Chancery Ceredig 32 H1
Chandler's Ford Hants 10 B3
Channel Tunnel Kent 21 H8
Channerwick Shetland 96 L6
Chantry Som 16 G4
Chantry Suff 31 D8
Chapel Fife 69 A11
Chapel Allerton Som 15 F10
Chapel Allerton W Yorks 51 F9
Chapel Amble Corn 3 B8
Chapel Brampton Northants 28 B4
Chapel Chorlton Staffs 34 B4
Chapel-en-le-Frith Derbys 44 D4
Chapel End Warks 35 F9
Chapel Green Warks 27 B11
Chapel Green Warks 35 G8
Chapel Haddlesey N Yorks 52 G1
Chapel Head Cambs 37 G9
Chapel Hill Aberds 89 E10
Chapel Hill Lincs 46 G6
Chapel Hill Mon 15 B11
Chapel Hill N Yorks 51 E9
Chapel Lawn Shrops 33 H9
Chapel-le-Dale N Yorks 50 B3
Chapel Milton Derbys 44 D4
Chapel of Garioch Aberds 83 A9
Chapel Row W Berks 18 E2
Chapel St Leonards Lincs 47 E9
Chapel Stile Cumb 56 F5
Chapelgate Lincs 37 C10
Chapelhall N Lanark 68 D6
Chapelhill Dumfries 60 D6
Chapelhill Highld 87 D11
Chapelhill N Ayrs 66 B5
Chapelhill Perth 76 D3
Chapelhill Perth 76 E5
Chapelknowe Dumfries 61 F9
Chapelton Angus 77 C9
Chapelton Devon 6 D4
Chapelton Highld 81 B11
Chapelton S Lanark 68 F5
Chapeltown Blackburn 50 H3
Chapeltown Moray 82 A4
Chapeltown S Yorks 45 C7
Chapmans Well Devon 6 G2
Chapmanslade Wilts 16 G5
Chapmore End Herts 29 G10
Chappel Essex 30 F5
Chard Som 8 D2
Chardstock Devon 8 D2
Charfield S Glos 16 B4
Charford Worcs 26 B6
Charing Kent 20 G6
Charing Cross Dorset 9 C10
Charing Heath Kent 20 G6
Charingworth Glos 27 E9
Charlbury Oxon 27 G10
Charlcombe Bath 16 E4
Charlecote Warks 27 C9
Charles Devon 6 C5
Charles Tye Suff 31 C7
Charlesfield Dumfries 61 G7
Charleston Angus 76 C6
Charleston Renfs 68 D3
Charlestown Aberdeen 83 C11
Charlestown Corn 3 D9
Charlestown Derbys 44 C4
Charlestown Dorset 8 G5
Charlestown Fife 69 B9
Charlestown Gtr Man 44 B2
Charlestown Highld 85 A13
Charlestown Highld 87 G9
Charlestown W Yorks 50 G5
Charlestown of Aberlour Moray 88 D2
Charlesworth Derbys 44 C4
Charleton Devon 5 G8
Charlton Hants 17 G10
Charlton Herts 29 F8
Charlton London 19 D11
Charlton Northants 28 E2
Charlton Northumb 62 E4
Charlton Som 16 F3
Charlton Telford 34 D1
Charlton W Sus 11 C7
Charlton Wilts 9 B8
Charlton Wilts 16 C6
Charlton Wilts 17 F8
Charlton Worcs 27 D7
Charlton Abbots Glos 27 F7
Charlton Adam Som 8 B4
Charlton-All-Saints Wilts 9 B10
Charlton Down Dorset 8 E5
Charlton Horethorne Som 8 B5
Charlton Kings Glos 26 F6
Charlton Mackerell Som 8 B4
Charlton Marshall Dorset 9 D7
Charlton Musgrove Som 8 B6
Charlton on Otmoor Oxon 28 G2
Charltons Redcar 59 E7
Charlwood Sur 19 G9
Charlynch Som 7 C11
Charminster Dorset 8 E5
Charmouth Dorset 8 E2
Charndon Bucks 28 F3
Charney Bassett Oxon 17 B10
Charnock Richard Lancs 50 H1
Charsfield Suff 31 C9
Chart Corner Kent 20 F4
Chart Sutton Kent 20 G5
Charter Alley Hants 18 F2
Charterhouse Som 15 F10
Charterville Allotments Oxon 27 G10
Chartham Kent 21 F8
Chartham Hatch Kent 21 F8
Chartridge Bucks 18 A6
Charvil Wokingham 18 D4
Charwelton Northants 28 C2
Chasetown Staffs 34 E6
Chastleton Oxon 27 F9
Chasty Devon 6 F2
Chatburn Lancs 50 E3
Chatcull Staffs 34 B3
Chatham Medway 20 E4
Chathill Northumb 71 H10
Chattenden Medway 20 D4
Chatteris Cambs 37 G9
Chattisham Suff 31 D7
Chatto Borders 62 B3
Chatton Northumb 71 H9
Chawleigh Devon 6 E6
Chawley Oxon 17 A11
Chawston Bedford 29 C8
Chawton Hants 18 H4
Cheadle Gtr Man 44 D2
Cheadle Staffs 34 A6
Cheadle Heath Gtr Man 44 D2
Cheadle Hulme Gtr Man 44 D2
Cheam London 19 E9
Cheapside Sur 19 F7
Chearsley Bucks 28 G4
Chebsey Staffs 34 C4
Checkendon Oxon 18 C3
Checkley Ches E 43 H10
Checkley Hereford 26 E2
Checkley Staffs 34 B6
Chedburgh Suff 30 C4
Cheddar Som 15 F10
Cheddington Bucks 28 G6
Cheddleton Staffs 44 G3
Cheddon Fitzpaine Som 8 B1
Chedglow Wilts 16 B6
Chedgrave Norf 39 F9
Chedington Dorset 8 D3
Chediston Suff 39 H9
Chedworth Glos 27 G7
Chedzoy Som 15 H9
Cheeklaw Borders 70 E6
Cheeseman's Green Kent 13 C9
Cheglinch Devon 6 B4
Cheldon Devon 7 E6
Chelford Ches E 44 E2
Chell Heath Stoke 44 G2
Chellaston Derby 35 B9
Chellington Bedford 28 C6
Chelmarsh Shrops 34 G3
Chelmer Village Essex 30 H4
Chelmondiston Suff 31 E9
Chelmorton Derbys 44 F5
Chelmsford Essex 30 H4
Chelsea London 19 D9
Chelsfield London 19 E11
Chelsworth Suff 30 D6
Cheltenham Glos 26 F6
Chelveston Northants 28 B6
Chelvey N Som 15 E10
Chelwood Bath 16 E3
Chelwood Common E Sus 12 D3
Chelwood Gate E Sus 12 D3
Chelworth Wilts 16 B6
Chelworth Green Wilts 17 B7
Chemistry Shrops 33 A11
Chenies Bucks 19 B7
Cheny Longville Shrops 33 G10
Chepstow = Cas-gwent Mon 15 B11
Chequerfield W Yorks 51 G10
Cherhill Wilts 17 D7
Cherington Glos 16 B6
Cherington Warks 27 E9
Cheriton Devon 7 B6
Cheriton Hants 10 B4
Cheriton Kent 21 H8
Cheriton Swansea 23 G9
Cheriton Bishop Devon 7 G6
Cheriton Fitzpaine Devon 7 F7
Cheriton or Stackpole Elidor Pembs 22 G4
Cherrington Telford 34 C2
Cherry Burton E Yorks 52 E5
Cherry Hinton Cambs 29 C11
Cherry Orchard Worcs 26 C5
Cherry Willingham Lincs 46 E4
Cherrybank Perth 76 E4
Chertsey Sur 19 E7
Cheselbourne Dorset 9 E6
Chesham Bucks 18 A6
Chesham Bois Bucks 18 B6
Cheshunt Herts 19 A10
Cheslyn Hay Staffs 34 E5
Chessington London 19 E8
Chester Ches W 43 F7
Chester-Le-Street Durham 58 A3
Chester Moor Durham 58 B3
Chesterblade Som 16 G3
Chesterfield Derbys 45 E7
Chesters Borders 62 A2
Chesters Borders 62 B2
Chesterton Cambs 29 B11
Chesterton Cambs 37 F7
Chesterton Glos 17 A7
Chesterton Oxon 28 F2
Chesterton Shrops 34 F3
Chesterton Staffs 44 H2
Chesterton Warks 27 C10
Chesterwood Northumb 62 G4
Chestfield Kent 21 E8
Cheston Devon 5 F7
Cheswardine Shrops 34 C3
Cheswick Northumb 71 F9
Chetnole Dorset 8 D5
Chettiscombe Devon 7 E8
Chettisham Cambs 37 G11
Chettle Dorset 9 C8
Chetton Shrops 34 F2
Chetwode Bucks 28 F3
Chetwynd Aston Telford 34 D3
Cheveley Cambs 30 B3
Chevening Kent 19 F11
Chevington Suff 30 C4
Chevithorne Devon 7 E8
Chew Magna Bath 16 E2
Chew Stoke Bath 16 E2
Chewton Keynsham Bath 16 E3
Chewton Mendip Som 16 F2
Chicheley M Keynes 28 D6
Chichester W Sus 11 D7
Chickerell Dorset 8 F5
Chicklade Wilts 9 A8
Chicksgrove Wilts 9 A8
Chidden Hants 10 C5
Chiddingfold Sur 18 H6
Chiddingly E Sus 12 E4
Chiddingstone Kent 19 G11
Chiddingstone Causeway Kent 20 G2
Chiddingstone Hoath Kent 12 B3
Chideock Dorset 8 E3
Chidham W Sus 11 D6
Chidswell W Yorks 51 G8
Chieveley W Berks 17 D11
Chignall St James Essex 30 H3
Chignall Smealy Essex 30 G3
Chigwell Essex 19 B11
Chigwell Row Essex 19 B11
Chilbolton Hants 17 H10
Chilcomb Hants 10 B4
Chilcombe Dorset 8 E4
Chilcompton Som 16 F3
Chilcote Leics 35 D8
Child Okeford Dorset 9 C7
Childer Thornton Ches W 42 E6
Childrey Oxon 17 C10
Child's Ercall Shrops 34 C2
Childswickham Worcs 27 E7
Childwall Mers 43 D7
Childwick Green Herts 29 G8
Chilfrome Dorset 8 E4
Chilgrove W Sus 11 C7
Chilham Kent 21 F7
Chilhampton Wilts 9 A9
Chilla Devon 6 F3
Chillaton Devon 4 C5
Chillenden Kent 21 F9
Chillerton IoW 10 F3
Chillesford Suff 31 C10
Chillingham Northumb 71 H9
Chillington Devon 5 G8
Chillington Som 8 C2
Chilmark Wilts 9 A8
Chilson Oxon 27 G10
Chilsworthy Corn 4 D5
Chilsworthy Devon 6 F2
Chilthorne Domer Som 8 C4
Chiltington E Sus 12 E2
Chilton Bucks 28 G3
Chilton Durham 58 D3
Chilton Oxon 17 C11
Chilton Cantelo Som 8 B4
Chilton Foliat Wilts 17 D10
Chilton Lane Durham 58 C4
Chilton Polden Som 15 H9
Chilton Street Suff 30 D4
Chilton Trinity Som 15 H8
Chilvers Coton Warks 35 F9
Chilwell Notts 35 B11
Chilworth Hants 10 C3
Chilworth Sur 19 G7
Chimney Oxon 17 A10
Chineham Hants 18 F3
Chingford London 19 B10
Chinley Derbys 44 D4
Chinley Head Derbys 44 D4
Chinnor Oxon 18 A4
Chipnall Shrops 34 B3
Chippenhall Green Suff 39 H8
Chippenham Cambs 30 B3
Chippenham Wilts 16 D6
Chipperfield Herts 19 A7
Chipping Herts 29 E10
Chipping Lancs 50 E2
Chipping Campden Glos 27 E8
Chipping Hill Essex 30 G5
Chipping Norton Oxon 27 F10
Chipping Ongar Essex 20 A2
Chipping Sodbury S Glos 16 C4
Chipping Warden Northants 27 D11
Chipstable Som 7 D9
Chipstead Kent 19 F11
Chipstead Sur 19 F9
Chirbury Shrops 33 F8
Chirk = Y Waun Wrex 33 B8
Chirk Bank Shrops 33 B8
Chirmorrie S Ayrs 54 B5
Chirnside Borders 71 E7
Chirnsidebridge Borders 71 E7
Chirton Wilts 17 F7
Chisbury Wilts 17 E9
Chiselborough Som 8 C3
Chiseldon Swindon 17 D8
Chiserley W Yorks 50 G6
Chislehampton Oxon 18 B2
Chislehurst London 19 D11
Chislet Kent 21 E9
Chiswell Green Herts 19 A8
Chiswick London 19 D9
Chiswick End Cambs 29 D10
Chisworth Derbys 44 C3
Chithurst W Sus 11 B7
Chittering Cambs 29 A11
Chitterne Wilts 16 G6
Chittlehamholt Devon 6 D5
Chittlehampton Devon 6 D5
Chittoe Wilts 16 E6
Chivenor Devon 6 C4
Chobham Sur 18 E6
Choicelee Borders 70 E6
Cholderton Wilts 17 G9
Cholesbury Bucks 28 H6
Chollerford Northumb 62 F5
Chollerton Northumb 62 F5
Cholmondeston Ches E 43 F9
Cholsey Oxon 18 C2
Cholstrey Hereford 25 C11
Chop Gate N Yorks 59 G6
Choppington Northumb 63 E8
Chopwell T&W 63 H7
Chorley Ches E 43 G8
Chorley Lancs 50 H1
Chorley Shrops 34 G2
Chorley Staffs 35 D6
Chorleywood Herts 19 B7
Chorlton cum Hardy Gtr Man 44 C2
Chorlton Lane Ches W 43 H7
Choulton Shrops 33 G9
Chowdene T&W 63 H8
Chowley Ches W 43 G7
Chrishall Essex 29 E11
Christchurch Cambs 37 F10
Christchurch Dorset 9 E10
Christchurch Glos 26 G2
Christchurch Newport 15 C9
Christian Malford Wilts 16 D6
Christleton Ches W 43 F7
Christmas Common Oxon 18 B4
Christon N Som 15 F9
Christon Bank Northumb 63 A8
Christow Devon 5 C9
Chryston N Lanark 68 C5
Chudleigh Devon 5 D9
Chudleigh Knighton Devon 5 D9
Chulmleigh Devon 6 E5
Chunal Derbys 44 C4
Church Lancs 50 G3
Church Aston Telford 34 D3
Church Brampton Northants 28 B4
Church Broughton Derbys 35 B8
Church Crookham Hants 18 F5
Church Eaton Staffs 34 D4
Church End C Beds 28 E6
Church End C Beds 28 F6
Church End C Beds 29 E8
Church End Cambs 37 E9
Church End Cambs 37 G8
Church End E Yorks 53 D6
Church End Essex 30 D2
Church End Essex 30 F4
Church End Hants 18 F3
Church End Lincs 37 B8
Church End Warks 35 F8
Church End Warks 35 F8
Church End Wilts 17 D7
Church Enstone Oxon 27 F10
Church Fenton N Yorks 51 F11
Church Green Devon 7 G10
Church Green Norf 39 F6
Church Gresley Derbys 35 D8
Church Hanborough Oxon 27 G11
Church Hill Ches W 43 F9
Church Houses N Yorks 59 G7
Church Knowle Dorset 9 F8
Church Laneham Notts 46 E2
Church Langton Leics 36 F3
Church Lawford Warks 35 H10
Church Lawton Ches E 44 G2
Church Leigh Staffs 34 B6
Church Lench Worcs 27 C7
Church Mayfield Staffs 35 A7
Church Minshull Ches E 43 F9
Church Norton W Sus 11 E7
Church Preen Shrops 33 F11
Church Pulverbatch Shrops 33 E10
Church Stoke Powys 33 F8
Church Stowe Northants 28 C3
Church Street Kent 20 D4
Church Stretton Shrops 33 F10
Church Town N Lincs 45 B11
Church Town Sur 19 F10
Church Village Rhondda 14 C6
Church Warsop Notts 45 F9
Churcham Glos 26 G4
Churchbank Shrops 33 H8
Churchbridge Staffs 34 E5
Churchdown Glos 26 G5
Churchend Essex 21 B7
Churchend Essex 30 F3
Churchend S Glos 16 B4
Churchfield W Mid 34 F6
Churchgate Street Essex 29 G11
Churchill Devon 6 B4
Churchill Devon 8 D2
Churchill N Som 15 F10
Churchill Oxon 27 F9
Churchill Worcs 26 C6
Churchill Worcs 34 H4
Churchinford Som 7 E11
Churchover Warks 35 G11
Churchstanton Som 7 E10
Churchstow Devon 5 G8
Churchtown Derbys 44 F6
Churchtown IoM 48 C4
Churchtown Lancs 49 E4
Churchtown Mers 49 H3
Churnsike Lodge Northumb 62 F2
Churston Ferrers Torbay 5 F10
Churt Sur 18 H5
Churton Ches W 43 G7
Churwell W Yorks 51 G8
Chute Standen Wilts 17 F10
Chwilog Gwyn 40 G6
Chyandour Corn 2 F3
Cilan Uchaf Gwyn 40 H4
Cilcain Flint 42 F4
Cilcennin Ceredig 24 B2
Cilfor Gwyn 41 G8
Cilfrew Neath 14 A3
Cilfynydd Rhondda 14 B6
Cilgerran Pembs 22 B6
Cilgwyn Carms 24 F4
Cilgwyn Gwyn 40 E6
Cilgwyn Pembs 22 C5
Ciliau Aeron Ceredig 23 A9
Cill Donnain W Isles 84 F2
Cille Bhrighde W Isles 84 G2
Cille Pheadair W Isles 84 G2
Cilmery Powys 25 C7
Cilsan Carms 23 D10
Ciltalgarth Gwyn 41 F10
Cilwendeg Pembs 23 C7
Cilybebyll Neath 14 A3
Cilycwm Carms 24 E4
Cimla Neath 14 B3
Cinderford Glos 26 G3
Cippyn Pembs 22 B6
Circebost W Isles 90 D6
Cirencester Glos 17 A7
Ciribhig W Isles 90 C6
City London 19 C10
City Powys 33 G8
City Dulas Anglesey 40 B6
Clachaig Argyll 73 E10
Clachan Argyll 72 B6
Clachan Argyll 72 H6
Clachan Argyll 74 F4
Clachan Argyll 79 G11
Clachan Highld 85 E10
Clachan W Isles 84 D2
Clachan na Luib W Isles 84 B3
Clachan of Campsie E Dunb 68 C5
Clachan of Glendaruel Argyll 73 E8
Clachan-Seil Argyll 72 B6
Clachan Strachur Argyll 73 C9
Clachaneasy Dumfries 54 B6
Clachanmore Dumfries 54 E3
Clachbreck Argyll 72 F6
Clachnabrain Angus 82 G5
Clachtoll Highld 92 G3
Clackmannan Clack 69 A8
Clacton-on-Sea Essex 31 G8
Cladach Chireboist W Isles 84 B2
Claddach-knockline W Isles 84 B2
Cladich Argyll 74 E3
Claggan Highld 79 G9
Claggan Highld 80 F3
Claigan Highld 84 C7
Claines Worcs 26 C5
Clandown Bath 16 F3
Clanfield Hants 10 C5
Clanfield Oxon 17 A9
Clanville Hants 17 G10
Claonaig Argyll 73 H7
Claonel Highld 93 J8
Clap Hill Kent 13 C9
Clapgate Dorset 9 D9
Clapgate Herts 29 F11
Clapham Bedford 29 C7
Clapham London 19 D9
Clapham N Yorks 50 C3
Clapham W Sus 11 D9
Clappers Borders 71 E8
Clappersgate Cumb 56 F5
Clapton Som 8 D3
Clapton-in-Gordano N Som 15 D10
Clapton-on-the-Hill Glos 27 G8
Clapworthy Devon 6 D5
Clara Vale T&W 63 G7
Clarach Ceredig 32 G2
Clarbeston Pembs 22 D5
Clarbeston Road Pembs 22 D5
Clarborough Notts 45 D11
Clardon Highld 94 D3
Clare Suff 30 D4
Clarebrand Dumfries 55 C10
Clarencefield Dumfries 60 G6
Clarilaw Borders 61 B11
Clark's Green Sur 19 H8
Clarkston E Renf 68 E4
Clashandorran Highld 87 G8
Clashcoig Highld 87 B9
Clashindarroch Aberds 88 E4
Clashmore Highld 87 C10
Clashmore Highld 92 F3
Clashnessie Highld 92 F3
Clashnoir Moray 82 A4
Clate Shetland 96 G7
Clathy Perth 76 F2
Clatt Aberds 83 A7
Clatter Powys 32 F5
Clatterford IoW 10 F3
Clatterin Bridge Aberds 83 F8
Clatworthy Som 7 C9
Claughton Lancs 49 E5
Claughton Lancs 50 C1
Claughton Mers 42 D6
Claverdon Warks 27 B8
Claverham N Som 15 E10
Clavering Essex 29 E11
Claverley Shrops 34 F3
Claverton Bath 16 E4
Clawdd-newydd Denb 42 G3
Clawthorpe Cumb 49 B5
Clawton Devon 6 G2
Claxby Lincs 46 C5
Claxby Lincs 47 E8
Claxton N Yorks 52 C2
Claxton Norf 39 E9
Clay Common Suff 39 G10
Clay Coton Northants 36 H1
Clay Cross Derbys 45 F7
Clay Hill W Berks 18 D2
Clay Lake Lincs 37 C8
Claybokie Aberds 82 D2
Claybrooke Magna Leics 35 G10
Claybrooke Parva Leics 35 G10
Claydon Oxon 27 C11
Claydon Suff 31 C8
Claygate Dumfries 61 F9
Claygate Kent 12 B6
Claygate Sur 19 E8
Claygate Cross Kent 20 F3
Clayhanger Devon 7 D9
Clayhanger W Mid 34 E6
Clayhidon Devon 7 E10
Clayhill E Sus 13 D7
Clayhill Hants 10 D2
Clayock Highld 94 E3
Claypole Lincs 46 H2
Clayton S Yorks 45 B8
Clayton Staffs 34 A4
Clayton W Sus 12 E1
Clayton W Yorks 51 F7
Clayton Green Lancs 50 G1
Clayton-le-Moors Lancs 50 F3
Clayton-le-Woods Lancs 50 G1
Clayton West W Yorks 44 A6
Clayworth Notts 45 D11
Cleadale Highld 78 C7
Cleadon T&W 63 G9
Clearbrook Devon 4 E6
Clearwell Glos 26 H2
Cleasby N Yorks 58 E3
Cleat Orkney 95 K5
Cleatlam Durham 58 E2
Cleator Cumb 56 E2
Cleator Moor Cumb 56 E2
Clebrig Highld 93 F8
Cleckheaton W Yorks 51 G7
Clee St Margaret Shrops 34 G1
Cleedownton Shrops 34 G1
Cleehill Shrops 34 H1
Cleethorpes NE Lincs 47 B7
Cleeton St Mary Shrops 34 H2
Cleeve N Som 15 E10
Cleeve Hill Glos 26 F6
Cleeve Prior Worcs 27 D7
Clegyrnant Powys 32 E5
Clehonger Hereford 25 E11
Cleish Perth 76 H3
Cleland N Lanark 69 E7
Clench Common Wilts 17 E8
Clenchwarton Norf 38 C1
Clent Worcs 34 H5
Cleobury Mortimer Shrops 34 H2
Cleobury North Shrops 34 G2
Cleongart Argyll 65 E7
Clephanton Highld 87 F11
Clerklands Borders 61 A11
Clestrain Orkney 95 H4
Cleuch Head Borders 61 B11
Cleughbrae Dumfries 60 F6
Clevancy Wilts 17 D7
Clevedon N Som 15 D10
Cleveley Oxon 27 F10
Cleveleys Lancs 49 E3
Cleverton Wilts 16 C6
Clevis Bridgend 14 D4
Clewer Som 15 F10
Cley next the Sea Norf 38 A6
Cliaid W Isles 84 H1
Cliasmol W Isles 90 G5
Cliburn Cumb 57 D7
Click Mill Orkney 95 F4
Cliddesden Hants 18 G3
Cliff End E Sus 13 E7
Cliffburn Angus 77 C9
Cliffe Medway 20 D4
Cliffe N Yorks 52 F2
Cliffe Woods Medway 20 D4
Clifford Hereford 25 D9
Clifford W Yorks 51 E10
Clifford Chambers Warks 27 C8
Clifford's Mesne Glos 26 F4
Cliffsend Kent 21 E10
Clifton Bristol 16 D2
Clifton C Beds 29 E8
Clifton Cumb 57 D7
Clifton Derbys 35 A7
Clifton Lancs 49 F4
Clifton N Yorks 51 E7
Clifton Northumb 63 E8
Clifton Nottingham 36 B1
Clifton Oxon 27 E11
Clifton S Yorks 45 C9
Clifton Stirling 74 D6
Clifton Worcs 26 D5
Clifton York 52 D1
Clifton Campville Staffs 35 D8
Clifton Green Gtr Man 43 B10
Clifton Hampden Oxon 18 B2
Clifton Reynes M Keynes 28 C6
Clifton upon Dunsmore Warks 35 H11
Clifton upon Teme Worcs 26 B4
Cliftoncote Borders 62 A4
Cliftonville Kent 21 D10
Climaen gwyn Neath 24 H4
Climping W Sus 11 D9
Climpy S Lanark 69 E8
Clink Som 16 G4
Clint N Yorks 51 D8
Clint Green Norf 38 D6
Clintmains Borders 70 G5
Cliobh W Isles 90 D5
Clippesby Norf 39 D10
Clipsham Rutland 36 D5
Clipston Northants 36 G3
Clipstone Notts 45 F9
Clitheroe Lancs 50 E3
Cliuthar W Isles 90 H6
Clive Shrops 33 C11
Clivocast Shetland 96 C8
Clixby Lincs 46 B5
Clocaenog Denb 42 G3
Clochan Moray 88 B4
Clock Face Mers 43 C8
Clockmill Borders 70 E6
Cloddiau Powys 33 E8
Clodock Hereford 25 F10
Clola Aberds 89 D10
Clophill C Beds 29 E7
Clopton Northants 37 G6
Clopton Suff 31 C9
Clopton Corner Suff 31 C9
Clopton Green Suff 30 C4
Close Clark IoM 48 E2
Closeburn Dumfries 60 D4
Closworth Som 8 C4
Clothall Herts 29 E9
Clotton Ches W 43 F8
Clough Foot W Yorks 50 G5
Cloughton N Yorks 59 G11
Cloughton Newlands N Yorks 59 G11
Clousta Shetland 96 H5
Clouston Orkney 95 G3
Clova Aberds 82 A6
Clova Angus 82 F5
Clove Lodge Durham 57 E11
Clovelly Devon 6 D2
Clovenfords Borders 70 G3
Clovenstone Aberds 83 B9
Clovullin Highld 74 A3
Clow Bridge Lancs 50 G4
Clowne Derbys 45 E8
Clows Top Worcs 26 A4
Cloy Wrex 33 A9
Cluanie Inn Highld 80 B2
Cluanie Lodge Highld 80 B2
Clun Shrops 33 G9
Clunbury Shrops 33 G9
Clunderwen Carms 22 E6
Clune Highld 81 A9
Clunes Highld 80 E4
Clungunford Shrops 33 H9
Clunie Aberds 89 C6
Clunie Perth 76 C4
Clunton Shrops 33 G9
Cluny Fife 76 H5
Cluny Castle Highld 81 D8
Clutton Bath 16 F3
Clutton Ches W 43 G7
Clwt-grugoer Conwy 42 F2
Clwt-y-bont Gwyn 41 D7
Clydach Mon 25 G9
Clydach Swansea 14 A2
Clydach Vale Rhondda 14 B5
Clydebank W Dunb 68 C3
Clydey Pembs 23 C7
Clyffe Pypard Wilts 17 D7
Clynder Argyll 73 E11
Clyne Neath 14 A4
Clynelish Highld 93 J11
Clynnog-fawr Gwyn 40 E6
Clyro Powys 25 D9
Clyst Honiton Devon 7 G8
Clyst Hydon Devon 7 F9
Clyst St George Devon 5 C10
Clyst St Lawrence Devon 7 F9
Clyst St Mary Devon 7 G8
Cnoc Amhlaigh W Isles 91 D10
Cnwch-coch Ceredig 32 H2
Coachford Aberds 88 D4
Coad's Green Corn 4 D3
Coal Aston Derbys 45 E7
Coalbrookdale Telford 34 E2
Coalbrookvale Bl Gwent 25 H8
Coalburn S Lanark 69 G7
Coalburns T&W 63 G7
Coalcleugh Northumb 57 B10
Coaley Glos 16 A4
Coalhall E Ayrs 67 E7
Coalhill Essex 20 B4
Coalpit Heath S Glos 16 C3
Coalport Telford 34 E2
Coalsnaughton Clack 76 H2
Coaltown of Balgonie Fife 76 H5
Coaltown of Wemyss Fife 76 H6
Coalville Leics 35 D10
Coalway Glos 26 G2
Coat Som 8 B3
Coatbridge N Lanark 68 D6
Coatdyke N Lanark 68 D6
Coate Swindon 17 C8
Coate Wilts 17 E7
Coates Cambs 37 F9
Coates Glos 16 A6
Coates Lancs 50 E4
Coates Notts 46 D2
Coates W Sus 11 C8
Coatham Redcar 59 D6
Coatham Mundeville Darl 58 D3
Coatsgate Dumfries 60 C6
Cobbaton Devon 6 D5
Cobbler's Green Norf 39 F8
Coberley Glos 26 G6
Cobham Kent 20 E3
Cobham Sur 19 E8
Cobholm Island Norf 39 E11
Cobleland Stirling 75 H8
Cobnash Hereford 25 B11
Coburty Aberds 89 B9
Cock Bank Wrex 42 H6
Cock Bridge Aberds 82 C4
Cock Clarks Essex 20 A5
Cockayne N Yorks 59 G7
Cockayne Hatley Cambs 29 D9
Cockburnspath Borders 70 C6
Cockenzie and Port Seton E Loth 70 C3
Cockerham Lancs 49 D4
Cockermouth Cumb 56 C3
Cockernhoe Green Herts 29 F8
Cockfield Durham 58 D2
Cockfield Suff 30 C6
Cockfosters London 19 B9
Cocking W Sus 11 C7
Cockington Torbay 5 E9
Cocklake Som 15 G10
Cockley Beck Cumb 56 F4
Cockley Cley Norf 38 E3
Cockshutt Shrops 33 C10
Cockthorpe Norf 38 A5
Cockwood Devon 5 C10
Cockyard Hereford 25 E11
Codda Corn 4 D2
Coddenham Suff 31 C8
Coddington Ches W 43 G7
Coddington Hereford 26 D4
Coddington Notts 46 G2
Codford St Mary Wilts 16 H6
Codford St Peter Wilts 16 H6
Codicote Herts 29 G9
Codmore Hill W Sus 11 B9
Codnor Derbys 45 H8
Codrington S Glos 16 D4
Codsall Staffs 34 E4
Codsall Wood Staffs 34 E4
Coed Duon = Blackwood Caerph 15 B7
Coed Mawr Gwyn 41 C7
Coed Morgan Mon 25 G10
Coed-Talon Flint 42 G5
Coed-y-bryn Ceredig 23 B8
Coed-y-paen Mon 15 B9
Coed-yr-ynys Powys 25 F8
Coed Ystumgwern Gwyn 32 C1
Coedely Rhondda 14 C6
Coedkernew Newport 15 C8
Coedpoeth Wrex 42 G5
Coedway Powys 33 D9
Coelbren Powys 24 G5
Coffinswell Devon 5 E9
Cofton Hackett Worcs 34 H6
Cogan V Glam 15 D7
Cogenhoe Northants 28 B5
Cogges Oxon 27 H10
Coggeshall Essex 30 F5
Coggeshall Hamlet Essex 30 F5
Coggins Mill E Sus 12 D4
Coig Peighinnean W Isles 91 A10
Coig Peighinnean Bhuirgh W Isles 91 B9
Coignafearn Lodge Highld 81 B8
Coilacriech Aberds 82 D5
Coilantogle Stirling 75 G8
Coilleag W Isles 84 G2
Coillore Highld 85 E8
Coity Bridgend 14 C5
Col W Isles 91 C9
Col Uarach W Isles 91 D9
Colaboll Highld 93 H8
Colan Corn 3 C7
Colaton Raleigh Devon 7 H9
Colbost Highld 84 D7
Colburn N Yorks 58 G2
Colby Cumb 57 D8
Colby IoM 48 E2
Colby Norf 39 B8
Colchester Essex 31 F7
Colcot V Glam 15 E7
Cold Ash W Berks 18 E2
Cold Ashby Northants 36 H2
Cold Ashton S Glos 16 D4
Cold Aston Glos 27 G8
Cold Blow Pembs 22 E6
Cold Brayfield M Keynes 28 C6
Cold Hanworth Lincs 46 D4
Cold Harbour Lincs 36 B5
Cold Hatton Telford 34 C2
Cold Hesledon Durham 58 B5
Cold Higham Northants 28 C3
Cold Kirby N Yorks 51 A11
Cold Newton Leics 36 E3
Cold Northcott Corn 4 C3
Cold Norton Essex 20 A5
Cold Overton Leics 36 D4
Coldbackie Highld 93 D9
Coldbeck Cumb 57 F9
Coldblow London 20 D2
Coldean Brighton 12 F2
Coldeast Devon 5 D9
Colden W Yorks 50 G5
Colden Common Hants 10 B3
Coldfair Green Suff 31 B11
Coldham Cambs 37 E10
Coldharbour Glos 16 A2
Coldharbour Kent 20 F2
Coldharbour Sur 19 G8
Coldingham Borders 71 D8
Coldrain Perth 76 G3
Coldred Kent 21 G9
Coldridge Devon 6 F5
Coldstream Angus 76 D6
Coldstream Borders 71 G7
Coldwaltham W Sus 11 C9
Coldwells Aberds 89 D11
Coldwells Croft Aberds 83 A7
Coldyeld Shrops 33 F9
Cole Som 8 A5
Cole Green Herts 29 G9
Cole Henley Hants 17 F11
Colebatch Shrops 33 G9
Colebrook Devon 7 F9
Colebrooke Devon 7 G6
Coleby Lincs 46 F3
Coleby N Lincs 52 H4
Coleford Devon 7 F6
Coleford Glos 26 G2
Coleford Som 16 G3
Colehill Dorset 9 D9
Coleman's Hatch E Sus 12 C3
Colemere Shrops 33 B10
Colemore Hants 10 A6
Coleorton Leics 35 D10
Colerne Wilts 16 D5
Cole's Green Suff 31 B9
Coles Green Suff 31 D7
Colesbourne Glos 26 G6
Colesden Bedford 29 C8
Coleshill Bucks 18 B6
Coleshill Oxon 17 B9
Coleshill Warks 35 G8
Colestocks Devon 7 F9
Colgate W Sus 11 A11
Colgrain Argyll 68 B2
Colinsburgh Fife 77 G7
Colinton Edin 69 D11
Colintraive Argyll 73 F9
Colkirk Norf 38 C5
Collace Perth 76 D5
Collafirth Shetland 96 G6
Collaton St Mary Torbay 5 F9
College Milton S Lanark 68 E5
Collessie Fife 76 F5
Collier Row London 20 B2
Collier Street Kent 20 G4
Collier's End Herts 29 F10
Collier's Green Kent 13 C6
Colliery Row T&W 58 B4
Collieston Aberds 89 F10
Collin Dumfries 60 F6
Collingbourne Ducis Wilts 17 F9
Collingbourne Kingston Wilts 17 F9
Collingham Notts 46 F2
Collingham W Yorks 51 E9
Collington Hereford 26 B3
Collingtree Northants 28 C4
Collins Green Warr 43 C8
Colliston Angus 77 C9
Collycroft Warks 35 G9
Collynie Aberds 89 E8
Collyweston Northants 36 E5
Colmonell S Ayrs 66 H4
Colmworth Bedford 29 C8
Coln Rogers Glos 27 H7
Coln St Aldwyn's Glos 27 H8
Coln St Dennis Glos 27 G7
Colnabaichin Aberds 82 C4
Colnbrook Slough 19 D7
Colne Cambs 37 H9
Colne Lancs 50 E4
Colne Edge Lancs 50 E4
Colne Engaine Essex 30 E5
Colney Norf 39 E7
Colney Heath Herts 29 H9
Colney Street Herts 19 A8
Colpy Aberds 89 E6
Colquhar Borders 70 F2
Colsterdale N Yorks 51 A7
Colsterworth Lincs 36 C5
Colston Bassett Notts 36 B2
Coltfield Moray 87 E14
Colthouse Cumb 56 G5
Coltishall Norf 39 D8
Coltness N Lanark 69 E7
Colton Cumb 56 H5
Colton N Yorks 51 E11
Colton Norf 39 E7
Colton Staffs 35 C6
Colton W Yorks 51 F9
Colva Powys 25 C9
Colvend Dumfries 55 D11
Colvister Shetland 96 D7
Colwall Green Hereford 26 D4
Colwall Stone Hereford 26 D4
Colwell Northumb 62 F5
Colwich Staffs 34 C6
Colwick Notts 36 A2
Colwinston V Glam 14 D5
Colworth W Sus 11 D8
Colwyn Bay = Bae Colwyn Conwy 41 C10
Colyford Devon 8 E1
Colyton Devon 8 E1
Combe Hereford 25 B10
Combe Oxon 27 G11
Combe W Berks 17 E10
Combe Common Sur 18 H6
Combe Down Bath 16 E4
Combe Florey Som 7 C10
Combe Hay Bath 16 F4
Combe Martin Devon 6 B4
Combe Moor Hereford 25 B10
Combe Raleigh Devon 7 F10
Combe St Nicholas Som 8 C2
Combeinteignhead Devon 5 D10
Comberbach Ches W 43 E9
Comberton Cambs 29 C10
Comberton Hereford 25 B11
Combpyne Devon 8 E1
Combridge Staffs 35 B6
Combrook Warks 27 C10
Combs Derbys 44 E4
Combs Suff 31 C7
Combs Ford Suff 31 C7
Combwich Som 15 G8
Comers Aberds 83 C8
Comins Coch Ceredig 32 G2
Commercial End Cambs 30 B2
Commins Capel Betws Ceredig 24 C3
Commins Coch Powys 32 E4
Common Edge Blackpool 49 F3
Common Side Derbys 45 E7
Commondale N Yorks 59 E7
Commonmoor Corn 4 E3
Commonside Ches W 43 E8
Compstall Gtr Man 44 C3
Compton Devon 5 E9
Compton Hants 10 B3
Compton Sur 18 G5
Compton Sur 18 G6
Compton W Berks 18 D2
Compton W Sus 11 C6
Compton Wilts 17 F8
Compton Abbas Dorset 9 C7
Compton Abdale Glos 27 G7
Compton Bassett Wilts 17 D7
Compton Beauchamp Oxon 17 C9
Compton Bishop Som 15 F9
Compton Chamberlayne Wilts 9 B9
Compton Dando Bath 16 E3
Compton Dundon Som 8 A3
Compton Martin Bath 15 F11
Compton Pauncefoot Som 8 B5
Compton Valence Dorset 8 E4
Comrie Fife 69 B9
Comrie Perth 75 E10
Conaglen House Highld 80 G2
Conchra Argyll 73 E9
Concraigie Perth 76 C4
Conder Green Lancs 49 D4
Conderton Worcs 26 E6
Condicote Glos 27 F8
Condorrat N Lanark 68 C6
Condover Shrops 33 E10
Coney Weston Suff 38 H5
Coneyhurst W Sus 11 B10
Coneysthorpe N Yorks 52 B3
Coneythorpe N Yorks 51 D9
Conford Hants 11 A7
Congash Highld 82 A2
Congdon's Shop Corn 4 D3
Congerstone Leics 35 E9
Congham Norf 38 C3
Congl-y-wal Gwyn 41 F9
Congleton Ches E 44 F2
Congresbury N Som 15 E10
Congreve Staffs 34 D5
Conicavel Moray 87 F12
Coningsby Lincs 46 G6
Conington Cambs 29 B10
Conington Cambs 37 G7
Conisbrough S Yorks 45 C9
Conisby Argyll 64 B3
Conisholme Lincs 47 C8
Coniston Cumb 56 G5
Coniston E Yorks 53 F7
Coniston Cold N Yorks 50 D5
Conistone N Yorks 50 C5
Connah's Quay Flint 42 F5
Connel Argyll 74 D2
Connel Park E Ayrs 67 E9
Connor Downs Corn 2 F4
Conon Bridge Highld 87 F8
Conon House Highld 87 F8
Cononley N Yorks 50 E5
Conordan Highld 85 E10
Consall Staffs 44 H3
Consett Durham 58 A2
Constable Burton N Yorks 58 G2
Constantine Corn 2 G6
Constantine Bay Corn 3 B7
Contin Highld 86 F7
Contlaw Aberdeen 83 C10
Conwy Conwy 41 C9
Conyer Kent 20 E6
Conyers Green Suff 30 B5
Cooden E Sus 12 F6
Cooil IoM 48 E3
Cookbury Devon 6 F3
Cookham Windsor 18 C5
Cookham Dean Windsor 18 C5
Cookham Rise Windsor 18 C5
Cookhill Worcs 27 C7
Cookley Suff 39 H9
Cookley Worcs 34 G4
Cookley Green Oxon 18 B3
Cookney Aberds 83 D10
Cookridge W Yorks 51 E8
Cooksbridge E Sus 12 E3
Cooksmill Green Essex 30 H3
Coolham W Sus 11 B10
Cooling Medway 20 D4
Coombe Corn 3 D8
Coombe Corn 6 E1
Coombe Hants 10 B5
Coombe Wilts 17 F8
Coombe Bissett Wilts 9 B10
Coombe Hill Glos 26 F5
Coombe Keynes Dorset 9 F7
Coombes W Sus 11 D10
Coopersale Common Essex 19 A11
Cootham W Sus 11 C9
Copdock Suff 31 D8
Copford Green Essex 30 F6
Copgrove N Yorks 51 C9
Copister Shetland 96 F6
Cople Bedford 29 D8
Copley Durham 58 D1
Coplow Dale Derbys 44 E5
Copmanthorpe York 52 E1
Coppathorne Corn 4 A3
Coppenhall Staffs 34 D5
Coppenhall Moss Ches E 43 G10
Copperhouse Corn 2 F4
Coppingford Cambs 37 G7
Copplestone Devon 7 F6
Coppull Lancs 43 A8
Coppull Moor Lancs 43 A8
Copsale W Sus 11 B10
Copster Green Lancs 50 F2
Copston Magna Warks 35 G10
Copt Heath W Mid 35 H7
Copt Hewick N Yorks 51 B9
Copt Oak Leics 35 D10
Copthorne Shrops 33 D10
Copthorne Sur 12 C2
Copy's Green Norf 38 B5
Copythorne Hants 10 C2
Corbets Tey London 20 C2
Corbridge Northumb 62 G5
Corby Northants 36 G4
Corby Glen Lincs 36 C5
Cordon N Ayrs 66 C3
Coreley Shrops 26 A3
Cores End Bucks 18 C6
Corfe Som 7 E11
Corfe Castle Dorset 9 F8
Corfe Mullen Dorset 9 E8
Corfton Shrops 33 G10
Corgarff Aberds 82 C4
Corhampton Hants 10 B5
Corlae Dumfries 67 G9
Corley Warks 35 G9
Corley Ash Warks 35 G8
Corley Moor Warks 35 G8
Cornaa IoM 48 D4
Cornabus Argyll 64 D4
Cornel Conwy 41 D9
Corner Row Lancs 49 F4
Corney Cumb 56 G3
Cornforth Durham 58 C4
Cornhill Aberds 88 C5
Cornhill-on-Tweed Northumb 71 G7
Cornholme W Yorks 50 G5
Cornish Hall End Essex 30 E3
Cornquoy Orkney 95 J6
Cornsay Durham 58 B2
Cornsay Colliery Durham 58 B2
Corntown Highld 87 F8
Corntown V Glam 14 D5
Cornwell Oxon 27 F9
Cornwood Devon 5 F7
Cornworthy Devon 5 F9
Corpach Highld 80 F2
Corpusty Norf 39 B7
Corran Highld 74 A3
Corran Highld 85 H13
Corranbuie Argyll 73 G7
Corrany IoM 48 D4
Corrie N Ayrs 66 B3
Corrie Common Dumfries 61 E8
Corriecravie N Ayrs 66 D2
Corriemoillie Highld 86 E6
Corriemulzie Lodge Highld 86 B6
Corrievarkie Lodge Perth 81 F7
Corrievorrie Highld 81 A9
Corrimony Highld 86 H6
Corringham Lincs 46 C2
Corringham Thurrock 20 C4
Corris Gwyn 32 E3
Corris Uchaf Gwyn 32 E3
Corrour Shooting Lodge Highld 80 G6
Corrow Argyll 74 G4
Corry Highld 85 F11
Corry of Ardnagrask Highld 87 G8
Corrykinloch Highld 92 G6
Corrymuckloch Perth 75 D11
Corrynachenchy Argyll 79 G9
Cors-y-Gedol Gwyn 32 C1
Corsback Highld 94 C4
Corscombe Dorset 8 D4
Corse Aberds 88 D6
Corse Glos 26 F4
Corse Lawn Worcs 26 E5
Corse of Kinnoir Aberds 88 D5
Corsewall Dumfries 54 C3
Corsham Wilts 16 D5
Corsindae Aberds 83 C8
Corsley Wilts 16 G5
Corsley Heath Wilts 16 G5
Corsock Dumfries 60 F3
Corston Bath 16 E3
Corston Wilts 16 C6
Corstorphine Edin 69 C10
Cortachy Angus 76 B6
Corton Suff 39 F11
Corton Wilts 16 G6
Corton Denham Som 8 B5
Coruanan Lodge Highld 80 G2
Corunna W Isles 84 B3
Corwen Denb 33 A6
Coryton Devon 4 C5
Coryton Thurrock 20 C4
Cosby Leics 35 F11
Coseley W Mid 34 F5
Cosgrove Northants 28 D4
Cosham Ptsmth 10 D5
Cosheston Pembs 22 F5
Cossall Notts 35 A10
Cossington Leics 36 D2
Cossington Som 15 G9
Costa Orkney 95 F4
Costessey Norf 39 D7
Costock Notts 36 C1
Coston Leics 36 C4
Cote Oxon 17 A10
Cotebrook Ches W 43 F8
Cotehill Cumb 56 A6
Cotes Cumb 57 H6
Cotes Leics 36 C1
Cotes Staffs 34 B4
Cotesbach Leics 35 G11
Cotgrave Notts 36 B2
Cothall Aberds 83 B10
Cotham Notts 45 H11
Cothelstone Som 7 C10
Cotherstone Durham 58 E1
Cothill Oxon 17 B11
Cotleigh Devon 7 F11
Cotmanhay Derbys 35 A10
Cotmaton Devon 7 H10
Coton Cambs 29 C11
Coton Northants 28 A3
Coton Staffs 34 B5
Coton Staffs 34 C4
Coton Clanford Staffs 34 C4
Coton Hill Shrops 33 D10
Coton Hill Staffs 34 B5
Coton in the Elms Derbys 35 D8
Cott Devon 5 E8
Cottam E Yorks 52 C5
Cottam Lancs 49 F5
Cottam Notts 46 E2
Cottartown Highld 87 H13
Cottenham Cambs 29 B11
Cotterdale N Yorks 57 G10
Cottered Herts 29 F10
Cotteridge W Mid 34 H6
Cotterstock Northants 36 F6
Cottesbrooke Northants 28 A4
Cottesmore Rutland 36 D5
Cotteylands Devon 7 E8
Cottingham E Yorks 52 F6
Cottingham Northants 36 F4
Cottingley W Yorks 51 F7
Cottisford Oxon 28 E2
Cotton Staffs 44 H4
Cotton Suff 31 B7
Cotton End Bedford 29 D7
Cottown Aberds 83 A7
Cottown Aberds 83 B9
Cottown Aberds 89 D8
Cotwalton Staffs 34 B5
Couch's Mill Corn 4 F2
Coughton Hereford 26 F2
Coughton Warks 27 B7
Coulaghailtro Argyll 72 G6
Coulags Highld 86 G2
Coulby Newham Mbro 58 E6
Coulderton Cumb 56 F1
Coulin Highld 86 F3
Coull Aberds 83 C7
Coull Argyll 64 B3
Coulport Argyll 73 E11
Coulsdon London 19 F9
Coulston Wilts 16 F6
Coulter S Lanark 69 G9
Coulton N Yorks 52 B2
Cound Shrops 34 E1
Coundon Durham 58 D3
Coundon W Mid 35 G9
Coundon Grange Durham 58 D3
Countersett N Yorks 57 H11
Countess Wilts 17 G8
Countess Wear Devon 5 C10
Countesthorpe Leics 36 F1
Countisbury Devon 7 B6
County Oak W Sus 12 C1
Coup Green Lancs 50 G1
Coupar Angus Perth 76 C5
Coupland Northumb 71 G8
Cour Argyll 65 D9
Courance Dumfries 60 D6
Court-at-Street Kent 13 C9
Court Henry Carms 23 D10
Courteenhall Northants 28 C4
Courtsend Essex 21 B7
Courtway Som 7 C11
Cousland Midloth 70 D2
Cousley Wood E Sus 12 C5
Cove Argyll 73 E11
Cove Borders 70 C6
Cove Devon 7 E8
Cove Hants 18 F5
Cove Highld 91 H13
Cove Bay Aberdeen 83 C11
Cove Bottom Suff 39 H10
Covehithe Suff 39 G11
Coven Staffs 34 E5
Coveney Cambs 37 G10
Covenham St Bartholomew Lincs 47 C7
Covenham St Mary Lincs 47 C7
Coventry W Mid 35 H9
Coverack Corn 3 H6
Coverham N Yorks 58 H2
Covesea Moray 88 A1
Covington Cambs 29 A7
Covington S Lanark 69 G8
Cow Ark Lancs 50 E2
Cowan Bridge Lancs 50 B2
Cowbeech E Sus 12 E5
Cowbit Lincs 37 D8
Cowbridge Lincs 47 H7
Cowbridge Som 7 B8
Cowbridge = Y Bont-Faen V Glam 14 D5
Cowdale Derbys 44 E4
Cowden Kent 12 B3
Cowdenbeath Fife 69 A10
Cowdenburn Borders 69 E11
Cowers Lane Derbys 45 H7
Cowes IoW 10 E3
Cowesby N Yorks 58 H5
Cowfold W Sus 11 B11
Cowgill Cumb 57 H9
Cowie Aberds 83 E10
Cowie Stirling 69 B7
Cowley Devon 7 G8
Cowley Glos 26 G6
Cowley London 19 C7
Cowley Oxon 18 A2
Cowleymoor Devon 7 E8
Cowling Lancs 50 H1
Cowling N Yorks 50 E5
Cowling N Yorks 58 H3
Cowlinge Suff 30 C4
Cowpe Lancs 50 G4
Cowpen Northumb 63 E8
Cowpen Bewley Stockton 58 D5
Cowplain Hants 10 C5
Cowshill Durham 57 B10
Cowslip Green N Som 15 E10
Cowstrandburn Fife 69 A9
Cowthorpe N Yorks 51 D10
Cox Common Suff 39 G9
Cox Green Windsor 18 D5
Cox Moor Notts 45 G9
Coxbank Ches E 34 A2
Coxbench Derbys 35 A9
Coxford Norf 38 C4
Coxford Soton 10 C2
Coxheath Kent 20 F4
Coxhill Kent 21 G9
Coxhoe Durham 58 C4
Coxley Som 15 G11
Coxwold N Yorks 51 B11
Coychurch Bridgend 14 D5
Coylton S Ayrs 67 D7
Coylumbridge Highld 81 B11
Coynach Aberds 82 C6
Coynachie Aberds 88 E4
Coytrahen Bridgend 14 C4
Crabadon Devon 5 F8
Crabbs Cross Worcs 27 B7
Crabtree W Sus 11 B11
Crackenthorpe Cumb 57 D8
Crackington Haven Corn 4 B2
Crackley Warks 27 A9
Crackleybank Shrops 34 D3
Crackpot N Yorks 57 G11
Cracoe N Yorks 50 C5
Craddock Devon 7 E9
Cradhlastadh W Isles 90 D5
Cradley Hereford 26 D4
Cradley Heath W Mid 34 G5
Crafthole Corn 4 F4
Cragg Vale W Yorks 50 G6
Craggan Highld 82 A2
Craggie Highld 87 H10
Craggie Highld 93 H11
Craghead Durham 58 A3
Crai Powys 24 F5
Craibstone Moray 88 C4
Craichie Angus 77 C8
Craig Dumfries 55 B9
Craig Dumfries 55 C9
Craig Highld 86 G3
Craig Castle Aberds 82 A6
Craig-cefn-parc Swansea 14 A2
Craig Penllyn V Glam 14 D5
Craig-y-don Conwy 41 B9
Craig-y-nos Powys 24 G5
Craiganor Lodge Perth 75 B9
Craigdam Aberds 89 E8
Craigdarroch Dumfries 60 D3
Craigdarroch Highld 86 F7
Craigdhu Highld 86 G7
Craigearn Aberds 83 B9
Craigellachie Moray 88 D2
Craigencross Dumfries 54 C3
Craigend Perth 76 E4
Craigend Stirling 68 B6
Craigendive Argyll 73 E9
Craigendoran Argyll 68 B2
Craigends Renfs 68 D3
Craigens Argyll 64 B3
Craigens E Ayrs 67 E8
Craighat Stirling 68 B3
Craighead Fife 77 G9
Craighlaw Mains Dumfries 54 C6
Craighouse Argyll 72 G4
Craigie Aberds 83 B11
Craigie Dundee 77 D7
Craigie Perth 76 C4
Craigie Perth 76 E4
Craigie S Ayrs 67 C7
Craigiefield Orkney 95 G5
Craigielaw E Loth 70 C3
Craiglockhart Edin 69 C11
Craigmalloch E Ayrs 67 G7
Craigmaud Aberds 89 C8
Craigmillar Edin 69 C11
Craigmore Argyll 73 G10
Craignant Shrops 33 B8
Craigneuk N Lanark 68 D6
Craigneuk N Lanark 68 E6
Craignure Argyll 79 H10
Craigo Angus 77 A9
Craigow Perth 76 G3
Craigrothie Fife 76 F6
Craigroy Moray 87 F14
Craigruie Stirling 75 E7
Craigston Castle Aberds 89 C7
Craigton Aberdeen 83 C10
Craigton Angus 76 B6
Craigton Angus 77 D8
Craigton Highld 87 B9
Craigtown Highld 93 D11
Craik Borders 61 C9
Crail Fife 77 G9
Crailing Borders 62 A2
Crailinghall Borders 62 A2
Craiselound N Lincs 45 C11
Crakehill N Yorks 51 B10
Crakemarsh Staffs 35 B6
Crambe N Yorks 52 C3
Cramlington Northumb 63 F8
Cramond Edin 69 C10
Cramond Bridge Edin 69 C10
Cranage Ches E 43 F10
Cranberry Staffs 34 B4
Cranborne Dorset 9 C9
Cranbourne Brack 18 D6
Cranbrook Devon 7 G9
Cranbrook Kent 13 C6
Cranbrook Common Kent 13 C6
Crane Moor S Yorks 45 B7
Crane's Corner Norf 38 D5
Cranfield C Beds 28 D6
Cranford London 19 D8
Cranford St Andrew Northants 36 H5
Cranford St John Northants 36 H5
Cranham Glos 26 G5
Cranham London 20 C2
Crank Mers 43 C8
Crank Wood Gtr Man 43 B9
Cranleigh Sur 19 H7
Cranley Suff 31 A8
Cranmer Green Suff 31 A7
Cranmore IoW 10 F2

Cranna Aberds 89 C6
Crannich Argyll 79 G8
Crannoch Moray 88 C4
Cranoe Leics 36 F3
Cransford Suff 31 B10
Cranshaws Borders 70 D5
Cranstal IoM 48 B4
Crantock Corn 3 C6
Cranwell Lincs 46 H4
Cranwich Norf 38 F3
Cranworth Norf 38 E5
Craobh Haven Argyll 72 C6
Crapstone Devon 4 E6
Crarae Argyll 73 D8
Crask Inn Highld 93 G8
Crask of Aigas Highld 86 G7
Craskins Aberds 83 C7
Craster Northumb 63 B8
Craswall Hereford 25 E9
Cratfield Suff 39 H9
Crathes Aberds 83 D9
Crathie Aberds 82 D4
Crathie Highld 81 D7
Crathorne N Yorks 58 F5
Craven Arms Shrops 33 G10
Crawcrook T&W 63 G7
Crawford Lancs 43 B7
Crawford S Lanark 60 A5
Crawfordjohn S Lanark 60 A4
Crawick Dumfries 60 B3
Crawley Hants 10 A3
Crawley Oxon 27 G10
Crawley W Sus 12 C1
Crawley Down W Sus 12 C2
Crawleyside Durham 57 B11
Crawshawbooth Lancs 50 G4
Crawton Aberds 83 F10
Cray N Yorks 50 B5
Cray Perth 76 A4
Crayford London 20 D2
Crayke N Yorks 52 B1
Crays Hill Essex 20 B4
Cray's Pond Oxon 18 C3
Creacombe Devon 7 E7
Creag Ghoraidh W Isles 84 D2
Creagan Argyll 74 C2
Creaguaineach Lodge Highld 80 G5
Creaksea Essex 20 B6
Creaton Northants 28 A4
Creca Dumfries 61 F8
Credenhill Hereford 25 D11
Crediton Devon 7 F7
Creebridge Dumfries 55 C7
Creech Heathfield Som 8 B1
Creech St Michael Som 8 B1
Creed Corn 3 E8
Creekmouth London 19 C11
Creeting Bottoms Suff 31 C8
Creeting St Mary Suff 31 C7
Creeton Lincs 36 C6
Creetown Dumfries 55 D7
Creg-ny-Baa IoM 48 D3
Creggans Argyll 73 C9
Cregneash IoM 48 F1
Cregrina Powys 25 C8
Creich Fife 76 E6
Creigiau Cardiff 14 C6
Cremyll Corn 4 F5
Creslow Bucks 28 F5
Cressage Shrops 34 E1
Cressbrook Derbys 44 E5
Cresselly Pembs 22 F5
Cressing Essex 30 F4
Cresswell Northumb 63 D8
Cresswell Staffs 34 B5
Cresswell Quay Pembs 22 F5
Creswell Derbys 45 E9
Cretingham Suff 31 B9
Cretshengan Argyll 72 G6
Crewe Ches E 43 G10
Crewe Ches W 43 G7
Crewgreen Powys 33 D9
Crewkerne Som 8 D3
Crianlarich Stirling 74 E6
Cribyn Ceredig 23 A10
Criccieth Gwyn 40 G6
Crich Derbys 45 G7
Crichie Aberds 89 D9
Crichton Midloth 70 D2
Crick Mon 15 B10
Crick Northants 28 A2
Crickadarn Powys 25 D7
Cricket Malherbie Som 8 C2
Cricket St Thomas Som 8 D2
Crickheath Shrops 33 C8
Crickhowell Powys 25 G9
Cricklade Wilts 17 B8
Cricklewood London 19 C9
Cridling Stubbs N Yorks 51 G11
Crieff Perth 75 E11
Criggion Powys 33 D8
Crigglestone W Yorks 51 H9
Crimond Aberds 89 C10
Crimonmogate Aberds 89 C10
Crimplesham Norf 38 E2
Crinan Argyll 72 D6
Cringleford Norf 39 E7
Cringles W Yorks 50 E6
Crinow Pembs 22 E6
Cripplesease Corn 2 F4
Cripplestyle Dorset 9 C9
Cripp's Corner E Sus 13 D6
Croasdale Cumb 56 E2
Crock Street Som 8 C2
Crockenhill Kent 20 E2
Crockernwell Devon 7 G6
Crockerton Wilts 16 G5
Crocketford or Ninemile Bar Dumfries 60 F4
Crockey Hill York 52 E2
Crockham Hill Kent 19 F11
Crockleford Heath Essex 31 F7
Crockness Orkney 95 J4
Croes-goch Pembs 22 C3
Croes-lan Ceredig 23 B8
Croes-y-mwyalch Torf 15 B9
Croeserw Neath 14 B4
Croesor Gwyn 41 F8
Croesyceiliog Carms 23 E9
Croesyceiliog Torf 15 B9
Croesywaun Gwyn 41 E7
Croft Leics 35 F11
Croft Lincs 47 F9
Croft Pembs 22 B6
Croft Warr 43 C9
Croft-on-Tees N Yorks 58 F3
Croftamie Stirling 68 B3
Croftmalloch W Loth 69 D8
Crofton W Yorks 51 H9
Crofton Wilts 17 E9
Crofts of Benachielt Highld 94 G3
Crofts of Haddo Aberds 89 E8
Crofts of Inverthernie Aberds 89 D7
Crofts of Meikle Ardo Aberds 89 D8
Crofty Swansea 23 G10
Croggan Argyll 79 J10
Croglin Cumb 57 B7
Croich Highld 86 B7
Crois Dughaill W Isles 84 F2
Cromarty Highld 87 E10
Cromblet Aberds 89 E7
Cromdale Highld 82 A2
Cromer Herts 29 F9
Cromer Norf 39 A8
Cromford Derbys 44 G6
Cromhall S Glos 16 B3
Cromhall Common S Glos 16 C3
Cromor W Isles 91 E9
Cromra Highld 81 D7
Cromwell Notts 45 F11
Cronberry E Ayrs 67 D9
Crondall Hants 18 G4
Cronk-y-Voddy IoM 48 D3
Cronton Mers 43 D7
Crook Cumb 56 G6
Crook Durham 58 C2
Crook of Devon Perth 76 G3
Crookedholm E Ayrs 67 C7
Crookes S Yorks 45 D7
Crookham Northumb 71 G8
Crookham W Berks 18 E2
Crookham Village Hants 18 F4
Crookhaugh Borders 69 H10
Crookhouse Borders 70 H6
Crooklands Cumb 49 A5
Cropredy Oxon 27 D11
Cropston Leics 36 D1
Cropthorne Worcs 26 D6
Cropton N Yorks 59 H8
Cropwell Bishop Notts 36 B2
Cropwell Butler Notts 36 B2
Cros W Isles 91 A10
Crosbost W Isles 91 E8
Crosby Cumb 56 C2
Crosby IoM 48 E3
Crosby N Lincs 46 A2
Crosby Garrett Cumb 57 F9
Crosby Ravensworth Cumb 57 E8
Crosby Villa Cumb 56 C2
Croscombe Som 16 G2
Cross Som 15 F10
Cross Ash Mon 25 G11
Cross-at-Hand Kent 20 G4
Cross Green Devon 4 C4
Cross Green Suff 30 C6
Cross Green Suff 30 C5
Cross Green Warks 27 C10
Cross-hands Carms 22 D6
Cross Hands Carms 23 E10
Cross Hands Pembs 22 E5
Cross Hill Derbys 45 H8
Cross Houses Shrops 33 E11
Cross in Hand E Sus 12 D4
Cross in Hand Leics 35 G11
Cross Inn Ceredig 23 A8
Cross Inn Ceredig 24 B2
Cross Inn Rhondda 14 C6
Cross Keys Kent 20 F2
Cross Lane Head Shrops 34 F3
Cross Lanes Corn 2 G5
Cross Lanes N Yorks 51 C11
Cross Lanes Wrex 43 H6
Cross o' th' hands Derbys 44 H6
Cross Oak Powys 25 F8
Cross of Jackston Aberds 89 E7
Cross Street Suff 39 H7
Cross Trickett's Dorset 9 D9
Crossaig Argyll 65 C9
Crossal Highld 85 E9
Crossapol Argyll 78 G2
Crossburn Falk 69 C7
Crossbush W Sus 11 D9
Crosscanonby Cumb 56 C2
Crossdale Street Norf 39 B8
Crossens Mers 49 H3
Crossflatts W Yorks 51 E7
Crossford Fife 69 B9
Crossford S Lanark 69 F7
Crossgate Lincs 37 C8
Crossgatehall E Loth 70 D2
Crossgates Fife 69 B10
Crossgates Powys 25 B7
Crossgill Lancs 50 C1
Crosshill E Ayrs 67 D7
Crosshill Fife 76 H4
Crosshill S Ayrs 66 F6
Crosshouse E Ayrs 67 C6
Crossings Cumb 61 F11
Crosskeys Caerph 15 B8
Crosskirk Highld 93 B13
Crosslanes Shrops 33 D9
Crosslee Borders 61 B9
Crosslee Renfs 68 D3
Crossmichael Dumfries 55 C10
Crossmoor Lancs 49 F4
Crossroads Aberds 83 D9
Crossroads E Ayrs 67 C7
Crossway Hereford 26 E3
Crossway Mon 25 G11
Crossway Powys 25 C7
Crossway Green Worcs 26 B5
Crossways Dorset 9 F6
Crosswell Pembs 22 C6
Crosswood Ceredig 24 A3
Crosthwaite Cumb 56 G6
Croston Lancs 49 H4
Crostwick Norf 39 D8
Crostwight Norf 39 C9
Crothair W Isles 90 D6
Crouch Kent 20 F3
Crouch Hill Dorset 8 C6
Crouch House Green Kent 19 G11
Croucheston Wilts 9 B9
Croughton Northants 28 E2
Crovie Aberds 89 B8
Crow Edge S Yorks 44 B5
Crow Hill Hereford 26 F3
Crowan Corn 2 F5
Crowborough E Sus 12 C4
Crowcombe Som 7 C10
Crowdecote Derbys 44 F5
Crowden Derbys 44 C4
Crowell Oxon 18 B4
Crowfield Northants 28 D3
Crowfield Suff 31 C8
Crowhurst E Sus 13 E6
Crowhurst Sur 19 G10
Crowhurst Lane End Sur 19 G10
Crowland Lincs 37 D8
Crowlas Corn 2 F4
Crowle N Lincs 45 A11
Crowle Worcs 26 C6
Crowmarsh Gifford Oxon 18 C3
Crown Corner Suff 31 A9
Crownhill Plym 4 F5
Crownland Suff 31 B7
Crownthorpe Norf 39 E6
Crowntown Corn 2 F5
Crows-an-wra Corn 2 G2
Crowshill Norf 38 E5
Crowsnest Shrops 33 E9
Crowthorne Brack 18 E5
Crowton Ches W 43 E8
Croxall Staffs 35 D7
Croxby Lincs 46 C5
Croxdale Durham 58 C3
Croxden Staffs 35 B6
Croxley Green Herts 19 B7
Croxton Cambs 29 B9
Croxton N Lincs 46 A4
Croxton Norf 38 G4
Croxton Staffs 34 B3
Croxton Kerrial Leics 36 C4
Croxtonbank Staffs 34 B3
Croy Highld 87 G10
Croy N Lanark 68 C6
Croyde Devon 6 C3
Croydon Cambs 29 D10
Croydon London 19 E10
Crubenmore Lodge Highld 81 D8
Cruckmeole Shrops 33 E10
Cruckton Shrops 33 D10
Cruden Bay Aberds 89 E10
Crudgington Telford 34 D2
Crudwell Wilts 16 B6
Crug Powys 25 A8
Crugmeer Corn 3 B8
Crugybar Carms 24 E3
Crulabhig W Isles 90 D6
Crumlin = Crymlyn Caerph 15 B8
Crumpsall Gtr Man 44 B2
Crundale Kent 21 G7
Crundale Pembs 22 E4
Cruwys Morchard Devon 7 E7
Crux Easton Hants 17 F11
Crwbin Carms 23 E9
Crya Orkney 95 H4
Cryers Hill Bucks 18 B5
Crymlyn = Crumlin Caerph 15 B8
Crymlyn Gwyn 41 C8
Crymych Pembs 22 C6
Crynant Neath 14 A3
Crynfryn Ceredig 24 B2
Cuaig Highld 85 C12
Cuan Argyll 72 B6
Cubbington Warks 27 B10
Cubeck N Yorks 57 H11
Cubert Corn 3 D6
Cubley S Yorks 44 B6
Cubley Common Derbys 35 B7
Cublington Bucks 28 F5
Cublington Hereford 25 E11
Cuckfield W Sus 12 D2
Cucklington Som 9 B6
Cuckney Notts 45 E9
Cuckoo Hill Notts 45 C11
Cuddesdon Oxon 18 A3
Cuddington Bucks 28 G4
Cuddington Ches W 43 E9
Cuddington Heath Ches W 43 H7
Cuddy Hill Lancs 49 F4
Cudham London 19 F11
Cudliptown Devon 4 D6
Cudworth S Yorks 45 B7
Cudworth Som 8 C2
Cuffley Herts 19 A10
Cuiashader W Isles 91 B10
Cuidhir W Isles 84 H1
Cuidhtinis W Isles 90 J5
Culbo Highld 87 E9
Culbokie Highld 87 F9
Culburnie Highld 86 G7
Culcabock Highld 87 G9
Culcairn Highld 87 E9
Culcharry Highld 87 F11
Culcheth Warr 43 C9
Culdrain Aberds 88 E5
Culduie Highld 85 D12
Culford Suff 30 A5
Culgaith Cumb 57 D8
Culham Oxon 18 B2
Culkein Highld 92 F3
Culkein Drumbeg Highld 92 F4
Culkerton Glos 16 B6
Cullachie Highld 81 A11
Cullen Moray 88 B5
Cullercoats T&W 63 F9
Cullicudden Highld 87 E9
Cullingworth W Yorks 51 F6
Cullipool Argyll 72 B6
Cullivoe Shetland 96 C7
Culloch Perth 75 F10
Culloden Highld 87 G10
Cullompton Devon 7 F9
Culmaily Highld 87 B11
Culmazie Dumfries 54 D6
Culmington Shrops 33 G10
Culmstock Devon 7 E10
Culnacraig Highld 92 J3
Culnaknock Highld 85 B10
Culpho Suff 31 D9
Culrain Highld 87 B8
Culross Fife 69 B8
Culroy S Ayrs 66 E6
Culsh Aberds 82 D5
Culsh Aberds 89 D8
Culshabbin Dumfries 54 D6
Culswick Shetland 96 J4
Cultercullen Aberds 89 F9
Cults Aberdeen 83 C10
Cults Aberds 88 E5
Cults Dumfries 55 E7
Culverstone Green Kent 20 E3
Culverthorpe Lincs 36 A6
Culworth Northants 28 D2
Culzie Lodge Highld 87 D8
Cumbernauld N Lanark 68 C6
Cumbernauld Village N Lanark 68 C6
Cumberworth Lincs 47 E9
Cuminestown Aberds 89 C8
Cumlewick Shetland 96 L6
Cummersdale Cumb 56 A5
Cummertrees Dumfries 61 G7
Cummingston Moray 88 B1
Cumnock E Ayrs 67 D8
Cumnor Oxon 17 A11
Cumrew Cumb 57 A7
Cumwhinton Cumb 56 A6
Cumwhitton Cumb 57 A7
Cundall N Yorks 51 B10
Cunninghamhead N Ayrs 67 B6
Cunnister Shetland 96 D7
Cupar Fife 76 F6
Cupar Muir Fife 76 F6
Cupernham Hants 10 B2
Curbar Derbys 44 E6
Curbridge Hants 10 C4
Curbridge Oxon 27 H10
Curdridge Hants 10 C4
Curdworth Warks 35 F7
Curland Som 8 C1
Curlew Green Suff 31 B10
Currarie S Ayrs 66 G4
Curridge W Berks 17 D11
Currie Edin 69 D10
Curry Mallet Som 8 B2
Curry Rivel Som 8 B2
Curtisden Green Kent 12 B6
Curtisknowle Devon 5 F8
Cury Corn 2 G5
Cushnie Aberds 89 B7
Cushuish Som 7 C10
Cusop Hereford 25 D9
Cutcloy Dumfries 55 F7
Cutcombe Som 7 C8
Cutgate Gtr Man 44 A2
Cutiau Gwyn 32 D2
Cutlers Green Essex 30 E2
Cutnall Green Worcs 26 B5
Cutsdean Glos 27 E7
Cutthorpe Derbys 45 E7
Cutts Shetland 96 K6
Cuxham Oxon 18 B3
Cuxton Medway 20 E4
Cuxwold Lincs 46 B5
Cwm Bl Gwent 25 H8
Cwm Denb 42 E3
Cwm Swansea 14 B2
Cwm-byr Carms 24 E3
Cwm-Cewydd Gwyn 32 D4
Cwm-cou Ceredig 23 B7
Cwm-Dulais Swansea 14 A2
Cwm-felin-fach Caerph 15 B7
Cwm Ffrwd-oer Torf 15 A8
Cwm-hesgen Gwyn 32 C3
Cwm-hwnt Rhondda 24 H6
Cwm Irfon Powys 24 D5
Cwm-Llinau Powys 32 E4
Cwm-mawr Carms 23 E10
Cwm-parc Rhondda 14 B5
Cwm Penmachno Conwy 41 F9
Cwm-y-glo Carms 23 E10
Cwm-y-glo Gwyn 41 D7
Cwmafan Neath 14 B3
Cwmaman Rhondda 14 B6
Cwmann Carms 23 B10
Cwmavon Torf 25 H9
Cwmbach Carms 23 D7
Cwmbach Carms 23 F9
Cwmbach Powys 25 C7
Cwmbach Powys 25 E8
Cwmbâch Rhondda 14 A6
Cwmbelan Powys 32 G5
Cwmbran = Cwmbrân Torf 15 B8
Cwmbrân = Cwmbran Torf 15 B8
Cwmbrwyno Ceredig 32 G3
Cwmcarn Caerph 15 B8
Cwmcarvan Mon 25 H11
Cwmcych Carms 23 C7
Cwmdare Rhondda 14 A5
Cwmderwen Powys 32 E5
Cwmdu Carms 24 E3
Cwmdu Powys 25 F8
Cwmdu Swansea 14 B2
Cwmduad Carms 23 C8
Cwmdwr Carms 24 E4
Cwmfelin Bridgend 14 C4
Cwmfelin M Tydf 14 A6
Cwmfelin Boeth Carms 22 E6
Cwmfelin Mynach Carms 23 D7
Cwmffrwd Carms 23 E9
Cwmgiedd Powys 24 G4
Cwmgors Neath 24 G4
Cwmgwili Carms 23 E10
Cwmgwrach Neath 14 A4
Cwmhiraeth Carms 23 C8
Cwmifor Carms 24 F3
Cwmisfael Carms 23 E9
Cwmllynfell Neath 24 G4
Cwmorgan Pembs 23 C7
Cwmpengraig Carms 23 C8
Cwmrhos Powys 25 F8
Cwmsychpant Ceredig 23 B9
Cwmtillery Bl Gwent 25 H9
Cwmwysg Powys 24 F5
Cwmyoy Mon 25 F9
Cwmystwyth Ceredig 24 A4
Cwrt Gwyn 32 E2
Cwrt-newydd Ceredig 23 B9
Cwrt-y-cadno Carms 24 D3
Cwrt-y-gollen Powys 25 G9
Cydweli = Kidwelly Carms 23 F9
Cyffordd Llandudno = Llandudno Junction Conwy 41 C9
Cyffylliog Denb 42 G3
Cyfronydd Powys 33 E7
Cymer Neath 14 B4
Cyncoed Cardiff 15 C7
Cynghordy Carms 24 D5
Cynheidre Carms 23 F9
Cynwyd Denb 33 A6
Cynwyl Elfed Carms 23 D8
Cywarch Gwyn 32 D4

D

Dacre Cumb 56 D6
Dacre N Yorks 51 C7
Dacre Banks N Yorks 51 C7
Daddry Shield Durham 57 C10
Dadford Bucks 28 E3
Dadlington Leics 35 F10
Dafarn Faig Gwyn 40 F6
Dafen Carms 23 F10
Daffy Green Norf 38 E5
Dagenham London 19 C11
Daglingworth Glos 26 H6
Dagnall Bucks 28 G6
Dail Beag W Isles 90 C7
Dail bho Dheas W Isles 91 A9
Dail bho Thuath W Isles 91 A9
Dail Mor W Isles 90 C7
Daill Argyll 64 B4
Dailly S Ayrs 66 F5
Dairsie or Osnaburgh Fife 77 F7
Daisy Hill Gtr Man 43 B9
Dalabrog W Isles 84 F2
Dalavich Argyll 73 B8
Dalbeattie Dumfries 55 C11
Dalblair E Ayrs 67 E9
Dalbog Angus 83 F7
Dalbury Derbys 35 B8
Dalby IoM 48 E2
Dalby N Yorks 52 B2
Dalchalloch Perth 75 A10
Dalchalm Highld 93 J12
Dalchenna Argyll 73 C9
Dalchirach Moray 88 E1
Dalchork Highld 93 H8
Dalchreichart Highld 80 B4
Dalchruin Perth 75 F10
Dalderby Lincs 46 F6
Dale Pembs 22 F3
Dale Abbey Derbys 35 B10
Dale Head Cumb 56 E6
Dale of Walls Shetland 96 H3
Dalelia Highld 79 E10
Daless Highld 87 H11
Dalfaber Highld 81 B11
Dalgarven N Ayrs 66 B5
Dalgety Bay Fife 69 B10
Dalginross Perth 75 E10
Dalguise Perth 76 C2
Dalhalvaig Highld 93 D11
Dalham Suff 30 B4
Dalinlongart Argyll 73 E10
Dalkeith Midloth 70 D2
Dallam Warr 43 C8
Dallas Moray 87 F14
Dalleagles E Ayrs 67 E8
Dallinghoo Suff 31 C9
Dallington E Sus 12 E5
Dallington Northants 28 B4
Dallow N Yorks 51 B7
Dalmadilly Aberds 83 B9
Dalmally Argyll 74 E4
Dalmarnock Glasgow 68 D5
Dalmary Stirling 75 H8
Dalmellington E Ayrs 67 F7
Dalmeny Edin 69 C10
Dalmigavie Highld 81 B9
Dalmigavie Lodge Highld 81 A9
Dalmore Highld 87 E9
Dalmuir W Dunb 68 C3
Dalnabreck Highld 79 E9
Dalnacardoch Lodge Perth 81 F9
Dalnacroich Highld 86 F6
Dalnaglar Castle Perth 76 A4
Dalnahaitnach Highld 81 A10
Dalnaspidal Lodge Perth 81 F8
Dalnavaid Perth 76 A3
Dalnavie Highld 87 D9
Dalnawillan Lodge Highld 93 E13
Dalness Highld 74 B4
Dalnessie Highld 93 H9
Dalqueich Perth 76 G3
Dalreavoch Highld 93 J10
Dalry N Ayrs 66 B5
Dalrymple E Ayrs 67 E6
Dalserf S Lanark 69 E7
Dalston Cumb 56 A5
Dalswinton Dumfries 60 E5
Dalton Dumfries 61 F7
Dalton Lancs 43 B7
Dalton N Yorks 51 B10
Dalton N Yorks 58 F2
Dalton Northumb 62 H5
Dalton Northumb 63 F7
Dalton S Yorks 45 C8
Dalton-in-Furness Cumb 49 B2
Dalton-le-Dale Durham 58 B5
Dalton-on-Tees N Yorks 58 F3
Dalton Piercy Hrtlpl 58 C5
Dalveich Stirling 75 E9
Dalvina Lo. Highld 93 E9
Dalwhinnie Highld 81 E8
Dalwood Devon 8 D1
Dalwyne S Ayrs 66 G6
Dam Green Norf 39 G6
Dam Side Lancs 49 E4
Damerham Hants 9 C10
Damgate Norf 39 E10
Damnaglaur Dumfries 54 F4
Damside Borders 69 F10
Danbury Essex 30 H4
Danby N Yorks 59 F8
Danby Wiske N Yorks 58 G4
Dandaleith Moray 88 D2
Danderhall Midloth 70 D2
Dane End Herts 29 F10
Danebridge Ches E 44 F3
Danehill E Sus 12 D3
Danemoor Green Norf 39 E6
Danesford Shrops 34 F3
Daneshill Hants 18 F3
Dangerous Corner Lancs 43 A8
Danskine E Loth 70 D4
Darcy Lever Gtr Man 43 B10
Darenth Kent 20 D2
Daresbury Halton 43 D8
Darfield S Yorks 45 B8
Darfoulds Notts 45 E9
Dargate Kent 21 E7
Darite Corn 4 E3
Darlaston W Mid 34 F5
Darley N Yorks 51 D8
Darley Bridge Derbys 44 F6
Darley Head N Yorks 51 D7
Darlingscott Warks 27 D9
Darlington Darl 58 E3
Darliston Shrops 34 B1
Darlton Notts 45 E11
Darnall S Yorks 45 D7
Darnick Borders 70 G4
Darowen Powys 32 E4
Darra Aberds 89 D7
Darracott Devon 6 C3
Darras Hall Northumb 63 F7
Darrington W Yorks 51 G10
Darsham Suff 31 B11
Dartford Kent 20 D2
Dartford Crossing Kent 20 D2
Dartington Devon 5 E8
Dartmeet Devon 5 D7
Dartmouth Devon 5 F9
Darton S Yorks 45 B7
Darvel E Ayrs 68 G4
Darwell Hole E Sus 12 E5
Darwen Blackburn 50 G2
Datchet Windsor 18 D6
Datchworth Herts 29 G9
Datchworth Green Herts 29 G9
Daubhill Gtr Man 43 B10
Daugh of Kinermony Moray 88 D2
Dauntsey Wilts 16 C6
Dava Moray 87 H13
Davenham Ches W 43 E9
Davenport Green Ches E 44 E2
Daventry Northants 28 B2
David's Well Powys 33 H6
Davidson's Mains Edin 69 C11
Davidstow Corn 4 C2
Davington Dumfries 61 C8
Daviot Aberds 83 A9
Daviot Highld 87 H10
Davoch of Grange Moray 88 C4
Davyhulme Gtr Man 43 C10
Dawley Telford 34 E2
Dawlish Devon 5 D10
Dawlish Warren Devon 5 D10
Dawn Conwy 41 C10
Daws Heath Essex 20 C5
Daw's House Corn 4 C4
Dawsmere Lincs 37 B10
Dayhills Staffs 34 B5
Daylesford Glos 27 F9
Ddôl-Cownwy Powys 32 D6
Ddrydwy Anglesey 40 C5
Deadwater Northumb 62 D2
Deaf Hill Durham 58 C4
Deal Kent 21 F10
Deal Hall Essex 21 B7
Dean Cumb 56 D2
Dean Devon 5 E8
Dean Devon 6 B4
Dean Dorset 9 C8
Dean Hants 10 C4
Dean Som 16 G3
Dean Prior Devon 5 E8
Dean Row Ches E 44 D2
Deanburnhaugh Borders 61 B9
Deane Gtr Man 43 B9
Deane Hants 18 F2
Deanich Lodge Highld 86 C6
Deanland Dorset 9 C8
Deans W Loth 69 D9
Deanscales Cumb 56 D2
Deanshanger Northants 28 E4
Deanston Stirling 75 G10
Dearham Cumb 56 C2
Debach Suff 31 C9
Debden Essex 19 B11
Debden Essex 30 E2
Debden Cross Essex 30 E2
Debenham Suff 31 B8
Dechmont W Loth 69 C9
Deddington Oxon 27 E11
Dedham Essex 31 E7
Dedham Heath Essex 31 E7
Deebank Aberds 83 D8
Deene Northants 36 F5
Deenethorpe Northants 36 F5
Deepcar S Yorks 44 C6
Deepcut Sur 18 F6
Deepdale Cumb 50 A3
Deeping Gate Lincs 37 E7
Deeping St James Lincs 37 E7
Deeping St Nicholas Lincs 37 D8
Deerhill Moray 88 C4
Deerhurst Glos 26 F5
Deerness Orkney 95 H6
Defford Worcs 26 D6
Defynnog Powys 24 F6
Deganwy Conwy 41 C9
Deighton N Yorks 58 F4
Deighton W Yorks 51 H7
Deighton York 52 E2
Deiniolen Gwyn 41 D7
Delabole Corn 4 C1
Delamere Ches W 43 F8
Delfrigs Aberds 89 F9
Dell Lodge Highld 82 B2
Delliefure Highld 87 H13
Delnabo Moray 82 B3
Delnadamph Aberds 82 C4
Delph Gtr Man 44 B3
Delves Durham 58 B2
Delvine Perth 76 C4
Dembleby Lincs 36 B6
Denaby Main S Yorks 45 C8
Denbigh = Dinbych Denb 42 F3
Denbury Devon 5 E9
Denby Derbys 45 H7
Denby Dale W Yorks 44 B6
Denchworth Oxon 17 B10
Dendron Cumb 49 B2
Denel End C Beds 29 E7
Denend Aberds 88 E6
Denford Northants 36 H5
Dengie Essex 20 A6
Denham Bucks 19 C7
Denham Suff 30 B4
Denham Suff 31 A8
Denham Street Suff 31 A8
Denhead Aberds 89 C9
Denhead Fife 77 F7
Denhead of Arbilot Angus 77 C8
Denhead of Gray Dundee 76 D6
Denholm Borders 61 B11
Denholme W Yorks 51 F6
Denholme Clough W Yorks 51 F6
Denio Gwyn 40 G5
Denmead Hants 10 C5
Denmore Aberdeen 83 B11
Denmoss Aberds 89 D6
Dennington Suff 31 B9
Denny Falk 69 B7
Denny Lodge Hants 10 D2
Dennyloanhead Falk 69 B7
Denshaw Gtr Man 44 A3
Denside Aberds 83 D10
Densole Kent 21 G9
Denston Suff 30 C4
Denstone Staffs 35 A7
Dent Cumb 57 H9
Denton Cambs 37 G7
Denton Darl 58 E3
Denton E Sus 12 F3
Denton Gtr Man 44 C3
Denton Kent 21 G9
Denton Lincs 36 B4
Denton N Yorks 51 E7
Denton Norf 39 G8
Denton Northants 28 C5
Denton Oxon 18 A2
Denton's Green Mers 43 C7
Denver Norf 38 E2
Denwick Northumb 63 B8
Deopham Norf 39 E6
Deopham Green Norf 38 F6
Depden Suff 30 C4
Depden Green Suff 30 C4
Deptford London 19 D10
Deptford Wilts 17 H7
Derby Derby 35 B9
Derbyhaven IoM 48 F2
Dereham Norf 38 D5
Deri Caerph 15 A7
Derril Devon 6 F2
Derringstone Kent 21 G9
Derrington Staffs 34 C4
Derriton Devon 6 F2
Derry Hill Wilts 16 D6
Derryguaig Argyll 78 H7
Derrythorpe N Lincs 46 B2
Dersingham Norf 38 B2
Dervaig Argyll 78 F7
Derwen Denb 42 G3
Derwenlas Powys 32 F3
Desborough Northants 36 G4
Desford Leics 35 E10
Detchant Northumb 71 G9
Detling Kent 20 F4
Deuddwr Powys 33 D8
Devauden Mon 15 B10
Devil's Bridge Ceredig 32 H3
Devizes Wilts 17 E7
Devol Invclyd 68 C2
Devonport Plym 4 F5
Devonside Clack 76 H2
Devoran Corn 3 F6
Dewar Borders 70 F2
Dewlish Dorset 9 E6
Dewsbury W Yorks 51 G8
Dewsbury Moor W Yorks 51 G8
Dewshall Court Hereford 25 E11
Dhoon IoM 48 D4
Dhoor IoM 48 C4
Dhowin IoM 48 B4
Dial Post W Sus 11 C10
Dibden Hants 10 D3
Dibden Purlieu Hants 10 D3
Dickleburgh Norf 39 G7
Didbrook Glos 27 E7
Didcot Oxon 18 C2
Diddington Cambs 29 B8
Diddlebury Shrops 33 G11
Didley Hereford 25 E11
Didling W Sus 11 C7
Didmarton Glos 16 C5
Didsbury Gtr Man 44 C2
Didworthy Devon 5 E7
Digby Lincs 46 G4
Digg Highld 85 B9
Diggle Gtr Man 44 B4
Digmoor Lancs 43 B7
Digswell Park Herts 29 G9
Dihewyd Ceredig 23 A9
Dilham Norf 39 C9
Dilhorne Staffs 34 A5
Dillarburn S Lanark 69 F7
Dillington Cambs 29 B8
Dilston Northumb 62 G5
Dilton Marsh Wilts 16 G5
Dilwyn Hereford 25 C11
Dinas Carms 23 C7
Dinas Gwyn 40 G4
Dinas Cross Pembs 22 C5
Dinas Dinlle Gwyn 40 E6
Dinas-Mawddwy Gwyn 32 D4
Dinas Powys V Glam 15 D7
Dinbych = Denbigh Denb 42 F3
Dinbych-y-Pysgod = Tenby Pembs 22 F6
Dinder Som 16 G2
Dinedor Hereford 26 E2
Dingestow Mon 25 G11
Dingle Mers 42 D6
Dingleden Kent 13 C7
Dingley Northants 36 G3
Dingwall Highld 87 F8
Dinlabyre Borders 61 D11
Dinmael Conwy 32 A6
Dinnet Aberds 82 D6
Dinnington S Yorks 45 D9
Dinnington Som 8 C3
Dinnington T&W 63 F8
Dinorwic Gwyn 41 D7
Dinton Bucks 28 G4
Dinton Wilts 9 A9
Dinwoodie Mains Dumfries 61 D7
Dinworthy Devon 6 E2
Dippen N Ayrs 66 D3
Dippenhall Sur 18 G5
Dipple Moray 88 C3
Dipple S Ayrs 66 F5
Diptford Devon 5 F8
Dipton Durham 58 A2
Dirdhu Highld 82 A2
Dirleton E Loth 70 B4
Dirt Pot Northumb 57 B10
Discoed Powys 25 B9
Diseworth Leics 35 C10
Dishes Orkney 95 F7
Dishforth N Yorks 51 B9
Disley Ches E 44 D3
Diss Norf 39 H7
Disserth Powys 25 C7
Distington Cumb 56 D2
Ditchampton Wilts 9 A9
Ditcheat Som 16 H3
Ditchingham Norf 39 F9
Ditchling E Sus 12 E2
Ditherington Shrops 33 D11
Dittisham Devon 5 F9
Ditton Halton 43 D7
Ditton Kent 20 F4
Ditton Green Cambs 30 C3
Ditton Priors Shrops 34 G2
Divach Highld 81 A6
Divlyn Carms 24 E4
Dixton Glos 26 E6
Dixton Mon 26 G2
Dobcross Gtr Man 44 B3
Dobwalls Corn 4 E3
Doc Penfro = Pembroke Dock Pembs 22 F4
Doccombe Devon 5 C8
Dochfour Ho. Highld 87 H9
Dochgarroch Highld 87 G9
Docking Norf 38 B3
Docklow Hereford 26 C2
Dockray Cumb 56 D5
Dockroyd W Yorks 50 F6
Dodburn Borders 61 C10
Doddinghurst Essex 20 B2
Doddington Cambs 37 F9
Doddington Kent 20 F6
Doddington Lincs 46 E3
Doddington Northumb 71 G8
Doddington Shrops 34 H2
Doddiscombsleigh Devon 5 C9
Dodford Northants 28 B3
Dodford Worcs 26 A6
Dodington S Glos 16 C4
Dodleston Ches W 42 F6
Dods Leigh Staffs 34 B6
Dodworth S Yorks 45 B7
Doe Green Warr 43 D8
Doe Lea Derbys 45 F8
Dog Village Devon 7 G8
Dogdyke Lincs 46 G6
Dogmersfield Hants 18 F4
Dogridge Wilts 17 C7
Dogsthorpe Pboro 37 E7
Dol-fôr Powys 32 E4
Dôl-y-Bont Ceredig 32 G2
Dol-y-cannau Powys 25 D9
Dolanog Powys 33 D6
Dolau Powys 25 B8
Dolau Rhondda 14 C5
Dolbenmaen Gwyn 41 F7
Dolfach Powys 32 E5
Dolfor Powys 33 G7
Dolgarrog Conwy 41 D9
Dolgellau Gwyn 32 D3
Dolgran Carms 23 C9
Dolhendre Gwyn 41 G10
Doll Highld 93 J11
Dollar Clack 76 H2
Dolley Green Powys 25 B9
Dollwen Ceredig 32 G2
Dolphin Flint 42 E4
Dolphinholme Lancs 49 D5
Dolphinton S Lanark 69 F10
Dolton Devon 6 E4
Dolwen Conwy 41 C10
Dolwen Powys 32 E5
Dolwyd Conwy 41 C10
Dolwyddelan Conwy 41 E9
Dolyhir Powys 25 C9
Doncaster S Yorks 45 B9
Dones Green Ches W 43 E9
Donhead St Andrew Wilts 9 B8
Donhead St Mary Wilts 9 B8
Donibristle Fife 69 B10
Donington Lincs 37 B8
Donington on Bain Lincs 46 D6
Donington South Ing Lincs 37 B8
Donisthorpe Leics 35 D9
Donkey Town Sur 18 E6
Donnington Glos 27 F8
Donnington Hereford 26 E4
Donnington Shrops 34 E1
Donnington Telford 34 D3
Donnington W Berks 17 E11
Donnington W Sus 11 D7
Donnington Wood Telford 34 D3
Donyatt Som 8 C2
Doonfoot S Ayrs 66 E6
Dorback Lodge Highld 82 B2
Dorchester Dorset 8 E5
Dorchester Oxon 18 B2
Dordon Warks 35 E8
Dore S Yorks 45 D7
Dores Highld 87 H8
Dorking Sur 19 G8
Dormansland Sur 12 B3
Dormanstown Redcar 59 D6
Dormington Hereford 26 D2
Dormston Worcs 26 C6
Dornal S Ayrs 54 B5
Dorney Bucks 18 D6
Dornie Highld 85 F13
Dornoch Highld 87 C10
Dornock Dumfries 61 G8
Dorrery Highld 94 E2
Dorridge W Mid 35 H7
Dorrington Lincs 46 G4
Dorrington Shrops 33 E10
Dorsington Warks 27 D8
Dorstone Hereford 25 D10
Dorton Bucks 28 G3
Dorusduain Highld 80 A1
Dosthill Staffs 35 F8
Dottery Dorset 8 E3
Doublebois Corn 4 E2
Dougarie N Ayrs 66 C1
Doughton Glos 16 B5
Douglas IoM 48 E3
Douglas S Lanark 69 G7
Douglas & Angus Dundee 77 D7
Douglas Water S Lanark 69 G7
Douglas West S Lanark 69 G7
Douglastown Angus 77 C7
Doulting Som 16 G3
Dounby Orkney 95 F3
Doune Highld 92 J7
Doune Stirling 75 G10
Doune Park Aberds 89 B7
Douneside Aberds 82 C6
Dounie Highld 87 B8
Dounreay Highld 93 C12
Dousland Devon 4 E6
Dovaston Shrops 33 C9
Dove Holes Derbys 44 E4
Dovenby Cumb 56 C2
Dover Kent 21 G10
Dovercourt Essex 31 E9
Doverdale Worcs 26 B5
Doveridge Derbys 35 B7
Doversgreen Sur 19 G9
Dowally Perth 76 C3
Dowbridge Lancs 49 F4
Dowdeswell Glos 26 G6
Dowlais M Tydf 25 H7
Dowland Devon 6 E4
Dowlish Wake Som 8 C2
Down Ampney Glos 17 B8
Down Hatherley Glos 26 F5
Down St Mary Devon 7 F6
Down Thomas Devon 4 F6
Downcraig Ferry N Ayrs 73 H10
Downderry Corn 4 F4
Downe London 19 E11
Downend IoW 10 F4
Downend S Glos 16 D3
Downend W Berks 17 D11
Downfield Dundee 76 D6
Downgate Corn 4 D4
Downham Essex 20 B4
Downham Lancs 50 E3
Downham Northumb 71 G7
Downham Market Norf 38 E2
Downhead Som 16 G3
Downhill Perth 76 D3
Downhill T&W 63 H9
Downholland Cross Lancs 42 B6
Downholme N Yorks 58 G2
Downies Aberds 83 D11
Downley Bucks 18 B5
Downside Som 16 G3
Downside Sur 19 F8
Downton Hants 10 E1
Downton Wilts 9 B10
Downton on the Rock Hereford 25 A11
Dowsby Lincs 37 C7
Dowsdale Lincs 37 D8
Dowthwaitehead Cumb 56 D5
Doxey Staffs 34 C5
Doxford Northumb 63 A7
Doxford Park T&W 58 A4
Doynton S Glos 16 D4
Draffan S Lanark 68 F6
Dragonby N Lincs 46 A3
Drakeland Corner Devon 5 F6
Drakemyre N Ayrs 66 A5
Drake's Broughton Worcs 26 D6
Drakes Cross Worcs 35 H6
Drakewalls Corn 4 D5
Draughton N Yorks 50 D6
Draughton Northants 36 H3
Drax N Yorks 52 G2
Draycote Warks 27 A11
Draycott Derbys 35 B10
Draycott Glos 27 E8
Draycott Som 15 F10
Draycott in the Clay Staffs 35 C7
Draycott in the Moors Staffs 34 A5
Drayford Devon 7 E6
Drayton Leics 36 F4
Drayton Lincs 37 B8
Drayton Norf 39 D7
Drayton Oxon 17 B11
Drayton Oxon 27 D11
Drayton Ptsmth 10 D5
Drayton Som 8 B3
Drayton Worcs 34 H5
Drayton Bassett Staffs 35 E7
Drayton Beauchamp Bucks 28 G6
Drayton Parslow Bucks 28 F5
Drayton St Leonard Oxon 18 B1
Dre-fach Carms 24 G3
Dre-fach Ceredig 23 B10
Drebley N Yorks 51 D6
Dreemskerry IoM 48 C4
Dreenhill Pembs 22 E4
Drefach Carms 23 C8
Drefach Carms 23 E10
Drefelin Carms 23 C8
Dreghorn N Ayrs 67 C6
Drellingore Kent 21 G9
Drem E Loth 70 C4
Dresden Stoke 34 A5
Dreumasdal W Isles 84 E2
Drewsteignton Devon 7 G6
Driby Lincs 47 E7
Driffield E Yorks 52 D6
Driffield Glos 17 B7
Drigg Cumb 56 G2
Drighlington W Yorks 51 G8
Drimnin Highld 79 F8
Drimpton Dorset 8 D3
Drimsynie Argyll 74 G4
Drinisiadar W Isles 90 H6
Drinkstone Suff 30 B6
Drinkstone Green Suff 30 B6
Drishaig Argyll 74 F4
Drissaig Argyll 73 B8
Drochil Borders 69 F10
Drointon Staffs 34 C6
Droitwich Spa Worcs 26 B5
Droman Highld 92 D4
Dron Perth 76 F4
Dronfield Derbys 45 E7
Dronfield Woodhouse Derbys 45 E7
Drongan E Ayrs 67 E7
Dronley Angus 76 D6
Droxford Hants 10 C5
Droylsden Gtr Man 44 C3
Druid Denb 32 A6
Druidston Pembs 22 E3
Druimarbin Highld 80 F2
Druimavuic Argyll 74 C3
Druimdrishaig Argyll 72 F6
Druimindarroch Highld 79 C9
Druimyeon More Argyll 65 C7
Drum Argyll 73 F8
Drum Perth 76 G3
Drumbeg Highld 92 F4
Drumblade Aberds 88 D5
Drumblair Aberds 89 D6
Drumbuie Dumfries 55 A8
Drumbuie Highld 85 E12
Drumburgh Cumb 61 H8
Drumburn Dumfries 60 G5
Drumchapel Glasgow 68 C4
Drumchardine Highld 87 G8
Drumchork Highld 91 J13
Drumclog S Lanark 68 G5
Drumderfit Highld 87 F9
Drumeldrie Fife 77 G7
Drumelzier Borders 69 G10
Drumfearn Highld 85 G11
Drumgask Highld 81 D8
Drumgley Angus 77 B7
Drumguish Highld 81 D9
Drumin Moray 88 E1
Drumlasie Aberds 83 C8
Drumlemble Argyll 65 G7
Drumligair Aberds 83 B11
Drumlithie Aberds 83 E9
Drummoddie Dumfries 54 E6
Drummond Highld 87 E9
Drummore Dumfries 54 F4
Drummuir Moray 88 D3
Drummuir Castle Moray 88 D3
Drumnadrochit Highld 81 A7
Drumnagorrach Moray 88 C5
Drumoak Aberds 83 D9
Drumpark Dumfries 60 E4
Drumphail Dumfries 54 C5
Drumrash Dumfries 55 B9
Drumrunie Highld 92 J4
Drums Aberds 89 F9
Drumsallie Highld 80 F1
Drumstinchall Dumfries 55 D11
Drumsturdy Angus 77 D7
Drumtochty Castle Aberds 83 F8
Drumtroddan Dumfries 54 E6
Drumuie Highld 85 D9
Drumuillie Highld 81 A11
Drumvaich Stirling 75 G9
Drumwhindle Aberds 89 E9
Drunkendub Angus 77 C9
Drury Flint 42 F5
Drury Square Norf 38 D5
Dry Doddington Lincs 46 H2
Dry Drayton Cambs 29 B10
Drybeck Cumb 57 E8
Drybridge Moray 88 B4
Drybridge N Ayrs 67 C6
Drybrook Glos 26 G3
Dryburgh Borders 70 G4
Dryhope Borders 61 A8
Drylaw Edin 69 C11
Drym Corn 2 F5
Drymen Stirling 68 B3
Drymuir Aberds 89 D9
Drynoch Highld 85 E9
Dryslwyn Carms 23 D10
Dryton Shrops 34 E1
Dubford Aberds 89 B8
Dubton Angus 77 B8
Duchally Highld 92 H6
Duchlage Argyll 68 B2
Duck Corner Suff 31 D10
Duckington Ches W 43 G7
Ducklington Oxon 27 H10
Duckmanton Derbys 45 E8
Duck's Cross Bedford 29 C8
Duddenhoe End Essex 29 E11
Duddingston Edin 69 C11
Duddington Northants 36 E5
Duddleswell E Sus 12 D3
Duddo Northumb 71 F8
Duddon Ches W 43 F8
Duddon Bridge Cumb 56 H4
Dudleston Shrops 33 B9
Dudleston Heath Shrops 33 B9
Dudley T&W 63 F8
Dudley W Mid 34 F5
Dudley Port W Mid 34 F5
Duffield Derbys 35 A9
Duffryn Neath 14 B4
Duffryn Newport 15 C8
Dufftown Moray 88 E3
Duffus Moray 88 B1
Dufton Cumb 57 D8
Duggleby N Yorks 52 C4
Duirinish Highld 85 E12
Duisdalemore Highld 85 G12
Duisky Highld 80 F2
Dukestown Bl Gwent 25 G8
Dukinfield Gtr Man 44 C3
Dulas Anglesey 40 B6
Dulcote Som 16 G2
Dulford Devon 7 F9
Dull Perth 75 C11
Dullatur N Lanark 68 C6
Dullingham Cambs 30 C3
Dulnain Bridge Highld 82 A1
Duloe Bedford 29 B8
Duloe Corn 4 F3
Dulsie Highld 87 G12
Dulverton Som 7 D8
Dulwich London 19 D10
Dumbarton W Dunb 68 C2
Dumbleton Glos 27 E7
Dumcrieff Dumfries 61 C7
Dumfries Dumfries 60 F5
Dumgoyne Stirling 68 B4
Dummer Hants 18 G2
Dumpford W Sus 11 B7
Dumpton Kent 21 E10
Dun Angus 77 B9
Dun Charlabhaigh W Isles 90 C6
Dunain Ho. Highld 87 G9
Dunalastair Perth 75 B10
Dunan Highld 85 F10
Dunans Argyll 73 D9
Dunball Som 15 G9
Dunbar E Loth 70 C5
Dunbeath Highld 94 H3
Dunbeg Argyll 79 H11
Dunblane Stirling 75 G10
Dunbog Fife 76 F5
Duncanston Highld 87 F8
Duncanstone Aberds 83 A7
Dunchurch Warks 27 A11
Duncote Northants 28 C3
Duncow Dumfries 60 E5
Duncraggan Stirling 75 G8
Duncrievie Perth 76 G4
Duncton W Sus 11 C8
Dundas Ho. Orkney 95 K5
Dundee Dundee 77 D7
Dundeugh Dumfries 67 H8
Dundon Som 8 A3
Dundonald S Ayrs 67 C6
Dundonnell Highld 86 C3
Dundonnell Hotel Highld 86 C3
Dundonnell House Highld 86 C4
Dundraw Cumb 56 B4
Dundreggan Highld 80 B5
Dundreggan Lodge Highld 80 B5
Dundrennan Dumfries 55 E10
Dundry N Som 16 E2
Dunecht Aberds 83 C9
Dunfermline Fife 69 B9
Dunfield Glos 17 B8
Dunford Bridge S Yorks 44 B5
Dungworth S Yorks 44 D6
Dunham Notts 46 E2
Dunham-on-the-Hill Ches W 43 E7
Dunham Town Gtr Man 43 D10
Dunhampton Worcs 26 B5
Dunholme Lincs 46 E4
Dunino Fife 77 F8
Dunipace Falk 69 B7
Dunira Perth 75 E10
Dunkeld Perth 76 C3
Dunkerton Bath 16 F4
Dunkeswell Devon 7 F10
Dunkeswick N Yorks 51 E9
Dunkirk Kent 21 F7
Dunkirk Norf 39 C8
Dunk's Green Kent 20 F3
Dunlappie Angus 83 G7
Dunley Hants 17 F11
Dunley Worcs 26 B4
Dunlichity Lodge Highld 87 H9
Dunlop E Ayrs 67 B7
Dunmaglass Lodge Highld 81 A7
Dunmore Argyll 72 G6
Dunmore Falk 69 B7
Dunnet Highld 94 C4
Dunnichen Angus 77 C8
Dunninald Angus 77 B10
Dunning Perth 76 F3
Dunnington E Yorks 53 D7
Dunnington Warks 27 C7
Dunnington York 52 D2
Dunnockshaw Lancs 50 G4
Dunollie Argyll 79 H11
Dunoon Argyll 73 F10
Dunragit Dumfries 54 D4
Dunrostan Argyll 72 E6
Duns Borders 70 E6
Duns Tew Oxon 27 F11
Dunsby Lincs 37 C7
Dunscore Dumfries 60 E4
Dunscroft S Yorks 45 B10
Dunsdale Redcar 59 E7
Dunsden Green Oxon 18 D4
Dunsfold Sur 19 H7
Dunsford Devon 5 C9
Dunshalt Fife 76 F5
Dunshillock Aberds 89 D9
Dunskey Ho. Dumfries 54 D3
Dunsley N Yorks 59 E9
Dunsmore Bucks 28 H5
Dunsop Bridge Lancs 50 D2
Dunstable C Beds 29 F7
Dunstall Staffs 35 C7
Dunstall Common Worcs 26 D5
Dunstall Green Suff 30 B4
Dunstan Northumb 63 B8
Dunstan Steads Northumb 63 A8
Dunster Som 7 B8
Dunston Lincs 46 F4
Dunston Norf 39 E8
Dunston Staffs 34 D5
Dunston T&W 63 G8
Dunsville S Yorks 45 B10
Dunswell E Yorks 53 F6
Dunsyre S Lanark 69 F9
Dunterton Devon 4 D4
Duntisbourne Abbots Glos 26 H6
Duntisbourne Leer Glos 26 H6
Duntisbourne Rouse Glos 26 H6
Duntish Dorset 8 D5
Duntocher W Dunb 68 C3
Dunton Bucks 28 F5
Dunton C Beds 29 D9
Dunton Norf 38 B4
Dunton Bassett Leics 35 F11
Dunton Green Kent 20 F2
Dunton Wayletts Essex 20 B3
Duntulm Highld 85 A9
Dunure S Ayrs 66 E5
Dunvant Swansea 23 G10
Dunvegan Highld 84 D7
Dunwich Suff 31 A11
Dunwood Staffs 44 G3
Dupplin Castle Perth 76 F3
Durdar Cumb 56 A6
Durgates E Sus 12 C5
Durham Durham 58 B3
Durisdeer Dumfries 60 C4
Durisdeermill Dumfries 60 C4
Durkar W Yorks 51 H9
Durleigh Som 15 H8
Durley Hants 10 C4
Durley Wilts 17 E9
Durnamuck Highld 86 B3
Durness Highld 92 C7
Durno Aberds 83 A9
Duror Highld 74 B2
Durran Argyll 73 C8
Durran Highld 94 D3
Durrington W Sus 11 D10
Durrington Wilts 17 G8
Dursley Glos 16 B4
Durston Som 8 B1
Durweston Dorset 9 D7
Dury Shetland 96 G6
Duston Northants 28 B4
Duthil Highld 81 A11
Dutlas Powys 33 H8
Duton Hill Essex 30 F3
Dutson Corn 4 C4
Dutton Ches W 43 E8
Duxford Cambs 29 D11
Duxford Oxon 17 B10
Dwygyfylchi Conwy 41 C9
Dwyran Anglesey 40 D6
Dyce Aberdeen 83 B10
Dye House Northumb 62 H5
Dyffryn Bridgend 14 B4
Dyffryn Carms 23 D8
Dyffryn Pembs 22 C4
Dyffryn Ardudwy Gwyn 32 C1
Dyffryn Castell Ceredig 32 G3
Dyffryn Ceidrych Carms 24 F4
Dyffryn Cellwen Neath 24 H5
Dyke Lincs 37 C7
Dyke Moray 87 F12
Dykehead Angus 76 A6
Dykehead N Lanark 69 E7
Dykehead Stirling 75 H8
Dykelands Aberds 83 G9
Dykends Angus 76 B5
Dykeside Aberds 89 D7
Dykesmains N Ayrs 66 B5
Dylife Powys 32 F4
Dymchurch Kent 13 D9
Dymock Glos 26 E4
Dyrham S Glos 16 D4
Dysart Fife 70 A2
Dyserth Denb 42 E3

E

Eachwick Northumb 63 F7
Eadar Dha Fhadhail W Isles 90 D5
Eagland Hill Lancs 49 E4
Eagle Lincs 46 F2
Eagle Barnsdale Lincs 46 F2
Eagle Moor Lincs 46 F2
Eaglescliffe Stockton 58 E5
Eaglesfield Cumb 56 D2
Eaglesfield Dumfries 61 F8
Eaglesham E Renf 68 E4
Eaglethorpe Northants 37 F6
Eairy IoM 48 E2
Eakley Lanes M Keynes 28 C5
Eakring Notts 45 F10
Ealand N Lincs 45 A11
Ealing London 19 C8
Eals Northumb 62 H2
Eamont Bridge Cumb 57 D7
Earby Lancs 50 E5
Earcroft Blackburn 50 G2
Eardington Shrops 34 F3
Eardisland Hereford 25 C11
Eardisley Hereford 25 D10
Eardiston Shrops 33 C9
Eardiston Worcs 26 B3
Earith Cambs 29 A10
Earl Shilton Leics 35 F10
Earl Soham Suff 31 B9
Earl Sterndale Derbys 44 F4
Earl Stonham Suff 31 C8
Earle Northumb 71 H8
Earley Wokingham 18 D4
Earlham Norf 39 E8
Earlish Highld 85 B8
Earls Barton Northants 28 B5
Earls Colne Essex 30 F5
Earl's Croome Worcs 26 D5
Earl's Green Suff 31 B7
Earlsdon W Mid 35 H9
Earlsferry Fife 77 H7
Earlsfield Lincs 36 B5
Earlsford Aberds 89 E8
Earlsheaton W Yorks 51 G8
Earlsmill Moray 87 F12
Earlston Borders 70 G4
Earlston E Ayrs 67 C7
Earlswood Mon 15 B10
Earlswood Sur 19 G9
Earlswood Warks 27 A8
Earnley W Sus 11 E7
Earsairidh W Isles 84 J2
Earsdon T&W 63 F9
Earsham Norf 39 G9
Earswick York 52 D2
Eartham W Sus 11 D8
Easby N Yorks 58 F2
Easby N Yorks 59 F6
Easdale Argyll 72 B6
Easebourne W Sus 11 B7
Easenhall Warks 35 H10
Eashing Sur 18 G6
Easington Bucks 28 G3
Easington Durham 58 B5
Easington E Yorks 53 H9
Easington Northumb 71 G10
Easington Oxon 18 B3
Easington Oxon 27 E11
Easington Redcar 59 E8
Easington Colliery Durham 58 B5
Easington Lane T&W 58 B4
Easingwold N Yorks 51 C11
Easole Street Kent 21 F9
Eassie Angus 76 C6
East Aberthaw V Glam 14 E6
East Adderbury Oxon 27 E11
East Allington Devon 5 G8
East Anstey Devon 7 D7
East Appleton N Yorks 58 G3
East Ardsley W Yorks 51 G9
East Ashling W Sus 11 D7
East Auchronie Aberds 83 C10
East Ayton N Yorks 59 H10
East Bank Bl Gwent 25 H9
East Barkwith Lincs 46 D5
East Barming Kent 20 F4
East Barnby N Yorks 59 E9
East Barnet London 19 B9
East Barns E Loth 70 C6
East Barsham Norf 38 B5
East Beckham Norf 39 B7
East Bedfont London 19 D7
East Bergholt Suff 31 E7
East Bilney Norf 38 D5
East Blatchington E Sus 12 F3
East Boldre Hants 10 D2
East Brent Som 15 F9
East Bridgford Notts 36 A2
East Buckland Devon 6 C5
East Budleigh Devon 7 H9
East Burrafirth Shetland 96 H5
East Burton Dorset 9 F7
East Butsfield Durham 58 B2
East Butterwick N Lincs 46 B2
East Cairnbeg Aberds 83 F9
East Calder W Loth 69 D9
East Carleton Norf 39 E7
East Carlton Northants 36 G4
East Carlton W Yorks 51 E8
East Chaldon Dorset 9 F6
East Challow Oxon 17 C10
East Chiltington E Sus 12 E2
East Chinnock Som 8 C3
East Chisenbury Wilts 17 F8
East Clandon Sur 19 F7
East Claydon Bucks 28 F4
East Clyne Highld 93 J12
East Coker Som 8 C4
East Combe Som 7 C10
East Common N Yorks 52 F2
East Compton Som 16 G3
East Cottingwith E Yorks 52 E3
East Cowes IoW 10 E4
East Cowick E Yorks 52 G2
East Cowton N Yorks 58 F4
East Cramlington Northumb 63 F8
East Cranmore Som 16 G3
East Creech Dorset 9 F8
East Croachy Highld 81 A8
East Croftmore Highld 81 B11
East Curthwaite Cumb 56 B5
East Dean E Sus 12 G4
East Dean Hants 10 B1
East Dean W Sus 11 C8
East Down Devon 6 B5
East Drayton Notts 45 E11
East Ella Hull 53 G6
East End Dorset 9 E8
East End E Yorks 53 G8
East End Hants 10 B5
East End Hants 10 E2
East End Hants 17 E11
East End Herts 29 F11
East End Kent 13 C7
East End N Som 15 D10
East End Oxon 27 G10
East Farleigh Kent 20 F4
East Farndon Northants 36 G3
East Ferry Lincs 46 C2
East Fortune E Loth 70 C4
East Garston W Berks 17 D10
East Ginge Oxon 17 C11
East Goscote Leics 36 D2
East Grafton Wilts 17 E9
East Grimstead Wilts 9 B11
East Grinstead W Sus 12 C2
East Guldeford E Sus 13 D8
East Haddon Northants 28 B3
East Hagbourne Oxon 18 C2
East Halton N Lincs 53 H7
East Ham London 19 C11
East Hanney Oxon 17 B11
East Hanningfield Essex 20 A4
East Hardwick W Yorks 51 H10
East Harling Norf 38 G5
East Harlsey N Yorks 58 G5
East Harnham Wilts 9 B10
East Harptree Bath 16 F2
East Hartford Northumb 63 F8
East Harting W Sus 11 C6
East Hatley Cambs 29 C9
East Hauxwell N Yorks 58 G2
East Haven Angus 77 D8
East Heckington Lincs 37 A7
East Hedleyhope Durham 58 B2
East Hendred Oxon 17 C11
East Herrington T&W 58 A4
East Heslerton N Yorks 52 B5
East Hoathly E Sus 12 E4
East Horrington Som 16 G2
East Horsley Sur 19 F7
East Horton Northumb 71 G9
East Huntspill Som 15 G9
East Hyde C Beds 29 G8
East Ilkerton Devon 6 B6
East Ilsley W Berks 17 C11
East Keal Lincs 47 F7
East Kennett Wilts 17 E8
East Keswick W Yorks 51 E9
East Kilbride S Lanark 68 E5
East Kirkby Lincs 47 F7
East Knapton N Yorks 52 B4
East Knighton Dorset 9 F7
East Knoyle Wilts 9 A7
East Kyloe Northumb 71 G9
East Lambrook Som 8 C3
East Lamington Highld 87 D10
East Langdon Kent 21 G10
East Langton Leics 36 F3
East Langwell Highld 93 J10
East Lavant W Sus 11 D7
East Lavington W Sus 11 C8
East Layton N Yorks 58 F2
East Leake Notts 36 C1
East Learmouth Northumb 71 G7
East Leigh Devon 6 F5
East Lexham Norf 38 D4
East Lilburn Northumb 62 A6
East Linton E Loth 70 C4
East Liss Hants 11 B6
East Looe Corn 4 F3
East Lound N Lincs 45 C11
East Lulworth Dorset 9 F7
East Lutton N Yorks 52 C5
East Lydford Som 8 A4
East Mains Aberds 83 D8
East Malling Kent 20 F4
East March Angus 77 D7
East Marden W Sus 11 C7
East Markham Notts 45 E11
East Marton N Yorks 50 D5
East Meon Hants 10 B5
East Mere Devon 7 E8
East Mersea Essex 31 G7
East Mey Highld 94 C5
East Molesey Sur 19 E8
East Morden Dorset 9 E8
East Morton W Yorks 51 E6
East Ness N Yorks 52 B2
East Newton E Yorks 53 F8
East Norton Leics 36 E3
East Nynehead Som 7 D10
East Oakley Hants 18 F2
East Ogwell Devon 5 D9
East Orchard Dorset 9 C7
East Ord Northumb 71 E8
East Panson Devon 6 G2
East Peckham Kent 20 G3
East Pennard Som 16 H2
East Perry Cambs 29 B8
East Portlemouth Devon 5 H8
East Prawle Devon 5 H8
East Preston W Sus 11 D9
East Putford Devon 6 E2
East Quantoxhead Som 7 B10
East Rainton T&W 58 B4
East Ravendale NE Lincs 46 C6
East Raynham Norf 38 C4
East Rhidorroch Lodge Highld 86 B5
East Rigton W Yorks 51 E9
East Rounton N Yorks 58 F5
East Row N Yorks 59 E9
East Rudham Norf 38 C4
East Runton Norf 39 A7
East Ruston Norf 39 C9
East Saltoun E Loth 70 D3
East Sleekburn Northumb 63 E8
East Somerton Norf 39 D10
East Stockwith Lincs 45 C11
East Stoke Dorset 9 F7
East Stoke Notts 45 H11
East Stour Dorset 9 B7
East Stourmouth Kent 21 E9
East Stowford Devon 6 D5
East Stratton Hants 18 H2
East Studdal Kent 21 G10
East Suisnish Highld 85 E10
East Taphouse Corn 4 E2
East-the-Water Devon 6 D3
East Thirston Northumb 63 D7
East Tilbury Thurrock 20 D3
East Tisted Hants 10 A6
East Torrington Lincs 46 D5
East Tuddenham Norf 39 D6
East Tytherley Hants 10 B1
East Tytherton Wilts 16 D6
East Village Devon 7 F7
East Wall Shrops 33 F11
East Walton Norf 38 D3
East Wellow Hants 10 B2
East Wemyss Fife 76 H6
East Whitburn W Loth 69 D8
East Williamston Pembs 22 F5
East Winch Norf 38 D2
East Winterslow Wilts 9 A11
East Wittering W Sus 11 E6
East Witton N Yorks 58 H2
East Woodburn Northumb 62 E5
East Woodhay Hants 17 E11
East Worldham Hants 18 H4
East Worlington Devon 7 E6
East Worthing W Sus 11 D10
Eastbourne E Sus 12 G5
Eastbridge Suff 31 B11
Eastburn W Yorks 50 E6
Eastbury London 19 B7
Eastbury W Berks 17 D10
Eastby N Yorks 50 D6
Eastchurch Kent 20 D6
Eastcombe Glos 16 A5
Eastcote London 19 C8
Eastcote Northants 28 C3
Eastcote W Mid 35 H7
Eastcott Corn 6 E1
Eastcott Wilts 17 F7
Eastcourt Wilts 16 B6
Eastcourt Wilts 17 E9
Easter Ardross Highld 87 D9
Easter Balmoral Aberds 82 D4
Easter Boleskine Highld 81 A7
Easter Compton S Glos 16 C2
Easter Cringate Stirling 68 B6
Easter Davoch Aberds 82 C6
Easter Earshaig Dumfries 60 C6
Easter Fearn Highld 87 C9
Easter Galcantray Highld 87 G11
Easter Howgate Midloth 69 D11
Easter Howlaws Borders 70 F6
Easter Kinkell Highld 87 F8
Easter Lednathie Angus 76 A6
Easter Milton Highld 87 F12
Easter Moniack Highld 87 G8
Easter Ord Aberdeen 83 C10
Easter Quarff Shetland 96 K6
Easter Rhynd Perth 76 F4
Easter Row Stirling 75 H10
Easter Silverford Aberds 89 B7
Easter Skeld Shetland 96 J5
Easter Whyntie Aberds 88 B6
Eastergate W Sus 11 D8
Easterhouse Glasgow 68 D5
Eastern Green W Mid 35 G8

Easterton Wilts 17 F7
Eastertown Som 15 F9
Eastertown of Auchleuchries Aberds 89 E10
Eastfield N Lanark 69 D7
Eastfield N Yorks 52 A6
Eastfield Hall Northumb 63 C8
Eastgate Durham 57 C11
Eastgate Norf 39 C7
Eastham Mers 42 D6
Eastham Ferry Mers 42 D6
Easthampstead Brack 18 E5
Eastheath Wokingham 18 E5
Easthope Shrops 34 F1
Easthorpe Essex 30 F6
Easthorpe Leics 36 B4
Easthorpe Notts 45 G11
Easthouses Midloth 70 D2
Eastington Devon 7 F6
Eastington Glos 26 H4
Eastington Glos 27 G8
Eastleach Martin Glos 27 H9
Eastleach Turville Glos 27 H8
Eastleigh Devon 6 D3
Eastleigh Hants 10 C3
Eastling Kent 20 F6
Eastmoor Derbys 45 E7
Eastmoor Norf 38 E3
Eastney Ptsmth 10 E5
Eastnor Hereford 26 E4
Eastoft N Lincs 52 H4
Eastoke Hants 10 E6
Easton Cambs 29 A8
Easton Cumb 61 F10
Easton Cumb 61 H8
Easton Devon 5 C8
Easton Dorset 8 G5
Easton Hants 10 A4
Easton Lincs 36 C5
Easton Norf 39 D7
Easton Som 15 G11
Easton Suff 31 C9
Easton Wilts 16 D5
Easton Grey Wilts 16 C5
Easton-in-Gordano N Som 15 D11
Easton Maudit Northants 28 C5
Easton on the Hill Northants 36 E6
Easton Royal Wilts 17 E9
Eastpark Dumfries 60 G6
Eastrea Cambs 37 F8
Eastriggs Dumfries 61 G8
Eastrington E Yorks 52 G3
Eastry Kent 21 F10
Eastville Bristol 16 D3
Eastville Lincs 47 G8
Eastwell Leics 36 C3
Eastwick Herts 29 G11
Eastwick Shetland 96 F5
Eastwood Notts 45 H8
Eastwood Southend 20 C5
Eastwood W Yorks 50 G5
Eathorpe Warks 27 B10
Eaton Ches E 44 F2
Eaton Ches W 43 F8
Eaton Leics 36 C3
Eaton Norf 39 E8
Eaton Notts 45 E11
Eaton Oxon 17 A11
Eaton Shrops 33 G9
Eaton Shrops 33 G11
Eaton Bishop Hereford 25 E11
Eaton Bray C Beds 28 F6
Eaton Constantine Shrops 34 E1
Eaton Green C Beds 28 F6
Eaton Hastings Oxon 17 B9
Eaton on Tern Shrops 34 C2
Eaton Socon Cambs 29 C8
Eavestone N Yorks 51 C8
Ebberston N Yorks 52 A4
Ebbesbourne Wake Wilts 9 B8
Ebbw Vale = Glyn Ebwy Bl Gwent 25 H8
Ebchester Durham 63 H7
Ebford Devon 5 C10
Ebley Glos 26 H5
Ebnal Ches W 43 H7
Ebrington Glos 27 D8
Ecchinswell Hants 17 F11
Ecclaw Borders 70 D6
Ecclefechan Dumfries 61 F7
Eccles Borders 70 F6
Eccles Gtr Man 43 C10
Eccles Kent 20 E4
Eccles on Sea Norf 39 C10
Eccles Road Norf 38 F6
Ecclesall S Yorks 45 D7
Ecclesfield S Yorks 45 C7
Ecclesgreig Aberds 83 G9
Eccleshall Staffs 34 C4
Eccleshill W Yorks 51 F7
Ecclesmachan W Loth 69 C9
Eccleston Ches W 43 F7
Eccleston Lancs 49 H5
Eccleston Mers 43 C7
Eccleston Park Mers 43 C7
Eccup W Yorks 51 E8
Echt Aberds 83 C9
Eckford Borders 70 H6
Eckington Derbys 45 E8
Eckington Worcs 26 D6
Ecton Northants 28 B5
Edale Derbys 44 D5
Edburton W Sus 11 C11
Edderside Cumb 56 B2
Edderton Highld 87 C10
Eddistone Devon 6 D1
Eddleston Borders 69 F11
Eden Park London 19 E10
Edenbridge Kent 19 G11
Edenfield Lancs 50 H3
Edenhall Cumb 57 C7
Edenham Lincs 37 C6
Edensor Derbys 44 F6
Edentaggart Argyll 68 A2
Edenthorpe S Yorks 45 B10
Edentown Cumb 61 H9
Ederline Argyll 73 C7
Edern Gwyn 40 G4
Edgarley Som 15 H11
Edgbaston W Mid 35 G6
Edgcott Bucks 28 F3
Edgcott Som 7 C7
Edge Shrops 33 E9
Edge End Glos 26 G2
Edge Green Ches W 43 G7
Edge Hill Mers 42 C6
Edgebolton Shrops 34 C1
Edgefield Norf 39 B6
Edgefield Street Norf 39 B6
Edgeside Lancs 50 G4
Edgeworth Glos 26 H6
Edgmond Telford 34 D3
Edgmond Marsh Telford 34 C3
Edgton Shrops 33 G9
Edgware London 19 B8
Edgworth Blackburn 50 H3
Edinample Stirling 75 E8
Edinbane Highld 85 C8
Edinburgh Edin 69 C11
Edingale Staffs 35 D8
Edingight Ho. Moray 88 C5
Edingley Notts 45 G10
Edingthorpe Norf 39 B9
Edingthorpe Green Norf 39 B9
Edington Som 15 H9
Edington Wilts 16 F6
Edintore Moray 88 D4
Edith Weston Rutland 36 E5
Edithmead Som 15 G9
Edlesborough Bucks 28 G6
Edlingham Northumb 63 C7
Edlington Lincs 46 E6
Edmondsham Dorset 9 C9
Edmondsley Durham 58 B3
Edmondthorpe Leics 36 D4
Edmonstone Orkney 95 F6
Edmonton London 19 B10
Edmundbyers Durham 58 A1
Ednam Borders 70 G6
Ednaston Derbys 35 A8
Edradynate Perth 75 B11
Edrom Borders 71 E7
Edstaston Shrops 33 B11
Edstone Warks 27 B8
Edvin Loach Hereford 26 C3
Edwalton Notts 36 B1
Edwardstone Suff 30 D6
Edwinsford Carms 24 E3
Edwinstowe Notts 45 F10
Edworth C Beds 29 D9
Edwyn Ralph Hereford 26 C3
Edzell Angus 83 G7
Efail Isaf Rhondda 14 C6
Efailnewydd Gwyn 40 G5
Efailwen Carms 22 D6
Efenechtyd Denb 42 G4
Effingham Sur 19 F8
Effirth Shetland 96 H5
Efford Devon 7 F7
Egdon Worcs 26 C6
Egerton Gtr Man 43 A10
Egerton Kent 20 G6
Egerton Forstal Kent 20 G5
Eggborough N Yorks 52 G1
Eggbuckland Plym 4 F6
Eggington C Beds 28 F6
Egginton Derbys 35 C8
Egglescliffe Stockton 58 E5
Eggleston Durham 57 D11
Egham Sur 19 D7
Egleton Rutland 36 E4
Eglingham Northumb 63 B7
Egloshayle Corn 3 B8
Egloskerry Corn 4 C3
Eglwys-Brewis V Glam 14 E6
Eglwys Cross Wrex 33 A10
Eglwys Fach Ceredig 32 F2
Eglwysbach Conwy 41 C10
Eglwyswen Pembs 22 C6
Eglwyswrw Pembs 22 C6
Egmanton Notts 45 F11
Egremont Cumb 56 E2
Egremont Mers 42 C6
Egton N Yorks 59 F9
Egton Bridge N Yorks 59 F9
Eight Ash Green Essex 30 F6
Eignaig Highld 79 G10
Eil Highld 81 B10
Eilanreach Highld 85 G13
Eilean Darach Highld 86 C4
Eileanach Lodge Highld 87 E8
Einacleite W Isles 90 E6
Eisgean W Isles 91 F8
Eisingrug Gwyn 41 G8
Elan Village Powys 24 B6
Elberton S Glos 16 C3
Elburton Plym 4 F6
Elcho Perth 76 E4
Elcombe Swindon 17 C8
Eldernell Cambs 37 F9
Eldersfield Worcs 26 E5
Elderslie Renfs 68 D3
Eldon Durham 58 D3
Eldrick S Ayrs 54 A5
Eldroth N Yorks 50 C3
Eldwick W Yorks 51 E7
Elfhowe Cumb 56 G6
Elford Northumb 71 G10
Elford Staffs 35 D7
Elgin Moray 88 B2
Elgol Highld 85 G10
Elham Kent 21 G8
Elie Fife 77 G7
Elim Anglesey 40 B5
Eling Hants 10 C2
Elishader Highld 85 B10
Elishaw Northumb 62 D4
Elkesley Notts 45 E10
Elkstone Glos 26 G6
Ellan Highld 81 A10
Elland W Yorks 51 G7
Ellary Argyll 72 F6
Ellastone Staffs 35 A7
Ellemford Borders 70 D6
Ellenbrook IoM 48 E3
Ellenhall Staffs 34 C4
Ellen's Green Sur 19 H7
Ellerbeck N Yorks 58 G5
Ellerburn N Yorks 52 A4
Ellerby N Yorks 59 E8
Ellerdine Heath Telford 34 C2
Ellerhayes Devon 7 F8
Elleric Argyll 74 C3
Ellerker E Yorks 52 G5
Ellerton E Yorks 52 F3
Ellerton Shrops 34 C3
Ellesborough Bucks 28 H5
Ellesmere Shrops 33 B10
Ellesmere Port Ches W 43 E7
Ellingham Norf 39 F9
Ellingham Northumb 71 H10
Ellingstring N Yorks 51 A7
Ellington Cambs 29 A8
Ellington Northumb 63 D8
Elliot Angus 77 D9
Ellisfield Hants 18 G3
Ellistown Leics 35 D10
Ellon Aberds 89 E9
Ellonby Cumb 56 C6
Ellough Suff 39 G10
Elloughton E Yorks 52 G5
Ellwood Glos 26 H2
Elm Cambs 37 E10
Elm Hill Dorset 9 B7
Elm Park London 20 C2
Elmbridge Worcs 26 B6
Elmdon Essex 29 E11
Elmdon W Mid 35 G7
Elmdon Heath W Mid 35 G7
Elmers End London 19 E10
Elmesthorpe Leics 35 F10
Elmfield IoW 10 E5
Elmhurst Staffs 35 D7
Elmley Castle Worcs 26 D6
Elmley Lovett Worcs 26 B5
Elmore Glos 26 G4
Elmore Back Glos 26 G4
Elmscott Devon 6 D1
Elmsett Suff 31 D7
Elmstead Market Essex 31 F7
Elmsted Kent 13 B10
Elmstone Kent 21 E9
Elmstone Hardwicke Glos 26 F6
Elmswell E Yorks 52 D5
Elmswell Suff 30 B6
Elmton Derbys 45 E9
Elphin Highld 92 H5
Elphinstone E Loth 70 C2
Elrick Aberds 83 C10
Elrig Dumfries 54 E6
Elsdon Northumb 62 D5
Elsecar S Yorks 45 C7
Elsenham Essex 30 F2
Elsfield Oxon 28 G2
Elsham N Lincs 46 A4
Elsing Norf 39 D6
Elslack N Yorks 50 E5
Elson Shrops 33 B9
Elsrickle S Lanark 69 F9
Elstead Sur 18 G6
Elsted W Sus 11 C7
Elsthorpe Lincs 37 C6
Elstob Durham 58 D4
Elston Notts 45 H11
Elston Wilts 17 G7
Elstone Devon 6 E5
Elstow Bedford 29 D7
Elstree Herts 19 B8
Elstronwick E Yorks 53 F8
Elswick Lancs 49 F4
Elsworth Cambs 29 B10
Elterwater Cumb 56 F5
Eltham London 19 D11
Eltisley Cambs 29 C9
Elton Cambs 37 F6
Elton Ches W 43 E7
Elton Derbys 44 F6
Elton Glos 26 G4
Elton Hereford 25 A11
Elton Notts 36 B3
Elton Stockton 58 E5
Elton Green Ches W 43 E7
Elvanfoot S Lanark 60 B5
Elvaston Derbys 35 B10
Elveden Suff 38 H4
Elvingston E Loth 70 C3
Elvington Kent 21 F9
Elvington York 52 E2
Elwick Hrtlpl 58 C5
Elwick Northumb 71 G10
Elworth Ches E 43 F10
Elworthy Som 7 C9
Ely Cambs 37 G11
Ely Cardiff 15 D7
Emberton M Keynes 28 D5
Embleton Cumb 56 C3
Embleton Northumb 63 A8
Embo Highld 87 B11
Embo Street Highld 87 B11
Emborough Som 16 F3
Embsay N Yorks 50 D6
Emersons Green S Glos 16 D3
Emery Down Hants 10 D1
Emley W Yorks 44 A6
Emmbrook Wokingham 18 E4
Emmer Green Reading 18 D4
Emmington Oxon 18 A4
Emneth Norf 37 E10
Emneth Hungate Norf 37 E11
Empingham Rutland 36 E5
Empshott Hants 11 A6
Emstrey Shrops 33 D11
Emsworth Hants 10 D6
Enborne W Berks 17 E11
Enchmarsh Shrops 33 F11
Enderby Leics 35 F11
Endmoor Cumb 49 A5
Endon Staffs 44 G3
Endon Bank Staffs 44 G3
Enfield London 19 B10
Enfield Wash London 19 B10
Enford Wilts 17 F8
Engamoor Shetland 96 H4
Engine Common S Glos 16 C3
Englefield W Berks 18 D3
Englefield Green Sur 18 D6
Englesea-brook Ches E 43 G10
English Bicknor Glos 26 G2
English Frankton Shrops 33 C10
Englishcombe Bath 16 E4
Enham Alamein Hants 17 G10
Enmore Som 8 A1
Ennerdale Bridge Cumb 56 E2
Enoch Dumfries 60 C4
Enochdhu Perth 76 A3
Ensay Argyll 78 G6
Ensbury Bmouth 9 E9
Ensdon Shrops 33 D10
Ensis Devon 6 D4
Enstone Oxon 27 F10
Enterkinfoot Dumfries 60 C4
Enterpen N Yorks 58 F5
Enville Staffs 34 G4
Eolaigearraidh W Isles 84 H2
Eorabus Argyll 78 J6
Eòropaidh W Isles 91 A10
Epperstone Notts 45 H10
Epping Essex 19 A11
Epping Green Essex 29 H11
Epping Green Herts 29 H9
Epping Upland Essex 19 A11
Eppleby N Yorks 58 E2
Eppleworth E Yorks 52 F6
Epsom Sur 19 E9
Epwell Oxon 27 D10
Epworth N Lincs 45 B11
Epworth Turbary N Lincs 45 B11
Erbistock Wrex 33 A9
Erbusaig Highld 85 F12
Erchless Castle Highld 86 G7
Erdington W Mid 35 F7
Eredine Argyll 73 C8
Eriboll Highld 92 D7
Ericstane Dumfries 60 B6
Eridge Green E Sus 12 C4
Erines Argyll 73 F7
Eriswell Suff 38 H3
Erith London 20 D2
Erlestoke Wilts 16 F6
Ermine Lincs 46 E3
Ermington Devon 5 F7
Erpingham Norf 39 B7
Errogie Highld 81 A7
Errol Perth 76 E5
Erskine Renfs 68 C3
Erskine Bridge Renfs 68 C3
Ervie Dumfries 54 C3
Erwarton Suff 31 E9
Erwood Powys 25 D7
Eryholme N Yorks 58 F4
Eryrys Denb 42 G5
Escomb Durham 58 D2
Escrick N Yorks 52 E2
Esgairdawe Carms 24 D3
Esgairgeiliog Powys 32 E3
Esh Durham 58 B2
Esh Winning Durham 58 B2
Esher Sur 19 E8
Esholt W Yorks 51 E7
Eshott Northumb 63 D8
Eshton N Yorks 50 D5
Esk Valley N Yorks 59 F9
Eskadale Highld 86 H7
Eskbank Midloth 70 D2
Eskdale Green Cumb 56 F3
Eskdalemuir Dumfries 61 D8
Eske E Yorks 53 E6
Eskham Lincs 47 C7
Esprick Lancs 49 F4
Essendine Rutland 36 D6
Essendon Herts 29 H9
Essich Highld 87 H9
Essington Staffs 34 E5
Esslemont Aberds 89 F9
Eston Redcar 59 E6
Eswick Shetland 96 H6
Etal Northumb 71 G8
Etchilhampton Wilts 17 E7
Etchingham E Sus 12 D6
Etchinghill Kent 21 H8
Etchinghill Staffs 34 D6
Ethie Castle Angus 77 C9
Ethie Mains Angus 77 C9
Etling Green Norf 38 D6
Eton Windsor 18 D6
Eton Wick Windsor 18 D6
Etteridge Highld 81 D8
Ettersgill Durham 57 D10
Ettingshall W Mid 34 F5
Ettington Warks 27 D9
Etton E Yorks 52 E5
Etton Pboro 37 E7
Ettrick Borders 61 B8
Ettrickbridge Borders 61 A9
Ettrickhill Borders 61 B8
Etwall Derbys 35 B8
Euston Suff 38 H4
Euximoor Drove Cambs 37 F10
Euxton Lancs 50 H1
Evanstown Bridgend 14 C5
Evanton Highld 87 E9
Evedon Lincs 46 H4
Evelix Highld 87 B10
Evenjobb Powys 25 B9
Evenley Northants 28 E2
Evenlode Glos 27 F9
Evenwood Durham 58 D2
Evenwood Gate Durham 58 D2
Everbay Orkney 95 F7
Evercreech Som 16 H3
Everdon Northants 28 C2
Everingham E Yorks 52 E4
Everleigh Wilts 17 F9
Everley N Yorks 59 H10
Eversholt C Beds 28 E6
Evershot Dorset 8 D4
Eversley Hants 18 E4
Eversley Cross Hants 18 E4
Everthorpe E Yorks 52 F5
Everton C Beds 29 C9
Everton Hants 10 E1
Everton Mers 42 C6
Everton Notts 45 C10
Evertown Dumfries 61 F9
Evesbatch Hereford 26 D3
Evesham Worcs 27 D7
Evington Leicester 36 E2
Ewden Village S Yorks 44 C6
Ewell Sur 19 E9
Ewell Minnis Kent 21 G9
Ewelme Oxon 18 B3
Ewen Glos 17 B7
Ewenny V Glam 14 D5
Ewerby Lincs 46 H5
Ewerby Thorpe Lincs 46 H5
Ewes Dumfries 61 D9
Ewesley Northumb 62 D6
Ewhurst Sur 19 G7
Ewhurst Green E Sus 13 D6
Ewhurst Green Sur 19 H7
Ewloe Flint 42 F6
Ewloe Grn. Flint 42 F5
Ewood Blackburn 50 G2
Eworthy Devon 6 G3
Ewshot Hants 18 G5
Ewyas Harold Hereford 25 F10
Exbourne Devon 6 F5
Exbury Hants 10 E3
Exebridge Devon 7 D8
Exelby N Yorks 58 H3
Exeter Devon 7 G8
Exford Som 7 C7
Exhall Warks 27 C8
Exley Head W Yorks 50 F6
Exminster Devon 5 C10
Exmouth Devon 5 C11
Exnaboe Shetland 96 M5
Exning Suff 30 B3
Exton Devon 5 C10
Exton Hants 10 B5
Exton Rutland 36 D5
Exton Som 7 C8
Exwick Devon 7 G8
Eyam Derbys 44 E6
Eydon Northants 28 C2
Eye Hereford 25 B11
Eye Pboro 37 E8
Eye Suff 31 A8
Eye Green Pboro 37 E8
Eyemouth Borders 71 D8
Eyeworth C Beds 29 D9
Eyhorne Street Kent 20 F5
Eyke Suff 31 C10
Eynesbury Cambs 29 C8
Eynort Highld 85 F8
Eynsford Kent 20 E2
Eynsham Oxon 27 H11
Eype Dorset 8 E3
Eyre Highld 85 C9
Eyre Highld 85 E10
Eythorne Kent 21 G9
Eyton Hereford 25 B11
Eyton Shrops 33 G9
Eyton Wrex 33 A9
Eyton upon the Weald Moors Telford 34 D2

F

Faccombe Hants 17 F10
Faceby N Yorks 58 F5
Facit Lancs 50 H4
Faddiley Ches E 43 G8
Fadmoor N Yorks 59 H7
Faerdre Swansea 14 A2
Failand N Som 15 D11
Failford S Ayrs 67 D7
Failsworth Gtr Man 44 B2
Fain Highld 86 D4
Fair Green Norf 38 D2
Fair Hill Cumb 57 C7
Fair Oak Hants 10 C3
Fair Oak Green Hants 18 E3
Fairbourne Gwyn 32 D2
Fairburn N Yorks 51 G10
Fairfield Derbys 44 E4
Fairfield Stockton 58 E5
Fairfield Worcs 27 D7
Fairfield Worcs 34 H5
Fairford Glos 17 A8
Fairhaven Lancs 49 G3
Fairlie N Ayrs 73 H11
Fairlight E Sus 13 E7
Fairlight Cove E Sus 13 E7
Fairmile Devon 7 G9
Fairmilehead Edin 69 D11
Fairoak Staffs 34 B3
Fairseat Kent 20 E3
Fairstead Essex 30 G4
Fairstead Norf 38 D2
Fairwarp E Sus 12 D3
Fairy Cottage IoM 48 D4
Fairy Cross Devon 6 D3
Fakenham Norf 38 C5
Fakenham Magna Suff 38 H5
Fala Midloth 70 D3
Fala Dam Midloth 70 D3
Falahill Borders 70 E2
Falcon Hereford 26 E3
Faldingworth Lincs 46 D4
Falfield S Glos 16 B3
Falkenham Suff 31 E9
Falkirk Falk 69 C7
Falkland Fife 76 G5
Falla Borders 62 B3
Fallgate Derbys 45 F7
Fallin Stirling 69 A7
Fallowfield Gtr Man 44 C2
Fallsidehill Borders 70 F5
Falmer E Sus 12 F2
Falmouth Corn 3 F7
Falsgrave N Yorks 59 H11
Falstone Northumb 62 E3
Fanagmore Highld 92 E4
Fangdale Beck N Yorks 59 G6
Fangfoss E Yorks 52 D3
Fankerton Falk 68 B6
Fanmore Argyll 78 G7
Fannich Lodge Highld 86 E5
Fans Borders 70 F5
Far Bank S Yorks 45 A10
Far Bletchley M Keynes 28 E5
Far Cotton Northants 28 C4
Far Forest Worcs 26 A4
Far Laund Derbys 45 H7
Far Sawrey Cumb 56 G5
Farcet Cambs 37 F8
Farden Shrops 34 H1
Fareham Hants 10 D4
Farewell Staffs 35 D6
Farforth Lincs 47 E7
Faringdon Oxon 17 B9
Farington Lancs 49 G5
Farlam Cumb 61 H11
Farlary Highld 93 J10
Farleigh N Som 15 E10
Farleigh Sur 19 E10
Farleigh Hungerford Som 16 F5
Farleigh Wallop Hants 18 G3
Farlesthorpe Lincs 47 E8
Farleton Cumb 49 A5
Farleton Lancs 50 C1
Farley Shrops 33 E9
Farley Staffs 35 A6
Farley Wilts 9 B11
Farley Green Sur 19 G7
Farley Hill Luton 29 F7
Farley Hill Wokingham 18 E4
Farleys End Glos 26 G4
Farlington N Yorks 52 C2
Farlow Shrops 34 G2
Farmborough Bath 16 E3
Farmcote Glos 27 F7
Farmcote Shrops 34 F3
Farmington Glos 27 G8
Farmoor Oxon 27 H11
Farmtown Moray 88 C5
Farnborough Hants 18 F5
Farnborough London 19 E11
Farnborough W Berks 17 C11
Farnborough Warks 27 D11
Farnborough Green Hants 18 F5
Farncombe Sur 18 G6
Farndish Bedford 28 B6
Farndon Ches W 43 G7
Farndon Notts 45 G11
Farnell Angus 77 B9
Farnham Dorset 9 C8
Farnham Essex 29 F11
Farnham N Yorks 51 C9
Farnham Suff 31 B10
Farnham Sur 18 G5
Farnham Common Bucks 18 C6
Farnham Green Essex 29 F11
Farnham Royal Bucks 18 C6
Farnhill N Yorks 50 E6
Farningham Kent 20 E2
Farnley N Yorks 51 E8
Farnley W Yorks 51 F8
Farnley Tyas W Yorks 44 A5
Farnsfield Notts 45 G10
Farnworth Gtr Man 43 B10
Farnworth Halton 43 D8
Farr Highld 81 C10
Farr Highld 87 H9
Farr Highld 93 C10
Farr House Highld 87 H9
Farringdon Devon 7 G9
Farrington Gurney Bath 16 F3
Farsley W Yorks 51 F8
Farthinghoe Northants 28 E2
Farthingloe Kent 21 G9
Farthingstone Northants 28 C3
Fartown W Yorks 51 H7
Farway Devon 7 G10
Fasag Highld 85 C13
Fascadale Highld 79 D8
Faslane Port Argyll 73 E11
Fasnacloich Argyll 74 C3
Fasnakyle Ho Highld 80 A5
Fassfern Highld 80 F2
Fatfield T&W 58 A4
Fattahead Aberds 89 C6
Faugh Cumb 57 A7
Fauldhouse W Loth 69 D8
Faulkbourne Essex 30 G4
Faulkland Som 16 F4
Fauls Shrops 34 B1
Faversham Kent 21 E7
Favillar Moray 88 E2
Fawdington N Yorks 51 B10
Fawfieldhead Staffs 44 F4
Fawkham Green Kent 20 E2
Fawler Oxon 27 G10
Fawley Bucks 18 C4
Fawley Hants 10 D3
Fawley W Berks 17 C10
Fawley Chapel Hereford 26 F2
Faxfleet E Yorks 52 G4
Faygate W Sus 11 A11
Fazakerley Mers 43 C6
Fazeley Staffs 35 E8
Fearby N Yorks 51 A7
Fearn Highld 87 D11
Fearn Lodge Highld 87 C9
Fearn Station Highld 87 D11
Fearnan Perth 75 C10
Fearnbeg Highld 85 C12
Fearnhead Warr 43 C9
Fearnmore Highld 85 B12
Featherstone Staffs 34 E5
Featherstone W Yorks 51 G10
Featherwood Northumb 62 C4
Feckenham Worcs 27 B7
Feering Essex 30 F5
Feetham N Yorks 57 G11
Feizor N Yorks 50 C3
Felbridge Sur 12 C2
Felbrigg Norf 39 B8
Felcourt Sur 12 B2
Felden Herts 19 A7
Felin-Crai Powys 24 F5
Felindre Carms 23 C8
Felindre Carms 23 D10
Felindre Carms 24 E3
Felindre Carms 24 F4
Felindre Ceredig 23 A10
Felindre Powys 33 G7
Felindre Swansea 14 A2
Felindre Farchog Pembs 22 C6
Felinfach Ceredig 23 A10
Felinfach Powys 25 E7
Felinfoel Carms 23 F10
Felingwm isaf Carms 23 D10
Felingwm uchaf Carms 23 D10
Felinwynt Ceredig 23 A7
Felixkirk N Yorks 51 A10
Felixstowe Suff 31 E9
Felixstowe Ferry Suff 31 E10
Felkington Northumb 71 F8
Felkirk W Yorks 45 A7
Fell Side Cumb 56 C5
Felling T&W 63 G8
Felmersham Bedford 28 C6
Felmingham Norf 39 C8
Felpham W Sus 11 E8
Felsham Suff 30 C6
Felsted Essex 30 F3
Feltham London 19 D8
Felthorpe Norf 39 D7
Felton Hereford 26 D2
Felton N Som 15 E11
Felton Northumb 63 C7
Felton Butler Shrops 33 D9
Feltwell Norf 38 F3
Fen Ditton Cambs 29 B11
Fen Drayton Cambs 29 B10
Fen End W Mid 35 H8
Fen Side Lincs 47 G7
Fenay Bridge W Yorks 51 H7
Fence Lancs 50 F4
Fence Houses T&W 58 A4
Fengate Norf 39 C7
Fengate Pboro 37 F8
Fenham Northumb 71 F9
Fenhouses Lincs 37 A8
Feniscliffe Blackburn 50 G2
Feniscowles Blackburn 50 G2
Feniton Devon 7 G10
Fenlake Bedford 29 D7
Fenny Bentley Derbys 44 G5
Fenny Bridges Devon 7 G10
Fenny Compton Warks 27 C11
Fenny Drayton Leics 35 F9
Fenny Stratford M Keynes 28 E5
Fenrother Northumb 63 D7
Fenstanton Cambs 29 B10
Fenton Cambs 37 H9
Fenton Lincs 46 E2
Fenton Lincs 46 G2
Fenton Stoke 34 A4
Fenton Barns E Loth 70 B4
Fenton Town Northumb 71 G8
Fenwick E Ayrs 67 B7
Fenwick Northumb 62 F6
Fenwick Northumb 71 F9
Fenwick S Yorks 52 H1
Feochaig Argyll 65 G8
Feock Corn 3 F7
Feolin Ferry Argyll 72 G3
Ferindonald Highld 85 H11
Feriniquarrie Highld 84 C6
Ferlochan Argyll 74 C2
Fern Angus 77 A7
Ferndale Rhondda 14 B6
Ferndown Dorset 9 D9
Ferness Highld 87 G12
Ferney Green Cumb 56 G6
Fernham Oxon 17 B9
Fernhill Heath Worcs 26 C5
Fernhurst W Sus 11 B7
Fernie Fife 76 F6
Ferniegair S Lanark 68 E6
Fernilea Highld 85 E8
Fernilee Derbys 44 E4
Ferrensby N Yorks 51 C9
Ferring W Sus 11 D9
Ferry Hill Cambs 37 G9
Ferry Point Highld 87 C10
Ferrybridge W Yorks 51 G10
Ferryden Angus 77 B10
Ferryhill Aberdeen 83 C11
Ferryhill Durham 58 C3
Ferryhill Station Durham 58 C4
Ferryside Carms 23 E8
Fersfield Norf 39 G6
Fersit Highld 80 F5
Ferwig Ceredig 22 B6
Feshiebridge Highld 81 C10
Fetcham Sur 19 F8
Fetterangus Aberds 89 C9
Fettercairn Aberds 83 F8
Fettes Highld 87 F8
Fewcott Oxon 28 F2
Fewston N Yorks 51 D7
Ffair-Rhos Ceredig 24 B4
Ffairfach Carms 24 F3
Ffaldybrenin Carms 24 D3
Ffarmers Carms 24 D3
Ffawyddog Powys 25 G9
Fforest Carms 23 F10
Fforest-fâch Swansea 14 B2
Ffos-y-ffin Ceredig 24 B1
Ffostrasol Ceredig 23 B8
Ffridd-Uchaf Gwyn 41 E7
Ffrith Wrex 42 G5
Ffrwd Gwyn 40 E6
Ffynnon ddrain Carms 23 D9
Ffynnon-oer Ceredig 23 A10
Ffynnongroyw Flint 42 D4
Fidden Argyll 78 J6
Fiddes Aberds 83 E10
Fiddington Glos 26 E6
Fiddington Som 7 B11
Fiddleford Dorset 9 C7
Fiddlers Hamlet Essex 19 A11
Field Staffs 34 B6
Field Broughton Cumb 49 A3
Field Dalling Norf 38 B6
Field Head Leics 35 E10
Fifehead Magdalen Dorset 9 B6
Fifehead Neville Dorset 9 C6
Fifield Oxon 27 G9
Fifield Wilts 17 F8
Fifield Windsor 18 D6
Fifield Bavant Wilts 9 B9
Figheldean Wilts 17 G8
Filands Wilts 16 C6
Filby Norf 39 D10
Filey N Yorks 53 A7
Filgrave M Keynes 28 D5
Filkins Oxon 17 A9
Filleigh Devon 6 D5
Filleigh Devon 7 E6
Fillingham Lincs 46 D3
Fillongley Warks 35 G8
Filton S Glos 16 D3
Fimber E Yorks 52 C4
Finavon Angus 77 B7
Finchairn Argyll 73 C8
Fincham Norf 38 E2
Finchampstead Wokingham 18 E4
Finchdean Hants 10 C6
Finchingfield Essex 30 E3
Finchley London 19 B9
Findern Derbys 35 B9
Findhorn Moray 87 E13
Findhorn Bridge Highld 81 A10
Findo Gask Perth 76 E3
Findochty Moray 88 B4
Findon Aberds 83 D11
Findon W Sus 11 D10
Findon Mains Highld 87 E9
Findrack Ho. Aberds 83 C8
Finedon Northants 28 A6
Fingal Street Suff 31 B9
Fingask Aberds 83 A9
Fingerpost Worcs 26 A4
Fingest Bucks 18 B4
Finghall N Yorks 58 H2
Fingland Cumb 61 H8
Fingland Dumfries 60 B3
Finglesham Kent 21 F10
Fingringhoe Essex 31 F7
Finlarig Stirling 75 D8
Finmere Oxon 28 E3
Finnart Perth 75 B8
Finningham Suff 31 B7
Finningley S Yorks 45 C10
Finnygaud Aberds 88 C5
Finsbury London 19 C10
Finstall Worcs 26 B6
Finsthwaite Cumb 56 H5
Finstock Oxon 27 G10
Finstown Orkney 95 G4
Fintry Aberds 89 C7
Fintry Dundee 77 D7
Fintry Stirling 68 B5
Finzean Aberds 83 D8
Fionnphort Argyll 78 J6
Fionnsbhagh W Isles 90 J5
Fir Tree Durham 58 C2
Firbeck S Yorks 45 D9
Firby N Yorks 52 C3
Firby N Yorks 58 H3
Firgrove Gtr Man 44 A3
Firsby Lincs 47 F8
Firsdown Wilts 9 A11
First Coast Highld 86 B2
Fishbourne IoW 10 E4
Fishbourne W Sus 11 D7
Fishburn Durham 58 C4
Fishcross Clack 75 H11
Fisher Place Cumb 56 E5
Fisherford Aberds 89 E6
Fisher's Pond Hants 10 B3
Fisherstreet W Sus 11 A8
Fisherton Highld 87 F10
Fisherton S Ayrs 66 E5
Fishguard = Abergwaun Pembs 22 C4
Fishlake S Yorks 45 A10
Fishleigh Barton Devon 6 D4
Fishponds Bristol 16 D3
Fishpool Glos 26 F3
Fishtoft Lincs 37 A9
Fishtoft Drove Lincs 47 H7
Fishtown of Usan Angus 77 B10
Fishwick Borders 71 E8
Fiskavaig Highld 85 E8
Fiskerton Lincs 46 E4
Fiskerton Notts 45 G11
Fitling E Yorks 53 F8
Fittleton Wilts 17 G8
Fittleworth W Sus 11 C9
Fitton End Cambs 37 D10
Fitz Shrops 33 D10
Fitzhead Som 7 D10
Fitzwilliam W Yorks 51 H10
Fiunary Highld 79 G9
Five Acres Glos 26 G2
Five Ashes E Sus 12 D4
Five Oak Green Kent 20 G3
Five Oaks Jersey 11
Five Oaks W Sus 11 B9
Five Roads Carms 23 F9
Fivecrosses Ches W 43 E8
Fivehead Som 8 B2
Flack's Green Essex 30 G4
Flackwell Heath Bucks 18 C5
Fladbury Worcs 26 D6
Fladdabister Shetland 96 K6
Flagg Derbys 44 F5
Flamborough E Yorks 53 B8
Flamstead Herts 29 G7
Flamstead End Herts 19 A10
Flansham W Sus 11 D8
Flanshaw W Yorks 51 G9
Flasby N Yorks 50 D5
Flash Staffs 44 F4
Flashader Highld 85 C8
Flask Inn N Yorks 59 F10
Flaunden Herts 19 A7
Flawborough Notts 36 A3
Flawith N Yorks 51 C10
Flax Bourton N Som 15 E11
Flaxby N Yorks 51 D9
Flaxholme Derbys 35 A9
Flaxley Glos 26 G3
Flaxpool Som 7 C10
Flaxton N Yorks 52 C2
Fleckney Leics 36 F2
Flecknoe Warks 28 B2
Fledborough Notts 46 E2
Fleet Hants 10 D6
Fleet Hants 18 F5
Fleet Lincs 37 C9
Fleet Hargate Lincs 37 C9
Fleetham Northumb 71 H10
Fleetlands Hants 10 D4
Fleetville Herts 29 H8
Fleetwood Lancs 49 E3
Flemingston V Glam 14 D6
Flemington S Lanark 68 E5
Flempton Suff 30 B5
Fleoideabhagh W Isles 90 J5
Fletchertown Cumb 56 B4
Fletching E Sus 12 D3
Flexbury Corn 6 F1
Flexford Sur 18 G6
Flimby Cumb 56 C2
Flimwell E Sus 12 C6
Flint = Y Fflint Flint 42 E5
Flint Mountain Flint 42 E5
Flintham Notts 45 H11
Flinton E Yorks 53 F8
Flintsham Hereford 25 C10
Flitcham Norf 38 C3
Flitton C Beds 29 E7
Flitwick C Beds 29 E7
Flixborough N Lincs 52 H4
Flixborough Stather N Lincs 46 A2
Flixton Gtr Man 43 C10
Flixton N Yorks 52 B6
Flixton Suff 39 G9
Flockton W Yorks 44 A6
Flodaigh W Isles 84 C3
Flodden Northumb 71 G8
Flodigarry Highld 85 A9
Flood's Ferry Cambs 37 F9
Flookburgh Cumb 49 B3
Florden Norf 39 F7
Flore Northants 28 B3
Flotterton Northumb 62 C5
Flowton Suff 31 D7
Flush House W Yorks 44 B5
Flushing Aberds 89 D10
Flushing Corn 3 F7
Flyford Flavell Worcs 26 C6
Foals Green Suff 31 A9
Fobbing Thurrock 20 C4
Fochabers Moray 88 C3
Fochriw Caerph 25 H8
Fockerby N Lincs 52 H4
Fodderletter Moray 82 A3
Fodderty Highld 87 F8
Foel Powys 32 D5
Foel-gastell Carms 23 E10
Foffarty Angus 77 C7
Foggathorpe E Yorks 52 F3
Fogo Borders 70 F6
Fogorig Borders 70 F6
Foindle Highld 92 E4
Folda Angus 76 A4
Fole Staffs 34 B6
Foleshill W Mid 35 G9
Folke Dorset 8 C5
Folkestone Kent 21 H9
Folkingham Lincs 37 B6
Folkington E Sus 12 F4
Folksworth Cambs 37 G7
Folkton N Yorks 53 B6
Folla Rule Aberds 89 E7
Follifoot N Yorks 51 D9
Folly Gate Devon 6 G4
Fonthill Bishop Wilts 9 A8
Fonthill Gifford Wilts 9 A8
Fontmell Magna Dorset 9 C7
Fontwell W Sus 11 D8
Foolow Derbys 44 E5
Foots Cray London 19 D11
Forbestown Aberds 82 B5
Force Mills Cumb 56 G5
Forcett N Yorks 58 E2
Ford Argyll 73 C7
Ford Bucks 28 H4
Ford Devon 6 D3
Ford Glos 27 F7
Ford Northumb 71 G8
Ford Shrops 33 D10
Ford Staffs 44 G4
Ford W Sus 11 D8
Ford Wilts 16 D5
Ford End Essex 30 G3
Ford Street Som 7 E10
Fordcombe Kent 12 B4
Fordell Fife 69 B10
Forden Powys 33 E8
Forder Grn. Devon 5 E8
Fordham Cambs 30 A3
Fordham Essex 30 F6
Fordham Norf 38 F2
Fordhouses W Mid 34 E5
Fordingbridge Hants 9 C10
Fordon E Yorks 52 B6
Fordoun Aberds 83 F9
Ford's Green Suff 31 B7
Fordstreet Essex 30 F6
Fordwells Oxon 27 G10
Fordwich Kent 21 F8
Fordyce Aberds 88 B5
Forebridge Staffs 34 C5
Forest Durham 57 C10
Forest Becks Lancs 50 D3
Forest Gate London 19 C11
Forest Green Sur 19 G8
Forest Hall Cumb 57 F7
Forest Head Cumb 61 H11
Forest Hill Oxon 28 H2
Forest Lane Head N Yorks 51 D9
Forest Lodge Argyll 74 C5
Forest Lodge Highld 82 B2
Forest Lodge Perth 81 F11
Forest Mill Clack 69 A8
Forest Row E Sus 12 C3
Forest Town Notts 45 F9
Forestburn Gate Northumb 62 D6
Foresterseat Moray 88 C1
Forestside W Sus 11 C6
Forfar Angus 77 B7
Forgandenny Perth 76 F3
Forge Powys 32 F3
Forge Side Torf 25 H9
Forgewood N Lanark 68 E6
Forgie Moray 88 C3
Forglen Ho. Aberds 89 C6
Formby Mers 42 B6
Forncett End Norf 39 F7
Forncett St Mary Norf 39 F7
Forncett St Peter Norf 39 F7
Forneth Perth 76 C3
Fornham All Saints Suff 30 B5
Fornham St Martin Suff 30 B5
Forres Moray 87 F13
Forrest Lodge Dumfries 67 H8
Forrestfield N Lanark 69 D7
Forsbrook Staffs 34 A5
Forse Highld 94 G4
Forse Ho. Highld 94 G4
Forsinain Highld 93 E12
Forsinard Highld 93 E11
Forsinard Station Highld 93 E11
Forston Dorset 8 E5
Fort Augustus Highld 80 C5
Fort George Guern 11
Fort George Highld 87 F10
Fort William Highld 80 F3
Forteviot Perth 76 F3
Forth S Lanark 69 E8
Forth Road Bridge Edin 69 C10
Forthampton Glos 26 E5
Fortingall Perth 75 C10
Forton Hants 17 G11
Forton Lancs 49 D4
Forton Shrops 33 D10
Forton Som 8 D2
Forton Staffs 34 C3
Forton Heath Shrops 33 D10
Fortrie Aberds 89 D6
Fortrose Highld 87 F10
Fortuneswell Dorset 8 G5
Forty Green Bucks 18 B6
Forty Hill London 19 B10
Forward Green Suff 31 C7
Fosbury Wilts 17 F10
Fosdyke Lincs 37 B9
Foss Perth 75 B10
Foss Cross Glos 27 H7
Fossebridge Glos 27 G7
Foster Street Essex 29 H11
Fosterhouses S Yorks 45 A10
Foston Derbys 35 B7
Foston Lincs 36 A4
Foston N Yorks 52 C2
Foston on the Wolds E Yorks 53 D7
Fotherby Lincs 47 C7
Fotheringhay Northants 37 F6
Foubister Orkney 95 H6
Foul Mile E Sus 12 E5
Foulby W Yorks 51 H9
Foulden Borders 71 E8
Foulden Norf 38 F3
Foulis Castle Highld 87 E8
Foulridge Lancs 50 E4
Foulsham Norf 38 C6
Fountainhall Borders 70 F3
Four Ashes Staffs 34 G4
Four Ashes Suff 31 A7
Four Crosses Powys 33 D8
Four Crosses Powys 33 E6
Four Crosses Wrex 42 G5
Four Elms Kent 19 G11
Four Forks Som 7 C11
Four Gotes Cambs 37 D10
Four Lane Ends Ches W 43 F8
Four Lanes Corn 2 F5
Four Marks Hants 10 A5
Four Mile Bridge Anglesey 40 C4
Four Oaks E Sus 13 D7
Four Oaks W Mid 35 F7
Four Oaks W Mid 35 G8
Four Roads Carms 23 F9
Four Roads IoM 48 F2
Four Throws Kent 13 D6
Fourlane Ends Derbys 45 G7
Fourlanes End Ches E 44 G2
Fourpenny Highld 87 B11
Fourstones Northumb 62 G4
Fovant Wilts 9 B9
Foveran Aberds 89 F9
Fowey Corn 4 F2
Fowley Common Warr 43 C9
Fowlis Angus 76 D6
Fowlis Wester Perth 76 E2
Fowlmere Cambs 29 D11
Fownhope Hereford 26 E2
Fox Corner Sur 18 F6
Fox Lane Hants 18 F5
Fox Street Essex 31 F7
Foxbar Renfs 68 D3
Foxcombe Hill Oxon 17 A11
Foxdale IoM 48 E2
Foxearth Essex 30 D5
Foxfield Cumb 56 H4
Foxham Wilts 16 D6
Foxhole Corn 3 D8
Foxhole Swansea 14 B2
Foxholes N Yorks 52 B6
Foxhunt Green E Sus 12 E4
Foxley Norf 38 C6
Foxley Wilts 16 C5
Foxt Staffs 44 H4
Foxton Cambs 29 D11
Foxton Durham 58 D4
Foxton Leics 36 F3
Foxup N Yorks 50 B4
Foxwist Green Ches W 43 F9
Foxwood Shrops 34 H2
Foy Hereford 26 F2
Foyers Highld 81 A6
Fraddam Corn 2 F4
Fraddon Corn 3 D8
Fradley Staffs 35 D7
Fradswell Staffs 34 B5
Fraisthorpe E Yorks 53 C7
Framfield E Sus 12 D3
Framingham Earl Norf 39 E8
Framingham Pigot Norf 39 E8
Framlingham Suff 31 B9
Frampton Dorset 8 E5
Frampton Lincs 37 B9
Frampton Cotterell S Glos 16 C3
Frampton Mansell Glos 16 A6
Frampton on Severn Glos 26 H4
Frampton West End Lincs 37 A8
Framsden Suff 31 C8
Framwellgate Moor Durham 58 B3
Franche Worcs 34 H4
Frankby Mers 42 D5
Frankley Worcs 34 G5
Frank's Bridge Powys 25 C8
Frankton Warks 27 A11
Frant E Sus 12 C4
Fraserburgh Aberds 89 B9
Frating Green Essex 31 F7
Fratton Ptsmth 10 E5
Freathy Corn 4 F4
Freckenham Suff 30 A3
Freckleton Lancs 49 G4
Freeby Leics 36 C4
Freehay Staffs 34 A6
Freeland Oxon 27 G11
Freester Shetland 96 H6
Freethorpe Norf 39 E10
Freiston Lincs 37 A9
Fremington Devon 6 C4
Fremington N Yorks 58 G1
Frenchay S Glos 16 D3
Frenchbeer Devon 5 C7
Frenich Stirling 75 G7
Frensham Sur 18 G5
Fresgoe Highld 93 C12
Freshfield Mers 42 B5
Freshford Bath 16 E4
Freshwater IoW 10 F2
Freshwater Bay IoW 10 F2
Freshwater East Pembs 22 G5
Fressingfield Suff 39 H8
Freston Suff 31 E8
Freswick Highld 94 D5
Fretherne Glos 26 H4
Frettenham Norf 39 D8
Freuchie Fife 76 G5
Freuchies Angus 76 A5
Freystrop Pembs 22 E4
Friar's Gate E Sus 12 C3
Friarton Perth 76 E4
Friday Bridge Cambs 37 E10
Friday Street E Sus 12 F5
Fridaythorpe E Yorks 52 D4
Friern Barnet London 19 B9
Friesland Argyll 78 F4
Friesthorpe Lincs 46 D4
Frieston Lincs 46 H3
Frieth Bucks 18 B4
Frilford Oxon 17 B11
Frilsham W Berks 18 D2
Frimley Sur 18 F5
Frimley Green Sur 18 F5
Frindsbury Medway 20 D4
Fring Norf 38 B3
Fringford Oxon 28 F3
Frinsted Kent 20 F5
Frinton-on-Sea Essex 31 F9
Friockheim Angus 77 C8
Friog Gwyn 32 D2
Frisby on the Wreake Leics 36 D2
Friskney Lincs 47 G8
Friskney Eaudike Lincs 47 G8
Friskney Tofts Lincs 47 G8
Friston E Sus 12 G4
Friston Suff 31 B11
Fritchley Derbys 45 G7
Frith Bank Lincs 47 H7
Frith Common Worcs 26 B3
Fritham Hants 9 C11
Frithelstock Devon 6 E3
Frithelstock Stone Devon 6 E3
Frithville Lincs 47 G7
Frittenden Kent 13 B7
Frittiscombe Devon 5 G9
Fritton Norf 39 E10
Fritton Norf 39 F8
Fritwell Oxon 28 F2
Frizinghall W Yorks 51 F7
Frizington Cumb 56 E2
Frocester Glos 16 A4
Frodesley Shrops 33 E11
Frodingham N Lincs 46 A2
Frodsham Ches W 43 E8
Frogden Borders 70 H6
Froggatt Derbys 44 E6
Froghall Staffs 44 H4
Frogmore Devon 5 G8
Frogmore Hants 18 F5
Frognall Lincs 37 D7
Frogshail Norf 39 B8
Frolesworth Leics 35 F11
Frome Som 16 G4
Frome St Quintin Dorset 8 D4
Fromes Hill Hereford 26 D3
Fron Denb 42 F3
Fron Gwyn 40 G5
Fron Gwyn 41 E7
Fron Powys 25 B7
Fron Powys 33 E8
Fron Powys 33 F7
Froncysyllte Wrex 33 A8
Frongoch Gwyn 32 B5
Frostenden Suff 39 G10
Frosterley Durham 58 C1
Frotoft Orkney 95 F5
Froxfield Wilts 17 E9
Froxfield Green Hants 10 B6
Froyle Hants 18 G4
Fryerning Essex 20 A3
Fryton N Yorks 52 B2
Fulbeck Lincs 46 G3
Fulbourn Cambs 30 C2
Fulbrook Oxon 27 G9
Fulford Som 7 D11
Fulford Staffs 34 B5
Fulford York 52 E2
Fulham London 19 D9
Fulking W Sus 11 C11
Full Sutton E Yorks 52 D3
Fullarton Glasgow 68 D5
Fullarton N Ayrs 66 C6
Fuller Street Essex 30 G4
Fuller's Moor Ches W 43 G7
Fullerton Hants 17 H10
Fulletby Lincs 46 E6
Fullwood E Ayrs 67 A7
Fulmer Bucks 18 C6
Fulmodestone Norf 38 B5
Fulnetby Lincs 46 E4
Fulstow Lincs 47 C7
Fulwell T&W 63 H9
Fulwood Lancs 49 F5
Fulwood S Yorks 45 D7
Fundenhall Norf 39 F7
Fundenhall Street Norf 39 F7
Funtington W Sus 11 D6
Funtley Hants 10 D4
Funtullich Perth 75 E10
Funzie Shetland 96 D8
Furley Devon 8 D1
Furnace Argyll 73 C9
Furnace Carms 23 F10
Furnace End Warks 35 F8
Furneaux Pelham Herts 29 F11
Furness Vale Derbys 44 D4
Furze Platt Windsor 18 C5
Furzehill Devon 7 B6
Fyfett Som 7 E11
Fyfield Essex 30 H2
Fyfield Glos 17 A9
Fyfield Hants 17 G9
Fyfield Oxon 17 B11
Fyfield Wilts 17 E8
Fylingthorpe N Yorks 59 F10
Fyvie Aberds 89 E7

G

Gabhsann bho Dheas W Isles 91 B9
Gabhsann bho Thuath W Isles 91 B9
Gablon Highld 87 B10
Gabroc Hill E Ayrs 67 A7
Gaddesby Leics 36 D2
Gadebridge Herts 29 H7
Gaer Powys 25 F8
Gaerllwyd Mon 15 B10
Gaerwen Anglesey 40 C6
Gagingwell Oxon 27 F11
Gaick Lodge Highld 81 E9
Gailey Staffs 34 D5
Gainford Durham 58 E2
Gainsborough Lincs 46 C2
Gainsborough Suff 31 D8
Gainsford End Essex 30 E4
Gairloch Highld 85 A13
Gairlochy Highld 80 E3
Gairney Bank Perth 76 H4
Gairnshiel Lodge Aberds 82 C4
Gaisgill Cumb 57 F8
Gaitsgill Cumb 56 B5
Galashiels Borders 70 G3
Galgate Lancs 49 D4
Galhampton Som 8 B5
Gallaberry Dumfries 60 E5
Gallachoille Argyll 72 E6
Gallanach Argyll 78 E5
Gallanach Argyll 79 J11
Gallantry Bank Ches E 43 G8
Gallatown Fife 69 A11
Galley Common Warks 35 F9
Galley Hill Cambs 29 B10
Galleyend Essex 20 A4
Galleywood Essex 20 A4
Gallin Perth 75 C8
Gallowfauld Angus 77 C7
Gallows Green Staffs 35 A6
Galltair Highld 85 F13
Galmisdale Highld 78 C7
Galmpton Devon 5 G7
Galmpton Torbay 5 F9
Galphay N Yorks 51 B8
Galston E Ayrs 67 C8
Galtrigill Highld 84 C6
Gamblesby Cumb 57 C8
Gamesley Derbys 44 C4
Gamlingay Cambs 29 C9
Gammersgill N Yorks 51 A6
Gamston Notts 45 E11
Ganarew Hereford 26 G2
Ganavan Argyll 79 H11
Gang Corn 4 E4
Ganllwyd Gwyn 32 C3
Gannochy Angus 83 F7
Gannochy Perth 76 E4
Gansclet Highld 94 F5
Ganstead E Yorks 53 F7
Ganthorpe N Yorks 52 B2
Ganton N Yorks 52 B5
Garbat Highld 86 E7
Garbhallt Argyll 73 D9
Garboldisham Norf 38 G6
Garden City Flint 42 F6
Garden Village W Yorks 51 F10
Garden Village Wrex 42 G6
Gardenstown Aberds 89 B7
Garderhouse Shetland 96 J5
Gardham E Yorks 52 E5
Gardin Shetland 96 G6
Gare Hill Som 16 G4
Garelochhead Argyll 73 D11
Garford Oxon 17 B11
Garforth W Yorks 51 F10
Gargrave N Yorks 50 D5
Gargunnock Stirling 68 A6
Garlic Street Norf 39 G8
Garlieston Dumfries 55 E7
Garlinge Green Kent 21 F8
Garlogie Aberds 83 C9
Garmond Aberds 89 C8
Garmony Argyll 79 G9
Garmouth Moray 88 B3
Garn-yr-erw Torf 25 G9
Garnant Carms 24 G3
Garndiffaith Torf 15 A8
Garndolbenmaen Gwyn 40 F6
Garnedd Conwy 41 E9
Garnett Bridge Cumb 57 G7
Garnfadryn Gwyn 40 G4
Garnkirk N Lanark 68 D5
Garnlydan Bl Gwent 25 G8
Garnswllt Swansea 24 H3
Garrabost W Isles 91 D10
Garraron Argyll 73 C7
Garras Corn 2 G6
Garreg Gwyn 41 F8
Garrick Perth 75 F11
Garrigill Cumb 57 B9
Garriston N Yorks 58 G2
Garroch Dumfries 55 A8
Garrogie Lodge Highld 81 B7
Garros Highld 85 B9
Garrow Perth 75 C11
Garryhorn Dumfries 67 G8
Garsdale Cumb 57 H9
Garsdale Head Cumb 57 G9
Garsdon Wilts 16 C6
Garshall Green Staffs 34 B5
Garsington Oxon 18 A2
Garstang Lancs 49 E4
Garston Mers 43 D7
Garswood Mers 43 C8
Gartcosh N Lanark 68 D5
Garth Bridgend 14 B4
Garth Gwyn 41 C7
Garth Powys 24 D6
Garth Shetland 96 H4
Garth Wrex 33 A8
Garth Row Cumb 57 G7
Garthamlock Glasgow 68 D5
Garthbrengy Powys 25 E7
Garthdee Aberdeen 83 C11
Gartheli Ceredig 23 A10
Garthmyl Powys 33 F7
Garthorpe Leics 36 C4
Garthorpe N Lincs 52 H4
Gartly Aberds 88 E5
Gartmore Stirling 75 H8
Gartnagrenach Argyll 72 H6
Gartness N Lanark 68 D6
Gartness Stirling 68 B4
Gartocharn W Dunb 68 B3
Garton E Yorks 53 F8
Garton-on-the-Wolds E Yorks 52 D5
Gartsherrie N Lanark 68 D6
Gartymore Highld 93 H13
Garvald E Loth 70 C4
Garvamore Highld 81 D7
Garvard Argyll 72 D2
Garvault Hotel Highld 93 F10
Garve Highld 86 E6
Garvestone Norf 38 E6
Garvock Aberds 83 F9
Garvock Invclyd 73 F11
Garway Hereford 25 F11
Garway Hill Hereford 25 F11
Gaskan Highld 79 D10
Gastard Wilts 16 E5
Gasthorpe Norf 38 G5
Gatcombe IoW 10 F3
Gate Burton Lincs 46 D2
Gate Helmsley N Yorks 52 D2
Gateacre Mers 43 D7
Gatebeck Cumb 57 H7
Gateford Notts 45 D9
Gateforth N Yorks 52 G1
Gatehead E Ayrs 67 C6
Gatehouse Northumb 62 E3
Gatehouse of Fleet Dumfries 55 D9
Gatelawbridge Dumfries 60 D5
Gateley Norf 38 C5
Gatenby N Yorks 58 H4
Gateshead T&W 63 G8
Gatesheath Ches W 43 F7
Gateside Aberds 83 B8
Gateside Angus 77 C7
Gateside E Renf 68 E3
Gateside Fife 76 G4
Gateside N Ayrs 67 A6
Gathurst Gtr Man 43 B8
Gatley Gtr Man 44 D2
Gattonside Borders 70 G4
Gatwick Airport W Sus 12 B1
Gaufron Powys 24 B6
Gaulby Leics 36 E2
Gauldry Fife 76 E6
Gaunt's Common Dorset 9 D9
Gautby Lincs 46 E5
Gavinton Borders 70 E6
Gawber S Yorks 45 B7
Gawcott Bucks 28 E3
Gawsworth Ches E 44 F2
Gawthorpe W Yorks 51 G8
Gawthrop Cumb 57 H8
Gawthwaite Cumb 49 A2
Gay Street W Sus 11 B9
Gaydon Warks 27 C10
Gayfield Orkney 95 C5
Gayhurst M Keynes 28 D5
Gayle N Yorks 57 H10
Gayles N Yorks 58 F2
Gayton Mers 42 D5
Gayton Norf 38 D3
Gayton Northants 28 C4
Gayton Staffs 34 C5
Gayton le Marsh Lincs 47 D8
Gayton le Wold Lincs 46 D6
Gayton Thorpe Norf 38 D3
Gaywood Norf 38 C2
Gazeley Suff 30 B4
Geanies House Highld 87 D11
Gearraidh Bhailteas W Isles 84 F2
Gearraidh Bhaird W Isles 91 E8
Gearraidh na h-Aibhne W Isles 90 D7
Gearraidh na Monadh W Isles 84 G2
Geary Highld 84 B7
Geddes House Highld 87 F11
Gedding Suff 30 C6
Geddington Northants 36 G4
Gedintailor Highld 85 E10
Gedling Notts 36 A2
Gedney Lincs 37 C10
Gedney Broadgate Lincs 37 C10
Gedney Drove End Lincs 37 C10
Gedney Dyke Lincs 37 C10
Gedney Hill Lincs 37 D9
Gee Cross Gtr Man 44 C3
Geilston Argyll 68 C2
Geirinis W Isles 84 D2
Geise Highld 94 D3
Geisiadar W Isles 90 D6
Geldeston Norf 39 F9
Gell Conwy 41 D10
Gelli Pembs 22 E5
Gelli Rhondda 14 B5
Gellideg M Tydf 25 H7
Gellifor Denb 42 F4
Gelligaer Caerph 15 B7
Gellilydan Gwyn 41 G8
Gellinudd Neath 14 A3
Gellyburn Perth 76 D3
Gellywen Carms 23 D7
Gelston Dumfries 55 D10
Gelston Lincs 36 A5
Gembling E Yorks 53 D7
Gentleshaw Staffs 35 D6
Geocrab W Isles 90 H6
George Green Bucks 19 C7
George Nympton Devon 6 D6
Georgefield Dumfries 61 D8
Georgeham Devon 6 C3
Georgetown Bl Gwent 25 H8
Gerlan Gwyn 41 D8
Germansweek Devon 6 G3
Germoe Corn 2 G4
Gerrans Corn 3 F7
Gerrards Cross Bucks 19 C7
Gestingthorpe Essex 30 E5
Geuffordd Powys 33 D8
Gib Hill Ches W 43 E9
Gibbet Hill Warks 35 G11
Gibbshill Dumfries 60 F3
Gidea Park London 20 C2
Gidleigh Devon 5 C7
Giffnock E Renf 68 E4
Gifford E Loth 70 D4
Giffordland N Ayrs 66 B5
Giffordtown Fife 76 F5
Giggleswick N Yorks 50 C4
Gilberdyke E Yorks 52 G4
Gilchriston E Loth 70 D3
Gilcrux Cumb 56 C3
Gildersome W Yorks 51 G8
Gildingwells S Yorks 45 D9
Gileston V Glam 14 E6
Gilfach Caerph 15 B7
Gilfach Goch Rhondda 14 C5
Gilfachrheda Ceredig 23 A9
Gillamoor N Yorks 59 H7
Gillar's Green Mers 43 C7
Gillen Highld 84 C7
Gilling East N Yorks 52 B2
Gilling West N Yorks 58 F2
Gillingham Dorset 9 B7
Gillingham Medway 20 E4
Gillingham Norf 39 F10
Gillock Highld 94 E4
Gillow Heath Staffs 44 G2
Gills Highld 94 C5
Gill's Green Kent 13 C6
Gilmanscleuch Borders 61 A9
Gilmerton Edin 69 D11
Gilmerton Perth 75 E11
Gilmonby Durham 57 E11
Gilmorton Leics 36 G1
Gilmourton S Lanark 68 F5
Gilsland Northumb 62 G2
Gilsland Spa Cumb 62 G2
Gilston Borders 70 E3
Gilston Herts 29 G11
Gilwern Mon 25 G9
Gimingham Norf 39 B8
Giosla W Isles 90 E6
Gipping Suff 31 B7
Gipsey Bridge Lincs 46 H6
Girdle Toll N Ayrs 66 B6
Girlsta Shetland 96 H6
Girsby N Yorks 58 F4
Girtford C Beds 29 C8
Girthon Dumfries 55 D9
Girton Cambs 29 B11
Girton Notts 46 F2
Girvan S Ayrs 66 G4
Gisburn Lancs 50 E4
Gisleham Suff 39 G11
Gislingham Suff 31 A7
Gissing Norf 39 G7
Gittisham Devon 7 G10
Gladestry Powys 25 C9
Gladsmuir E Loth 70 C3
Glais Swansea 14 A3
Glaisdale N Yorks 59 F8
Glame Highld 85 D10
Glamis Angus 76 C6
Glan Adda Gwyn 41 C7
Glan Conwy Conwy 41 C10
Glan-Conwy Conwy 41 E10
Glan-Duar Carms 23 B10
Glan-Dwyfach Gwyn 40 F6
Glan Gors Anglesey 40 C6
Glan-rhyd Gwyn 40 E6
Glan-traeth Anglesey 40 C4
Glan-y-don Flint 42 E4
Glan-y-nant Powys 32 G5
Glan-y-wern Gwyn 41 G8
Glan-yr-afon Anglesey 41 B8
Glan-yr-afon Gwyn 32 A5
Glan-yr-afon Gwyn 32 A6
Glanaman Carms 24 G3
Glandford Norf 38 A6
Glandwr Pembs 22 D6
Glandy Cross Carms 22 D6
Glandyfi Ceredig 32 F2
Glangrwyney Powys 25 G9
Glanmule Powys 33 F7
Glanrafon Ceredig 32 G2
Glanrhyd Gwyn 40 G4
Glanrhyd Pembs 22 B6
Glanton Northumb 62 B6
Glanton Pike Northumb 62 B6
Glanvilles Wootton Dorset 8 D5
Glapthorn Northants 36 F6
Glapwell Derbys 45 F8
Glas-allt Shiel Aberds 82 E4
Glasbury Powys 25 E8
Glaschoil Highld 87 H13
Glascoed Denb 42 E2
Glascoed Mon 15 A9
Glascoed Powys 33 D7
Glascorrie Aberds 82 D5
Glascote Staffs 35 E8
Glascwm Powys 25 C8
Glasdrum Argyll 74 C3
Glasfryn Conwy 42 G2
Glasgow Glasgow 68 D4
Glashvin Highld 85 B9
Glasinfryn Gwyn 41 D7
Glasnacardoch Highld 79 B9
Glasnakille Highld 85 G10
Glasphein Highld 84 D6
Glaspwll Powys 32 F3
Glassburn Highld 86 H6
Glasserton Dumfries 55 F7
Glassford S Lanark 68 F6
Glasshouse Hill Glos 26 F4
Glasshouses N Yorks 51 C7
Glasslie Fife 76 G5
Glasson Cumb 61 G8
Glasson Lancs 49 D4
Glassonby Cumb 57 C7
Glasterlaw Angus 77 B8
Glaston Rutland 36 E4
Glastonbury Som 15 H11
Glatton Cambs 37 G7
Glazebrook Warr 43 C9
Glazebury Warr 43 C9
Glazeley Shrops 34 G3
Gleadless S Yorks 45 D7
Gleadsmoss Ches E 44 F2
Gleann Tholàstaidh W Isles 91 C10
Gleaston Cumb 49 B2
Gleiniant Powys 32 F5
Glemsford Suff 30 D5
Glen Dumfries 55 D8
Glen Dumfries 60 F4
Glen Auldyn IoM 48 C4
Glen Bernisdale Highld 85 D9
Glen Ho Borders 69 G11
Glen Mona IoM 48 D4
Glen Nevis House Highld 80 F3
Glen Parva Leics 36 F1
Glen Sluain Argyll 73 D9
Glen Tanar House Aberds 82 D6
Glen Trool Lodge Dumfries 55 A7
Glen Village Falk 69 C7
Glen Vine IoM 48 E3
Glenamachrie Argyll 74 E2
Glenbarr Argyll 65 E7
Glenbeg Highld 79 E8
Glenbeg Highld 82 A2
Glenbervie Aberds 83 E9
Glenboig N Lanark 68 D6
Glenborrodale Highld 79 E9
Glenbranter Argyll 73 D10
Glenbreck Borders 60 A6
Glenbrein Lodge Highld 81 B6
Glenbrittle House Highld 85 F9
Glenbuchat Lodge Aberds 82 B5
Glenbuck E Ayrs 68 H6
Glenburn Renfs 68 D3
Glencalvie Lodge Highld 86 C7
Glencanisp Lodge Highld 92 G4
Glencaple Dumfries 60 G5
Glencarron Lodge Highld 86 F3
Glencarse Perth 76 E4
Glencassley Castle Highld 92 J7
Glenceitlein Highld 74 C4
Glencoe Highld 74 B3
Glencraig Fife 76 H4
Glencripesdale Highld 79 F9
Glencrosh Dumfries 60 E3
Glendavan Ho. Aberds 82 C6
Glendevon Perth 76 G2
Glendoe Lodge Highld 80 C6
Glendoebeg Highld 80 C6
Glendoick Perth 76 E5
Glendoll Lodge Angus 82 F4
Glendoune S Ayrs 66 G4
Glenduckie Fife 76 F5
Glendye Lodge Aberds 83 E8
Gleneagles Hotel Perth 76 F2
Gleneagles House Perth 76 G2
Glenegedale Argyll 64 C4
Glenelg Highld 85 G13
Glenernie Moray 87 G13
Glenfarg Perth 76 F4
Glenfarquhar Lodge Aberds 83 E9
Glenferness House Highld 87 G12
Glenfeshie Lodge Highld 81 D10
Glenfield Leics 35 E11
Glenfinnan Highld 79 C11
Glenfoot Perth 76 F4
Glenfyne Lodge Argyll 74 F5
Glengap Dumfries 55 D9
Glengarnock N Ayrs 66 A6
Glengorm Castle Argyll 78 F7
Glengrasco Highld 85 D9
Glenhead Farm Angus 76 A5
Glenhoul Dumfries 67 H9

Glenhurich Highld 79 E11
Glenkerry Borders 61 B8
Glenkiln Dumfries 60 F4
Glenkindie Aberds 82 B6
Glenlatterach Moray 88 C1
Glenlee Dumfries 55 A9
Glenlichorn Perth 75 F10
Glenlivet Moray 82 A3
Glenlochsie Perth 82 F2
Glenloig N Ayrs 66 C2
Glenluce Dumfries 54 D5
Glenmallan Argyll 74 H5
Glenmarksie Highld 86 F6
Glenmassan Argyll 73 E10
Glenmavis N Lanark 68 D6
Glenmaye IoM 48 E2
Glenmidge Dumfries 60 E4
Glenmore Argyll 73 B7
Glenmore Highld 85 D9
Glenmore Lodge Highld 82 C1
Glenmoy Angus 77 A7
Glenogil Angus 77 A7
Glenprosen Lodge Angus 82 G4
Glenprosen Village Angus 82 G5
Glenquiech Angus 77 A7
Glenreasdell Mains Argyll 73 H7
Glenree N Ayrs 66 D2
Glenridding Cumb 56 E5
Glenrossal Highld 92 J7
Glenrothes Fife 76 G5
Glensanda Highld 79 G11
Glensaugh Aberds 83 F8
Glenshero Lodge Highld 81 D7
Glenstockadale Dumfries 54 C3
Glenstriven Argyll 73 F9
Glentaggart S Lanark 69 H7
Glentham Lincs 46 C4
Glentirranmuir Stirling 68 A5
Glenton Aberds 83 A8
Glentress Borders 69 G11
Glentromie Lodge Highld 81 D9
Glentrool Village Dumfries 54 B6
Glentruan IoM 48 B4
Glentruim House Highld 81 D8
Glentworth Lincs 46 D3
Glenuig Highld 79 D9
Glenurquhart Highld 87 E10
Glespin S Lanark 69 H7
Gletness Shetland 96 H6
Glewstone Hereford 26 F2
Glinton Pboro 37 E7
Glooston Leics 36 F3
Glororum Northumb 71 G10
Glossop Derbys 44 C4
Gloster Hill Northumb 63 C8
Gloucester Glos 26 G5
Gloup Shetland 96 C7
Glusburn N Yorks 50 E6
Glutt Lodge Highld 93 F12
Glutton Bridge Staffs 44 F4
Glympton Oxon 27 F11
Glyn-Ceiriog Wrex 33 B8
Glyn-cywarch Gwyn 41 G8
Glyn Ebwy = Ebbw Vale Bl Gwent 25 H8
Glyn-neath = Glynedd Neath 24 H5
Glynarthen Ceredig 23 B8
Glynbrochan Powys 32 G5
Glyncoch Rhondda 14 B6
Glyncorrwg Neath 14 B4
Glynde E Sus 12 F3
Glyndebourne E Sus 12 E3
Glyndyfrdwy Denb 33 A7
Glynedd = Glyn-neath Neath 24 H5
Glynogwr Bridgend 14 C5
Glyntaff Rhondda 14 C6
Glyntawe Powys 24 G5
Gnosall Staffs 34 C4
Gnosall Heath Staffs 34 C4
Goadby Leics 36 F3
Goadby Marwood Leics 36 C3
Goat Lees Kent 21 G7
Goatacre Wilts 17 D7
Goathill Dorset 8 C5
Goathland N Yorks 59 F9
Goathurst Som 8 A1
Gobernuisgach Lodge Highld 92 E7
Gobhaig W Isles 90 G5
Gobowen Shrops 33 B9
Godalming Sur 18 G6
Godley Gtr Man 44 C3
Godmanchester Cambs 29 A9
Godmanstone Dorset 8 E5
Godmersham Kent 21 F7
Godney Som 15 G10
Godolphin Cross Corn 2 F5
Godre'r-graig Neath 24 H4
Godshill Hants 9 C10
Godshill IoW 10 F4
Godstone Sur 19 F10
Godwinscroft Hants 9 E10
Goetre Mon 25 H10
Goferydd Anglesey 40 B4
Goff's Oak Herts 19 A10
Gogar Edin 69 C10
Goginan Ceredig 32 G2
Golan Gwyn 41 F7
Golant Corn 4 F2
Golberdon Corn 4 D4
Golborne Gtr Man 43 C9
Golcar W Yorks 51 H7
Gold Hill Norf 37 F11
Goldcliff Newport 15 C9
Golden Cross E Sus 12 E4
Golden Green Kent 20 G3
Golden Grove Carms 23 E10
Golden Hill Hants 10 E1
Golden Pot Hants 18 G4
Golden Valley Glos 26 F6
Goldenhill Stoke 44 G2
Golders Green London 19 C9
Goldhanger Essex 30 H6
Golding Shrops 33 E11
Goldington Bedford 29 C7
Goldsborough N Yorks 51 D9
Goldsborough N Yorks 59 E9
Goldsithney Corn 2 F4
Goldsworthy Devon 6 D2
Goldthorpe S Yorks 45 B8
Gollanfield Highld 87 F11
Golspie Highld 93 J11
Golval Highld 93 C11
Gomeldon Wilts 17 H8
Gomersal W Yorks 51 G8
Gomshall Sur 19 G7
Gonalston Notts 45 H10
Gonfirth Shetland 96 G5
Good Easter Essex 30 G3
Gooderstone Norf 38 E3
Goodleigh Devon 6 C5
Goodmanham E Yorks 52 E4
Goodnestone Kent 21 E7
Goodnestone Kent 21 F9
Goodrich Hereford 26 G2
Goodrington Torbay 5 F9
Goodshaw Lancs 50 G4
Goodwick = Wdig Pembs 22 C4
Goodworth Clatford Hants 17 G10
Goole E Yorks 52 G3
Goonbell Corn 2 E6
Goonhavern Corn 3 D6
Goose Eye W Yorks 50 E6
Goose Green Gtr Man 43 B8
Goose Green Norf 39 G7
Goose Green W Sus 11 C10
Gooseham Corn 6 E1
Goosey Oxon 17 B10
Goosnargh Lancs 50 F1
Goostrey Ches E 43 E10
Gorcott Hill Warks 27 B7
Gord Shetland 96 L6
Gordon Borders 70 F5
Gordonbush Highld 93 J11
Gordonsburgh Moray 88 B4
Gordonstoun Moray 88 B1
Gordonstown Aberds 88 C5
Gordonstown Aberds 89 E7
Gore Kent 21 F10
Gore Cross Wilts 17 F7
Gore Pit Essex 30 G5
Gorebridge Midloth 70 D2
Gorefield Cambs 37 D10
Gorey Jersey 11
Gorgie Edin 69 C11
Goring Oxon 18 C3
Goring-by-Sea W Sus 11 D10
Goring Heath Oxon 18 D3
Gorleston-on-Sea Norf 39 E11
Gornalwood W Mid 34 F5
Gorrachie Aberds 89 C7
Gorran Churchtown Corn 3 E8
Gorran Haven Corn 3 E9
Gorrenberry Borders 61 D10
Gors Ceredig 32 H2
Gorse Hill Swindon 17 C8
Gorsedd Flint 42 E4
Gorseinon Swansea 23 G10
Gorseness Orkney 95 G5
Gorsgoch Ceredig 23 A9
Gorslas Carms 23 E10
Gorsley Glos 26 F3
Gorstan Highld 86 E6
Gorstanvorran Highld 79 D11
Gorsteyhill Staffs 43 G10
Gorsty Hill Staffs 35 C7
Gortantaoid Argyll 64 A4
Gorton Gtr Man 44 C2
Gosbeck Suff 31 C8
Gosberton Lincs 37 B8
Gosberton Clough Lincs 37 C7
Gosfield Essex 30 F4
Gosford Hereford 26 B2
Gosforth Cumb 56 F2
Gosforth T&W 63 G8
Gosmore Herts 29 F8
Gosport Hants 10 E5
Gossabrough Shetland 96 E7
Gossington Glos 16 A4
Goswick Northumb 71 F9
Gotham Notts 35 B11
Gotherington Glos 26 F6
Gott Shetland 96 J6
Goudhurst Kent 12 C6
Goulceby Lincs 46 E6
Gourdas Aberds 89 D7
Gourdon Aberds 83 F10
Gourock Invclyd 73 F11
Govan Glasgow 68 D4
Govanhill Glasgow 68 D4
Goveton Devon 5 G8
Govilon Mon 25 G9
Gowanhill Aberds 89 B10
Gowdall E Yorks 52 G2
Gowerton Swansea 23 G10
Gowkhall Fife 69 B9
Gowthorpe E Yorks 52 D3
Goxhill E Yorks 53 E7
Goxhill N Lincs 53 G7
Goxhill Haven N Lincs 53 G7
Goytre Neath 14 C3
Grabhair W Isles 91 F8
Graby Lincs 37 C6
Grade Corn 2 H6
Graffham W Sus 11 C8
Grafham Cambs 29 B8
Grafham Sur 19 G7
Grafton Hereford 25 E11
Grafton N Yorks 51 C10
Grafton Oxon 17 A9
Grafton Shrops 33 D10
Grafton Worcs 26 B2
Grafton Flyford Worcs 26 C6
Grafton Regis Northants 28 D4
Grafton Underwood Northants 36 G5
Grafty Green Kent 20 G5
Graianrhyd Denb 42 G5
Graig Conwy 41 C10
Graig Denb 42 E3
Graig-fechan Denb 42 G4
Grain Medway 20 D5
Grainsby Lincs 46 C6
Grainthorpe Lincs 47 C7
Grampound Corn 3 E8
Grampound Road Corn 3 D8
Gramsdal W Isles 84 C3
Granborough Bucks 28 F4
Granby Notts 36 B3
Grandborough Warks 27 B11
Grandtully Perth 76 B2
Grange Cumb 56 E4
Grange E Ayrs 67 C7
Grange Medway 20 E4
Grange Mers 42 D5
Grange Perth 76 E5
Grange Crossroads Moray 88 C4
Grange Hall Moray 87 E13
Grange Hill Essex 19 B11
Grange Moor W Yorks 51 H8
Grange of Lindores Fife 76 F5
Grange-over-Sands Cumb 49 B4
Grange Villa Durham 58 A3
Grangemill Derbys 44 G6
Grangemouth Falk 69 B8
Grangepans Falk 69 B9
Grangetown Cardiff 15 D7
Grangetown Redcar 59 D6
Granish Highld 81 B11
Gransmoor E Yorks 53 D7
Granston Pembs 22 C3
Grantchester Cambs 29 C11
Grantham Lincs 36 B5
Grantley N Yorks 51 C8
Grantlodge Aberds 83 B9
Granton Dumfries 60 C6
Granton Edin 69 C11
Grantown-on-Spey Highld 82 A2
Grantshouse Borders 71 D7
Grappenhall Warr 43 D9
Grasby Lincs 46 B4
Grasmere Cumb 56 F5
Grasscroft Gtr Man 44 B3
Grassendale Mers 43 D6
Grassholme Durham 57 D11
Grassington N Yorks 50 C6
Grassmoor Derbys 45 F8
Grassthorpe Notts 45 F11
Grateley Hants 17 G9
Gratwich Staffs 34 B6
Graveley Cambs 29 B9
Graveley Herts 29 F9
Gravelly Hill W Mid 35 F7
Gravels Shrops 33 E9
Graven Shetland 96 F6
Graveney Kent 21 E7
Gravesend Herts 29 F11
Gravesend Kent 20 D3
Grayingham Lincs 46 C3
Grayrigg Cumb 57 G7
Grays Thurrock 20 D3
Grayshott Hants 18 H5
Grayswood Sur 11 A8
Graythorp Hrtlpl 58 D6
Grazeley Wokingham 18 E3
Greasbrough S Yorks 45 C8
Greasby Mers 42 D5
Great Abington Cambs 30 D2
Great Addington Northants 28 A6
Great Alne Warks 27 C8
Great Altcar Lancs 42 B6
Great Amwell Herts 29 G10
Great Asby Cumb 57 E8
Great Ashfield Suff 30 B6
Great Ayton N Yorks 59 E6
Great Baddow Essex 20 A4
Great Bardfield Essex 30 E3
Great Barford Bedford 29 C8
Great Barr W Mid 34 F6
Great Barrington Glos 27 G9
Great Barrow Ches W 43 F7
Great Barton Suff 30 B5
Great Barugh N Yorks 52 B3
Great Bavington Northumb 62 E5
Great Bealings Suff 31 D9
Great Bedwyn Wilts 17 E9
Great Bentley Essex 31 F8
Great Billing Northants 28 B5
Great Bircham Norf 38 B3
Great Blakenham Suff 31 C8
Great Blencow Cumb 56 C6
Great Bolas Telford 34 C2
Great Bookham Sur 19 F8
Great Bourton Oxon 27 D11
Great Bowden Leics 36 G3
Great Bradley Suff 30 C3
Great Braxted Essex 30 G5
Great Bricett Suff 31 C7
Great Brickhill Bucks 28 E6
Great Bridge W Mid 34 F5
Great Bridgeford Staffs 34 C4
Great Brington Northants 28 B3
Great Bromley Essex 31 F7
Great Broughton Cumb 56 C2
Great Broughton N Yorks 59 F6
Great Budworth Ches W 43 E9
Great Burdon Darl 58 E4
Great Burgh Sur 19 F9
Great Burstead Essex 20 B3
Great Busby N Yorks 58 F6
Great Canfield Essex 30 G2
Great Carlton Lincs 47 D8
Great Casterton Rutland 36 E6
Great Chart Kent 13 B8
Great Chatwell Staffs 34 D3
Great Chesterford Essex 30 D2
Great Cheverell Wilts 16 F6
Great Chishill Cambs 29 E11
Great Clacton Essex 31 G8
Great Cliff W Yorks 51 H9
Great Clifton Cumb 56 D2
Great Coates NE Lincs 46 B6
Great Comberton Worcs 26 D6
Great Corby Cumb 56 A6
Great Cornard Suff 30 D5
Great Cowden E Yorks 53 E8
Great Coxwell Oxon 17 B9
Great Crakehall N Yorks 58 G3
Great Cransley Northants 36 H4
Great Cressingham Norf 38 E4
Great Crosby Mers 42 C6
Great Cubley Derbys 35 B7
Great Dalby Leics 36 D3
Great Denham Bedford 29 D7
Great Doddington Northants 28 B5
Great Dunham Norf 38 D4
Great Dunmow Essex 30 F3
Great Durnford Wilts 17 H8
Great Easton Essex 30 F3
Great Easton Leics 36 F4
Great Eccleston Lancs 49 E4
Great Edstone N Yorks 52 A3
Great Ellingham Norf 38 F6
Great Elm Som 16 G4
Great Eversden Cambs 29 C10
Great Fencote N Yorks 58 G3
Great Finborough Suff 31 C7
Great Fransham Norf 38 D4
Great Gaddesden Herts 29 G7
Great Gidding Cambs 37 G7
Great Givendale E Yorks 52 D4
Great Glemham Suff 31 B10
Great Glen Leics 36 F2
Great Gonerby Lincs 36 B4
Great Gransden Cambs 29 C9
Great Green Norf 39 G8
Great Green Suff 30 C6
Great Habton N Yorks 52 B3
Great Hale Lincs 37 A7
Great Hallingbury Essex 30 G2
Great Hampden Bucks 18 A5
Great Harrowden Northants 28 A5
Great Harwood Lancs 50 F3
Great Haseley Oxon 18 A3
Great Hatfield E Yorks 53 E7
Great Haywood Staffs 34 C6
Great Heath W Mid 35 G9
Great Heck N Yorks 52 G1
Great Henny Essex 30 E5
Great Hinton Wilts 16 F6
Great Hockham Norf 38 F5
Great Holland Essex 31 G9
Great Horkesley Essex 30 E6
Great Hormead Herts 29 F10
Great Horton W Yorks 51 F7
Great Horwood Bucks 28 E4
Great Houghton Northants 28 C4
Great Houghton S Yorks 45 B8
Great Hucklow Derbys 44 E5
Great Kelk E Yorks 53 D7
Great Kimble Bucks 28 H5
Great Kingshill Bucks 18 B5
Great Langton N Yorks 58 G3
Great Leighs Essex 30 G4
Great Lever Gtr Man 43 B10
Great Limber Lincs 46 B5
Great Linford M Keynes 28 D5
Great Livermere Suff 30 A5
Great Longstone Derbys 44 E6
Great Lumley Durham 58 B3
Great Lyth Shrops 33 E10
Great Malvern Worcs 26 D4
Great Maplestead Essex 30 E5
Great Marton Blackpool 49 F3
Great Massingham Norf 38 C3
Great Melton Norf 39 E7
Great Milton Oxon 18 A3
Great Missenden Bucks 18 A5
Great Mitton Lancs 50 F3
Great Mongeham Kent 21 F10
Great Moulton Norf 39 F7
Great Munden Herts 29 F10
Great Musgrave Cumb 57 E9
Great Ness Shrops 33 D9
Great Notley Essex 30 F4
Great Oakley Essex 31 F8
Great Oakley Northants 36 G4
Great Offley Herts 29 F8
Great Ormside Cumb 57 E9
Great Orton Cumb 56 A5
Great Ouseburn N Yorks 51 C10
Great Oxendon Northants 36 G3
Great Oxney Green Essex 30 H3
Great Palgrave Norf 38 D4
Great Parndon Essex 29 H11
Great Paxton Cambs 29 B9
Great Plumpton Lancs 49 F3
Great Plumstead Norf 39 D9
Great Ponton Lincs 36 B5
Great Preston W Yorks 51 G10
Great Raveley Cambs 37 G8
Great Rissington Glos 27 G8
Great Rollright Oxon 27 E10
Great Ryburgh Norf 38 C5
Great Ryle Northumb 62 B6
Great Ryton Shrops 33 E10
Great Saling Essex 30 F4
Great Salkeld Cumb 57 C7
Great Sampford Essex 30 E3
Great Sankey Warr 43 D8
Great Saxham Suff 30 B4
Great Shefford W Berks 17 D10
Great Shelford Cambs 29 C11
Great Smeaton N Yorks 58 F4
Great Snoring Norf 38 B5
Great Somerford Wilts 16 C6
Great Stainton Darl 58 D4
Great Stambridge Essex 20 B5
Great Staughton Cambs 29 B8
Great Steeping Lincs 47 F8
Great Stonar Kent 21 F10
Great Strickland Cumb 57 D7
Great Stukeley Cambs 29 A9
Great Sturton Lincs 46 E6
Great Sutton Ches W 43 E6
Great Sutton Shrops 33 G11
Great Swinburne Northumb 62 F5
Great Tew Oxon 27 F10
Great Tey Essex 30 F5
Great Thurkleby N Yorks 51 B10
Great Thurlow Suff 30 C3
Great Torrington Devon 6 E3
Great Tosson Northumb 62 C6
Great Totham Essex 30 G5
Great Totham Essex 30 G5
Great Tows Lincs 46 C6
Great Urswick Cumb 49 B2
Great Wakering Essex 20 C6
Great Waldingfield Suff 30 D6
Great Walsingham Norf 38 B5
Great Waltham Essex 30 G3
Great Warley Essex 20 B2
Great Washbourne Glos 26 E6
Great Weldon Northants 36 G5
Great Welnetham Suff 30 C5
Great Wenham Suff 31 E7
Great Whittington Northumb 62 F6
Great Wigborough Essex 30 G6
Great Wilbraham Cambs 30 C2
Great Wishford Wilts 17 H7
Great Witcombe Glos 26 G6
Great Witley Worcs 26 B4
Great Wolford Warks 27 E9
Great Wratting Suff 30 D3
Great Wymondley Herts 29 F9
Great Wyrley Staffs 34 E5
Great Wytheford Shrops 34 D1
Great Yarmouth Norf 39 E11
Great Yeldham Essex 30 E4
Greater Doward Hereford 26 G2
Greatford Lincs 37 D6
Greatgate Staffs 35 A6
Greatham Hants 11 A6
Greatham Hrtlpl 58 D5
Greatham W Sus 11 C9
Greatstone on Sea Kent 13 D9
Greatworth Northants 28 D2
Greave Lancs 50 G4
Greeba IoM 48 D3
Green Denb 42 F3
Green End Bedford 29 C8
Green Hammerton N Yorks 51 D10
Green Lane Powys 33 F7
Green Ore Som 16 F2
Green St Green London 19 E11
Green Street Herts 19 B8
Greenbank Shetland 96 C7
Greenburn W Loth 69 D8
Greendikes Northumb 71 H9
Greenfield C Beds 29 E7
Greenfield Flint 42 E4
Greenfield Gtr Man 44 B3
Greenfield Highld 80 C4
Greenfield Oxon 18 B4
Greenford London 19 C8
Greengairs N Lanark 68 C6
Greenham W Berks 17 E11
Greenhaugh Northumb 62 E3
Greenhead Northumb 62 G2
Greenhill Falk 69 C7
Greenhill Kent 21 E8
Greenhill Leics 35 D10
Greenhill London 19 C8
Greenhills N Ayrs 67 A6
Greenhithe Kent 20 D2
Greenholm E Ayrs 67 C8
Greenholme Cumb 57 F7
Greenhouse Borders 61 A11
Greenhow Hill N Yorks 51 C7
Greenigoe Orkney 95 H5
Greenland Highld 94 D4
Greenlands Bucks 18 C4
Greenlaw Aberds 89 C6
Greenlaw Borders 70 F6
Greenlea Dumfries 60 F6
Greenloaning Perth 75 G11
Greenmount Gtr Man 43 A10
Greenmow Shetland 96 L6
Greenock Invclyd 73 F11
Greenock West Invclyd 73 F11
Greenodd Cumb 49 A3
Greenrow Cumb 56 A3
Greens Norton Northants 28 D3
Greenside T&W 63 G7
Greensidehill Northumb 62 B5
Greenstead Green Essex 30 F5
Greensted Essex 20 A2
Greenwich London 19 D10
Greet Glos 27 E7
Greete Shrops 26 A2
Greetham Lincs 47 E7
Greetham Rutland 36 D5
Greetland W Yorks 51 G6
Gregg Hall Cumb 56 G6
Gregson Lane Lancs 50 G1
Greinetobht W Isles 84 A3
Greinton Som 15 H10
Gremista Shetland 96 J6
Grenaby IoM 48 E2
Grendon Northants 28 B5
Grendon Warks 35 E8
Grendon Common Warks 35 F8
Grendon Green Hereford 26 C2
Grendon Underwood Bucks 28 F3
Grenofen Devon 4 D5
Grenoside S Yorks 45 C7
Greosabhagh W Isles 90 H6
Gresford Wrex 42 G6
Gresham Norf 39 B7
Greshornish Highld 85 C8
Gressenhall Norf 38 D5
Gressingham Lancs 50 C1
Gresty Green Ches E 43 G10
Greta Bridge Durham 58 E1
Gretna Dumfries 61 G9
Gretna Green Dumfries 61 G9
Gretton Glos 27 E7
Gretton Northants 36 F4
Gretton Shrops 33 F11
Grewelthorpe N Yorks 51 B8
Grey Green N Lincs 45 B11
Greygarth N Yorks 51 B7
Greynor Carms 23 F10
Greysouthen Cumb 56 D2
Greystoke Cumb 56 C6
Greystone Angus 77 C8
Greystone Dumfries 60 F5
Greywell Hants 18 F4
Griais W Isles 91 C9
Grianan W Isles 91 D9
Gribthorpe E Yorks 52 F3
Gridley Corner Devon 6 G2
Griff Warks 35 G9
Griffithstown Torf 15 B8
Grimbister Orkney 95 G4
Grimblethorpe Lincs 46 D6
Grimeford Village Lancs 43 A9
Grimethorpe S Yorks 45 B8
Griminis W Isles 84 C2
Grimister Shetland 96 D6
Grimley Worcs 26 B5
Grimness Orkney 95 J5
Grimoldby Lincs 47 D7
Grimpo Shrops 33 C9
Grimsargh Lancs 50 F1
Grimsbury Oxon 27 D11
Grimsby NE Lincs 46 A6
Grimscote Northants 28 C3
Grimscott Corn 6 F1
Grimsthorpe Lincs 36 C6
Grimston E Yorks 53 F8
Grimston Leics 36 C2
Grimston Norf 38 C3
Grimston York 52 D2
Grimstone Dorset 8 E5
Grinacombe Moor Devon 6 G3
Grindale E Yorks 53 B7
Grindigar Orkney 95 H6
Grindiscol Shetland 96 K6
Grindle Shrops 34 E3
Grindleford Derbys 44 E6
Grindleton Lancs 50 E3
Grindley Staffs 34 C6
Grindley Brook Shrops 33 A11
Grindlow Derbys 44 E5
Grindon Northumb 71 F8
Grindon Staffs 44 G4
Grindonmoor Gate Staffs 44 G4
Gringley on the Hill Notts 45 C11
Grinsdale Cumb 61 H9
Grinshill Shrops 33 C11
Grinton N Yorks 58 G1
Griomsidar W Isles 91 E8
Grishipoll Argyll 78 F4
Grisling Common E Sus 12 D3
Gristhorpe N Yorks 53 A6
Griston Norf 38 F5
Gritley Orkney 95 H6
Grittenham Wilts 17 C7
Grittleton Wilts 16 C5
Grizebeck Cumb 49 A2
Grizedale Cumb 56 G5
Grobister Orkney 95 F7
Groby Leics 35 E11
Groes Conwy 42 F3
Groes Neath 14 C3
Groes-faen Rhondda 14 C6
Groes-lwyd Powys 33 D8
Groesffordd Marli Denb 42 E3
Groeslon Gwyn 40 E6
Groeslon Gwyn 41 D7
Grogport Argyll 65 D9
Gromford Suff 31 C10
Gronant Flint 42 D3
Groombridge E Sus 12 C4
Grosmont Mon 25 F11
Grosmont N Yorks 59 F9
Groton Suff 30 D6
Grougfoot Falk 69 C9
Grouville Jersey 11
Grove Dorset 8 G6
Grove Kent 21 E9
Grove Notts 45 E11
Grove Oxon 17 B11
Grove Park London 19 D11
Grove Vale W Mid 34 F6
Grovesend Swansea 23 F10
Grudie Highld 86 E6
Gruids Highld 93 J8
Gruinard House Highld 86 B2
Grula Highld 85 F8
Gruline Argyll 79 G8
Grunasound Shetland 96 K5
Grundisburgh Suff 31 C9
Grunsagill Lancs 50 D3
Gruting Shetland 96 J4
Grutness Shetland 96 N6
Gualachulain Highld 74 C4
Gualin Ho. Highld 92 D6
Guardbridge Fife 77 F7
Guarlford Worcs 26 D5
Guay Perth 76 C3
Guestling Green E Sus 13 E7
Guestling Thorn E Sus 13 E7
Guestwick Norf 39 C6
Guestwick Green Norf 39 C6
Guide Blackburn 50 G3
Guide Post Northumb 63 E8
Guilden Morden Cambs 29 D9
Guilden Sutton Ches W 43 F7
Guildford Sur 18 G6
Guildtown Perth 76 D4
Guilsborough Northants 28 A3
Guilsfield Powys 33 D8
Guilton Kent 21 F9
Guineaford Devon 6 C4
Guisborough Redcar 59 E7
Guiseley W Yorks 51 E7
Guist Norf 38 C5
Guith Orkney 95 E6
Guiting Power Glos 27 F7
Gulberwick Shetland 96 K6
Gullane E Loth 70 B3
Gulval Corn 2 F3
Gulworthy Devon 4 D5
Gumfreston Pembs 22 F6
Gumley Leics 36 F2
Gummow's Shop Corn 3 D7
Gun Hill E Sus 12 E4
Gunby E Yorks 52 F3
Gunby Lincs 36 C5
Gundleton Hants 10 A5
Gunn Devon 6 C5
Gunnerside N Yorks 57 G11
Gunnerton Northumb 62 F5
Gunness N Lincs 46 A2
Gunnislake Corn 4 D5
Gunnista Shetland 96 J7
Gunthorpe Norf 38 B6
Gunthorpe Notts 36 A2
Gunthorpe Pboro 37 E7
Gunville IoW 10 F3
Gunwalloe Corn 2 G5
Gurnard IoW 10 E3
Gurnett Ches E 44 E3
Gurney Slade Som 16 G3
Gurnos Powys 24 H4
Gussage All Saints Dorset 9 C9
Gussage St Michael Dorset 9 C8
Guston Kent 21 G10
Gutcher Shetland 96 D7
Guthrie Angus 77 B8
Guyhirn Cambs 37 E9
Guyhirn Gull Cambs 37 E9
Guy's Head Lincs 37 C10
Guy's Marsh Dorset 9 B7
Guyzance Northumb 63 C8
Gwaenysgor Flint 42 D3
Gwalchmai Anglesey 40 C5
Gwaun-Cae-Gurwen Neath 24 G4
Gwaun-Leision Neath 24 G4
Gwbert Ceredig 22 B6
Gweek Corn 2 G6
Gwehelog Mon 15 A9
Gwenddwr Powys 25 D7
Gwennap Corn 2 F6
Gwenter Corn 2 H6
Gwernaffield Flint 42 F5
Gwernesney Mon 15 A10
Gwernogle Carms 23 C10
Gwernymynydd Flint 42 F5
Gwersyllt Wrex 42 G6
Gwespyr Flint 42 D4
Gwithian Corn 2 E4
Gwredog Anglesey 40 B6
Gwyddelwern Denb 42 H3
Gwyddgrug Carms 23 C9
Gwydyr Uchaf Conwy 41 D9
Gwynfryn Wrex 42 G5
Gwystre Powys 25 B7
Gwytherin Conwy 41 D10
Gyfelia Wrex 42 H6
Gyffin Conwy 41 C9
Gyre Orkney 95 H4
Gyrn-goch Gwyn 40 F6

H

Habberley Shrops 33 E9
Habergham Lancs 50 F4
Habrough NE Lincs 46 A5
Haceby Lincs 36 B6
Hacheston Suff 31 C10
Hackbridge London 19 E9
Hackenthorpe S Yorks 45 D8
Hackford Norf 39 E6
Hackforth N Yorks 58 G3
Hackland Orkney 95 F4
Hackleton Northants 28 C5
Hackness N Yorks 59 G10
Hackness Orkney 95 J4
Hackney London 19 C10
Hackthorn Lincs 46 D3
Hackthorpe Cumb 57 D7
Haconby Lincs 37 C7
Hacton London 20 C2
Hadden Borders 70 G6
Haddenham Bucks 28 H4
Haddenham Cambs 37 H10
Haddington E Loth 70 C4
Haddington Lincs 46 F3
Haddiscoe Norf 39 F10
Haddon Cambs 37 F7
Haddon Ches E 44 F3
Hade Edge W Yorks 44 B5
Hademore Staffs 35 E7
Hadfield Derbys 44 C4
Hadham Cross Herts 29 G11
Hadham Ford Herts 29 F11
Hadleigh Essex 20 C5
Hadleigh Suff 31 D7
Hadley Telford 34 D2
Hadley End Staffs 35 C7
Hadlow Kent 20 G3
Hadlow Down E Sus 12 D4
Hadnall Shrops 33 D11
Hadstock Essex 30 D2
Hady Derbys 45 E7
Hadzor Worcs 26 B6
Haffenden Quarter Kent 13 B7
Hafod-Dinbych Conwy 41 E10
Hafod-lom Conwy 41 C10
Haggate Lancs 50 F4
Haggbeck Cumb 61 F10
Haggerston Northumb 71 F9
Haggrister Shetland 96 F5
Hagley Hereford 26 D2
Hagley Worcs 34 G5
Hagworthingham Lincs 47 F7
Haigh Gtr Man 43 B9
Haigh S Yorks 44 A6
Haigh Moor W Yorks 51 G8
Haighton Green Lancs 50 F1
Hail Weston Cambs 29 B8
Haile Cumb 56 F2
Hailes Glos 27 E7
Hailey Herts 29 G10
Hailey Oxon 27 G10
Hailsham E Sus 12 F4
Haimer Highld 94 D3
Hainault London 19 B11
Hainford Norf 39 D8
Hainton Lincs 46 D5
Hairmyres S Lanark 68 E5
Haisthorpe E Yorks 53 C7
Hakin Pembs 22 F3
Halam Notts 45 G10
Halbeath Fife 69 B10
Halberton Devon 7 E9
Halcro Highld 94 D4
Hale Gtr Man 43 D10
Hale Halton 43 D7
Hale Hants 9 C10
Hale Bank Halton 43 D7
Hale Street Kent 20 G3
Halebarns Gtr Man 43 D10
Hales Norf 39 F9
Hales Staffs 34 B3
Hales Place Kent 21 F8
Halesfield Telford 34 E3
Halesgate Lincs 37 C9
Halesowen W Mid 34 G5
Halesworth Suff 39 H9
Halewood Mers 43 D7
Halford Shrops 33 G10
Halford Warks 27 D9
Halfpenny Furze Carms 23 E7
Halfpenny Green Staffs 34 F4
Halfway Carms 24 E3
Halfway Carms 24 E5
Halfway W Berks 17 E11
Halfway Bridge W Sus 11 B8
Halfway House Shrops 33 D9
Halfway Houses Kent 20 D6
Halifax W Yorks 51 G6
Halket E Ayrs 67 A7
Halkirk Highld 94 E3
Halkyn Flint 42 E5
Hall Dunnerdale Cumb 56 G4
Hall Green W Mid 35 G7
Hall Green W Yorks 51 H9
Hall Grove Herts 29 G9
Hall of Tankerness Orkney 95 H6
Hall of the Forest Shrops 33 G8
Halland E Sus 12 E3
Hallaton Leics 36 F3
Hallatrow Bath 16 F3
Hallbankgate Cumb 61 H11
Hallen S Glos 15 C11
Halliburton Borders 70 F5
Hallin Highld 84 C7
Halling Medway 20 E4
Hallington Lincs 47 D7
Hallington Northumb 62 F5
Halliwell Gtr Man 43 A10
Halloughton Notts 45 G10
Hallow Worcs 26 C5
Hallrule Borders 61 B11
Halls E Loth 70 C5
Hall's Green Herts 29 F9
Hallsands Devon 5 H9
Hallthwaites Cumb 56 H3
Hallworthy Corn 4 C2
Hallyburton House Perth 76 D5
Hallyne Borders 69 F10
Halmer End Staffs 43 H10
Halmore Glos 16 A3
Halmyre Mains Borders 69 F10
Halnaker W Sus 11 D8
Halsall Lancs 42 A6
Halse Northants 28 D2
Halse Som 7 D10
Halsetown Corn 2 F4
Halsham E Yorks 53 G8
Halsinger Devon 6 C4
Halstead Essex 30 E5
Halstead Kent 19 E11
Halstead Leics 36 E3
Halstock Dorset 8 D4
Haltham Lincs 46 F6
Haltoft End Lincs 47 H7
Halton Bucks 28 G5
Halton Halton 43 D8
Halton Lancs 49 C5
Halton Northumb 62 G5
Halton W Yorks 51 F9
Halton Wrex 33 B9
Halton East N Yorks 50 D6
Halton Gill N Yorks 50 B4
Halton Holegate Lincs 47 F8
Halton Lea Gate Northumb 62 H2
Halton West N Yorks 50 D4
Haltwhistle Northumb 62 G3
Halvergate Norf 39 E10
Halwell Devon 5 F8
Halwill Devon 6 G3
Halwill Junction Devon 6 F3
Ham Devon 7 F11
Ham Glos 16 B3
Ham Highld 94 C4
Ham Kent 21 F10
Ham London 19 D8
Ham Shetland 96 K1
Ham Wilts 17 E10
Ham Common Dorset 9 B7
Ham Green Hereford 26 D4
Ham Green Kent 13 D7
Ham Green Kent 20 E5
Ham Green N Som 15 D11
Ham Green Worcs 27 B7
Ham Street Som 8 A4
Hamble-le-Rice Hants 10 D3
Hambleden Bucks 18 C4
Hambledon Hants 10 C5
Hambledon Sur 18 H6
Hambleton Lancs 49 E3
Hambleton N Yorks 52 F1
Hambridge Som 8 B2
Hambrook S Glos 16 D3
Hambrook W Sus 11 D6
Hameringham Lincs 47 F7
Hamerton Cambs 37 H7
Hametoun Shetland 96 K1
Hamilton S Lanark 68 E6
Hammer W Sus 11 A7
Hammerpot W Sus 11 D9
Hammersmith London 19 D9
Hammerwich Staffs 35 E6
Hammerwood E Sus 12 C3
Hammond Street Herts 19 A10
Hammoon Dorset 9 C7
Hamnavoe Shetland 96 E4
Hamnavoe Shetland 96 E6
Hamnavoe Shetland 96 F6
Hamnavoe Shetland 96 K5
Hampden Park E Sus 12 F5
Hamperden End Essex 30 E2
Hampnett Glos 27 G7
Hampole S Yorks 45 A9
Hampreston Dorset 9 E9
Hampstead London 19 C9
Hampstead Norreys W Berks 18 D2
Hampsthwaite N Yorks 51 D8
Hampton London 19 E8
Hampton Shrops 34 G3
Hampton Worcs 27 D7
Hampton Bishop Hereford 26 E2
Hampton Heath Ches W 43 H7
Hampton in Arden W Mid 35 G8
Hampton Loade Shrops 34 G3
Hampton Lovett Worcs 26 B5
Hampton Lucy Warks 27 C9
Hampton on the Hill Warks 27 B9
Hampton Poyle Oxon 28 G2
Hamrow Norf 38 C5
Hamsey E Sus 12 E3
Hamsey Green London 19 F10
Hamstall Ridware Staffs 35 D7
Hamstead IoW 10 E3
Hamstead W Mid 34 F6
Hamstead Marshall W Berks 17 E11
Hamsterley Durham 58 C2
Hamsterley Durham 63 H7
Hamstreet Kent 13 C9
Hamworthy Poole 9 E8
Hanbury Staffs 35 C7
Hanbury Worcs 26 B6
Hanbury Woodend Staffs 35 C7
Hanby Lincs 36 B6
Hanchurch Staffs 34 A4
Handbridge Ches W 43 F7
Handcross W Sus 12 D1
Handforth Ches E 44 D2
Handley Ches W 43 G7
Handsacre Staffs 35 D6
Handsworth S Yorks 45 D8
Handsworth W Mid 34 F6
Handy Cross Devon 6 D3
Hanford Stoke 34 A4
Hanging Langford Wilts 17 H7
Hangleton W Sus 11 D9
Hanham S Glos 16 D3
Hankelow Ches E 43 H9
Hankerton Wilts 16 B6
Hankham E Sus 12 F5
Hanley Stoke 44 H2
Hanley Castle Worcs 26 D5
Hanley Child Worcs 26 B3
Hanley Swan Worcs 26 D5
Hanley William Worcs 26 B3
Hanlith N Yorks 50 C5
Hanmer Wrex 33 B10
Hannah Lincs 47 E9
Hannington Hants 18 F2
Hannington Northants 28 A5
Hannington Swindon 17 B8
Hannington Wick Swindon 17 B8
Hansel Village S Ayrs 67 C6
Hanslope M Keynes 28 D5
Hanthorpe Lincs 37 C6
Hanwell London 19 C8
Hanwell Oxon 27 D11
Hanwood Shrops 33 E10
Hanworth London 19 D8
Hanworth Norf 39 B7
Happendon S Lanark 69 G7
Happisburgh Norf 39 B9
Happisburgh Common Norf 39 C9
Hapsford Ches W 43 E7
Hapton Lancs 50 F3
Hapton Norf 39 F7
Harberton Devon 5 F8
Harbertonford Devon 5 F8
Harbledown Kent 21 F8
Harborne W Mid 34 G6
Harborough Magna Warks 35 H10
Harbottle Northumb 62 C5
Harbury Warks 27 C10
Harby Leics 36 B3
Harby Notts 46 E2
Harcombe Devon 7 G10
Harden W Mid 34 E6
Harden W Yorks 51 F6
Hardenhuish Wilts 16 D6
Hardgate Aberds 83 C9
Hardham W Sus 11 C9
Hardingham Norf 38 E6
Hardingstone Northants 28 C4
Hardington Som 16 F4
Hardington Mandeville Som 8 C4
Hardington Marsh Som 8 D4
Hardley Hants 10 D3
Hardley Street Norf 39 E9
Hardmead M Keynes 28 D6
Hardrow N Yorks 57 G10
Hardstoft Derbys 45 F8
Hardway Hants 10 D5
Hardway Som 8 A6
Hardwick Bucks 28 G5
Hardwick Cambs 29 C10
Hardwick Norf 38 D2
Hardwick Norf 39 G8
Hardwick Northants 28 B5
Hardwick Notts 45 E10
Hardwick Oxon 27 H10
Hardwick Oxon 28 F2
Hardwick W Mid 35 F6
Hardwicke Glos 26 F6
Hardwicke Glos 26 G4
Hardwicke Hereford 25 D9
Hardy's Green Essex 30 F6
Hare Green Essex 31 F7
Hare Hatch Wokingham 18 D5
Hare Street Herts 29 F10
Hareby Lincs 47 F7
Hareden Lancs 50 D2
Harefield London 19 B7
Harehills W Yorks 51 F9
Harehope Northumb 62 A6
Haresceugh Cumb 57 B8
Harescombe Glos 26 G5
Haresfield Glos 26 G5
Hareshaw N Lanark 69 D7
Hareshaw Head Northumb 62 E4
Harewood W Yorks 51 E9
Harewood End Hereford 26 F2
Harford Carms 24 D3
Harford Devon 5 F7
Hargate Norf 39 F7
Hargatewall Derbys 44 E5
Hargrave Ches W 43 F7
Hargrave Northants 29 A7
Hargrave Suff 30 C4
Harker Cumb 61 G9
Harkland Shetland 96 E6
Harkstead Suff 31 E8
Harlaston Staffs 35 D8
Harlaw Ho. Aberds 83 A9
Harlaxton Lincs 36 B4
Harle Syke Lancs 50 F4
Harlech Gwyn 41 G7
Harlequin Notts 36 B2
Harlescott Shrops 33 D11
Harlesden London 19 C9
Harleston Devon 5 G8
Harleston Norf 39 G8
Harleston Suff 31 C7
Harlestone Northants 28 B4
Harley S Yorks 45 C7
Harley Shrops 34 E1
Harleyholm S Lanark 69 G8
Harlington C Beds 29 E7
Harlington London 19 D7
Harlington S Yorks 45 B8
Harlosh Highld 85 D7
Harlow Essex 29 G11
Harlow Hill N Yorks 51 D8
Harlow Hill Northumb 62 G6
Harlthorpe E Yorks 52 F3
Harlton Cambs 29 C10
Harman's Cross Dorset 9 F8
Harmby N Yorks 58 H2
Harmer Green Herts 29 G9
Harmer Hill Shrops 33 C10
Harmondsworth London 19 D7
Harmston Lincs 46 F3
Harnham Northumb 62 F6
Harnhill Glos 17 A7
Harold Hill London 20 B2
Harold Wood London 20 B2
Haroldston West Pembs 22 E3
Haroldswick Shetland 96 B8
Harome N Yorks 52 A2
Harpenden Herts 29 G8
Harpford Devon 7 G9
Harpham E Yorks 53 C6
Harpley Norf 38 C3
Harpley Worcs 26 B3
Harpole Northants 28 B3
Harpsdale Highld 94 E3
Harpsden Oxon 18 C4
Harpswell Lincs 46 D3
Harpur Hill Derbys 44 E4
Harpurhey Gtr Man 44 B2
Harraby Cumb 56 A6
Harrapool Highld 85 F11
Harrier Shetland 96 J1
Harrietfield Perth 76 E2
Harrietsham Kent 20 F5
Harrington Cumb 56 D1
Harrington Lincs 47 E7
Harrington Northants 36 G3
Harringworth Northants 36 F5
Harris Highld 78 B6
Harrogate N Yorks 51 D9
Harrold Bedford 28 C6
Harrow London 19 C8
Harrow on the Hill London 19 C8
Harrow Street Suff 30 E6
Harrow Weald London 19 B8
Harrowbarrow Corn 4 E4
Harrowden Bedford 29 D7
Harrowgate Hill Darl 58 E3
Harston Cambs 29 C11
Harston Leics 36 B4
Harswell E Yorks 52 E4
Hart Hrtlpl 58 C5
Hart Common Gtr Man 43 B9
Hart Hill Luton 29 F8
Hart Station Hrtlpl 58 C5
Hartburn Northumb 62 E6
Hartburn Stockton 58 E5
Hartest Suff 30 C5
Hartfield E Sus 12 C3
Hartford Cambs 29 A9
Hartford Ches W 43 E9
Hartford End Essex 30 G3
Hartfordbridge Hants 18 F4
Hartforth N Yorks 58 F2
Harthill Ches W 43 G8
Harthill N Lanark 69 D8
Harthill S Yorks 45 D8
Hartington Derbys 44 F5
Hartland Devon 6 D1
Hartlebury Worcs 26 A5
Hartlepool Hrtlpl 58 C6
Hartley Cumb 57 F9
Hartley Kent 13 C6
Hartley Kent 20 E3
Hartley Northumb 63 F9
Hartley Westpall Hants 18 F3
Hartley Wintney Hants 18 F4
Hartlip Kent 20 E5
Hartoft End N Yorks 59 G8
Harton N Yorks 52 C3
Harton Shrops 33 G10
Harton T&W 63 G9
Hartpury Glos 26 F4
Hartshead W Yorks 51 G7
Hartshill Warks 35 F9
Hartshorne Derbys 35 C9
Hartsop Cumb 56 E6
Hartwell Northants 28 C4
Hartwood N Lanark 69 E7
Harvieston Stirling 68 B4
Harvington Worcs 27 D7
Harvington Cross Worcs 27 D7
Harwell Oxon 17 C11
Harwich Essex 31 E9
Harwood Durham 57 C10
Harwood Gtr Man 43 A10
Harwood Dale N Yorks 59 G10
Harworth Notts 45 C10
Hasbury W Mid 34 G5
Hascombe Sur 18 G6
Haselbech Northants 36 H3
Haselbury Plucknett Som 8 C3
Haseley Warks 27 B9
Haselor Warks 27 C8
Hasfield Glos 26 F5
Hasguard Pembs 22 F3
Haskayne Lancs 42 B6
Hasketon Suff 31 C9
Hasland Derbys 45 F7
Haslemere Sur 11 A8
Haslingden Lancs 50 G3
Haslingfield Cambs 29 C11
Haslington Ches E 43 G10
Hassall Ches E 43 G10
Hassall Green Ches E 43 G10
Hassell Street Kent 21 G7
Hassendean Borders 61 A11
Hassingham Norf 39 E9
Hassocks W Sus 12 E1
Hassop Derbys 44 E6
Hastigrow Highld 94 D4
Hastingleigh Kent 13 B9
Hastings E Sus 13 F7
Hastingwood Essex 29 H11
Hastoe Herts 28 H6
Haswell Durham 58 B4
Haswell Plough Durham 58 B4
Hatch C Beds 29 D8
Hatch Hants 18 F3
Hatch Wilts 9 B8
Hatch Beauchamp Som 8 B2
Hatch End London 19 B8
Hatch Green Som 8 C2
Hatchet Gate Hants 10 D2
Hatching Green Herts 29 G8
Hatchmere Ches W 43 E8
Hatcliffe NE Lincs 46 B6
Hatfield Hereford 26 C2
Hatfield Herts 29 H9
Hatfield S Yorks 45 B10
Hatfield Worcs 26 C5
Hatfield Broad Oak Essex 30 G2
Hatfield Garden Village Herts 29 H9
Hatfield Heath Essex 30 G2
Hatfield Hyde Herts 29 G9
Hatfield Peverel Essex 30 G4
Hatfield Woodhouse S Yorks 45 B10
Hatford Oxon 17 B10
Hatherden Hants 17 F10
Hatherleigh Devon 6 F4
Hathern Leics 35 C10
Hatherop Glos 27 H8
Hathersage Derbys 44 D6
Hathershaw Gtr Man 44 B3
Hatherton Ches E 43 H9
Hatherton Staffs 34 D5
Hatley St George Cambs 29 C9
Hatt Corn 4 E4
Hattingley Hants 18 H3
Hatton Aberds 89 E10
Hatton Derbys 35 C8
Hatton Lincs 46 E5
Hatton Shrops 33 F10
Hatton Warks 27 B9
Hatton Warr 43 D8
Hatton Castle Aberds 89 D7
Hatton Heath Ches W 43 F7
Hatton of Fintray Aberds 83 B10
Hattoncrook Aberds 89 F8
Haugh E Ayrs 67 D7
Haugh Gtr Man 44 A3
Haugh Lincs 47 E8
Haugh Head Northumb 71 H9
Haugh of Glass Moray 88 E4
Haugh of Urr Dumfries 55 C11
Haugham Lincs 47 D7
Haughley Suff 31 B7
Haughley Green Suff 31 B7
Haughs of Clinterty Aberdeen 83 B10
Haughton Notts 45 E10
Haughton Shrops 33 C9
Haughton Shrops 34 D1
Haughton Shrops 34 E3
Haughton Shrops 34 F2
Haughton Staffs 34 C4
Haughton Castle Northumb 62 F5
Haughton Green Gtr Man 44 C3
Haughton Moss Ches E 43 G8
Haultwick Herts 29 F10
Haunn Argyll 78 G6
Haunn W Isles 84 G2
Haunton Staffs 35 D8
Hauxley Northumb 63 C8
Hauxton Cambs 29 C11
Havant Hants 10 D6
Haven Hereford 25 C11
Haven Bank Lincs 46 G6
Haven Side E Yorks 53 G7
Havenstreet IoW 10 E4
Havercroft W Yorks 45 A7
Haverfordwest = Hwlffordd Pembs 22 E4
Haverhill Suff 30 D3
Haverigg Cumb 49 B1
Havering-atte-Bower London 20 B2
Haveringland Norf 39 C7
Haversham M Keynes 28 D5
Haverthwaite Cumb 49 A3
Haverton Hill Stockton 58 D5
Hawarden = Penarlâg Flint 42 F6
Hawcoat Cumb 49 B2
Hawen Ceredig 23 B8
Hawes N Yorks 57 H10
Hawes' Green Norf 39 F8
Hawes Side Blackpool 49 F3
Hawford Worcs 26 B5
Hawick Borders 61 B11
Hawk Green Gtr Man 44 D3
Hawkchurch Devon 8 D2
Hawkedon Suff 30 C4
Hawkenbury Kent 12 C4
Hawkenbury Kent 13 B7
Hawkeridge Wilts 16 F5
Hawkerland Devon 7 H9
Hawkes End W Mid 35 G9
Hawkesbury S Glos 16 C4
Hawkesbury Warks 35 G9
Hawkesbury Upton S Glos 16 C4
Hawkhill Northumb 63 B8
Hawkhurst Kent 13 C6
Hawkinge Kent 21 H9
Hawkley Hants 10 B6
Hawkridge Som 7 C7
Hawkshead Cumb 56 G5
Hawkshead Hill Cumb 56 G5
Hawksland S Lanark 69 G7
Hawkswick N Yorks 50 B5
Hawksworth Notts 36 A3
Hawksworth W Yorks 51 E7
Hawksworth W Yorks 51 F8
Hawkwell Essex 20 B5
Hawley Hants 18 F5
Hawley Kent 20 D2
Hawling Glos 27 F7
Hawnby N Yorks 59 H6
Haworth W Yorks 50 F6
Hawstead Suff 30 C5
Hawthorn Durham 58 B5
Hawthorn Rhondda 15 C7
Hawthorn Wilts 16 E5
Hawthorn Hill Brack 18 D5
Hawthorn Hill Lincs 46 G6
Hawthorpe Lincs 36 C6
Hawton Notts 45 G11
Haxby York 52 D2
Haxey N Lincs 45 C11
Hay Green Norf 37 D11
Hay-on-Wye = Y Gelli Gandryll Powys 25 D9
Hay Street Herts 29 F10
Haydock Mers 43 C8
Haydon Dorset 8 C5
Haydon Bridge Northumb 62 G4
Haydon Wick Swindon 17 C8
Haye Corn 4 E4
Hayes London 19 C8
Hayes London 19 E11
Hayfield Derbys 44 D4
Hayfield Fife 69 A11
Hayhill E Ayrs 67 E7
Hayhillock Angus 77 C8
Hayle Corn 2 F4
Haynes C Beds 29 D7
Haynes Church End C Beds 29 D7
Hayscastle Pembs 22 D3
Hayscastle Cross Pembs 22 D4
Hayshead Angus 77 C9
Hayton Aberdeen 83 C11
Hayton Cumb 56 B3
Hayton Cumb 61 H11
Hayton E Yorks 52 E4
Hayton Notts 45 D11
Hayton's Bent Shrops 33 G11
Haytor Vale Devon 5 D8
Haywards Heath W Sus 12 D2
Haywood S Yorks 45 A9
Haywood Oaks Notts 45 G10
Hazel Grove Gtr Man 44 D3
Hazel Street Kent 12 C5
Hazelbank S Lanark 69 F7
Hazelbury Bryan Dorset 8 D6
Hazeley Hants 18 F4
Hazelhurst Gtr Man 44 B3
Hazelslade Staffs 34 D6
Hazelton Glos 27 G7
Hazelton Walls Fife 76 E6
Hazelwood Derbys 45 H7
Hazlemere Bucks 18 B5
Hazlerigg T&W 63 F8
Hazlewood N Yorks 51 D6
Hazon Northumb 63 C7
Heacham Norf 38 B2
Head of Muir Falk 69 B7
Headbourne Worthy Hants 10 A3
Headbrook Hereford 25 C10
Headcorn Kent 13 B7
Headingley W Yorks 51 F8
Headington Oxon 28 H2
Headlam Durham 58 E2
Headless Cross Worcs 27 B7
Headley Hants 18 E2
Headley Hants 18 H5
Headley Sur 19 F9
Headon Notts 45 E11
Heads S Lanark 68 F6
Heads Nook Cumb 61 H10
Heage Derbys 45 G7
Healaugh N Yorks 51 E10
Healaugh N Yorks 58 G1
Heald Green Gtr Man 44 D2
Heale Devon 6 B5
Heale Som 16 G3
Healey Gtr Man 50 H4
Healey N Yorks 51 A7
Healey Northumb 62 H6
Healing NE Lincs 46 A6
Heamoor Corn 2 F3
Heanish Argyll 78 G3
Heanor Derbys 45 H8
Heanton Punchardon Devon 6 C4
Heapham Lincs 46 D2
Hearthstane Borders 69 H10
Heasley Mill Devon 7 C6
Heast Highld 85 G11
Heath Cardiff 15 D7
Heath Derbys 45 F8
Heath and Reach C Beds 28 F6
Heath End Hants 18 E2
Heath End Sur 18 G5
Heath End Warks 27 B9
Heath Hayes Staffs 34 D6
Heath Hill Shrops 34 D3
Heath House Som 15 G10
Heath Town W Mid 34 F5
Heathcote Derbys 44 F5
Heather Leics 35 D9
Heatherfield Highld 85 D9
Heathfield Devon 5 D9
Heathfield E Sus 12 D4
Heathfield Som 7 D10
Heathhall Dumfries 60 F5
Heathrow Airport London 19 D7
Heathstock Devon 8 D1
Heathton Shrops 34 F4
Heatley Warr 43 D10
Heaton Lancs 49 C4
Heaton Staffs 44 F3
Heaton T&W 63 G8
Heaton W Yorks 51 F7
Heaton Moor Gtr Man 44 C2
Heaverham Kent 20 F2
Heaviley Gtr Man 44 D3
Heavitree Devon 7 G8
Hebburn T&W 63 G9
Hebden N Yorks 50 C6
Hebden Bridge W Yorks 50 G5
Hebron Anglesey 40 B6
Hebron Carms 22 D6
Hebron Northumb 63 E7
Heck Dumfries 60 E6
Heckfield Hants 18 E4
Heckfield Green Suff 39 H7
Heckfordbridge Essex 30 F6
Heckington Lincs 37 A7
Heckmondwike W Yorks 51 G8
Heddington Wilts 16 E6
Heddle Orkney 95 G4
Heddon-on-the-Wall Northumb 63 G7
Hedenham Norf 39 F9
Hedge End Hants 10 C3
Hedgerley Bucks 18 C6
Hedging Som 8 B2
Hedley on the Hill Northumb 62 H6
Hednesford Staffs 34 D6
Hedon E Yorks 53 G7
Hedsor Bucks 18 C6
Hedworth T&W 63 G9
Hegdon Hill Hereford 26 C2
Heggerscales Cumb 57 E10
Heglibister Shetland 96 H5
Heighington Darl 58 D3
Heighington Lincs 46 F4
Heights of Brae Highld 87 E8
Heights of Kinlochewe Highld 86 E3
Heilam Highld 92 C7
Heiton Borders 70 G6
Hele Devon 6 B4
Hele Devon 7 F8
Helensburgh Argyll 73 E11
Helford Corn 3 G6
Helford Passage Corn 3 G6
Helhoughton Norf 38 C4
Helions Bumpstead Essex 30 D3
Hellaby S Yorks 45 C9
Helland Corn 4 D1
Hellesdon Norf 39 D8
Hellidon Northants 28 C2
Hellifield N Yorks 50 D4
Hellingly E Sus 12 E4
Hellington Norf 39 E9
Hellister Shetland 96 J5
Helm Northumb 63 D7
Helmdon Northants 28 D2
Helmingham Suff 31 C8
Helmington Row Durham 58 C2
Helmsdale Highld 93 H13
Helmshore Lancs 50 G3
Helmsley N Yorks 52 A2
Helperby N Yorks 51 C10
Helperthorpe N Yorks 52 B5
Helpringham Lincs 37 A7
Helpston Pboro 37 E7
Helsby Ches W 43 E7
Helsey Lincs 47 E9
Helston Corn 2 G5
Helstone Corn 4 C1
Helton Cumb 57 D7
Helwith Bridge N Yorks 50 C4
Hemblington Norf 39 D9
Hemel Hempstead Herts 29 H7
Hemingbrough N Yorks 52 F2
Hemingby Lincs 46 E6
Hemingford Abbots Cambs 29 A9
Hemingford Grey Cambs 29 A9
Hemingstone Suff 31 C8
Hemington Leics 35 C10
Hemington Northants 37 G6
Hemington Som 16 F4
Hemley Suff 31 D9
Hemlington Mbro 58 E6
Hemp Green Suff 31 B10
Hempholme E Yorks 53 D6
Hempnall Norf 39 F8
Hempnall Green Norf 39 F8
Hempriggs House Highld 94 F5
Hempstead Essex 30 E3
Hempstead Medway 20 E4
Hempstead Norf 39 B7
Hempstead Norf 39 C10
Hempsted Glos 26 G5
Hempton Norf 38 C5
Hempton Oxon 27 E11
Hemsby Norf 39 D10
Hemswell Lincs 46 C3
Hemswell Cliff Lincs 46 D3
Hemsworth W Yorks 45 A8
Hemyock Devon 7 E10
Hen-feddau fawr Pembs 23 C7
Henbury Bristol 16 D2
Henbury Ches E 44 E2
Hendon London 19 C9
Hendon T&W 63 H10
Hendre Flint 42 F4
Hendre-ddu Conwy 41 D10
Hendreforgan Rhondda 14 C5
Hendy Carms 23 F10
Heneglwys Anglesey 40 C6
Henfield W Sus 11 C11
Henford Devon 6 G2
Henghurst Kent 13 C8
Hengoed Caerph 15 B7
Hengoed Powys 25 C9
Hengoed Shrops 33 B8
Hengrave Suff 30 B5
Henham Essex 30 F2
Heniarth Powys 33 E7
Henlade Som 8 B1
Henley Shrops 33 H11
Henley Som 8 A3
Henley Suff 31 C8
Henley W Sus 11 B7
Henley-in-Arden Warks 27 B8
Henley-on-Thames Oxon 18 C4
Henley's Down E Sus 12 E6
Henllan Ceredig 23 B8
Henllan Denb 42 F3
Henllan Amgoed Carms 22 D6
Henllys Torf 15 B8
Henlow C Beds 29 E8
Hennock Devon 5 C9
Henny Street Essex 30 E5
Henryd Conwy 41 C9
Henry's Moat Pembs 22 D5
Hensall N Yorks 52 G1
Henshaw Northumb 62 G3
Hensingham Cumb 56 E1
Henstead Suff 39 G10
Henstridge Som 8 C6
Henstridge Ash Som 8 B6
Henstridge Marsh Som 8 B6
Henton Oxon 18 A4
Henton Som 15 G10
Henwood Corn 4 D3
Heogan Shetland 96 J6
Heol-las Swansea 14 B2
Heol Senni Powys 24 F6
Heol-y-Cyw Bridgend 14 C5
Hepburn Northumb 62 A6
Hepple Northumb 62 C5
Hepscott Northumb 63 E8
Heptonstall W Yorks 50 G5
Hepworth Suff 30 A6
Hepworth W Yorks 44 B5
Herbrandston Pembs 22 F3
Hereford Hereford 26 D2
Heriot Borders 70 E2
Hermiston Edin 69 C10
Hermitage Borders 61 D11
Hermitage Dorset 8 D5
Hermitage W Berks 18 D2
Hermitage W Sus 11 D6
Hermon Anglesey 40 D5
Hermon Carms 23 C8
Hermon Carms 24 F3
Hermon Pembs 23 C7
Herne Kent 21 E8
Herne Bay Kent 21 E8
Herner Devon 6 D4
Hernhill Kent 21 E7
Herodsfoot Corn 4 E3
Herongate Essex 20 B3
Heronsford S Ayrs 54 A4
Herriard Hants 18 G3
Herringfleet Suff 39 F10
Herringswell Suff 30 A4
Hersden Kent 21 E9
Hersham Corn 6 F1
Hersham Sur 19 E8
Herstmonceux E Sus 12 E5
Herston Orkney 95 J5
Hertford Herts 29 G10
Hertford Heath Herts 29 G10
Hertingfordbury Herts 29 G10
Hesket Newmarket Cumb 56 C5
Hesketh Bank Lancs 49 G4
Hesketh Lane Lancs 50 E2
Heskin Green Lancs 49 H5
Hesleden Durham 58 C5
Hesleyside Northumb 62 E4
Heslington York 52 D2
Hessay York 51 D11
Hessenford Corn 4 F4
Hessett Suff 30 B6
Hessle E Yorks 52 G6
Hest Bank Lancs 49 C4
Heston London 19 D8
Hestwall Orkney 95 G3
Heswall Mers 42 D5
Hethe Oxon 28 F2
Hethersett Norf 39 E7
Hethersgill Cumb 61 G10
Hethpool Northumb 71 H7
Hett Durham 58 C3
Hetton N Yorks 50 D5
Hetton-le-Hole T&W 58 B4
Hetton Steads Northumb 71 G9
Heugh Northumb 62 F6
Heugh-head Aberds 82 B5
Heveningham Suff 31 A10
Hever Kent 12 B3
Heversham Cumb 49 A4
Hevingham Norf 39 C7
Hewas Water Corn 3 E8
Hewelsfield Glos 16 A2
Hewish N Som 15 E10
Hewish Som 8 D3
Heworth York 52 D2
Hexham Northumb 62 G5
Hextable Kent 20 D2
Hexton Herts 29 E8
Hexworthy Devon 5 D7
Hey Lancs 50 E4
Heybridge Essex 20 B3
Heybridge Essex 30 H5
Heybridge Basin Essex 30 H5
Heybrook Bay Devon 4 G6
Heydon Cambs 29 D11

Kinlocheil Highld 80 F1
Kinlochewe Highld 86 E3
Kinlochleven Highld 74 A4
Kinlochmoidart Highld 79 D10
Kinlochmorar Highld 79 B11
Kinlochmore Highld 74 A4
Kinlochspelve Argyll 79 J9
Kinloid Highld 79 C9
Kinloss Moray 87 E13
Kinmel Bay Conwy 42 D2
Kinmuck Aberds 83 B10
Kinmundy Aberds 83 B10
Kinnadie Aberds 89 D9
Kinnaird Perth 76 E5
Kinnaird Castle Angus 77 B9
Kinneff Aberds 83 F10
Kinnelhead Dumfries 60 C6
Kinnell Angus 77 B9
Kinnerley Shrops 33 C9
Kinnersley Hereford 25 D10
Kinnersley Worcs 26 D5
Kinnerton Powys 25 B9
Kinnesswood Perth 76 G4
Kinninvie Durham 58 D1
Kinnordy Angus 76 B6
Kinoulton Notts 36 B2
Kinross Perth 76 G4
Kinrossie Perth 76 D4
Kinsbourne Green Herts 29 G8
Kinsey Heath Ches E 34 A2
Kinsham Hereford 25 B10
Kinsham Worcs 26 E6
Kinsley W Yorks 45 A8
Kinson Bmouth 9 E9
Kintbury W Berks 17 E10
Kintessack Moray 87 E12
Kintillo Perth 76 F4
Kintocher Aberds 83 C7
Kinton Hereford 25 A11
Kinton Shrops 33 D9
Kintore Aberds 83 B9
Kintour Argyll 64 C5
Kintra Argyll 64 D4
Kintra Argyll 78 J6
Kintraw Argyll 73 C7
Kinuachdrachd Argyll 72 D6
Kinveachy Highld 81 B11
Kinver Staffs 34 G4
Kippax W Yorks 51 F10
Kippen Stirling 68 A5
Kippford or Scaur Dumfries 55 D11
Kirbister Orkney 95 F7
Kirbister Orkney 95 H4
Kirbuster Orkney 95 F3
Kirby Bedon Norf 39 E8
Kirby Bellars Leics 36 D3
Kirby Cane Norf 39 F9
Kirby Cross Essex 31 F9
Kirby Grindalythe N Yorks 52 C5
Kirby Hill N Yorks 51 C9
Kirby Hill N Yorks 58 F2
Kirby Knowle N Yorks 58 H5
Kirby-le-Soken Essex 31 F9
Kirby Misperton N Yorks 52 B3
Kirby Muxloe Leics 35 E11
Kirby Row Norf 39 F9
Kirby Sigston N Yorks 58 G5
Kirby Underdale E Yorks 52 D4
Kirby Wiske N Yorks 51 A9
Kirdford W Sus 11 B9
Kirk Highld 94 E4
Kirk Bramwith S Yorks 45 A10
Kirk Deighton N Yorks 51 D9
Kirk Ella E Yorks 52 G6
Kirk Hallam Derbys 35 A10
Kirk Hammerton N Yorks 51 D10
Kirk Ireton Derbys 44 G6
Kirk Langley Derbys 35 B8
Kirk Merrington Durham 58 C3
Kirk Michael IoM 48 C3
Kirk of Shotts N Lanark 69 D7
Kirk Sandall S Yorks 45 B10
Kirk Smeaton N Yorks 51 H11
Kirk Yetholm Borders 71 H7
Kirkabister Shetland 96 K6
Kirkandrews Dumfries 55 E9
Kirkandrews upon Eden Cumb 61 H9
Kirkbampton Cumb 61 H9
Kirkbean Dumfries 60 H5
Kirkbride Cumb 61 H8
Kirkbuddo Angus 77 C8
Kirkburn Borders 69 G11
Kirkburn E Yorks 52 D5
Kirkburton W Yorks 44 A5
Kirkby Lincs 46 C4
Kirkby Mers 43 C7
Kirkby N Yorks 59 F6
Kirkby Fleetham N Yorks 58 G3
Kirkby Green Lincs 46 G4
Kirkby In Ashfield Notts 45 G9
Kirkby-in-Furness Cumb 49 A2
Kirkby la Thorpe Lincs 46 H5
Kirkby Lonsdale Cumb 50 B2
Kirkby Malham N Yorks 50 C4
Kirkby Mallory Leics 35 E10
Kirkby Malzeard N Yorks 51 B8
Kirkby Mills N Yorks 59 H8
Kirkby on Bain Lincs 46 F6
Kirkby Overflow N Yorks 51 E9
Kirkby Stephen Cumb 57 F9
Kirkby Thore Cumb 57 D8
Kirkby Underwood Lincs 37 C6
Kirkby Wharfe N Yorks 51 E11
Kirkbymoorside N Yorks 59 H7
Kirkcaldy Fife 69 A11
Kirkcambeck Cumb 61 G11
Kirkcarswell Dumfries 55 E10
Kirkcolm Dumfries 54 C3
Kirkconnel Dumfries 60 B3
Kirkconnell Dumfries 60 G5
Kirkcowan Dumfries 54 C6
Kirkcudbright Dumfries 55 D9
Kirkdale Mers 42 C6
Kirkfieldbank S Lanark 69 F7
Kirkgunzeon Dumfries 55 C11
Kirkham Lancs 49 F4
Kirkham N Yorks 52 C3
Kirkhamgate W Yorks 51 G8
Kirkharle Northumb 62 E6
Kirkheaton Northumb 62 F6
Kirkheaton W Yorks 51 H7
Kirkhill Angus 77 A9
Kirkhill Highld 87 G8
Kirkhill Midloth 69 D11
Kirkhill Moray 88 E2
Kirkhope Borders 61 A9
Kirkhouse Borders 70 G2
Kirkiboll Highld 93 D8
Kirkibost Highld 85 G10
Kirkinch Angus 76 C6
Kirkinner Dumfries 55 D7
Kirkintilloch E Dunb 68 C5
Kirkland Cumb 56 E2
Kirkland Cumb 57 C8
Kirkland Dumfries 60 B3
Kirkland Dumfries 60 D4
Kirkleatham Redcar 59 D6
Kirklevington Stockton 58 F5
Kirkley Suff 39 F11
Kirklington N Yorks 51 A9
Kirklington Notts 45 G10
Kirklinton Cumb 61 G10
Kirkliston Edin 69 C10
Kirkmaiden Dumfries 54 F4
Kirkmichael Perth 76 B3
Kirkmichael S Ayrs 66 F6
Kirkmuirhill S Lanark 68 F6
Kirknewton Northumb 71 G8
Kirknewton W Loth 69 D10
Kirkney Aberds 88 E5
Kirkoswald Cumb 57 B7
Kirkoswald S Ayrs 66 F5
Kirkpatrick Durham Dumfries 60 F3
Kirkpatrick-Fleming Dumfries 61 F8
Kirksanton Cumb 49 A1
Kirkstall W Yorks 51 F8
Kirkstead Lincs 46 F5
Kirkstile Aberds 88 E5
Kirkstyle Highld 94 C5
Kirkton Aberds 83 A8
Kirkton Aberds 89 D6
Kirkton Angus 77 C7
Kirkton Angus 77 D7
Kirkton Borders 61 B11
Kirkton Dumfries 60 E5
Kirkton Fife 76 E6
Kirkton Highld 85 F13
Kirkton Highld 86 G2
Kirkton Highld 87 B10
Kirkton Highld 87 F10
Kirkton Perth 76 F2
Kirkton S Lanark 60 A5
Kirkton Stirling 75 G8
Kirkton Manor Borders 69 G11
Kirkton of Airlie Angus 76 B6
Kirkton of Auchterhouse Angus 76 D6
Kirkton of Auchterless Aberds 89 D7
Kirkton of Barevan Highld 87 G11
Kirkton of Bourtie Aberds 89 F8
Kirkton of Collace Perth 76 D4
Kirkton of Craig Angus 77 B10
Kirkton of Culsalmond Aberds 89 E6
Kirkton of Durris Aberds 83 D9
Kirkton of Glenbuchat Aberds 82 B5
Kirkton of Glenisla Angus 76 A5
Kirkton of Kingoldrum Angus 76 B6
Kirkton of Largo Fife 77 G7
Kirkton of Lethendy Perth 76 C4
Kirkton of Logie Buchan Aberds 89 F9
Kirkton of Maryculter Aberds 83 D10
Kirkton of Menmuir Angus 77 A8
Kirkton of Monikie Angus 77 D8
Kirkton of Oyne Aberds 83 A8
Kirkton of Rayne Aberds 83 A8
Kirkton of Skene Aberds 83 C10
Kirkton of Tough Aberds 83 B8
Kirktonhill Borders 70 E3
Kirktown Aberds 89 C10
Kirktown of Alvah Aberds 89 B6
Kirktown of Deskford Moray 88 B5
Kirktown of Fetteresso Aberds 83 E10
Kirktown of Mortlach Moray 88 E3
Kirktown of Slains Aberds 89 F10
Kirkurd Borders 69 F10
Kirkwall Orkney 95 G5
Kirkwhelpington Northumb 62 E5
Kirmington N Lincs 46 A5
Kirmond le Mire Lincs 46 C5
Kirn Argyll 73 F10
Kirriemuir Angus 76 B6
Kirstead Green Norf 39 F8
Kirtlebridge Dumfries 61 F8
Kirtleton Dumfries 61 E8
Kirtling Cambs 30 C3
Kirtling Green Cambs 30 C3
Kirtlington Oxon 27 G11
Kirtomy Highld 93 C10
Kirton Lincs 37 B9
Kirton Notts 45 F10
Kirton Suff 31 E9
Kirton End Lincs 37 A8
Kirton Holme Lincs 37 A8
Kirton in Lindsey N Lincs 46 C3
Kislingbury Northants 28 C3
Kites Hardwick Warks 27 B11
Kittisford Som 7 D9
Kittle Swansea 23 H10
Kitt's Green W Mid 35 G7
Kitt's Moss Gtr Man 44 D2
Kittybrewster Aberdeen 83 C11
Kitwood Hants 10 A5
Kivernoll Hereford 25 E11
Kiveton Park S Yorks 45 D8
Knaith Lincs 46 D2
Knaith Park Lincs 46 D2
Knap Corner Dorset 9 B7
Knaphill Sur 18 F6
Knapp Perth 76 D5
Knapp Som 8 B2
Knapthorpe Notts 45 G11
Knapton Norf 39 B9
Knapton York 52 D1
Knapton Green Hereford 25 C11
Knapwell Cambs 29 B10
Knaresborough N Yorks 51 D9
Knarsdale Northumb 57 A8
Knauchland Moray 88 C5
Knaven Aberds 89 D8
Knayton N Yorks 58 H5
Knebworth Herts 29 F9
Knedlington E Yorks 52 G3
Kneesall Notts 45 F11
Kneesworth Cambs 29 D10
Kneeton Notts 45 H11
Knelston Swansea 23 H9
Knenhall Staffs 34 B5
Knettishall Suff 38 G5
Knightacott Devon 6 C5
Knightcote Warks 27 C10
Knightley Dale Staffs 34 C4
Knighton Devon 4 G6
Knighton Leicester 36 E1
Knighton = Tref-y-Clawdd Powys 25 A9
Knighton Staffs 34 A3
Knighton Staffs 34 C3
Knightswood Glasgow 68 D4
Knightwick Worcs 26 C4
Knill Hereford 25 B9
Knipton Leics 36 B4
Knitsley Durham 58 B2
Kniveton Derbys 44 G6
Knock Argyll 79 H8
Knock Cumb 57 D8
Knock Moray 88 C5
Knockally Highld 94 H3
Knockan Highld 92 H5
Knockandhu Moray 82 A4
Knockando Moray 88 D1
Knockando Ho. Moray 88 D2
Knockbain Highld 87 F9
Knockbreck Highld 84 B7
Knockbrex Dumfries 55 E8
Knockdee Highld 94 D3
Knockdolian S Ayrs 66 H4
Knockenkelly N Ayrs 66 D3
Knockentiber E Ayrs 67 C6
Knockespock Ho. Aberds 83 A7
Knockfarrel Highld 87 F8
Knockglass Dumfries 54 D3
Knockholt Kent 19 F11
Knockholt Pound Kent 19 F11
Knockie Lodge Highld 80 B6
Knockin Shrops 33 C9
Knockinlaw E Ayrs 67 C7
Knocklearn Dumfries 60 F3
Knocknaha Argyll 65 G7
Knocknain Dumfries 54 C2
Knockrome Argyll 72 F4
Knocksharry IoM 48 D2
Knodishall Suff 31 B11
Knolls Green Ches E 44 E2
Knolton Wrex 33 B9
Knolton Bryn Wrex 33 B9
Knook Wilts 16 G6
Knossington Leics 36 E4
Knott End-on-Sea Lancs 49 E3
Knotting Bedford 29 B7
Knotting Green Bedford 29 B7
Knottingley W Yorks 51 G11
Knotts Cumb 56 D6
Knotts Lancs 50 D3
Knotty Ash Mers 43 C7
Knotty Green Bucks 18 B6
Knowbury Shrops 26 A2
Knowe Dumfries 54 B6
Knowehead Dumfries 67 G9
Knowes of Elrick Aberds 88 C6
Knowesgate Northumb 62 E5
Knoweton N Lanark 68 E6
Knowhead Aberds 89 C9
Knowl Hill Windsor 18 D5
Knowle Bristol 16 D3
Knowle Devon 6 C3
Knowle Devon 7 F9
Knowle Devon 7 H9
Knowle Shrops 26 A2
Knowle W Mid 35 H7
Knowle Green Lancs 50 F2
Knowle Park W Yorks 51 E6
Knowlton Dorset 9 C9
Knowlton Kent 21 F9
Knowsley Mers 43 C7
Knowstone Devon 7 D7
Knox Bridge Kent 13 B6
Knucklas Powys 25 A9
Knuston Northants 28 B6
Knutsford Ches E 43 E10
Knutton Staffs 44 H2
Knypersley Staffs 44 G2
Kuggar Corn 2 H6
Kyle of Lochalsh Highld 85 F12
Kyleakin Highld 85 F12
Kylerhea Highld 85 F12
Kylesknoydart Highld 79 B11
Kylesku Highld 92 F5
Kylesmorar Highld 79 B11
Kylestrome Highld 92 F5
Kyllachy House Highld 81 A9
Kynaston Shrops 33 C9
Kynnersley Telford 34 D2
Kyre Magna Worcs 26 B3

L

La Fontenelle Guern 11
La Planque Guern 11
Labost W Isles 91 C7
Lacasaidh W Isles 91 E8
Lacasdal W Isles 91 D9
Laceby NE Lincs 46 B6
Lacey Green Bucks 18 B5
Lach Dennis Ches W 43 E10
Lackford Suff 30 A4
Lacock Wilts 16 E6
Ladbroke Warks 27 C11
Laddingford Kent 20 G3
Lade Bank Lincs 47 G7
Ladock Corn 3 D7
Lady Orkney 95 D7
Ladybank Fife 76 F6
Ladykirk Borders 71 F7
Ladysford Aberds 89 B9
Laga Highld 79 E9
Lagalochan Argyll 73 B7
Lagavulin Argyll 64 D5
Lagg Argyll 72 F4
Lagg N Ayrs 66 D2
Laggan Argyll 64 C3
Laggan Highld 79 D10
Laggan Highld 80 D4
Laggan Highld 81 D8
Laggan S Ayrs 54 A5
Lagganulva Argyll 78 G7
Laide Highld 91 H13
Laigh Fenwick E Ayrs 67 B7
Laigh Glengall S Ayrs 66 E6
Laighmuir E Ayrs 67 B7
Laindon Essex 20 C3
Lair Highld 86 G3
Lairg Highld 93 J8
Lairg Lodge Highld 93 J8
Lairg Muir Highld 93 J8
Lairgmore Highld 87 H8
Laisterdyke W Yorks 51 F7
Laithes Cumb 56 C6
Lake IoW 10 F4
Lake Wilts 17 H8
Lakenham Norf 39 E8
Lakenheath Suff 38 G3
Lakesend Norf 37 F11
Lakeside Cumb 56 H5
Laleham Sur 19 E7
Laleston Bridgend 14 D4
Lamarsh Essex 30 E5
Lamas Norf 39 C8
Lambden Borders 70 F6
Lamberhurst Kent 12 C5
Lamberhurst Quarter Kent 12 C5
Lamberton Borders 71 E8
Lambeth London 19 D10
Lambhill Glasgow 68 D4
Lambley Northumb 62 H2
Lambley Notts 45 H10
Lamborough Hill Oxon 17 A11
Lambourn W Berks 17 D10
Lambourne End Essex 19 B11
Lambs Green W Sus 19 H9
Lambston Pembs 22 E4
Lambton T&W 58 A3
Lamerton Devon 4 D5
Lamesley T&W 63 H8
Laminess Orkney 95 E7
Lamington Highld 87 D10
Lamington S Lanark 69 G8
Lamlash N Ayrs 66 C3
Lamloch Dumfries 67 G8
Lamonby Cumb 56 C6
Lamorna Corn 2 G3
Lamorran Corn 3 E7
Lampardbrook Suff 31 B9
Lampeter = Llanbedr Pont Steffan Ceredig 23 B10
Lampeter Velfrey Pembs 22 E6
Lamphey Pembs 22 F5
Lamplugh Cumb 56 D2
Lamport Northants 28 A4
Lamyatt Som 16 H3
Lana Devon 6 G2
Lanark S Lanark 69 F7
Lancaster Lancs 49 C4
Lanchester Durham 58 B2
Lancing W Sus 11 D10
Landbeach Cambs 29 B11
Landcross Devon 6 D3
Landerberry Aberds 83 C9
Landford Wilts 10 C1
Landford Manor Wilts 10 B1
Landimore Swansea 23 G9
Landkey Devon 6 C4
Landore Swansea 14 B2
Landrake Corn 4 E4
Landscove Devon 5 E8
Landshipping Pembs 22 E5
Landshipping Quay Pembs 22 E5
Landulph Corn 4 E5
Landwade Suff 30 B3
Lane Corn 3 C7
Lane End Bucks 18 B5
Lane End Cumb 56 G3
Lane End Dorset 9 E7
Lane End Hants 10 B4
Lane End IoW 10 F5
Lane End Lancs 50 E4
Lane Ends Lancs 50 D3
Lane Ends Lancs 50 F3
Lane Ends N Yorks 50 E5
Lane Head Derbys 44 E5
Lane Head Durham 58 E2
Lane Head Gtr Man 43 C9
Lane Head W Yorks 44 B5
Lane Side Lancs 50 G3
Laneast Corn 4 C3
Laneham Notts 46 E2
Lanehead Durham 57 B10
Lanehead Northumb 62 E3
Lanercost Cumb 61 G11
Laneshaw Bridge Lancs 50 E5
Lanfach Caerph 15 B8
Langar Notts 36 B3
Langbank Renfs 68 C2
Langbar N Yorks 51 D6
Langburnshiels Borders 61 C11
Langcliffe N Yorks 50 C4
Langdale Highld 93 E9
Langdale End N Yorks 59 G10
Langdon Corn 4 C4
Langdon Beck Durham 57 C10
Langdon Hills Essex 20 C3
Langdyke Fife 76 G6
Langenhoe Essex 31 G7
Langford C Beds 29 D8
Langford Devon 7 F9
Langford Essex 30 H5
Langford Notts 46 G2
Langford Oxon 17 A9
Langford Budville Som 7 D10
Langham Essex 31 E7
Langham Norf 38 A6
Langham Rutland 36 D4
Langham Suff 30 B6
Langhaugh Borders 69 G11
Langho Lancs 50 F3
Langholm Dumfries 61 E9
Langleeford Northumb 62 A5
Langley Ches E 44 E3
Langley Hants 10 D3
Langley Herts 29 F9
Langley Kent 20 F5
Langley Northumb 62 G4
Langley Slough 19 D7
Langley W Sus 11 B7
Langley Warks 27 B8
Langley Burrell Wilts 16 D6
Langley Common Derbys 35 B8
Langley Heath Kent 20 F5
Langley Lower Green Essex 29 E11
Langley Marsh Som 7 D9
Langley Park Durham 58 B3
Langley Street Norf 39 E9
Langley Upper Green Essex 29 E11
Langney E Sus 12 F5
Langold Notts 45 D9
Langore Corn 4 C4
Langport Som 8 B3
Langrick Lincs 46 H6
Langridge Bath 16 E4
Langridge Ford Devon 6 D4
Langrigg Cumb 56 B3
Langrish Hants 10 B6
Langsett S Yorks 44 B6
Langshaw Borders 70 G4
Langside Perth 75 F10
Langskaill Orkney 95 D5
Langstone Hants 10 D6
Langstone Newport 15 B9
Langthorne N Yorks 58 G3
Langthorpe N Yorks 51 C9
Langthwaite N Yorks 58 F1
Langtoft E Yorks 52 C6
Langtoft Lincs 37 D7
Langton Durham 58 E2
Langton Lincs 46 F6
Langton Lincs 47 E7
Langton N Yorks 52 C3
Langton by Wragby Lincs 46 E5
Langton Green Kent 12 C4
Langton Green Suff 31 A8
Langton Herring Dorset 8 F5
Langton Matravers Dorset 9 G9
Langtree Devon 6 E3
Langwathby Cumb 57 C7
Langwell Ho. Highld 94 H3
Langwell Lodge Highld 92 J4
Langwith Derbys 45 E9
Langwith Junction Derbys 45 F9
Langworth Lincs 46 E4
Lanivet Corn 3 C9
Lanlivery Corn 4 F1
Lanner Corn 2 F6
Lanreath Corn 4 F2
Lansallos Corn 4 F2
Lansdown Glos 26 F6
Lanteglos Highway Corn 4 F2
Lanton Borders 62 A2
Lanton Northumb 71 G8
Lapford Devon 7 F6
Laphroaig Argyll 64 D4
Lapley Staffs 34 D4
Lapworth Warks 27 A8
Larachbeg Highld 79 G9
Larbert Falk 69 B7
Larden Green Ches E 43 G8
Largie Aberds 88 E6
Largiemore Argyll 73 E8
Largoward Fife 77 G7
Largs N Ayrs 73 H11
Largybeg N Ayrs 66 D3
Largymore N Ayrs 66 D3
Larkfield Invclyd 73 F11
Larkhall S Lanark 68 E6
Larkhill Wilts 17 G8
Larling Norf 38 G5
Larriston Borders 61 D11
Lartington Durham 58 E1
Lary Aberds 82 C5
Lasham Hants 18 G3
Lashenden Kent 13 B7
Lassington Glos 26 F4
Lassodie Fife 69 A10
Lastingham N Yorks 59 G8
Latcham Som 15 G10
Latchford Herts 29 F10
Latchford Warr 43 D9
Latchingdon Essex 20 A5
Latchley Corn 4 D5
Lately Common Warr 43 C9
Lathbury M Keynes 28 D5
Latheron Highld 94 G3
Latheronwheel Highld 94 G3
Latheronwheel Ho. Highld 94 G3
Lathones Fife 77 G7
Latimer Bucks 19 B7
Latteridge S Glos 16 C3
Lattiford Som 8 B5
Latton Wilts 17 B7
Latton Bush Essex 29 H11
Lauchintilly Aberds 83 B9
Lauder Borders 70 F4
Laugharne Carms 23 E8
Laughterton Lincs 46 E2
Laughton E Sus 12 E3
Laughton Leics 36 G2
Laughton Lincs 37 B6
Laughton Lincs 46 C2
Laughton Common S Yorks 45 D9
Laughton en le Morthen S Yorks 45 D9
Launcells Corn 4 A3
Launceston Corn 4 C4
Launton Oxon 28 F3
Laurencekirk Aberds 83 F9
Laurieston Dumfries 55 C9
Laurieston Falk 69 C8
Lavendon M Keynes 28 C6
Lavenham Suff 30 D6
Laverhay Dumfries 61 D7
Laversdale Cumb 61 G10
Laverstock Wilts 9 A10
Laverstoke Hants 17 G11
Laverton Glos 27 E7
Laverton N Yorks 51 B8
Laverton Som 16 F4
Lavister Wrex 42 G6
Law S Lanark 69 E7
Lawers Perth 75 D9
Lawers Perth 75 E10
Lawford Essex 31 E7
Lawhitton Corn 4 C4
Lawkland N Yorks 50 C3
Lawley Telford 34 E2
Lawnhead Staffs 34 C4
Lawrenny Pembs 22 F5
Lawshall Suff 30 C5
Lawton Hereford 25 C11
Laxey IoM 48 D4
Laxfield Suff 31 A9
Laxfirth Shetland 96 H6
Laxfirth Shetland 96 J6
Laxford Bridge Highld 92 E5
Laxo Shetland 96 G6
Laxobigging Shetland 96 F6
Laxton E Yorks 52 G3
Laxton Northants 36 F5
Laxton Notts 45 F11
Laycock W Yorks 50 E6
Layer Breton Essex 30 G6
Layer de la Haye Essex 30 G6
Layer Marney Essex 30 G6
Layham Suff 31 D7
Laylands Green W Berks 17 E10
Laytham E Yorks 52 F3
Layton Blackpool 49 F3
Lazenby Redcar 59 D6
Lazonby Cumb 57 C7
Le Planel Guern 11
Le Skerne Haughton Darl 58 E4
Le Villocq Guern 11
Lea Derbys 45 G7
Lea Hereford 26 F3
Lea Lincs 46 D2
Lea Shrops 33 E10
Lea Shrops 33 G9
Lea Wilts 16 C6
Lea Marston Warks 35 F7
Lea Town Lancs 49 F4
Leabrooks Derbys 45 G8
Leac a Li W Isles 90 H6
Leachkin Highld 87 G9
Leadburn Midloth 69 E11
Leaden Roding Essex 30 G2
Leadenham Lincs 46 G3
Leadgate Cumb 57 B9
Leadgate Durham 58 A2
Leadgate T&W 63 H7
Leadhills S Lanark 60 B4
Leafield Oxon 27 G10
Leagrave Luton 29 F7
Leake N Yorks 58 G5
Leake Commonside Lincs 47 G7
Lealholm N Yorks 59 F8
Lealt Argyll 72 D5
Lealt Highld 85 B10
Leamington Hastings Warks 27 B11
Leamonsley Staffs 35 E7
Leamside Durham 58 B4
Leanaig Highld 87 F8
Leargybreck Argyll 72 F4
Leasgill Cumb 49 A4
Leasingham Lincs 46 H4
Leasingthorne Durham 58 D3
Leasowe Mers 42 C5
Leatherhead Sur 19 F8
Leatherhead Common Sur 19 F8
Leathley N Yorks 51 E8
Leaton Shrops 33 D10
Leaveland Kent 21 F7
Leavening N Yorks 52 C3
Leaves Green London 19 E11
Leazes Durham 63 H7
Lebberston N Yorks 53 A6
Lechlade-on-Thames Glos 17 B9
Leck Lancs 50 B2
Leckford Hants 17 H10
Leckfurin Highld 93 D10
Leckgruinart Argyll 64 B3
Leckhampstead Bucks 28 E4
Leckhampstead W Berks 17 D11
Leckhampstead Thicket W Berks 17 D11
Leckhampton Glos 26 G6
Leckie Highld 86 E3
Leckmelm Highld 86 B4
Leckwith V Glam 15 D7
Leconfield E Yorks 52 E6
Ledaig Argyll 74 D2
Ledburn Bucks 28 F6
Ledbury Hereford 26 E4
Ledcharrie Stirling 75 E8
Ledgemoor Hereford 25 C11
Ledicot Hereford 25 B11
Ledmore Highld 92 H5
Lednagullin Highld 93 C10
Ledsham Ches W 42 E6
Ledsham W Yorks 51 G10
Ledston W Yorks 51 G10
Ledston Luck W Yorks 51 F10
Ledwell Oxon 27 F11
Lee Argyll 78 J7
Lee Devon 6 B3
Lee Hants 10 C2
Lee Lancs 50 D1
Lee Shrops 33 B10
Lee Brockhurst Shrops 33 C11
Lee Clump Bucks 18 A6
Lee Mill Devon 5 F7
Lee Moor Devon 5 E6
Lee-on-the-Solent Hants 10 D4
Leeans Shetland 96 J5
Leebotten Shetland 96 L6
Leebotwood Shrops 33 F10
Leece Cumb 49 C2
Leechpool Pembs 22 E4
Leeds Kent 20 F5
Leeds W Yorks 51 F8
Leedstown Corn 2 F5
Leek Staffs 44 G3
Leek Wootton Warks 27 B9
Leekbrook Staffs 44 G3
Leeming N Yorks 58 H3
Leeming Bar N Yorks 58 G3
Lees Derbys 35 B8
Lees Gtr Man 44 B3
Lees W Yorks 50 F6
Leeswood Flint 42 G5
Legbourne Lincs 47 D7
Legerwood Borders 70 F4
Legsby Lincs 46 D5
Leicester Leicester 36 E1
Leicester Forest East Leics 35 E11
Leigh Dorset 8 D5
Leigh Glos 26 F5
Leigh Gtr Man 43 B9
Leigh Kent 20 G2
Leigh Shrops 33 E9
Leigh Sur 19 G9
Leigh Wilts 17 B7
Leigh Worcs 26 C4
Leigh Beck Essex 20 C5
Leigh Common Som 8 B6
Leigh Delamere Wilts 16 D5
Leigh Green Kent 13 C8
Leigh on Sea Southend 20 C5
Leigh Park Hants 10 D6
Leigh Sinton Worcs 26 C4
Leigh upon Mendip Som 16 G3
Leigh Woods N Som 16 D2
Leighswood W Mid 35 E6
Leighterton Glos 16 B5
Leighton N Yorks 51 B7
Leighton Powys 33 E8
Leighton Shrops 34 E2
Leighton Som 16 G4
Leighton Bromswold Cambs 37 H7
Leighton Buzzard C Beds 28 F6
Leinthall Earls Hereford 25 B11
Leinthall Starkes Hereford 25 B11
Leintwardine Hereford 25 A11
Leire Leics 35 F11
Leirinmore Highld 92 C7
Leiston Suff 31 B11
Leitfie Perth 76 C5
Leith Edin 69 C11
Leitholm Borders 70 F6
Lelant Corn 2 F4
Lelley E Yorks 53 F8
Lem Hill Worcs 26 A4
Lemmington Hall Northumb 63 B7
Lempitlaw Borders 70 G6
Lenchwick Worcs 27 D7
Lendalfoot S Ayrs 66 H4
Lendrick Lodge Stirling 75 G8
Lenham Kent 20 F5
Lenham Heath Kent 20 G6
Lennel Borders 71 F7
Lennoxtown E Dunb 68 C5
Lenton Lincs 36 B6
Lenton Nottingham 36 B1
Lentran Highld 87 G8
Lenwade Norf 39 D6
Leny Ho. Stirling 75 G9
Lenzie E Dunb 68 C5
Leoch Angus 76 D6
Leochel-Cushnie Aberds 83 B7
Leominster Hereford 25 C11
Leonard Stanley Glos 16 A5
Leorin Argyll 64 D4
Lepe Hants 10 E3
Lephin Highld 84 D6
Lephinchapel Argyll 73 D8
Lephinmore Argyll 73 D8
Leppington N Yorks 52 C3
Lepton W Yorks 51 H8
Lerryn Corn 4 F2
Lerwick Shetland 96 J6
Lesbury Northumb 63 B8
Leslie Aberds 83 A7
Leslie Fife 76 G5
Lesmahagow S Lanark 69 G7
Lesnewth Corn 4 B2
Lessendrum Aberds 88 D5
Lessingham Norf 39 C9
Lessonhall Cumb 56 A4
Leswalt Dumfries 54 C3
Letchmore Heath Herts 19 B8
Letchworth Herts 29 E9
Letcombe Bassett Oxon 17 C10
Letcombe Regis Oxon 17 C10
Letham Angus 77 C8
Letham Falk 69 B7
Letham Fife 76 F6
Letham Perth 76 E3
Letham Grange Angus 77 C9
Lethenty Aberds 89 D8
Letheringham Suff 31 C9
Letheringsett Norf 39 B6
Lettaford Devon 5 C8
Lettan Orkney 95 D8
Letterewe Highld 86 D2
Letterfearn Highld 85 F13
Letterfinlay Highld 80 D4
Lettermorar Highld 79 C10
Lettermore Argyll 78 G7
Letters Highld 86 C4
Letterston Pembs 22 D4
Lettoch Highld 82 B2
Lettoch Highld 87 H13
Letton Hereford 25 A10
Letton Hereford 25 D10
Letton Green Norf 38 E5
Letty Green Herts 29 G9
Letwell S Yorks 45 D9
Leuchars Fife 77 E7
Leuchars Ho. Moray 88 B2
Leumrabhagh W Isles 91 F8
Levan Invclyd 73 F11
Levaneap Shetland 96 G6
Levedale Staffs 34 D4
Leven E Yorks 53 E7
Leven Fife 76 G6
Levencorroch N Ayrs 66 D3
Levens Cumb 57 H6
Levens Green Herts 29 F10
Levenshulme Gtr Man 44 C2
Levenwick Shetland 96 L6
Leverburgh = An t-Ob W Isles 90 J5
Leverington Cambs 37 D10
Leverton Lincs 47 H8
Leverton Highgate Lincs 47 H8
Leverton Lucasgate Lincs 47 H8
Leverton Outgate Lincs 47 H8
Levington Suff 31 E9
Levisham N Yorks 59 G9
Levishie Highld 80 B6
Lew Oxon 27 H10
Lewannick Corn 4 C3
Lewdown Devon 4 C5
Lewes E Sus 12 E3
Leweston Pembs 22 D4
Lewisham London 19 D10
Lewiston Highld 81 A7
Lewistown Bridgend 14 C5
Lewknor Oxon 18 B4
Leworthy Devon 6 C5
Leworthy Devon 6 F2
Lewtrenchard Devon 4 C5
Lexden Essex 30 F6
Ley Aberds 83 B7
Ley Corn 4 E2
Leybourne Kent 20 F3
Leyburn N Yorks 58 G2
Leyfields Staffs 35 E8
Leyhill Bucks 18 A6
Leyland Lancs 49 G5
Leylodge Aberds 83 B9
Leymoor W Yorks 51 H7
Leys Aberds 89 C10
Leys Perth 76 D5
Leys Castle Highld 87 G9
Leys of Cossans Angus 76 C6
Leysdown-on-Sea Kent 21 D7
Leysmill Angus 77 C9
Leysters Pole Hereford 26 B2
Leyton London 19 C10
Leytonstone London 19 C10
Lezant Corn 4 D4
Leziate Norf 38 D2
Lhanbryde Moray 88 B2
Liatrie Highld 86 H5
Libanus Powys 24 F6
Libberton S Lanark 69 F8
Liberton Edin 69 D11
Liceasto W Isles 90 H6
Lichfield Staffs 35 E7
Lickey Worcs 34 H5
Lickey End Worcs 26 A6
Lickfold W Sus 11 B8
Liddel Orkney 95 K5
Liddesdale Highld 79 F10
Liddington Swindon 17 C9
Lidgate Suff 30 C4
Lidget S Yorks 45 B10
Lidget Green W Yorks 51 F7
Lidgett Notts 45 F10
Lidlington C Beds 28 E6
Lidstone Oxon 27 F10
Lieurary Highld 94 D2
Liff Angus 76 D6
Lifton Devon 4 C4
Liftondown Devon 4 C4
Lighthorne Warks 27 C10
Lightwater Sur 18 E6
Lightwood Stoke 34 A5
Lightwood Green Ches E 34 A2
Lightwood Green Wrex 33 A9
Lilbourne Northants 36 H1
Lilburn Tower Northumb 62 A6
Lilleshall Telford 34 D3
Lilley Herts 29 F8
Lilley W Berks 17 D11
Lilliesleaf Borders 61 A11
Lillingstone Dayrell Bucks 28 E4
Lillingstone Lovell Bucks 28 D4
Lillington Dorset 8 C5
Lillington Warks 27 B10
Lilliput Poole 9 E9
Lilstock Som 7 B10
Lilyhurst Shrops 34 D3
Limbury Luton 29 F7
Limebrook Hereford 25 B10
Limefield Gtr Man 44 A2
Limekilnburn S Lanark 68 E6
Limekilns Fife 69 B9
Limerigg Falk 69 C7
Limerstone IoW 10 F3
Limington Som 8 B4
Limpenhoe Norf 39 E9
Limpley Stoke Wilts 16 E4
Limpsfield Sur 19 F11
Limpsfield Chart Sur 19 F11
Linby Notts 45 G9
Linchmere W Sus 11 A7
Lincluden Dumfries 60 F5
Lincoln Lincs 46 E3
Lincomb Worcs 26 B5
Lincombe Devon 5 F8
Lindal in Furness Cumb 49 B2
Lindale Cumb 49 A4
Lindean Borders 70 G3
Lindfield W Sus 12 D2
Lindford Hants 18 H5
Lindifferon Fife 76 F6
Lindley W Yorks 51 H7
Lindley Green N Yorks 51 E8
Lindores Fife 76 F5
Lindridge Worcs 26 B3
Lindsell Essex 30 F3
Lindsey Suff 30 D6
Linford Hants 9 D10
Linford Thurrock 20 D3
Lingague IoM 48 E2
Lingards Wood W Yorks 44 A4
Lingbob W Yorks 51 F6
Lingdale Redcar 59 E7
Lingen Hereford 25 B10
Lingfield Sur 12 B2
Lingreabhagh W Isles 90 J5
Lingwood Norf 39 E9
Linicro Highld 85 B8
Linkenholt Hants 17 F10
Linkhill Kent 13 D7
Linkinhorne Corn 4 D4
Linklater Orkney 95 K5
Linksness Orkney 95 H3
Linktown Fife 69 A11
Linley Shrops 33 F9
Linley Green Hereford 26 C3
Linlithgow W Loth 69 C9
Linlithgow Bridge W Loth 69 C8
Linshiels Northumb 62 C4
Linsiadar W Isles 90 D7
Linsidemore Highld 87 B8
Linslade C Beds 28 F6
Linstead Parva Suff 39 H9
Linstock Cumb 61 H10
Linthwaite W Yorks 44 A5
Lintlaw Borders 71 E7
Lintmill Moray 88 B5
Linton Borders 70 H6
Linton Cambs 30 D2
Linton Derbys 35 D8
Linton Hereford 26 F3
Linton Kent 20 G4
Linton N Yorks 50 C5
Linton Northumb 63 D8
Linton W Yorks 51 E9
Linton-on-Ouse N Yorks 51 C10
Linwood Hants 9 D10
Linwood Lincs 46 D5
Linwood Renfs 68 D3
Lionacleit W Isles 84 D2
Lional W Isles 91 A10
Liphook Hants 11 A7
Liscard Mers 42 C6
Liscombe Som 7 C7
Liskeard Corn 4 E3
L'Islet Guern 11
Liss Hants 11 B6
Liss Forest Hants 11 B6
Lissett E Yorks 53 D7
Lissington Lincs 46 D5
Lisvane Cardiff 15 C7
Liswerry Newport 15 C9
Litcham Norf 38 D4
Litchborough Northants 28 C3
Litchfield Hants 17 F11
Litherland Mers 42 C6
Litlington Cambs 29 D10
Litlington E Sus 12 F4
Little Abington Cambs 30 D2
Little Addington Northants 28 A6
Little Alne Warks 27 B8
Little Altcar Mers 42 B6
Little Asby Cumb 57 F8
Little Assynt Highld 92 G4
Little Aston Staffs 35 E6
Little Atherfield IoW 10 F3
Little Ayre Orkney 95 J4
Little-ayre Shetland 96 G5
Little Ayton N Yorks 59 E6
Little Baddow Essex 30 H4
Little Badminton S Glos 16 C5
Little Ballinluig Perth 76 B2
Little Bampton Cumb 61 H8
Little Bardfield Essex 30 E3
Little Barford Bedford 29 C8
Little Barningham Norf 39 B7
Little Barrington Glos 27 G9
Little Barrow Ches W 43 E7
Little Barugh N Yorks 52 B3
Little Bavington Northumb 62 F5
Little Bealings Suff 31 D9
Little Bedwyn Wilts 17 E9
Little Bentley Essex 31 F8
Little Berkhamsted Herts 29 H9
Little Billing Northants 28 B5
Little Birch Hereford 26 E2
Little Blakenham Suff 31 D8
Little Blencow Cumb 56 C6
Little Bollington Ches E 43 D10
Little Bookham Sur 19 F8
Little Bowden Leics 36 G3
Little Bradley Suff 30 C3
Little Brampton Shrops 33 G9
Little Brechin Angus 77 A8
Little Brickhill M Keynes 28 E6
Little Brington Northants 28 B3
Little Bromley Essex 31 F7
Little Broughton Cumb 56 C2
Little Budworth Ches W 43 F8
Little Burstead Essex 20 B3
Little Bytham Lincs 36 D6
Little Carlton Lincs 47 D7
Little Carlton Notts 45 G11
Little Casterton Rutland 36 E6
Little Cawthorpe Lincs 47 D7
Little Chalfont Bucks 18 B6
Little Chart Kent 20 G6
Little Chesterford Essex 30 D2
Little Cheverell Wilts 16 F6
Little Chishill Cambs 29 E11
Little Clacton Essex 31 G9
Little Clifton Cumb 56 D2
Little Colp Aberds 89 D7
Little Comberton Worcs 26 D6
Little Common E Sus 12 F6
Little Compton Warks 27 E9
Little Cornard Suff 30 E5
Little Cowarne Hereford 26 C3
Little Coxwell Oxon 17 B9
Little Crakehall N Yorks 58 G3
Little Cressingham Norf 38 F4
Little Crosby Mers 42 B6
Little Dalby Leics 36 D3
Little Dawley Telford 34 E2
Little Dens Aberds 89 D10
Little Dewchurch Hereford 26 E2
Little Downham Cambs 37 G11
Little Driffield E Yorks 52 D6
Little Dunham Norf 38 D4
Little Dunkeld Perth 76 C3
Little Dunmow Essex 30 F3
Little Easton Essex 30 F3
Little Eaton Derbys 35 A9
Little Eccleston Lancs 49 E4
Little Ellingham Norf 38 F6
Little End Essex 20 A2
Little Eversden Cambs 29 C10
Little Faringdon Oxon 17 A9
Little Fencote N Yorks 58 G3
Little Fenton N Yorks 51 F11
Little Finborough Suff 31 C7
Little Fransham Norf 38 D5
Little Gaddesden Herts 28 G6
Little Gidding Cambs 37 G7
Little Glemham Suff 31 C10
Little Glenshee Perth 76 D2
Little Gransden Cambs 29 C9
Little Green Som 16 G4
Little Grimsby Lincs 47 C7
Little Gruinard Highld 86 C2
Little Habton N Yorks 52 B3
Little Hadham Herts 29 F11
Little Hale Lincs 37 A7
Little Hallingbury Essex 29 G11
Little Hampden Bucks 18 A5
Little Harrowden Northants 28 A5
Little Haseley Oxon 18 A3
Little Hatfield E Yorks 53 E7
Little Hautbois Norf 39 C8
Little Haven Pembs 22 E3
Little Hay Staffs 35 E7
Little Hayfield Derbys 44 D4
Little Haywood Staffs 34 C6
Little Heath W Mid 35 G9
Little Hereford Hereford 26 B2
Little Horkesley Essex 30 E6
Little Horsted E Sus 12 E3
Little Horton W Yorks 51 F7
Little Horwood Bucks 28 E4
Little Houghton Northants 28 C5
Little Houghton S Yorks 45 B8
Little Hucklow Derbys 44 E5
Little Hulton Gtr Man 43 B10
Little Humber E Yorks 53 G7
Little Hungerford W Berks 18 D2
Little Irchester Northants 28 B6
Little Kimble Bucks 28 H5
Little Kineton Warks 27 C10
Little Kingshill Bucks 18 B5
Little Langdale Cumb 56 F5
Little Langford Wilts 17 H7
Little Laver Essex 30 H2
Little Leigh Ches W 43 E9
Little Leighs Essex 30 G4
Little Lever Gtr Man 43 B10
Little London Bucks 28 G3
Little London E Sus 12 E4
Little London Hants 17 G10
Little London Hants 18 F3
Little London Lincs 37 C10
Little London Lincs 37 C8
Little London Norf 39 C7
Little London Powys 32 G6
Little Longstone Derbys 44 E5
Little Lynturk Aberds 83 B7
Little Malvern Worcs 26 D4
Little Maplestead Essex 30 E5
Little Marcle Hereford 26 E3
Little Marlow Bucks 18 C5
Little Marsden Lancs 50 F4
Little Massingham Norf 38 C3
Little Melton Norf 39 E7
Little Mill Mon 15 A9
Little Milton Oxon 18 A3
Little Missenden Bucks 18 B6
Little Musgrave Cumb 57 E9
Little Ness Shrops 33 D10
Little Neston Ches W 42 E5
Little Newcastle Pembs 22 D4
Little Newsham Durham 58 E2
Little Oakley Essex 31 F9
Little Oakley Northants 36 G4
Little Orton Cumb 61 H9
Little Ouseburn N Yorks 51 C10
Little Paxton Cambs 29 B8
Little Petherick Corn 3 B8
Little Pitlurg Moray 88 D4
Little Plumpton Lancs 49 F3
Little Plumstead Norf 39 D9
Little Ponton Lincs 36 B5
Little Raveley Cambs 37 H8
Little Reedness E Yorks 52 G4
Little Ribston N Yorks 51 D9
Little Rissington Glos 27 G8
Little Ryburgh Norf 38 C5
Little Ryle Northumb 62 B6
Little Salkeld Cumb 57 C7
Little Sampford Essex 30 E3
Little Sandhurst Brack 18 E5
Little Saxham Suff 30 B4
Little Scatwell Highld 86 F6
Little Sessay N Yorks 51 B10
Little Shelford Cambs 29 C11
Little Singleton Lancs 49 F3
Little Skillymarno Aberds 89 C9
Little Smeaton N Yorks 51 H11
Little Snoring Norf 38 B5
Little Sodbury S Glos 16 C4
Little Somborne Hants 10 A2
Little Somerford Wilts 16 C6
Little Stainforth N Yorks 50 C4
Little Stainton Darl 58 D4
Little Stanney Ches W 43 E7
Little Staughton Bedford 29 B8
Little Steeping Lincs 47 F8
Little Stoke Staffs 34 B5
Little Stonham Suff 31 B8
Little Stretton Leics 36 E2
Little Stretton Shrops 33 F10
Little Strickland Cumb 57 E7
Little Stukeley Cambs 37 H8
Little Sutton Ches W 42 E6
Little Tew Oxon 27 F10
Little Thetford Cambs 37 H11
Little Thirkleby N Yorks 51 B10
Little Thurlow Suff 30 C3
Little Thurrock Thurrock 20 D3
Little Torboll Highld 87 B10
Little Torrington Devon 6 E3
Little Totham Essex 30 G5
Little Toux Aberds 88 C5
Little Town Cumb 56 E4
Little Town Lancs 50 F2
Little Urswick Cumb 49 B2
Little Wakering Essex 20 C6
Little Walden Essex 30 D2
Little Waldingfield Suff 30 D6
Little Walsingham Norf 38 B5
Little Waltham Essex 30 G4
Little Warley Essex 20 B3
Little Weighton E Yorks 52 F5
Little Weldon Northants 36 G5
Little Welnetham Suff 30 B5
Little Wenlock Telford 34 E2
Little Whittingham Green Suff 39 H8
Little Wilbraham Cambs 30 C2
Little Wishford Wilts 17 H7
Little Witley Worcs 26 B4
Little Wittenham Oxon 18 B2
Little Wolford Warks 27 E9
Little Wratting Suff 30 D3
Little Wymington Bedford 28 B6
Little Wymondley Herts 29 F9
Little Wyrley Staffs 34 E6
Little Yeldham Essex 30 E4
Littlebeck N Yorks 59 F9
Littleborough Gtr Man 50 H5
Littleborough Notts 46 D2
Littlebourne Kent 21 F9
Littlebredy Dorset 8 F4
Littlebury Essex 30 E2
Littlebury Green Essex 29 E11
Littledean Glos 26 G3
Littleferry Highld 87 B11
Littleham Devon 5 C11
Littleham Devon 6 D3
Littlehampton W Sus 11 D9
Littlehempston Devon 5 E9
Littlehoughton Northumb 63 B8
Littlemill Aberds 82 D5
Littlemill E Ayrs 67 E7
Littlemill Highld 87 F12
Littlemill Northumb 63 B8
Littlemoor Dorset 8 F5
Littlemore Oxon 18 A2
Littleover Derby 35 B9
Littleport Cambs 38 G1
Littlestone on Sea Kent 13 D9
Littlethorpe Leics 35 F11
Littlethorpe N Yorks 51 C9
Littleton Ches W 43 F7
Littleton Hants 10 A3
Littleton Perth 76 D5
Littleton Som 8 A3
Littleton Sur 18 G6
Littleton Sur 19 E7
Littleton Drew Wilts 16 C5
Littleton-on-Severn S Glos 16 C2
Littleton Pannell Wilts 17 F7
Littletown Durham 58 B4
Littlewick Green Windsor 18 D5
Littleworth Bedford 29 D7
Littleworth Glos 16 A5
Littleworth Oxon 17 B10
Littleworth Staffs 34 D6
Littleworth Worcs 26 C5
Litton Derbys 44 E5
Litton N Yorks 50 B5
Litton Som 16 F2
Litton Cheney Dorset 8 E4
Liurbost W Isles 91 E8
Liverpool Mers 42 C6
Liverpool Airport Mers 43 D7
Liversedge W Yorks 51 G8
Liverton Devon 5 D9
Liverton Redcar 59 E8
Livingston W Loth 69 D9
Livingston Village W Loth 69 D9
Lixwm Flint 42 E4
Lizard Corn 2 H6
Llaingoch Anglesey 40 B4
Llaithddu Powys 33 G6
Llan Powys 32 E4
Llan Ffestiniog Gwyn 41 F9
Llan-y-pwll Wrex 42 G6
Llanaber Gwyn 32 D2
Llanaelhaearn Gwyn 40 F5
Llanafan Ceredig 24 A3
Llanafan-fawr Powys 24 C6
Llanallgo Anglesey 40 B6
Llanandras = Presteigne Powys 25 B10
Llanarmon Gwyn 40 G6
Llanarmon Dyffryn Ceiriog Wrex 33 B7
Llanarmon-yn-Ial Denb 42 G4
Llanarth Ceredig 23 A9
Llanarth Mon 25 G10
Llanarthne Carms 23 D10
Llanasa Flint 42 D4
Llanbabo Anglesey 40 B5
Llanbadarn Fawr Ceredig 32 G2
Llanbadarn Fynydd Powys 33 H7
Llanbadarn-y-Garreg Powys 25 D8
Llanbadoc Mon 15 B9
Llanbadrig Anglesey 40 A5
Llanbeder Newport 15 B9
Llanbedr Gwyn 32 C1
Llanbedr Powys 25 D8
Llanbedr Powys 25 F9
Llanbedr-Dyffryn-Clwyd Denb 42 G4
Llanbedr Pont Steffan = Lampeter Ceredig 23 B10
Llanbedr-y-cennin Conwy 41 D9
Llanbedrgoch Anglesey 40 B6
Llanbedrog Gwyn 40 G5
Llanberis Gwyn 41 D7
Llanbethêry V Glam 14 E6
Llanbister Powys 25 A8
Llanblethian V Glam 14 D5
Llanboidy Carms 23 D7
Llanbradach Caerph 15 B7
Llanbrynmair Powys 32 E5
Llancarfan V Glam 14 D6
Llancayo Mon 15 A9
Llancloudy Hereford 25 F11
Llancynfelyn Ceredig 32 F2
Llandaff Cardiff 15 D7
Llandanwg Gwyn 32 C1
Llandarcy Neath 14 B3
Llandawke Carms 23 E7
Llanddaniel Fab Anglesey 40 C6
Llanddarog Carms 23 E10
Llanddeiniol Ceredig 24 A2
Llanddeiniolen Gwyn 41 D7
Llandderfel Gwyn 32 B5
Llanddeusant Anglesey 40 B5
Llanddeusant Carms 24 F4
Llanddew Powys 25 E7
Llanddewi Swansea 23 H9
Llanddewi-Brefi Ceredig 24 C3
Llanddewi Rhydderch Mon 25 G10
Llanddewi Velfrey Pembs 22 E6
Llanddewi'r Cwm Powys 25 D7
Llanddoged Conwy 41 D10
Llanddona Anglesey 41 C7
Llanddowror Carms 23 E7
Llanddulas Conwy 42 E2
Llanddwywe Gwyn 32 C1
Llanddyfynan Anglesey 41 C7
Llandefaelog Fach Powys 25 E7
Llandefaelog-tre'r-graig Powys 25 F8
Llandefalle Powys 25 E8
Llandegai Gwyn 41 C7
Llandegfan Anglesey 41 C7
Llandegla Denb 42 G4
Llandegley Powys 25 B8
Llandegveth Mon 15 B9
Llandegwning Gwyn 40 G4
Llandeilo Carms 24 F3
Llandeilo Graban Powys 25 D7
Llandeilo'r Fan Powys 24 E5
Llandeloy Pembs 22 D3
Llandenny Mon 15 A10
Llandevenny Mon 15 C10
Llandewednock Corn 2 H6
Llandewi Ystradenny Powys 25 B8
Llandinabo Hereford 26 F2
Llandinam Powys 32 G6
Llandissilio Pembs 22 D6
Llandogo Mon 15 A11
Llandough V Glam 14 D5
Llandough V Glam 15 D7
Llandovery = Llanymddyfri Carms 24 E4
Llandow V Glam 14 D5
Llandre Carms 24 D3
Llandre Ceredig 32 G2
Llandrillo Denb 32 B6
Llandrillo-yn-Rhos Conwy 41 B10
Llandrindod = Llandrindod Wells Powys 25 B7
Llandrindod Wells = Llandrindod Powys 25 B7
Llandrinio Powys 33 D8
Llandudno Conwy 41 B9
Llandudno Junction = Cyffordd Llandudno Conwy 41 C9
Llandwrog Gwyn 40 E6
Llandybie Carms 24 G3
Llandyfaelog Carms 23 E9
Llandyfan Carms 24 G3
Llandyfriog Ceredig 23 B8
Llandyfrydog Anglesey 40 B6
Llandygwydd Ceredig 23 B7
Llandynan Denb 42 H4
Llandyrnog Denb 42 F4
Llandysilio Powys 33 D8
Llandyssil Powys 33 F7
Llandysul Ceredig 23 B9
Llanedeyrn Cardiff 15 C8
Llanedi Carms 23 F10
Llaneglwys Powys 25 E7
Llanegryn Gwyn 32 E1
Llanegwad Carms 23 D10
Llaneilian Anglesey 40 A6
Llanelian-yn-Rhos Conwy 41 C10
Llanelidan Denb 42 G4
Llanelieu Powys 25 E8
Llanellen Mon 25 G10
Llanelli Carms 23 G10
Llanelltyd Gwyn 32 D3
Llanelly Mon 25 G9
Llanelly Hill Mon 25 G9
Llanelwedd Powys 25 C7
Llanelwy = St Asaph Denb 42 E3
Llanenddwyn Gwyn 32 C1
Llanengan Gwyn 40 H4
Llanerchymedd Anglesey 40 B6
Llanerfyl Powys 33 E6
Llanfachraeth Anglesey 40 B5
Llanfachreth Gwyn 32 C4
Llanfaelog Anglesey 40 C5
Llanfaelrhys Gwyn 40 H4
Llanfaenor Mon 25 G11
Llanfaes Anglesey 41 C8
Llanfaes Powys 25 F7
Llanfaethlu Anglesey 40 B5
Llanfaglan Gwyn 40 D6
Llanfair Gwyn 32 C1
Llanfair-ar-y-bryn Carms 24 E5
Llanfair Caereinion Powys 33 E7
Llanfair Clydogau Ceredig 24 C3
Llanfair-Dyffryn-Clwyd Denb 42 G4
Llanfair Kilgheddin Mon 25 H10
Llanfair-Nant-Gwyn Pembs 22 C6
Llanfair Talhaiarn Conwy 42 E2
Llanfair Waterdine Shrops 33 H8
Llanfair-ym-Muallt = Builth Wells Powys 25 C7
Llanfairfechan Conwy 41 C8
Llanfairpwll-gwyngyll Anglesey 41 C7
Llanfairyneubwll Anglesey 40 C5
Llanfairynghornwy Anglesey 40 A5
Llanfallteg Carms 22 E6
Llanfaredd Powys 25 C7
Llanfarian Ceredig 32 H1
Llanfechain Powys 33 C7
Llanfechan Powys 24 C6
Llanfechell Anglesey 40 A5
Llanfendigaid Gwyn 32 E1
Llanferres Denb 42 F4
Llanfflewyn Anglesey 40 B5
Llanfihangel-ar-arth Carms 23 C9
Llanfihangel-Crucorney Mon 25 F10
Llanfihangel Glyn Myfyr Conwy 42 H2
Llanfihangel Nant Bran Powys 24 E6
Llanfihangel-nant-Melan Powys 25 C8
Llanfihangel Rhydithon Powys 25 B8
Llanfihangel Rogiet Mon 15 C10
Llanfihangel Tal-y-llyn Powys 25 F8
Llanfihangel-uwch-Gwili Carms 23 D9
Llanfihangel-y-Creuddyn Ceredig 32 H2
Llanfihangel-y-pennant Gwyn 32 E2
Llanfihangel-y-pennant Gwyn 41 F7
Llanfihangel-y-traethau Gwyn 41 G7
Llanfihangel-yn-Ngwynfa Powys 33 D6
Llanfihangel yn Nhowyn Anglesey 40 C5
Llanfilo Powys 25 E8
Llanfoist Mon 25 G9
Llanfor Gwyn 32 B5
Llanfrechfa Torf 15 B9
Llanfrothen Gwyn 41 F8
Llanfrynach Powys 25 F7
Llanfwrog Anglesey 40 B5
Llanfwrog Denb 42 G4
Llanfyllin Powys 33 D7
Llanfynydd Carms 23 D10
Llanfynydd Flint 42 G5
Llanfyrnach Pembs 23 C7
Llangadfan Powys 32 D6
Llangadog Carms 24 F4
Llangadwaladr Anglesey 40 D5
Llangadwaladr Powys 33 B7
Llangaffo Anglesey 40 D6
Llangain Carms 23 E8
Llangammarch Wells Powys 24 D6
Llangan V Glam 14 D5
Llangarron Hereford 26 F2
Llangasty Talyllyn Powys 25 F8
Llangathen Carms 23 D10
Llangattock Powys 25 G9
Llangattock Lingoed Mon 25 F10
Llangattock nigh Usk Mon 25 H10
Llangattock-Vibon-Avel Mon 25 G11
Llangedwyn Powys 33 C7
Llangefni Anglesey 40 C6
Llangeinor Bridgend 14 C5
Llangeitho Ceredig 24 C3
Llangeler Carms 23 C8
Llangelynin Gwyn 32 E1
Llangendeirne Carms 23 E9
Llangennech Carms 23 F10
Llangennith Swansea 23 G9
Llangenny Powys 25 G9
Llangernyw Conwy 41 D10
Llangian Gwyn 40 H4
Llanglydwen Carms 22 D6
Llangoed Anglesey 41 C8
Llangoedmor Ceredig 22 B6
Llangollen Denb 33 A8
Llangolman Pembs 22 D6
Llangors Powys 25 F8
Llangovan Mon 25 H11
Llangower Gwyn 32 B5
Llangrannog Ceredig 23 A8
Llangristiolus Anglesey 40 C6
Llangrove Hereford 26 G2
Llangua Mon 25 F10
Llangunllo Powys 25 A9
Llangunnor Carms 23 E9
Llangurig Powys 32 H5
Llangwm Conwy 32 A5
Llangwm Mon 15 A10
Llangwm Pembs 22 F4
Llangwnnadl Gwyn 40 G4
Llangwyfan Denb 42 F4
Llangwyfan-isaf Anglesey 40 D5
Llangwyllog Anglesey 40 C6
Llangwyryfon Ceredig 24 A2
Llangybi Ceredig 24 C3
Llangybi Gwyn 40 F6
Llangybi Mon 15 B9
Llangyfelach Swansea 14 B2
Llangynhafal Denb 42 F4
Llangynidr Powys 25 G8
Llangynin Carms 23 E7
Llangynog Carms 23 E8
Llangynog Powys 33 C6
Llangynwyd Bridgend 14 C4
Llanhamlach Powys 25 F7
Llanharan Rhondda 14 C6
Llanharry Rhondda 14 C6
Llanhennock Mon 15 B9
Llanhiledd = Llanhilleth Bl Gwent 15 A8
Llanhilleth = Llanhiledd Bl Gwent 15 A8
Llanidloes Powys 32 G5
Llaniestyn Gwyn 40 G4
Llanifyny Powys 32 G4
Llanigon Powys 25 E9
Llanilar Ceredig 24 A3
Llanilid Rhondda 14 C5
Llanilltud Fawr = Llantwit Major V Glam 14 E5
Llanishen Cardiff 15 C7
Llanishen Mon 15 A10
Llanllawddog Carms 23 D9
Llanllechid Gwyn 41 D8
Llanllowell Mon 15 B9
Llanllugan Powys 33 E6
Llanllwch Carms 23 E8
Llanllwchaiarn Powys 33 F7
Llanllwni Carms 23 C9
Llanllyfni Gwyn 40 E6
Llanmadoc Swansea 23 G9
Llanmaes V Glam 14 E5
Llanmartin Newport 15 C9
Llanmihangel V Glam 14 D5
Llanmorlais Swansea 23 G10
Llannefydd Conwy 42 E2
Llannon Carms 23 F10
Llannor Gwyn 40 G5
Llanon Ceredig 24 B2
Llanover Mon 25 H10
Llanpumsaint Carms 23 D9
Llanreithan Pembs 22 D3
Llanrhaeadr Denb 42 F3
Llanrhaeadr-ym-Mochnant Powys 33 C7
Llanrhian Pembs 22 C3
Llanrhidian Swansea 23 G9
Llanrhos Conwy 41 B9
Llanrhyddlad Anglesey 40 B5
Llanrhystud Ceredig 24 B2
Llanrosser Hereford 25 E9
Llanrothal Hereford 25 G11
Llanrug Gwyn 41 D7
Llanrumney Cardiff 15 C8
Llanrwst Conwy 41 D10
Llansadurnen Carms 23 E7
Llansadwrn Anglesey 41 C7
Llansadwrn Carms 24 E3
Llansaint Carms 23 F8
Llansamlet Swansea 14 B2
Llansannan Conwy 42 F2
Llansannor V Glam 14 D5
Llansantffraed Ceredig 24 B2
Llansantffraed Powys 25 F8
Llansantffraed Cwmdeuddwr Powys 24 B6
Llansantffraed-in-Elvel Powys 25 C7
Llansantffraid-ym-Mechain Powys 33 C8
Llansawel Carms 24 E3
Llansilin Powys 33 C8
Llansoy Mon 15 A10
Llanspyddid Powys 25 F7
Llanstadwell Pembs 22 F4
Llansteffan Carms 23 E8
Llanstephan Powys 25 D8
Llantarnam Torf 15 B9
Llanteg Pembs 22 E6
Llanthony Mon 25 F9
Llantilio Crossenny Mon 25 G10
Llantilio Pertholey Mon 25 G10
Llantood Pembs 22 B6
Llantrisant Anglesey 40 B5
Llantrisant Mon 15 B9
Llantrisant Rhondda 14 C6
Llantrithyd V Glam 14 D6
Llantwit Fardre Rhondda 14 C6
Llantwit Major = Llanilltud Fawr V Glam 14 E5
Llanuwchllyn Gwyn 41 G10
Llanvaches Newport 15 B10

Ollerton Shrops 34 C2
Olmarch Ceredig 24 C3
Olney M Keynes 28 C5
Olrig Ho. Highld 94 D3
Olton W Mid 35 G7
Olveston S Glos 16 C3
Olwen Ceredig 23 B10
Ombersley Worcs 26 B5
Ompton Notts 45 F10
Onchan IoM 48 E3
Onecote Staffs 44 G4
Onen Mon 25 G11
Ongar Hill Norf 38 C1
Ongar Street Hereford 25 B10
Onibury Shrops 33 H10
Onich Highld 74 A3
Onllwyn Neath 24 G5
Onneley Staffs 34 A3
Onslow Village Sur 18 G6
Onthank E Ayrs 67 B7
Openwoodgate Derbys 45 H7
Opinan Highld 85 A12
Opinan Highld 91 H13
Orange Lane Borders 70 F6
Orange Row Norf 37 C11
Orasaigh W Isles 91 F8
Orbliston Moray 88 C3
Orbost Highld 84 D7
Orby Lincs 47 F8
Orchard Hill Devon 6 D3
Orchard Portman Som 8 B1
Orcheston Wilts 17 G7
Orcop Hereford 25 F11
Orcop Hill Hereford 25 F11
Ord Highld 85 G11
Ordhead Aberds 83 B8
Ordie Aberds 82 C6
Ordiequish Moray 88 C3
Ordsall Notts 45 D10
Ore E Sus 13 E7
Oreton Shrops 34 G2
Orford Suff 31 D11
Orford Warr 43 C9
Orgreave Staffs 35 D7
Orlestone Kent 13 C8
Orleton Hereford 25 B11
Orleton Worcs 26 B3
Orlingbury Northants 28 A5
Ormesby Redcar 59 E6
Ormesby St Margaret Norf 39 D10
Ormesby St Michael Norf 39 D10
Ormiclate Castle W Isles 84 E2
Ormiscaig Highld 91 H13
Ormiston E Loth 70 D3
Ormsaigbeg Highld 78 E7
Ormsaigmore Highld 78 E7
Ormsary Argyll 72 F6
Ormsgill Cumb 49 B1
Ormskirk Lancs 43 B7
Orpington London 19 E11
Orrell Gtr Man 43 B8
Orrell Mers 42 C6
Orrisdale IoM 48 C3
Orroland Dumfries 55 E10
Orsett Thurrock 20 C3
Orslow Staffs 34 D4
Orston Notts 36 A3
Orthwaite Cumb 56 C4
Ortner Lancs 49 D5
Orton Cumb 57 F8
Orton Northants 36 H4
Orton Longueville Pboro 37 F7
Orton-on-the-Hill Leics 35 E9
Orton Waterville Pboro 37 F7
Orwell Cambs 29 C10
Osbaldeston Lancs 50 F2
Osbaldwick York 52 D2
Osbaston Shrops 33 C9
Osbournby Lincs 37 B6
Oscroft Ches W 43 F8
Ose Highld 85 D8
Osgathorpe Leics 35 D10
Osgodby Lincs 46 C4
Osgodby N Yorks 52 F2
Osgodby N Yorks 53 A6
Oskaig Highld 85 E10
Oskamull Argyll 78 G7
Osmaston Derby 35 B9
Osmaston Derbys 35 A8
Osmington Dorset 8 F6
Osmington Mills Dorset 8 F6
Osmotherley N Yorks 58 G5
Ospisdale Highld 87 C10
Ospringe Kent 21 E7
Ossett W Yorks 51 G8
Ossington Notts 45 F11
Ostend Essex 20 B6
Oswaldkirk N Yorks 52 B2
Oswaldtwistle Lancs 50 G3
Oswestry Shrops 33 C8
Otford Kent 20 F2
Otham Kent 20 F4
Othery Som 8 A2
Otley Suff 31 C9
Otley W Yorks 51 E8
Otter Ferry Argyll 73 E8
Otterbourne Hants 10 B3
Otterburn N Yorks 50 D4
Otterburn Northumb 62 D4
Otterburn Camp Northumb 62 D4
Otterham Corn 4 B2
Otterhampton Som 15 G8
Ottershaw Sur 19 E7
Otterswick Shetland 96 E7
Otterton Devon 7 H9
Ottery St Mary Devon 7 G10
Ottinge Kent 21 G8
Ottringham E Yorks 53 G8
Oughterby Cumb 61 H8
Oughtershaw N Yorks 50 A4
Oughterside Cumb 56 B3
Oughtibridge S Yorks 45 C7
Oughtrington Warr 43 D9
Oulston N Yorks 51 B11
Oulton Cumb 56 A4
Oulton Norf 39 C7
Oulton Staffs 34 B5
Oulton Suff 39 F11
Oulton W Yorks 51 G9
Oulton Broad Suff 39 F11
Oulton Street Norf 39 C7
Oundle Northants 36 G6
Ousby Cumb 57 C8
Ousdale Highld 94 H2
Ousden Suff 30 C4
Ousefleet E Yorks 52 G4
Ouston Durham 58 A3
Ouston Northumb 62 F6
Out Newton E Yorks 53 G9
Out Rawcliffe Lancs 49 E4
Outertown Orkney 95 G3
Outgate Cumb 56 G5
Outhgill Cumb 57 F9
Outlane W Yorks 51 H6
Outwell Norf 37 E11
Outwick Hants 9 C10
Outwood Sur 19 G10
Outwood W Yorks 51 G9
Outwoods Staffs 34 D3
Ovenden W Yorks 51 G6
Ovenscloss Borders 70 G3
Over Cambs 29 A10
Over Ches W 43 F9
Over S Glos 16 C2
Over Compton Dorset 8 C4
Over Green W Mid 35 F7
Over Haddon Derbys 44 F6
Over Hulton Gtr Man 43 B9
Over Kellet Lancs 49 B5
Over Kiddington Oxon 27 F11
Over Knutsford Ches E 43 E10
Over Monnow Mon 26 G2
Over Norton Oxon 27 F10
Over Peover Ches E 43 E10
Over Silton N Yorks 58 G5
Over Stowey Som 7 C10
Over Stratton Som 8 C3
Over Tabley Ches E 43 D10
Over Wallop Hants 17 H9
Over Whitacre Warks 35 F8
Over Worton Oxon 27 F11
Overbister Orkney 95 D7
Overbury Worcs 26 E6
Overcombe Dorset 8 F5
Overgreen Derbys 45 E7
Overleigh Som 15 H10
Overley Green Warks 27 C7
Overpool Ches W 43 E6
Overscaig Hotel Highld 92 G7
Overseal Derbys 35 D8
Oversland Kent 21 F7
Overstone Northants 28 B5
Overstrand Norf 39 A8
Overthorpe Northants 27 D11
Overton Aberdeen 83 B10
Overton Ches W 43 E8
Overton Dumfries 60 G5
Overton Hants 18 G2
Overton Lancs 49 D4
Overton N Yorks 52 D1
Overton Shrops 26 A2
Overton Swansea 23 H9
Overton W Yorks 51 H8
Overton = Owrtyn Wrex 33 A9
Overton Bridge Wrex 33 A9
Overtown N Lanark 69 E7
Oving Bucks 28 F4
Oving W Sus 11 D8
Ovingdean Brighton 12 F2
Ovingham Northumb 62 G6
Ovington Durham 58 E2
Ovington Essex 30 D4
Ovington Hants 10 A4
Ovington Norf 38 E5
Ovington Northumb 62 G6
Ower Hants 10 C2
Owermoigne Dorset 9 F6
Owlbury Shrops 33 F9
Owler Bar Derbys 44 E6
Owlerton S Yorks 45 D7
Owl's Green Suff 31 B9
Owlswick Bucks 28 H4
Owmby Lincs 46 B4
Owmby-by-Spital Lincs 46 D4
Owrtyn = Overton Wrex 33 A9
Owslebury Hants 10 B4
Owston Leics 36 E3
Owston S Yorks 45 A9
Owston Ferry N Lincs 46 B2
Owstwick E Yorks 53 F8
Owthorne E Yorks 53 G9
Owthorpe Notts 36 B2
Oxborough Norf 38 E3
Oxcombe Lincs 47 E7
Oxen Park Cumb 56 H5
Oxenholme Cumb 57 H7
Oxenhope W Yorks 50 F6
Oxenton Glos 26 E6
Oxenwood Wilts 17 F10
Oxford Oxon 28 H2
Oxhey Herts 19 B8
Oxhill Warks 27 D10
Oxley W Mid 34 E5
Oxley Green Essex 30 G6
Oxley's Green E Sus 12 D5
Oxnam Borders 62 B3
Oxshott Sur 19 E8
Oxspring S Yorks 44 B6
Oxted Sur 19 F10
Oxton Borders 70 E3
Oxton Notts 45 G10
Oxwich Swansea 23 H9
Oxwick Norf 38 C5
Oykel Bridge Highld 92 J6
Oyne Aberds 83 A8

P

Pabail Iarach W Isles 91 D10
Pabail Uarach W Isles 91 D10
Pace Gate N Yorks 51 D7
Packington Leics 35 D9
Padanaram Angus 77 B7
Padbury Bucks 28 E4
Paddington London 19 C9
Paddlesworth Kent 21 H8
Paddock Wood Kent 12 B5
Paddockhaugh Moray 88 C2
Paddockhole Dumfries 61 E8
Padfield Derbys 44 C4
Padiham Lancs 50 F3
Padog Conwy 41 E10
Padside N Yorks 51 D7
Padstow Corn 3 B8
Padworth W Berks 18 E3
Page Bank Durham 58 C3
Pagham W Sus 11 E7
Paglesham Churchend Essex 20 B6
Paglesham Eastend Essex 20 B6
Paibeil W Isles 84 B2
Paible W Isles 90 H5
Paignton Torbay 5 E9
Pailton Warks 35 G10
Painscastle Powys 25 D8
Painshawfield Northumb 62 G6
Painsthorpe E Yorks 52 D4
Painswick Glos 26 H5
Pairc Shiaboist W Isles 90 C7
Paisley Renfs 68 D3
Pakefield Suff 39 F11
Pakenham Suff 30 B6
Pale Gwyn 32 B5
Palestine Hants 17 G9
Paley Street Windsor 18 D5
Palfrey W Mid 34 F6
Palgowan Dumfries 54 A6
Palgrave Suff 39 H7
Pallion T&W 63 H9
Palmarsh Kent 13 C10
Palnackie Dumfries 55 D11
Palnure Dumfries 55 C7
Palterton Derbys 45 F8
Pamber End Hants 18 F3
Pamber Green Hants 18 F3
Pamber Heath Hants 18 E3
Pamphill Dorset 9 D8
Pampisford Cambs 29 D11
Pan Orkney 95 J4
Panbride Angus 77 D8
Pancrasweek Devon 6 F1
Pandy Gwyn 32 E2
Pandy Mon 25 F10
Pandy Powys 32 E5
Pandy Wrex 33 B7
Pandy Tudur Conwy 41 D10
Panfield Essex 30 F4
Pangbourne W Berks 18 D3
Pannal N Yorks 51 D9
Panshanger Herts 29 G9
Pant Shrops 33 C8
Pant-glâs Powys 32 F3
Pant-glas Carms 23 D10
Pant-glas Gwyn 40 F6
Pant-glas Shrops 33 B8
Pant-lasau Swansea 14 B2
Pant Mawr Powys 32 G4
Pant-teg Carms 23 D9
Pant-y-Caws Carms 22 D6
Pant-y-dwr Powys 32 H5
Pant-y-ffridd Powys 33 E7
Pant-y-Wacco Flint 42 E4
Pant-yr-awel Bridgend 14 C5
Pantgwyn Carms 23 D10
Pantgwyn Ceredig 23 B7
Panton Lincs 46 E5
Pantperthog Gwyn 32 E3
Pantyffynnon Carms 24 G3
Pantymwyn Flint 42 F4
Panxworth Norf 39 D9
Papcastle Cumb 56 C3
Papigoe Highld 94 E5
Papil Shetland 96 K5
Papley Orkney 95 J5
Papple E Loth 70 C4
Papplewick Notts 45 G9
Papworth Everard Cambs 29 B9
Papworth St Agnes Cambs 29 B9
Par Corn 4 F1
Parbold Lancs 43 A7
Parbrook Som 16 H2
Parbrook W Sus 11 B9
Parc Gwyn 41 G10
Parc-Seymour Newport 15 B10
Parc-y-rhôs Carms 23 B10
Parcllyn Ceredig 23 A7
Pardshaw Cumb 56 D2
Parham Suff 31 B10
Park Dumfries 60 D5
Park Corner Oxon 18 C3
Park Corner Windsor 18 C5
Park End Mbro 58 E6
Park End Northumb 62 F4
Park Gate Hants 10 D4
Park Hill N Yorks 51 C9
Park Hill Notts 45 G10
Park Street W Sus 11 A10
Parkend Glos 26 H3
Parkeston Essex 31 E9
Parkgate Ches W 42 E5
Parkgate Dumfries 60 E6
Parkgate Kent 13 C7
Parkgate Sur 19 G9
Parkham Devon 6 D2
Parkham Ash Devon 6 D2
Parkhill Ho. Aberds 83 B10
Parkhouse Mon 15 A10
Parkhouse Green Derbys 45 F8
Parkhurst IoW 10 E3
Parkmill Swansea 23 H10
Parkneuk Aberds 83 F9
Parkstone Poole 9 E9
Parley Cross Dorset 9 E9
Parracombe Devon 6 B5
Parrog Pembs 22 C5
Parsley Hay Derbys 44 F5
Parson Cross S Yorks 45 C7
Parson Drove Cambs 37 E9
Parsonage Green Essex 30 H4
Parsonby Cumb 56 C3
Parson's Heath Essex 31 F7
Partick Glasgow 68 D4
Partington Gtr Man 43 C10
Partney Lincs 47 F8
Parton Cumb 56 D1
Parton Dumfries 55 B9
Parton Glos 26 F5
Partridge Green W Sus 11 C10
Parwich Derbys 44 G5
Passenham Northants 28 E4
Paston Norf 39 B9
Patchacott Devon 6 G3
Patcham Brighton 12 F2
Patching W Sus 11 D9
Patchole Devon 6 B5
Pateley Bridge N Yorks 51 C7
Paternoster Heath Essex 30 G6
Path of Condie Perth 76 F3
Pathe Som 8 A2
Pathhead Aberds 77 A10
Pathhead E Ayrs 67 E9
Pathhead Fife 69 A11
Pathhead Midloth 70 D2
Pathstruie Perth 76 F3
Patna E Ayrs 67 E7
Patney Wilts 17 F7
Patrick IoM 48 D2
Patrick Brompton N Yorks 58 G3
Patrington E Yorks 53 G9
Patrixbourne Kent 21 F8
Patterdale Cumb 56 E5
Pattingham Staffs 34 F4
Pattishall Northants 28 C3
Pattiswick Green Essex 30 F5
Patton Bridge Cumb 57 G7
Paul Corn 2 G3
Paulerspury Northants 28 D4
Paull E Yorks 53 G7
Paulton Bath 16 F3
Pavenham Bedford 28 C6
Pawlett Som 15 G9
Pawston Northumb 71 G7
Paxford Glos 27 E8
Paxton Borders 71 E8
Payhembury Devon 7 F9
Paythorne Lancs 50 D4
Peacehaven E Sus 12 F3
Peak Dale Derbys 44 E4
Peak Forest Derbys 44 E5
Peakirk Pboro 37 E7
Pearsie Angus 76 B6
Pease Pottage W Sus 12 C1
Peasedown St John Bath 16 F4
Peasemore W Berks 17 D11
Peasenhall Suff 31 B10
Peaslake Sur 19 G7
Peasley Cross Mers 43 C8
Peasmarsh E Sus 13 D7
Peaston E Loth 70 D3
Peastonbank E Loth 70 D3
Peat Inn Fife 77 G7
Peathill Aberds 89 B9
Peatling Magna Leics 36 F1
Peatling Parva Leics 36 G1
Peaton Shrops 33 G11
Peats Corner Suff 31 B8
Pebmarsh Essex 30 E5
Pebworth Worcs 27 D8
Pecket Well W Yorks 50 G5
Peckforton Ches E 43 G8
Peckham London 19 D10
Peckleton Leics 35 E10
Pedlinge Kent 13 C10
Pedmore W Mid 34 G5
Pedwell Som 15 H10
Peebles Borders 69 F11
Peel IoM 48 D2
Peel Common Hants 10 D4
Peel Park S Lanark 68 E5
Peening Quarter Kent 13 D7
Pegsdon C Beds 29 E8
Pegswood Northumb 63 E8
Pegwell Kent 21 E10
Peinchorran Highld 85 E10
Peinlich Highld 85 C9
Pelaw T&W 63 G8
Pelcomb Bridge Pembs 22 E4
Pelcomb Cross Pembs 22 E4
Peldon Essex 30 G6
Pellon W Yorks 51 G6
Pelsall W Mid 34 E6
Pelton Durham 58 A3
Pelutho Cumb 56 B3
Pelynt Corn 4 F3
Pemberton Gtr Man 43 B8
Pembrey Carms 23 F9
Pembridge Hereford 25 C10
Pembroke = Penfro Pembs 22 F4
Pembroke Dock = Doc Penfro Pembs 22 F4
Pembury Kent 12 B5
Pen-bont Rhydybeddau Ceredig 32 G2
Pen-clawdd Swansea 23 G10
Pen-ffordd Pembs 22 D5
Pen-groes-oped Mon 25 H10
Pen-llyn Anglesey 40 B5
Pen-lon Anglesey 40 D6
Pen-sarn Gwyn 32 C1
Pen-sarn Gwyn 40 F6
Pen-twyn Mon 26 H2
Pen-y-banc Carms 24 F3
Pen-y-bont Carms 23 D8
Pen-y-bont Gwyn 32 C2
Pen-y-bont Gwyn 32 E3
Pen-y-bont Powys 33 C8
Pen-y-bont ar Ogwr = Bridgend Bridgend 14 D5
Pen-y-bryn Gwyn 32 D2
Pen-y-bryn Pembs 22 B6
Pen-y-cae Powys 24 G5
Pen-y-cae-mawr Mon 15 B10
Pen-y-cefn Flint 42 E4
Pen-y-clawdd Mon 25 H11
Pen-y-coedcae Rhondda 14 C6
Pen-y-fai Bridgend 14 C4
Pen-y-garn Carms 23 C10
Pen-y-garn Ceredig 32 G2
Pen-y-garnedd Anglesey 41 C7
Pen-y-gop Conwy 32 A5
Pen-y-graig Gwyn 40 G3
Pen-y-groes Carms 23 E10
Pen-y-groeslon Gwyn 40 G4
Pen-y-Gwryd Hotel Gwyn 41 E8
Pen-y-stryt Denb 42 G4
Pen-yr-heol Mon 25 G11
Pen-yr-Heolgerrig M Tydf 25 H7
Penallt Mon 26 G2
Penally Pembs 22 G6
Penalt Hereford 26 F2
Penare Corn 3 E8
Penarlâg = Hawarden Flint 42 F6
Penarth V Glam 15 D7
Penbryn Ceredig 23 A7
Pencader Carms 23 C9
Pencaenewydd Gwyn 40 F6
Pencaitland E Loth 70 D3
Pencarnisiog Anglesey 40 C5
Pencarreg Carms 23 B10
Pencelli Powys 25 F7
Pencoed Bridgend 14 C5
Pencombe Hereford 26 C2
Pencoyd Hereford 26 F2
Pencraig Hereford 26 F2
Pencraig Powys 32 C6
Pendeen Corn 2 F2
Penderyn Rhondda 24 H6
Pendine Carms 23 F7
Pendlebury Gtr Man 43 B10
Pendleton Lancs 43 F3
Pendock Worcs 26 E4
Pendoggett Corn 3 B9
Pendomer Som 8 C4
Pendoylan V Glam 14 D6
Pendre Bridgend 14 C5
Penegoes Powys 32 E3
Penfro = Pembroke Pembs 22 F4
Pengam Caerph 15 B7
Penge London 19 D10
Pengenffordd Powys 25 E8
Pengorffwysfa Anglesey 40 A6
Pengover Green Corn 4 E3
Penhale Corn 2 H5
Penhale Corn 3 D8
Penhalvaen Corn 2 F6
Penhill Swindon 17 C8
Penhow Newport 15 B10
Penhurst E Sus 12 E5
Peniarth Gwyn 32 E2
Penicuik Midloth 69 D11
Peniel Carms 23 D9
Peniel Denb 42 F3
Penifiler Highld 85 D9
Peninver Argyll 65 F8
Penisarwaun Gwyn 41 D7
Penistone S Yorks 44 B6
Penjerrick Corn 3 F6
Penketh Warr 43 D8
Penkill S Ayrs 66 G5
Penkridge Staffs 34 D5
Penley Wrex 33 B10
Penllergaer Swansea 14 B2
Penllyn V Glam 14 D5
Penmachno Conwy 41 E9
Penmaen Swansea 23 H10
Penmaenan Conwy 41 C9
Penmaenmawr Conwy 41 C9
Penmaenpool Gwyn 32 D2
Penmark V Glam 14 E6
Penmarth Corn 2 F6
Penmon Anglesey 41 B8
Penmore Mill Argyll 78 F7
Penmorfa Ceredig 23 A8
Penmorfa Gwyn 41 F7
Penmynydd Anglesey 41 C7
Penn Bucks 18 B6
Penn W Mid 34 F4
Penn Street Bucks 18 B6
Pennal Gwyn 32 E3
Pennan Aberds 89 B8
Pennant Ceredig 24 B2
Pennant Denb 32 B6
Pennant Denb 42 G3
Pennant Powys 32 F4
Pennant Melangell Powys 32 C6
Pennar Pembs 22 F4
Pennard Swansea 23 H10
Pennerley Shrops 33 F9
Pennington Cumb 49 B2
Pennington Gtr Man 43 C9
Pennington Hants 10 E2
Penny Bridge Cumb 49 A3
Pennycross Argyll 79 J8
Pennygate Norf 39 C9
Pennygown Argyll 79 G8
Pennymoor Devon 7 E7
Pennywell T&W 63 H9
Penparc Ceredig 23 B7
Penparc Pembs 22 C3
Penparcau Ceredig 32 G1
Penperlleni Mon 15 A9
Penpillick Corn 4 F1
Penpol Corn 3 F7
Penpoll Corn 4 F2
Penpont Dumfries 60 D4
Penpont Powys 24 F6
Penrhôs Mon 25 G11
Penrherber Carms 23 C7
Penrhiw goch Carms 23 E10
Penrhiw-llan Ceredig 23 B8
Penrhiw-pâl Ceredig 23 B8
Penrhiwceiber Rhondda 14 B6
Penrhos Gwyn 40 G5
Penrhos Powys 24 G4
Penrhosfeilw Anglesey 40 B4
Penrhyn Bay Conwy 41 B10
Penrhyn-coch Ceredig 32 G2
Penrhyndeudraeth Gwyn 41 G8
Penrhynside Conwy 41 B10
Penrice Swansea 23 H9
Penrith Cumb 57 C7
Penrose Corn 3 B7
Penruddock Cumb 56 D6
Penryn Corn 3 F6
Pensarn Carms 23 E9
Pensarn Conwy 42 E2
Pensax Worcs 26 B4
Pensby Mers 42 D5
Penselwood Som 9 A6
Pensford Bath 16 E3
Penshaw T&W 58 A4
Penshurst Kent 12 B4
Pensilva Corn 4 E3
Penston E Loth 70 C3
Pentewan Corn 3 E9
Pentir Gwyn 41 D7
Pentire Corn 3 C6
Pentlow Essex 30 D5
Pentney Norf 38 D3
Penton Mewsey Hants 17 G10
Pentraeth Anglesey 41 C7
Pentre Carms 23 E10
Pentre Powys 33 F8
Pentre Powys 33 G6
Pentre Rhondda 14 B5
Pentre Shrops 33 D9
Pentre Wrex 33 A8
Pentre Wrex 33 B7
Pentre-bâch Ceredig 23 B10
Pentre-bach Powys 24 E6
Pentre Berw Anglesey 40 C6
Pentre-bont Conwy 41 E9
Pentre-celyn Denb 42 G4
Pentre-Celyn Powys 32 E4
Pentre-chwyth Swansea 14 B2
Pentre-cwrt Carms 23 C8
Pentre Dolau-Honddu Powys 24 D6
Pentre-dwr Swansea 14 B2
Pentre-galar Pembs 22 C6
Pentre-Gwenlais Carms 24 G3
Pentre Gwynfryn Gwyn 32 C1
Pentre Halkyn Flint 42 E5
Pentre-Isaf Conwy 41 D10
Pentre Llanrhaeadr Denb 42 F3
Pentre-llwyn-llŵyd Powys 24 C6
Pentre-llyn Ceredig 24 A3
Pentre-llyn cymmer Conwy 42 G2
Pentre Meyrick V Glam 14 D5
Pentre-poeth Newport 15 C8
Pentre-rhew Ceredig 24 C3
Pentre-tafarn-y-fedw Conwy 41 D10
Pentre-ty-gwyn Carms 24 E5
Pentrebach M Tydf 14 A6
Pentrebach Swansea 24 H3
Pentrebeirdd Powys 33 D7
Pentrecagal Carms 23 B8
Pentredwr Denb 42 H4
Pentrefelin Carms 23 D10
Pentrefelin Ceredig 24 D3
Pentrefelin Conwy 41 C10
Pentrefelin Gwyn 41 G7
Pentrefoelas Conwy 41 E10
Pentregat Ceredig 23 A8
Pentreheyling Shrops 33 F8
Pentre'r Felin Conwy 41 D10
Pentre'r-felin Powys 24 E6
Pentrich Derbys 45 G7
Pentridge Dorset 9 C9
Pentyrch Cardiff 15 C7
Penuchadre V Glam 14 D4
Penuwch Ceredig 24 B2
Penwithick Corn 3 D9
Penwyllt Powys 24 G5
Penybanc Carms 24 G3
Penybont Powys 25 B8
Penybontfawr Powys 33 C6
Penycae Wrex 42 H5
Penycwm Pembs 22 D3
Penyffordd Flint 42 F6
Penyffridd Gwyn 41 E7
Penygarnedd Powys 33 C7
Penygraig Rhondda 14 B5
Penygroes Gwyn 40 E6
Penygroes Pembs 22 C6
Penyrheol Caerph 15 C7
Penysarn Anglesey 40 A6
Penywaun Rhondda 14 A5
Penzance Corn 2 F3
Peopleton Worcs 26 C6
Peover Heath Ches E 43 E10
Peper Harow Sur 18 G6
Perceton N Ayrs 67 B6
Percie Aberds 83 D7
Percyhorner Aberds 89 B9
Periton Som 7 B8
Perivale London 19 C8
Perkinsville Durham 58 A3
Perlethorpe Notts 45 E10
Perranarworthal Corn 3 F6
Perranporth Corn 3 D6
Perranuthnoe Corn 2 G4
Perranzabuloe Corn 3 D6
Perry Barr W Mid 35 F6
Perry Green Herts 29 G11
Perry Green Wilts 16 C6
Perry Street Kent 20 D3
Perryfoot Derbys 44 D5
Pershall Staffs 34 B4
Pershore Worcs 26 D6
Pert Angus 83 G8
Pertenhall Bedford 29 B7
Perth Perth 76 E4
Perthy Shrops 33 B9
Perton Staffs 34 F4
Pertwood Wilts 16 H5
Peter Tavy Devon 4 D6
Peterborough Pboro 37 F7
Peterburn Highld 91 J12
Peterchurch Hereford 25 E10
Peterculter Aberdeen 83 C10
Peterhead Aberds 89 D11
Peterlee Durham 58 B5
Peter's Green Herts 29 G8
Peters Marland Devon 6 E3
Petersfield Hants 10 B6
Peterston super-Ely V Glam 14 D6
Peterstone Wentlooge Newport 15 C8
Peterstow Hereford 26 F2
Petertown Orkney 95 H4
Petham Kent 21 F8
Petrockstow Devon 6 F4
Pett E Sus 13 E7
Pettaugh Suff 31 C8
Petteridge Kent 12 B5
Pettinain S Lanark 69 F8
Pettistree Suff 31 C9
Petton Devon 7 D9
Petton Shrops 33 C10
Petts Wood London 19 E11
Petty Aberds 89 E7
Pettycur Fife 69 B11
Pettymuick Aberds 89 F9
Petworth W Sus 11 B8
Pevensey E Sus 12 F5
Pevensey Bay E Sus 12 F5
Pewsey Wilts 17 E8
Philham Devon 6 D1
Philiphaugh Borders 70 H3
Phillack Corn 2 F4
Philleigh Corn 3 F7
Philpstoun W Loth 69 C9
Phocle Green Hereford 26 F3
Phoenix Green Hants 18 F4
Pica Cumb 56 D2
Piccotts End Herts 29 H7
Pickering N Yorks 52 A3
Picket Piece Hants 17 G10
Picket Post Hants 9 D10
Pickhill N Yorks 51 A9
Picklescott Shrops 33 F10
Pickletillem Fife 77 E7
Pickmere Ches E 43 E9
Pickney Som 7 D10
Pickstock Telford 34 C3
Pickwell Devon 6 B3
Pickwell Leics 36 D3
Pickworth Lincs 36 B6
Pickworth Rutland 36 D5
Picton Ches W 43 E7
Picton Flint 42 D4
Picton N Yorks 58 F5
Piddinghoe E Sus 12 F3
Piddington Northants 28 C5
Piddington Oxon 28 G3
Piddlehinton Dorset 8 E6
Piddletrenthide Dorset 8 E6
Pidley Cambs 37 H9
Piercebridge Darl 58 E3
Pierowall Orkney 95 D5
Pigdon Northumb 63 E7
Pikehall Derbys 44 G5
Pilgrims Hatch Essex 20 B2
Pilham Lincs 46 C2
Pill N Som 15 D11
Pillaton Corn 4 E4
Pillerton Hersey Warks 27 D10
Pillerton Priors Warks 27 D9
Pilleth Powys 25 B9
Pilley Hants 10 E2
Pilley S Yorks 45 B7
Pilling Lancs 49 E4
Pilling Lane Lancs 49 E3
Pillowell Glos 26 H3
Pillwell Dorset 9 C6
Pilning S Glos 16 C2
Pilsbury Derbys 44 F5
Pilsdon Dorset 8 E3
Pilsgate Pboro 37 E6
Pilsley Derbys 44 E6
Pilsley Derbys 45 F8
Pilton Devon 6 C4
Pilton Northants 36 G6
Pilton Rutland 36 E5
Pilton Som 16 G2
Pilton Green Swansea 23 H9
Pimperne Dorset 9 D8
Pin Mill Suff 31 E9
Pinchbeck Lincs 37 C8
Pinchbeck Bars Lincs 37 C7
Pinchbeck West Lincs 37 C8
Pincheon Green S Yorks 52 H2
Pinehurst Swindon 17 C8
Pinfold Lancs 43 A6
Pinged Carms 23 F9
Pinhoe Devon 7 G8
Pinkneys Grn. Windsor 18 C5
Pinley W Mid 35 H9
Pinminnoch S Ayrs 66 G4
Pinmore S Ayrs 66 G5
Pinmore Mains S Ayrs 66 G5
Pinner London 19 C8
Pinvin Worcs 26 D6
Pinwherry S Ayrs 66 H4
Pinxton Derbys 45 G8
Pipe and Lyde Hereford 26 D2
Pipe Gate Shrops 34 A3
Piperhill Highld 87 F11
Piper's Pool Corn 4 C3
Pipewell Northants 36 G4
Pippacott Devon 6 C4
Pipton Powys 25 E8
Pirbright Sur 18 F6
Pirnmill N Ayrs 66 B1
Pirton Herts 29 E8
Pirton Worcs 26 D5
Pisgah Ceredig 32 H2
Pisgah Stirling 75 G10
Pishill Oxon 18 C4
Pistyll Gwyn 40 F5
Pitagowan Perth 81 G10
Pitblae Aberds 89 B9
Pitcairngreen Perth 76 E3
Pitcalnie Highld 87 D11
Pitcaple Aberds 83 A9
Pitch Green Bucks 18 A4
Pitch Place Sur 18 F6
Pitchcombe Glos 26 H5
Pitchcott Bucks 28 F4
Pitchford Shrops 33 E11
Pitcombe Som 8 A5
Pitcorthie Fife 77 G8
Pitcox E Loth 70 C5
Pitcur Perth 76 D5
Pitfichie Aberds 83 B8
Pitforthie Aberds 83 F10
Pitgrudy Highld 87 B10
Pitkennedy Angus 77 B8
Pitkevy Fife 76 G5
Pitkierie Fife 77 G8
Pitlessie Fife 76 G6
Pitlochry Perth 76 B2
Pitmachie Aberds 83 A8
Pitmain Highld 81 C9
Pitmedden Aberds 89 F8
Pitminster Som 7 E11
Pitmuies Angus 77 C8
Pitmunie Aberds 83 B8
Pitney Som 8 B3
Pitscottie Fife 77 F7
Pitsea Essex 20 C4
Pitsford Northants 28 B4
Pitsmoor S Yorks 45 D7
Pitstone Bucks 28 G6
Pitstone Green Bucks 28 G6
Pittendreich Moray 88 B1
Pittentrail Highld 93 J10
Pittenweem Fife 77 G8
Pittington Durham 58 B4
Pittodrie Aberds 83 A8
Pitton Wilts 9 A11
Pittswood Kent 20 G3
Pittulie Aberds 89 B9
Pity Me Durham 58 B3
Pityme Corn 3 B8
Pityoulish Highld 81 B11
Pixey Green Suff 39 H8
Pixham Sur 19 F8
Pixley Hereford 26 E3
Place Newton N Yorks 52 B4
Plaidy Aberds 89 C7
Plains N Lanark 68 D6
Plaish Shrops 33 F11
Plaistow W Sus 11 A9
Plaitford Wilts 10 C1
Plank Lane Gtr Man 43 C9
Plas-canol Gwyn 32 D1
Plas Gogerddan Ceredig 32 G2
Plas Llwyngwern Powys 32 E3
Plas Nantyr Wrex 33 B7
Plas-yn-Cefn Denb 42 E3
Plastow Green Hants 18 E2
Platt Kent 20 F3
Platt Bridge Gtr Man 43 B9
Platts Common S Yorks 45 B7
Plawsworth Durham 58 B3
Plaxtol Kent 20 F3
Play Hatch Oxon 18 D4
Playden E Sus 13 D8
Playford Suff 31 D9
Playing Place Corn 3 E7
Playley Green Glos 26 E4
Plealey Shrops 33 E10
Plean Stirling 69 B7
Pleasington Blackburn 50 G2
Pleasley Derbys 45 F9
Pleckgate Blackburn 50 F2
Plenmeller Northumb 62 G3
Pleshey Essex 30 G3
Plockton Highld 85 E13
Plocrapol W Isles 90 H6
Ploughfield Hereford 25 D10
Plowden Shrops 33 G9
Ploxgreen Shrops 33 E9
Pluckley Kent 20 G6
Pluckley Thorne Kent 13 B8
Plumbland Cumb 56 C3
Plumley Ches E 43 E10
Plumpton Cumb 57 C6
Plumpton E Sus 12 E2
Plumpton Green E Sus 12 E2
Plumpton Head Cumb 57 C7
Plumstead London 19 D11
Plumstead Norf 39 B7
Plumtree Notts 36 B2
Plungar Leics 36 B3
Plush Dorset 8 D6
Plwmp Ceredig 23 A8
Plymouth Plym 4 F5
Plympton Plym 4 F6
Plymstock Plym 4 F6
Plymtree Devon 7 F9
Pockley N Yorks 59 H7
Pocklington E Yorks 52 E4
Pode Hole Lincs 37 C8
Podimore Som 8 B4
Podington Bedford 28 B6
Podmore Staffs 34 B3
Point Clear Essex 31 G7
Pointon Lincs 37 B7
Pokesdown Bmouth 9 E10
Pol a Charra W Isles 84 G2
Polbae Dumfries 54 B5
Polbain Highld 92 H2
Polbathic Corn 4 F4
Polbeth W Loth 69 D9
Polchar Highld 81 C10
Pole Elm Worcs 26 D5
Polebrook Northants 37 G6
Polegate E Sus 12 F4
Poles Highld 87 B10
Polesworth Warks 35 E8
Polgigga Corn 2 G2
Polglass Highld 92 J3
Polgooth Corn 3 D8
Poling W Sus 11 D9
Polkerris Corn 4 F1
Polla Highld 92 D6
Pollington E Yorks 52 H2
Polloch Highld 79 E10
Pollok Glasgow 68 D4
Pollokshields Glasgow 68 D4
Polmassick Corn 3 E8
Polmont Falk 69 C8
Polnessan E Ayrs 67 E7
Polnish Highld 79 C10
Polperro Corn 4 F3
Polruan Corn 4 F2
Polsham Som 15 G11
Polstead Suff 30 E6
Poltalloch Argyll 73 D7
Poltimore Devon 7 G8
Polton Midloth 69 D11
Polwarth Borders 70 E6
Polyphant Corn 4 C3
Polzeath Corn 3 B8
Ponders End London 19 B10
Pondersbridge Cambs 37 F8
Pondtail Hants 18 F5
Ponsanooth Corn 3 F6
Ponsworthy Devon 5 D8
Pont Aber Carms 24 F4
Pont Aber-Geirw Gwyn 32 C3
Pont-ar-gothi Carms 23 D10
Pont ar Hydfer Powys 24 F5
Pont-ar-llechau Carms 24 F4
Pont Cwm Pydew Denb 32 B6
Pont Cyfyng Conwy 41 E9
Pont Cysyllte Wrex 33 A8
Pont Dolydd Prysor Gwyn 41 G9
Pont-faen Powys 24 E6
Pont Fronwydd Gwyn 32 C4
Pont-gareg Pembs 22 B6
Pont-Henri Carms 23 F9
Pont-Llogel Powys 32 D6
Pont Pen-y-benglog Gwyn 41 D8
Pont Rhyd-goch Conwy 41 D8
Pont-Rhyd-sarn Gwyn 32 C4
Pont Rhyd-y-cyff Bridgend 14 C4
Pont-rhyd-y-groes Ceredig 24 A4
Pont-rug Gwyn 41 D7
Pont Senni = Sennybridge Powys 24 F6
Pont-siân Ceredig 23 B9
Pont-y-gwaith Rhondda 14 B6
Pont-y-Pŵl = Pontypool Torf 15 A8
Pont-y-pant Conwy 41 E9
Pont y Pennant Gwyn 32 C5
Pont yr Afon-Gam Gwyn 41 F9
Pont-yr-hafod Pembs 22 D4
Pontamman Carms 24 G3
Pontantwn Carms 23 E9
Pontardawe Neath 14 A3
Pontarddulais Swansea 23 F10
Pontarsais Carms 23 D9
Pontblyddyn Flint 42 F5
Pontbren Araeth Carms 24 F3
Pontbren Llwyd Rhondda 24 H6
Pontefract W Yorks 51 G10
Ponteland Northumb 63 F7
Ponterwyd Ceredig 32 G3
Pontesbury Shrops 33 E9
Pontfadog Wrex 33 B8
Pontfaen Pembs 22 C5
Pontgarreg Ceredig 23 A8
Ponthir Torf 15 B9
Ponthirwaun Ceredig 23 B7
Pontllanfraith Caerph 15 B7
Pontlliw Swansea 14 A2
Pontllyfni Gwyn 40 E6
Pontlottyn Caerph 25 H8
Pontneddfechan Powys 24 H6
Pontnewydd Torf 15 B8
Pontrhydfendigaid Ceredig 24 B4
Pontrhydyfen Neath 14 B3
Pontrilas Hereford 25 F10
Pontrobert Powys 33 D7
Ponts Green E Sus 12 E5
Pontshill Hereford 26 F3
Pontsticill M Tydf 25 G7
Pontwgan Conwy 41 C9
Pontyates Carms 23 F9
Pontyberem Carms 23 E10
Pontyclun Rhondda 14 C6
Pontycymer Bridgend 14 B5
Pontyglasier Pembs 22 C6
Pontypool = Pont-y-Pŵl Torf 15 A8
Pontypridd Rhondda 14 C6
Pontywaun Caerph 15 B8
Pooksgreen Hants 10 C2
Pool Corn 2 E5
Pool W Yorks 51 E8
Pool o' Muckhart Clack 76 G3
Pool Quay Powys 33 D8
Poole Poole 9 E9
Poole Keynes Glos 16 B6
Poolend Staffs 44 G3
Poolewe Highld 91 J13
Pooley Bridge Cumb 56 D6
Poolfold Staffs 44 G2
Poolhill Glos 26 F4
Poolsbrook Derbys 45 E8
Pootings Kent 19 G11
Pope Hill Pembs 22 E4
Popeswood Brack 18 E5
Popham Hants 18 G2
Poplar London 19 C10
Popley Hants 18 F3
Porchester Nottingham 36 A1
Porchfield IoW 10 E3
Porin Highld 86 F6
Poringland Norf 39 E8
Porkellis Corn 2 F5
Porlock Som 7 B7
Porlock Weir Som 7 B7
Port Ann Argyll 73 E8
Port Appin Argyll 74 C2
Port Arthur Shetland 96 K5
Port Askaig Argyll 64 B5
Port Bannatyne Argyll 73 G9
Port Carlisle Cumb 61 G8
Port Charlotte Argyll 64 C3
Port Clarence Stockton 58 D5
Port Driseach Argyll 73 F8
Port e Vullen IoM 48 C4
Port Ellen Argyll 64 D4
Port Elphinstone Aberds 83 B9
Port Erin IoM 48 F1
Port Erroll Aberds 89 E10
Port-Eynon Swansea 23 H9
Port Gaverne Corn 3 A9
Port Glasgow Invclyd 68 C2
Port Henderson Highld 85 A12
Port Isaac Corn 3 A8
Port Lamont Argyll 73 F9
Port Lion Pembs 22 F4
Port Logan Dumfries 54 E3
Port Mholair W Isles 91 D10
Port Mor Highld 78 D7
Port Mulgrave N Yorks 59 E8
Port Nan Giùran W Isles 91 D10
Port nan Long W Isles 84 A3
Port Nis W Isles 91 A10
Port of Menteith Stirling 75 G8
Port Quin Corn 3 A8
Port Ramsay Argyll 79 G11
Port St Mary IoM 48 F2
Port Sunlight Mers 42 D6
Port Talbot Neath 14 B3
Port Tennant Swansea 14 B2
Port Wemyss Argyll 64 C2
Port William Dumfries 54 E6
Portachoillan Argyll 72 H6
Portavadie Argyll 73 G8
Portbury N Som 15 D11
Portchester Hants 10 D5
Portclair Highld 80 B6
Portencalzie Dumfries 54 B3
Portencross N Ayrs 66 B4
Portesham Dorset 8 F5
Portessie Moray 88 B4
Portfield Gate Pembs 22 E4
Portgate Devon 4 C5
Portgordon Moray 88 B3
Portgower Highld 93 H13
Porth Corn 3 C7
Porth Rhondda 14 B6
Porth Navas Corn 3 G6
Porth Tywyn = Burry Port Carms 23 F9
Porth-y-waen Shrops 33 C8
Porthaethwy = Menai Bridge Anglesey 41 C7
Porthallow Corn 3 G6
Porthallow Corn 4 F3
Porthcawl Bridgend 14 D4
Porthcothan Corn 3 B7
Porthcurno Corn 2 G2
Porthgain Pembs 22 C3
Porthill Shrops 33 D10
Porthkerry V Glam 14 E6
Porthleven Corn 2 G5
Porthllechog Anglesey 40 A6
Porthmadog Gwyn 41 G7
Porthmeor Corn 2 F3
Portholland Corn 3 E8
Porthoustock Corn 3 G7
Porthpean Corn 3 D9
Porthtowan Corn 2 E5
Porthyrhyd Carms 23 E10
Porthyrhyd Carms 24 E4
Portincaple Argyll 73 D11
Portington E Yorks 52 F3
Portinnisherrich Argyll 73 B8
Portinscale Cumb 56 D4
Portishead N Som 15 D10
Portkil Argyll 73 E11
Portknockie Moray 88 B4
Portlethen Aberds 83 D11
Portling Dumfries 55 D11
Portloe Corn 3 F8
Portmahomack Highld 87 C12
Portmeirion Gwyn 41 G7
Portmellon Corn 3 E9
Portmore Hants 10 E2
Portnacroish Argyll 74 C2
Portnahaven Argyll 64 C2
Portnalong Highld 85 E8
Portnaluchaig Highld 79 C9
Portnancon Highld 92 C7
Portnellan Stirling 75 E7
Portobello Edin 70 C2
Porton Wilts 17 H8
Portpatrick Dumfries 54 D3
Portreath Corn 2 E5
Portree Highld 85 D9
Portscatho Corn 3 F7
Portsea Ptsmth 10 D5
Portskerra Highld 93 C11
Portskewett Mon 15 C11
Portslade Brighton 12 F1
Portslade-by-Sea Brighton 12 F1
Portsmouth Ptsmth 10 D5
Portsmouth W Yorks 50 G5
Portsonachan Argyll 74 E3
Portsoy Aberds 88 B5
Portswood Soton 10 C3
Porttanachy Moray 88 B3
Portuairk Highld 78 E7
Portway Hereford 25 E11
Portway Worcs 27 A7
Portwrinkle Corn 4 F4
Poslingford Suff 30 D4
Postbridge Devon 5 D7
Postcombe Oxon 18 B4
Postling Kent 13 C10
Postwick Norf 39 E8
Potholm Dumfries 61 E9
Potsgrove C Beds 28 F6
Pott Row Norf 38 C3
Pott Shrigley Ches E 44 E3
Potten End Herts 29 H7
Potter Brompton N Yorks 52 B5
Potter Heigham Norf 39 D10
Potter Street Essex 29 H11
Potterhanworth Lincs 46 F4
Potterhanworth Booths Lincs 46 F4
Potterne Wilts 16 F6
Potterne Wick Wilts 17 F7
Potternewton W Yorks 51 F9
Potters Bar Herts 19 A9
Potter's Cross Staffs 34 G4
Potterspury Northants 28 D4
Potterton Aberds 83 B11
Potterton W Yorks 51 F10
Potto N Yorks 58 F5
Potton C Beds 29 D9
Poughill Corn 6 F1
Poughill Devon 7 F7
Poulshot Wilts 16 F6
Poulton Glos 17 A8
Poulton Mers 42 C6
Poulton-le-Fylde Lancs 49 F3
Pound Bank Worcs 26 A4
Pound Green E Sus 12 D4
Pound Green IoW 10 F2
Pound Green Worcs 34 H3
Pound Hill W Sus 12 C1
Poundfield E Sus 12 C4
Poundland S Ayrs 66 H4
Poundon Bucks 28 F3
Poundsgate Devon 5 D8
Poundstock Corn 4 B3
Powburn Northumb 62 B6
Powderham Devon 5 C10
Powerstock Dorset 8 E4
Powfoot Dumfries 61 G7
Powick Worcs 26 C5
Powmill Perth 76 H3
Poxwell Dorset 8 F6
Poyle Slough 19 D7
Poynings W Sus 12 E1
Poyntington Dorset 8 C5
Poynton Ches E 44 D3
Poynton Green Telford 34 D1
Poystreet Green Suff 30 C6
Praa Sands Corn 2 G4
Pratt's Bottom London 19 E11
Praze Corn 2 F4
Praze-an-Beeble Corn 2 F5
Predannack Wollas Corn 2 H5
Prees Shrops 34 B1
Prees Green Shrops 34 B1
Prees Heath Shrops 34 B1
Prees Higher Heath Shrops 34 B1
Prees Lower Heath Shrops 34 B1
Preesall Lancs 49 E3
Preesgweene Shrops 33 B8
Prenderguest Borders 71 E8
Prendwick Northumb 62 B6
Prengwyn Ceredig 23 B9
Prenteg Gwyn 41 F7
Prenton Mers 42 D6
Prescot Mers 43 C7
Prescott Shrops 33 C10
Pressen Northumb 71 G7
Prestatyn Denb 42 D3
Prestbury Ches E 44 E3
Prestbury Glos 26 F6
Presteigne = Llanandras Powys 25 B10
Presthope Shrops 34 F1
Prestleigh Som 16 G3
Preston Borders 70 E6
Preston Brighton 12 F2
Preston Devon 5 D9
Preston Dorset 8 F6
Preston E Loth 70 C4
Preston E Yorks 53 F7
Preston Glos 17 A7
Preston Glos 26 E3
Preston Herts 29 F8
Preston Kent 21 E9
Preston Kent 21 E7
Preston Lancs 49 G5
Preston Northumb 71 H10
Preston Rutland 36 E4
Preston Shrops 33 D11
Preston Wilts 17 D7
Preston Wilts 17 D9
Preston Bagot Warks 27 B8
Preston Bissett Bucks 28 F3
Preston Bowyer Som 7 D10
Preston Brockhurst Shrops 33 C11
Preston Brook Halton 43 D8
Preston Candover Hants 18 G3
Preston Capes Northants 28 C2
Preston Crowmarsh Oxon 18 B3
Preston Gubbals Shrops 33 D10
Preston on Stour Warks 27 C9
Preston on the Hill Halton 43 D8
Preston on Wye Hereford 25 D10
Preston Plucknett Som 8 C4
Preston St Mary Suff 30 C6
Preston-under-Scar N Yorks 58 G1
Preston upon the Weald Moors Telford 34 D2
Preston Wynne Hereford 26 D2
Prestonmill Dumfries 60 H5
Prestonpans E Loth 70 C2
Prestwich Gtr Man 44 B2
Prestwick Northumb 63 F7
Prestwick S Ayrs 67 D6
Prestwood Bucks 18 A5
Price Town Bridgend 14 B5
Prickwillow Cambs 38 G1
Priddy Som 15 F11
Priest Hutton Lancs 49 B5
Priest Weston Shrops 33 F8
Priesthaugh Borders 61 C10
Primethorpe Leics 35 F11
Primrose Green Norf 39 D6
Primrose Valley N Yorks 53 B7
Primrosehill Herts 19 A7
Princes Gate Pembs 22 E6
Princes Risborough Bucks 18 A5
Princethorpe Warks 27 A11
Princetown Caerph 25 G8
Princetown Devon 5 D6
Prion Denb 42 F3
Prior Muir Fife 77 F8
Prior Park Northumb 71 E8
Priors Frome Hereford 26 E2
Priors Hardwick Warks 27 C11
Priors Marston Warks 27 C11
Priorslee Telford 34 D3
Priory Wood Hereford 25 D9
Priston Bath 16 E3
Pristow Green Norf 39 G7
Prittlewell Southend 20 C5
Privett Hants 10 B5
Prixford Devon 6 C4
Probus Corn 3 E7
Proncy Highld 87 B10
Prospect Cumb 56 B3
Prudhoe Northumb 62 G6
Ptarmigan Lodge Stirling 74 G6
Pubil Perth 75 C7
Puckeridge Herts 29 F10
Puckington Som 8 C2
Pucklechurch S Glos 16 D3
Pucknall Hants 10 B2
Puckrup Glos 26 E5
Puddinglake Ches W 43 F10
Puddington Ches W 42 E6
Puddington Devon 7 E7
Puddledock Norf 39 F6
Puddletown Dorset 9 E6
Pudleston Hereford 26 C2
Pudsey W Yorks 51 F8
Pulborough W Sus 11 C9
Puleston Telford 34 C3
Pulford Ches W 43 G6
Pulham Dorset 8 D6
Pulham Market Norf 39 G7
Pulham St Mary Norf 39 G8
Pulloxhill C Beds 29 E7
Pumpherston W Loth 69 D9
Pumsaint Carms 24 D3
Puncheston Pembs 22 D5
Puncknowle Dorset 8 F4
Punnett's Town E Sus 12 D5
Purbrook Hants 10 D5
Purewell Dorset 9 E10
Purfleet Thurrock 20 D2
Puriton Som 15 G9
Purleigh Essex 20 A5
Purley London 19 E10
Purley W Berks 18 D3
Purlogue Shrops 33 H8
Purls Bridge Cambs 37 G10
Purse Caundle Dorset 8 C5
Purslow Shrops 33 G9
Purston Jaglin W Yorks 51 H10
Purton Glos 16 A3
Purton Glos 16 A3
Purton Wilts 17 C7
Purton Stoke Wilts 17 B7
Pury End Northants 28 D4
Pusey Oxon 17 B10
Putley Hereford 26 E3
Putney London 19 D9
Putsborough Devon 6 B3
Puttenham Herts 28 G5
Puttenham Sur 18 G6
Puxton N Som 15 E10
Pwll Carms 23 F9
Pwll-glas Denb 42 G4
Pwll-trap Carms 23 E7
Pwll-y-glaw Neath 14 B3
Pwllcrochan Pembs 22 F4
Pwllgloyw Powys 25 E7
Pwllheli Gwyn 40 G5
Pwllmeyric Mon 15 B11
Pye Corner Newport 15 C9
Pye Green Staffs 34 D5
Pyecombe W Sus 12 E1
Pyewipe NE Lincs 46 A6
Pyle = Y Pîl Bridgend 14 C4
Pyle IoW 10 G3
Pylle Som 16 H3
Pymoor Cambs 37 G10
Pyrford Sur 19 F7
Pyrton Oxon 18 B3
Pytchley Northants 28 A5
Pyworthy Devon 6 F2

Q

Quabbs Shrops 33 G8
Quadring Lincs 37 B8
Quainton Bucks 28 G4
Quarley Hants 17 G9
Quarndon Derbys 35 A9
Quarrier's Homes Invclyd 68 D2
Quarrington Lincs 37 A6
Quarrington Hill Durham 58 C4
Quarry Bank W Mid 34 G5
Quarryford E Loth 70 D4
Quarryhill Highld 87 C10
Quarrywood Moray 88 B1
Quarter S Lanark 68 E6
Quatford Shrops 34 F3
Quatt Shrops 34 G3
Quebec Durham 58 B2
Quedgeley Glos 26 G5
Queen Adelaide Cambs 38 G1
Queen Camel Som 8 B4
Queen Charlton Bath 16 E3
Queen Dart Devon 7 E7
Queen Oak Dorset 9 A6
Queen Street Kent 20 G3
Queen Street Wilts 17 C7
Queenborough Kent 20 D6
Queenhill Worcs 26 E5
Queen's Head Shrops 33 C9
Queen's Park Bedford 29 D7
Queen's Park Northants 28 B4
Queensbury W Yorks 51 F7
Queensferry Edin 69 C10
Queensferry Flint 42 F6
Queenstown Blackpool 49 F3
Queenzieburn N Lanark 68 C5
Quemerford Wilts 17 E7
Quendale Shetland 96 M5
Quendon Essex 30 E2
Queniborough Leics 36 D2
Quenington Glos 17 A8
Quernmore Lancs 49 D5
Quethiock Corn 4 E4
Quholm Orkney 95 G3
Quicks Green W Berks 18 D2
Quidenham Norf 38 G6
Quidhampton Hants 18 F2
Quidhampton Wilts 9 A10
Quilquox Aberds 89 E9
Quina Brook Shrops 33 B11
Quindry Orkney 95 J5
Quinton Northants 28 C4
Quinton W Mid 34 G5
Quintrell Downs Corn 3 C7
Quixhill Staffs 35 A7
Quoditch Devon 6 G3
Quoig Perth 75 E11
Quorndon Leics 36 D1
Quothquan S Lanark 69 G8
Quoyloo Orkney 95 F3
Quoyness Orkney 95 H3
Quoys Shetland 96 B8
Quoys Shetland 96 G6

R

Raasay Ho. Highld 85 E10
Rabbit's Cross Kent 20 G4
Raby Mers 42 E6
Rachan Mill Borders 69 G10
Rachub Gwyn 41 D8
Rackenford Devon 7 E7
Rackham W Sus 11 C9
Rackheath Norf 39 D8
Racks Dumfries 60 F6
Rackwick Orkney 95 D5
Rackwick Orkney 95 J3
Radbourne Derbys 35 B8
Radcliffe Gtr Man 43 B10
Radcliffe Northumb 63 C8
Radcliffe on Trent Notts 36 B2
Radclive Bucks 28 E3
Radcot Oxon 17 B9
Raddery Highld 87 F10
Radernie Fife 77 G7
Radford Semele Warks 27 B10
Radipole Dorset 8 F5
Radlett Herts 19 B8
Radley Oxon 18 B2
Radmanthwaite Notts 45 F9
Radmoor Shrops 34 C2
Radmore Green Ches E 43 G8
Radnage Bucks 18 B4
Radstock Bath 16 F3
Radstone Northants 28 D2
Radway Warks 27 D10
Radway Green Ches E 43 G10
Radwell Bedford 29 C7
Radwell Herts 29 E9
Radwinter Essex 30 E3
Radyr Cardiff 15 C7
Rafford Moray 87 F13
Ragdale Leics 36 D2
Raglan Mon 25 H11
Ragnall Notts 46 E2
Rahane Argyll 73 E11
Rainford Mers 43 B7
Rainford Junction Mers 43 B7
Rainham London 20 C2
Rainham Medway 20 E5
Rainhill Mers 43 C7
Rainhill Stoops Mers 43 C8
Rainow Ches E 44 E3
Rainton N Yorks 51 B9
Rainworth Notts 45 G9
Raisbeck Cumb 57 F8
Raise Cumb 57 B9
Rait Perth 76 E5
Raithby Lincs 47 D7
Raithby Lincs 47 F7
Rake W Sus 11 B7
Rakewood Gtr Man 44 A3
Ram Carms 23 B10
Ram Lane Kent 20 G6
Ramasaig Highld 84 D6
Rame Corn 2 F6
Rame Corn 4 G5
Rameldry Mill Bank Fife 76 G6
Ramnageo Shetland 96 C8
Rampisham Dorset 8 D4
Rampside Cumb 49 C2
Rampton Cambs 29 B11
Rampton Notts 45 E11
Ramsbottom Gtr Man 50 H3
Ramsbury Wilts 17 D9
Ramscraigs Highld 94 H3
Ramsdean Hants 10 B6
Ramsdell Hants 18 F2
Ramsden Oxon 27 G10
Ramsden Bellhouse Essex 20 B4
Ramsden Heath Essex 20 B4
Ramsey Cambs 37 G8
Ramsey Essex 31 E9
Ramsey IoM 48 C4
Ramsey Forty Foot Cambs 37 G9
Ramsey Heights Cambs 37 G8
Ramsey Island Essex 30 H6
Ramsey Mereside Cambs 37 G8
Ramsey St Mary's Cambs 37 G8
Ramseycleuch Borders 61 B8
Ramsgate Kent 21 E10
Ramsgill N Yorks 51 B7
Ramshorn Staffs 44 H4
Ramsnest Common Sur 11 A8
Ranais W Isles 91 E9
Ranby Lincs 46 E6
Ranby Notts 45 D10
Rand Lincs 46 E5
Randwick Glos 26 H5
Ranfurly Renfs 68 D2
Rangag Highld 94 F3
Rangemore Staffs 35 C7
Rangeworthy S Glos 16 C3
Rankinston E Ayrs 67 E7
Ranmoor S Yorks 45 D7
Ranmore Common Sur 19 F8
Rannerdale Cumb 56 E3
Rannoch Station Perth 75 B7
Ranochan Highld 79 C11
Ranskill Notts 45 D10
Ranton Staffs 34 C4
Ranworth Norf 39 D9
Raploch Stirling 68 A6
Rapness Orkney 95 D6
Rascal Moor E Yorks 52 F4
Rascarrel Dumfries 55 E10
Rashiereive Aberds 89 F9
Raskelf N Yorks 51 B10
Rassau Bl Gwent 25 G8
Rastrick W Yorks 51 G7
Ratagan Highld 85 G14
Ratby Leics 35 E11
Ratcliffe Culey Leics 35 F9
Ratcliffe on Soar Leics 35 C10
Ratcliffe on the Wreake Leics 36 D2
Rathen Aberds 89 B10
Rathillet Fife 76 E6
Rathmell N Yorks 50 D4
Ratho Edin 69 C10
Ratho Station Edin 69 C10
Rathven Moray 88 B4
Ratley Warks 27 D10
Ratlinghope Shrops 33 F10
Rattar Highld 94 C4
Ratten Row Lancs 49 E4
Rattery Devon 5 E8
Rattlesden Suff 30 C6
Rattray Perth 76 C4
Raughton Head Cumb 56 B5
Raunds Northants 28 A6
Ravenfield S Yorks 45 C8
Ravenglass Cumb 56 G2
Raveningham Norf 39 F9
Ravenscar N Yorks 59 F10
Ravenscraig Invclyd 73 F11
Ravensdale IoM 48 C3
Ravensden Bedford 29 C7
Ravenseat N Yorks 57 F10
Ravenshead Notts 45 G9
Ravensmoor Ches E 43 G9
Ravensthorpe Northants 28 A3
Ravensthorpe W Yorks 51 G8
Ravenstone Leics 35 D10
Ravenstone M Keynes 28 C5
Ravenstonedale Cumb 57 F9
Ravenstown Cumb 49 B3
Ravenstruther S Lanark 69 F8
Ravensworth N Yorks 58 F2
Raw N Yorks 59 F10
Rawcliffe E Yorks 52 G2
Rawcliffe York 52 D1
Rawcliffe Bridge E Yorks 52 G2
Rawdon W Yorks 51 F8
Rawmarsh S Yorks 45 C8
Rawreth Essex 20 B4
Rawridge Devon 7 F11
Rawtenstall Lancs 50 G4
Raxton Aberds 89 E8
Raydon Suff 31 E7
Raylees Northumb 62 D5
Rayleigh Essex 20 B5
Rayne Essex 30 F4
Rayners Lane London 19 C8
Raynes Park London 19 E9
Reach Cambs 30 B2
Read Lancs 50 F3
Reading Reading 18 D4
Reading Street Kent 13 C8
Reagill Cumb 57 E8
Rearquhar Highld 87 B10
Rearsby Leics 36 D2
Reaster Highld 94 D4
Reawick Shetland 96 J5
Reay Highld 93 C12
Rechullin Highld 85 C13
Reculver Kent 21 E9
Red Dial Cumb 56 B4
Red Hill Worcs 26 C5
Red Houses Jersey 11
Red Lodge Suff 30 A3
Red Rail Hereford 26 F2
Red Rock Gtr Man 43 B8
Red Roses Carms 23 E7
Red Row Northumb 63 D8
Red Street Staffs 44 G2
Red Wharf Bay Anglesey 41 B7
Redberth Pembs 22 F5
Redbourn Herts 29 G8
Redbourne N Lincs 46 C3
Redbrook Mon 26 G2
Redbrook Wrex 33 A11
Redburn Highld 87 E8
Redburn Highld 87 G12
Redburn Northumb 62 G3
Redcar Redcar 59 D7
Redcastle Angus 77 B9
Redcastle Highld 87 G8
Redcliff Bay N Som 15 D10
Redding Falk 69 C8
Reddingmuirhead Falk 69 C8
Reddish Gtr Man 44 C2
Redditch Worcs 27 B7
Rede Suff 30 C5
Redenhall Norf 39 G8
Redesdale Camp Northumb 62 D4
Redesmouth Northumb 62 E4
Redford Aberds 83 F9
Redford Angus 77 C8
Redford Durham 58 C1
Redfordgreen Borders 61 B9
Redgorton Perth 76 E3
Redgrave Suff 38 H6
Redhill Aberds 83 C9
Redhill Aberds 89 E6
Redhill N Som 15 E11
Redhill Sur 19 F9
Redhouse Argyll 73 G7
Redhouses Argyll 64 B4
Redisham Suff 39 G10
Redland Bristol 16 D2
Redland Orkney 95 F4
Redlingfield Suff 31 A8
Redlynch Som 8 A6
Redlynch Wilts 9 B11
Redmarley D'Abitot Glos 26 E4
Redmarshall Stockton 58 D4
Redmile Leics 36 B3
Redmire N Yorks 58 G1
Redmoor Corn 4 E1
Rednal Shrops 33 C9
Redpath Borders 70 G4
Redpoint Highld 85 B12
Redruth Corn 2 E5
Redvales Gtr Man 44 B2
Redwick Newport 15 C10
Redwick S Glos 15 C11
Redworth Darl 58 D3
Reed Herts 29 E10
Reedham Norf 39 E10
Reedness E Yorks 52 G3
Reeds Beck Lincs 46 F6
Reepham Lincs 46 E4
Reepham Norf 39 C6
Reeth N Yorks 58 G1
Regaby IoM 48 C4
Regoul Highld 87 F11
Reiff Highld 92 H2
Reigate Sur 19 F9
Reighton N Yorks 53 B7
Reighton Gap N Yorks 53 B7
Reinigeadal W Isles 90 G7
Reiss Highld 94 E5
Rejerrah Corn 3 D6
Releath Corn 2 F5
Relubbus Corn 2 F4
Relugas Moray 87 G12
Remenham Wokingham 18 C4
Remenham Hill Wokingham 18 C4
Remony Perth 75 C10
Rempstone Notts 36 C1
Rendcomb Glos 27 H7
Rendham Suff 31 B10
Rendlesham Suff 31 C10
Renfrew Renfs 68 D4
Renhold Bedford 29 C7
Renishaw Derbys 45 E8
Rennington Northumb 63 B8
Renton W Dunb 68 C2
Renwick Cumb 57 B7
Repps Norf 39 D10
Repton Derbys 35 C9
Reraig Highld 85 F13
Rescobie Angus 77 B8
Resipole Highld 79 E10
Resolis Highld 87 E9
Resolven Neath 14 A4
Reston Borders 71 D7
Reswallie Angus 77 B8
Retew Corn 3 D8
Retford Notts 45 D11
Rettendon Essex 20 B4
Rettendon Place Essex 20 B4
Revesby Lincs 46 F6
Revesby Bridge Lincs 47 F7
Rew Street IoW 10 E3
Rewe Devon 7 G8
Reydon Suff 39 H10
Reydon Smear Suff 39 H10
Reymerston Norf 38 E6
Reynalton Pembs 22 F5
Reynoldston Swansea 23 G9
Rezare Corn 4 D4
Rhôs Carms 23 C8
Rhôs Neath 14 A3
Rhŷd-y-foel Conwy 42 E2
Rhaeadr Gwy = Rhayader Powys 24 B6
Rhandirmwyn Carms 24 D4
Rhayader = Rhaeadr Gwy Powys 24 B6
Rhedyn Gwyn 40 G4
Rhemore Highld 79 F8
Rhencullen IoM 48 C3
Rhes-y-cae Flint 42 E4
Rhewl Denb 42 F4
Rhewl Denb 42 H4
Rhian Highld 93 H8
Rhicarn Highld 92 G3
Rhiconich Highld 92 D5
Rhicullen Highld 87 D9
Rhidorroch Ho. Highld 86 B4
Rhifail Highld 93 E10
Rhigos Rhondda 24 H6
Rhilochan Highld 93 J10
Rhiroy Highld 86 C4
Rhisga = Risca Caerph 15 B8
Rhiw Gwyn 40 H4
Rhiwabon = Ruabon Wrex 33 A9
Rhiwbina Cardiff 15 C7
Rhiwbryfdir Gwyn 41 F8
Rhiwderin Newport 15 C8
Rhiwlas Gwyn 32 B5
Rhiwlas Gwyn 41 D7
Rhiwlas Powys 33 B7
Rhodes Gtr Man 44 B2
Rhodes Minnis Kent 21 G8
Rhodesia Notts 45 E9

Rho–Sly 149

Rhodiad Pembs 22 D2
Rhondda Rhondda 14 B5
Rhonehouse or Kelton Hill Dumfries 55 D10
Rhoose = Y Rhws V Glam 14 E6
Rhos-fawr Gwyn 40 G5
Rhos-goch Powys 25 D8
Rhos-hill Pembs 22 B6
Rhos-on-Sea Conwy 41 B10
Rhos-y-brithdir Powys 33 C7
Rhos-y-garth Ceredig 24 A3
Rhos-y-gwaliau Gwyn 32 B5
Rhos-y-llan Gwyn 40 G4
Rhos-y-Madoc Wrex 33 A9
Rhos-y-meirch Powys 25 B9
Rhosaman Carms 24 G4
Rhosbeirio Anglesey 40 A5
Rhoscefnhir Anglesey 41 C7
Rhoscolyn Anglesey 40 C4
Rhoscrowther Pembs 22 F4
Rhosesmor Flint 42 F5
Rhosgadfan Gwyn 41 E7
Rhosgoch Anglesey 40 B6
Rhoshirwaun Gwyn 40 H3
Rhoslan Gwyn 40 F6
Rhoslefain Gwyn 32 E1
Rhosllanerchrugog Wrex 42 H5
Rhosmaen Carms 24 F3
Rhosmeirch Anglesey 40 C6
Rhosneigr Anglesey 40 C5
Rhosnesni Wrex 42 G6
Rhosrobin Wrex 42 G6
Rhossili Swansea 23 H9
Rhosson Pembs 22 D2
Rhostryfan Gwyn 40 E6
Rhostyllen Wrex 42 H6
Rhosybol Anglesey 40 B6
Rhu Argyll 73 E11
Rhu Argyll 73 G7
Rhuallt Denb 42 E3
Rhuddall Heath Ches W 43 F8
Rhuddlan Ceredig 23 B9
Rhuddlan Denb 42 E3
Rhue Highld 86 B3
Rhulen Powys 25 D8
Rhunahaorine Argyll 65 D8
Rhuthun = Ruthin Denb 42 G4
Rhyd Gwyn 41 F8
Rhyd Powys 32 E5
Rhyd-Ddu Gwyn 41 E7
Rhyd-moel-ddu Powys 33 H6
Rhyd-Rosser Ceredig 24 B2
Rhyd-uchaf Gwyn 32 B5
Rhyd-wen Gwyn 32 D3
Rhyd-y-clafdy Gwyn 40 G5
Rhyd-y-fro Neath 24 H4
Rhyd-y-gwin Swansea 14 A2
Rhyd-y-meirch Mon 25 H10
Rhyd-y-meudwy Denb 42 G4
Rhyd-y-pandy Swansea 14 A2
Rhyd-y-sarn Gwyn 41 F8
Rhyd-yr-onen Gwyn 32 E2
Rhydaman = Ammanford Carms 24 G3
Rhydargaeau Carms 23 D9
Rhydcymerau Carms 23 C10
Rhydd Worcs 26 D5
Rhydding Neath 14 B3
Rhydfudr Ceredig 24 B2
Rhydlewis Ceredig 23 B8
Rhydlios Gwyn 40 G3
Rhydlydan Conwy 41 E10
Rhydness Powys 25 D8
Rhydowen Ceredig 23 B9
Rhydspence Hereford 25 D9
Rhydtalog Flint 42 G5
Rhydwyn Anglesey 40 B5
Rhydycroesau Powys 33 B8
Rhydyfelin Ceredig 32 H1
Rhydyfelin Rhondda 14 C6
Rhydymain Gwyn 32 C4
Rhydymwyn Flint 42 F5
Rhyl = Y Rhyl Denb 42 D3
Rhymney = Rhymni Caerph 25 H8
Rhymni = Rhymney Caerph 25 H8
Rhynd Fife 77 E7
Rhynd Perth 76 E4
Rhynie Aberds 82 A6
Rhynie Highld 87 D11
Ribbesford Worcs 26 A4
Ribblehead N Yorks 50 B3
Ribbleton Lancs 50 F1
Ribchester Lancs 50 F2
Ribigill Highld 93 D8
Riby Lincs 46 B5
Riby Cross Roads Lincs 46 B5
Riccall N Yorks 52 F2
Riccarton E Ayrs 67 C7
Richards Castle Hereford 25 B11
Richings Park Bucks 19 D7
Richmond London 19 D8
Richmond N Yorks 58 F2
Rickarton Aberds 83 E10
Rickinghall Suff 38 H6
Rickleton T&W 58 A3
Rickling Essex 29 E11
Rickmansworth Herts 19 B7
Riddings Cumb 61 F10
Riddings Derbys 45 G8
Riddlecombe Devon 6 E5
Riddlesden W Yorks 51 E6
Riddrie Glasgow 68 D5
Ridge Dorset 9 F8
Ridge Hants 10 C2
Ridge Wilts 9 A8
Ridge Green Sur 19 G10
Ridge Lane Warks 35 F8
Ridgebourne Powys 25 B7
Ridgehill N Som 15 E11
Ridgeway Cross Hereford 26 D4
Ridgewell Essex 30 D4
Ridgewood E Sus 12 E3
Ridgmont C Beds 28 E6
Riding Mill Northumb 62 G6
Ridleywood Wrex 43 G7
Ridlington Norf 39 B9
Ridlington Rutland 36 E4
Ridsdale Northumb 62 E5
Riechip Perth 76 C3
Riemore Perth 76 C3
Rienachait Highld 92 F3
Rievaulx N Yorks 59 H6
Rift House Hrtlpl 58 C5
Rigg Dumfries 61 G8
Riggend N Lanark 68 C6
Rigsby Lincs 47 E8
Rigside S Lanark 69 G7
Riley Green Lancs 50 G2
Rileyhill Staffs 35 D7
Rilla Mill Corn 4 D3
Rillington N Yorks 52 B4
Rimington Lancs 50 E4
Rimpton Som 8 B5
Rimswell E Yorks 53 G9
Rinaston Pembs 22 D4
Ringasta Shetland 96 M5
Ringford Dumfries 55 D9
Ringinglow S Yorks 44 D6
Ringland Norf 39 D7
Ringles Cross E Sus 12 D3
Ringmer E Sus 12 E3
Ringmore Devon 5 G7
Ringorm Moray 88 D2
Ring's End Cambs 37 E9
Ringsfield Suff 39 G10
Ringsfield Corner Suff 39 G10
Ringshall Herts 28 G6
Ringshall Suff 31 C7
Ringshall Stocks Suff 31 C7
Ringstead Norf 38 A3
Ringstead Northants 36 H5
Ringwood Hants 9 D10
Ringwould Kent 21 G10
Rinmore Aberds 82 B6
Rinnigill Orkney 95 J4
Rinsey Corn 2 G4
Riof W Isles 90 D6
Ripe E Sus 12 E4
Ripley Derbys 45 G7
Ripley Hants 9 E10
Ripley N Yorks 51 C8
Ripley Sur 19 F7
Riplingham E Yorks 52 F5
Ripon N Yorks 51 B9
Rippingale Lincs 37 C6
Ripple Kent 21 G10
Ripple Worcs 26 E5
Ripponden W Yorks 50 H6
Rireavach Highld 86 B3
Risabus Argyll 64 D4
Risbury Hereford 26 C2
Risby Suff 30 B4
Risca = Rhisga Caerph 15 B8
Rise E Yorks 53 E7
Riseden E Sus 12 C5
Risegate Lincs 37 C8
Riseholme Lincs 46 E3
Riseley Bedford 29 B7
Riseley Wokingham 18 E4
Rishangles Suff 31 B8
Rishton Lancs 50 F3
Rishworth W Yorks 50 H6
Rising Bridge Lancs 50 G3
Risley Derbys 35 B10
Risley Warr 43 C9
Risplith N Yorks 51 C8
Rispond Highld 92 C7
Rivar Wilts 17 E10
Rivenhall End Essex 30 G5
River Bank Cambs 30 B2
Riverhead Kent 20 F2
Rivington Lancs 43 A9
Roa Island Cumb 49 C2
Roachill Devon 7 D7
Road Green Norf 39 F8
Roade Northants 28 C4
Roadhead Cumb 61 F11
Roadmeetings S Lanark 69 F7
Roadside Highld 94 D3
Roadside of Catterline Aberds 83 F10
Roadside of Kinneff Aberds 83 F10
Roadwater Som 7 C9
Roag Highld 85 D7
Roath Cardiff 15 D7
Roberton Borders 61 B10
Roberton S Lanark 69 H8
Robertsbridge E Sus 12 D6
Roberttown W Yorks 51 G7
Robeston Cross Pembs 22 F3
Robeston Wathen Pembs 22 E5
Robin Hood W Yorks 51 G9
Robin Hood's Bay N Yorks 59 F10
Roborough Devon 4 E6
Roborough Devon 6 E4
Roby Mers 43 C7
Roby Mill Lancs 43 B8
Rocester Staffs 35 B7
Roch Pembs 22 D3
Roch Gate Pembs 22 D3
Rochdale Gtr Man 44 A2
Roche Corn 3 C8
Rochester Medway 20 E4
Rochester Northumb 62 D4
Rochford Essex 20 B5
Rock Corn 3 B8
Rock Northumb 63 A8
Rock W Sus 11 C10
Rock Worcs 26 A4
Rock Ferry Mers 42 D6
Rockbeare Devon 7 G9
Rockbourne Hants 9 C10
Rockcliffe Cumb 61 G9
Rockcliffe Dumfries 55 D11
Rockfield Highld 87 C12
Rockfield Mon 25 G11
Rockford Hants 9 D10
Rockhampton S Glos 16 B3
Rockingham Northants 36 F4
Rockland All Saints Norf 38 F5
Rockland St Mary Norf 39 E9
Rockland St Peter Norf 38 F5
Rockley Wilts 17 D8
Rockwell End Bucks 18 C4
Rockwell Green Som 7 D10
Rodborough Glos 16 A5
Rodbourne Swindon 17 C8
Rodbourne Wilts 16 C6
Rodbourne Cheney Swindon 17 C8
Rodd Hereford 25 B10
Roddam Northumb 62 A6
Rodden Dorset 8 F5
Rode Som 16 F5
Rode Heath Ches E 44 G2
Rodeheath Ches E 44 F2
Roden Telford 34 D1
Rodhuish Som 7 C9
Rodington Telford 34 D1
Rodley Glos 26 G4
Rodley W Yorks 51 F8
Rodmarton Glos 16 B6
Rodmell E Sus 12 F3
Rodmersham Kent 20 E6
Rodney Stoke Som 15 F10
Rodsley Derbys 35 A8
Rodway Som 15 H8
Rodwell Dorset 8 G5
Roe Green Herts 29 E10
Roecliffe N Yorks 51 C9
Roehampton London 19 D9
Roesound Shetland 96 G5
Roffey W Sus 11 A10
Rogart Highld 93 J10
Rogart Station Highld 93 J10
Rogate W Sus 11 B7
Rogerstone Newport 15 C8
Roghadal W Isles 90 J5
Rogiet Mon 15 C10
Rogue's Alley Cambs 37 E9
Roke Oxon 18 B3
Roker T&W 63 H10
Rollesby Norf 39 D10
Rolleston Leics 36 E3
Rolleston Notts 45 G11
Rolleston-on-Dove Staffs 35 C8
Rolston E Yorks 53 E8
Rolvenden Kent 13 C7
Rolvenden Layne Kent 13 C7
Romaldkirk Durham 57 D11
Romanby N Yorks 58 G4
Romannobridge Borders 69 F10
Romansleigh Devon 7 D6
Romford London 20 C2
Romiley Gtr Man 44 C3
Romsey Hants 10 B2
Romsey Town Cambs 29 C11
Romsley Shrops 34 G3
Romsley Worcs 34 H5
Ronague IoM 48 E2
Rookhope Durham 57 B11
Rookley IoW 10 F4
Rooks Bridge Som 15 F9
Roos E Yorks 53 F8
Roosebeck Cumb 49 C2
Rootham's Green Bedford 29 C8
Rootpark S Lanark 69 E8
Ropley Hants 10 A5
Ropley Dean Hants 10 A5
Ropsley Lincs 36 B5
Rora Aberds 89 C10
Rorandle Aberds 83 B8
Rorrington Shrops 33 E9
Roscroggan Corn 2 E5
Rose Corn 3 D6
Rose Ash Devon 7 D6
Rose Green W Sus 11 E8
Rose Grove Lancs 50 F4
Rose Hill E Sus 12 E3
Rose Hill Lancs 50 F4
Rose Hill Suff 31 D8
Roseacre Kent 20 F4
Roseacre Lancs 49 F4
Rosebank S Lanark 69 F7
Rosebrough Northumb 71 H10
Rosebush Pembs 22 D5
Rosecare Corn 4 B2
Rosedale Abbey N Yorks 59 G8
Roseden Northumb 62 A6
Rosefield Highld 87 F11
Rosehall Highld 92 J7
Rosehaugh Mains Highld 87 F9
Rosehearty Aberds 89 B9
Rosehill Shrops 34 B2
Roseisle Moray 88 B1
Roselands E Sus 12 F5
Rosemarket Pembs 22 F4
Rosemarkie Highld 87 F10
Rosemary Lane Devon 7 E10
Rosemount Perth 76 C4
Rosenannon Corn 3 C8
Rosewell Midloth 69 D11
Roseworth Stockton 58 D5
Roseworthy Corn 2 F5
Rosgill Cumb 57 E7
Roshven Highld 79 D10
Roskhill Highld 85 D7
Roskill House Highld 87 F9
Rosley Cumb 56 B5
Roslin Midloth 69 D11
Rosliston Derbys 35 D8
Rosneath Argyll 73 E11
Ross Dumfries 55 E9
Ross Northumb 71 G10
Ross Perth 75 E10
Ross-on-Wye Hereford 26 F3
Rossett Wrex 42 G6
Rossett Green N Yorks 51 D9
Rossie Ochill Perth 76 F3
Rossie Priory Perth 76 D5
Rossington S Yorks 45 C10
Rosskeen Highld 87 E9
Rossland Renfs 68 C3
Roster Highld 94 G4
Rostherne Ches E 43 D10
Rosthwaite Cumb 56 E4
Roston Derbys 35 A7
Rosyth Fife 69 B10
Rothbury Northumb 62 C6
Rotherby Leics 36 D2
Rotherfield E Sus 12 D4
Rotherfield Greys Oxon 18 C4
Rotherfi eld Peppard Oxon 18 C4
Rotherham S Yorks 45 C8
Rothersthorpe Northants 28 C4
Rotherwick Hants 18 F4
Rothes Moray 88 D2
Rothesay Argyll 73 G9
Rothiebrisbane Aberds 89 E7
Rothienorman Aberds 89 E7
Rothiesholm Orkney 95 F7
Rothley Leics 36 D1
Rothley Northumb 62 E6
Rothley Shield East Northumb 62 D6
Rothmaise Aberds 89 E6
Rothwell Lincs 46 C5
Rothwell Northants 36 G4
Rothwell W Yorks 51 G9
Rothwell Haigh W Yorks 51 G9
Rotsea E Yorks 53 D6
Rottal Angus 82 G5
Rotten End Suff 31 B10
Rottingdean Brighton 12 F2
Rottington Cumb 56 E1
Roud IoW 10 F4
Rough Close Staffs 34 B5
Rough Common Kent 21 F8
Rougham Norf 38 C4
Rougham Suff 30 B6
Rougham Green Suff 30 B6
Roughburn Highld 80 E5
Roughlee Lancs 50 E4
Roughley W Mid 35 F7
Roughsike Cumb 61 F11
Roughton Lincs 46 F6
Roughton Norf 39 B8
Roughton Shrops 34 F3
Roughton Moor Lincs 46 F6
Roundhay W Yorks 51 F9
Roundstonefoot Dumfries 61 C7
Roundstreet Common W Sus 11 B9
Roundway Wilts 17 E7
Rous Lench Worcs 27 C7
Rousdon Devon 8 E1
Routenburn N Ayrs 73 G10
Routh E Yorks 53 E6
Row Corn 4 D1
Row Cumb 56 H6
Row Heath Essex 31 G8
Rowanburn Dumfries 61 F10
Rowardennan Stirling 74 H6
Rowde Wilts 16 E6
Rowen Conwy 41 C9
Rowfoot Northumb 62 G2
Rowhedge Essex 31 F7
Rowhook W Sus 11 A10
Rowington Warks 27 B9
Rowland Derbys 44 E6
Rowlands Castle Hants 10 C6
Rowlands Gill T&W 63 H7
Rowledge Sur 18 G5
Rowlestone Hereford 25 F10
Rowley E Yorks 52 F5
Rowley Shrops 33 E9
Rowley Hill W Yorks 44 A5
Rowley Regis W Mid 34 G5
Rowly Sur 19 G7
Rowney Green Worcs 27 A7
Rownhams Hants 10 C2
Rowrah Cumb 56 E2
Rowsham Bucks 28 G5
Rowsley Derbys 44 F6
Rowstock Oxon 17 C11
Rowston Lincs 46 G4
Rowton Ches W 43 F7
Rowton Shrops 33 D9
Rowton Telford 34 D2
Roxburgh Borders 70 G6
Roxby N Lincs 52 H5
Roxby N Yorks 59 E8
Roxton Bedford 29 C8
Roxwell Essex 30 H3
Royal Leamington Spa Warks 27 B10
Royal Oak Darl 58 D3
Royal Oak Lancs 43 B7
Royal Tunbridge Wells Kent 12 C4
Royal Wootton Bassett Wilts 17 C7
Roybridge Highld 80 E4
Roydhouse W Yorks 44 A6
Roydon Essex 29 H11
Roydon Norf 38 C3
Roydon Norf 39 G6
Roydon Hamlet Essex 29 H11
Royston Herts 29 D10
Royston S Yorks 45 A7
Royton Gtr Man 44 B3
Rozel Jersey 11
Ruabon = Rhiwabon Wrex 33 A9
Ruaig Argyll 78 G3
Ruan Lanihorne Corn 3 E7
Ruan Minor Corn 2 H6
Ruarach Highld 80 A1
Ruardean Glos 26 G3
Ruardean Woodside Glos 26 G3
Rubery Worcs 34 H5
Ruckcroft Cumb 57 B7
Ruckhall Hereford 25 E11
Ruckinge Kent 13 C9
Ruckland Lincs 47 E7
Ruckley Shrops 33 E11
Rudbaxton Pembs 22 D4
Rudby N Yorks 58 F5
Ruddington Notts 36 B1
Rudford Glos 26 F4
Rudge Shrops 34 F4
Rudge Som 16 F5
Rudgeway S Glos 16 C3
Rudgwick W Sus 11 A9
Rudhall Hereford 26 F3
Rudheath Ches W 43 E9
Rudley Green Essex 20 A5
Rudry Caerph 15 C7
Rudston E Yorks 53 C6
Rudyard Staffs 44 G3
Rufford Lancs 49 H4
Rufforth York 51 D11
Rugby Warks 35 H11
Rugeley Staffs 34 D6
Ruglen S Ayrs 66 F5
Ruilick Highld 87 G8
Ruishton Som 8 B1
Ruisigearraidh W Isles 90 J4
Ruislip London 19 C7
Ruislip Common London 19 C7
Rumbling Bridge Perth 76 H3
Rumburgh Suff 39 G9
Rumford Corn 3 B7
Rumney Cardiff 15 D8
Runcorn Halton 43 D8
Runcton W Sus 11 D7
Runcton Holme Norf 38 E2
Rundlestone Devon 5 D6
Runfold Sur 18 G5
Runhall Norf 39 E6
Runham Norf 39 D10
Runham Norf 39 E11
Runnington Som 7 D10
Runsell Green Essex 30 H4
Runswick Bay N Yorks 59 E9
Runwell Essex 20 B4
Ruscombe Wokingham 18 D4
Rush Green London 20 C2
Rush-head Aberds 89 D8
Rushall Hereford 26 E3
Rushall Norf 39 G7
Rushall W Mid 34 E6
Rushall Wilts 17 F8
Rushbrooke Suff 30 B5
Rushbury Shrops 33 F11
Rushden Herts 29 E10
Rushden Northants 28 B6
Rushenden Kent 20 D6
Rushford Norf 38 G5
Rushlake Green E Sus 12 E5
Rushmere Suff 39 G10
Rushmere St Andrew Suff 31 D9
Rushmoor Sur 18 G5
Rushock Worcs 26 A5
Rusholme Gtr Man 44 C2
Rushton Ches W 43 F8
Rushton Northants 36 G4
Rushton Shrops 34 E2
Rushton Spencer Staffs 44 F3
Rushwick Worcs 26 C5
Rushyford Durham 58 D3
Ruskie Stirling 75 G9
Ruskington Lincs 46 G4
Rusland Cumb 56 H5
Rusper W Sus 19 H9
Ruspidge Glos 26 G3
Russell's Water Oxon 18 C4
Russel's Green Suff 31 A9
Rusthall Kent 12 C4
Rustington W Sus 11 D9
Ruston N Yorks 52 A5
Ruston Parva E Yorks 53 C6
Ruswarp N Yorks 59 F9
Rutherford Borders 70 G5
Rutherglen S Lanark 68 D5
Ruthernbridge Corn 3 C9
Ruthin = Rhuthun Denb 42 G4
Ruthrieston Aberdeen 83 C11
Ruthven Aberds 88 D5
Ruthven Angus 76 C5
Ruthven Highld 81 D9
Ruthven Highld 87 H11
Ruthven House Angus 76 C6
Ruthvoes Corn 3 C8
Ruthwell Dumfries 60 G6
Ruyton-XI-Towns Shrops 33 C9
Ryal Northumb 62 F6
Ryal Fold Blackburn 50 G2
Ryall Dorset 8 E3
Ryarsh Kent 20 F3
Rydal Cumb 56 F5
Ryde IoW 10 E4
Rye E Sus 13 D8
Rye Foreign E Sus 13 D7
Rye Harbour E Sus 13 E8
Rye Park Herts 29 G10
Rye Street Worcs 26 E4
Ryecroft Gate Staffs 44 F3
Ryehill E Yorks 53 G8
Ryhall Rutland 36 D6
Ryhill W Yorks 45 A7
Ryhope T&W 58 A5
Rylstone N Yorks 50 D5
Ryme Intrinseca Dorset 8 C4
Ryther N Yorks 52 F1
Ryton Glos 26 E4
Ryton N Yorks 52 B3
Ryton Shrops 34 E3
Ryton T&W 63 G7
Ryton-on-Dunsmore Warks 27 A10

S

Sabden Lancs 50 F3
Sacombe Herts 29 G10
Sacriston Durham 58 B3
Sadberge Darl 58 E4
Saddell Argyll 65 E8
Saddington Leics 36 F2
Saddle Bow Norf 38 D2
Saddlescombe W Sus 12 E1
Sadgill Cumb 57 F6
Saffron Walden Essex 30 E2
Sageston Pembs 22 F5
Saham Hills Norf 38 E5
Saham Toney Norf 38 E5
Saighdinis W Isles 84 B3
Saighton Ches W 43 F7
St Abbs Borders 71 D8
St. Abb's Haven Borders 71 D8
St Agnes Corn 2 D6
St Agnes Scilly 2 D2
St Albans Herts 29 H8
St Allen Corn 3 D7
St Andrews Fife 77 F8
St Andrew's Major V Glam 15 D7
St Anne Ald 11
St Annes Lancs 49 G3
St Ann's Dumfries 60 D6
St Ann's Chapel Corn 4 D5
St Ann's Chapel Devon 5 G7
St Anthony-in-Meneage Corn 3 G6
St Anthony's Hill E Sus 12 F5
St Arvans Mon 15 B11
St Asaph = Llanelwy Denb 42 E3
St Athan V Glam 14 E6
St Aubin Jersey 11
St Austell Corn 3 D9
St Bees Cumb 56 E1
St Blazey Corn 4 F1
St Boswells Borders 70 G4
St Brelade Jersey 11
St Breock Corn 3 B8
St Breward Corn 4 D1
St Briavels Glos 16 A2
St Bride's Pembs 22 E3
St Brides Major V Glam 14 D4
St Bride's Netherwent Mon 15 C10
St Brides super Ely V Glam 14 D6
St Brides Wentlooge Newport 15 C8
St Budeaux Plym 4 F5
St Buryan Corn 2 G3
St Catherine Bath 16 D4
St Catherine's Argyll 73 C10
St Clears = Sanclêr Carms 23 E7
St Cleer Corn 4 E3
St Clement Corn 3 E7
St Clements Jersey 11
St Clether Corn 4 C3
St Colmac Argyll 73 G9
St Columb Major Corn 3 C8
St Columb Minor Corn 3 C7
St Columb Road Corn 3 D8
St Combs Aberds 89 B10
St Cross South Elmham Suff 39 G8
St Cyrus Aberds 77 A10
St David's = Tyddewi Pembs 22 D2
St David's Perth 76 E2
St Day Corn 2 E6
St Dennis Corn 3 D8
St Devereux Hereford 25 E11
St Dogmaels Pembs 22 B6
St Dogwells Pembs 22 D4
St Dominick Corn 4 E5
St Donat's V Glam 14 E5
St Edith's Wilts 16 E6
St Endellion Corn 3 B8
St Enoder Corn 3 D7
St Erme Corn 3 D7
St Erney Corn 4 F4
St Erth Corn 2 F4
St Ervan Corn 3 B7
St Eval Corn 3 C7
St Ewe Corn 3 E8
St Fagans Cardiff 15 D7
St Fergus Aberds 89 C10
St Fillans Perth 75 E9
St Florence Pembs 22 F5
St Genny's Corn 4 B2
St George Conwy 42 E2
St George's V Glam 14 D6
St Germans Corn 4 F4
St Giles Lincs 46 E3
St Giles in the Wood Devon 6 E4
St Giles on the Hth. Devon 6 G2
St Harmon Powys 24 A6
St Helen Auckland Durham 58 D2
St Helena Warks 35 E8
St Helen's E Sus 13 E7
St Helens IoW 10 F5
St Helens Mers 43 C8
St Helier Jersey 11
St Helier London 19 E9
St Hilary Corn 2 F4
St Hilary V Glam 14 D6
Saint Hill W Sus 12 C2
St Illtyd Bl Gwent 15 A8
St Ippollytts Herts 29 F8
St Ishmael's Pembs 22 F3
St Issey Corn 3 B8
St Ive Corn 4 E4
St Ives Cambs 29 A10
St Ives Corn 2 E4
St Ives Dorset 9 D10
St James South Elmham Suff 39 G9
St Jidgey Corn 3 C8
St John Corn 4 F5
St John's IoM 48 D2
St John's Jersey 11
St John's Sur 18 F6
St John's Worcs 26 C5
St John's Chapel Durham 57 C10
St John's Fen End Norf 37 D11
St John's Highway Norf 37 D11
St John's Town of Dalry Dumfries 55 A9
St Judes IoM 48 C3
St Just in Roseland Corn 3 F7
St Just Corn 2 F2
St Katherine's Aberds 89 E7
St Keverne Corn 3 G6
St Kew Corn 3 B9
St Kew Highway Corn 3 B9
St Keyne Corn 4 E3
St Lawrence Corn 3 C9
St Lawrence Essex 20 A6
St Lawrence IoW 10 G4
St Leonard's Bucks 28 H6
St Leonards Dorset 9 D10
St Leonards E Sus 13 F6
Saint Leonards S Lanark 68 E5
St Levan Corn 2 G2
St Lythans V Glam 15 D7
St Mabyn Corn 3 B9
St Madoes Perth 76 E4
St Margaret South Elmham Suff 39 G9
St Margaret's Hereford 25 E10
St Margarets Herts 29 G10
St Margaret's at Cliffe Kent 21 G10
St. Margaret's Hope Orkney 95 J5
St Mark's IoM 48 E2
St Martin Corn 4 F3
St Martins Corn 2 G6
St Martin's Jersey 11
St Martins Perth 76 D4
St Martin's Shrops 33 B9
St Mary Bourne Hants 17 F11
St Mary Church V Glam 14 D6
St Mary Cray London 19 E11
St Mary Hill V Glam 14 D5
St Mary Hoo Medway 20 D5
St Mary in the Marsh Kent 13 D9
St Mary's Jersey 11
St Mary's Orkney 95 H5
St Mary's Bay Kent 13 D9
St Maughans Mon 25 G11
St Mawes Corn 3 F7
St Mawgan Corn 3 C7
St Mellion Corn 4 E4
St Mellons Cardiff 15 C8
St Merryn Corn 3 B7
St Mewan Corn 3 D8
St Michael Caerhays Corn 3 E8
St Michael Penkevil Corn 3 E7
St Michael South Elmham Suff 39 G9
St Michael's Kent 13 C7
St Michaels Worcs 26 B2
St Michael's on Wyre Lancs 49 E4
St Minver Corn 3 B8
St Monans Fife 77 G8
St Neot Corn 4 E2
St Neots Cambs 29 B8
St Newlyn East Corn 3 D7
St Nicholas Pembs 22 C3
St Nicholas V Glam 14 D6
St Nicholas at Wade Kent 21 E9
St Ninians Stirling 68 A6
St Osyth Essex 31 G8
St Osyth Heath Essex 31 G8
St Ouens Jersey 11
St Owens Cross Hereford 26 F2
St Paul's Cray London 19 E11
St Paul's Walden Herts 29 F8
St Peter Port Guern 11
St Peter's Jersey 11
St Peter's Kent 21 E10
St Petrox Pembs 22 G4
St Pinnock Corn 4 E3
St Quivox S Ayrs 67 D6
St Ruan Corn 2 H6
St Sampson Guern 11
St Stephen Corn 3 D8
St Stephen's Corn 4 C4
St Stephens Corn 4 F5
St Stephens Herts 29 H8
St Teath Corn 4 C1
St Thomas Devon 7 G8
St Tudy Corn 4 D1
St Twynnells Pembs 22 G4
St Veep Corn 4 F2
St Vigeans Angus 77 C9
St Wenn Corn 3 C8
St Weonards Hereford 25 F11
Saintbury Glos 27 E8
Salcombe Devon 5 H8
Salcombe Regis Devon 7 H10
Salcott Essex 30 G6
Sale Gtr Man 43 C10
Sale Green Worcs 26 C6
Saleby Lincs 47 E8
Salehurst E Sus 12 D6
Salem Carms 24 F3
Salem Ceredig 32 G2
Salen Argyll 79 G8
Salen Highld 79 E9
Salesbury Lancs 50 F2
Salford C Beds 28 E6
Salford Gtr Man 44 C2
Salford Oxon 27 F9
Salford Priors Warks 27 C7
Salfords Sur 19 G9
Salhouse Norf 39 D9
Saline Fife 69 A9
Salisbury Wilts 9 B10
Sallachan Highld 74 A2
Sallachy Highld 86 H2
Sallachy Highld 93 J8
Salle Norf 39 C7
Salmonby Lincs 47 E7
Salmond's Muir Angus 77 D8
Salperton Glos 27 F7
Salph End Bedford 29 C7
Salsburgh N Lanark 69 D7
Salt Staffs 34 C5
Salt End E Yorks 53 G7
Saltaire W Yorks 51 F7
Saltash Corn 4 F5
Saltburn Highld 87 E10
Saltburn-by-the-Sea Redcar 59 D7
Saltby Leics 36 C4
Saltcoats Cumb 56 G2
Saltcoats N Ayrs 66 B5
Saltdean Brighton 12 F2
Salter Lancs 50 C2
Salterforth Lancs 50 E4
Salterswall Ches W 43 F9
Saltfleet Lincs 47 C8
Saltfleetby All Saints Lincs 47 C8
Saltfleetby St Clements Lincs 47 C8
Saltfleetby St Peter Lincs 47 D8
Saltford Bath 16 E3
Salthouse Norf 39 A6
Saltmarshe E Yorks 52 G3
Saltney Flint 43 F6
Salton N Yorks 52 B3
Saltwick Northumb 63 F7
Saltwood Kent 21 H8
Salum Argyll 78 G3
Salvington W Sus 11 D10
Salwarpe Worcs 26 B5
Salwayash Dorset 8 E3
Sambourne Warks 27 B7
Sambrook Telford 34 C3
Samhla W Isles 84 B2
Samlesbury Lancs 50 F1
Samlesbury Bottoms Lancs 50 G2
Sampford Arundel Som 7 E10
Sampford Brett Som 7 B9
Sampford Courtenay Devon 6 F5
Sampford Peverell Devon 7 E9
Sampford Spiney Devon 4 D6
Sampool Bridge Cumb 56 H6
Samuelston E Loth 70 C3
Sanachan Highld 85 D13
Sanaigmore Argyll 64 A3
Sanclêr = St Clears Carms 23 E7
Sancreed Corn 2 G3
Sancton E Yorks 52 F5
Sand Highld 86 B2
Sand Shetland 96 J5
Sand Hole E Yorks 52 F4
Sand Hutton N Yorks 52 D2
Sandaig Highld 85 H12
Sandal Magna W Yorks 51 H9
Sandale Cumb 56 B4
Sandbach Ches E 43 F10
Sandbank Argyll 73 E10
Sandbanks Poole 9 F9
Sandend Aberds 88 B5
Sanderstead London 19 E10
Sandfields Glos 26 F6
Sandford Cumb 57 E9
Sandford Devon 7 F7
Sandford Dorset 9 F8
Sandford IoW 10 F4
Sandford N Som 15 F10
Sandford S Lanark 68 F6
Sandford Shrops 34 B1
Sandford on Thames Oxon 18 A2
Sandford Orcas Dorset 8 B5
Sandford St Martin Oxon 27 F11
Sandfordhill Aberds 89 D11
Sandgate Kent 21 H8
Sandgreen Dumfries 55 D8
Sandhaven Aberds 89 B9
Sandhead Dumfries 54 E3
Sandhills Sur 18 H6
Sandhoe Northumb 62 G5
Sandholme E Yorks 52 F4
Sandholme Lincs 37 B9
Sandhurst Brack 18 E5
Sandhurst Glos 26 F5
Sandhurst Kent 13 D6
Sandhurst Cross Kent 13 D6
Sandhutton N Yorks 51 A9
Sandiacre Derbys 35 B10
Sandilands Lincs 47 D9
Sandilands S Lanark 69 G7
Sandiway Ches W 43 E9
Sandleheath Hants 9 C10
Sandling Kent 20 F4
Sandlow Green Ches E 43 F10
Sandness Shetland 96 H3
Sandon Essex 20 A4
Sandon Herts 29 E10
Sandon Staffs 34 B5
Sandown IoW 10 F4
Sandplace Corn 4 F3
Sandridge Herts 29 G8
Sandridge Wilts 16 E6
Sandringham Norf 38 C2
Sandsend N Yorks 59 E9
Sandside Ho. Highld 93 C12
Sandsound Shetland 96 J5
Sandtoft N Lincs 45 B11
Sandway Kent 20 F5
Sandwell W Mid 34 G6
Sandwich Kent 21 F10
Sandwick Cumb 56 E6
Sandwick Orkney 95 K5
Sandwick Shetland 96 L6
Sandwith Cumb 56 E1
Sandy C Beds 29 D8
Sandy Carms 23 F9
Sandy Bank Lincs 46 G6
Sandy Haven Pembs 22 F3
Sandy Lane Wilts 16 E6
Sandy Lane Wrex 33 A9
Sandycroft Flint 42 F6
Sandyford Dumfries 61 D8
Sandyford Stoke 44 G2
Sandygate IoM 48 C3
Sandyhills Dumfries 55 D11
Sandylands Lancs 49 C4
Sandypark Devon 5 C8
Sandysike Cumb 61 G9
Sangobeg Highld 92 C7
Sangomore Highld 92 C7
Sanna Highld 78 E7
Sanndabhaig W Isles 84 D3
Sanndabhaig W Isles 91 D9
Sannox N Ayrs 66 B3
Sanquhar Dumfries 60 C3
Santon N Lincs 46 A3
Santon Bridge Cumb 56 F3
Santon Downham Suff 38 G4
Sapcote Leics 35 F10
Sapey Common Hereford 26 B4
Sapiston Suff 38 H5
Sapley Cambs 29 A9
Sapperton Glos 16 A6
Sapperton Lincs 36 B6
Saracen's Head Lincs 37 C9
Sarclet Highld 94 F5
Sardis Carms 23 F10
Sarn Bridgend 14 C5
Sarn Powys 33 F8
Sarn Bach Gwyn 40 H5
Sarn Meyllteyrn Gwyn 40 G4
Sarnau Carms 23 E8
Sarnau Ceredig 23 A8
Sarnau Gwyn 32 B5
Sarnau Powys 25 E7
Sarnau Powys 33 D8
Sarnesfield Hereford 25 C10
Saron Carms 23 C8
Saron Carms 24 G3
Saron Denb 42 F3
Saron Gwyn 40 E6
Saron Gwyn 41 D7
Sarratt Herts 19 B7
Sarre Kent 21 E9
Sarsden Oxon 27 F9
Sarsgrum Highld 92 C6
Satley Durham 58 B2
Satron N Yorks 57 G11
Satterleigh Devon 6 D5
Satterthwaite Cumb 56 G5
Satwell Oxon 18 C4
Sauchen Aberds 83 B8
Saucher Perth 76 D4
Sauchie Clack 69 A7
Sauchieburn Aberds 83 G8
Saughall Ches W 42 E6
Saughtree Borders 61 D11
Saul Glos 26 H4
Saundby Notts 45 D11
Saundersfoot Pembs 22 F6
Saunderton Bucks 18 A4
Saunton Devon 6 C3
Sausthorpe Lincs 47 F7
Saval Highld 93 J8
Savary Highld 79 G9
Savile Park W Yorks 51 G6
Sawbridge Warks 28 B2
Sawbridgeworth Herts 29 G11
Sawdon N Yorks 59 H10
Sawley Derbys 35 B10
Sawley Lancs 50 E3
Sawley N Yorks 51 C8
Sawston Cambs 29 D11
Sawtry Cambs 37 G7
Saxby Leics 36 D4
Saxby Lincs 46 D4
Saxby All Saints N Lincs 52 H5
Saxelbye Leics 36 C3
Saxham Street Suff 31 B7
Saxilby Lincs 46 E2
Saxlingham Norf 38 B6
Saxlingham Green Norf 39 F8
Saxlingham Nethergate Norf 39 F8
Saxlingham Thorpe Norf 39 F8
Saxmundham Suff 31 B10
Saxon Street Cambs 30 C3
Saxondale Notts 36 B2
Saxtead Suff 31 B9
Saxtead Green Suff 31 B9
Saxthorpe Norf 39 B7
Saxton N Yorks 51 F10
Sayers Common W Sus 12 E1
Scackleton N Yorks 52 B2
Scadabhagh W Isles 90 H6
Scaftworth Notts 45 C10
Scagglethorpe N Yorks 52 B4
Scaitcliffe Lancs 50 G3
Scalasaig Argyll 72 D2
Scalby E Yorks 52 G4
Scalby N Yorks 59 G11
Scaldwell Northants 28 A4
Scale Houses Cumb 57 B7
Scaleby Cumb 61 G10
Scaleby Hill Cumb 61 G10
Scales Cumb 49 B2
Scales Cumb 56 D5
Scales Lancs 49 F4
Scalford Leics 36 C3
Scaling Redcar 59 E8
Scallastle Argyll 79 H9
Scalloway Shetland 96 K6
Scalpay W Isles 90 H7
Scalpay Ho. Highld 85 F11
Scalpsie Argyll 73 H9
Scamadale Highld 79 B10
Scamblesby Lincs 46 E6
Scamodale Highld 79 D11
Scampston N Yorks 52 B4
Scampton Lincs 46 E3
Scapa Orkney 95 H5
Scapegoat Hill W Yorks 51 H6
Scar Orkney 95 D7
Scarborough N Yorks 59 H11
Scarcliffe Derbys 45 F8
Scarcroft W Yorks 51 E9
Scarcroft Hill W Yorks 51 E9
Scardroy Highld 86 F5
Scarff Shetland 96 E4
Scarfskerry Highld 94 C4
Scargill Durham 58 E1
Scarinish Argyll 78 G3
Scarisbrick Lancs 43 A6
Scarning Norf 38 D5
Scarrington Notts 36 A3
Scartho NE Lincs 46 B6
Scarwell Orkney 95 F3
Scatness Shetland 96 M5
Scatraig Highld 87 H10
Scawby N Lincs 46 B3
Scawsby S Yorks 45 B9
Scawton N Yorks 51 A11
Scayne's Hill W Sus 12 D2
Scethrog Powys 25 F8
Scholar Green Ches E 44 G2
Scholes W Yorks 44 B5
Scholes W Yorks 51 F9
Scholes W Yorks 51 G7
School Green Ches W 43 F9
Scleddau Pembs 22 C4
Sco Ruston Norf 39 C8
Scofton Notts 45 D10
Scole Norf 39 H7
Scolpaig W Isles 84 A2
Scone Perth 76 E4
Sconser Highld 85 E10
Scoonie Fife 76 G6
Scoor Argyll 78 K7
Scopwick Lincs 46 G4
Scoraig Highld 86 B3
Scorborough E Yorks 52 E6
Scorrier Corn 2 E6
Scorton Lancs 49 E5
Scorton N Yorks 58 F3
Scotbheinn W Isles 84 C3
Scotby Cumb 61 H10
Scotch Corner N Yorks 58 F3
Scotforth Lancs 49 D4
Scothern Lincs 46 E4
Scotland Gate Northumb 63 E8
Scotlandwell Perth 76 G4
Scots' Gap Northumb 62 E6
Scotsburn Highld 87 D10
Scotscalder Station Highld 94 E2
Scotscraig Fife 77 E7
Scotston Aberds 83 F9
Scotston Perth 76 C2
Scotstoun Glasgow 68 D4
Scotstown Highld 79 E11
Scotswood T&W 63 G7
Scottas Highld 85 H12
Scotter Lincs 46 B2
Scotterthorpe Lincs 46 B2
Scottlethorpe Lincs 37 C6
Scotton Lincs 46 C2
Scotton N Yorks 51 D9
Scotton N Yorks 58 G2
Scottow Norf 39 C8
Scoughall E Loth 70 B5
Scoulag Argyll 73 H10
Scoulton Norf 38 E5
Scourie Highld 92 E4
Scourie More Highld 92 E4
Scousburgh Shetland 96 M5
Scrabster Highld 94 C2
Scrafield Lincs 47 F7
Scrainwood Northumb 62 C5
Scrane End Lincs 37 A9
Scraptoft Leics 36 E2
Scratby Norf 39 D11
Scrayingham N Yorks 52 C3
Scredington Lincs 37 A6
Scremby Lincs 47 F8
Scremerston Northumb 71 F9
Screveton Notts 36 A3
Scrivelsby Lincs 46 F6
Scriven N Yorks 51 D9
Scrooby Notts 45 C10
Scropton Derbys 35 B7
Scrub Hill Lincs 46 G6
Scruton N Yorks 58 G3
Sculcoates Hull 53 F6
Sculthorpe Norf 38 B4
Scunthorpe N Lincs 46 A2
Scurlage Swansea 23 H9
Sea Palling Norf 39 C10
Seaborough Dorset 8 D3
Seacombe Mers 42 C6
Seacroft Lincs 47 F9
Seacroft W Yorks 51 F9
Seadyke Lincs 37 B9
Seafield S Ayrs 66 D6
Seafield W Loth 69 D9
Seaford E Sus 12 G3
Seaforth Mers 42 C6
Seagrave Leics 36 D2
Seaham Durham 58 B5
Seahouses Northumb 71 G11
Seal Kent 20 F2
Sealand Flint 42 F6
Seale Sur 18 G5
Seamer N Yorks 52 A6
Seamer N Yorks 58 E5
Seamill N Ayrs 66 B5
Searby Lincs 46 B4
Seasalter Kent 21 E7
Seascale Cumb 56 F2
Seathorne Lincs 47 F9
Seathwaite Cumb 56 E4
Seathwaite Cumb 56 G4
Seatoller Cumb 56 E4
Seaton Corn 4 F4
Seaton Cumb 56 C2
Seaton Devon 8 F1
Seaton Durham 58 A4
Seaton E Yorks 53 E7
Seaton Northumb 63 F9
Seaton Rutland 36 F5
Seaton Burn T&W 63 F8
Seaton Carew Hrtlpl 58 D6
Seaton Delaval Northumb 63 F9
Seaton Ross E Yorks 52 E3
Seaton Sluice Northumb 63 F9
Seatown Aberds 88 B5
Seatown Dorset 8 E3
Seave Green N Yorks 59 F6
Seaview IoW 10 E5
Seaville Cumb 56 A3
Seavington St Mary Som 8 C3
Seavington St Michael Som 8 C3
Sebergham Cumb 56 B5
Seckington Warks 35 E8
Second Coast Highld 86 B2
Sedbergh Cumb 57 G8
Sedbury Glos 15 B11
Sedbusk N Yorks 57 G10
Sedgeberrow Worcs 27 E7
Sedgebrook Lincs 36 B4
Sedgefield Durham 58 D4
Sedgeford Norf 38 B3
Sedgehill Wilts 9 B7
Sedgley W Mid 34 F5
Sedgwick Cumb 57 H7
Sedlescombe E Sus 13 E6
Sedlescombe Street E Sus 13 E6
Seend Wilts 16 E6
Seend Cleeve Wilts 16 E6
Seer Green Bucks 18 B6
Seething Norf 39 F9
Sefton Mers 42 B6
Seghill Northumb 63 F8
Seifton Shrops 33 G10
Seighford Staffs 34 C4
Seilebost W Isles 90 H5
Seion Gwyn 41 D7
Seisdon Staffs 34 F4
Seisiadar W Isles 91 D10
Selattyn Shrops 33 B8
Selborne Hants 10 A6
Selby N Yorks 52 F2
Selham W Sus 11 B8
Selhurst London 19 E10
Selkirk Borders 70 H3
Sellack Hereford 26 F2
Sellafirth Shetland 96 D7
Sellibister Orkney 95 D8
Sellindge Kent 13 C9
Sellindge Lees Kent 13 C10
Selling Kent 21 F7
Sells Green Wilts 16 E6
Selly Oak W Mid 34 G6
Selmeston E Sus 12 F4
Selsdon London 19 E10
Selsey W Sus 11 E7
Selsfield Common W Sus 12 C2
Selsted Kent 21 G9
Selston Notts 45 G8
Selworthy Som 7 B8
Semblister Shetland 96 H5
Semer Suff 30 D6
Semington Wilts 16 E5
Semley Wilts 9 B7
Send Sur 19 F7
Send Marsh Sur 19 F7
Senghenydd Caerph 15 B7
Sennen Corn 2 G2
Sennen Cove Corn 2 G2
Sennybridge = Pont Senni Powys 24 F6
Serlby Notts 45 D10
Sessay N Yorks 51 B10
Setchey Norf 38 D2
Setley Hants 10 D2
Setter Shetland 96 E6
Setter Shetland 96 H5
Setter Shetland 96 J7
Settiscarth Orkney 95 G4
Settle N Yorks 50 C4
Settrington N Yorks 52 B4
Seven Kings London 19 C11
Seven Sisters Neath 24 H5
Sevenhampton Glos 27 F7
Sevenoaks Kent 20 F2
Sevenoaks Weald Kent 20 F2
Severn Beach S Glos 15 C11
Severn Stoke Worcs 26 D5
Severnhampton Swindon 17 B9
Sevington Kent 13 B9
Sewards End Essex 30 E2
Sewardstone Essex 19 B10
Sewardstonebury Essex 19 B10
Sewerby E Yorks 53 C7
Seworgan Corn 2 F6
Sewstern Leics 36 C4
Sezincote Glos 27 E8
Sgarasta Mhor W Isles 90 H5
Sgiogarstaigh W Isles 91 A10
Shabbington Bucks 28 H3
Shackerstone Leics 35 E9
Shackleford Sur 18 G6
Shade W Yorks 50 G5
Shadforth Durham 58 B4
Shadingfield Suff 39 G10
Shadoxhurst Kent 13 C8
Shadsworth Blackburn 50 G3
Shadwell Norf 38 G5
Shadwell W Yorks 51 F9
Shaftesbury Dorset 9 B7
Shafton S Yorks 45 A7
Shalbourne Wilts 17 E10
Shalcombe IoW 10 F2
Shalden Hants 18 G3
Shaldon Devon 5 D10
Shalfleet IoW 10 F3
Shalford Essex 30 F4
Shalford Sur 19 G7
Shalford Green Essex 30 F4
Shallowford Devon 6 B6
Shalmsford Street Kent 21 F7
Shalstone Bucks 28 E3
Shamley Green Sur 19 G7
Shandon Argyll 73 E11
Shandwick Highld 87 D11
Shangton Leics 36 F3
Shankhouse Northumb 63 F8
Shanklin IoW 10 F4
Shanquhar Aberds 88 E5
Shanzie Perth 76 B5
Shap Cumb 57 E7
Shapwick Dorset 9 D8
Shapwick Som 15 H10
Shardlow Derbys 35 B10
Shareshill Staffs 34 E5
Sharlston W Yorks 51 H9
Sharlston Common W Yorks 51 H9
Sharnbrook Bedford 28 C6
Sharnford Leics 35 F10
Sharoe Green Lancs 49 F5
Sharow N Yorks 51 B9
Sharp Street Norf 39 C9
Sharpenhoe C Beds 29 E7
Sharperton Northumb 62 C5
Sharpness Glos 16 A3
Sharpthorne W Sus 12 C2
Sharrington Norf 38 B6
Shatterford Worcs 34 G3
Shaugh Prior Devon 4 E6
Shavington Ches E 43 G10
Shaw Gtr Man 44 B3
Shaw W Berks 17 E11
Shaw Wilts 16 E5
Shaw Green Lancs 49 H5
Shaw Mills N Yorks 51 C8
Shawbury Shrops 34 C1
Shawdon Hall Northumb 62 B6
Shawell Leics 35 G11
Shawford Hants 10 B3
Shawforth Lancs 50 G4
Shawhead Dumfries 60 F4
Shawhill Dumfries 61 G8
Shawton S Lanark 68 F5
Shawtonhill S Lanark 68 F5
Shear Cross Wilts 16 G5
Shearington Dumfries 60 G6
Shearsby Leics 36 F2
Shebbear Devon 6 F3
Shebdon Staffs 34 C3
Shebster Highld 93 C13
Sheddens E Renf 68 E4
Shedfield Hants 10 C4
Sheen Staffs 44 F5
Sheepscar W Yorks 51 F9
Sheepscombe Glos 26 G5
Sheepstor Devon 5 E6
Sheepwash Devon 6 F3
Sheepway N Som 15 D10
Sheepy Magna Leics 35 E9
Sheepy Parva Leics 35 E9
Sheering Essex 30 G2
Sheerness Kent 20 D6
Sheet Hants 11 B6
Sheffield S Yorks 45 D7
Sheffield Bottom W Berks 18 E3
Sheffield Green E Sus 12 D3
Shefford C Beds 29 E8
Shefford Woodlands W Berks 17 D10
Sheigra Highld 92 C4
Sheinton Shrops 34 E2
Shelderton Shrops 33 H10
Sheldon Derbys 44 F5
Sheldon Devon 7 F10
Sheldon W Mid 35 G7
Sheldwich Kent 21 F7
Shelf W Yorks 51 G7
Shelfanger Norf 39 G7
Shelfield W Mid 34 E6
Shelfield Warks 27 B8
Shelford Notts 36 A2
Shellacres Northumb 71 F7
Shelley Essex 20 A2
Shelley Suff 31 E7
Shelley W Yorks 44 A6
Shellingford Oxon 17 B10
Shellow Bowells Essex 30 H3
Shelsley Beauchamp Worcs 26 B4
Shelsley Walsh Worcs 26 B4
Shelthorpe Leics 35 D11
Shelton Bedford 29 B7
Shelton Norf 39 F8
Shelton Notts 36 A3
Shelton Shrops 33 D10
Shelton Green Norf 39 F8
Shelve Shrops 33 F9
Shelwick Hereford 26 D2
Shenfield Essex 20 B3
Shenington Oxon 27 D10
Shenley Herts 19 A8
Shenley Brook End M Keynes 28 E5
Shenley Church End M Keynes 28 E5
Shenleybury Herts 19 A8
Shenmore Hereford 25 E10
Shennanton Dumfries 54 C6
Shenstone Staffs 35 E7
Shenstone Worcs 26 A5
Shenton Leics 35 E9
Shenval Highld 80 A6
Shenval Moray 82 A4
Shepeau Stow Lincs 37 D9
Shephall Herts 29 F9
Shepherd's Green Oxon 18 C4
Shepherd's Port Norf 38 B2
Shepherdswell Kent 21 G9
Shepley W Yorks 44 B5
Shepperdine S Glos 16 B3
Shepperton Sur 19 E7
Shepreth Cambs 29 D10
Shepshed Leics 35 D10
Shepton Beauchamp Som 8 C3
Shepton Mallet Som 16 G3
Shepton Montague Som 8 A5
Shepway Kent 20 F4
Sheraton Durham 58 C5
Sherborne Dorset 8 C5
Sherborne Glos 27 G8
Sherborne St John Hants 18 F3
Sherbourne Warks 27 B9
Sherburn Durham 58 B4
Sherburn N Yorks 52 B5
Sherburn Hill Durham 58 B4
Sherburn in Elmet N Yorks 51 F10
Shere Sur 19 G7
Shereford Norf 38 C4
Sherfield English Hants 10 B1
Sherfield on Loddon Hants 18 F3
Sherford Devon 5 G8
Sheriff Hutton N Yorks 52 C2
Sheriffhales Shrops 34 D3
Sheringham Norf 39 A7
Sherington M Keynes 28 D5
Shernal Green Worcs 26 B6
Shernborne Norf 38 B3
Sherrington Wilts 16 H6
Sherston Wilts 16 C5
Sherwood Green Devon 6 D4
Shettleston Glasgow 68 D5
Shevington Gtr Man 43 B8
Shevington Moor Gtr Man 43 A8
Shevington Vale Gtr Man 43 B8
Sheviock Corn 4 F4
Shide IoW 10 F3
Shiel Bridge Highld 80 B1
Shieldaig Highld 85 A13
Shieldaig Highld 85 C13
Shieldhill Dumfries 60 E6
Shieldhill Falk 69 C7
Shieldhill S Lanark 69 F9
Shielfoot Highld 79 E9
Shielhill Angus 77 B7
Shielhill Invclyd 73 F11
Shifford Oxon 17 A10
Shifnal Shrops 34 E3
Shilbottle Northumb 63 C7
Shildon Durham 58 D3
Shillingford Devon 7 D8
Shillingford Oxon 18 B2
Shillingford St George Devon 5 C10
Shillingstone Dorset 9 C7
Shillington C Beds 29 E8
Shillmoor Northumb 62 C4
Shilton Oxon 27 H9
Shilton Warks 35 G10
Shilvington Northumb 63 E7
Shimpling Norf 39 G7
Shimpling Suff 30 C5
Shimpling Street Suff 30 C5
Shincliffe Durham 58 B3
Shiney Row T&W 58 A4
Shinfield Wokingham 18 E4
Shingham Norf 38 E3
Shingle Street Suff 31 D10
Shinner's Bridge Devon 5 E8
Shinness Highld 93 H8
Shipbourne Kent 20 F2
Shipdham Norf 38 E5
Shipham Som 15 F10
Shiphay Torbay 5 E9
Shiplake Oxon 18 D4
Shipley Derbys 35 A10
Shipley Northumb 63 B7
Shipley Shrops 34 F4
Shipley W Sus 11 B10
Shipley W Yorks 51 F7
Shipley Shiels Northumb 62 D3
Shipmeadow Suff 39 G9
Shippea Hill Sta. Cambs 38 G2
Shippon Oxon 17 B11
Shipston-on-Stour Warks 27 D9
Shipton Glos 27 G7
Shipton N Yorks 52 D1
Shipton Shrops 34 F1
Shipton Bellinger Hants 17 G9
Shipton Gorge Dorset 8 E3
Shipton Green W Sus 11 D7
Shipton Moyne Glos 16 C5
Shipton on Cherwell Oxon 27 G11
Shipton Solers Glos 27 G7
Shipton-under-Wychwood Oxon 27 G9
Shiptonthorpe E Yorks 52 E4
Shirburn Oxon 18 B3
Shirdley Hill Lancs 42 A6
Shirebrook Derbys 45 F9
Shiregreen S Yorks 45 C7
Shirehampton Bristol 15 D11
Shiremoor T&W 63 F9
Shirenewton Mon 15 B10
Shireoaks Notts 45 D9
Shirkoak Kent 13 C8
Shirl Heath Hereford 25 C11
Shirland Derbys 45 G7
Shirley Derbys 35 A8
Shirley London 19 E10
Shirley Soton 10 C3
Shirley W Mid 35 H7
Shirrell Heath Hants 10 C4
Shirwell Devon 6 C4
Shirwell Cross Devon 6 C4
Shiskine N Ayrs 66 D2
Shobdon Hereford 25 B11
Shobnall Staffs 35 C8
Shobrooke Devon 7 F7
Shoby Leics 36 D2
Shocklach Ches W 43 H7
Shoeburyness Southend 20 C6
Sholden Kent 21 F10
Sholing Soton 10 C3
Shoot Hill Shrops 33 D10
Shop Corn 3 B7
Shop Corn 6 E1
Shop Corner Suff 31 E9
Shore Mill Highld 87 E10
Shoreditch London 19 C10
Shoreham Kent 20 E2
Shoreham-By-Sea W Sus 11 D11
Shoresdean Northumb 71 F8
Shoreswood Northumb 71 F8
Shoreton Highld 87 E9
Shorncote Glos 17 B7
Shorne Kent 20 D3
Short Heath W Mid 34 E5
Shortacombe Devon 4 C6
Shortgate E Sus 12 E3
Shortlanesend Corn 3 E7
Shortlees E Ayrs 67 C7
Shortstown Bedford 29 D7
Shorwell IoW 10 F3
Shoscombe Bath 16 F4
Shotatton Shrops 33 C9
Shotesham Norf 39 F8
Shotgate Essex 20 B4
Shotley Suff 31 E9
Shotley Bridge Durham 58 A1
Shotley Gate Suff 31 E9
Shotleyfield Northumb 58 A1
Shottenden Kent 21 F7
Shottermill Sur 11 A7
Shottery Warks 27 C8
Shotteswell Warks 27 D11
Shottisham Suff 31 D10
Shottle Derbys 45 H7
Shottlegate Derbys 45 H7
Shotton Durham 58 C5
Shotton Flint 42 F6
Shotton Northumb 71 G7
Shotton Colliery Durham 58 B4
Shotts N Lanark 69 D7
Shotwick Ches W 42 E6
Shouldham Norf 38 E2
Shouldham Thorpe Norf 38 E2
Shoulton Worcs 26 C5
Shover's Green E Sus 12 C5
Shrawardine Shrops 33 D10
Shrawley Worcs 26 B5
Shrewley Common Warks 27 B9
Shrewsbury Shrops 33 D10
Shrewton Wilts 17 G7
Shripney W Sus 11 D8
Shrivenham Oxon 17 C9
Shropham Norf 38 F5
Shrub End Essex 30 F6
Shucknall Hereford 26 D2
Shudy Camps Cambs 30 D3
Shulishadermor Highld 85 D9
Shurdington Glos 26 G6
Shurlock Row Windsor 18 D5
Shurrery Highld 93 D13
Shurrery Lodge Highld 93 D13
Shurton Som 7 B11
Shustoke Warks 35 F8
Shute Devon 7 F7
Shute Devon 8 E1
Shutford Oxon 27 D10
Shuthonger Glos 26 E5
Shutlanger Northants 28 C4
Shuttington Warks 35 E8
Shuttlewood Derbys 45 E8
Siabost bho Dheas W Isles 90 C7
Siabost bho Thuath W Isles 90 C7
Siadar W Isles 91 B8
Siadar Iarach W Isles 91 B8
Siadar Uarach W Isles 91 B8
Sibbaldbie Dumfries 61 E7
Sibbertoft Northants 36 G2
Sibdon Carwood Shrops 33 G10
Sibford Ferris Oxon 27 E10
Sibford Gower Oxon 27 E10
Sible Hedingham Essex 30 E4
Sibsey Lincs 47 G7
Sibson Cambs 37 F6
Sibson Leics 35 E9
Sibthorpe Notts 45 H11
Sibton Suff 31 B10
Sibton Green Suff 31 A10
Sicklesmere Suff 30 B5
Sicklinghall N Yorks 51 E9
Sid Devon 7 H10
Sidbury Devon 7 G10
Sidbury Shrops 34 G2
Sidcot N Som 15 F10
Sidcup London 19 D11
Siddick Cumb 56 C2
Siddington Ches E 44 E2
Siddington Glos 17 B7
Sidemoor Worcs 26 A6
Sidestrand Norf 39 B8
Sidford Devon 7 G10
Sidlesham W Sus 11 E7
Sidley E Sus 12 F6
Sidlow Sur 19 G9
Sidmouth Devon 7 H10
Sigford Devon 5 D8
Sigglesthorne E Yorks 53 E7
Sighthill Edin 69 C10
Sigingstone V Glam 14 D5
Signet Oxon 27 G9
Silchester Hants 18 E3
Sildinis W Isles 91 F7
Sileby Leics 36 D1
Silecroft Cumb 49 A1
Silfield Norf 39 F7
Silian Ceredig 23 A10
Silk Willoughby Lincs 37 A6
Silkstone S Yorks 44 B6
Silkstone Common S Yorks 44 B6
Silloth Cumb 56 A3
Sills Northumb 62 C4
Sillyearn Moray 88 C5
Siloh Carms 24 E4
Silpho N Yorks 59 G10
Silsden W Yorks 50 E6
Silsoe C Beds 29 E7
Silver End Essex 30 G5
Silverburn Midloth 69 D11
Silverdale Lancs 49 B4
Silverdale Staffs 44 H2
Silvergate Norf 39 C7
Silverhill E Sus 13 E6
Silverley's Green Suff 39 H8
Silverstone Northants 28 D3
Silverton Devon 7 F8
Silvington Shrops 34 H2
Silwick Shetland 96 J4
Simmondley Derbys 44 C4
Simonburn Northumb 62 F4
Simonsbath Som 7 C6
Simonstone Lancs 50 F3
Simprim Borders 71 F7
Simpson M Keynes 28 E5
Simpson Cross Pembs 22 E3
Sinclair's Hill Borders 71 E7
Sinclairston E Ayrs 67 E7
Sinderby N Yorks 51 A9
Sinderhope Northumb 57 A10
Sindlesham Wokingham 18 E4
Singdean Borders 61 C11
Singleborough Bucks 28 E4
Singleton Lancs 49 F3
Singleton W Sus 11 C7
Singlewell Kent 20 D3
Sinkhurst Green Kent 13 B7
Sinnahard Aberds 82 B6
Sinnington N Yorks 59 H8
Sinton Green Worcs 26 B5
Sipson London 19 D7
Sirhowy Bl Gwent 25 G8
Sisland Norf 39 F9
Sissinghurst Kent 13 C6
Sisterpath Borders 70 F6
Siston S Glos 16 D3
Sithney Corn 2 G5
Sittingbourne Kent 20 E5
Six Ashes Staffs 34 G3
Six Hills Leics 36 C2
Six Mile Bottom Cambs 30 C2
Sixhills Lincs 46 D5
Sixpenny Handley Dorset 9 C8
Sizewell Suff 31 B11
Skail Highld 93 E10
Skaill Orkney 95 E5
Skaill Orkney 95 G3
Skaill Orkney 95 H6
Skares E Ayrs 67 E8
Skateraw E Loth 70 C6
Skaw Shetland 96 G7
Skeabost Highld 85 D9
Skeabrae Orkney 95 F3
Skeeby N Yorks 58 F3
Skeffington Leics 36 E3
Skeffling E Yorks 53 H9
Skegby Notts 45 F8
Skegness Lincs 47 F9
Skelberry Shetland 96 M5
Skelbo Highld 87 B10
Skelbrooke S Yorks 45 A9
Skeldyke Lincs 37 B9
Skellingthorpe Lincs 46 E3
Skellister Shetland 96 H6
Skellow S Yorks 45 A9
Skelmanthorpe W Yorks 44 A6
Skelmersdale Lancs 43 B7
Skelmonae Aberds 89 E8
Skelmorlie N Ayrs 73 G10
Skelmuir Aberds 89 D9
Skelpick Highld 93 D10
Skelton Cumb 56 C6
Skelton E Yorks 52 G3
Skelton N Yorks 58 F1
Skelton Redcar 59 E7
Skelton York 52 D1
Skelton-on-Ure N Yorks 51 C9
Skelwick Orkney 95 D5
Skelwith Bridge Cumb 56 F5
Skendleby Lincs 47 F8
Skene Ho. Aberds 83 C9
Skenfrith Mon 25 F11
Skerne E Yorks 52 D6
Skeroblingarry Argyll 65 F8
Skerray Highld 93 C9
Skerton Lancs 49 C4
Sketchley Leics 35 F10
Sketty Swansea 14 B2
Skewen Neath 14 B3
Skewsby N Yorks 52 B2
Skeyton Norf 39 C8
Skiag Bridge Highld 92 G5
Skibo Castle Highld 87 C10
Skidbrooke Lincs 47 C8
Skidbrooke North End Lincs 47 C8
Skidby E Yorks 52 F6
Skilgate Som 7 D8
Skillington Lincs 36 C4
Skinburness Cumb 61 H7
Skinflats Falk 69 B8
Skinidin Highld 84 D7
Skinnet Highld 93 C8
Skinningrove Redcar 59 D8
Skipness Argyll 73 H7
Skippool Lancs 49 E3
Skipsea E Yorks 53 D7
Skipsea Brough E Yorks 53 D7
Skipton N Yorks 50 D5
Skipton-on-Swale N Yorks 51 B9
Skipwith N Yorks 52 F2
Skirbeck Lincs 37 A9
Skirbeck Quarter Lincs 37 A9
Skirlaugh E Yorks 53 F7
Skirling Borders 69 G9
Skirmett Bucks 18 C4
Skirpenbeck E Yorks 52 D3
Skirwith Cumb 57 C8
Skirza Highld 94 D5
Skulamus Highld 85 F11
Skullomie Highld 93 C9
Skyborry Green Shrops 25 A9
Skye of Curr Highld 82 A1
Skyreholme N Yorks 51 C6
Slackhall Derbys 44 D4
Slackhead Moray 88 B4
Slad Glos 26 H5
Slade Devon 6 B4
Slade Pembs 22 E4
Slade Green London 20 D2
Slaggyford Northumb 57 A8
Slaidburn Lancs 50 D3
Slaithwaite W Yorks 44 A4
Slaley Northumb 62 H5
Slamannan Falk 69 C7
Slapton Bucks 28 F6
Slapton Devon 5 G9
Slapton Northants 28 D3
Slatepit Dale Derbys 45 F7
Slattocks Gtr Man 44 B2
Slaugham W Sus 12 D1
Slaughterford Wilts 16 D5
Slawston Leics 36 F3
Sleaford Hants 18 H5
Sleaford Lincs 46 H4
Sleagill Cumb 57 E7
Sleapford Telford 34 D2
Sledge Green Worcs 26 E5
Sledmere E Yorks 52 C5
Sleightholme Durham 57 E11
Sleights N Yorks 59 F9
Slepe Dorset 9 E8
Slickly Highld 94 D4
Sliddery N Ayrs 66 D2
Sligachan Hotel Highld 85 F9
Slimbridge Glos 16 A4
Slindon Staffs 34 B4
Slindon W Sus 11 D8
Slinfold W Sus 11 A10
Sling Gwyn 41 D8
Slingsby N Yorks 52 B2
Slioch Aberds 88 E5
Slip End C Beds 29 G7
Slip End Herts 29 E9
Slipton Northants 36 H5
Slitting Mill Staffs 34 D6
Slochd Highld 81 A10
Slockavullin Argyll 73 D7
Sloley Norf 39 C8
Sloothby Lincs 47 E8
Slough Slough 18 D6
Slough Green W Sus 12 D1
Sluggan Highld 81 A10
Slumbay Highld 85 E13
Slyfield Sur 18 F6

Thistleton Rutland 36 D5
Thistley Green Suff 38 H2
Thixendale N Yorks 52 C4
Thockrington Northumb 62 F5
Tholomas Drove Cambs 37 E9
Tholthorpe N Yorks 51 C10
Thomas Chapel Pembs 22 F6
Thomas Close Cumb 56 B6
Thomastown Aberds 88 E5
Thompson Norf 38 F5
Thomshill Moray 88 C2
Thong Kent 20 D3
Thongsbridge W Yorks 44 B5
Thoralby N Yorks 58 H1
Thoresway Lincs 46 C5
Thorganby Lincs 46 C6
Thorganby N Yorks 52 E2
Thorgill N Yorks 59 G8
Thorington Suff 31 A11
Thorington Street Suff 31 E7
Thorlby N Yorks 50 D5
Thorley Herts 29 G11
Thorley Street Herts 29 G11
Thorley Street IoW 10 F2
Thormanby N Yorks 51 B10
Thornaby-on-Tees Stockton 58 E5
Thornage Norf 38 B6
Thornborough Bucks 28 E4
Thornborough N Yorks 51 B8
Thornbury Devon 6 F3
Thornbury Hereford 26 C3
Thornbury S Glos 16 B3
Thornbury W Yorks 51 F7
Thornby Northants 36 H2
Thorncliffe Staffs 44 G4
Thorncombe Dorset 8 D2
Thorncombe Dorset 9 D7
Thorncombe Street Sur 19 G7
Thorncote Green C Beds 29 D8
Thorncross IoW 10 F3
Thorndon Suff 31 B8
Thorndon Cross Devon 6 G4
Thorne S Yorks 45 A10
Thorne St Margaret Som 7 D9
Thorner W Yorks 51 E9
Thorney Notts 46 E2
Thorney Pboro 37 E8
Thorney Crofts E Yorks 53 G8
Thorney Green Suff 31 B7
Thorney Hill Hants 9 E10
Thorney Toll Pboro 37 E9
Thornfalcon Som 8 B1
Thornford Dorset 8 C5
Thorngumbald E Yorks 53 G8
Thornham Norf 38 A3
Thornham Magna Suff 31 A8
Thornham Parva Suff 31 A8
Thornhaugh Pboro 37 E6
Thornhill Cardiff 15 C7
Thornhill Cumb 56 F2
Thornhill Derbys 44 D5
Thornhill Dumfries 60 D4
Thornhill Soton 10 C3
Thornhill Stirling 75 H9
Thornhill W Yorks 51 H8
Thornhill Edge W Yorks 51 H8
Thornhill Lees W Yorks 51 H8
Thornholme E Yorks 53 C7
Thornley Durham 58 C4
Thornley Durham 58 C2
Thornliebank E Renf 68 E4
Thorns Suff 30 C4
Thorns Green Ches E 43 D10
Thornsett Derbys 44 D4
Thornthwaite Cumb 56 D4
Thornthwaite N Yorks 51 D7
Thornton Angus 76 C6
Thornton Bucks 28 E4
Thornton E Yorks 52 E3
Thornton Fife 76 H5
Thornton Lancs 49 E3
Thornton Leics 35 E10
Thornton Lincs 46 F6
Thornton Mbro 58 E5
Thornton Mers 42 B6
Thornton Northumb 71 F8
Thornton Pembs 22 F4
Thornton W Yorks 51 F7
Thornton Curtis N Lincs 53 H6
Thornton Heath London 19 E10
Thornton Hough Mers 42 D6
Thornton in Craven N Yorks 50 E5
Thornton-le-Beans N Yorks 58 G4
Thornton-le-Clay N Yorks 52 C2
Thornton-le-Dale N Yorks 52 A4
Thornton le Moor Lincs 46 C4
Thornton-le-Moor N Yorks 58 H4
Thornton-le-Moors Ches W 43 E7
Thornton-le-Street N Yorks 58 H5
Thornton Rust N Yorks 57 H11
Thornton Steward N Yorks 58 H2
Thornton Watlass N Yorks 58 H3
Thorntonhall S Lanark 68 E4
Thorntonloch E Loth 70 C6
Thorntonpark Northumb 71 F8
Thornwood Common Essex 19 A11
Thornydykes Borders 70 F5
Thoroton Notts 36 A3
Thorp Arch W Yorks 51 E10
Thorpe Derbys 44 G5
Thorpe E Yorks 52 E5
Thorpe Lincs 47 D8
Thorpe N Yorks 50 C6
Thorpe Norf 39 F10
Thorpe Notts 45 H11
Thorpe Sur 19 E7
Thorpe Abbotts Norf 39 H7
Thorpe Acre Leics 35 C11
Thorpe Arnold Leics 36 C3
Thorpe Audlin W Yorks 51 H10
Thorpe Bassett N Yorks 52 B4
Thorpe Bay Southend 20 C6
Thorpe by Water Rutland 36 F4
Thorpe Common Suff 31 E9
Thorpe Constantine Staffs 35 E8
Thorpe Culvert Lincs 47 F8
Thorpe End Norf 39 D8
Thorpe Fendykes Lincs 47 F8
Thorpe Green Essex 31 F8
Thorpe Green Suff 30 C6
Thorpe Hesley S Yorks 45 C7
Thorpe in Balne S Yorks 45 A9
Thorpe in the Fallows Lincs 46 D3
Thorpe Langton Leics 36 F3
Thorpe Larches Durham 58 D4
Thorpe-le-Soken Essex 31 F8
Thorpe le Street E Yorks 52 E4
Thorpe Malsor Northants 36 H4
Thorpe Mandeville Northants 28 D2
Thorpe Market Norf 39 B8
Thorpe Marriot Norf 39 D7
Thorpe Morieux Suff 30 C6
Thorpe on the Hill Lincs 46 F3
Thorpe St Andrew Norf 39 E8
Thorpe St Peter Lincs 47 F8
Thorpe Salvin S Yorks 45 D9
Thorpe Satchville Leics 36 D3
Thorpe Thewles Stockton 58 D5
Thorpe Tilney Lincs 46 G5
Thorpe Underwood N Yorks 51 D10
Thorpe Waterville Northants 36 G6
Thorpe Willoughby N Yorks 52 F1
Thorpeness Suff 31 C11
Thorrington Essex 31 F7
Thorverton Devon 7 F8
Thrandeston Suff 39 H7
Thrapston Northants 36 H5
Thrashbush N Lanark 68 D6
Threapland Cumb 56 C3
Threapland N Yorks 50 C5
Threapwood Ches W 43 H7
Threapwood Staffs 34 A6
Three Ashes Hereford 26 F2
Three Bridges W Sus 12 C1
Three Burrows Corn 2 E6
Three Chimneys Kent 13 C7
Three Cocks Powys 25 E8
Three Crosses Swansea 23 G10
Three Cups Corner E Sus 12 D5
Three Holes Norf 37 E11
Three Leg Cross E Sus 12 C5
Three Legged Cross Dorset 9 D9
Three Oaks E Sus 13 E7
Threehammer Common Norf 39 D9
Threekingham Lincs 37 B6
Threemile Cross Wokingham 18 E4
Threemilestone Corn 3 E6
Threemiletown W Loth 69 C9
Threlkeld Cumb 56 D5
Threshfield N Yorks 50 C5
Thrigby Norf 39 D10
Thringarth Durham 57 D11
Thringstone Leics 35 D10
Thrintoft N Yorks 58 G4
Thriplow Cambs 29 D11
Throckenholt Lincs 37 E9
Throcking Herts 29 E10
Throckley T&W 63 G7
Throckmorton Worcs 26 D6
Throphill Northumb 63 E7
Thropton Northumb 62 C6
Throsk Stirling 69 A7
Throwleigh Devon 6 G5
Throwley Kent 20 F6
Thrumpton Notts 35 B11
Thrumster Highld 94 F5
Thrunton Northumb 62 B6
Thrupp Glos 16 A5
Thrupp Oxon 27 G11
Thrushelton Devon 4 C5
Thrussington Leics 36 D2
Thruxton Hants 17 G9
Thruxton Hereford 25 E11
Thrybergh S Yorks 45 C8
Thulston Derbys 35 B10
Thundergay N Ayrs 66 B1
Thundersley Essex 20 C4
Thundridge Herts 29 G10
Thurcaston Leics 36 D1
Thurcroft S Yorks 45 D8
Thurgarton Norf 39 B7
Thurgarton Notts 45 H10
Thurgoland S Yorks 44 B6
Thurlaston Leics 35 F11
Thurlaston Warks 27 A11
Thurlbear Som 8 B1
Thurlby Lincs 37 D7
Thurlby Lincs 46 F3
Thurleigh Bedford 29 C7
Thurlestone Devon 5 G7
Thurloxton Som 8 A1
Thurlstone S Yorks 44 B6
Thurlton Norf 39 F10
Thurlwood Ches E 44 G2
Thurmaston Leics 36 E2
Thurnby Leics 36 E2
Thurne Norf 39 D10
Thurnham Kent 20 F5
Thurnham Lancs 49 D4
Thurning Norf 39 C6
Thurning Northants 37 G6
Thurnscoe S Yorks 45 B8
Thurnscoe East S Yorks 45 B8
Thursby Cumb 56 A5
Thursford Norf 38 B5
Thursley Sur 18 H6
Thurso Highld 94 D3
Thurso East Highld 94 D3
Thurstaston Mers 42 D5
Thurston Suff 30 B6
Thurstonfield Cumb 61 H9
Thurstonland W Yorks 44 A5
Thurton Norf 39 E9
Thurvaston Derbys 35 B8
Thuxton Norf 38 E6
Thwaite N Yorks 57 G10
Thwaite Suff 31 B8
Thwaite St Mary Norf 39 F9
Thwaites W Yorks 51 E6
Thwaites Brow W Yorks 51 E6
Thwing E Yorks 53 B6
Tibbermore Perth 76 E3
Tibberton Glos 26 F4
Tibberton Telford 34 C2
Tibberton Worcs 26 C6
Tibenham Norf 39 G7
Tibshelf Derbys 45 F8
Tibthorpe E Yorks 52 D5
Ticehurst E Sus 12 C5
Tichborne Hants 10 A4
Tickencote Rutland 36 E5
Tickenham N Som 15 D10
Tickhill S Yorks 45 C9
Ticklerton Shrops 33 F10
Ticknall Derbys 35 C9
Tickton E Yorks 53 E6
Tidcombe Wilts 17 F9
Tiddington Oxon 18 A3
Tiddington Warks 27 C9
Tidebrook E Sus 12 D5
Tideford Corn 4 F4
Tideford Cross Corn 4 E4
Tidenham Glos 16 B2
Tideswell Derbys 44 E5
Tidmarsh W Berks 18 D3
Tidmington Warks 27 E9
Tidpit Hants 9 C9
Tidworth Wilts 17 G9
Tiers Cross Pembs 22 E4
Tiffield Northants 28 C3
Tifty Aberds 89 D7
Tigerton Angus 77 A8
Tigh-na-Blair Perth 75 F10
Tighnabruaich Argyll 73 F8
Tighnafiline Highld 91 J13
Tigley Devon 5 E8
Tilbrook Cambs 29 B7
Tilbury Thurrock 20 D3
Tilbury Juxta Clare Essex 30 D4
Tile Cross W Mid 35 G7
Tile Hill W Mid 35 H8
Tilehurst Reading 18 D3
Tilford Sur 18 G5
Tilgate W Sus 12 C1
Tilgate Forest Row W Sus 12 C1
Tillathrowie Aberds 88 E4
Tilley Shrops 33 C11
Tillicoultry Clack 76 H2
Tillingham Essex 20 A6
Tillington Hereford 25 D11
Tillington W Sus 11 B8
Tillington Common Hereford 25 D11
Tillyarblet Angus 83 G7
Tillybirloch Aberds 83 C8
Tillycorthie Aberds 89 F9
Tillydrine Aberds 83 D8
Tillyfour Aberds 83 B7
Tillyfourie Aberds 83 B8
Tillygarmond Aberds 83 D8
Tillygreig Aberds 89 F8
Tillykerrie Aberds 89 F8
Tilmanstone Kent 21 F10
Tilney All Saints Norf 38 D1
Tilney High End Norf 38 D1
Tilney St Lawrence Norf 37 D11
Tilshead Wilts 17 G7
Tilstock Shrops 33 B11
Tilston Ches W 43 G7
Tilstone Fearnall Ches W 43 F8
Tilsworth C Beds 28 F6
Tilton on the Hill Leics 36 E3
Timberland Lincs 46 G5
Timbersbrook Ches E 44 F2
Timberscombe Som 7 B8
Timble N Yorks 51 D7
Timperley Gtr Man 43 D10
Timsbury Bath 16 F3
Timsbury Hants 10 B2
Timsgearraidh W Isles 90 D5
Timworth Green Suff 30 B5
Tincleton Dorset 9 E6
Tindale Cumb 62 H2
Tingewick Bucks 28 E3
Tingley W Yorks 51 G8
Tingrith C Beds 29 E7
Tingwall Orkney 95 F4
Tinhay Devon 4 C4
Tinshill W Yorks 51 F8
Tinsley S Yorks 45 C8
Tintagel Corn 4 C1
Tintern Parva Mon 15 A11
Tintinhull Som 8 C4
Tintwistle Derbys 44 C4
Tinwald Dumfries 60 E6
Tinwell Rutland 36 E6
Tipperty Aberds 89 F9
Tipsend Norf 37 F11
Tipton W Mid 34 F5
Tipton St John Devon 7 G9
Tiptree Essex 30 G5
Tir-y-dail Carms 24 G3
Tirabad Powys 24 D5
Tiraghoil Argyll 78 J6
Tirley Glos 26 F5
Tirphil Caerph 15 A7
Tirril Cumb 57 D7
Tisbury Wilts 9 B8
Tisman's Common W Sus 11 A9
Tissington Derbys 44 G5
Titchberry Devon 6 D1
Titchfield Hants 10 D4
Titchmarsh Northants 36 H6
Titchwell Norf 38 A3
Tithby Notts 36 B2
Titley Hereford 25 B10
Titlington Northumb 63 B7
Titsey Sur 19 F11
Tittensor Staffs 34 B4
Tittleshall Norf 38 C4
Tiverton Ches W 43 F8
Tiverton Devon 7 E8
Tivetshall St Margaret Norf 39 G7
Tivetshall St Mary Norf 39 G7
Tividale W Mid 34 F5
Tivy Dale S Yorks 44 B6
Tixall Staffs 34 C5
Tixover Rutland 36 E5
Toab Orkney 95 H6
Toab Shetland 96 M5
Toadmoor Derbys 45 G7
Tobermory Argyll 79 F8
Toberonochy Argyll 72 C6
Tobha Mor W Isles 84 E2
Tobhtarol W Isles 90 D6
Tobson W Isles 90 D6
Tocher Aberds 89 E6
Tockenham Wilts 17 D7
Tockenham Wick Wilts 17 C7
Tockholes Blackburn 50 G2
Tockington S Glos 16 C3
Tockwith N Yorks 51 D10
Todber Dorset 9 B7
Todding Hereford 33 H10
Toddington C Beds 29 F7
Toddington Glos 27 E7
Todenham Glos 27 E9
Todhills Cumb 61 G9
Todlachie Aberds 83 B8
Todmorden W Yorks 50 G5
Todrig Borders 61 B10
Todwick S Yorks 45 D8
Toft Cambs 29 C10
Toft Lincs 37 D6
Toft Hill Durham 58 D2
Toft Hill Lincs 46 F6
Toft Monks Norf 39 F10
Toft next Newton Lincs 46 D4
Toftrees Norf 38 C4
Tofts Highld 94 D5
Toftwood Norf 38 D5
Togston Northumb 63 C8
Tokavaig Highld 85 G11
Tokers Green Oxon 18 D4
Tolastadh a Chaolais W Isles 90 D6
Tolastadh bho Thuath W Isles 91 C10
Toll Bar S Yorks 45 B9
Toll End W Mid 34 F5
Toll of Birness Aberds 89 E10
Tolland Som 7 C10
Tollard Royal Wilts 9 C8
Tollbar End W Mid 35 H9
Toller Fratrum Dorset 8 E4
Toller Porcorum Dorset 8 E4
Tollerton N Yorks 51 C11
Tollerton Notts 36 B2
Tollesbury Essex 30 G6
Tolleshunt D'Arcy Essex 30 G6
Tolleshunt Major Essex 30 G6
Tolm W Isles 91 D9
Tolpuddle Dorset 9 E6
Tolvah Highld 81 D10
Tolworth London 19 E8
Tomatin Highld 81 A10
Tombreck Highld 87 H9
Tomchrasky Highld 80 B4
Tomdoun Highld 80 C3
Tomich Highld 80 A5
Tomich Highld 87 D9
Tomich House Highld 87 G8
Tomintoul Aberds 82 D3
Tomintoul Moray 82 B3
Tomnaven Moray 88 E4
Tomnavoulin Moray 82 A4
Ton-Pentre Rhondda 14 B5
Tonbridge Kent 20 G2
Tondu Bridgend 14 C4
Tonfanau Gwyn 32 E1
Tong Shrops 34 E3
Tong W Yorks 51 F8
Tong Norton Shrops 34 E3
Tonge Leics 35 C10
Tongham Sur 18 G5
Tongland Dumfries 55 D9
Tongue Highld 93 D8
Tongue End Lincs 37 D7
Tongwynlais Cardiff 15 C7
Tonna Neath 14 B3
Tonwell Herts 29 G10
Tonypandy Rhondda 14 B5
Tonyrefail Rhondda 14 C6
Toot Baldon Oxon 18 A2
Toot Hill Essex 20 A2
Toothill Hants 10 C2
Top of Hebers Gtr Man 44 B2
Topcliffe N Yorks 51 B10
Topcroft Norf 39 F8
Topcroft Street Norf 39 F8
Toppesfield Essex 30 E4
Toppings Gtr Man 43 A10
Topsham Devon 5 C10
Torbay Torbay 5 F10
Torbeg N Ayrs 66 D2
Torboll Farm Highld 87 B10
Torbrex Stirling 68 A6
Torbryan Devon 5 E9
Torcross Devon 5 G9
Tore Highld 87 F9
Torinturk Argyll 73 G7
Torksey Lincs 46 E2
Torlum W Isles 84 C2
Torlundy Highld 80 F3
Tormarton S Glos 16 D4
Tormisdale Argyll 64 C2
Tormitchell S Ayrs 66 G5
Tormore N Ayrs 66 C1
Tornagrain Highld 87 G10
Tornahaish Aberds 82 C4
Tornaveen Aberds 83 C8
Torness Highld 81 A7
Toronto Durham 58 C2
Torpenhow Cumb 56 C4
Torphichen W Loth 69 C8
Torphins Aberds 83 C8
Torpoint Corn 4 F5
Torquay Torbay 5 E10
Torquhan Borders 70 F3
Torran Argyll 73 C7
Torran Highld 85 D10
Torran Highld 87 D10
Torrance E Dunb 68 C5
Torrans Argyll 78 J7
Torranyard N Ayrs 67 B6
Torre Torbay 5 E10
Torridon Highld 86 F2
Torridon Ho. Highld 85 C13
Torrin Highld 85 F10
Torrisdale Highld 93 C9
Torrisdale-Square Argyll 65 E8
Torrish Highld 93 H12
Torrisholme Lancs 49 C4
Torroble Highld 93 J8
Torry Aberdeen 83 C11
Torry Aberds 88 E4
Torryburn Fife 69 B9
Torterston Aberds 89 D10
Torthorwald Dumfries 60 F6
Tortington W Sus 11 D9
Tortworth S Glos 16 B4
Torvaig Highld 85 D9
Torver Cumb 56 G4
Torwood Falk 69 B7
Torworth Notts 45 D10
Tosberry Devon 6 D1
Toscaig Highld 85 E12
Toseland Cambs 29 B9
Tosside N Yorks 50 D3
Tostock Suff 30 B6
Totaig Highld 84 C7
Totaig Highld 85 F13
Tote Highld 85 D9
Totegan Highld 93 C11
Tothill Lincs 47 D8
Totland IoW 10 F2
Totnes Devon 5 E9
Toton Notts 35 B11
Totronald Argyll 78 F4
Totscore Highld 85 B8
Tottenham London 19 B10
Tottenhill Norf 38 D2
Tottenhill Row Norf 38 D2
Totteridge London 19 B9
Totternhoe C Beds 28 F6
Tottington Gtr Man 43 A10
Totton Hants 10 C2
Touchen End Windsor 18 D5
Tournaig Highld 91 J13
Toux Aberds 89 C9
Tovil Kent 20 F4
Tow Law Durham 58 C2
Toward Argyll 73 G10
Towcester Northants 28 D3
Towednack Corn 2 F3
Tower End Norf 38 D2
Towersey Oxon 28 H4
Towie Aberds 82 B6
Towie Aberds 89 B8
Towiemore Moray 88 D3
Town End Cambs 37 F10
Town End Cumb 49 A4
Town Row E Sus 12 C4
Town Yetholm Borders 71 H7
Townend W Dunb 68 C3
Towngate Lincs 37 D7
Townhead Cumb 57 C7
Townhead Dumfries 55 E9
Townhead S Ayrs 66 F5
Townhead S Yorks 44 B5
Townhead of Greenlaw Dumfries 55 C10
Townhill Fife 69 B10
Townsend Bucks 28 H4
Townsend Herts 29 H8
Townshend Corn 2 F4
Towthorpe York 52 D2
Towton N Yorks 51 F10
Towyn Conwy 42 E2
Toxteth Mers 42 D6
Toynton All Saints Lincs 47 F7
Toynton Fen Side Lincs 47 F7
Toynton St Peter Lincs 47 F8
Toy's Hill Kent 19 F11
Trabboch E Ayrs 67 D7
Traboe Corn 2 G6
Tradespark Highld 87 F11
Tradespark Orkney 95 H5
Trafford Park Gtr Man 43 C10
Trallong Powys 24 F6
Tranent E Loth 70 C3
Tranmere Mers 42 D6
Trantlebeg Highld 93 D11
Trantlemore Highld 93 D11
Tranwell Northumb 63 E7
Trapp Carms 24 G3
Traprain E Loth 70 C4
Traquair Borders 70 G2
Trawden Lancs 50 F5
Trawsfynydd Gwyn 41 G9
Tre-Gibbon Rhondda 24 H6
Tre-Taliesin Ceredig 32 F2
Tre-vaughan Carms 23 D8
Tre-wyn Mon 25 F10
Trealaw Rhondda 14 B6
Treales Lancs 49 F4
Trearddur Anglesey 40 C4
Treaslane Highld 85 C8
Trebanog Rhondda 14 B6
Trebanos Neath 14 A3
Trebartha Corn 4 D3
Trebarwith Corn 4 C1
Trebetherick Corn 3 B8
Treborough Som 7 C9
Trebudannon Corn 3 C7
Trebullett Corn 4 D4
Treburley Corn 4 D4
Trebyan Corn 4 E1
Trecastle Powys 24 F5
Trecenydd Caerph 15 C7
Trecwn Pembs 22 C4
Trecynon Rhondda 14 A5
Tredavoe Corn 2 G3
Treddiog Pembs 22 D3
Tredegar Bl Gwent 25 H8
Tredegar Newydd = New Tredegar Caerph 15 A7
Tredington Glos 26 F6
Tredington Warks 27 D9
Tredinnick Corn 3 B8
Tredomen Powys 25 E8
Tredunnock Mon 15 B9
Tredustan Powys 25 E8
Treen Corn 2 G2
Treeton S Yorks 45 D8
Tref-y-Clawdd = Knighton Powys 25 A9
Trefaldwyn = Montgomery Powys 33 F8
Trefasser Pembs 22 C3
Trefdraeth Anglesey 40 C6
Trefdraeth = Newport Pembs 22 C5
Trefecca Powys 25 E8
Trefechan Ceredig 32 G1
Trefeglwys Powys 32 F5
Trefenter Ceredig 24 B3
Treffgarne Pembs 22 D4
Treffynnon = Holywell Flint 42 E4
Treffynnon Pembs 22 D3
Trefgarn Owen Pembs 22 D3
Trefil Bl Gwent 25 G8
Trefilan Ceredig 23 A10
Trefin Pembs 22 C3
Treflach Shrops 33 C8
Trefnanney Powys 33 D8
Trefnant Denb 42 E3
Trefonen Shrops 33 C8
Trefor Anglesey 40 B5
Trefor Gwyn 40 F5
Treforest Rhondda 14 C6
Trefriw Conwy 41 D9
Trefynwy = Monmouth Mon 26 G2
Tregadillett Corn 4 C3
Tregaian Anglesey 40 C6
Tregare Mon 25 G11
Tregaron Ceredig 24 C3
Tregarth Gwyn 41 D8
Tregeare Corn 4 C3
Tregeiriog Wrex 33 B7
Tregele Anglesey 40 A5
Tregidden Corn 3 G6
Treglemais Pembs 22 D3
Tregole Corn 4 B2
Tregonetha Corn 3 C8
Tregony Corn 3 E8
Tregoss Corn 3 C8
Tregoyd Powys 25 E9
Tregroes Ceredig 23 B9
Tregurrian Corn 3 C7
Tregynon Powys 33 F6
Trehafod Rhondda 14 B6
Treharris M Tydf 14 B6
Treherbert Rhondda 14 B5
Trekenner Corn 4 D4
Treknow Corn 4 C1
Trelan Corn 2 H6
Trelash Corn 4 B2
Trelassick Corn 3 D7
Trelawnyd Flint 42 E3
Trelech Carms 23 C7
Treleddyd-fawr Pembs 22 D2
Trelewis M Tydf 15 B7
Treligga Corn 4 C1
Trelights Corn 3 B8
Trelill Corn 3 B9
Trelissick Corn 3 F7
Trellech Mon 26 H2
Trelleck Grange Mon 15 A10
Trelogan Flint 42 D4
Trelystan Powys 33 E8
Tremadog Gwyn 41 F7
Tremail Corn 4 C2
Tremain Ceredig 23 B7
Tremaine Corn 4 C3
Tremar Corn 4 E3
Trematon Corn 4 F4
Tremeirchion Denb 42 E3
Trenance Corn 3 C7
Trenarren Corn 3 E9
Trench Telford 34 D2
Treneglos Corn 4 C3
Trenewan Corn 4 F2
Trent Dorset 8 C4
Trent Vale Stoke 34 A4
Trentham Stoke 34 A4
Trentishoe Devon 6 B5
Treoes V Glam 14 D5
Treorchy = Treorci Rhondda 14 B5
Treorci = Treorchy Rhondda 14 B5
Tre'r-ddôl Ceredig 32 F2
Trerulefoot Corn 4 F4
Tresaith Ceredig 23 A7
Tresawle Corn 3 E7
Trescott Staffs 34 F4
Trescowe Corn 2 F4
Tresham Glos 16 B4
Tresillian Corn 3 E7
Tresinwen Pembs 22 B4
Treskinnick Cross Corn 4 B3
Tresmeer Corn 4 C3
Tresparrett Corn 4 B2
Tresparrett Posts Corn 4 B2
Tressait Perth 75 A11
Tresta Shetland 96 D8
Tresta Shetland 96 H5
Treswell Notts 45 E11
Trethosa Corn 3 D8
Trethurgy Corn 3 D9
Tretio Pembs 22 D2
Tretire Hereford 26 F2
Tretower Powys 25 F8
Treuddyn Flint 42 G5
Trevalga Corn 4 C1
Trevalyn Wrex 43 G6
Trevanson Corn 3 B8
Trevarren Corn 3 C8
Trevarrian Corn 3 C7
Trevarrick Corn 3 E8
Trevaughan Carms 22 E6
Treveighan Corn 4 D1
Trevellas Corn 2 D6
Treverva Corn 3 F6
Trevethin Torf 15 A8
Trevigro Corn 4 E4
Treviscoe Corn 3 D8
Trevone Corn 3 B7
Trewarmett Corn 4 C1
Trewassa Corn 4 C2
Trewellard Corn 2 F2
Trewen Corn 4 C3
Trewennack Corn 2 G5
Trewern Powys 33 D8
Trewethern Corn 3 B9
Trewidland Corn 4 F3
Trewint Corn 4 B2
Trewint Corn 4 C3
Trewithian Corn 3 F7
Trewoofe Corn 2 G3
Trewoon Corn 3 D8
Treworga Corn 3 E7
Treworlas Corn 3 F7
Treyarnon Corn 3 B7
Treyford W Sus 11 C7
Trezaise Corn 3 D8
Triangle W Yorks 50 G6
Triffleton Pembs 22 D4
Trimdon Durham 58 C4
Trimdon Colliery Durham 58 C4
Trimdon Grange Durham 58 C4
Trimingham Norf 39 B8
Trimley Lower Street Suff 31 E9
Trimley St Martin Suff 31 E9
Trimley St Mary Suff 31 E9
Trimpley Worcs 34 H3
Trimsaran Carms 23 F9
Trimstone Devon 6 B3
Trinafour Perth 75 A10
Trinant Caerph 15 A8
Tring Herts 28 G6
Tring Wharf Herts 28 G6
Trinity Angus 77 A9
Trinity Jersey 11
Trisant Ceredig 32 H3
Trislaig Highld 80 F2
Trispen Corn 3 D7
Tritlington Northumb 63 D8
Trochry Perth 76 C2
Trodigal Argyll 65 F7
Troed-rhiwdalar Powys 24 C6
Troedyraur Ceredig 23 B8
Troedyrhiw M Tydf 14 A6
Tromode IoM 48 E3
Trondavoe Shetland 96 F5
Troon Corn 2 F5
Troon S Ayrs 66 C6
Trosaraidh W Isles 84 G2
Trossachs Hotel Stirling 75 G8
Troston Suff 30 A5
Trottiscliffe Kent 20 E3
Trotton W Sus 11 B7
Troutbeck Cumb 56 D5
Troutbeck Cumb 56 F6
Troutbeck Bridge Cumb 56 F6
Trow Green Glos 26 H2
Trowbridge Wilts 16 F5
Trowell Notts 35 B10
Trowle Common Wilts 16 F5
Trowley Bottom Herts 29 G7
Trows Borders 70 G5
Trowse Newton Norf 39 E8
Trudoxhill Som 16 G4
Trull Som 7 D11
Trumaisgearraidh W Isles 84 A3
Trumpan Highld 84 B7
Trumpet Hereford 26 E3
Trumpington Cambs 29 C11
Trunch Norf 39 B8
Trunnah Lancs 49 E3
Truro Corn 3 E7
Trusham Devon 5 C9
Trusley Derbys 35 B8
Trusthorpe Lincs 47 D9
Trysull Staffs 34 F4
Tubney Oxon 17 B11
Tuckenhay Devon 5 F9
Tuckhill Shrops 34 G3
Tuckingmill Corn 2 E5
Tuddenham Suff 30 A4
Tuddenham St Martin Suff 31 D8
Tudeley Kent 20 G3
Tudhoe Durham 58 C3
Tudorville Hereford 26 F2
Tudweiliog Gwyn 40 G4
Tuesley Sur 18 G6
Tuffley Glos 26 G5
Tufton Hants 17 G11
Tufton Pembs 22 D5
Tugby Leics 36 E3
Tugford Shrops 34 G1
Tullibardine Perth 76 F2
Tullibody Clack 75 H11
Tullich Argyll 73 B9
Tullich Highld 81 A8
Tullich Muir Highld 87 D10
Tulliemet Perth 76 B2
Tulloch Aberds 83 F9
Tulloch Aberds 89 E8
Tulloch Perth 76 E3
Tulloch Castle Highld 87 E8
Tullochgorm Argyll 73 D8
Tulloes Angus 77 C8
Tullybannocher Perth 75 E10
Tullybelton Perth 76 D3
Tullyfergus Perth 76 C5
Tullymurdoch Perth 76 B4
Tullynessle Aberds 83 B7
Tumble Carms 23 E10
Tumby Woodside Lincs 46 G6
Tummel Bridge Perth 75 B10
Tunga W Isles 91 D9
Tunstall E Yorks 53 F9
Tunstall Kent 20 E5
Tunstall Lancs 50 B2
Tunstall N Yorks 58 G3
Tunstall Norf 39 E10
Tunstall Stoke 44 G2
Tunstall Suff 31 C10
Tunstall T&W 58 A4
Tunstead Derbys 44 E5
Tunstead Gtr Man 44 B4
Tunstead Norf 39 C8
Tunworth Hants 18 G3
Tupsley Hereford 26 D2
Tupton Derbys 45 F7
Tur Langton Leics 36 F3
Turgis Green Hants 18 F3
Turin Angus 77 B8
Turkdean Glos 27 G8
Turleigh Wilts 16 E5
Turn Lancs 50 H4
Turnastone Hereford 25 E10
Turnberry S Ayrs 66 F5
Turnditch Derbys 44 H6
Turners Hill W Sus 12 C2
Turners Puddle Dorset 9 E7
Turnford Herts 19 A10
Turnhouse Edin 69 C10
Turnworth Dorset 9 D7
Turriff Aberds 89 C7
Turton Bottoms Blackburn 50 H3
Turves Cambs 37 F9
Turvey Bedford 28 C6
Turville Bucks 18 B4
Turville Heath Bucks 18 B4
Turweston Bucks 28 E3
Tushielaw Borders 61 B9
Tutbury Staffs 35 C8
Tutnall Worcs 26 A6
Tutshill Glos 15 B11
Tuttington Norf 39 C8
Tutts Clump W Berks 18 D2
Tuxford Notts 45 E11
Twatt Orkney 95 F3
Twatt Shetland 96 H5
Twechar E Dunb 68 C6
Tweedmouth Northumb 71 E8
Tweedsmuir Borders 60 A6
Twelve Heads Corn 3 E6
Twemlow Green Ches E 43 F10
Twenty Lincs 37 C7
Twerton Bath 16 E4
Twickenham London 19 D8
Twigworth Glos 26 F5
Twineham W Sus 12 E1
Twinhoe Bath 16 F4
Twinstead Essex 30 E5
Twinstead Green Essex 30 E5
Twiss Green Warr 43 C9
Twiston Lancs 50 E4
Twitchen Devon 7 C6
Twitchen Shrops 33 H9
Two Bridges Devon 5 D7
Two Dales Derbys 44 F6
Two Mills Ches W 42 E6
Twycross Leics 35 E9
Twyford Bucks 28 F3
Twyford Derbys 35 C9
Twyford Hants 10 B3
Twyford Leics 36 D3
Twyford Lincs 36 C5
Twyford Norf 38 C6
Twyford Wokingham 18 D4
Twyford Common Hereford 26 E2
Twyn-y-Sheriff Mon 25 H11
Twynholm Dumfries 55 D9
Twyning Glos 26 E5
Twyning Green Glos 26 E6
Twynllanan Carms 24 F4
Twynmynydd Carms 24 G3
Twywell Northants 36 H5
Ty-draw Conwy 41 E10
Ty-hen Carms 23 D8
Ty-hen Gwyn 40 G3
Ty-mawr Anglesey 40 B6
Ty Mawr Carms 23 B10
Ty Mawr Cwm Conwy 42 H2
Ty-nant Conwy 32 A5
Ty-nant Gwyn 32 C5
Ty-uchaf Powys 32 C6
Tyberton Hereford 25 E10
Tyburn W Mid 35 F7
Tycroes Carms 24 G3
Tycrwyn Powys 33 D7
Tydd Gote Lincs 37 D10
Tydd St Giles Cambs 37 D10
Tydd St Mary Lincs 37 D10
Tyddewi = St David's Pembs 22 D2
Tyddyn-mawr Gwyn 41 F7
Tye Green Essex 29 H11
Tye Green Essex 30 E2
Tye Green Essex 30 F4
Tyldesley Gtr Man 43 B9
Tyler Hill Kent 21 E8
Tylers Green Bucks 18 B6
Tylorstown Rhondda 14 B6
Tylwch Powys 32 G5
Tyn-y-celyn Wrex 33 B7
Tyn-y-coed Shrops 33 C8
Tyn-y-fedwen Powys 33 B7
Tyn-y-ffridd Powys 33 B7
Tyn-y-graig Powys 25 C7
Ty'n-y-groes Conwy 41 C9
Ty'n-y-maes Gwyn 41 D8
Tyn-y-pwll Anglesey 40 B6
Ty'n-yr-eithin Ceredig 24 B3
Tyncelyn Ceredig 24 B3
Tyndrum Stirling 74 D6
Tyne Tunnel T&W 63 G9
Tyneham Dorset 9 F7
Tynehead Midloth 70 E2
Tynemouth T&W 63 G9
Tynewydd Rhondda 14 B5
Tyninghame E Loth 70 C5
Tynron Dumfries 60 D4
Tynygongl Anglesey 41 B7
Tynygraig Ceredig 24 B3
Tŷ'r-felin-isaf Conwy 41 D10
Tyrie Aberds 89 B9
Tyringham M Keynes 28 D5
Tythecott Devon 6 E3
Tythegston Bridgend 14 D4
Tytherington Ches E 44 E3
Tytherington S Glos 16 C3
Tytherington Som 16 G4
Tytherington Wilts 16 G6
Tytherleigh Devon 8 D2
Tywardreath Corn 4 F1
Tywyn Conwy 41 C9
Tywyn Gwyn 32 E1

U

Uachdar W Isles 84 C2
Uags Highld 85 E12
Ubbeston Green Suff 31 A10
Ubley Bath 15 F11
Uckerby N Yorks 58 F3
Uckfield E Sus 12 D3
Uckington Glos 26 F6
Uddingston S Lanark 68 D5
Uddington S Lanark 69 G7
Udimore E Sus 13 E7
Udny Green Aberds 89 F8
Udny Station Aberds 89 F9
Udston S Lanark 68 E5
Udstonhead S Lanark 68 F6
Uffcott Wilts 17 D8
Uffculme Devon 7 E9
Uffington Lincs 37 E6
Uffington Oxon 17 C10
Uffington Shrops 33 D11
Ufford Pboro 37 E6
Ufford Suff 31 C9
Ufton Warks 27 B10
Ufton Nervet W Berks 18 E3
Ugadale Argyll 65 F8
Ugborough Devon 5 F7
Uggeshall Suff 39 G10
Ugglebarnby N Yorks 59 F9
Ughill S Yorks 44 C6
Ugley Essex 30 F2
Ugley Green Essex 30 F2
Ugthorpe N Yorks 59 E8
Uidh W Isles 84 J1
Uig Argyll 73 E10
Uig Highld 84 C6
Uig Highld 85 B8
Uigen W Isles 90 D5
Uigshader Highld 85 D9
Uisken Argyll 78 K6
Ulbster Highld 94 F5
Ulceby Lincs 47 E8
Ulceby N Lincs 46 A5
Ulceby Skitter N Lincs 46 A5
Ulcombe Kent 20 G5
Uldale Cumb 56 C4
Uley Glos 16 B4
Ulgham Northumb 63 D8
Ullapool Highld 86 B4
Ullenhall Warks 27 B8
Ullenwood Glos 26 G6
Ulleskelf N Yorks 51 E11
Ullesthorpe Leics 35 G11
Ulley S Yorks 45 D8
Ullingswick Hereford 26 D2
Ullinish Highld 85 E8
Ullock Cumb 56 D2
Ulnes Walton Lancs 49 H5
Ulpha Cumb 56 G3
Ulrome E Yorks 53 D7
Ulsta Shetland 96 E6
Ulva House Argyll 78 H7
Ulverston Cumb 49 B2
Ulwell Dorset 9 F9
Umberleigh Devon 6 D5
Unapool Highld 92 F5
Unasary W Isles 84 F2
Underbarrow Cumb 56 G6
Undercliffe W Yorks 51 F7
Underhoull Shetland 96 C7
Underriver Kent 20 F2
Underwood Notts 45 G8
Undy Mon 15 C10
Unifirth Shetland 96 H4
Union Cottage Aberds 83 D10
Union Mills IoM 48 E3
Union Street E Sus 12 C6
Unstone Derbys 45 E7
Unstone Green Derbys 45 E7
Unthank Cumb 56 C6
Unthank Cumb 57 B8
Unthank End Cumb 56 C6
Up Cerne Dorset 8 D5
Up Exe Devon 7 F8
Up Hatherley Glos 26 F6
Up Holland Lancs 43 B8
Up Marden W Sus 11 C6
Up Nately Hants 18 F3
Up Somborne Hants 10 A2
Up Sydling Dorset 8 D5
Upavon Wilts 17 F8
Upchurch Kent 20 E5
Upcott Hereford 25 C10
Upend Cambs 30 C3
Upgate Norf 39 D7
Uphall W Loth 69 C9
Uphall Station W Loth 69 C9
Upham Devon 7 F7
Upham Hants 10 B4
Uphampton Worcs 26 B5
Uphill N Som 15 F9
Uplawmoor E Renf 68 E3
Upleadon Glos 26 F4
Upleatham Redcar 59 E7
Uplees Kent 20 E6
Uploders Dorset 8 E4
Uplowman Devon 7 E9
Uplyme Devon 8 E2
Upminster London 20 C2
Upnor Medway 20 D4
Upottery Devon 7 F11
Upper Affcot Shrops 33 G10
Upper Ardchronie Highld 87 C9
Upper Arley Worcs 34 G3
Upper Arncott Oxon 28 G3
Upper Astrop Northants 28 E2
Upper Badcall Highld 92 E4
Upper Basildon W Berks 18 D2
Upper Beeding W Sus 11 C10
Upper Benefield Northants 36 G5
Upper Bighouse Highld 93 D11
Upper Boddington Northants 27 C11
Upper Borth Ceredig 32 G2
Upper Boyndlie Aberds 89 B9
Upper Brailes Warks 27 E10
Upper Breakish Highld 85 F11
Upper Breinton Hereford 25 D11
Upper Broadheath Worcs 26 C5
Upper Broughton Notts 36 C2
Upper Bucklebury W Berks 18 E2
Upper Burnhaugh Aberds 83 D10
Upper Caldecote C Beds 29 D8
Upper Catesby Northants 28 C2
Upper Chapel Powys 25 D7
Upper Church Village Rhondda 14 C6
Upper Chute Wilts 17 F9
Upper Clatford Hants 17 G10
Upper Clynnog Gwyn 40 F6
Upper Cumberworth W Yorks 44 B6
Upper Cwm-twrch Powys 24 G4
Upper Cwmbran Torf 15 B8
Upper Dallachy Moray 88 B3
Upper Dean Bedford 29 B7
Upper Denby W Yorks 44 B6
Upper Denton Cumb 62 G2
Upper Derraid Highld 87 H13
Upper Dicker E Sus 12 F4
Upper Dovercourt Essex 31 E9
Upper Druimfin Argyll 79 F8
Upper Dunsforth N Yorks 51 C10
Upper Eathie Highld 87 E10
Upper Elkstone Staffs 44 G4
Upper End Derbys 44 E4
Upper Farringdon Hants 18 H4
Upper Framilode Glos 26 G4
Upper Glenfintaig Highld 80 E4
Upper Gornal W Mid 34 F5
Upper Gravenhurst C Beds 29 E8
Upper Green Mon 25 G10
Upper Green W Berks 17 E10
Upper Grove Common Hereford 26 F2
Upper Hackney Derbys 44 F6
Upper Hale Sur 18 G5
Upper Halistra Highld 84 C7
Upper Halling Medway 20 E3
Upper Hambleton Rutland 36 E5
Upper Hardres Court Kent 21 F8
Upper Hartfield E Sus 12 C3
Upper Haugh S Yorks 45 C8
Upper Heath Shrops 34 G1
Upper Hellesdon Norf 39 D8
Upper Helmsley N Yorks 52 D2
Upper Hergest Hereford 25 C9
Upper Heyford Northants 28 C3
Upper Heyford Oxon 27 F11
Upper Hill Hereford 25 C11
Upper Hopton W Yorks 51 H7
Upper Horsebridge E Sus 12 E4
Upper Hulme Staffs 44 F4
Upper Inglesham Swindon 17 B9
Upper Inverbrough Highld 87 H11
Upper Killay Swansea 23 G10
Upper Knockando Moray 88 D1
Upper Lambourn W Berks 17 C10
Upper Leigh Staffs 34 B6
Upper Lenie Highld 81 A7
Upper Lochton Aberds 83 D8
Upper Longdon Staffs 35 D6
Upper Lybster Highld 94 G4
Upper Lydbrook Glos 26 G3
Upper Maes-coed Hereford 25 E10
Upper Midway Derbys 35 C8
Upper Milovaig Highld 84 D6
Upper Minety Wilts 17 B7
Upper Mitton Worcs 26 A5
Upper North Dean Bucks 18 B5
Upper Obney Perth 76 D3
Upper Ollach Highld 85 E10
Upper Padley Derbys 44 E6
Upper Pollicott Bucks 28 G4
Upper Poppleton York 52 D1
Upper Quinton Warks 27 D8
Upper Ratley Hants 10 B2
Upper Rissington Glos 27 G9
Upper Rochford Worcs 26 B3
Upper Sandaig Highld 85 G12
Upper Sanday Orkney 95 H6
Upper Sapey Hereford 26 B3
Upper Saxondale Notts 36 B2
Upper Seagry Wilts 16 C6
Upper Shelton C Beds 28 D6
Upper Sheringham Norf 39 A7
Upper Skelmorlie N Ayrs 73 G11
Upper Slaughter Glos 27 F8
Upper Soudley Glos 26 G3
Upper Stondon C Beds 29 E8
Upper Stowe Northants 28 C3
Upper Stratton Swindon 17 C8
Upper Street Hants 9 C10
Upper Street Norf 39 D9
Upper Street Norf 39 D9
Upper Street Suff 31 E8
Upper Strensham Worcs 26 E6
Upper Sundon C Beds 29 F7
Upper Swell Glos 27 F8
Upper Tean Staffs 34 B6
Upper Tillyrie Perth 76 G4
Upper Tooting London 19 D9
Upper Tote Highld 85 C10
Upper Town N Som 15 E11
Upper Treverward Shrops 33 H8
Upper Tysoe Warks 27 D10
Upper Upham Wilts 17 D9
Upper Wardington Oxon 27 D11
Upper Weald M Keynes 28 E4
Upper Weedon Northants 28 C3
Upper Wield Hants 18 H3
Upper Winchendon Bucks 28 G4
Upper Witton W Mid 35 F6
Upper Woodend Aberds 83 B8
Upper Woodford Wilts 17 H8
Upper Wootton Hants 18 F2
Upper Wyche Hereford 26 D4
Upperby Cumb 56 A6
Uppermill Gtr Man 44 B3
Uppersound Shetland 96 J6
Upperthong W Yorks 44 B5
Upperthorpe N Lincs 45 B11
Upperton W Sus 11 B8
Uppertown Derbys 45 F7
Uppertown Highld 94 C5
Uppertown Orkney 95 J5
Uppingham Rutland 36 F4
Uppington Shrops 34 E2
Upsall N Yorks 58 H5
Upshire Essex 19 A11
Upstreet Kent 21 E9
Upthorpe Suff 30 A6
Upton Cambs 37 H7
Upton Ches W 43 F7
Upton Corn 6 F1
Upton Dorset 8 F6
Upton Dorset 9 E8
Upton Hants 10 C2
Upton Hants 17 F10
Upton Leics 35 F9
Upton Lincs 46 D2
Upton Mers 42 D5
Upton Norf 39 D9
Upton Northants 28 B4
Upton Notts 45 E11
Upton Notts 45 G11
Upton Oxon 18 C2
Upton Pboro 37 E7
Upton Slough 18 D6
Upton Som 7 D8
Upton W Yorks 45 A8
Upton Bishop Hereford 26 F3
Upton Cheyney S Glos 16 E3
Upton Cressett Shrops 34 F2
Upton Cross Corn 4 D3
Upton Grey Hants 18 G3
Upton Hellions Devon 7 F7
Upton Lovell Wilts 16 G6
Upton Magna Shrops 34 D1
Upton Noble Som 16 H4
Upton Pyne Devon 7 G8
Upton St Leonard's Glos 26 G5
Upton Scudamore Wilts 16 G5
Upton Snodsbury Worcs 26 C6
Upton upon Severn Worcs 26 D5
Upton Warren Worcs 26 B6
Upwaltham W Sus 11 C8
Upware Cambs 30 A2
Upwell Norf 37 E10
Upwey Dorset 8 F5
Upwood Cambs 37 G8
Uradale Shetland 96 K6
Urafirth Shetland 96 F5
Urchfont Wilts 17 F7
Urdimarsh Hereford 26 D2
Ure Shetland 96 F4
Ure Bank N Yorks 51 B9
Urgha W Isles 90 H6
Urishay Common Hereford 25 E10
Urlay Nook Stockton 58 E4
Urmston Gtr Man 43 C10
Urpeth Durham 58 A3
Urquhart Highld 87 F8
Urquhart Moray 88 B2
Urra N Yorks 59 F6
Urray Highld 87 F8
Ushaw Moor Durham 58 B3
Usk = Brynbuga Mon 15 A9
Usselby Lincs 46 C4
Usworth T&W 63 H9
Utkinton Ches W 43 F8
Utley W Yorks 50 E6
Uton Devon 7 G7
Utterby Lincs 47 C7
Uttoxeter Staffs 35 B6
Uwchmynydd Gwyn 40 H3
Uxbridge London 19 C7
Uyeasound Shetland 96 C7
Uzmaston Pembs 22 E4

V

Valley Anglesey 40 C4
Valley Truckle Corn 4 C1
Valleyfield Dumfries 55 D9
Valsgarth Shetland 96 B8
Valtos Highld 85 B10
Van Powys 32 G5
Vange Essex 20 C4
Varteg Torf 25 H9
Vatten Highld 85 D7
Vaul Argyll 78 G3
Vaynor M Tydf 25 G7
Veensgarth Shetland 96 J6
Velindre Powys 25 E8
Vellow Som 7 C9
Veness Orkney 95 F6
Venn Green Devon 6 E2
Venn Ottery Devon 7 G9
Vennington Shrops 33 E9
Venny Tedburn Devon 7 G7
Ventnor IoW 10 G4
Vernham Dean Hants 17 F10
Vernham Street Hants 17 F10
Vernolds Common Shrops 33 G10
Verwood Dorset 9 D9
Veryan Corn 3 F8
Vicarage Devon 7 H11
Vickerstown Cumb 49 C1
Victoria Corn 3 C8
Victoria S Yorks 44 B5
Vidlin Shetland 96 G6
Viewpark N Lanark 68 D6
Vigo Village Kent 20 E3
Vinehall Street E Sus 13 D6
Vine's Cross E Sus 12 E4
Viney Hill Glos 26 H3
Virginia Water Sur 18 E6
Virginstow Devon 6 G2
Vobster Som 16 G4
Voe Shetland 96 E5
Voe Shetland 96 G6
Vowchurch Hereford 25 E10
Voxter Shetland 96 F5
Voy Orkney 95 G3

W

Wackerfield Durham 58 D2
Wacton Norf 39 F7
Wadbister Shetland 96 J6
Wadborough Worcs 26 D6
Waddesdon Bucks 28 G4
Waddingham Lincs 46 C3
Waddington Lancs 50 E3
Waddington Lincs 46 F3
Wadebridge Corn 3 B8
Wadeford Som 8 C2
Wadenhoe Northants 36 G6
Wadesmill Herts 29 G10
Wadhurst E Sus 12 C5
Wadshelf Derbys 45 E7
Wadsley S Yorks 45 C7
Wadsley Bridge S Yorks 45 C7
Wadworth S Yorks 45 C9
Waen Denb 42 F4
Waen Denb 42 F2
Waen Fach Powys 33 D8
Waen Goleugoed Denb 42 E3
Wag Highld 93 G13
Wainfleet All Saints Lincs 47 G8
Wainfleet Bank Lincs 47 G8
Wainfleet St Mary Lincs 47 G9
Wainfleet Tofts Lincs 47 G8
Wainhouse Corner Corn 4 B2
Wainscott Medway 20 D4
Wainstalls W Yorks 50 G6
Waitby Cumb 57 F9
Waithe Lincs 46 B6
Wake Lady Green N Yorks 59 G7
Wakefield W Yorks 51 G9
Wakerley Northants 36 F5
Wakes Colne Essex 30 F5
Walberswick Suff 31 A11
Walberton W Sus 11 D8
Walbottle T&W 63 G7
Walcot Lincs 37 B6
Walcot N Lincs 52 G4
Walcot Shrops 33 G9
Walcot Swindon 17 C8
Walcot Telford 34 D1
Walcot Green Norf 39 G7
Walcote Leics 36 G1
Walcote Warks 27 C8
Walcott Lincs 46 G5
Walcott Norf 39 B9
Walden N Yorks 50 A6
Walden Head N Yorks 50 A5
Walden Stubbs N Yorks 52 H1
Waldersey Cambs 37 E10
Walderslade Medway 20 E4
Walderton W Sus 11 C6
Walditch Dorset 8 E3
Waldley Derbys 35 B7
Waldridge Durham 58 A3
Waldringfield Suff 31 D9
Waldringfield Heath Suff 31 D9
Waldron E Sus 12 E4
Wales S Yorks 45 D8
Walesby Lincs 46 C5
Walesby Notts 45 E10
Walford Hereford 25 A10
Walford Hereford 26 F2
Walford Shrops 33 C10
Walford Heath Shrops 33 D10
Walgherton Ches E 43 H9
Walgrave Northants 28 A5
Walhampton Hants 10 E2
Walk Mill Lancs 50 F4
Walkden Gtr Man 43 B10
Walker T&W 63 G8
Walker Barn Ches E 44 E3
Walker Fold Lancs 50 E2
Walkerburn Borders 70 G2
Walkeringham Notts 45 C11
Walkerith Lincs 45 C11
Walkern Herts 29 F9
Walker's Green Hereford 26 D2
Walkerville N Yorks 58 G3
Walkford Dorset 9 E11
Walkhampton Devon 4 E6
Walkington E Yorks 52 F5
Walkley S Yorks 45 D7
Wall Northumb 62 G5
Wall Staffs 35 E7
Wall Bank Shrops 33 F11
Wall Heath W Mid 34 G4
Wall under Heywood Shrops 33 F11
Wallaceton Dumfries 60 E4
Wallacetown S Ayrs 66 D6
Wallacetown S Ayrs 66 F5
Wallands Park E Sus 12 E3
Wallasey Mers 42 C6
Wallcrouch E Sus 12 C5
Wallingford Oxon 18 C3
Wallington Hants 10 D4
Wallington Herts 29 E9
Wallington London 19 E9
Wallis Pembs 22 D5
Walliswood Sur 19 H8
Walls Shetland 96 J4
Wallsend T&W 63 G8
Wallston V Glam 15 D7
Wallyford E Loth 70 C2
Walmer Kent 21 F10
Walmer Bridge Lancs 49 G4
Walmersley Gtr Man 44 A2
Walmley W Mid 35 F7
Walpole Suff 31 A10
Walpole Cross Keys Norf 37 D11
Walpole Highway Norf 37 D11
Walpole Marsh Norf 37 D10
Walpole St Andrew Norf 37 D11
Walpole St Peter Norf 37 D11
Walsall W Mid 34 F6
Walsall Wood W Mid 34 E6
Walsden W Yorks 50 G5
Walsgrave on Sowe W Mid 35 G9
Walsham le Willows Suff 30 A6
Walshaw Gtr Man 43 A10
Walshford N Yorks 51 D10
Walsoken Cambs 37 D10
Walston S Lanark 69 F9
Walsworth Herts 29 E9
Walters Ash Bucks 18 B5
Walterston V Glam 14 D6
Walterstone Hereford 25 F10
Waltham Kent 21 G8
Waltham NE Lincs 46 B6
Waltham Abbey Essex 19 A10
Waltham Chase Hants 10 C4
Waltham Cross Herts 19 A10
Waltham on the Wolds Leics 36 C4
Waltham St Lawrence Windsor 18 D5
Walthamstow London 19 C10
Walton Cumb 61 G11
Walton Derbys 45 F7
Walton Leics 36 G1
Walton M Keynes 28 E5
Walton Mers 42 C6
Walton Pboro 37 E7
Walton Powys 25 C9
Walton Som 15 H10
Walton Staffs 34 B4
Walton Suff 31 E9
Walton Telford 34 D1
Walton W Yorks 51 E10
Walton W Yorks 51 H9
Walton Warks 27 C9
Walton Cardiff Glos 26 E6
Walton East Pembs 22 D5
Walton-in-Gordano N Som 15 D10
Walton-le-Dale Lancs 50 G1
Walton-on-Thames Sur 19 E8
Walton on the Hill Staffs 34 C5
Walton on the Hill Sur 19 F9
Walton-on-the-Naze Essex 31 F9
Walton on the Wolds Leics 36 D1
Walton-on-Trent Derbys 35 D8
Walton West Pembs 22 E3
Walwen Flint 42 E5
Walwick Northumb 62 F5
Walworth Darl 58 E3
Walworth Gate Darl 58 D3
Walwyn's Castle Pembs 22 E3
Wambrook Som 8 D1
Wanborough Sur 18 G6
Wanborough Swindon 17 C9
Wandsworth London 19 D9
Wangford Suff 39 H10
Wanlockhead Dumfries 60 B4
Wansford E Yorks 53 D6
Wansford Pboro 37 F6
Wanstead London 19 C11
Wanstrow Som 16 G4
Wanswell Glos 16 A3
Wantage Oxon 17 C10
Wapley S Glos 16 D4
Wappenbury Warks 27 B10
Wappenham Northants 28 D3
Warbleton E Sus 12 E5
Warblington Hants 10 D6
Warborough Oxon 18 B2
Warboys Cambs 37 G9
Warbreck Blackpool 49 F3
Warbstow Corn 4 B3
Warburton Gtr Man 43 D10
Warcop Cumb 57 E9
Ward End W Mid 35 G7
Ward Green Suff 31 B7
Warden Kent 21 D7
Warden Northumb 62 G5
Wardhill Orkney 95 F7
Wardington Oxon 27 D11
Wardlaw Borders 61 B8
Wardle Ches E 43 G9
Wardle Gtr Man 50 H5
Wardley Rutland 36 E4
Wardlow Derbys 44 E5
Wardy Hill Cambs 37 G10
Ware Herts 29 G10
Ware Kent 21 E9
Wareham Dorset 9 F8
Warehorne Kent 13 C8
Waren Mill Northumb 71 G10
Warenford Northumb 71 H10
Warenton Northumb 71 G10
Wareside Herts 29 G10
Waresley Cambs 29 C9
Waresley Worcs 26 A5
Warfield Brack 18 D5
Warfleet Devon 5 F9
Wargrave Wokingham 18 D4
Warham Norf 38 A5
Warhill Gtr Man 44 C3
Wark Northumb 62 F4
Wark Northumb 71 G7
Warkleigh Devon 6 D5
Warkton Northants 36 H4
Warkworth Northants 27 D11
Warkworth Northumb 63 C8
Warlaby N Yorks 58 G4
Warland W Yorks 50 G5
Warleggan Corn 4 E2
Warlingham Sur 19 F10
Warmfield W Yorks 51 G9
Warmingham Ches E 43 F10
Warmington Northants 37 F6
Warmington Warks 27 D11
Warminster Wilts 16 G5
Warmlake Kent 20 F5
Warmley S Glos 16 D3
Warmley Tower S Glos 16 D3
Warmonds Hill Northants 28 B6
Warmsworth S Yorks 45 B9
Warmwell Dorset 9 F6
Warndon Worcs 26 C5
Warnford Hants 10 B5
Warnham W Sus 11 A10
Warninglid W Sus 11 B11
Warren Ches E 44 E2
Warren Pembs 22 G4
Warren Heath Suff 31 D9
Warren Row Windsor 18 C5
Warren Street Kent 20 F6
Warrington M Keynes 28 C5
Warrington Warr 43 D9
Warsash Hants 10 D3
Warslow Staffs 44 G4
Warter E Yorks 52 D4
Warthermarske N Yorks 51 B8
Warthill N Yorks 52 D2
Wartling E Sus 12 F5
Wartnaby Leics 36 C3
Warton Lancs 49 B4
Warton Lancs 49 G4
Warton Northumb 62 C6
Warton Warks 35 E8
Warwick Warks 27 B9
Warwick Bridge Cumb 61 H10
Warwick on Eden Cumb 61 H10
Wasbister Orkney 95 E4
Wasdale Head Cumb 56 F3
Wash Common W Berks 17 E11
Washaway Corn 3 C9
Washbourne Devon 5 F8
Washfield Devon 7 E8
Washfold N Yorks 58 F1
Washford Som 7 B9
Washford Pyne Devon 7 E7
Washingborough Lincs 46 E4
Washington T&W 63 H9
Washington W Sus 11 C10
Wasing W Berks 18 E2
Waskerley Durham 58 B1
Wasperton Warks 27 C9
Wasps Nest Lincs 46 F4
Wass N Yorks 52 B1
Watchet Som 7 B9
Watchfield Oxon 17 B9
Watchfield Som 15 G9
Watchgate Cumb 57 G7
Watchhill Cumb 56 B3
Watcombe Torbay 5 E10
Watendlath Cumb 56 E4
Water Devon 5 C8
Water Lancs 50 G4
Water End E Yorks 52 F3
Water End Herts 19 A9
Water End Herts 29 G7
Water Newton Cambs 37 F7
Water Orton Warks 35 F7
Water Stratford Bucks 28 E3
Water Yeat Cumb 56 H4
Waterbeach Cambs 29 B11
Waterbeck Dumfries 61 F8
Waterden Norf 38 B4
Waterfall Staffs 44 G4
Waterfoot E Renf 68 E4
Waterfoot Lancs 50 G4
Waterford Hants 10 E2
Waterford Herts 29 G10
Waterhead Cumb 56 F5
Waterhead Dumfries 61 D7
Waterheads Borders 69 E11
Waterhouses Durham 58 B2
Waterhouses Staffs 44 G4
Wateringbury Kent 20 F3
Waterloo Gtr Man 44 B3
Waterloo Highld 85 F11
Waterloo Mers 42 C6
Waterloo N Lanark 69 E7
Waterloo Norf 39 D8
Waterloo Perth 76 D3
Waterloo Poole 9 E9
Waterloo Shrops 33 B11
Waterloo Port Gwyn 40 D6
Waterlooville Hants 10 D5
Watermeetings S Lanark 60 B5
Watermillock Cumb 56 D6
Waterperry Oxon 28 H3
Waterrow Som 7 D9
Water's Nook Gtr Man 43 B9
Waters Upton Telford 34 D2
Watersfield W Sus 11 C9
Waterside Aberds 89 F10
Waterside Blackburn 50 G3
Waterside Cumb 56 B4
Waterside E Ayrs 67 B7
Waterside E Ayrs 67 F7
Waterside E Dunb 68 C5
Waterside E Renf 68 E4
Waterstock Oxon 28 H3
Waterston Pembs 22 F4
Watford Herts 19 B8
Watford Northants 28 B3
Watford Gap Staffs 35 E7
Wath N Yorks 51 B9
Wath N Yorks 51 C7
Wath N Yorks 52 B2
Wath Brow Cumb 56 E2
Wath upon Dearne S Yorks 45 B8
Watlington Norf 38 D2
Watlington Oxon 18 B3
Watnall Notts 45 H9
Watten Highld 94 E4
Wattisfield Suff 31 A7
Wattisham Suff 31 C7
Wattlesborough Heath Shrops 33 D9
Watton E Yorks 52 D6
Watton Norf 38 E5
Watton at Stone Herts 29 G10
Wattston N Lanark 68 C6
Wattstown Rhondda 14 B6
Wauchan Highld 80 E1
Waulkmill Lodge Orkney 95 H4
Waun Powys 32 E4
Waun-y-clyn Carms 23 F9
Waunarlwydd Swansea 14 B2
Waunclunda Carms 24 E3
Waunfawr Gwyn 41 E7
Waungron Swansea 23 F10
Waunlwyd Bl Gwent 25 H8
Wavendon M Keynes 28 E6
Waverbridge Cumb 56 B4
Waverton Ches W 43 F7
Waverton Cumb 56 B4
Wavertree Mers 43 D6
Wawne E Yorks 53 F6
Waxham Norf 39 C10
Waxholme E Yorks 53 G9
Way Kent 21 E10
Way Village Devon 7 E7
Wayfield Medway 20 E4
Wayford Som 8 D3
Waymills Shrops 34 A1
Wayne Green Mon 25 G11
Wdig = Goodwick Pembs 22 C4
Weachyburn Aberds 89 C6
Weald Oxon 17 A10
Wealdstone London 19 C8
Weardley W Yorks 51 E8
Weare Som 15 F10
Weare Giffard Devon 6 D3
Wearhead Durham 57 C10
Weasdale Cumb 57 F8
Weasenham All Saints Norf 38 C4
Weasenham St Peter Norf 38 C4
Weatherhill Sur 12 B2
Weaverham Ches W 43 E9
Weaverthorpe N Yorks 52 B5
Webheath Worcs 27 B7
Wedderlairs Aberds 89 E8
Wedderlie Borders 70 E5
Weddington Warks 35 F9
Wedhampton Wilts 17 F7
Wedmore Som 15 G10
Wednesbury W Mid 34 F5
Wednesfield W Mid 34 E5
Weedon Bucks 28 G5
Weedon Bec Northants 28 C3
Weedon Lois Northants 28 D3
Weeford Staffs 35 E7
Week Devon 7 E6
Week St Mary Corn 4 B3
Weeke Hants 10 A3
Weekley Northants 36 G4
Weel E Yorks 53 F6
Weeley Essex 31 F8
Weeley Heath Essex 31 F8
Weem Perth 75 C11
Weeping Cross Staffs 34 C5
Weethley Gate Warks 27 C7
Weeting Norf 38 G3
Weeton E Yorks 53 G9
Weeton Lancs 49 F3

Weeton N Yorks 51 E8
Weetwood Hall 71 H9
Weir Lancs 50 G4
Weir Quay Devon 4 E5
Welborne Norf 39 E6
Welborn Lincs 46 G3
Welburn N Yorks 51 F6
Welburn N Yorks 52 C3
Welby Lincs 36 B5
Welches Dam Cambs 37 G10
Welcombe Devon 6 E1
Weld Bank Lancs 50 G1
Weldon Northumb 63 D7
Welford Northants 36 G2
Welford W Berks 26 B2
Welford-on-Avon Warks 27 C8
Welham Leics 36 F3
Welham Notts 45 D11
Welham Green Herts 29 H9
Well Hants 18 G4
Well Lincs 47 E8
Well N Yorks 51 A8
Well End Bucks 18 C5
Well Heads W Yorks 51 F6
Well Hill Kent 19 E11
Well Town Devon 7 F8
Welland Worcs 26 D4
Wellbank Angus 77 D7
Welldale Dumfries 61 G7
Wellesbourne Warks 27 C9
Welling London 19 D11
Wellingborough Northants 28 B5
Wellingham Norf 38 C4
Wellingore Lincs 46 G3
Wellington Cumb 56 F2
Wellington Hereford 25 D11
Wellington Som 7 D10
Wellington Telford 34 D2
Wellington Heath Hereford 26 D4
Wellington Hill W Yorks 51 F9
Wellow Bath 16 F4
Wellow IoW 10 F2
Wellow Notts 45 F10
Wellpond Green Herts 29 F11
Wells Som 16 G2
Wells Green Ches E 43 G9
Wells-Next-The-Sea Norf 38 A5
Wellsborough Leics 35 E9
Wellswood Torbay 5 E10
Wellwood Fife 69 B9
Welney Norf 37 F11
Welsh Bicknor Hereford 26 G2
Welsh End Shrops 33 B11
Welsh Frankton Shrops 33 B9
Welsh Hook Pembs 22 D4
Welsh Newton Hereford 25 G11
Welsh St Donats V Glam 14 D6
Welshampton Shrops 33 B10
Welshpool = Y Trallwng Powys 33 E8
Welton Cumb 56 B5
Welton E Yorks 52 G5
Welton Lincs 46 E4
Welton Northants 28 B2
Welton Hill Lincs 46 D4
Welton le Marsh Lincs 47 F8
Welton le Wold Lincs 46 D6
Welwick E Yorks 53 G9
Welwyn Herts 29 G9
Welwyn Garden City Herts 29 G9
Wem Shrops 33 C11
Wembdon Som 15 H8
Wembley London 19 C8
Wembury Devon 4 G6
Wembworthy Devon 6 F5
Wemyss Bay Invclyd 73 G10
Wenallt Ceredig 24 A3
Wenallt S Glam 32 A5
Wendens Ambo Essex 30 E2
Wendlebury Oxon 28 G2
Wendling Norf 38 D5
Wendover Bucks 28 H5
Wendron Corn 2 F5
Wendy Cambs 29 D10
Wenfordbridge Corn 4 D1
Wenhaston Suff 39 H10
Wennington Cambs 29 A9
Wennington London 20 C2
Wennington Lancs 50 C2
Wensley Derbys 44 F6
Wensley N Yorks 58 H1
Wentbridge W Yorks 51 H10
Wentnor Shrops 33 F9
Wentworth Cambs 37 H10
Wentworth S Yorks 45 C7
Wenvoe V Glam 15 D7
Weobley Hereford 25 C11
Weobley Marsh Hereford 25 C11
Wereham Norf 38 E2
Wergs W Mid 34 E4
Wern Powys 32 G5
Wern Powys 33 D8
Wernffrwd Swansea 23 G10
Wernyrheolydd Mon 25 G10
Werrington Corn 4 C4
Werrington Pboro 37 E7
Werrington Staffs 44 H3
Wervin Ches W 43 E7
Wesham Lancs 49 F4
Wessington Derbys 45 G7
West Acre Norf 38 D3
West Adderbury Oxon 27 E11
West Allerdean Northumb 71 F8
West Alvington Devon 5 G8
West Amesbury Wilts 17 G8
West Anstey Devon 7 D7
West Ashby Lincs 46 E6
West Ashling W Sus 11 D7
West Ashton Wilts 16 F5
West Auckland Durham 58 D2
West Ayton N Yorks 52 A5
West Bagborough Som 7 C10
West Barkwith Lincs 46 D5
West Barnby N Yorks 59 E9
West Barns E Loth 70 C5
West Barsham Norf 38 B5
West Bay Dorset 8 E3
West Beckham Norf 39 B7
West Bedfont Sur 19 D7
West Benhar N Lanark 69 D7
West Bergholt Essex 30 F6
West Bexington Dorset 8 F4
West Bilney Norf 38 D2
West Blatchington Brighton 12 F1
West Bowling W Yorks 51 F7
West Bradford Lancs 50 E3
West Bradley Som 16 H2
West Bretton W Yorks 44 A6
West Bridgford Notts 36 B1
West Bromwich W Mid 34 F6
West Buckland Devon 6 C5
West Buckland Som 7 D10
West Burrafirth Shetland 96 H4
West Burton N Yorks 58 H1
West Burton W Sus 11 C8
West Butterwick N Lincs 46 B2
West Byfleet Sur 19 E7
West Caister Norf 39 D11
West Calder W Loth 69 D9
West Challow Oxon 17 C10

West Chelborough Dorset 8 D4
West Chevington Northumb 63 D8
West Chiltington W Sus 11 C9
West Chiltington Common W Sus 11 C9
West Chinnock Som 8 C3
West Chisenbury Wilts 17 F8
West Clandon Sur 19 F7
West Cliffe Kent 21 G10
West Clyne Highld 93 J11
West Coker Som 8 C4
West Compton Dorset 8 E4
West Compton Som 16 G2
West Cowick E Yorks 52 G2
West Cranmore Som 16 G3
West Cross Swansea 14 C2
West Cullerly Aberds 83 C9
West Curry Corn 6 G1
West Curthwaite Cumb 56 B5
West Darlochan Argyll 65 F7
West Dean W Sus 11 C7
West Dean Wilts 10 B1
West Deeping Lincs 37 E7
West Derby Mers 43 C6
West Dereham Norf 38 E2
West Didsbury Gtr Man 44 C2
West Ditchburn Northumb 63 A7
West Down Devon 6 B4
West Drayton London 19 D7
West Drayton Notts 45 E11
West Ella E Yorks 52 G6
West End Bedford 28 C6
West End E Yorks 52 F5
West End E Yorks 53 F7
West End Hants 10 C3
West End Lancs 50 D1
West End N Som 15 D7
West End N Yorks 51 D7
West End Norf 39 D11
West End Oxon 17 A11
West End S Lanark 69 F8
West End Suff 39 G10
West End Sur 18 E6
West End W Sus 11 C11
West End Wilts 9 B8
West End Wilts 16 D5
West End Green Hants 18 E3
West Farleigh Kent 20 F4
West Felton Shrops 33 C9
West Fenton E Loth 70 B3
West Ferry Dundee 77 D7
West Firle E Sus 12 F3
West Ginge Oxon 17 C11
West Grafton Wilts 17 E9
West Green Hants 18 F4
West Greenskares Aberds 89 B7
West Grimstead Wilts 9 B11
West Grinstead W Sus 11 B10
West Haddlesey N Yorks 52 G1
West Haddon Northants 28 A3
West Hagbourne Oxon 18 C2
West Hagley Worcs 34 G5
West Hall Cumb 61 G11
West Hallam Derbys 35 A10
West Halton N Lincs 52 G5
West Ham London 19 C11
West Handley Derbys 45 E7
West Hanney Oxon 17 B11
West Hanningfield Essex 20 B4
West Hardwick W Yorks 51 H10
West Harnham Wilts 9 B10
West Harptree Bath 16 F2
West Hatch Som 8 B1
West Hatch Wilts 9 B8
West Head Norf 38 E1
West Heath Ches E 44 F2
West Heath Hants 18 F2
West Helmsdale Highld 93 H13
West Hendred Oxon 17 C11
West Heslerton N Yorks 52 B5
West Hill Devon 7 G9
West Hill E Yorks 53 C7
West Hill N Som 15 D10
West Hoathly W Sus 12 C2
West Holme Dorset 9 F7
West Horndon Essex 20 C3
West Horrington Som 16 G2
West Horsley Sur 19 F7
West Horton Northumb 71 G9
West Hougham Kent 21 G9
West Houlland Shetland 96 H4
West-houses Derbys 45 G8
West Huntington York 52 D2
West Hythe Kent 13 C10
West Ilsley W Berks 17 C11
West Itchenor W Sus 11 D6
West Keal Lincs 47 F7
West Kennett Wilts 17 E8
West Kilbride N Ayrs 66 B5
West Kingsdown Kent 20 E3
West Kington Wilts 16 D5
West Kinharrachie Aberds 89 E9
West Kirby Mers 42 D5
West Knapton N Yorks 52 B4
West Knighton Dorset 8 F6
West Knoyle Wilts 9 A7
West Kyloe Northumb 71 F9
West Lambrook Som 8 C3
West Langdon Kent 21 G10
West Langwell Highld 93 J9
West Lavington W Sus 11 B7
West Lavington Wilts 17 F7
West Layton N Yorks 58 F2
West Lea Durham 58 B5
West Leake Notts 35 C11
West Learmouth Northumb 71 G7
West Leigh Devon 6 F5
West Lexham Norf 38 D4
West Lilling N Yorks 52 C2
West Linton Borders 69 E10
West Liss Hants 11 A6
West Littleton S Glos 16 D4
West Looe Corn 4 F3
West Luccombe Som 7 B8
West Lulworth Dorset 9 F7
West Lydford Som 8 A4
West Lyng Som 8 B2
West Lynn Norf 38 D2
West Malling Kent 20 F3
West Malvern Worcs 26 D4
West Marden W Sus 11 C6
West Marina E Sus 13 F6
West Markham Notts 45 E11
West Marsh NE Lincs 46 A6
West Marton N Yorks 50 D4
West Meon Hants 10 B5
West Mersea Essex 31 G7
West Milton Dorset 8 E4
West Minster Kent 20 D6
West Molesey Sur 19 E8
West Monkton Som 8 B1
West Moors Dorset 9 D9
West Morriston Borders 70 F5
West Muir Angus 77 A8

West Ness N Yorks 52 B2
West Newton E Yorks 53 F8
West Newton Norf 38 C2
West Norwood London 19 D10
Westacott Devon 6 C4
Westbere Kent 21 E8
Westborough Lincs 36 A4
Westbourne Suff 31 D8
Westbourne W Sus 11 D6
Westbrook W Berks 17 D11
Westbury Bucks 28 E3
Westbury Shrops 33 E9
Westbury Wilts 16 F5
Westbury Leigh Wilts 16 F5
Westbury-on-Severn Glos 26 G3
Westbury on Trym Bristol 16 D2
Westbury-sub-Mendip Som 15 G11
Westby Lancs 49 F3
Westcliff-on-Sea Southend 20 C5
Westcombe Som 16 G3
Westcote Glos 27 F9
Westcott Bucks 28 G4
Westcott Devon 7 F9
Westcott Sur 19 G8
Westcott Barton Oxon 27 F11
Westdean E Sus 12 G4
Westdene Brighton 12 F1
Wester Aberchalder Highld 81 A7
Wester Balgedie Perth 76 G4
Wester Culbeuchly Aberds 89 B6
Wester Dechmont W Loth 69 D9
Wester Denoon Angus 76 C6
Wester Fintray Aberds 83 B10
Wester Gruinards Highld 87 B8
Wester Lealty Highld 87 D9
Wester Milton Highld 87 F12
Wester Newburn Fife 77 G7
Wester Quarff Shetland 96 K6
Wester Skeld Shetland 96 J4
Westerdale Highld 94 E3
Westerdale N Yorks 59 F7
Westerfield Shetland 96 H6
Westerfield Suff 31 D8
Westergate W Sus 11 D8
Westerham Kent 19 F11
Westerhope T&W 63 G7
Westerleigh S Glos 16 D4
Westerton Angus 77 B9
Westerton Durham 58 C3
Westerton W Sus 11 D7
Westerwick Shetland 96 J4
Westfield Cumb 56 D1
Westfield E Sus 13 E7
Westfield Hereford 26 D4
Westfield Highld 94 D2
Westfield N Lanark 68 C6
Westfield Norf 38 E5
Westfield W Loth 69 C8
Westfields Dorset 8 D6
Westfields of Rattray Perth 76 C4
Westgate Durham 57 C11
Westgate N Lincs 45 B11
Westgate Norf 38 A5
Westgate on Sea Kent 21 D10
Westhall Aberds 83 A8
Westhall Suff 39 G10
Westham Dorset 8 G5
Westham E Sus 12 F5
Westham Som 15 G10
Westhampnett W Sus 11 D7
Westhay Som 15 G10
Westhead Lancs 43 B7
Westhide Hereford 26 D2
Westhill Aberds 83 C10
Westhill Highld 87 G10
Westhope Hereford 25 C11
Westhope Shrops 33 G10
Westhorpe Lincs 37 B8
Westhorpe Suff 31 B7
Westhoughton Gtr Man 43 B9
Westhouse N Yorks 50 B2
Westhumble Sur 19 F8
Westing Shetland 96 C7
Westlake Devon 5 F7
Westleigh Devon 6 D3
Westleigh Devon 7 E9
Westleigh Gtr Man 43 B9
Westleton Suff 31 B11
Westley Shrops 33 E9
Westley Suff 30 B5
Westley Waterless Cambs 30 C3
Westlington Bucks 28 G4
Westlinton Cumb 61 G9
Westmarsh Kent 21 E9
Westmeston E Sus 12 E2
Westmill Herts 29 F10
Westminster London 19 D10
Westmuir Angus 76 B6
Westness Orkney 95 F4
Westnewton Cumb 56 B3
Westnewton Northumb 71 G8
Weston Bath 16 E4
Weston Ches E 43 G10
Weston Devon 7 H10
Weston Dorset 8 G5
Weston Halton 43 D8
Weston Hants 10 B6
Weston Herts 29 E9
Weston Lincs 37 C8
Weston N Yorks 51 E7
Weston Northants 28 D2
Weston Notts 45 F11
Weston Shrops 33 C11
Weston Shrops 34 C1
Weston Staffs 34 C5
Weston W Berks 17 D10
Weston Beggard Hereford 26 D2
Weston by Welland Northants 36 F3
Weston Colville Cambs 30 C3
Weston Coyney Stoke 34 A5
Weston Favell Northants 28 B4
Weston Green Cambs 30 C3
Weston Green Norf 39 D7
Weston Heath Shrops 34 D3
Weston Hills Lincs 37 C8
Weston-in-Gordano N Som 15 D10
Weston Jones Staffs 34 C3
Weston Longville Norf 39 D7
Weston Lullingfields Shrops 33 C10
Weston-on-the-Green Oxon 28 G2
Weston-on-Trent Derbys 35 C10
Weston Patrick Hants 18 G3
Weston Rhyn Shrops 33 B8
Weston-Sub-Edge Glos 27 D8
Weston-super-Mare N Som 15 E9
Weston Turville Bucks 28 G5
Weston under Lizard Staffs 34 D4
Weston under Penyard Hereford 26 F3
Weston under Wetherley Warks 27 B10
Weston Underwood Derbys 35 A8
Weston Underwood M Keynes 28 C5
Westoncommon Shrops 33 C10
Westonzoyland Som 8 A2
Westow N Yorks 52 C3
Westport Argyll 65 F7
Westport Som 8 C2
Westray Orkney 95 C5
Westrigg W Loth 69 D8
Westruther Borders 70 F5
Westry Cambs 37 F9
Westville Notts 45 H9
Westward Cumb 56 B4
Westward Ho! Devon 6 D3
Westwell Kent 20 G6
Westwell Oxon 27 H9
Westwell Leacon Kent 20 G6
Westwick Cambs 29 B11
Westwick Durham 58 E1
Westwick Norf 39 C8
Westwood Devon 7 G9
Westwood Wilts 16 F5
Westwoodside N Lincs 45 C11
Wetheral Cumb 56 A6
Wetherby W Yorks 51 E10
Wetherden Suff 31 B7
Wetheringsett Suff 31 B8
Wethersfield Essex 30 E4
Wethersta Shetland 96 G5
Wetherup Street Suff 31 B8
Wetley Rocks Staffs 44 H3
Wettenhall Ches E 43 F9
Wetton Staffs 44 G5
Wetwang E Yorks 52 D5
Wetwood Staffs 34 B3
Wexcombe Wilts 17 F9
Wexham Street Bucks 18 C6
Weybourne Norf 39 A7
Weybourne Sur 18 G5
Weybread Suff 39 G8
Weybridge Sur 19 E7
Weycroft Devon 8 E2
Weydale Highld 94 D3
Weyhill Hants 17 G10
Weymouth Dorset 8 G5
Whaddon Bucks 28 E5
Whaddon Cambs 29 D10
Whaddon Glos 26 G5
Whaddon Wilts 9 B10
Whale Cumb 57 D7
Whaley Derbys 45 E9
Whaley Bridge Derbys 44 D4
Whaley Thorns Derbys 45 E9
Whaligoe Highld 94 F5
Whalley Lancs 50 F3
Whalton Northumb 63 E7
Wham N Yorks 50 C3
Whaplode Lincs 37 C9
Whaplode Drove Lincs 37 D9
Whaplode St Catherine Lincs 37 C9
Wharfe N Yorks 50 C3
Wharles Lancs 49 F4
Wharncliffe Side S Yorks 44 C6
Wharram le Street N Yorks 52 C4
Wharton Ches W 43 F9
Wharton Green Ches W 43 F9
Whashton N Yorks 58 F2
Whatcombe Dorset 9 D7
Whatcote Warks 27 D10
Whatfield Suff 31 D7
Whatley Som 8 D2
Whatley Som 16 G4
Whatlington E Sus 13 E6
Whatstandwell Derbys 45 G7
Whatton Notts 36 B3
Whauphill Dumfries 55 E7
Whaw N Yorks 57 F11
Wheatacre Norf 39 F10
Wheatcroft Derbys 45 G7
Wheathampstead Herts 29 G8
Wheathill Shrops 34 G2

Wheatley Devon 7 G8
Wheatley Hants 18 G4
Wheatley Oxon 28 H2
Wheatley S Yorks 45 B9
Wheatley W Yorks 51 G6
Wheatley Hill Durham 58 C4
Wheaton Aston Staffs 34 D4
Wheddon Cross Som 7 C8
Wheedlemont Aberds 82 A6
Wheelerstreet Sur 18 G6
Wheelock Ches E 43 G10
Wheelock Heath Ches E 43 G10
Wheelton Lancs 50 G2
Wheen Angus 82 F5
Wheldrake York 52 E2
Whelford Glos 17 B8
Whelpley Hill Herts 28 H6
Whempstead Herts 29 F10
Whenby N Yorks 52 C2
Whepstead Suff 30 C5
Wherstead Suff 31 D8
Wherwell Hants 17 G10
Wheston Derbys 44 E5
Whetsted Kent 20 G3
Whetstone Leics 35 F11
Whicham Cumb 49 A1
Whichford Warks 27 E10
Whickham T&W 63 G8
Whiddon Down Devon 6 G5
Whigstreet Angus 77 C7
Whilton Northants 28 B3
Whim Farm Borders 69 E11
Whimble Devon 6 F2
Whimple Devon 7 G9
Whimpwell Green Norf 39 C9
Whinburgh Norf 38 E6
Whinnieliggate Dumfries 55 D10
Whinnyfold Aberds 89 E10
Whippingham IoW 10 E4
Whipsnade C Beds 29 G7
Whipton Devon 7 G8
Whirlow S Yorks 45 D7
Whisby Lincs 46 F3
Whissendine Rutland 36 D4
Whissonsett Norf 38 C5
Whistlefield Argyll 73 D10
Whistlefield Argyll 73 D11
Whistley Green Wokingham 18 D4
Whiston Mers 43 C7
Whiston Northants 28 B5
Whiston S Yorks 45 D8
Whiston Staffs 34 D4
Whiston Staffs 44 H4
Whitbeck Cumb 49 A1
Whitbourne Hereford 26 C4
Whitburn T&W 63 G10
Whitburn W Loth 69 D8
Whitburn Colliery T&W 63 G10
Whitby Ches W 43 E6
Whitby N Yorks 59 E9
Whitbyheath Ches W 43 E6
Whitchurch Bath 16 E3
Whitchurch Bucks 28 F4
Whitchurch Cardiff 15 C7
Whitchurch Devon 4 D6
Whitchurch Hants 17 G11
Whitchurch Hereford 26 G2
Whitchurch Oxon 18 D3
Whitchurch Pembs 22 D2
Whitchurch Shrops 33 A11
Whitchurch Canonicorum Dorset 8 E2
Whitchurch Hill Oxon 18 D3
Whitcombe Dorset 8 F6
Whitcott Keysett Shrops 33 G8
White Coppice Lancs 50 H2
White Lackington Dorset 8 E6
White Ladies Aston Worcs 26 C6
White Lund Lancs 49 C4
White Ness Shetland 96 J5
White Notley Essex 30 G4
White Pit Lincs 47 E7
White Post Notts 45 G10
White Rocks Hereford 25 F11
White Roding Essex 30 G2
White Waltham Windsor 18 D5
Whiteacen Moray 88 D2
Whiteacre Heath Warks 35 F8
Whitebridge Highld 81 B6
Whitebrook Mon 26 H2
Whiteburn Borders 70 F4
Whitecairn Dumfries 54 D6
Whitecairns Aberds 83 B11
Whitecastle S Lanark 69 F8
Whitechapel Lancs 50 E1
Whitecleat Orkney 95 H6
Whitecraig E Loth 70 C2
Whitecroft Glos 26 H3
Whitecross Corn 3 C8
Whitecross Falk 69 C8
Whiteface Highld 87 C10
Whitefarland N Ayrs 66 B1
Whitefaulds S Ayrs 66 F5
Whitefield Gtr Man 44 B2
Whitefield Perth 76 D4
Whiteford Aberds 83 A9
Whitegate Ches W 43 F9
Whitehall Blackburn 50 G2
Whitehall W Sus 11 B10
Whitehall Village Orkney 95 F7
Whitehaven Cumb 56 E1
Whitehill Hants 11 A6
Whitehills Aberds 89 B6
Whitehills S Lanark 68 E5
Whitehough Derbys 44 D4
Whitehouse Aberds 83 B8
Whitehouse Argyll 73 G7
Whiteinch Glasgow 68 D4
Whitekirk E Loth 70 B4
Whitelaw S Lanark 68 E5
Whiteleas T&W 63 G9
Whiteley Bank IoW 10 F4
Whiteley Green Ches E 44 E3
Whiteley Village Sur 19 E7
Whitemans Green W Sus 12 D2
Whitemire Moray 87 F12
Whitemoor Corn 3 D8
Whitemore Staffs 44 F2
Whitenap Hants 10 B2
Whiteoak Green Oxon 27 G10
Whiteparish Wilts 9 B11
Whiterashes Aberds 89 F8
Whiterow Highld 94 F5
Whiteshill Glos 26 H5
Whiteside Northumb 62 G2
Whiteside W Loth 69 D8
Whitesmith E Sus 12 E4
Whitestaunton Som 8 C1
Whitestone Devon 7 G7
Whitestone Devon 6 B4
Whitestone Warks 35 G9
Whitestones Aberds 89 C8
Whitestreet Green Suff 30 E6
Whitewall Corner N Yorks 52 B3
Whiteway Glos 26 G6
Whiteway Glos 16 D4
Whitewell Aberds 89 B9
Whitewell Lancs 50 E2
Whitewell Bottom Lancs 50 G4
Whiteworks Devon 5 D7
Whitfield Kent 21 G10
Whitfield Northants 28 E3
Whitfield Northumb 62 H3
Whitfield S Glos 16 B3
Whitford Devon 8 E1
Whitford Flint 42 E4
Whitgift E Yorks 52 G4
Whitgreave Staffs 34 C4
Whithorn Dumfries 55 E7
Whiting Bay N Ayrs 66 D3
Whitington Norf 38 E3
Whitkirk W Yorks 51 F9
Whitland Carms 22 E6
Whitletts S Ayrs 67 D6
Whitley N Yorks 52 G1
Whitley Reading 18 D4

Whitley Wilts 16 E5
Whitley Bay T&W 63 F9
Whitley Chapel Northumb 62 H5
Whitley Lower W Yorks 51 H8
Whitley Row Kent 19 F11
Whitlock's End W Mid 35 H7
Whitminster Glos 26 H4
Whitmore Staffs 34 A4
Whitnage Devon 7 E9
Whitnash Warks 27 B10
Whitney-on-Wye Hereford 25 D9
Whitrigg Cumb 56 A4
Whitrigg Cumb 61 H8
Whitsbury Hants 9 C10
Whitsome Borders 71 E7
Whitson Newport 15 C9
Whitstable Kent 21 E7
Whitstone Corn 6 G1
Whittingham Northumb 62 B6
Whittingslow Shrops 33 G10
Whittington Glos 27 F7
Whittington Lancs 50 B2
Whittington Norf 38 F3
Whittington Shrops 33 B9
Whittington Staffs 34 G3
Whittington Staffs 35 E7
Whittington Warks 35 F8
Whittington Worcs 26 C5
Whittington Corner Ches E 44 F2
Whittle-le-Woods Lancs 50 G1
Whittlebury Northants 28 D3
Whittlesey Cambs 37 F8
Whittlesford Cambs 29 D11
Whittlestone Head Blackburn 50 H3
Whitton Borders 70 H6
Whitton N Lincs 52 G5
Whitton Northumb 62 C6
Whitton Powys 25 B9
Whitton Shrops 26 A2
Whitton Stockton 58 D4
Whitton Suff 31 D8
Whittonditch Wilts 17 D10
Whittonstall Northumb 62 H6
Whitway Hants 17 F11
Whitwell Derbys 45 E9
Whitwell Herts 29 F8
Whitwell IoW 10 G4
Whitwell N Yorks 58 G3
Whitwell Rutland 36 E5
Whitwell-on-the-Hill N Yorks 52 C3
Whitwell Street Norf 39 C7
Whitwick Leics 35 D10
Whitwood W Yorks 51 G10
Whitworth Lancs 50 H4
Whixall Shrops 33 B11
Whixley N Yorks 51 D10
Whoberley W Mid 35 H9
Whorlton Durham 58 E2
Whorlton N Yorks 58 F5
Whygate Northumb 62 F3
Whyle Hereford 26 B2
Whyteleafe Sur 19 F10
Wibdon Glos 16 B2
Wibsey W Yorks 51 F7
Wibtoft Leics 35 G10
Wichenford Worcs 26 B4
Wichling Kent 20 F6
Wick Bmouth 9 E10
Wick Devon 7 F10
Wick Highld 94 E5
Wick S Glos 16 D4
Wick Shetland 96 J6
Wick V Glam 14 D5
Wick W Sus 11 D9
Wick Wilts 9 B10
Wick Worcs 26 D6
Wick Wokingham 18 E5
Wick Hill Wokingham 18 E4
Wick St Lawrence N Som 15 E9
Wicken Cambs 30 A2
Wicken Northants 28 E4
Wicken Green Village Norf 38 B4
Wickenby Lincs 46 D4
Wickersley S Yorks 45 C8
Wickford Essex 20 B4
Wickham Hants 10 C4
Wickham W Berks 17 D10
Wickham Bishops Essex 30 G5
Wickham Market Suff 31 C10
Wickham Skeith Suff 31 B7
Wickham St Paul Essex 30 E5
Wickhambreaux Kent 21 E9
Wickhambrook Suff 30 C4
Wickhamford Worcs 27 D7
Wickhampton Norf 39 E10
Wicklewood Norf 39 E6
Wickmere Norf 39 B7
Wickwar S Glos 16 C4
Widdington Essex 30 E2
Widdrington Northumb 63 D8
Widdrington Station Northumb 63 D8
Wide Open T&W 63 F8
Widecombe in the Moor Devon 5 D8
Widegates Corn 4 F3
Widemouth Bay Corn 6 F1
Widewall Orkney 95 J5
Widford Essex 30 H4
Widford Herts 29 G11
Widham Wilts 17 C7
Widmer End Bucks 18 B5
Widmerpool Notts 36 C2
Widnes Halton 43 D8
Wigan Gtr Man 43 B8
Wiggaton Devon 7 G10
Wiggenhall St Germans Norf 38 D1
Wiggenhall St Mary Magdalen Norf 38 D1
Wiggenhall St Mary the Virgin Norf 38 D1
Wigginton Herts 28 G6
Wigginton Oxon 27 E10
Wigginton Staffs 35 E8
Wigginton York 52 D1
Wigglesworth N Yorks 50 D4
Wiggonby Cumb 56 A4
Wiggonholt W Sus 11 C9
Wighill N Yorks 51 E10
Wighton Norf 38 B5
Wigley Hants 10 C2
Wigmore Hereford 25 B11
Wigmore Medway 20 E5
Wigsley Notts 46 E2
Wigsthorpe Northants 36 G6
Wigston Leics 36 F2
Wigthorpe Notts 45 D9
Wigtoft Lincs 37 B8
Wigton Cumb 56 B4
Wigtown Dumfries 55 D7
Wigtwizzle S Yorks 44 C6
Wike W Yorks 51 E9
Wike Well End S Yorks 45 A10
Wilberfoss E Yorks 52 D3
Wilberlee W Yorks 44 A4
Wilburton Cambs 29 A11
Wilby Norf 38 F6
Wilby Northants 28 B5
Wilby Suff 31 A9
Wilcot Wilts 17 E8
Wilcott Shrops 33 D9
Wilcrick Newport 15 C10
Wilday Green Derbys 45 E7
Wildboarclough Ches E 44 F3
Wilden Bedford 29 C7
Wilden Worcs 26 A5
Wildhern Hants 17 F10
Wildhill Herts 29 H9
Wildmoor Worcs 34 H5
Wildsworth Lincs 46 C2
Wilford Nottingham 36 B1

Wilkesley Ches E 34 A2
Wilkhaven Highld 87 C12
Wilkieston W Loth 69 D10
Willand Devon 7 E9
Willaston Ches E 43 G9
Willaston Ches W 42 E6
Willen M Keynes 28 D5
Willenhall W Mid 34 F5
Willenhall W Mid 35 H9
Willerby E Yorks 52 F6
Willerby N Yorks 52 B6
Willersey Glos 27 D8
Willersley Hereford 25 D10
Willesborough Kent 13 B9
Willesborough Lees Kent 13 B9
Willesden London 19 C9
Willett Som 7 C10
Willey Shrops 34 F2
Willey Warks 35 G10
Willey Green Sur 18 F6
Williamscot Oxon 27 D11
Willian Herts 29 E9
Willingale Essex 30 H2
Willingdon E Sus 12 F4
Willingham Cambs 29 A11
Willingham by Stow Lincs 46 D2
Willington Bedford 29 D8
Willington Derbys 35 C8
Willington Durham 58 C2
Willington T&W 63 G9
Willington Warks 27 E9
Willington Corner Ches W 43 F8
Willisham Tye Suff 31 C7
Willitoft E Yorks 52 F3
Williton Som 7 B9
Willoughbridge Staffs 34 A3
Willoughby Lincs 47 E8
Willoughby Warks 28 B2
Willoughby-on-the-Wolds Notts 36 C2
Willoughby Waterleys Leics 36 F1
Willoughton Lincs 46 C3
Willows Grn. Essex 30 G4
Willsbridge S Glos 16 D3
Willsworthy Devon 4 C6
Wilmcote Warks 27 C8
Wilmington Bath 16 E3
Wilmington Devon 8 E1
Wilmington E Sus 12 F4
Wilmington Kent 20 D2
Wilmslow Ches E 44 D2
Wilnecote Staffs 35 E8
Wilpshire Lancs 50 F2
Wilsden W Yorks 51 F6
Wilsford Lincs 36 A6
Wilsford Wilts 9 A10
Wilsford Wilts 17 F8
Wilsill N Yorks 51 C7
Wilsley Pound Kent 13 C6
Wilsom Hants 18 H4
Wilson Leics 35 C10
Wilsontown S Lanark 69 E8
Wilstead Bedford 29 D7
Wilsthorpe Lincs 37 D6
Wilstone Herts 28 G6
Wilton Borders 61 B10
Wilton Cumb 56 E2
Wilton N Yorks 52 A4
Wilton Redcar 59 E6
Wilton Wilts 9 A9
Wilton Wilts 17 E9
Wimbish Essex 30 E2
Wimbish Green Essex 30 E3
Wimblebury Staffs 34 D6
Wimbledon London 19 D9
Wimblington Cambs 37 F10
Wimborne Minster Dorset 9 E9
Wimborne St Giles Dorset 9 C9
Wimbotsham Norf 38 E2
Wimpole Cambs 29 C10
Wimpstone Warks 27 D9
Wincanton Som 8 B6
Wincham Ches W 43 E9
Winchburgh W Loth 69 C9
Winchcombe Glos 27 F7
Winchelsea E Sus 13 E7
Winchelsea Beach E Sus 13 E7
Winchester Hants 10 B3
Winchet Hill Kent 13 B6
Winchfield Hants 18 F4
Winchmore Hill Bucks 18 B6
Winchmore Hill London 19 B10
Wincle Ches E 44 F3
Wincobank S Yorks 45 C7
Windermere Cumb 56 G6
Winderton Warks 27 D10
Windhill Highld 87 G8
Windhouse Shetland 96 D6
Windlehurst Gtr Man 44 D3
Windlesham Sur 18 E6
Windley Derbys 35 A9
Windmill Hill E Sus 12 E5
Windmill Hill Som 8 C2
Windrush Glos 27 G8
Windsor N Lincs 45 B11
Windsor Windsor 18 D6
Windsoredge Glos 16 A5
Windygates Fife 76 G6
Windyknowe W Loth 69 D8
Windywalls Borders 70 G6
Wineham W Sus 11 B11
Winestead E Yorks 53 G8
Winewall Lancs 50 E5
Winfarthing Norf 39 G7
Winford IoW 10 F4
Winford N Som 15 E11
Winforton Hereford 25 D9
Winfrith Newburgh Dorset 9 F7
Wing Bucks 28 F5
Wing Rutland 36 E4
Wingate Durham 58 C4
Wingates Gtr Man 43 B9
Wingates Northumb 63 D7
Wingerworth Derbys 45 F7
Wingfield C Beds 29 F7
Wingfield Suff 39 H8
Wingfield Wilts 16 F5
Wingham Kent 21 F9
Wingmore Kent 21 G8
Wingrave Bucks 28 G5
Winkburn Notts 45 G11
Winkfield Brack 18 D6
Winkfield Row Brack 18 D5

Winkhill Staffs 44 G4
Winklebury Hants 18 F3
Winkleigh Devon 6 F5
Winksley N Yorks 51 B8
Winkton Dorset 9 E10
Winlaton T&W 63 G7
Winless Highld 94 E5
Winmarleigh Lancs 49 E4
Winnall Hants 10 B3
Winnersh Wokingham 18 D4
Winscales Cumb 56 D2
Winscombe N Som 15 F10
Winsford Ches W 43 F9
Winsford Som 7 C8
Winsham Som 8 D2
Winshill Staffs 35 C8
Winskill Cumb 57 C7
Winslade Hants 18 G3
Winsley Wilts 16 E5
Winslow Bucks 28 F4
Winson Glos 27 H7
Winson Green W Mid 35 G6
Winsor Hants 10 C2
Winster Cumb 56 G6
Winster Derbys 44 F6
Winston Durham 58 E2
Winston Suff 31 B8
Winston Green Suff 31 B8
Winstone Glos 26 H6
Winswell Devon 6 E3
Winter Gardens Essex 20 C4
Winterborne Clenston Dorset 9 D7
Winterborne Herringston Dorset 8 F5
Winterborne Houghton Dorset 9 D7
Winterborne Kingston Dorset 9 E7
Winterborne Monkton Dorset 8 F5
Winterborne Stickland Dorset 9 D7
Winterborne Whitechurch Dorset 9 D7
Winterborne Zelston Dorset 9 E7
Winterbourne S Glos 16 C3
Winterbourne W Berks 17 D11
Winterbourne Abbas Dorset 8 E5
Winterbourne Bassett Wilts 17 D8
Winterbourne Dauntsey Wilts 9 A10
Winterbourne Down S Glos 16 D3
Winterbourne Earls Wilts 9 A10
Winterbourne Gunner Wilts 9 A10
Winterbourne Monkton Wilts 17 D8
Winterbourne Steepleton Dorset 8 F5
Winterbourne Stoke Wilts 17 G7
Winterburn N Yorks 50 D5
Winteringham N Lincs 52 G5
Winterley Ches E 43 G10
Wintersett W Yorks 51 H9
Wintershill Hants 10 C4
Winterton N Lincs 52 H5
Winterton-on-Sea Norf 39 D10
Winthorpe Lincs 47 F9
Winthorpe Notts 46 G2
Winton Bmouth 9 E9
Winton Cumb 57 E9
Winton N Yorks 58 G5
Wintringham N Yorks 52 B5
Winwick Cambs 37 G7
Winwick Northants 28 A3
Winwick Warr 43 C9
Wirksworth Derbys 44 G6
Wirksworth Moor Derbys 45 G7
Wirswall Ches E 33 A11
Wisbech Cambs 37 E10
Wisbech St Mary Cambs 37 E10
Wisborough Green W Sus 11 B9
Wiseton Notts 45 D11
Wishaw N Lanark 68 E6
Wishaw Warks 35 F7
Wisley Sur 19 F7
Wispington Lincs 46 E6
Wissenden Kent 13 B8
Wissett Suff 39 H9
Wistanstow Shrops 33 G10
Wistanswick Shrops 34 C2
Wistaston Ches E 43 G9
Wistaston Green Ches E 43 G9
Wiston Pembs 22 E5
Wiston S Lanark 69 G8
Wiston W Sus 11 C10
Wistow Cambs 37 G8
Wistow N Yorks 52 F1
Wiswell Lancs 50 F3
Witcham Cambs 37 G10
Witchampton Dorset 9 D8
Witchford Cambs 37 H10
Witham Essex 30 G5
Witham Friary Som 16 G4
Witham on the Hill Lincs 37 D6
Withcall Lincs 46 D6
Withdean Brighton 12 F2
Witherenden Hill E Sus 12 D5
Witheridge Devon 7 E7
Witherley Leics 35 F9
Withern Lincs 47 D8
Withernsea E Yorks 53 G9
Withernwick E Yorks 53 E8
Withersdale Street Suff 39 G8
Withersfield Suff 30 D3
Witherslack Cumb 49 A4
Withiel Corn 3 C8
Withiel Florey Som 7 C8
Withington Glos 27 G7
Withington Gtr Man 44 C2
Withington Hereford 26 D2
Withington Shrops 34 D1
Withington Staffs 34 B6
Withington Green Ches E 44 E2
Withleigh Devon 7 E8
Withnell Lancs 50 G2
Withybrook Warks 35 G10
Withycombe Som 7 B9
Withycombe Raleigh Devon 5 C11
Withyham E Sus 12 C3
Withypool Som 7 C7
Witley Sur 18 H6
Witnesham Suff 31 C8
Witney Oxon 27 G10
Wittersham Kent 13 D7
Witton Angus 83 F7
Witton Worcs 26 B5
Witton Bridge Norf 39 B9
Witton Gilbert Durham 58 B3
Witton-le-Wear Durham 58 C2
Witton Park Durham 58 C2
Wiveliscombe Som 7 D9
Wivelrod Hants 18 H3
Wivelsfield E Sus 12 D2
Wivelsfield Green E Sus 12 E2
Wivenhoe Essex 31 F7
Wivenhoe Cross Essex 31 F7
Wiveton Norf 38 A6
Wix Essex 31 F8
Wixford Warks 27 C7
Wixhill Shrops 34 C1
Wixoe Suff 30 D4
Woburn C Beds 28 E6
Woburn Sands M Keynes 28 E6
Wokefield Park W Berks 18 E3
Woking Sur 19 F7
Wokingham Wokingham 18 E5
Wolborough Devon 5 D9
Wold Newton E Yorks 52 B6
Wold Newton NE Lincs 46 C6
Woldingham Sur 19 F10
Wolfclyde S Lanark 69 G9
Wolferton Norf 38 C2
Wolfhill Perth 76 D4
Wolf's Castle Pembs 22 D4
Wolfsdale Pembs 22 D4
Woll Borders 61 A10
Wollaston Northants 28 B6
Wollaston Shrops 33 D9
Wollaton Nottingham 35 B11
Wollerton Shrops 34 B2
Wollescote W Mid 34 G5
Wolsingham Durham 58 C1
Wolstanton Staffs 44 H2
Wolston Warks 35 H10
Wolvercote Oxon 27 H11
Wolverhampton W Mid 34 F5
Wolverley Shrops 33 B10
Wolverley Worcs 34 H4
Wolverton Hants 18 F2
Wolverton M Keynes 28 D5
Wolverton Warks 27 B9
Wolverton Common Hants 18 F2
Wolvesnewton Mon 15 B10
Wolvey Warks 35 G10
Wolviston Stockton 58 D5
Wombleton N Yorks 59 H7
Wombourne Staffs 34 F4
Wombwell S Yorks 45 B7
Womenswold Kent 21 F9
Womersley N Yorks 51 H11
Wonastow Mon 25 G11
Wonersh Sur 19 G7
Wonson Devon 5 C7
Wonston Hants 17 H11
Wooburn Bucks 18 C6
Wooburn Green Bucks 18 C6
Wood Dalling Norf 39 C6
Wood End Herts 29 F10
Wood End Warks 27 A8
Wood End Warks 35 F8
Wood Enderby Lincs 46 F6
Wood Field Sur 19 F8
Wood Green London 19 B10
Wood Hayes W Mid 34 E5
Wood Lanes Ches E 44 D3
Wood Norton Norf 38 C6
Wood Street Norf 39 C9
Wood Street Sur 18 F6
Wood Walton Cambs 37 G8

Woodacott Devon 6 F2
Woodale N Yorks 50 B6
Woodbank Argyll 65 G7
Woodbastwick Norf 39 D9
Woodbeck Notts 45 E11
Woodborough Notts 45 H10
Woodborough Wilts 17 F8
Woodbridge Dorset 8 C6
Woodbridge Suff 31 D9
Woodbury Devon 5 C11
Woodbury Salterton Devon 5 C11
Woodchester Glos 16 A5
Woodchurch Kent 13 C8
Woodchurch Mers 42 D5
Woodcombe Som 7 B8
Woodcote Oxon 18 C3
Woodcott Hants 17 F11
Woodcroft Glos 15 B11
Woodcutts Dorset 9 C8
Woodditton Cambs 30 C3
Woodeaton Oxon 28 G2
Woodend Cumb 56 G3
Woodend Northants 28 D3
Woodend W Sus 11 D7
Woodend Green Northants 28 D3
Woodfalls Wilts 9 B10
Woodfield Oxon 28 F2
Woodfield S Ayrs 66 D6
Woodford Corn 6 E1
Woodford Devon 5 F8
Woodford Glos 16 B3
Woodford Gtr Man 44 D2
Woodford London 19 B11
Woodford Northants 36 H5
Woodford Bridge London 19 B11
Woodford Halse Northants 28 C2
Woodgate Norf 38 D6
Woodgate W Mid 34 G5
Woodgate W Sus 11 D8
Woodgate Worcs 26 B6
Woodgreen Hants 9 C10
Woodhall Herts 29 G9
Woodhall Invclyd 68 C2
Woodhall N Yorks 57 H11
Woodhall Spa Lincs 46 F5
Woodham Sur 19 E7
Woodham Ferrers Essex 20 B4
Woodham Mortimer Essex 20 A5
Woodham Walter Essex 30 H5
Woodhaven Fife 77 E7
Woodhead Aberds 89 E7
Woodhey Gtr Man 50 H3
Woodhill Shrops 34 G3
Woodhorn Northumb 63 E8
Woodhouse Leics 35 D11
Woodhouse S Yorks 45 D8
Woodhouse W Yorks 51 F8
Woodhouse W Yorks 51 G10
Woodhouse Eaves Leics 35 D11
Woodhouse Park Gtr Man 44 D2
Woodhouselee Midloth 69 D11
Woodhouselees Dumfries 61 F9
Woodhouses Staffs 35 D7
Woodhurst Cambs 37 H9
Woodingdean Brighton 12 F2
Woodland Devon 5 E8
Woodland Durham 58 D1
Woodlands Aberds 83 D9
Woodlands Dorset 9 D9
Woodlands Hants 10 C2
Woodlands Highld 87 E8
Woodlands N Yorks 51 D9
Woodlands S Yorks 45 B9
Woodlands Park Windsor 18 D5
Woodlands St Mary W Berks 17 D10
Woodlane Staffs 35 C7
Woodleigh Devon 5 G8
Woodlesford W Yorks 51 G9
Woodley Gtr Man 44 C3
Woodley Wokingham 18 D4
Woodmancote Glos 16 A5
Woodmancote Glos 26 F6
Woodmancote Glos 27 F7
Woodmancote W Sus 11 D6
Woodmancote W Sus 12 E1
Woodmancott Hants 18 G2
Woodmansey E Yorks 52 F6
Woodmansterne Sur 19 F9
Woodminton Wilts 9 B9
Woodnesborough Kent 21 F10
Woodnewton Northants 37 F6
Woodplumpton Lancs 49 F5
Woodrising Norf 38 E5
Wood's Green E Sus 12 C5
Woodseaves Shrops 34 B2
Woodseaves Staffs 34 C3
Woodsend Wilts 17 D9
Woodsetts S Yorks 45 D9
Woodsford Dorset 9 E6
Woodside Aberds 83 C11
Woodside Aberds 89 D10
Woodside Brack 18 D6
Woodside Fife 77 G7
Woodside Hants 10 E2
Woodside Herts 29 H9
Woodside Perth 76 D5
Woodside of Arbeadie Aberds 83 D9
Woodstock Oxon 27 G11
Woodstock Pembs 22 D5
Woodthorpe Derbys 45 E8
Woodthorpe Leics 35 D11
Woodthorpe Lincs 47 D8
Woodthorpe York 52 E1
Woodton Norf 39 F8
Woodtown Devon 6 D3
Woodtown Devon 6 D3
Woodvale Mers 49 H3
Woodville Derbys 35 D9
Woodwalton Cambs 37 G8
Woodyates Dorset 9 C9
Woofferton Shrops 26 B2
Wookey Som 15 G11
Wookey Hole Som 15 G11
Woolacombe Devon 6 B3
Woolage Green Kent 21 G9
Woolaston Glos 16 B2
Woolavington Som 15 G9
Woolbeding W Sus 11 B7
Wooldale W Yorks 44 B5
Wooler Northumb 71 H8
Woolfardisworthy Devon 6 D2
Woolfardisworthy Devon 7 F7
Woolfords Cottages S Lanark 69 E9
Woolhampton W Berks 18 E2
Woolhope Hereford 26 E3
Woolhope Cockshoot Hereford 26 E3
Woolland Dorset 8 D6
Woollaton Devon 6 E3
Woolley Bath 16 E4
Woolley Cambs 37 H7
Woolley Corn 6 E1
Woolley Derbys 45 F7
Woolley W Yorks 45 A7
Woolmer Green Herts 29 G9
Woolmere Green Worcs 26 B6
Woolpit Suff 30 B6
Woolscott Warks 27 B11
Woolsington T&W 63 G7
Woolstanwood Ches E 43 G9
Woolstaston Shrops 33 F10
Woolsthorpe Lincs 36 C4
Woolsthorpe Lincs 36 B5
Woolston Devon 5 G8
Woolston Shrops 33 C9
Woolston Shrops 33 G10
Woolston Soton 10 C3
Woolston Warr 43 D9
Woolstone M Keynes 28 E5
Woolstone Oxon 17 C9
Woolton Mers 43 D7
Woolton Hill Hants 17 E11
Woolverstone Suff 31 E8
Woolverton Som 16 F4
Woolwich London 19 D11
Woolwich Ferry London 19 D11
Woonton Hereford 25 C10
Wooperton Northumb 62 A6
Woore Shrops 34 A3

Wootten Green Suff 31 A9
Wootton Bedford 29 D7
Wootton Hants 9 E11
Wootton Hereford 25 C10
Wootton Kent 21 G9
Wootton N Lincs 52 H6
Wootton Northants 28 C4
Wootton Oxon 27 G11
Wootton Oxon 27 H11
Wootton Shrops 33 C9
Wootton Shrops 33 H10
Wootton Staffs 34 C4
Wootton Staffs 44 H5
Wootton Bridge IoW 10 E4
Wootton Common IoW 10 E4
Wootton Courtenay Som 7 B8
Wootton Fitzpaine Dorset 8 E2
Wootton Rivers Wilts 17 E8
Wootton St Lawrence Hants 18 F2
Wootton Wawen Warks 27 B8
Worcester Worcs 26 C5
Worcester Park London 19 E9
Wordsley W Mid 34 G4
Worfield Shrops 34 F3
Work Orkney 95 G5
Workington Cumb 56 D1
Worksop Notts 45 E9
World's End W Berks 17 D11
Worle N Som 15 E9
Worleston Ches E 43 G9
Worlingham Suff 39 F10
Worlington Suff 30 A3
Worlingworth Suff 31 B9
Wormald Green N Yorks 51 C9
Wormbridge Hereford 25 E11
Wormegay Norf 38 D2
Wormelow Tump Hereford 25 E11
Wormhill Derbys 44 E5
Wormingford Essex 30 E6
Worminghall Bucks 28 H3
Wormington Glos 27 E7
Worminster Som 16 G2
Wormit Fife 77 E6
Wormleighton Warks 27 C11
Wormley Herts 29 H10
Wormley Sur 18 H6
Wormley West End Herts 29 H10
Wormshill Kent 20 F5
Wormsley Hereford 25 D11
Worplesdon Sur 18 F6
Worrall S Yorks 44 C6
Worsbrough S Yorks 45 B7
Worsbrough Common S Yorks 45 B7
Worsley Gtr Man 43 B10
Worstead Norf 39 C9
Worsthorne Lancs 50 F4
Worston Lancs 50 E3
Worswell Devon 4 G6
Worth Kent 21 F10
Worth W Sus 12 C2
Worth Matravers Dorset 9 G8
Wortham Suff 39 H6
Worthen Shrops 33 E9
Worthenbury Wrex 43 H7
Worthing Norf 38 D5
Worthing W Sus 11 D10
Worthington Leics 35 C10
Worting Hants 18 F3
Wortley S Yorks 45 C7
Wortley W Yorks 51 F8
Worton N Yorks 57 H11
Worton Wilts 16 F6
Wortwell Norf 39 G8
Wotherton Shrops 33 E8
Wotter Devon 5 E6
Wotton Sur 19 G8
Wotton-under-Edge Glos 16 B4
Wotton Underwood Bucks 28 G3
Woughton on the Green M Keynes 28 E5
Wouldham Kent 20 E4
Wrabness Essex 31 E8
Wrafton Devon 6 C3
Wragby Lincs 46 E5
Wragby W Yorks 51 H10
Wragholme Lincs 47 C7
Wramplingham Norf 39 E7
Wrangaton Devon 5 F7
Wrangbrook W Yorks 45 A8
Wrangham Aberds 89 E6
Wrangle Lincs 47 G8
Wrangle Bank Lincs 47 G8
Wrangle Lowgate Lincs 47 G8
Wrangway Som 7 E10
Wrantage Som 8 B2
Wrawby N Lincs 46 B4
Wraxall Dorset 8 D4
Wraxall N Som 15 D10
Wraxall Som 16 H3
Wray Lancs 50 C2
Wraysbury Windsor 19 D7
Wrayton Lancs 50 B2
Wrea Green Lancs 49 F3
Wreay Cumb 56 B6
Wreay Cumb 56 D6
Wrecclesham Sur 18 G5
Wrecsam = Wrexham Wrex 42 G6
Wrekenton T&W 63 H8
Wrelton N Yorks 59 H8
Wrenbury Ches E 43 H8
Wreningham Norf 39 F7
Wrentham Suff 39 G10
Wrenthorpe W Yorks 51 G9
Wrentnall Shrops 33 E10
Wressle E Yorks 52 F3
Wressle N Lincs 46 B3
Wrestlingworth C Beds 29 D9
Wretham Norf 38 F5
Wretton Norf 38 E2
Wrexham = Wrecsam Wrex 42 G6
Wrexham Industrial Estate Wrex 42 H6
Wribbenhall Worcs 34 H3
Wrightington Bar Lancs 43 A8
Wrinehill Staffs 43 H10
Wrington N Som 15 E10
Writhlington Bath 16 F4
Writtle Essex 30 H3
Wrockwardine Telford 34 D2
Wroot N Lincs 45 B11
Wrotham Kent 20 F3
Wrotham Heath Kent 20 F3
Wroughton Swindon 17 C8
Wroxall IoW 10 G4
Wroxall Warks 27 A9
Wroxeter Shrops 34 E1
Wroxham Norf 39 D9
Wroxton Oxon 27 D11
Wyaston Derbys 35 A7
Wyberton Lincs 37 A9
Wyboston Bedford 29 C8
Wybunbury Ches E 43 H10
Wychbold Worcs 26 B6
Wyck Hants 18 H4
Wyck Rissington Glos 27 F8
Wycoller Lancs 50 F5
Wycomb Leics 36 C3
Wycombe Marsh Bucks 18 B5
Wyddial Herts 29 E10
Wye Kent 21 G7
Wyesham Mon 26 G2
Wyfordby Leics 36 D3
Wyke Dorset 9 A6
Wyke Shrops 34 E2
Wyke Sur 18 F6
Wyke W Yorks 51 G7
Wyke Regis Dorset 8 G5
Wykeham N Yorks 52 A4
Wykeham N Yorks 52 B5
Wyken W Mid 35 G9
Wykey Shrops 33 C9
Wylam Northumb 63 G7
Wylde Green W Mid 35 F7
Wyllie Caerph 15 B7
Wylye Wilts 17 H7
Wymering Ptsmth 10 D5
Wymeswold Leics 36 C2
Wymington Bedford 28 B6
Wymondham Leics 36 D4
Wymondham Norf 39 E7

Wyndham Bridgend 14 B5
Wynford Eagle Dorset 8 E4
Wyng Orkney 95 J4
Wynyard Village Stockton 58 D5
Wyre Piddle Worcs 26 D6
Wysall Notts 36 C2
Wythall Worcs 35 H6
Wytham Oxon 27 H11
Wythburn Cumb 56 E5
Wythenshawe Gtr Man 44 D2
Wythop Mill Cumb 56 D3
Wyverstone Suff 31 B7
Wyverstone Street Suff 31 B7
Wyville Lincs 36 C4
Wyvis Lodge Highld 86 D7

Y

Y Bala = Bala Gwyn 32 B5
Y Barri = Barry V Glam 15 E7
Y Bont-Faen = Cowbridge V Glam 14 D5
Y Drenewydd = Newtown Powys 33 F7
Y Felinheli Gwyn 41 D7
Y Fflint = Flint Flint 42 E5
Y-Ffrith Denb 42 D3
Y Gelli Gandryll = Hay-on-Wye Powys 25 D9
Y Mwmbwls = The Mumbles Swansea 14 C2
Y Pil = Pyle Bridgend 14 C4
Y Rhws = Rhoose V Glam 14 E6
Y Rhyl = Rhyl Denb 42 D3
Y Trallwng = Welshpool Powys 33 E8
Y Waun = Chirk Wrex 33 B8
Yaddlethorpe N Lincs 46 B2
Yafford IoW 10 F3
Yafforth N Yorks 58 G4
Yalding Kent 20 G3
Yanworth Glos 27 G7
Yapham E Yorks 52 D3
Yapton W Sus 11 D8
Yarburgh Lincs 47 C7
Yarcombe Devon 8 D1
Yard Som 7 C9
Yardley W Mid 35 G7
Yardley Gobion Northants 28 D4
Yardley Hastings Northants 28 C5
Yardro Powys 25 C9
Yarkhill Hereford 26 D3
Yarlet Staffs 34 C5
Yarlington Som 8 B5
Yarlside Cumb 49 C2
Yarm Stockton 58 E5
Yarmouth IoW 10 F2
Yarnbrook Wilts 16 F5
Yarnfield Staffs 34 B4
Yarnscombe Devon 6 D4
Yarnton Oxon 27 G11
Yarpole Hereford 25 B11
Yarrow Borders 70 H2
Yarrow Feus Borders 70 H2
Yarsop Hereford 25 D11
Yarwell Northants 37 F6
Yate S Glos 16 C4
Yateley Hants 18 E5
Yatesbury Wilts 17 D7
Yattendon W Berks 18 D2
Yatton Hereford 25 B11
Yatton N Som 15 E10
Yatton Keynell Wilts 16 D5
Yaverland IoW 10 F5
Yaxham Norf 38 D6
Yaxley Cambs 37 F7
Yaxley Suff 31 A8
Yazor Hereford 25 D11
Yeading London 19 C8
Yeadon W Yorks 51 E8
Yealand Conyers Lancs 49 B5
Yealand Redmayne Lancs 49 B5
Yealmpton Devon 5 F6
Yearby Redcar 59 D7
Yearsley N Yorks 52 B1
Yeaton Shrops 33 D10
Yeaveley Derbys 35 A7
Yedingham N Yorks 52 B4
Yeldon Bedford 29 B7
Yelford Oxon 27 H10
Yelling Cambs 29 B9
Yelvertoft Northants 36 H1
Yelverton Devon 4 E6
Yelverton Norf 39 E8
Yenston Som 8 B6
Yeo Mill Devon 7 D7
Yeoford Devon 7 G6
YeoLmbridge Corn 4 C4
Yeovil Som 8 C4
Yeovil Marsh Som 8 C4
Yeovilton Som 8 B4
Yerbeston Pembs 22 F5
Yesnaby Orkney 95 G3
Yetlington Northumb 62 C6
Yetminster Dorset 8 C4
Yettington Devon 7 H9
Yetts o' Muckhart Clack 76 G3
Yieldshields S Lanark 69 E7
Yiewsley London 19 C7
Ynys-meudwy Neath 14 A3
Ynysboeth Rhondda 14 B6
Ynysddu Caerph 15 B7
Ynysgyfflog Gwyn 32 D2
Ynyshir Rhondda 14 B6
Ynyslas Ceredig 32 F2
Ynystawe Swansea 14 A2
Ynysybwl Rhondda 14 B6
Yockenthwaite N Yorks 50 B5
Yockleton Shrops 33 D9
Yokefleet E Yorks 52 G4
Yoker W Dunb 68 D4
Yonder Bognie Aberds 88 D5
York York 52 D2
York Town Sur 18 E5
Yorkletts Kent 21 E7
Yorkley Glos 26 H3
Youlgreave Derbys 44 F6
Youlstone Devon 6 E1
Youlthorpe E Yorks 52 D3
Youlton N Yorks 51 C10
Young Wood Lincs 46 E5
Young's End Essex 30 G4
Yoxall Staffs 35 D7
Yoxford Suff 31 B10
Yr Hôb = Hope Flint 42 G6
Yr Wyddgrug = Mold Flint 42 F5
Ysbyty-Cynfyn Ceredig 32 H3
Ysbyty Ifan Conwy 41 E10
Ysbyty Ystwyth Ceredig 32 H3
Ysceifiog Flint 42 E4
Yspitty Carms 23 G10
Ystalyfera Neath 14 A3
Ystrad Rhondda 14 B5
Ystrad Aeron Ceredig 23 A10
Ystrad-mynach Caerph 15 B7
Ystradfellte Powys 24 H6
Ystradffin Carms 24 D4
Ystradgynlais Powys 24 H4
Ystradmeurig Ceredig 24 B4
Ystradowen Carms 24 G4
Ystradowen V Glam 14 D6
Ystumtuen Ceredig 32 H3
Ythanbank Aberds 89 E9
Ythanwells Aberds 89 E6
Ythsie Aberds 89 E8

Z

Zeal Monachorum Devon 6 F6
Zeals Wilts 9 A6
Zelah Corn 3 D7
Zennor Corn 2 F3